CHEER UP!

'To Everything in Life': the British over-glamorisation of Gitta Alpár in *Everything in Life* (1936)

CHEER UP!

British Musical Films, 1929–1945

Adrian Wright

THE BOYDELL PRESS

© Adrian Wright 2020

All Rights Reserved. Except as permitted under current legislation
no part of this work may be photocopied, stored in a retrieval system,
published, performed in public, adapted, broadcast,
transmitted, recorded or reproduced in any form or by any means,
without the prior permission of the copyright owner

The right of Adrian Wright to be identified as
the author of this work has been asserted in accordance with
sections 77 and 78 of the Copyright, Designs and Patents Act 1988

First published 2020
The Boydell Press, Woodbridge

ISBN 978 1 78327 499 4

The Boydell Press is an imprint of Boydell & Brewer Ltd
PO Box 9, Woodbridge, Suffolk IP12 3DF, UK
and of Boydell & Brewer Inc.
668 Mt Hope Avenue, Rochester, NY 14620–2731, USA
website: www.boydellandbrewer.com

A CIP catalogue record for this book is available
from the British Library

The publisher has no responsibility for the continued existence or accuracy of URLs for
external or third-party internet websites referred to in this book, and does not guarantee
that any content on such websites is, or will remain, accurate or appropriate

This publication is printed on acid-free paper

Printed and bound in Great Britain by
TJ International Ltd, Padstow, Cornwall

This is for the 'extras'

Contents

List of Illustrations xi
Preface and Acknowledgements xiii

1929
Auld Lang Syne • Under the Greenwood Tree • Dark Red Roses
• The Co-Optimists • Splinters 1

1930
Comets • Elstree Calling • Raise the Roof • Song of Soho • Harmony Heaven
• The Flame of Love • The Loves of Robert Burns • Just for a Song • Greek
Street • Piccadilly Nights • The Brat (The Nipper) • The Yellow Mask •
Spanish Eyes • Big Business • Why Sailors Leave Home 9

1931
City of Song • Sally in Our Alley • Gipsy Blood • Out of the Blue
• Sunshine Susie • The Love Race • The Beggar Student • Congress Dances 26

1932
The Blue Danube • Lord Babs • In a Monastery Garden • Goodnight, Vienna
• The First Mrs Fraser • Indiscretions of Eve • His Lordship • Lucky Girl •
Jack's the Boy • Love on the Spot • Monte Carlo Madness • The Love Contract
• Love on Wheels • The Maid of the Mountains • Looking on the Bright Side
• Marry Me • Happy Ever After • Tell Me Tonight • Sleepless Nights • Say It
with Music • Where Is This Lady? • The Midshipmaid • For the Love of Mike
• Born Lucky 35

1933
Yes, Mr Brown • The Little Damozel • The Good Companions • Soldiers of
the King • King of the Ritz • Radio Parade • The Only Girl • Facing the Music
• Waltz Time • Maid Happy • Falling for You • Britannia of Billingsgate •
Prince of Arcadia • Bitter Sweet • Early to Bed • This Week of Grace •
The Song You Gave Me • The Girl from Maxim's • This is the Life • Going Gay
• That's a Good Girl • You Made Me Love You • A Southern Maid •
I Adore You • For Love of You • Aunt Sally 56

1934

Lily of Killarney • Say It with Flowers • On the Air • Jack Ahoy! • Waltzes from Vienna • Happy • Boots! Boots! • The Queen's Affair • Love, Life and Laughter • The Unfinished Symphony • Two Hearts in Waltz Time • Princess Charming • Evergreen • Those Were the Days • The Broken Melody • How's Chances? • Over the Garden Wall • Music Hall • Danny Boy • Song at Eventide • Give Her a Ring • Chu Chin Chow • Blossom Time • My Song for You • Gay Love • There Goes Susie • Sing As We Go • Love-Mirth-Melody • Romance in Rhythm • My Song Goes Round the World • Mister Cinders • Evensong • The Broken Rosary • The Kentucky Minstrels • My Heart Is Calling • Road House • Spring in the Air • Radio Parade of 1935 • Temptation   81

1935

His Majesty and Co. • Things Are Looking Up • In Town Tonight • Oh, Daddy! • Street Song • Radio Pirates • Variety • Off the Dole • Heat Wave • Hello Sweetheart • Squibs • The Divine Spark • Look Up and Laugh • Dance Band • Cock o' the North • Charing Cross Road • Me and Marlborough • The Student's Romance • Heart's Desire • Jimmy Boy • The Deputy Drummer • Car of Dreams • Honeymoon for Three • A Fire Has Been Arranged • Invitation to the Waltz • Music Hath Charms • No Limit • Father O'Flynn • First a Girl • I Give My Heart • Hyde Park Corner • Come Out of the Pantry • She Shall Have Music • Two Hearts in Harmony   118

1936

Stars on Parade • Ball at Savoy • Limelight • Sunshine Ahead • Cheer Up! • Queen of Hearts • When Knights Were Bold • Soft Lights and Sweet Music • Jack of All Trades • Public Nuisance No. 1 • Beloved Impostor • Faithful • King of Hearts • Happy Days Are Here Again • Forget-Me-Not • Melody of My Heart • It's Love Again • Shipmates o' Mine • Men of Yesterday • Everything Is Rhythm • She Knew What She Wanted • A Star Fell from Heaven • The Robber Symphony • Dodging the Dole • Annie Laurie • Calling the Tune • Guilty Melody • Keep Your Seats, Please • Rhythm in the Air • Song of Freedom • Gypsy Melody • The Beloved Vagabond • Southern Roses • Land Without Music • Everybody Dance • Live Again • The Last Waltz • Dreams Come True • This'll Make You Whistle • Everything in Life • Variety Parade • Sporting Love • Pagliacci • Murder at the Cabaret   148

1937

Café Colette • Wake Up Famous • London Melody • Please Teacher • Head Over Heels • Moonlight Sonata • Kathleen Mavourneen • Feather Your Nest • Mayfair Melody • Variety Hour • Calling All Stars • The Show Goes On •

CONTENTS ix

The Street Singer • The Gang Show • Rose of Tralee • O-Kay for Sound • Glamorous Night • Song of the Forge • Take My Tip • Sunset in Vienna • Big Fella • The Penny Pool • Let's Make a Night of It • Talking Feet • Sing As You Swing • The Lilac Domino • Keep Fit • The Girl in the Taxi • Gangway • Command Performance • Over She Goes • The Minstrel Boy • The Last Rose of Summer • Rhythm Racketeer • Shooting Stars • Saturday Night Revue • Paradise for Two • The Sky's the Limit • Intimate Relations • Melody and Romance • Mad About Money   187

1938

Lily of Laguna • The Singing Cop • Sweet Devil • Sailing Along • I See Ice • Thistledown • Chips • On Velvet • Around the Town • We're Going to Be Rich • Mountains o' Mourne • Little Dolly Daydream • Kicking the Moon Around • Break the News • Stepping Toes • Follow Your Star • Hold My Hand • Lassie from Lancashire • Calling All Crooks • Penny Paradise • Save a Little Sunshine • Yes, Madam? • It's in the Air • Keep Smiling • My Irish Molly   224

1939

The Mikado • Me and My Pal • Let's Be Famous • Trouble Brewing • The Lambeth Walk • Music Hall Parade • Shipyard Sally • Discoveries • Come on George! • Lucky to Me   246

1940

The Proud Valley • Laugh It Off • Band Waggon • Let George Do It! • Pack Up Your Troubles • Old Mother Riley in Society • Garrison Follies • Somewhere in England • Crook's Tour • Under Your Hat • Sailors Three • Spare a Copper • Cavalcade of Variety   257

1941

Danny Boy • Turned Out Nice Again • Facing the Music • He Found a Star • I Thank You • Gert and Daisy's Weekend • Bob's Your Uncle • Hi Gang! • South American George   274

1942

Somewhere in Camp • Let the People Sing • Gert and Daisy Clean Up • Much Too Shy • Rose of Tralee • We'll Smile Again • Somewhere on Leave • We'll Meet Again • King Arthur Was a Gentleman • The Balloon Goes Up   282

1943

It's That Man Again • Variety Jubilee • Get Cracking • The Dummy Talks • Happidrome • I'll Walk Beside You • Miss London Ltd • Theatre Royal • Rhythm Serenade • Somewhere in Civvies • Up with the Lark • Down Melody Lane • It's in the Bag • Battle for Music • Bell-Bottom George 294

1944

Demobbed • Bees in Paradise • Heaven is Round the Corner • Candles at Nine • One Exciting Night • Champagne Charlie • Give Me the Stars • Fiddlers Three • My Ain Folk • Dreaming • He Snoops to Conquer 306

1945

Flight from Folly • For You Alone • I'll Be Your Sweetheart • I Didn't Do It • Waltz Time • Home Sweet Home 318

Notes to the Text 329
Select Bibliography 342
Index of Film Titles 344
General Index 349

Illustrations

1.	*Everything in Life* (1936)	Frontispiece
2.	*Just for a Song* (1930)	18
3.	*Greek Street* (1930)	20
4.	*The Yellow Mask* (1930)	22
5.	*His Lordship* (1932)	41
6.	*Marry Me* (1932)	48
7.	*Born Lucky* (1932)	54
8.	*The Little Damozel* (1933)	58
9.	*Britannia of Billingsgate* (1933)	67
10.	*Early to Bed* (1933)	72
11.	*Princess Charming* (1934)	92
12.	*Over the Garden Wall* (1934)	99
13.	*Temptation* (1934)	117
14.	*Squibs* (1935)	126
15.	*Two Hearts in Harmony* (1935)	147
16.	*Cheer Up!* (1936)	153
17.	*The Robber Symphony* (1936)	169
18.	*Southern Roses* (1936)	178
19.	*Everybody Dance* (1936)	181
20.	*Big Fella* (1937)	206
21.	*Keep Fit* (1937)	213
22.	*Sailing Along* (1938)	227
23.	*We're Going to Be Rich* (1938)	233
24.	*Let's Be Famous* (1939)	249
25.	*Band Waggon* (1940)	262
26.	*He Found a Star* (1941)	277
27.	*We'll Smile Again* (1942)	289
28.	*King Arthur Was a Gentleman* (1942)	292
29.	*Champagne Charlie* (1944)	311
30.	*I'll Be Your Sweetheart* (1945)	321

All illustrations are courtesy of Paul Guinery.

Every effort has been made to trace the copyright holders of the illustrations; apologies are offered for any omission, and the publishers will be pleased to add any necessary acknowledgement in subsequent editions.

Preface and Acknowledgements

After serving in the RAF during the Great War, Herbert Wilcox, destined to be one of the most prolific producers and directors in the British film industry, worked as a salesman with silent films to sell. The business of making films would be his lifelong obsession. Wilcox's greatest contribution to the medium, Anna Neagle, recalled how on the threshold of his career,

> He spent many weary months plodding round grey, windy streets and waiting in the draughty foyers of run-down cinemas to see the managers. He knew the sort of people who 'went to the pictures' not in the very few lush cinemas of London's West End but in the shabby places across the country which were the bread-and-butter of the film makers.

Herbert Wilcox was travelling by train, revisiting the industrial north with Anna Neagle and actor Michael Wilding, scheduled for personal appearances. The films Wilcox made with them held up an image of metropolitan sophistication, ersatz glamour and romance that a vast proportion of their audiences could only have dreamed of. As the train sped past the dreary, blackened landscape,

> with rows and rows of small brick houses, Herbert touched Michael's arm and pointed through the train window. 'Never forget, Michael,' he said. 'The people who live in those houses are the people we are making films for, they *need* entertainment.'[1]

I have spent too many years looking for a book about British musical films that is not only informative but attempts a long-overdue critical reassessment of the genre. Perhaps that book already exists. I have not found it. The lack of attention paid to these films in the mountain of literature about cinema, much of it too academic for digestible words, suggests that they are, perhaps with a handful of exceptions, unworthy of remembrance or reconsideration, and cannot be accepted as art of the meanest kind. The veil has too often been drawn. One of the characters in the 1945 film *I'll Be Your Sweetheart* refers to the sort of musical numbers that crop up on almost every page of *Cheer Up!* as 'gutter music', presumably even lower on the intellectual scale than Noël Coward's 'cheap music'. We should at least remember that in *Private Lives* Coward hit a nail on the head by recognising cheap music's potency.

---

1   Anna Neagle, *There's Always Tomorrow* (London: W. H. Allen, 1974), p. 75.

Perhaps the time is right for such cheap gutter music to make itself heard again. In recent years many musical films of the 1930s and 1940s have resurfaced via modern technology, on DVD and on YouTube, making them accessible to a new generation of cineastes. The advent of a television channel, Talking Pictures, devoted to the showing of 'old' films, has revealed many long-lost delights to an even wider audience, now able to gasp at the naïve choreography of Bernard Vorhaus's *Street Song* or the manic destructiveness of Frank Randle. Perhaps this is the appropriate moment for a book that considers this too-long overlooked history, critically and affectionately.

I believe that *Cheer Up!* is the first attempt at a detailed reassessment of over 320 British musical films made from the beginning of sound up to the end of World War II. It makes no claim to be a cinematic history of that period, and is neither completely comprehensive nor encyclopedic. It is not a history of the various British film studios that produced musical films. It is not a history of technical advances in film-making during the period.

Many other books that deal (usually only in part, and often with a pronounced lack of enthusiasm) with this genre scatter references to specific films throughout the text. *Cheer Up!* presents the films made between 1929 and September 1945 in the chronological order prescribed by Denis Gifford in his *British Film Catalogue*. Gifford's decision to catalogue films 'chronologically in order of their initial exhibition' seems eminently sensible, although, as he states, 'It is common for films to be dated by their dates of release [although] this practice has not been followed here.' Gifford defines the 'initial exhibition' date thus: 'by date of first advertisement, first review, notice, or listing in contemporary publications; by date of first Trade Show; by date of showing to the British Board of Film Censors', etc. His sequencing of films is 'divided into years, and then into months. Days of the month are not shown, and the films should not be taken as chronologically arranged within the monthly divisions.'[2] This, then, is the sequencing used throughout *Cheer Up!*.

This allows for a linear approach, making the possibility of narrative in a book that at first glance may seem to be merely a collection of essays (if that is not too pretentious a description). In theory, the reader is perhaps better able to follow, with the help of the attendant index, the genre's progress. In this way, *Cheer Up!* is intended as a book that can be read rather than as a reference work. Like many of the pictures it discusses, I hope it lacks pretension.

Be warned: your favourite picture may not be showing. Deciding what films should or should not be included has been a formidable challenge, involving the inevitable difficulty of determining what the British musical film might be. For our purposes, the definition remains flexible. It will be immediately apparent to anyone idling through these pages that some films easily qualify. Who will question the

---

2 Denis Gifford, *The British Film Catalogue 1895–1985: A Reference Guide* (London: David and Charles, 1986), p. 9.

inclusion of a Jessie Matthews picture, or a George Formby, as a musical film? Some may. After all, in Matthews's films the songs tend to emerge from character or situation (in a descriptive word relished by film academics, they are 'diegetic'), but Formby's songs happen because he finds a ukulele, often in the most surprising locations. In many of the films included here, the songs have absolutely nothing to do with the plot, but this has not been used as a reason to exclude them. For some of the entries, one song (even a snatch at one) has been enough to pass it for certification. Some of the titles even qualify as 'film musicals' rather than 'musical films'.

The amount of production information given, and information about the musical content of a picture, varies from title to title. Films lasting under sixty minutes have been excluded. Although presented as home-grown products, several 'British' pictures were made in foreign studios. Audiences for these may have been unaware that they were watching 'bilinguals' or 'trilinguals' made in various versions in different languages. These were sometimes denied official classification as British films. In her monumental history of British film-making in the 1930s, Rachael Low sternly refuses to consider them as domestic product. I have policed entries less stringently, and waved them in. When dealing with what might be considered a 'series' of films starring major British performers, the book does not necessarily include every one of them.

Any author is indebted to others, and those who have helped me towards cheering up will know who they are. I am indebted to the film historian and biographer Roger Mellor, who has consistently provided encouragement and advice as I climbed the hill of this book. My thanks are due to Dr Jo Botting and the staff of the British Film Institute, and those of other libraries. Paul Guinery has generously allowed me access to his quite extraordinary archive of sheet music. Michael King's technical advice has been indispensable. My editor Michael Middeke has believed in this book from its inception, and I have to thank him and the staff at Boydell, including Megan Milan and Nick Bingham, for seeing it through. I have also had the inestimable benefit of a perceptive and assiduous copy-editor in Ingalo Thomson. Any idiocies that remain are, as John Hanson once sang (but never in a British musical film), 'mine alone'.

My apologies are extended to those who search in vain for the film of their choice, although the apology is not humble. As the witty chronicler of British music-hall, Michael Kilgarriff, writes in the introduction to his gargantuan guide to popular song between 1860 and 1920, *Sing Us One of the Old Songs*, 'This compilation may have its shortcomings, but as The Great Macdermott used to sing, "It's Better Than Nothing At All".

Adrian Wright
Norfolk, 2019

adrianwright.online

1929

At times, this is R. C. Sherriff's *Journey's End* with songs and frocks
Splinters

Auld Lang Syne
Under the Greenwood Tree
Dark Red Roses

The Co-Optimists
Splinters

SEPTEMBER

Returning from Hollywood in February, the producer-director Herbert Wilcox proclaimed that talkies were now the essential American entertainment. It was an example that British studios would ignore at their peril, and a rush to sound, rather than a persistence with silence, ensued with remarkable rapidity. The impact of Hollywood's *The Jazz Singer* when shown in London and Glasgow in 1928 spurred domestic cinemas to install the American Western Electric System. By March 1929 the Elstree studios of British International Pictures (BIP) were made ready for the talking, and singing, and dancing, picture. The impact of sound was particularly relevant to musical film. Drama and comedy had managed well enough on screen without it, but the inability to incorporate sound had, understandably, somewhat limited the making of the musical film.

From the silent years of the 1920s through to their filmic decline in the 1950s, operetta and what might be called 'classical' music played their part in British pictures. Ivor Novello bookends the period, being the star of one of the very first musical films and the creator and composer of one of the last. The absurdity of attempting a silent film version of a nineteenth-century opera may not have occurred to those responsible for the 1922 *The Bohemian Girl*. It is likely that Novello was cast as the gypsy Thaddeus – a Polish officer in disguise – purely on his good looks; there is certainly an argument for Novello being the Welsh answer to Rudolph Valentino. On this occasion, the *New York Tribune* reported that 'Ivor Novello seems bored with the whole thing, though there has never been such a gorgeous profile on the screen since Francis X. Bushman's.'[1]

With no distracting dialogue, audiences were at least free to feast on that profile. Patrons arriving late at showings, having no hints of what the story might be about, must have been even more puzzled than those who would later treat the talkies with equal disrespect, only leaving the cinema when they realised 'This is where I came in'. The most obvious problem with Harley Knoles and Rosina Henley's screenplay for *The Bohemian Girl* was that Balfe's music, including his parlour-room hit 'I Dreamt I Dwelt in Marble Halls', was nowhere to be heard. Silent filming of a drama or comedy was one thing; silent filming of a musical work another. There seemed little reason to adapt the piece, especially since Balfe's librettist, Alfred Bunn, was a hack writer of melodrama. Such an accusation might justifiably be made of some who would contribute screenplays to British musical films after the arrival of sound.

Films may have been silent, but British studios were already plundering opera. In the same year as *The Bohemian Girl*, Gaumont offered the British public a series of 'Tense Moments from Opera', featuring the juicier portions of *Samson and Delilah*, *Rigoletto* and a host of other stage works including two Irish bed-mates of *The Bohemian Girl*, Julius Benedict's *The Lily of Killarney* and William Wallace's *Maritana*. The most 'tense moments' may have been in wondering if audiences were going to sit through such stuff. In 1923 the popular star Lilian Hall Davis played the heroine in a silent *I Pagliacci*.

Also in 1923 Herbert Wilcox produced and directed *Chu Chin Chow*, classified as British although shot in Berlin. *Variety* was initially impressed, applauding 'The finest spectacle yet produced by a British firm',[2] but subsequently changed its tune, denouncing it as 'crudely directed' and noting a cast 'made up of crepe-adorned characters whose comedy falls short and whose inability to express pathos is pathetic'.[3]

Throughout the 1920s, Phonofilm, the invention of Lee de Forest, was turning out shorts at its Clapham studio, plundering drama (Sybil Thorndike in extracts from Shaw's *St Joan*) and opera singers (as early as 1922 'the coloured prima donna' from the New York Met, Abbie Mitchell, was featured in 'Songs of Yesterday'); anything, in fact, that might divert the public and not take too long. A Phonofilm of cross-talking act Ben Bard and Jack Pearl has credible clarity. In 1926 Phonofilm caught Betty Chester, one of the 'Co-Optimists' concert-party, singing 'Pig-Tail Alley', Gwen Farrar and Billy Mayerl joining up for 'I've Got A Sweetie On The Radio', and Paul England (a busy, if forgotten, early film performer) and Dorothy Boyd in the exhilarating 'I'm Knee-Deep In Daisies And Head Over Heels In Love With You'.

In 1927 John E. Blakeley's 'Cameo Operas' series featured extracts in condensed versions of works that could be synchronised in cinemas with live singers and orchestras; how many managements took advantage of this troublesome possibility is unknown. The same year, the Edwardian favourite *The Arcadians*, vaguely remembered for its genteel Lionel Monckton score, was an early success for director Victor Saville, but with the arrival of sound British studios turned more purposely to operetta and classical music with *City of Song*, made in three language versions (a trilingual) and exhibited in Britain in January 1931 following its Vienna debut in October 1930 as *Die Singende Stadt*.

Charitably, we may see the early development of the British musical film, already in the shadow of the phenomenally successful Al Jolson's singing fool, as a period of experiment. There may be an argument for seeing the development of the British musical film through most of the years up to 1945 as a continuation of that experiment.

It is generally agreed that Alfred Hitchcock's *Blackmail* is the first British talkie, stealing a march on the new medium in June 1929. The legitimacy of *Blackmail*'s claim to pre-eminence may yet be challenged. Hitchcock's understanding with BIP was that he would direct a *silent* film; on the sly, he made a *talkie*. Alongside his major achievement, others worked at sound film more modestly, producing musical shorts. The essential brevity of a song, and its ability to deliver 'light' entertainment, provided ideal fodder for the 'musical' short. Electrocord Films was busy, filming artists miming to gramophone records, offering such delights as 'The Gay Caballero' and 'I'll Take You Home Again, Kathleen'. Butcher's Films, destined to be a major force in British musical films, had 115 Electrocord machines installed in British cinemas by the end of 1929. Other synchronising systems included Filmophone, Syntok Talking Films and British Phonotone. These cumbersome developments were doomed to be short-lived.

Meanwhile, musical shorts poured forth, as in BIP's nine-minute *An Arabian Night* featuring Paul England as an upstanding Englishman and Alma Vane as an alluring princess, presumably promising an out-of-the-ordinary nocturnal Eastern delight. Mr England was joined by Mimi Crawford for *In an Old World Garden*, their love-making among ghosts lasting one minute longer than the previous Arabian night. BIP pushed the boat out with the twelve-minute *Chelsea Nights*, in which Crawford was teamed with the continental Carl Brisson. In the rush to be fashionably heard, films originally intended and released as silent were recalled by studios to have sound added. The quality of much of such works may be imagined. In 1929 over 200 films shown were sound films. At the start of 1931, 685 picture-houses in Britain had sound equipment; by the beginning of 1932 these had grown to 3,537.

The emergence of some sort of musical film with sound glimmers feebly in *Auld Lang Syne*, silent when listed in April, but singing, after its aural facelift, in September. In several ways the picture established a template that would remain in place for at least the next sixteen years. At the end of World War II musical films were still being produced with titles 'inspired' by songs of the long ago: *My Ain Folk* (1944) and Harry Dacre's 1899 *I'll Be Your Sweetheart* (1945). *Auld Lang Syne* may be seen as the first example in sound pictures as a vehicle for its star, the eminent Scots entertainer of the music-halls, Harry Lauder. This, too, was a trait that the British musical film would inevitably follow, providing platforms for a panoply of performers as yet undreamed of, among them Gracie Fields, Jessie Matthews and George Formby, along with their supporting casts.

British films also needed plots, and these, when it came to the musical film, tended to the conservative. During these birth pangs of the genre, the idea that a musical film should be in any way thought-provoking seems not to have been seriously considered. For *Auld Lang Syne*, George Pearson, Hugh E. Wright and Patrick L. Mannock's screenplay had Lauder as Sandy McTavish, leaving bonny Scotland in search of his two children. Worryingly, he discovers that they have not turned out as he might have imagined. Despite his disappointment, McTavish finds time to sing 'Keep Right On To The End Of The Road', 'I Love A Lassie', 'It's A Fine Thing To Sing', 'A Wee Deoch An' Doris' and, inevitably, the title song – only made possible by the addition of sound after the silent version was revisited.

Auld Lang Syne also points to the future in its use of non-diegetic music, pulling in songs that do not arise naturally from the drama but are inserted into it, having little and often nothing to do with the propulsion of story or furthering our understanding of character. In this way, the musical content of a film such as Stanley Lupino's 1936 *Cheer Up!* (one of the jolliest to be found in this volume) may be said to be diegetic, as is *The Sound of Music* or *Camelot*.

Made at Cricklewood Studios by Welsh-Pearson-Elder, *Auld Lang Syne*, produced and directed by one of the most gentlemanly of old-school British directors George Pearson, may stake a claim as one of the first British sound musical films, but in essence it belongs to the earlier age. Pearson made it as a silent, subsequently adding the songs with Lauder miming, courtesy of the RCA sound-on-film technique. As Rachael Low (a sage to whom anyone writing about the genre must turn) explains, 'However clever, this was neither a talkie nor a true sound film. The company [Welsh-Pearson-Elder] unwisely continued to make silent pictures, closing shortly afterwards.'[4] The British film industry, often uncertain as to which way to turn, was suffused with such curiosities in its post-natal state.

British International Pictures was to be a trail-blazer in establishing British musical films. The rustic romance **Under the Greenwood Tree** was unusual in being one of the very few of the genre to be based on what we might see as a 'classical' literary source, Thomas Hardy's 1872 novel. Originally made as a silent, BIP's film was presented to the public with sound, its music attributed to Hubert Bath and played by the studios' own British International Symphony Orchestra, arranged and conducted by BIP's resident musical director John Reynders. The quality of the film's creators was not in question, with Harry Lachman as director, and a screenplay by Monckton Hoffe and Frank Launder from an adaptation by Lachman and Rex Taylor. So seriously was the subject considered that Sidney Gilliat (who would go on to make films with Launder through to the 1960s) was credited as literary adviser; very few productions owned up to having such personnel. Admired for the cinematography of Claude Friese-Greene, and for Marguerite Allan's performance as Fanny Day, the saga of parochial church politics in 1870 Dorset was

OCTOBER

The British Sound Film Productions' melodramatic 'Drama of Today', *Dark Red Roses*, made at the soon-to-be-burned-down Wembley Park studios, was a Phonofilm deploying the de Forest recording system. It had much to recommend it: a 'domestic horror'[5] based on a short story by Stacy Aumonier, handsomely designed by Oscar Friedrich Werndorff, and directed by Sinclair Hill. Stewart Rome, one of the most popular silent film actors, played sculptor David Cardew, who thinks his marriage to Laura (Frances Doble) is threatened by the arrival of a handsome cellist. When she suggests that David sculpts the young man's hands, David plans to trap the interloper's hands in a plaster cast and cut them off. The screenplay by Leslie Howard Gordon and Harcourt Templeman was enlivened by Hill's encouraging the cast, including the charming child siblings Jack and Jill Clayton, to extemporise. The film's title was turned into a vocal valse by the prolific theatre composer Philip Braham and lyricist T. Barry.

One of the earliest examples of a British musical film that wedded criminality with music, it also offered an opportunity to glimpse the Ballets Russes, with Anton Dolin, Lydia Lopokova and George Balanchine performing Mussorgsky's 'Persian Dance' to Balanchine's choreography. Glimmers of ballet would infiltrate the British musical film throughout the period. They persist as late as 1944 in the fleeting but delicate Players' Theatre-like ballet sequence of *Champagne Charlie*.

NOVEMBER

In its need for available product, it was inevitable that British studios would instinctively turn to theatre, increasingly throughout the 1930s to musical comedy, revue, music-hall and that now thoroughly outdated art of concert party, of which *The Co-Optimists* remains the only genuine example on film. The Co-Optimists (its title joined 'co-operation' with 'optimism') was the most successful concert party or, as it was billed, 'pierrotic entertainment' of all time, and the only one to achieve a ten-year run in London, beginning in 1921. Its players through its best years included Stanley Holloway doing 'Sam, Pick Up Thy Musket', Phyllis Monkman, avuncular comedian Davy Burnaby, and the show's co-creators, performer Laddie Cliff and composer Melville Gideon.

Gideon had a rare, immediately recognisable style, languid, reminiscent, melancholic, and quite unlike any other composer working in musical films in the 1930s. Unfortunately, by the time Gordon Craig Productions got around to making its film version, the Co-Optimists had already been at it for eight years, and the quality of the numbers used for the film was some way off the finest that Gideon (often with Cliff) had written. No one performed them better than Gideon, accompanying himself at the piano. If only the film had used some of his best: 'I'm Tickled To Death I'm Single', 'Little Lacquer Lady', 'I've Fallen In Love With A Voice' and the lingering 'You Forgot To Remember'. A more enterprising idea would have been a musical biopic of the man himself. In 1931 Gideon was bankrupted for the third time, owing income tax and £7,000, with assets of just over £10 and a set of dress studs. He died two years later.

Produced by New Era at Twickenham, devised by Gideon and Cliff and directed by Cliff and Edwin Greenwood, *The Co-Optimists* suffered from unimaginative camerawork which failed to translate the show's theatricality. The numbers included were 'Bow Wow', Holloway singing 'London Town', 'My Girl's Face', 'It's For You', 'Maybe Me, Maybe You', 'If It Weren't For The Likes Of Us Chaps', 'Wung Lung Too', 'You've Gotta Beat Out The Rhythm', 'When The Rich Man Rides By', 'Till The Wheel Comes Off', 'Down Love Lane' and 'My Lady's Eyes'.

The *Bioscope* tactfully reported that the picture was 'shown in a form which will be appreciated in every English-speaking country',[6] but *Variety* discovered 'a species of lightly factitious, well-mannered and definitely British song and dance entertainment […] drab and lifeless. It's an optical monotone that could never get by except in houses regularly presenting foreign films.'[7] The *Observer* foresaw no international success, for 'the readers of *Punch* and A. A. Milne, the followers of the Gilbert and Sullivan tradition, will find much to please them in a twodimensional copy of [this] entertainment, a mechanically able record of their songs and turns' in a piece that was 'neither fully theatrical nor fully photographic. There is no stress either way, and to be successful a film must have stress.'[8]

Sadly, no one thought of getting the other, and in many ways more fascinating, British concert party, The Fol de Rols, into a British studio; it long outlived the Co-Optimists, surviving from 1911 to 1976. Along the way it employed many artists who went on to substantial careers, among them Arthur Askey, the Western Brothers, and Elsie and Doris Waters.

DECEMBER

Splinters paved the way for future British musical films, even if too few lived up to its promise. This is a wonderful piece, produced by Herbert Wilcox (among the best of his productions) for British and Dominions, and directed by Jack Raymond. Written by W. P. Lipscomb, it is built around the true story of the concert party begun by serving soldiers at the West Front in France in 1916. When the conflict ended, the show went on to further success, promising '16 Soldiers and Every Soldier an Artiste', 'Supported by a Beauty Chorus of 40 – and Every One a Perfect

Gentleman'. It is particularly interesting to have a film that highlights the Splinters' company of female impersonators. Gentility and elegance was their essential; these were not Danny La Rue-type performers, and bore no resemblance to the more outré drag artists that may be familiar to us. It is the context of their dragging-up that is emphasised here, this collection of young, able servicemen happy to dress and act and sing and dance as females and at any moment be ready for battle. In this extraordinary situation, *Splinters* remains an important manifestation of gender identification.

As war rages outside, upper-crust officers decide that a concert party made up from the ranks is the very thing to keep up morale, and ex-pro Private Jones (Hal Jones) is charged with setting it up. 'There's a fellow in my unit who played Hamlet,' says one of the gentry officers. 'Would he be any good?' asks another. Probably not, for the men need diversion, laughter and song and, difficult in the circumstances with no female in sight, glamour. The suggestion of a singer who sings songs about 'tarts' is unwelcomed, but Jones auditions for performers, providing a consistently amusing sequence, accompanied by no less than Carroll Gibbons on piano. Beyond the stilted officers, the casting is a joy, not least in the sublime Sydney Howard, one of the most idiosyncratic and underrated of actors, with the consistent demeanour of an over-anxious child who mimics life. The recurring theme of his double-act with Nelson Keys is beautifully done.

The storyline – putting on a show – may be the most predictable, but the achievement here is to make us believe that this is happening during World War I. In fact, the film is so convincing that we have to pull ourselves back from believing that war really is raging outside. This, it *must* be, is realism. The whizzbangs coming over No Man's Land, the filthy uniforms, the privations of the men's quarters, the very sounds of war, the cramped dug-outs – all too real to be studio-bound – although we know better. They serve, too, to accentuate the poignancy and sense of shared experience that suffuses the whole, bringing the comic and musical sequences more effectively into focus. Even the appearance of what is obviously a model aeroplane doesn't kill the illusion. The battle scenes might easily have been inserted from existent footage, but are not, and are beautifully choreographed by Raymond across a war-scarred landscape that might have inspired a Paul Nash painting. At times, this is R. C. Sherriff's *Journey's End* with songs and frocks.

The first night of the *Splinters* concert party proves a great success, with its line of male pierrots, pointing a way forward to the opening sequence of television's *It Ain't Half Hot, Mum*, with Jones, sprightly and agreeable, dancing into their midst and singing of 'Lanky Carrie From Lancashire'. The unexpected moment comes with the appearance of Private Stone (Reg Stone). This is female impersonation without parody. Not surprisingly, the rows of testosterone-charged soldiers out front seem bewitched as he sings the charming 'I'll Be Getting Along'. The flirtation is blatant and endearing. Off-stage, the ultra-innocent Howard and Keys make the mistake of visiting Stone in his make-shift dressing-room, but he sucks on his pipe, tears off his wig and sends them packing. Stone returns for another number, the tempting 'Encore', telling the soldier-audience 'So kiss me half to death, and when I get my breath, I'll whisper dear, once more, encore …'. The slyness of this invitation to sexual repetition is remarkably obvious for 1929.

A lost-in-translation sketch between an attractive French girl (Stone) and British soldier (Jones) has as much innuendo, closing with a neat duet 'That's What I'm Trying To Say'. A smithy scena has a blacksmith (Wilfred Temple) singing 'At Greta Green', the boys and 'girls' filling the stage around him. At the last, the quiet before the storm, Jones turns pensively to 'Since I Fell In Love With You', but already war is at the door, and the show has to be abandoned. Stone and the Beauty Chorus scramble into their uniforms, putting them on over their stage clothes, giving a new meaning to 'battledress'. With a resonance far beyond that which may (possibly) have been appreciated at the time of its making, *Splinters* ends with everybody, no matter what their inclination or sexual orientation, coming together. Whatever deficiencies it displays, such as the halting speed of its dialogue (understandable at the beginning of sound), ninety years on this remains a remarkable achievement. In 1931 Walter Forde directed a sequel, *Splinters in the Navy*, reuniting Stone, Howard and Jones, followed by the 1937 *Splinters in the Air*, directed by Alfred Goulding.

1930

It is against the decadence of the Weimar Republic, starkly evoked in the Orpheum scenes, rather than the background of imperial Russia, that this picture unfolds   *The Flame of Love*

Comets
Elstree Calling
Raise the Roof
Song of Soho
Harmony Heaven
The Flame of Love
The Loves of Robert Burns
Just for a Song

Greek Street
Piccadilly Nights
The Brat (The Nipper)
The Yellow Mask
Spanish Eyes
Big Business
Why Sailors Leave Home

FEBRUARY

One immediate result, which could have been foreseen, of the introduction of sound-films, is necessarily to place at a disadvantage any film that is derived from musical sources. To quote an outstanding instance, who would want to see *The Arcadians* on the screen with an unsynchronised ballet and a loose fitting if they could have it with every bar of the well-remembered music infallibly accompanying the movements of the pretty Arcadians in their dances, or the antics of the comedians? The advent of mechanical synchronisation reads as a warning to keep away from all operas, 'grand' or light, from all musical comedies, from ballet, and leave such luxuries to the new devices with which the old ones cannot compete in accurate fitting. After all, there are plenty of other stories in the world.[1]

In its rush to make a sound picture that might 'place at a disadvantage any film that is derived from musical sources', the Alpha Film Corporation came up with *Comets*, in its way a prototype of the sort of revue-based compendium that British studios served up until the end of World War II, even feeding upon its own by using material from earlier compendiums to fill out the running time of new compendiums. Produced by Maurice J. Wilson and directed by Sasha Geneen, *Comets* was not without interest, featuring popular violinist Albert Sandler, celebrated clowns Noni and Horace, Heather Thatcher, piano entertainer Rex Evans, Flora le Breton (in 1929 she had appeared in a short, performing 'Poor Little Locked-Up Me'), and Gus McNaughton in the first of many appearances in British musical films. From music-hall, Billy Merson brought his biggest success 'The Spaniard

That Blighted My Life'. This was perhaps eclipsed by Charles Laughton and Elsa Lanchester performing 'Frankie and Johnny', and Miss Lanchester singing the Temperance ditty 'Please Sell No More Drink To My Father'. Alpha made only one other film, the 1930 *Infatuation* starring Jeanne de Casalis, and quit the field.

What might British International Pictures' *Elstree Calling* have been had Adrian Brunel's direction been allowed to reach the screen? It seems a very early example of the manhandling of a director's work on a British sound picture (its certificate described it as 'synchronised'). Strangely, this concoction of variety turns passes itself off as a film about presenting its acts on *television*, a word that at the time for many represented fantasy. Admittedly, in July 1930 the BBC made an essentially embryonic television transmission of Pirandello's *The Man with the Flower in His Mouth* (the BBC can't have been worried about the viewing figures), but the developments in cinema were just as current, more fast-moving and more exciting in every way.

Nevertheless, the dinner-jacketed compere of *Elstree Calling* Tommy Handley, acting as a sort of master of ceremonies talking almost straight to camera, could with some justification exclaim 'Wonders will never cease'. The spectacle that followed didn't always live up to this. A fleeting glimpse of the studio floor at Elstree, and it's straight into Teddy Brown on xylophone, behind him a gargantuan supersized cardboard version of himself, the jest pushed home by tasteless comments about Brown's size.

The curiously compiled light entertainment continues with a frantic tap-dancing routine by The Three Eddies, black men blacked up as grotesque parodies of their race. Bridging the gap between acts is that friendliest of cockney characters Gordon Harker trying to get a television picture out of the most unpromising apparatus, or plum-voiced Donald Calthrop in a mercilessly unfunny running gag about Shakespeare, or a spoof murder sequence directed and subsequently remembered in embarrassment by Alfred Hitchcock. These fill-ins hit the studio floor with resounding dullness before the acts eat up most of the running time.

The West End is plundered for Helen Burnell's number 'My Heart Is Saying' from the then current stage show *The House That Jack Built*. A rare opportunity to see what a London revue of the period would have looked like, 'My Heart Is Saying' is an odd experience, with Burnell's voodoo-like contortions and the uncoordinated movements of the Charlot Girls suggesting that British choreography (on film, as well as on stage) had some way to go to match Hollywood. Burnell returns with lanky and likeable Jack Hulbert for an Ivor Novello song 'The Thought Never Entered My Head', with no less peculiar dancing.

The Charlot Girls are *en travesti* in soldierly mood for another badly organised dance sequence. There seems no reason why cinema audiences should have been expected to sit through such stuff, when they would probably have seen better at the local Hippodrome. At times the film seems to be sending its audience back to the stage, not least with the inclusion of two music-hall performers, Will Fyffe Jnr ('and now for a little Scotch', says Handley in introduction, delivering another of the scriptwriter's deadly lines) and the irrepressible Lily Morris. 'How Can A Fellow Be Happy When Happiness Costs Such A Lot?' asks Fyffe, along the way scattering hoary jokes about the meanness of the Scotsman, but he seems throughout to be playing to the front row of a theatre's stalls. Morris does rather better with two of her staple numbers, 'He's Only A Working Man' and 'Why Am I Always The Bridesmaid?', but for all her skills these come over as curiosities that by 1930 were past their best (she had introduced the last in 1917).

The presentation of these music-hall veterans is in no way cinematic, but the style persists whenever music-hall artists were put on screen in British musical films: witness the appearances of Florrie Forde and Marie Kendall in *Say It with Flowers*. Basically, cinema could not bring about the intimate inter-reaction between the stage artist and the live audience, and may be said only to have overcome the problem in 1944, in Cavalcanti's masterful *Champagne Charlie*. This Ealing biopic about two music-hall greats remains a little-appreciated work, but is the most exuberant of the attempts to recreate an atmosphere of the old halls and the vigour of their performers, and – culminating in its star Tommy Trinder looking straight into the audience's eye as he invites it to join a toast to the long dead days of music-hall – the finest evocation of this lost art.

But still Elstree insists on calling, through those Charlot Girls (just as slackly choreographed as before) explaining that 'A Lady's Maid Is Always In The Know', presumably to audiences who had few servant problems. Teddy Brown, big as before, comes back doing an impersonation of a train, but the cameraman seems not to know the scene is over, leaving Brown staring vacantly at the camera long after an editor should have cut him short.

Variety claimed that *Elstree Calling* 'has everything such a film needs, and does nothing with it […] the material is old where it is not amateurish' and 'many things start well and then do not come off'.[2] More kindly, *Bioscope* hailed 'a very successful attempt to present together so varied and brilliant a collection of popular artists'.[3] Subsequently, a less effusive verdict fell somewhere between these two, noting that Handley's references at the start of proceedings about the piece 'being drawn from Hollywood, Shoreditch and Ashby-de-la-Zouch' made no excuses for an essentially English production 'homelier, tattier and, on balance, prettier than the streamlined Revues, Parades and Follies with which Hollywood celebrated the coming of sound'.

Betty Balfour had been one of the most successful silent stars of British cinema in the 1920s, following her debut *Nothing Else Matters* (1920). Its director George Pearson described it as 'the eternal search for happiness' set in a music-hall world where a comic's life collapses. *Bioscope* suggested that 'low comedy methods never fail to appeal to a film audience'. Pearson then directed her in *Mary-Find-the-Gold*, by which time he had realised the potential of her perky screen personality. The screenwriter Eliot Stannard suggested the character of Squibs, the name suggestive of explosive fireworks, as ideal for Balfour. Clifford Seyler's comedy *Squibs* had played London during the Great War, and in 1921 Pearson's film adaptation proved an enormous success. All rights, except for America, were taken up after the movie exhibited in 1921, sparking something of a Squibs mania; Madame Tussaud made a waxwork of her.

Between them, Pearson and Balfour wasted no time exploiting the popularity of the cockney flower-girl (something owed to Shaw's *Pygmalion*), the following year turning out three sequels, *Squibs Wins the Calcutta Sweep*, which mixed murder with comedy, *Squibs M. P.* and *Squibs' Honeymoon*. In 1924 Balfour was named 'top British star' by readers of the *Daily News*, and 'top world star' by the *Daily Mirror* three years later. One of Balfour's most notable silents was *Love Life and Laughter*, written, produced and directed by Pearson, and considered one of the finest works of its period. *The Times* thought she 'once again proves she is the cleverest comedienne now playing in British films', alongside the *Evening News*' assertion that 'what few people there are who have not fallen beneath the spell of her pretty face, clever comedy, and sympathetic interpretation of human feelings must surely be captured by now'. In 1927 a pre-London tour of a stage musical built around her, *Up with the Lark*, suggested that she was not its ideal leading lady, and she was replaced.

As the new decade approached, all seemed set fair for Balfour's transition to talking pictures. The Austrian-British production of Hitchcock's *Champagne*, also known as *Bright Eyes*, was a collaboration between BIP and Sascha-Film, and at least had sound effects. *Variety* proclaimed it 'a lot of blithering drivel [...] Cheapest grind audiences may sit through this English made, and they are the only ones that will'.[4] On the cusp between silence and sound, Balfour was *The Vagabond Queen*, a sort of parody of *The Prisoner of Zenda*. In fact, her character wasn't far removed from that of Squibs, a London drudge standing in for a glamorous princess whose life is in danger. *Variety* thought it 'well worn'.[5] At the trade show, the subtitles got more laughs than the comedy itself. The film probably had personality disorders of its own, having been made in Germany as a silent in 1929, with some sound added the following year, and subsequently reissued as a partial talkie in 1931.

Balfour's first full talkie, BIP's **Raise the Roof**, was meant to establish her as a singing as well as speaking personality, but its backstage romance co-written by director Walter Summers and Philip Macdonald offered little opportunities, with Balfour as an actress named Maisie working in a touring musical, whose boss (Maurice Evans) falls for her. His father plans to sabotage the show's success, but Maisie squares it, getting her man, a successful musical and reconciliation with her boyfriend's father. The music was by Harry Carlton and Jay Whidden, William Helmore, and BIP's musical director Idris Lewis. The recording of speech and music was poor, but *Bioscope* detected that 'recent productions seem to suggest that the "backstage" story is likely to rival in public favour the everlasting Wild West drama, and for British audiences this story of theatrical life in the small towns of England should have a special appeal.'[6] Nevertheless, Balfour's role in it didn't raise much excitement, and Balfour and BIP parted company.

MARCH

BIP determinedly pursued musical film production at Elstree throughout the year, making what was effectively the first to be constructed around an established star, hitherto of silents. Danish matinee idol Carl Brisson was already assured box office when **Song of Soho** premiered. The product of three distinguished writers, Arthur Wimperis, Frank Launder and American Randall Faye, it had Brisson as an ex-foreign legionnaire at loose in Soho alongside his mate Nobby, helping his girl (Edna Davies) make a success of her local restaurant. When he is mistakenly accused of having killed a prostitute, his innocence is confirmed by a blind beggar who provides an alibi by having known the songs the legionnaire sang. If the plot was to hold up, Brisson's numbers needed to be catchy, and the songwriting team of Harry Carlton and Jay Whidden succeeded with 'Camille', 'There's Something About You That's Different', 'Lady Of The Moon' and 'Mademoiselle From Montparnasse'. *Song of Soho*, based on an original idea by its director Harry Lachman and Val Valentine, can certainly claim to be the first musical film set in that now tidied-away milieu. Its idea of twinning a light musical piece with a crime story was another first. *Bioscope* reported that 'Though the story is never tedious it is often unconvincing.'[7] It was however successful enough to encourage two more Brisson films in British studios, *Prince of Arcadia* and *Two Hearts in Waltz Time*, but these were made for the less-prestigious Nettlefold-Fogwell studios.

Song of Soho's screenwriters were also responsible for **Harmony Heaven**, but any spark of originality the Brisson vehicle had exhibited was missing in this pedestrian account of backstage romance directed by Thomas Bentley, who would work long and hard at the coal face of British films. Although it was originally released with some colour sequences, a coldness pervades it, with dull and ugly sets, and obvious difficulties with taming the sound.

At a time when West End musical stars were in abundance, it seems odd that John Maxwell's production should have hired none of them. Were Ivor Novello, Fred Astaire (then in London), Bobby Howes, and such not available? Was it, more commendably, that Maxwell's idea was to create film stars from rough clay? Was it that prominent stage performers simply weren't interested in making films? There is enough evidence to suggest that they regarded them as a lower form of art, not to be taken seriously. There must have been better screen material than its frail leading man, Stuart Hall, although there is something quite touching about his presence. The chorus girl he ends up with was played by Polly Ward, whose career would include *The Kentucky Minstrels*, *Shipmates o' Mine* and (most delightfully) *Hold My Hand*. With these young players at the helm, *Harmony Heaven*, as the first of countless backstage British musical films, has a good deal to answer for.

To its credit, it doesn't drag in disassociated variety acts to spin out the running time, and has some decently organised dance routines arranged by *The Flame of Love*'s choreographer Alexander Oumansky. For British cinema audiences, *Harmony Heaven* offered its first insight into a theatrical rehearsal as a big new London show is being prepared. Eager male dancers in an assortment of natty home-knits enjoy watching auditionee Bob Farrell (Hall) hoping to get into the production by singing a composition of his own, 'Nobody Knows Where The Fairies Play'. He is roundly mocked, despite having introduced himself with a truly Hollywood bravado: 'I'm not a dancer, but I've got a song here that'll make this show a success.' Rejected, he is rescued by pretty Billie Breeze (Ward), taken back to her flat, fed (a good idea in the circumstances), and has to listen to some peppy music on the gramophone. She advises him to 'write a real song that a real man would sing to a real girl that he was in love with'. Hall confirms our suspicions by replying, 'I don't think it's going to be so difficult, *now*.'

With new-found confidence, Bob sings his new number 'That's All That Matters' to a mystified broker's man who thinks he's being propositioned. It's one of the unexpected side-swipes at homosexuality; another comes when Bill Shine, uncredited as a somewhat effeminate chorus boy, can't come up with a manly voice, and Bob, sensing his opportunity, gets the job. From here on, there are sequences that – unlikely as it seems – propel the film into surrealism, as when a moustachioed baritone dressed in bathing costume sings 'What's The Good Of Moonlight When There's No One To Love?', backed by the chorus in what appears to be Edwardian beachwear. Oumansky follows up with a strange routine to the 'Raggedy Romp' involving head-bandaged men in bath-chairs. Now, *Harmony Heaven* (yes, it's the show within the film) is a hit, conducted from the pit by John Reynders, in fact the musical director for British International Pictures.

When the swanky leading man falls by the wayside, Bob is pushed on to sing the show's theme song, helped by the chorus, the girls dressed as so many Bo-Peeps and the men jumping about in jodhpurs and cowboy hats. A brief burst of 'The Prehistoric Blues' at a soirée hosted by Lady Violet (Trilby Clarke) makes us wish the number wasn't cut short. Her ladyship is after Bob, but she is no competition for Billie, in whose arms he ends. By this time Oumansky has staged another ambitious routine up down and along a massive staircase with the company looking like metallic tin soldiers, furiously tap-dancing as the cameras attempt Busby Berkeley-like aerial shots. American songwriters Edward Brandt and Charlie Pola provided the generous score.

The Flame of Love was fanned by Anna May Wong, the Chinese-American actress who had just played a doomed innocent in *Piccadilly* (1929), made by BIP originally as a silent but with sound added the following year. For the critic Hugh Castle, Ewald André Dupont's film was no more than 'typical' of the British studios, 'one of the world's worst', and as late as the 1980s Leslie Halliwell was telling readers that the film was 'no longer watchable with a straight face'.[8] Posterity has disagreed, to the extent that *Piccadilly* is sometimes cited as high art, personifying its period and creating in its female star one of its first vividly manufactured icons of cinema.

Appropriately for a movie issued trilingually, the follow-up to *Piccadilly* was an international affair, with all three versions – English, French and German – made at Elstree, repackaged for France as *Hai Tang* and for Germany as *Der Weg zur Schande* (*The Road to Dishonour*). Wong played in all three versions, produced by Richard Eichberg and co-directed by Walter Summers. The complications of producing different language editions with changing personnel must have been considerable. For the French version, Marcel Vibert and Robert Ancelin were drafted in as leading men, and Jean Kemm imported to assist with direction at the BIP studios already buzzing with talented émigrés, many working on *The Flame of Life*. Producer and director Eichberg was German, as were Willi Herrmann and Werner Schlichting working alongside British art director Clarence Elder on décor, as were cinematographers Heinrich Gärtner (tidied into Henry Gartner for his British career), Bruno Mondi and Otto Baecker, with scenario and dialogue by Irish Monckton Hoffe, who would go on to work on several British film musicals, and by the Austrian Adolf Lantz and Polish Ludwig Wolff.

Prominent among the émigré team assembled by BIP was Vienna-born composer Hans May, already established – as were all the émigré participants – in silents. One of the least remembered of composers, May had a long and productive career, totalling fifty-six features as well as two London stage musicals, the 'Venetian' *Carissima* (1948) and *Wedding in Paris* (1954). His fifty-second 'overture in the dark' for *The Flame of Love* heralds a solidly musical film. As Geoff Brown has understood, 'As a true child of Vienna, Hans May's default mode as a composer was always the melodic, the charming, the sentimental'.[9] May's canvas is substantial, whether focusing on the almond-eyed purity of Hai-Tang's singing, seeing her writhe through a dance sequence dressed in a dazzlingly beaded and tasselled costume, or having Hai Tang's lover, the dewy-eyed Lt Boris (John Longden) singing the praises of old Russia at the piano. The authenticity of the moment is enhanced by the fact that Longden isn't dubbed, and can't sing. May adjusts brilliantly to the extravagant royal levee in honour of the Grand Duke, whose first sight of Hai Tang over-excites him. The American censors would not be happy with the Grand Duke's lustful intentions, or Lt Boris's physical adoration of her.

The sexual situation is frankly stated. British audiences must have gaped at the ensuing scenes in the Orpheum, a rowdy house where the showgirls dress as prancing horses, drink, smoke and show acres of thigh. How must this have gone down at the Alexandra Cinema, Newton Abbot? Clearly, this is a culture to which Hai Tang must never subscribe. At these moments *The Flame of Love* is at its best, notable for the excess it disarmingly portrays. When it flags, as in the cabaret presented to the Grand Duke, there is room for an act already seen in *Elstree Calling*, the Balalaika Choral Orchestra with attendant Cossacks and plate-spinning acrobats. Such padding swerves the film off course from its central love theme, which suffers from the same affliction that had affected BIP's *Atlantic* (1929) – painfully slow dialogue. With the new commodity of sound, the placement and enunciation of the script was over-emphasised, inevitably creating a melodramatic air. This was unhelpful in a screenplay that had Wong telling Longden, 'The day will come when you and I will go a different way. It must be so.'

Thankfully, words are mostly unnecessary when Wong fills the screen, cross-legged, shimmering and gently stroking a balalaika, her long fingers winding about her body in some strange reptilian rite. It has to be said that when Wong speaks, much of the mystical allure vanishes. We can sympathise with Lt Boris at her unexpected death in the final moments of the film; he will come to realise, as we have, that such purity and steadfastness stands little chance of survival in a wicked world. It is against the decadence of the Weimar Republic, starkly evoked in the Orpheum scenes, rather than the background of imperial Russia, that this picture unfolds. In its subversive way, it reflects Hai Tang's predicament, being of a race misunderstood by Caucasians, back at the 1930 audience. It is for us to decide if the wonder that surrounded Wong at that time had more than a smidgen of curiosity value. Her death is perhaps too obliging, her last supplication to an alien society. For *Bioscope*, the film 'makes effective drama of a very conventional kind, and holds the interest, though it can hardly be said to raise the emotions, as all the characters belong to the stage rather than to real life'.[10]

The Loves of Robert Burns was producer Herbert Wilcox's first biopic talkie; there had been a silent *Nell Gwynne* (Dorothy Gish) in 1926. The Scot's biography came with the usual Wilcox trumpeting – 'All-Talking, Singing and Dance [sic]' – although historians are unsure of how much of a dancer Burns was. Wilcox's career included various biopics, with subjects including Nell Gwynne (or Gwyn as the 1934 version had it), Peg of Old Drury, Queen Victoria (basically his 1937 film remade the following year with the same star), Odette and Florence Nightingale. It was no accident that these roles would be played by Wilcox's wife Anna Neagle. The stars of *The Loves of Robert Burns* had rather less pulling power. Joseph Hislop, a British singer who had sung in international opera houses, had the voice and looks to carry off an impersonation of the Scots poet, but it was generally agreed that the script by Wilcox, Reginald Berkeley and Maclean Rogers was weak. Some complained that it was more concerned with Burns's romantic assignations than his verses, but it was, after all, called *The Loves* not *The Poems* of

Robert Burns. Cinemagoers weren't keen, and Hislop never made another film. As a producer, Wilcox went on to compile an impressive list of musical and semi-musical features, most featuring Neagle. Some of the most commercially successful of these had to wait until the 1940s, when the strangely suburban sophistication of such flimsy concoctions as Neagle's films shared with Michael Wilding met with popular approval. For now, beyond the pleasing voice of Hislop singing Scots ballads, *The Loves of Robert Burns* was of little significance, although not bereft of admirers. The *Daily Mail* declared it 'deeply moving' and Hislop's film debut 'a triumph' in what was 'striking proof of the English talking film's capacity'.

Not all musical films emanated from BIP. Gainsborough and Ideal's **Just for a Song**, partly made in Pathécolor at Islington, was notable for starring two veterans of silents, Lilian Hall Davis and Roy Royston, as a young couple hoping to make a success on the music-halls. Michael Balcon assembled a strong cast that included Cyril Ritchard as a praying mantis of an agent, Constance Carpenter and the always welcome Syd Crossley, using a script co-written by director Gareth Gundrey, based on a story by Desmond Carter. Royston had starred in many shorts including the 'Hurricanes' series of comedies, as well as establishing himself as a West End and Broadway leading man. *Bioscope* thought the film 'exceptionally well played'.[11]

Hall Davis was in a class of her own, her fragility and intensity appreciated by Alfred Hitchcock, who cast her in two 1928 movies, *The Ring* and *The Farmer's Wife*. A few images from her silent career remain, but making her talkie debut in a musical must have tested her. *Just for a Song* had some delightful stage set designs, and its theatrical milieu allowed for the Mangan Tillerettes, and Syd Seymour and His Mad Hatters. Harry Carlton and Jay Whidden contributed songs, such as 'Oh, Lover True' and (poignant in the circumstances) 'Ashes Of Dreams', overseen by Gainsborough's musical supervisor Louis Levy. *Just for a Song* also included the charming 'Jack and Jill' sequence with Royston and Carpenter in fairy-tale mood. Much admired by critics and public alike, Hall Davis's transition to talkies may have been hampered by a mental instability. Suffering from neurasthenia, and with her film career declining, she committed suicide in October 1933. A concerned neighbour fetched a policeman, PC Putt, who found her in the kitchen of her brother, her head in the oven, her throat cut.

MAY

The majority of Sinclair Hill's work as director had been in silents from 1920, prior to joining Gaumont-British. His *Dark Red Roses* (1929) was a candidate for the first British musical sound film, followed by **Greek Street**. Hill's contributions to the genre were among the decade's best, *Britannia of Billingsgate* (1933) and *My Old*

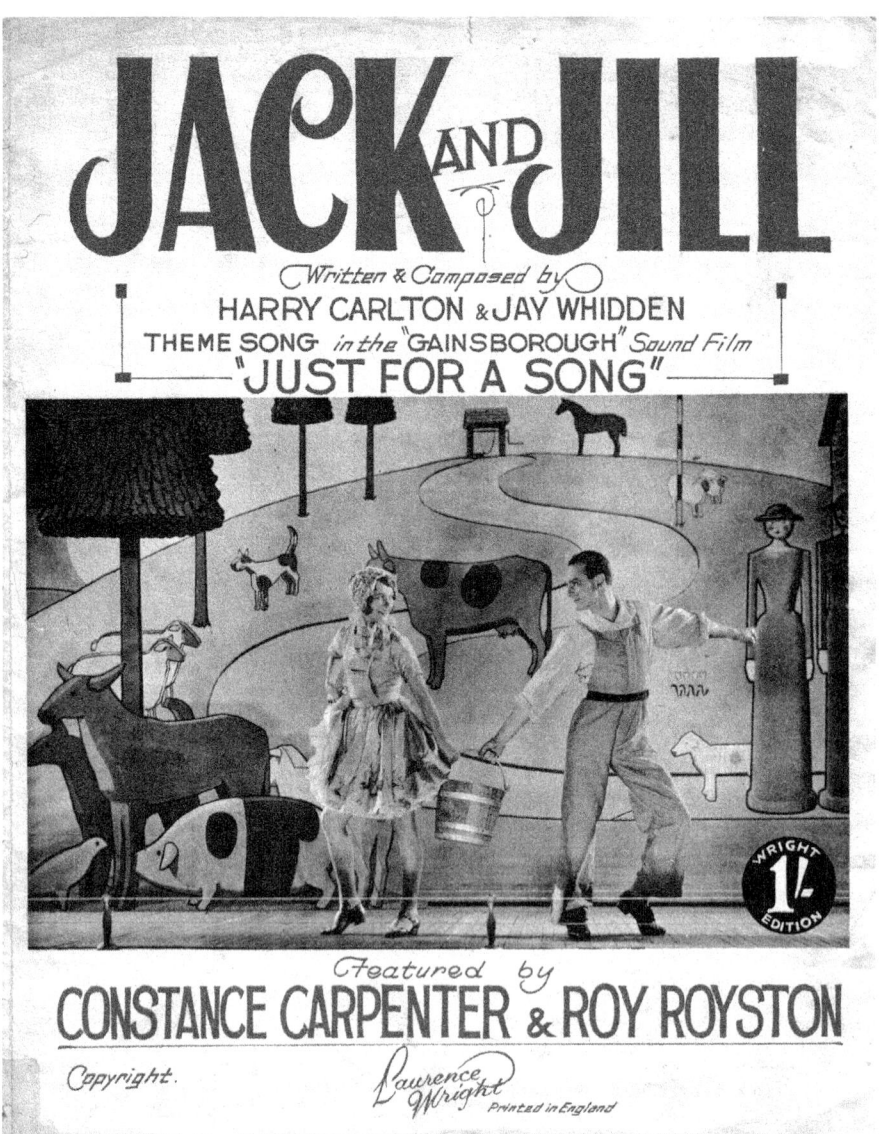

Nursery delights up the hill in Gainsborough's *Just for a Song* (1930)

Dutch (1934) among them. Meanwhile, *Greek Street*, tantalisingly renamed *Latin Love* for the American market, was not without merit, although Ralph Gilbert Bettinson and Leslie Howard Gordon's screenplay, based on a storyline by Robert Stevenson, was set in what even at this early time of the talkies was regarded as the natural hiding place of the British musical film: backstage. Stevenson went on to a highly successful career in London and Hollywood. One of his last hurrahs in Britain was the glorious *Young Man's Fancy* (1939), a non-musical that seemed quite capable of becoming one. His British reputation as scriptwriter and director was eclipsed with his work on Disney's *Mary Poppins*.

Hill had two strong leads for *Greek Street*. Sari Maritza's career between Britain, Hollywood and Germany was short if not always sweet; doubting her ability as an actress, she retired in 1934. She had also endured some odd casting, having played the somewhat dim-witted Lily Bell in the non-musical *The Water Gipsies* (1932). When shooting for *Greek Street* began early February, the first section to be filmed was a bedroom scene with Maritza in a boudoir, 'all curls and peignoir'.[12] *Greek Street*'s leading man was William Freshman, cast as Soho café proprietor Rikki who is enamoured of the singer Anna. Her career turns a corner under the dubious influence of a nightclub impresario (Martin Lewis) but good sense prevails, reuniting Anna and Rikki at fade-out.

Music was partly credited to 'Trytel', a name that was frequently seen in the opening credits of the period. It served as a warning. A Dutch composer, W. L. Trytel produced scores that numbered among them some John Baxter productions, as well as second-drawer efforts such as *Lily of Killarney*, *The Broken Melody* (whose musical sequences verge on the embarrassing), *Street Song* and *Squibs*. His compositions for Twickenham studios inevitably produced 'a rambling and irrelevant accompaniment, churning on regardless of change of shot, sequence or mood'.[13] The score by Trytel and Stanelli (part of a variety act 'The Fiddle Fanatic') included the song 'Within My Arms' and 'I've A Little Love Song', words by Max Gartman. The reception for Maritza was a little muted, her role achieved 'without creating anything in the nature of a sensation' in a movie that while 'not a super [was] an excellent little picture, as clean as a whistle and as full of action as Soho itself'.[14]

Almost everything about **Piccadilly Nights** was in the minor key, and it was the sole musical film made by Kingsway General Productions, produced and directed by Albert H. Arch, whose speciality seems to have been travelogues of Scotland. Chanteuse Billie (Billie Rutherford) pops up between variety turns that included popular bands of the time organised by Maurice Winnick and Ralph Goldsmith. Billie becomes a star when she replaces a leading lady too inebriated to appear. It was a stretch at eighty-six minutes. Harry Shalson's 'For You and Me' was featured.

Exemplifying the imported continental female star: Sari Maritza in
Greek Street (1930)

Betty Balfour's uneasy switch to sound pictures was not much helped by presenting her yet again as another Squibs-type heroine in *The Nipper*, renamed ***The Brat***. Having parted company with BIP, the 1920s silent star set up her own production company, Betty Balfour Pictures. Filming at Elstree was made more complex by the decision to go trilingual; the source was itself French. Louis Mercanton directed a screenplay by Reginald Berkeley and Donovan Parsons from Michael Carré and A.

Acremont's play *La Môme*. In line with the bitter-sweet storyline, the brave little cockney, 'The Nipper', works as a singer in a public house. She is taken up by Max Nicholson (John Stuart), whose house she has inadvisably burgled. Per the Balfour formula, Nipper ends up much as she began, more Dog and Duck than West End.

Balfour's publicity team promised that the star would 'sing some of the jolliest songs ever – five or six of them', but there was little enthusiasm for *The Brat*, or the spattering of songs that included 'We're Uncomfortable', 'Back To Gay Paree' (redolent of a Marie Lloyd number, 'The Coster Girl In Paris'), 'We Shan't Be Happy Till Mother's Gone Away', and the wonderfully titled 'Come And Have A Cocktail At The Cock-A-Doodle-Do'. The dancing wasn't anything to write home about either. Balfour had so obviously underrated the audience's intelligence, and failed to understand what opportunities film offered. She must have been disappointed by *Bioscope*'s decision that this was 'not of the type of which great films are made' or that it was 'transparently a vehicle merely for the old Betty, the Betty Balfour of *Squibs* humour'. Old Betty also had to cope with the backhanded compliment that it was 'doubtful whether Betty Balfour was ever better than in this low comedy performance'.[15] It would be four years before Balfour returned to the studios, playing a secondary fiddle to the star of *Evergreen*.

AUGUST

The rest of the year yielded little that was remarkable. Audiences expecting BIP's ***The Yellow Mask*** to be a celluloid copy of the musical that had closed in London two years earlier after a reasonably successful run were in for disappointment. On stage, the piece had good provenance: a book by Edgar Wallace based on his play *Traitor's Gate*, songs by American Vernon Duke and lyricist Desmond Carter. At BIP, producer John Maxwell hired a little army of writers to provide a screenplay: Val Valentine, Miles Malleson, George Arthurs, Walter C. Mycroft and Worton David. They successfully emasculated the original script, leaving the bones of a comedy about a Chinaman, Li-San, planning to steal a precious Chinese jewel from the crown jewels, pursued by the captain of the guard and his girlfriend and a comical detective, Sam Slider.

With its scenic set-pieces, *The Yellow Mask* seemed admirably suited for cinematic treatment, but even the direction of Harry Lachman could not meld the elements satisfactorily. At the Adelphi Theatre, Slider had been played by little Bobby Howes, a brightly comical actor who could be persuaded into singing (after a fashion) but never took to dancing. Howes's career in musical films would not take fire until 1932 when he became associated with some of the lightest and most delightful of British musical comedy pictures. Now, Sam Slider, renamed Sam Slipper by the film's five screenwriters, was played by Lupino Lane. Lane's remarkable career in Hollywood as the most charming and brilliantly elastic of

Inscrutable oriental goings-on in *The Yellow Mask* (1930)

performers should have had him etched into film history forever, but his return to the British studios coincided with the decline in his reputation. Warwick Ward repeated his stage performance as Li-San, and Winnie Collins her role as Molly Vane, remembered from the Adelphi show for her numbers shared with Howes, 'Eggs And Bacon' and 'I'm Wonderful'. BIP's version squandered the sophisticated delights of Duke's score, making do with 'Personality' (written by Lupino Lane and Donald M'Cullough and composed by Francis M. Collinson); 'Song Of The

Guards' by Dave Comer and Val Valentine; 'A Million Dreams' written by Val Valentine and composed by Herman Darewski; and 'I Left My Heart With You' by Hugh Wade, Billy Noble and Campbell Williams.

The bilingual *Spanish Eyes*, made at the cramped Twickenham Studios, run by the industrious Julius Hagen as 'a miniature mass production machine',[16] was a co-production of an originally French piece by the colourful theatrical impresario Julian Wylie ('the chorus girls' best friend' according to a *Pathé Gazette* tribute) and Ulargui. Its director was Wylie's brother, G. B. Samuelson, whose career would be eked out working for his own production unit and such companies as Westminster Films, New Era, and Majestic Films. Its leading players were the Welsh actress Edna Davies, Anthony Ireland, Dennis Noble and Donald Calthrop. The picture would by now be forgotten were it not for a backstage drama that eclipsed it.

The filming of this gypsy romance was done overnight after the day crew filming *Bedrock* had gone home. At this time, it was common practice at Twickenham for the studio to run around the clock, one film being made by day and another by night, with exhausted personnel sometimes working on both. For *Spanish Eyes* Wylie had also hired the Piccadilly Theatre, filling it with an audience of extras and recording some dance sequences that used some of the dancers in the Piccadilly's current show, *Here Comes the Bride*. One of these was a young hopeful, Annie Foy Tipping, known as Nita Foy.

Early in the morning of 1 April, Calthrop, seeing how exhausted Tipping was, invited the young dancer to his dressing-room (officially out of bounds) for a drink. She was dressed in a crinoline-like costume of tulle, ready for a ballet sequence, when she brushed against a heater with unguarded filaments. Calthrop had turned away for a moment when he heard her cry out. He described her as being enveloped in a wall of flame. A doctor was called but was slow in arriving. Tipping subsequently died in hospital, and a verdict of accidental death given at Richmond's Coroners' Court. During this process, Samuelson was criticised for not having responded to the tragedy, claiming that he had been vaguely aware of screaming but put it down to mice frightening the girls. He was perhaps exaggerating when he explained at the inquest that at times he had up to 3,000 girls to look after. The coroner somewhat waspishly replied, 'I have seen some of your films, Mr Samuelson, and I think this will be a lesson to you.'

SEPTEMBER

Also made at Twickenham, **Big Business** was the work of Oscar M. Sheridan who produced, directed and (with H. W. David) wrote it. Promoted as 'A Movietone Song and Dance Show', it is described by David Quinlan as a 'lacklustre musical' that is 'merely a peg on which to hang a series of music-hall acts'.[17] At least it includes one of the top British cabaret entertainers of the decade Leslie Hutchinson, 'Hutch', performing Sheridan and David's 'Always Your Humble Servant'. Otherwise, *Big Business* was one of the first musical productions to involve acts that scarcely deserved to be immortalised. It did, however, give American-born Frances Day, the most patently seductive British blonde of the 1930s, her first film role in a string of productions that never made it into the first class. Somehow, the camera never managed to make the most of her, either under-using her talents, as in the otherwise delightful *Oh, Daddy!*, or matching her with Arthur Riscoe, with whom she shared a successful stage partnership that never quite takes fire on screen.

In 1932 Pathé captured her with Carroll Gibbons and his Savoy Hotel Orpheans performing 'I'm For You, A Hundred Per Cent'. It's a sublime fragment that not only confirms Day's innate humanity, but reminds us of the fragility of life itself. There were countless such bands (but few as good) as Gibbons's in the 1930s. What happened to the men who had played in them when the fashion for their music faded? It's the close-ups of the men's faces as Day sings that stays with you, the arrival of Howard Jones on sax, the sensation that something significant is happening between these people joined together, that retains an ability to move us. It is a reminder of what Day expressed in *Oh, Daddy!*, the importance of hanging on to happiness.

'Oh de-ar, deee-arr, deeee-arr'. If Leslie Fuller had a catchphrase, perhaps this was it. Fuller, late of a much-appreciated concert party at Margate, had already claimed prime place as the British sound picture's very first low comedian. The attempt to establish him as such wasn't built on sand. ***Why Sailors Leave Home***, his third film for British International Pictures, was essentially backed by the same team in place for his first two, *Not So Quiet on the Western Front* (May 1930) and *Kiss Me, Sergeant* (August 1930). No one could accuse BIP of not backing its bets. All three were directed by comedy expert Monty Banks, not yet a major director for British musical films; he would go on to work with and for Gracie Fields (he married her), George Formby, Stanley Lupino and Bobby Howes.

Fuller's first three sound pictures used the husband-and-wife writers and performers Syd Courtenay and Lola Harvey, and all three used the delightful Olivette, sometimes known as Nina Olivette. The musical content seems to have involved a great number of people. A sophisticated approach to film-making was something that BIP, Banks and co. didn't seem particularly concerned with at this time. *Not So Quiet on the Western Front* had been made in four days, and there's little to suggest that *Why Sailors* took any longer. Armed with his battery of funny sticking-out-his-bottom walks, grimacing and mugging, and with his patently stagey performance emphasised by his heavy make-up (a little square of black on the upper lid of his eyes), Fuller is hard put to get an audience to keep watching after the first five minutes, and a supposedly witty number from Peter Bernard, 'Imagine My Embarrassment', in which Bill joins, doesn't help matters.

Desertion would, however, be a mistake, because there's a good reason for persisting: Fuller's a very funny man. When good-hearted but none too bright sailor Bill Biggles arrives in a foreign port, he remembers the local sheikh owes him a favour for having saved his life. Once in the harem, the screenplay shifts gear, with absurdly heightened dialogue for the locals, to which Fuller responds with glorious inappropriateness. Courtenay doubles as screenwriter and sheikh, informing Bill, 'I was educated at Eaton and Oxford.' 'Now, isn't that funny?' says Bill. 'I was at Borstal and Dartmoor.' Fuller makes even the most hackneyed gags chime. 'Are you fearless?' he's asked. 'Well, I once jumped off a bus without ringing the bell, and I walked out of Woolworth's without buying anything.' Courtenay bats these absurdities with relish, and introduces Bill to his queue of wives.

Observing the proceedings are two male attendants (one of them a portly and effeminate eunuch). 'I don't like the way you walk,' says Bill, advising him to change his ways or 'I'll cut your rations down.' There are several such gay touches in Banks's armoury. Meanwhile, the harem girls do a routine choreographed by Alexander Oumansky, fresh from *Harmony Heaven* and *Kiss Me, Sergeant*. This precedes the arrival of screenwriter Harvey as a matronly, plummy-voiced senior of the harem, ridiculously over-elocuted, who warns Bill, now officially acting as the sheikh, that changes need to be made. There must be '50% increase in pin money ... no Sunday work ... no overtime ... and double pay for night-shifts', a list of demands greeted with a huge gathering of double-take.

Harvey then introduces Olivette as the secretary of the Amalgamated Union of Royal Wives, a tiny, skinny, pigeon-toed little creature, who barks out instructions to an astounded Bill. His answer is to join her in an apache-dance. It's a brilliant routine, partly because of being so unexpected. Olivette must surely have been known to Fuller from his music-hall days (she would appear with him again in films, as in the 1937 *Boys Will Be Girls*). The apache routine over, the film tails off when Bill's sailor-mates burst into the harem, presumably to give Bernard the chance to sing the unremarkable 'When I Want To Be Loved I Want To Be Loved'. The sheikh frees the girls from the harem, to the random delight of the sailors. As Bill escapes by boat, the company on shore rhapsodise in front of a painted backcloth.

1931

No female star in British studios had glimmered as convincingly

Sally in Our Alley

City of Song
Sally in Our Alley
Gipsy Blood
Out of the Blue

Sunshine Susie
The Love Race
The Beggar Student
Congress Dances

JANUARY

City of Song, renamed *Farewell to Love* for America, was a co-production trilingual from Associated Sound Film Industries, made at Wembley and in parts in Naples. The German original, *Die Singende Stadt*, premiered in Vienna in October 1930, with Brigitte Helm playing opposite the singing star of the moment, Jan Kiepura. The original intention was that the British version would be in colour. *City of Song* only narrowly escaped being classed as foreign. It was obvious that whatever else British film-makers did when abroad, making a foreign country look attractive to foreigners was not one of them. Many of the films made in this early period were homeless, crossing the seas to be remade in different languages. The tedious and surely unsatisfactory business of having to re-shoot in different languages, with changed personnel, did little to spur creative thought.

Casts turning up for that day's *City of Song* schedule were mixing with a smorgasbord of nationalities. The director, Carmine Gallone, was Italian, the producer Arnold Pressburger Austrian, and the production supervisor Bernard Vorhaus American; the screenwriters were Hungarian Hans Székely and British Miles Malleson, who for good measure wrote a role for himself as a stage doorman. The original cinematographer was the Hungarian Arpad Viragh, who contracted typhoid during the shooting and died on location in Capri; he was succeeded by the German Curt Courant. The film editor Lars Moen was of Danish-American descent.

Based on a storyline by C. H. Dand, the plot is an early example of the theatrically themed formula that, with various alterations and variations, threaded through many British (and American) musical films of the decade. Visiting Naples, wealthy, sophisticated Claire Winter (Betty Stockfeld) is attracted to the Neopolitan singer Giovanni Cavallone (Jan Kiepura), as much by his looks as his voice. She returns with him to London and a high-society milieu. Cavallone turns his back on her and the chance of success as a performer in England, returning to the arms of his childhood sweetheart Carmela. Their reunion is a little dampened by his donning of a beret.

Today, much of *City of Song* looks rudimentary, but it was admired at its debut (the *Bioscope* thought it 'an artistic triumph'[1]). In every way the British edition suggests that domestic studios still had much to learn if they were to produce well-crafted work, while Kiepura's hesitant struggle with a foreign language makes you sympathise with his predicament. There was, after all, no British singer who could have stood in for Kiepura; without him, the film is meaningless.

At the conclusion of the German version, we see Claire, isolated and thoughtful, after Cavallone has left her, but accompanied by a male companion, as the voice of Cavallone plays on the gramophone. In the British version of the trilingual we see only the hand of the man when he takes the needle from the record as it spins to an end. We are left wondering which Claire misses most, the man or the voice.

One of the great tenors of his generation, Kiepura had the looks and singing voice to earn him a substantial movie career at a time when a voice struggled against poor sound reproduction. His subsequent projects included *Tell Me Tonight*, made in Germany, *My Song for You* made at Shepherd's Bush, and *My Heart Is Calling*, made at Beaconsfield and again directed by Gallone, but not registered as British. British cinemagoers, perhaps on a damp afternoon in Truro, can only have wondered at the depiction of the British way of life as lived by Claire and her champagne-swigging cronies? In one scene Gallone fixates the camera on a waterfall of the stuff, suggesting the excesses of the Weimar Republic. Along with so many other films of the time, Gallone in *City of Song* turns a mirror from the depression from which Britain was suffering.

JULY

Filming for **Sally in Our Alley** began on 23 March, in the same month in which its star underwent a screen test. The film would be interesting if it had done no more than launch the screen career of Gracie Fields; but in its own right it isn't unremarkable. Her arrival signalled a weather change in what British musical films might achieve. It disqualified the apparently unimaginative use of the medium in such films as *Elstree Calling* and *Harmony Heaven*, with a star that could lift sometimes indifferent material. David Shipman refers to *Sally in Our Alley* as 'a cheap little effort' in which Fields 'only glimmered', but up till then no female star in British studios had glimmered as convincingly. The film marked the start of a career that would last successfully until the outbreak of war and go on to include one of her best roles in the Hollywood non-musical *Holy Matrimony*, based on Arnold Bennett's novel *Buried Alive*.[2]

Made at Beaconsfield by Associated Talking Pictures, *Sally in Our Alley* was a determined effort by Fields's husband Archie Pitts to kick-start her career in pictures. Based on Charles McEvoy's 1920s play *The Likes of Her*, it was skilfully adapted in a novelettish manner by Miles Malleson (recently partly responsible for *City of Song*) and Alma Reville, skilled screenwriter and wife of Alfred Hitchcock. The director was Maurice Elvey, already with over a hundred silents to his credit. He went on to many other musical films of the period including the Cicely Courtneidge *Soldiers of the King*, the Evelyn Laye *Princess Charming*, the Jan Kiepura *My Song for You* and the Violet Loraine *Road House*. The opening credits for *Sally in Our Alley* offer no information about its music, an essential component and a major reason for the film's popularity, lacking any acknowledgement of Will E. Haines, Leo Towers, Harry Leon and A. P. Herbert.

As Sally Winch, Fields plays across the emotional spectrum with complete conviction. A waitress at old Sam Bilson's coffee gaff, she is in love with George Miles (Ian Hunter), but he sustains injuries as a soldier and decides it is best that Sally thinks him dead. Rumours reach her that he is alive and married. He isn't married, but he is walking again, and determined to start a new life. On the rebound, Sally agrees to marry kindly Sam (some onlookers thought this mirrored the marriage of Fields and Pitts), who assures her, 'I'll do my best to make you happy.' It doesn't work. Sally leaves him, along the way giving shelter to the physically and mentally abused Florrie Small, played by Florence Desmond.

The dramatic heart of the film is the confrontation between Sally and the deceitful Florrie, as Sally breaks down Florrie's emotional wall, enduring Florrie's orgy of plate-smashing. The tension between them is superbly caught. For a moment it seems that Sally will be seduced into higher society when she's asked to entertain at a posh party for the Duchess of Wexford. She has a great success (why wouldn't she?), even getting the Duchess to join in the chorus of 'Fred Fanakapan'. She's admired. They cheer. But as soon as her turn is done, she is cold-shouldered. The point is starkly made: the divide between the classes cannot be bridged. When the smart girls at the party dress her up like a Paris modèle, you sense that Sally thinks it's ridiculous, that whatever she wears at Sam's gaff is perfectly satisfactory. The message may not have been lost on working-class cinemagoers. The good news is that Sally and George are reunited at last, and at no time has she sold her soul. The question was, could the subsequent cinematic exploitation of Fields retain her ingenuousness?

No effort was spared to bring off a major event for the British industry. Production clientele were imported from Hollywood: Otto Ludwig to cut the rushes, Bob Martin to supervise the cinematography. Elvey assembled a first-rate supporting cast without a weak link, including Gibb McLaughlin, veteran of many cameos, mournfully propping up the bar at Sam's, and Fred Groves as a gentle non-starter admirer of our Sally. The film is notable for its songs, too – songs that emerge from the story such as 'Fall In And Follow The Band', with its Punch and Judy Bank Holiday jollity. All sorts of incidental delights contribute, as when little Ian Wilson (in at the birth of the British talkie, and still going strong into the 1960s) arrives with the haddock. Basil Dean recalled that 'The film critics prophesised its success even while condemning it for its indifferent story (there they were wrong, for the McEvoy play had already proved itself), uncertain direction and poor recording. Their prophecy was fulfilled.'[3]

Bioscope was decidedly unenthusiastic. Fields 'ought to have been better advised concerning the story she should accept. She might, with advantage, have confined herself to a definite comedy role, for she must not be allowed to forget that she is a comedienne and not a tragedienne.' She was, of course, both. Perhaps Desmond had provided 'the brightest piece of acting'. There was more: as a tragic sweetheart Fields was 'not convincing' in a 'slender and unconvincing story relying entirely upon stellar appeal' with Fields 'not ideally cast'.[4] This problem, the balance between drama and comedy and song, was one that would plague Fields throughout her film career. The *Manchester Guardian* praised Fields as 'rough, abrupt and real. Somehow […] she manages to be herself, and that is unique', despite the fact that 'Instead of realising that here he has a singer to lift a film out of the rut' the producer 'cuts down her singing'.[5]

NOVEMBER

The diva of BIP's first 'talkie' opera film reportedly always referred to it as *The Bloody Gipsy*, more properly known as **Gipsy Blood**, an adaptation by director Cecil Lewis and musical director Malcolm Sargent of Bizet's *Carmen*. Some of the credit should attach to another major figure of British studios at the time, Walter C. Mycroft, the film's 'scenario editor'. Not surprisingly for one of the world's most-performed operas, *Carmen* had already made it into cinema in 1907 when Chronophone Films (with sound) filmed some of its more popular tunes; more adventurously, Chronophone also managed a complete *Faust*. Presumably not intended for those of a nervous disposition, a 1922 series titled 'Tense Moments from Opera' was produced by Master Film Company, the tense moments from *Carmen* performed by Patricia Fitzgerald. The rather more exotically named Zeda Pascha was the gypsy heroine in John E. Blakeley's 1927 collection 'Cameo Operas', which had to be synchronised with orchestra and live singers in cinemas.

The spirit of Spain, the torrid heat and even more torrid sexual frisson upsetting the characters of the opera needs to be hastily established if the drama is to carry any force. The entrance of Carmen is a crucial moment: this, after all, is the minx with whom one is going to have to spend the evening. We first see BIP's self-confessed 'bloody gipsy', the internationally renowned opera singer Marguerite Namara, spitting out the pips of some exotic fruit; we can only assume that her stage performances were riveting.

Her Don José, Thomas Burke, never seems to integrate with what is happening around him, although his singing (more impressive than Namara's) wakes things up, and seems to have been recorded live, with him standing on tip-toe at the approach of a high note. There can have been few to rival Burke's tragic hero in manly bearing, and his acting is probably no worse than anyone else's here. Labelled 'the Lancashire Caruso', he was more colourful than the film he found himself in. At Covent Garden he sang opposite Nellie Melba, who would accept no substitute, and performed before Puccini. If he sang 'Here is the flower that once you gave me' to the composer as directly as he sings it in *Gipsy Blood*, little wonder that Puccini said 'Never have I heard my music so beautifully sung' – a compliment inscribed on Burke's tombstone. His evident distraction at certain moments may in part be excused by the fact that he had recently lost £100,000 in the Wall Street crash. Lance Fairfax's rigid Escamillo is no competition for Burke's testosterone-fuelled presence, and Fairfax's toreador's outfit does absolutely nothing for him.

Nervous as to what an opera-shy public might make of the film, BIP decided there was just so much of *Carmen* the audience would take, and deleted ten minutes of film it considered less appealing than Bizet's lollipop melodies. Cinematic opera has hardly worked well in any of the decades that followed, although *Bioscope* was hopeful that 'It is now possible for those who, not being musical enthusiasts, are somewhat bored by a big operatic performance, to view a filmic condensation'.[6] They might have stayed longer awake for a stage performance, where the musical sounds would be natural, colour plentiful, and the performances more interesting. It was an understatement that Namara 'at no time suggests the fiery Latin lass'.[7] The *Manchester Guardian* thought that 'In America they do these things better', for there was 'no thrill, and the actors move slowly and often too much'. The pronounced English accents and scenes of women going into church bareheaded didn't ring true, but 'Dialogue, song, and the musical score […] have been remarkably well blended'.[8]

Not much good seems to have come from BIP taking the trouble to do some location shooting in Spain and, back at Elstree, Carmen's homeland looked incredibly artificial, cardboardy and cramped.

On the occasion of the final transmission of BBC radio's *Mrs Dale's Diary*, its titular star was asked by a reporter if, given the chance, she would have her stage and film career all over again? 'No,' she replied, 'not for all the tea in China. Not for all the tea in China. *No, no, no.* Definitely no.' Charles Simon, the actor playing Mrs Dale's doctor husband about whom she was always worrying, told an interviewer that the show's star had 'an open-hearted, generous disposition, but [was] bedevilled all her life by a set of complicated nervous disorders which nearly wrecked her career on several occasions and resulted in the loss of friends and all society'.[9] Many listeners tuning in to the daily Home Service soap opera would have been unaware that Jessie Matthews, a rather cosier Mrs Dale than the actress she had replaced (Ellis Powell), had been the British film studios' biggest name of the

1930s. Already a prominent stage performer by the end of the 1920s via shows by Berlin, Coward, Porter, and Rodgers and Hart, she surprised many by not only breaking into pictures but, for a space of six years between 1933 and 1938, conquering them as well as, almost uniquely for a British artist, gaining a reputation in America.

She had been glimpsed on screen before *Out of the Blue*, but no one would have remembered her three prior appearances in silents filmed at Isleworth in 1923, as an uncredited Pan in a dance sequence for *The Beloved Vagabond*, an uncredited village girl in *Straws in the Wind* and an uncredited royal prince in G. B. Samuelson's patriotic tableau *This England*, intended for the 1924 British National Film Week. *Out of the Blue* was based on the 1930 London musical comedy *Little Tommy Tucker*, its score by Vivian Ellis and Arthur Schwartz. A showpiece for popular leading man Gene Gerrard and for Frances Day, it had a moderate run with a last night on 31 January 1931.

In these days no time was lost in turning stage into film product, complete with Gerrard and a few other original cast members. Matthews, cast as Tommy Tucker, subsequently denounced the film as 'a disaster' that 'should never have left the boards'. With little to do, she suggests a vitality itching for release, and in a last-minute explosion of high kicks she seems almost to be auditioning for the 'Dancing On The Ceiling' number from *Evergreen*. In kindly mood, *Bioscope* praised the film as 'sparkling but unintellectual', containing 'so much enjoyable wit, pleasing singing and clever nonsense'.[10]

Adapted for the screen by Frank Miller, R. P. Weston and Bert Lee, *Out of the Blue* was shot at Elstree through August and September. BIP promoted Gerrard as one of their prime performers, but it was probably unwise to have him also direct the film, in which he played radio announcer Bill Coverdale who was engaged to Angela Tucker (Kay Hammond) but more inclined to Angela's sister Tommy. In his first assignment as director of a talkie, one can imagine the difficulties Gerrard must have faced in an industry grappling with new developments. He was supervised by J. O. C. (John) Orton, who was clearly unable to enliven the lax comedy sequences, Gerrard's careless performance, and the emasculation of Ellis's original score that retained the title number, 'Let's Be Sentimental' and 'I'm Glad I Met You'.

DECEMBER

A cheeky smiling sun welcomes us to Gainsborough's *Sunshine Susie*, according to Rachael Low 'one of the most profitable of the period and although not the first British musical it was certainly the best so far'.[11] Perhaps Low confuses the already muddled situation with multi-language productions by claiming this as British product, when it was as German as its star Renate Müller. Effectively, it was a translation of the original film *Die Privatsekretärin*, based on a play by Franz Schulz, whose work for British musical films included *Marry Me*, *Love on Wheels*, *The Lucky Number*, *Blossom Time* and *Two Hearts in Waltz Time*. Produced by Michael Balcon and directed by Victor Saville, *Sunshine Susie* had a screenplay by Saville, Robert Stevenson and Angus Macphail, although 'the development of some of the episodes is not accomplished with the same artistry as the original'.[12]

British audiences were lucky to have the original Susie repeat her role for them. For the remakes, France made do with Marie Glory in the renamed *Dactylo*; in Italy Elsa Merlini played *La Segretaria Privata*. In Britain, the film was said to have been seen by ten million cinemagoers, many of them entranced by its winning song 'Today I Feel So Happy'. Desmond Carter's thrown-off lyric was the perfect accompaniment to Paul Abrahám's simplistic melody. Abrahám had recently come to prominence with his 1930 operetta *Viktoria und ihr Husar*. Although a British production ran successfully at the Palace Theatre in 1931, there would be no British film version, but his subsequent *Bal im Savoy* turned up as a British film in 1936.

Abrahám's music is pleasant and stylish, and especially inventive – and probably a shock to British audiences in its extended musical sequences, as when Susie first arrives in Vienna, staying at a pension for businesswomen, or in the choreographed scene of the typewriting girls. Who, anyway, could resist Müller's cry of joy as she flings open her window, joined by all the other girls in all the other windows. There's an uncluttered simplicity when she explains 'Just Because I Lost My Heart To You'. Inevitably, some of the sun has gone behind a cloud since the film first appeared. It's a surprisingly dark, slightly Teutonic affair, wrapped in Alexander Vetchinsky's décor.

For Jack Hulbert, following the revue snippets in *Elstree Calling*, *Sunshine Susie* was his film debut in a musical proper. He probably seemed more amusing in 1931, and his fooling is apt to be tiresome. As for his dancing during his number 'I've Got A Rich Aunt', it serves as a warning to the public as to what sort of choreography they were going to be subjected to for the next ten years, as he loops about the studio; Stanley Lupino was equally prone to such balletic moments. It cannot be denied that a naïve charm carries off the choreography.

Bioscope was in no doubt that this was 'Unquestionably the best musical film yet turned out by a British concern'. Hopes were high that this might mark the beginning of a change in the way British musical films were constructed, for 'A feature of *Sunshine Susie* is to be the manner in which the musical numbers will be introduced as an essential part of the story.'[13]

The *Observer*'s critic thought it lagged too late behind what foreign filmmakers were doing, comparing badly with Lubitsch (USA), René Clair (France), and Erik Charell (Germany), although '*Sunshine Susie* is undoubtedly a new break in British production along sound movie lines [in which] Jack Hulbert at last finds his feet as a film comedian.'[14] For all this, the film does not make for easy viewing. Low notes that it was 'shot in short takes with synchronous sound, a fact which is only too obvious in some of the songs',[15] rather like a rehearsal for *Singin' in the Rain*. The film nevertheless makes the most of Müller, and an encouraged Balcon quickly mounted another vehicle for her, *Marry Me*. Watching *Sunshine Susie* today, its jollity is the weaker for the sense of impending doom hovering over the heavy Germanic settings, and knowing that Abrahám, and Müller (dead at the age of 31), would fall into the hands of the Nazis. Her last film was the 1937 anti-Semitic *Togger*.

BIP speedily followed up Stanley Lupino's first film comedy *Love Lies* with **The Love Race**, an adaptation of his most recent stage success that had run successfully in London and only closed a few months before filming at Elstree began. Misleadingly billed as a musical comedy, the movie emasculated the theatre score by composer Jack Clarke and lyricist Desmond Carter, leaving what was patently a farce with one song and a dash of mock opera. Perhaps Edwin Greenwood's scenario decided that the songs would hold back the comic propulsion. This was a family affair, directed by Lupino Lane with Stanley Lupino as Jack Powley, heir to a motor racing business. Its theatrical origins are plain to see on screen, but Stanley holds it together, his pop-eyes, his frog-like dancing, his store of double-takes, and willingness to put over corny material. 'Must you drink as much as you do?' asks his father. 'Well, Dad', he replies, 'it's not my fault. I had a whisky and soda on St Swithin's Day.'

He is well supported by the superb farceur Wallace Lupino's Mr Fish, while Jack Hobbs, replacing on-stage Laddie Cliff, jogs along at Stanley's side. They join with the guests at a smart party in 'Dance Your Blues Away', its choreographer (perhaps wisely) uncredited. The observant will recognise some of the moves in Stanley's 1936 *Cheer Up!*. As the complexities of the character's relationships unravels, there is a cod-melodramatic sequence, played to the hilt by all concerned, the sort of thing that Jack Waller and Joseph Tunbridge did better. Along the way, female underwear cascades from suitcases, before Lupino Lane himself makes a momentary director's cameo à la Alfred Hitchcock (it's a typical Lupino trick sequence). There's considerable enjoyment to be had by the madcap goings-on, not least when the chief culprits pop up in court in time to the music. If nothing else, *The Love Race* confirms Stanley Lupino's place in the decade's musical films, which he went on to consolidate in such delights as *Sleepless Nights*, the perfectly formed *Cheer Up!*, *Over She Goes* and *Hold My Hand*. Few worked harder than Stanley to keep the British public cheerful.

Produced at Beaconsfield as a bilingual by John Harvel for Amalgamated Films Association, **The Beggar Student** was adapted by John Stafford and Hans Zerlett from Millöcker's operetta *Der Bettelstudent*; AFA's only other British-made film would be the 1932 *Where Is This Lady?*. Neither was noticeably successful. Both were directed by Victor Hanbury, whose other operetta-type assignments included *There Goes Susie* and *Ball at Savoy*. Some of these later projects attracted bigger names than did the second-drawer *The Beggar Student*. In nineteenth-century Cracow, Polish Colonel Ollendorff (Frederick Lloyd) loves Tania (Shirley Dale), but her mother, Countess Novalska (Margaret Halstan) disapproves. A Ruritanian plot of disguise and misunderstanding winds to a foregone conclusion in the well-trodden manner of Heidelberg-type confections, helped by Lance Fairfax (late of *Gipsy Blood*) as romantic interest.

Congress Dances sounded and looked British, and its delightful German star Lilian Harvey managed a bright British accent (not difficult, she had been born in Hornsey as Helene Lilian Muriel Pape), but it surfaced in Britain in one of three language versions made at the Babelsberg Studios outside Berlin. For the British edition, Harvey's original leading man Willy Fritsch was replaced by the more anglicised Conrad Veidt. Caught on the cusp of change, *Congress Dances* was denied British classification, English versions of movies produced by the German UFA no longer being allowable as British, in the same way that films in the German language were no longer classified as German if made outside Germany. At this time, the making of multi-language versions (MLVs) was still considered a practicable policy, with the chairman of Gaumont-British, Isidore Ostrer, instigating the mating of his company with UFA to produce Anglo-German pictures. Harvey's charm survived all three MLVs of *Congress Dances*, her no more than mildly competent singing voice no impediment to Werner R. Heymann's song 'Just Once For All Time' (English lyric by Rowland Leigh), brimming with happiness and quintessentially of its period. The film's success was enormous, helping Harvey on to other films in Hollywood and then, briefly, Britain, for *Invitation to the Waltz*. But *Congress Dances* had never been truly British.

1932

Who could not be moved as Laurie's room and Gracie's room slide towards one another for the lovers' embrace?

Looking on the Bright Side

The Blue Danube
Lord Babs
In a Monastery Garden
Goodnight, Vienna
The First Mrs Fraser
Indiscretions of Eve
His Lordship
Lucky Girl
Jack's the Boy
Love on the Spot
Monte Carlo Madness
The Love Contract

Love on Wheels
The Maid of the Mountains
Looking on the Bright Side
Marry Me
Happy Ever After
Tell Me Tonight
Sleepless Nights
Say It with Music
Where Is This Lady?
The Midshipmaid
For the Love of Mike
Born Lucky

JANUARY

If the publicity department of British and Dominions was to be believed, the year could not have got off to a more scintillating beginning, with 'A Sensational Picture of Gay, Care-Free Budapest. Haunting Music and a Love Story That Will Thrill You'. This seems to have borne little relationship to the bilingual produced and directed by the already prolific Herbert Wilcox, **The Blue Danube**, having discarded its working titles, *Rhapsody* and *Shuttlecoq*. The cast was probably not at fault. Brigitte Helm, a refugee from Fritz Lang's silent *Metropolis*, played Countess Gabrielle, to whom Sandor (Joseph Schildkraut) is attracted. He leaves his simple gypsy dancer lover Yutka, played by Wilcox's then favourite Chili Bouchier (billed here as Dorothy Bouchier), for the Countess, before learning the error of his ways. The screenplay was by Miles Malleson, worked up from a story by Doris Zinkeisen, who frequently designed costumes for Wilcox's productions.

His idea of a musical film with minimal dialogue was commendable, but the results were generally considered lamentable except by flocking cinemagoers in Sydney, proving that there is no accounting for taste. The *MFB* (*Monthly Film Bulletin*) suggested that the film, 'very dated', 'must not be looked on as a typical Wilcox production', criticising the poor sound and cinematography, but much about *The Blue Danube* suggests it *was* typical of his work. The fact that it badly served its three stars – never mind that it also involved the legendary Léonide Massine, partnered by Nikitina – was inexcusable. Helm, Schildkraut (a sort of Hungarian Ivor Novello) and Bouchier had already been teamed for Wilcox's *Carnival* the previous year, so must have known what they were in for. Prominent in both films was the Hungarian Alfred Rode and his Royal Tzigane Band, remembered by Bouchier as 'a wild looking bunch from the Hungarian woods, and I found it imprudent to get too close to them after a long day in the studio under the hot lights. They played with tempestuous abandon …'[1] Their selection inevitably included Strauss's famous waltz (a lollipop for the audience Wilcox knew he was playing to), a dash of Liszt , and a song to a guitar composed by Rode, all performed 'in a manner that sets one's blood to pounding'.

There was a polite thumbs-down from *Bioscope*, which was disappointed that 'An attempt to set a serious plot against such lavishly fantastic backgrounds has all but failed, and, indeed, should not have been attempted, because the story of itself is inevitably overwhelmed by the beauty of the "Blue Danube" music.' Helm was side-swiped, for 'she has little more to do in this picture than could have been accomplished by a simple extra'. The photography 'leaves much to be desired' and the recording was 'not too good'.[2]

The *New York Times* regretted 'a sorry tale of poor editing, incoherence and an overwrought performance by Joseph Schildkraut', deciding that 'there is nothing in the film's acting, direction or tempo to arouse enthusiasm'.[3] Over twenty years later, much the same might be said of Wilcox's manhandling of Novello's *King's Rhapsody*, 'ludicrously inept' and 'killed stone dead by casting [Anna Neagle and Errol Flynn] and wide screen'.[4] By then, Wilcox had long given up trying to make a star of Bouchier, and had moved on to the more marketable Anna Neagle.

FEBRUARY

Although the British composer Vivian Ellis wrote that 'I have never been asked to write a major musical picture in this country', his contribution to the British musical film was far from negligible. His autobiography, unusually informative for a theatrical figure, reveals his attitude to writing music for films at the time of *Jack's the Boy*, when lyricist Douglas Furber handed him a lyric 'The Flies Crawled Up The Window' for a Jack Hulbert number. As Ellis wrote twenty-three years later:

> In those days the sound in talkies was not as efficient as it is today. In music, one was inclined to hear the melody and miss the accompanying harmonies. The taste of the film public, too, was relatively simple, to put it kindly. I sought a tune that would please a backward child of twelve. In as many minutes I jotted down a sixteen-bar

chorus containing a choice of two chords, two arpeggios, and a five-finger exercise. 'That,' I jeered, 'is exactly what they want.' It was.[5]

It's from Ellis that we learn how Walter Forde always had a piano on the studio floor – Forde played it between shots – but, as Ellis suggests, 'nobody in pictures would dream of behaving normally.'[6] There was little sign of normal behaviour in Gainsborough's **Lord Babs**. The provenance was fine: Michael Balcon producing, and Forde directing a screenplay by Clifford Grey (doubling as lyricist) and Angus Macphail, from Keble Howard's 1927 novel of the same name, subtitled 'a tragical farce'. Keble had already provided material for three silents, *Miss Charity* and *The God in the Garden* in 1921, and *King of the Castle* in 1925. The music was by Ellis, and the cast headed by Bobby Howes, who was on the road to becoming one of the best-known light comedians in British musical films. The lightest of confections, *Lord Babs* followed the adventures of a ship's steward who unexpectedly inherits a title and finds himself engaged to Helen (Pat Paterson), daughter of Ambrose Parker (Alfred Drayton, who attracted the best notices). To escape this attachment, his lordship reverts to childhood.

Contemporary critics were excited by the spectacle of Howes misbehaving in a perambulator. Complaining of its 'rather feeble story', *Bioscope* thought Howes's regressive behaviour the strongest thing in the film, but 'though the situation has some possibilities, Walter Forde has carried it to inordinate lengths, which develop eventually to ordinary rush-about comedy.'[7] *Kine Weekly* applauded Howes as 'a bright and engaging comedian, and his antics as the baby are sure to command the laughs', while admitting that Drayton stole the picture.[8] A more recent BFI showing of the once-lost film drew a different response, exposing 'twenty minutes of the most cringe-making antics you could see in a cinema'.[9]

MARCH

Principally a straight melodrama and musically thin (although an irresistibly silly snatch of Chopin and the inevitable Albert Ketèlbey sneak in to this retrospective), **In a Monastery Garden** is surprisingly enjoyable. Considering the cramped conditions at Twickenham studios, producer Julius Hagen, his designers and director Maurice Elvey conjure a spaciousness that suits the switches from vaulting monastic institution to outdoor café to concert hall. It is competently cast, with John Stuart as composer Michael, and Hugh Williams as his by-no-means-so-talented composer brother Paul. Both are in love with Roma Romano (Joan Maude), who is inconveniently promised to psychotic Cesare Bonelli (the nippy Dino Galvani). Unwisely, Bonelli is already involved with Nina, a shrewish ballerina. She murders Bonelli, but Michael is accused of the crime and sentenced to life imprisonment, eventually retiring to a monastery. The field is clear for Paul not only to marry Roma but to pass himself off as the composer of his brother's music, through which Paul has become famous. Conscience ultimately dictates that Paul (accompanied by Roma) confesses to his now-monkish brother. Michael forgives him, but decides not to return to the world outside the monastery walls.

The story was conceived by H. Fowler Mear, who had written for silents since 1917, and whose copious musical film-writing credits during the decade include *Lily of Killarney*, *Say It with Flowers*, *The Broken Melody*, John Baxter's *Music Hall* and *Stepping Toes*, *D'Ye Ken John Peel?* and *Squibs*. The dialogue is credited to Michael Barringer, a prolific screenwriter between 1928 and 1947. The opening minutes are unpromising: shots held too long of someone (supposedly Stuart) playing Albert Ketèlbey's 'In a Monastery Garden' (what else?) on a massive organ (a little over the top for a monastery, surely?). Sanctified religiosity fills the air, until the commencement of the flashback that explains why Paul has come to see his brother. It is then that the neatness of this unpretentious little film has its effect. Both Stuart and Williams give creditable performances through what may seem a pedantic progress, as do the rest of the cast. Joan Maude, who was once photographed by Bassano, displays a series of extraordinarily ornate outfits that must have had British housewives agog. Elvey makes the most of her lowering eyes, which now and again fix directly on the cinema audience. At Maude's memorial service, an admirer said of her, 'One cannot forget her beautiful eyes, with which she looked at the world with humour and understanding'.[10] In the monastery garden, her accent veers alarmingly between Italian and cut-glass RADA; some days at the studio were obviously better than others.

Gina Malo has rather more chances as 'that dancing woman' Nina, behaving badly at a café with an elderly male escort, shooting her lover and then, very unwisely during her solo turn in *Les Sylphides*, breaking down *en pointe* and confessing her crime. For this event, Hagen persuaded Marie Rambert to lend some of her dancers. Malo's Ophelia-like madness at the most inappropriate terpsichorean moment is one of the most amusing sequences. It was, however, all too little for the *New York Times*'s critic, condemning the film as 'stodgily directed and unimaginatively photographed'. The funereal pace meant that the audience suffered 'the punishment of hearing the same problem threshed over and over again', so that 'Whatever dramatic import the scenario may have had is lost in the meandering treatment it has been accorded'.[11]

Goodnight, Vienna was an early collaboration between Eric Maschwitz (writing as Holt Marvell) and composer George Posford, who between them went on to write several stage musicals. This tale of love in Vienna began life as a radio production. Maschwitz recalled how Herbert Wilcox listened in, rang Maschwitz and bought the film rights for a paltry £200, resulting in what Wilcox claimed was 'the first musical "talkie" to be made in this country'.[12]

It wasn't, but it was one of the most successful so far, and notable as the first time

Wilcox worked with Jack Buchanan and Anna Neagle. Lanky, suave, lazy-voiced, a lounge-lizard with a penchant for the most casual of choreography, Buchanan was already an established star, with eight silents behind him, and ahead of him a list of lightly enjoyable musical films that would carry him through to the beginning of the war, by which time the highly likeable performer was something of an anachronism. Now, *Bioscope* thought he would 'please his many admirers, though as he is called upon to do such little dancing – in which he excels – it is problematical if one more suited to the role could not have been found'.[13]

Neagle had already appeared on screen as Ann Eagle, with a small role in the 1930 comedy *Should a Doctor Tell?* and the 1932 *The Chinese Bungalow*. Wilcox's enthusiasm for Neagle was such that he placed her under long-term contract, assiduously building her reputation during the decade. In some ways, it was a strange mix. Astonishingly, for she could hardly be described as a brilliant actress, Wilcox had her star in biopics of Queen Victoria (twice, the same film more or less made over), Nell Gwyn, Florence Nightingale, Odette and Amy Johnson. Some of these impersonations bore more than a passing resemblance to one another. Each was accompanied by her armoury of mannerisms that too often made do for characterisation, while her singing roles provoked some budgerigar-trilling, but to everything she brought a dignity and zest.

Her less than convincing attempts at sophistication, accentuated in the 'Park Lane' type movies Wilcox put her into in later years, suggested an altogether less confident persona behind the impersonations. As David Shipman notes, none of this prevented Neagle having 'her very special place in British show business; although her abilities as actress, singer or dancer are really rather like painting with numbers, her genteel charm is considerable enough to have endeared her to great sections of the public'.[14] All things considered, *Goodnight, Vienna* was the sort of piece that suited her admirably, making few demands of her or her audience.

APRIL

Spring 1932 offered two minor diversions, the first from Sterling Films, made at Wembley, directed by Sinclair Hill and Thorold Dickinson. Produced by Louis Zimmerman, *The First Mrs Fraser* has a screenplay by Leslie Howard Gordon and Peter Ellis, worked up from St John Greer Ervine's 1929 play. Henry Ainley headlines the 'romantic drama with music',[15] playing James Fraser, married to Elsie (Joan Barry, who had dubbed Anny Ondra in Hitchcock's *Blackmail*). Elsie, set on marrying a peer of the realm, wants rid of James. Fortunately, James's first wife Janet (Dorothy Dix) still loves him, persuades him of the unsuitability of Wife No. 2, and gets him back. Music was provided by a Frances Day on the verge of stardom, the Gaucho Tango Orchestra, and Billy Cotton. Composer Philip Braham supervised the music.

MAY

For BIP, Cecil Lewis, creator of British sound cinema's first 'full' opera *Gipsy Blood*, wrote and directed ***Indiscretions of Eve***, snapping up glamorous Hungarian Steffi Duna, then in London appearing in the Noël Coward revue *Words and Music*, as the heroine who earns a living by 'wax modelling' for shop window dummies. Wealthy Sir Peter Martin (Fred Conyngham) is infatuated, but Eve is already engaged to the manager at the factory. Inevitably, she breaks free and becomes Lady Peter. Duna was almost immediately off to Hollywood, but in 1936 was in the Richard Tauber vehicle *Pagliacci*. Lewis wrote a score that included 'She's Only Wax', 'Is That Love?', 'Such A Nice Young Man' and 'Heading For Paradise'. Xylophonist Teddy Brown and the popular Marius B. Winter's Orchestra offered musical diversion.

Film Pictorial's review of Michael Powell's ***His Lordship*** was discouraging.

> This is the type of production that does not improve Britain's film prestige. It opens slowly and never at any time does it seem to be on the track of improving. Each minute becomes drearier and drearier; the yawns around us become more and more frequent and the depression ends eventually, about seventy-five minutes after it began. We gather it was supposed to be a comedy. You've probably heard of *The Comedy of Errors* …? This was the other one![16]

Powell's Westminster Films' 'musical extravaganza' quota quickie, one of several made in collaboration with producer Jerry Jackson, was one of the more adventurous of the decade. Now, the melting-pot that made up the British musical film was stirred in a manner that only someone of Powell's imagination could orchestrate, but this member of the aristocracy was unlikely to have popular appeal. Ralph Smart's screenplay, based on Oliver Madox Hueffer's novel *The Right Honourable*, concerned cockney plumber and peer of the realm Bert Gibbs (Jerry Verno). His girlfriend Leninia (Polly Ward) is a staunch communist. To keep up social pretences, Gibbs agrees to be seen as the romantic escort of a tempestuous Russian film star Ilya Myona (Janet Megrew), but is reconciled with Leninia by final fade-out. Music and lyrics have been variously attributed to Eric Maschwitz, V. C. Clinton-Baddeley, Walter Leigh (who would collaborate with Clinton-Baddeley on the operetta *Jolly Roger* the following year), Paul Bergen, Richard Addinsell, Ronald Hill and Leslie Holmes – a feast of talent that few British films of the time could muster. Steve Chibnall celebrates *His Lordship* as a picture that

> alienated critics and audiences by taking Verno's plausible working-class character and placing him in implausible situations. Powell had done much the same thing in *My Friend the King*, but this time he added gloriously absurd song-and-dance sequences that parodied contemporary tastes in musical talkies. In its plot and treat-

Hire purchase romance for Polly Ward and Jerry Verno in *His Lordship* (1932)

ment, *His Lordship* again held up a distorting mirror to the popular British cinema of the day with its class masquerades and phony sophistication. Its topsy-turvy world of social pretence and frustrated romance punctuated by musical interludes is reminiscent of a Gilbert and Sullivan operetta.[17]

Chibnall's perceptiveness is out of line with much of the film's contemporary reception. When it premiered in London, it was laughed off-screen. *Kinematograph Weekly* complained that 'This effort, which starts off as a musical comedy, drifts into burlesque, then finishes up in a rich satirical vein, is neither flesh, fowl, or good red herring.'[18] Along the way, Verno and Ward duetted in 'We'll Furnish It With Love' by Leslie Holmes and Clay Keyes.

JUNE

Whatever success **Lucky Girl** enjoyed on stage was squandered in its conversion to BIP's film, between Shaftesbury Avenue and Elstree.[19] The stage version, based on Reginald Berkeley's play *Mr Abdulla*, was the work of trusted hands Douglas Furber, R. P. Weston and Bert Lee, with a score mainly by America's Phil Charig. One of the stage production's stars, Gene Gerrard, was jointly responsible for the 'screen version' with Frank Miller, with whom he co-directed. On stage, Gerrard had played second fiddle to Clifford Mollison's King Stephen of Karaslavia, but he now stepped up to play the king, with Gus McNaughton as his sidekick, the 'efficiency expert' Hudson Greener. Charig and his composing helpers had got lost along the way; new music and lyrics were credited to actor-singer Arthur Margetson. These included 'There Is Another Island', 'For All Or Nothing' and 'All My Life'.

The result is unappealing. If Margetson was indeed responsible for the score, his work was disappointingly insipid: listen to Gerrard carolling his (wasted) leading lady Molly Lamont in 'Peeping Round The Corner', or their dreadful 'island' duet set among garden greenery where Lamont has been innocently strumming her guitar. The plot follows tired tracks. King Stephen's country is bankrupt, and identity confusion abounds when he hits London posing as Mr Abdullah. From this performance it's impossible to tell why Gerrard was so popular, or how anyone would have found him even faintly entertaining. An abundance of poor acting and ludicrous false beards crowds in, not helped by an embarrassing dance sequence à la oriental for Gerrard and McNaughton and young society ladies. Charitably, no choreographer is credited. A nadir is reached in an attempt at comedy with the two men encased in body armour. As for the dialogue, Lamont speaks no lie when she tells Gerrard, 'You do say the most ridiculous things.'

Jack's the Boy, and British cinemagoers throughout the 1930s needed no more information. There was only one Jack: Hulbert. His Christian name saw him through a hugely successful career in pictures: *Jack Ahoy* (1934), *Bulldog Jack* (1935) and *Jack of All Trades* (1936), never mind *The Camels Are Coming* (1934) – he played a character called Jack in that, too – and others, including several (not to be missed) with wife Cicely Courtneidge, with whom he enjoyed a professional partnership that lasted until old, old age. By now, Jack was one of the best-known actors in British sound films, having cut his teeth (somewhere above that extraordinary chin) on *Elstree Calling* and going on to bigger success in *The Ghost Train* and *Sunshine Susie*. He could not have wished for a stronger follow-up than Gainsborough's hugely enjoyable *Jack's the Boy*, produced by Michael Balcon and directed unobtrusively by Walter Forde (who seems to let Hulbert do his own thing). It was Hulbert's idea, worked up with Douglas Furber, and with a screenplay by W. P. Lipscomb and Sidney Gilliat. Records show that 11–12 million saw the picture, whose plot is of the simplest. Here, Jack is the son of the head of Scotland Yard, Commissioner Brown (Peter Gawthorne, one of the most genially authoritative performers known to casting directors). Jack eschews responsibility by getting plastered in nightclubs and singing endless choruses of Douglas Furber and Vivian Ellis's elemental 'The Flies Crawled Up The Window'.

> The flies crawled up the window
> That's all they had to do
> They went up by the thousand
> And came back two by two.
> The flies crawled up the window
> They said 'We love to roam
> So once more up the window
> And then we'll all go home

Ellis recalled that the film's cost was 'comparatively negligible and the result was an unqualified success from the point of view of both Press and box office, who do not always see eye to eye'. He confessed himself ashamed of 'The Flies Crawled Up The Window', but it sold a quarter of a million records. 'It was the easiest money I ever earned.'[20]

To his father's surprise, Jack turns his back on unalloyed pleasure and joins the police force, learning by default (he moves on a Punch and Judy show in the street) during a spate of jewel robberies. He meets the owner of the Loch Lomond café Mrs Bobday (Courtneidge at her sprightliest and most wide-eyed), and together, culminating in a Madame Tussauds finale, they hunt down the miscreants. En route, Courtneidge supervises the table-laying at a celebration ('If You Are Out To Give A Party') and joins Hulbert in a delightful cod ballet arranged by choreographer Philip Buchel and (as always) Jack. The romantic meeting with Ivy Bradley (Winifred Shotter) is shoe-horned in, encapsulated in the charming 'I Want To Cling To Ivy'.

There is something about the immediacy of this picture that remains as fresh as when it was filmed almost ninety years ago. This is as much down to Hulbert as to Forde (who had distinguished himself playing similar characters in silent comedies). We should not forget that Hulbert has claim to be the pre-eminent light comedian of British sound; it's obvious that he *owns* the picture. His involvement in its genesis was total, fired by his conviction that what people wanted to see was a 'tough adventure, and a hero doing mad things, but coming out on top at the end'. Low classifies *Jack's the Boy* as

> a comedy with songs rather than a musical. It recognised that this tall, amiable performer with his long legs and long chin, and his ability to toss off a pleasing song and a casual-seeming dance, needed an image for the public to identify.[21]

JULY

Love on the Spot was in good hands, produced by Basil Dean, screenplay by John Paddy Carstairs – although Reginald Purdell was credited for dialogue – and directed by Graham Cutts. Carstairs would work consistently in films into the 1960s, ultimately directing vehicles for Norman Wisdom, Tommy Steele and Charlie Drake. Cutts would have a considerable success later in the year with *Looking on the Bright Side*, going on to direct *Car of Dreams, Oh, Daddy!* and *Over She Goes*. Made at Ealing by Associated Talking Pictures, *Love on the Spot* began as a novel by Sapper. American actress Rosemary Ames made her screen debut as Joan Prior, daughter of a veteran crook, played by Aubrey Mather. Joan is disappointed when the young man she has fallen for (Richard Dolman) falls victim to her father's crookery. It's just as well that the young man is as much a crook as Joan and her father, and all three decide to go straight at fade-out. Ernest Irving was its musical director.

Many of the remaining films of the year had foreign origins; however busy British studios were, they seemed unbothered about developing home-grown writers. The policy of multi-language versions remained an option, as with the bilingual ***Monte Carlo Madness*** made in Berlin by UFA, whose recent achievements included *The Blue Angel* and *Congress Dances*, produced by writers and technicians whose skills often outstripped those of their British counterparts. Welcome as such product was, the BBFC did not recognise such films as British, but classified them as foreign, and therefore technically outside the scope of this book. This did not prevent a sizeable dose of Germanic escapism getting into British cinemas. Few cinemagoers worried themselves about provenance.

Produced by Erich Pommer and directed by Hanns Schwarz, *Monte Carlo Madness* had a screenplay by Frank Schulz, Hans Müller and Rowland V. Lee, based on a novel by Fritz Reck-Malleczewen, and starred Hans Albers, and Sari Maritza who replaced Anna Sten for the English edition. In translation, the movie couldn't successfully shake off the decidedly Teutonic atmosphere of the German original *Bomben auf Monte Carlo*. By this time, UFA was coming under pressure from the Nazis to tailor its films to official government policy, and the whiff of a decadent Weimar Republic wafts over all. Neither is the film as musical as some sources imply, although Werner R. Heymann's score is inventive enough here and there. Within a few years, British audiences would surely have been unwelcoming to Nazi comedy, no matter how prettily dressed up, and Albers would become an actor too closely associated with Hitler's party for comfort.

Basically another import, British and Dominions' **The Love Contract** was a Herbert Wilcox production, in effect a remake of Excelsior-Film's *Chauffeur Antoinette* exhibited in Berlin in January 1932. The screenplay/translation was the work of several hands, including director Herbert Selpin, Roger Blum, George C. Klaren and Heinz Goldberg, worked from Jean de Létraz's original play. Dependable straight man Owen Nares played a financier who is partly responsible for Antoinette having lost her house and fortune. Resourcefully, she becomes his chauffeur and, after various complexities, regains her house and gets her man. Winifred Shotter starred in the role originally played by Charlotte Ander. The music is by Ralph Benatzky, best known for such operettas as *Casanova* (based on the music of Johann Strauss II) and *Im weissen Rössel* (*White Horse Inn*).

More love arrived, this time propelled by **Love on Wheels**, produced at Elstree by Michael Balcon, and directed for Gainsborough by Victor Saville. A follow-up for Jack Hulbert after the success of *Jack's the Boy*, it linked him to glamorous Leonora Corbett in a romantic comedy tied up with adventures around (and shot in) Selfridge's department store. The 'foreign' story was the work of Frank Schulz (*Sunshine Susie, Monte Carlo Madness*) and Ernst Angel, made into a screenplay by trusted hands Angus Macphail and Robert Stevenson, with dialogue attributed to Douglas Furber, also credited as lyricist for the songs, with music by Jean Gilbert: 'The Same Old Bus', 'I Hunger For You', 'Wear Gloves', 'Little Girl', 'Find The Lady' and 'Two In A Bar'. The German art director was Alexander Vetchinsky, whose designs enhanced several British musical films including *Sunshine Susie, Marry Me, Soldiers of the King, Aunt Sally*, and *Shipyard Sally*.

SEPTEMBER

The onset of autumn brought BIP's **The Maid of the Mountains**, adapted for the screen by director Lupino Lane, Douglas Furber, Frank Miller, Victor Kendall and Edwin Greenwood from the Frederick Lonsdale–Fraser-Simson British musical hit of the Great War. Another attempt by Lane to re-establish his reputation in Britain, it wasn't the ideal vehicle. Low complained that 'He made much of his Hollywood experience but some of the sound films he directed in Britain during the thirties show that as a director he did not adapt his style to the new demands of the sound film, but continued to employ the techniques of the stage and the silent film.' What was more, his version was 'slow and stagy, with jokes held interminably, using close-ups and illustrative reference shots in the manner of silent film.'[22]

This waddling warhorse of an operetta on film, with its lush waltzing insistence that 'Love Will Find A Way', was far removed from the vocal and physical splendour of the original 1917 stage production with leading lady Jose Collins (now matronly, she would star in Stanley Lupino's *Facing the Music* the following year). BIP's maid was Australian Nancy Brown, who would go on to play in *Facing the Music* and *A Southern Maid*. Her leading man was Harry Welchman, the epitome of the manly hero of stage musicals in London, including *The Desert Song*, *The New Moon* and *The Vagabond King*, and on Broadway. An ideal choice for the irresistible brigand Baldasarre to Brown's maid, Welchman now starred in his first sound picture, followed up by the 1933 *A Southern Maid*.

If more vigour was needed, it arrived with Gracie Fields's **Looking on the Bright Side**, made at Ealing by Associated Talking Pictures and without doubt the brightest of the year. It is difficult to over-emphasise the significance of Fields's presence throughout the 1930s. Where else is this total naturalness, Fields's ability to directly communicate from the screen to the two and sixpennies, to be found? In a grey Britain, she was not a role model – who else in the real world, after all, could sing and lark and be as socially outrageous? – but it must be that women saw in her a vision of what they might achieve. She emits a strength, a stoicism, that underpins everything she touches. It's a remarkable thing to witness, perhaps most noticeable at this early point of her career, before the industry sucked so much naturalness out of her. Luckily, co-directors Basil Dean and Graham Cutts had other excellent components on hand, not least songs that, despite not being listed or attributed in the credits, hold the piece together: 'After Tonight We Say Good-Bye' (Leo Towers and Harry Leon); 'You're More Than The Whole World To Me' (Will E. Haines, Maurice Beresford and Frank Sumner); 'He's Dead But He Won't Lie Down' (Haines, Beresford and Jimmy Harper); and 'I Hate You' by Harry Parr Davies, a number he had written for Fields's stage act. Music is at the heart of this movie, and here it's managed beautifully, arranged by Carroll Gibbons, with uncredited stock music from J. S. Zamecnik.

It gives point to the essential community spirit celebrated so exuberantly in the opening scenes, when eager young composer Laurie (Richard Dolman), obliged to work as a hairdresser, receives printed copies of his new song. Soon his tenement building is seething with crowds assuring him that they too are looking on the bright side. This is early Ealing territory, story and dialogue by Dean and Archie Pitts, a hymn to social cohesion. Plucky Gracie encourages Laurie in everything he does, and gives him the title for another hit song, but Laurie is lured away by a rival who tells him 'You make me feel like a flame', before – in a hugely touching finale – being reunited with tearful Gracie. It is impossible to imagine the film without Fields. The *Manchester Guardian* reported, 'She is herself so completely that even the scenes of the heaviest sentiment she puts across with unflagging verve.'[23]

The closing moments are pure magic, the superimposing of Laurie's happy chorus song vying with his manic playing of the piano. The camera tracks Gracie clambering, as fast as she can, up the steps of the tenement until she is in reach of his window. Who could not be moved as Laurie's room and Gracie's room slide toward one another for the lovers' embrace?

Dean considered that 'for all its crudities' the film

> did give Gracie ample opportunity to indulge a riotous sense of fun, interspersed with slabs of unashamed English sentiment which pleased the popular audience mightily. One paper seized upon its robust quality, declaring that here was a 'gloriously British talkie, one that Dickens might have devised if he had lived today' – a useful box office comment but decidedly unfair to Dickens. And the *Manchester Guardian* (of all papers) headlined its notice 'A British Triumph'. A Gracie Fields Triumph would have been more appropriate. In the event the film played to enormous business in every part of Great Britain and the Commonwealth, except the West End of London – that stronghold was for later conquest.[24]

OCTOBER

The use of foreign product continued with Gainsborough's translation of the German-made *Mädchen zum Heiraten* into Michael Balcon's **Marry Me**, directed at Islington by its original German director William Thiele. Nine writers were credited with the British adaptation of István Zágon's play, but there was no attempt to relocate its story to Britain for the trouble-strewn romance between Renate Müller as Ann Linden, an assistant in a gramophone shop, and her boss Robert Hart, played by Ian Hunter. The score by composer Michael Krausz, with English lyrics by Desmond Carter and Frank Eyton, included the title song, 'Wonderful Me' and what was presumably a stab at revisiting the spirit of Müller's *Sunshine Susie*, 'A Little Sunshine'. The casting was solid enough, with music-hall veteran George Robey in prime place.

The next two films released in October were made in Germany. **Happy Ever After** was directed by Paul Martin and Robert Stevenson for Universum Film Aktiengesellschaft (UFA). In effect, patrons of the local kinema at Bexhill-on-Sea were sitting through *Ein Blondes Traum*, possibly misled by the predominantly British cast list. The German original was worked up from a scenario by Walter Reisch and Billy Wilder, and Lilian Harvey was held over to repeat her winning performance as Jou-Jou for the British audience. Her career is one of the most interesting of the period. Helene Lilian Muriel Pape was born in London to a German father and English mother. She went on to become a major German cinema star via her partnership with Willy Fritsch, begun in the 'silent' operetta *Chaste Susanne* in 1926, and in 1931 had set down the legendary version of 'Just Once For All Time'

Foreign product at work: 'Sunshine Susie' Renate Müller in the
Gaumont-British *Marry Me* (1932)

in *Congress Dances*. With her somewhat cool but mischievously elfin qualities, she was never fully accepted by British cinemagoers as one of their own.

Her co-stars for *Happy Ever After* were two British big beasts, the husband and wife team of Jack Hulbert and Cicely Courtneidge[25] (playing Illustrated Ida), joined here by Sonnie Hale. For such talents, rooted as they were in the British tradition, the making of a bilingual could easily tip over into artistic nightmare. Courtneidge's idiosyncratic style must have seemed foreign. Remembering his year working in German studios, and how tedious was the business of shooting a remake in a different language, co-director Robert Stevenson recognised her dilemma: 'If you imagine what it was like for Cicely Courtneidge to be directed in an allegedly funny scene through a German interpreter by a Jugo Slav director [Paul Martin] who could not speak English, you will realise what a monstrous Tower of Babel a multilingual film studio becomes.'[26]

In fact, under producer Erich Pommer's jurisdiction, the studios at Babelsberg were run on strict martial lines, in what Stevenson described as 'an astonishing military atmosphere'. The various impossibilities arising from the production of other language versions were seemingly unending, not least that 'in questions of sex, the continental story often appears to the English public brutal and ill-mannered, and the romantic lover, whom the continentals consider a hero, often appears to an English audience a cad.'[27]

The usual frictions on the studio floor were more likely to develop during the making of the bi or trilingual. During *Happy Ever After*, Hulbert's behaviour was 'very difficult and has upset everybody a bit, which is pretty easy to do as they don't speak our language.'[28] Nevertheless, British audiences probably put up with Hulbert and Douglas Furber's screenplay (most probably much adapted on the floor once in Germany) with its two male stars as window cleaners (Hulbert and Sonnie Hale) who help turn Jou-Jou into a star. In the circumstances, its theme song 'Keep On The Bright Side' struck a hopeful note, with Harvey singing 'In A Year, In A Day' and 'Truly Rural Gentleman'.

Tell Me Tonight, another bilingual made in Germany under the auspices of Cine-Allianz, was written around Jan Kiepura. When the film surfaced in the States as *Be Mine Tonight* the following year, the *New York Times* reported, 'Much is made very charmingly out of little [in a] most agreeable blending of melody, romance and humour. It is an artistically photographed production, some of the outdoor scenes being particularly inviting, and instead of the chanting of the brooding blues or tawdry airs one hears excerpts from *Rigoletto*, *La Traviata* and other operas, including a pleasing theme song.'[29]

Kiepura had been exported to Switzerland as the singer Enrico Ferraro who obligingly switches identity with a refugee Kotetsky (Sonnie Hale, retained in Germany after *Happy Ever After*), along the way discovering romance with Mathilde (Magda Schneider). Mischa Spoliansky wrote the title song, subsequently furnished with an English lyric by Frank Eyton, and later recorded by the likes of David Whitfield and Mario Lanza. Now, Kiepura sang its definitive version, along with 'Che Gelida Manina', 'Ach So Fromm', 'La Danza', 'O Sole Mio' and 'My Heart Is Full Of Sunshine'. Directed at Babelsberg by Anatole Litvak, the English screenplay was by John Orton. Dependable Edmund Gwenn and Athene Seyler were among the distinguished British contingent sent to Germany to help convince British audiences that they were watching a domestic film, but *Tell Me Tonight* was refused classification as home-grown.

NOVEMBER

British cinemagoer Gladys Langford's reaction to Stanley Lupino's *Sleepless Nights* was unequivocal. 'I never saw such piffle. No wonder no one wants English films.'[30]

Gladys had a point, especially when they were held up against this year's Hollywood product: Bing Crosby in *The Big Broadcast*, Cary Grant in *This Is the Night*, the Ernst Lubitsch-driven *One Hour with You* starring Maurice Chevalier and Jeanette McDonald, the brilliant Eddie Cantor as *The Kid from Spain* (made at a cost unimaginable to makers of British films), and a leading lady, Marion Davies, knocking her British equivalents into a far-off corner as the chorus-girl hailed as *Blondie of the Follies*. Comparison with much British product was undoubtedly odious, but was no bar to BIP's production of Lupino's new vehicle directed by Thomas Bentley, whose reputation rests on a few titles, among which his sound version of Dickens's *The Old Curiosity Shop*, despite its insufficiencies, can hold its own (he had already made two silent versions). Bentley had also been responsible for *Harmony Heaven*, which in no way suggested a deft touch with musical film.

Lupino's reputation has hardly outlived his early death, but he was an agreeable comedian, turning his hand to providing ideas and stories for his movies, even as producer and songwriter. His fooling may be an acquired taste, his usually temporarily disastrous amorous adventures with impossibly beautiful women difficult to take seriously (he was no Valentino), his frog-like dancing at least matching his pop-eyed response to all life threw at him, and his apparent ability to be happy when carousing in the most unlikely-looking nightclubs and high-class venues. At some point most of his films inhabit these supposed realities. Unrealistic as they are, they sustain Lupino's cheerful personality.

Even Gladys might agree (although I doubt it) that *Sleepless Nights* gets off to a decent start, with its continuous echoing of Noel Gay's 'I Don't Want To Go To Bed', in Lupino's insistent lyric. It's clear that our hero likes the hedonistic life, as he races away in a taxi at heaven knows what ungodly hour of the morning, rushing from one of those luxurious nightclubs along with the evening-dressed clientele madly dancing their way into the street, watched by postmen and milkmen, so caught up in the enjoyment that they join in. Even model animals (a neat little trick) join in the fun.

Tireless reporter Guy Raynor (Lupino) hasn't been to bed for three days but is sent to Nice in pursuit of a golden trophy, incidentally providing him with a sweetheart in Marjorie Drew (Polly Ward). Victor Kendall's screenplay, probably liable to Lupino's interpolations of corny humour, is serviceable enough, and the score brings brightness, with Ward singing 'With All My Heart', and two duets, 'It's Happened' and 'Just One More'. Born Byno Poluski, Ward had a career that saw out the 1930s, signing off in 1938 with the rather more effective Stanley Lupino picture *Hold My Hand*.

It's tempting to compare the 'Just One More' number, when Lupino and Ward dance their way around a yacht, with what an afloat Astaire and Rogers might have done in such a location. Here, the choreographer, if that is not too strong a definition, is Ralph Reader, and the routine is rudimentary; indeed, much of it looks as if it was made up on the spot. Curiously, there's a hint of gayness when two effeminate sailors break out into dance (hastily clipped either by the director or editor) and when a foreign chef does a bit of a turn. Otherwise, it's Lupino's froggy steps and his trademarked balletic leaps across the deck (although he hasn't the body for it) that take the eye. After such folly, a plot seems unnecessary. When at last hero and heroine are allowed to go to bed as the closing credits arrive, there is subtext of sorts in the 'I Don't Want To Go To Bed' motif. Space is found for some blatant product placement, with a dress show sequence featuring 'Display Frocks by British Celanese Ltd.' A similar exhibition of ladies' fashion can be found in Lupino's *Cheer Up!*.

Producer Herbert Wilcox was not one to let a contemporary craze go unheeded. An early example of what might be termed 'bandleader' films, **Say It with Music**, made by British and Dominions at Elstree, was constructed around the music of Jack Payne and his orchestra, directed by Jack Raymond, late of *Splinters* and soon to be director for *Come Out of the Pantry* and *When Knights Were Bold*. William Pollock's screenplay incorporated the BBC Dance Band, with Payne playing himself, a bandleader who helps bring a promising composer back from amnesia. The somewhat starless cast featured in its most minor roles Anna Lee and William Hartnell. As well as the Irving Berlin title song, the score contained Ray Noble's 'Good Morning Mr Sun', 'Love Is The Sweetest Thing', 'I'll Do My Best To Make You Happy' and 'Sing And Smile Your Cares Away'. Payne would go on to the much less sumptuous *Sunshine Ahead*, made by the always-strapped-for-cash John Baxter in 1935.

It was back to foreign product with John Stafford's production of **Where Is This Lady?**, previously known as Billy Wilder's *Es war einmail ein Walzer (Once There Was a Waltz)*, in which Marta Eggerth played Steffi Pirzinger opposite the Rudi

Moebius of Rolf von Goth. Eggerth's other British work included *My Heart Is Calling* and *Unfinished Symphony* (both 1934) and *The Divine Spark* (1935). Directed by Laszlo Vajda and Victor Hanbury, the British screenplay of *Where Is This Lady?* was by Stafford and Sydney Blow, filmed at Elstree by its German star with home-grown Owen Nares and Wendy Barrie in the other leads. Here was another flag of all nations set in Vienna, where a couple find success in turning a bank into a nightclub. The radiant Eggerth and a score specially written by Franz Lehár set the picture apart. Lehár had already provided music for the German-made *Die grosse Attraktion* (1931) and would go on to write for the 1933 *Grossfürstin Alexandra*, although his music for films was not considered among his best.

Based on a stage production seen at the Shaftesbury Theatre the previous year, Michael Balcon's **The Midshipmaid**, made at Shepherd's Bush, had a scenario by Stafford Dickens made up from Ian Hay and Stephen King-Hall's original play. What had basically been a farce reappeared with musical embellishments, including a breezy nautical overture arranged by Gaumont-British musical director Louis Levy, and one number from Noel Gay and Clifford Grey, 'One Little Kiss From You', shared between its over-the-title star Jessie Matthews, tyro John Mills and Basil Sydney. Director Albert de Courville made the best of the somewhat tedious storyline concerning the efforts of Sir Percy Newbiggin (Fred Kerr) to introduce rigorous economies into the Navy, on which mission Sir Percy is sent to Malta with his daughter Celia (Matthews).

de Courville had a reputation as a taskmaster director, remembered tactfully by Balcon as 'One of the most capricious men I have ever met, though with extraordinary if erratic charm.'[31] Michael Thornton colourfully relates that Matthews 'spent that autumn of 1932 racing between the two film sets [for *The Midshipmaid* and *The Good Companions*] at Shepherd's Bush and driving home to Hampton in the small hours [having worked from early morning]. One night she felt so exhausted that she fell asleep with her head against the car horn and woke the entire neighbourhood for miles around. But she was too tired to care.'

The pressures on Matthews were already considerable, complicated by personality disorders that clouded her career. Unhappy as she may have been in working with de Courville, on screen she maintains a pertness, despite exaggerated vowels that must have caused tittering among some cinemagoers. Helpfully, some time is taken up with the staging of an on-board concert by the naval crew preparing for 'a potpourri of musical blancmange'. The lower ratings include a frustrated bandmaster (Edwin Lawrence) and po-faced A. W. Baskcomb as Pook, in sequences that recall the atmosphere of *Splinters*. Outside of the concert, de Courville has assembled a collection of naval officers, most prominently Mills and Anthony Bushell, while the social divide between this privileged personnel and the less-educated sailors is sharply realised in several amusing scenes that remain watchable.

DECEMBER

'For the love of Mike' may well have been one of the reactions to *For the Love of Mike*, based on the Saville Theatre stage production that had only shut up shop in May. Monty Banks's production for BIP retained the show's librettist Clifford Grey as screenwriter, now joined by Frank Launder. Bobby Howes repeated his stage role of frolicsome private secretary Bob Seymour. Most happily, the music is by Jack Waller and Joseph Tunbridge, who would provide the British musical with a string of frothy musicals throughout the 1930s. Here, Howes has two of their best numbers, 'Got A Date With An Angel' and 'Sing Brothers'. Also retained from the stage production is Arthur Riscoe as a leering private eye, and in minor roles the glorious Lady (Viola) Tree, and (a regular in Waller and Tunbridge films) Wylie Watson. Meanwhile, Banks could not resist a cameo appearance as a chef, assisted by the Carlyle Cousins, during 'Sing Brothers', but it's a clumsy incidental in a film that too often looks as if it's been put together in haste. On the dance floor, Australian Fred Leslie and Ivy Schilling may have deserved the soubriquet 'London's Fred and Adele Astaire', but in this instance Leslie's routines are undisciplined; a few more rehearsals might have helped.

Banks's handling of much of the too-drawn-out comedy is decidedly slack, and Riscoe's antics veer to the tiresome. Happily, relief is at hand courtesy of the supporting players. It's a rare opportunity to see Tree, who made only a handful of films, as the out-of-her-social-depth Mrs Miller, balancing on a shooting stick or revealing rather too much back or delighting in her social status ('The peacocks 'as arrived'). She's at her best when matched by Watson's timid vicar, confessing that he's 'a happy little chappie full of glee', twanging his cello in response to Tree's plea for him to 'give us the vulgar boatman'. 'I'm far from well,' he tells her. 'No, not since I caught a chill between Michaelmas and Epiphany.'

In the star part, Howes's over-elocuted speaking marks him out as a male equivalent of Jessie Matthews, while his comedy technique is stretched to the limit; much of this is simple silliness. The sleep-walking scene is ineffective, the idea being more successfully worked in Waller and Tunbridge's *Please Teacher*. Jerky camerawork, poor sound recording, untidy movement and clumsy editing have their way, so that one seizes on the slightest amusement. As they are the last to leave a party, Watson's Revd James tells Tree, 'The first shall be last and the last shall be first.' 'Oh really!' she exclaims, 'I didn't know you were interested in horse racing.' Not a sparkling witticism, perhaps, but in *For the Love of Mike* it does well enough.

Michael Powell's ninth film was received with some bewilderment. *Kinematograph Weekly* suggested 'the treatment shows some imagination, if the stars shine but dimly'.[32] Mops, the chirping cockney sparrow at the heart of Westminster Films' **Born Lucky**, is in the line of chirping cockney sparrow Amelia 'Squibs' Hopkins,

Accomplished dramatic and musical actress Rene Ray awaits a celestial event in *Born Lucky* (1932)

as played by Betty Balfour in George Pearson's 1921 silent *Squibs*. The 1932 Mops, more waif-like than Balfour, was Rene Ray, co-starring with John Longden and Talbot O'Farrell.

Produced by Jerome Jackson and filmed at Wembley's Fox-British studios, *Born Lucky* had a screenplay by Ralph Smart based on Oliver Sandys's novel *Mops*. Mops is the wafer-like soubrette of a tatty touring concert party run by her caring protector Turnips (O'Farrell). Out of work, Mops and Turnips find employment in the hop-fields of Kent, where Mops meets Frank (Longden) whom she assumes is a tramp. He isn't; he's a playwright getting 'copy' for his next project. Working as a maid to Lady Chard (Helen Ferrars), Mops meets Frank again. He orchestrates her getting the leading role in his new musical show. She becomes a star, and happiness ensues.

Steve Chibnall notes one of the problems that *Born Lucky* faced as a quota quickie, for 'this musical was even longer than *His Lordship* and would have been a real squeeze to accommodate on most suburban double bills without unauthorised trimming'. More, 'Although Miss Ray was herself a rising star, her film failed to clean up the mess left by *His Lordship*.'[33]

1933

This is the most thrilling finale of the decade's musical films
Britannia of Billingsgate

Yes, Mr Brown
The Little Damozel
The Good Companions
Soldiers of the King
King of the Ritz
Radio Parade
The Only Girl
Facing the Music
Waltz Time
Maid Happy
Falling for You
Britannia of Billingsgate
Prince of Arcadia

Bitter Sweet
Early to Bed
This Week of Grace
The Song You Gave Me
The Girl from Maxim's
This is the Life
Going Gay
That's a Good Girl
You Made Me Love You
A Southern Maid
I Adore You
For Love of You
Aunt Sally

JANUARY

Globe-trotting cinemagoers may have gazed up at the new Jack Buchanan entertainment *Yes, Mr Brown* and recalled that they had already seen it in Germany, France and Italy masquerading under various titles. It probably didn't matter to British audiences, who must have pretty well known what they were in for if one of their favourite artistes was above the title. Made at Elstree for British and Dominions, Herbert Wilcox's production (a stretch at 94 minutes) was directed by Buchanan, working on Douglas Furber's screenplay adapted from Paul Franck and Ludwig Hirschfeld's stage musical *Geschäft mit Amerika*. Paul Abrahám, composer of Renate Müller's 'Today I Feel So Happy', wrote the score with Furber as British lyricist, including 'Leave A Little To Me', 'If You Would Learn To Live', and the title song.

In Vienna, Nicholas Baumann (Buchanan) temporarily loses his wife Clary (Margot Grahame) when they argue over a dog. Having planned to impress his American boss Mr Brown (Hartley Power), Nicholas gets his secretary Ann (Elsie Randolph, making her debut in her professional partnership with Buchanan) to take her place. To everyone's satisfaction, Mr Brown marries Ann, while Nicholas and Clary are reunited. The reviews were reasonable, with *Variety* finding that 'There seems to be no limit to the entertaining talents of Jack Buchanan. He not only stars in this picture, but directed it in a manner which establishes him as an expert', citing 'A generous production, directed in good taste, marred occasionally by defective lighting, but not enough to interfere with the fact that it is another successful British picture.'[1] *Picturegoer* was less effusive, discovering 'a far cry from *Goodnight, Vienna*, with its polished technique and sophistry, to this naïve and conventional marital upset play.'[2] Whatever the critical reaction, Buchanan's stylish insouciance was now embedded in the British psyche, and would serve him well on stage and screen. Besides which, *any* film featuring the inimitable Vera Pearce deserves attention.

FEBRUARY

For Herbert Wilcox, an adaptation of **The Little Damozel** began to consolidate the ascendancy of his *Goodnight, Vienna* leading lady Anna Neagle over his previously favoured Chili Bouchier. He had sat in the gallery for the first night of Monckton Hoffe's stage play and may have seen the 1916 silent film version starring Barbara Conrad as cabaret chanteuse Julie Alardy. During a chance meeting with Hoffe in the lavatory of the Savoy Hotel, Wilcox introduced himself to the playwright, and left having negotiated the film rights. It must have seemed an ideal vehicle for his new star. Neagle was cast opposite Canadian James Rennie as Recky Poole. The press attempted to interest its readers in yet another flimsy and highly unlikely sequence of events, explaining that it

> concerns the affairs of a little cabaret girl, sophisticated and alluring, but whose character reveals greater depths of sweetness when she marries Recky (Rennie), a good-looking wastrel, unaware that he had been paid a considerable sum of money to make her his wife. The role of the cabaret girl calls for an actress with the ability to convince the onlooker of her change of character and also requires an artist who can both sing and dance. This was no easy role to fill, but Herbert Wilcox, determined to back his faith in Neagle, gave her this important part. This charming actress gives a really splendid performance, and the opening of the film, showing Miss Neagle as the cabaret artiste, gives her the opportunity to sing some delightful numbers. It is interesting to record that *The Little Damozel* played to absolute capacity during its London season, despite the strong opposition of [the much more sophisticated American filming of Noël Coward's patriotic epic] *Cavalcade*.[3]

In one week 42,000 Mancunians paid to see Neagle's new romantic extravaganza, 'a deliberate attempt to create a more sophisticated and glamorous image for her but she continued to look demure even decked out in a daring black negligee'.[4] The *Observer* detected in Neagle 'a curious inner clarity independent of

Anna Neagle in daring mood as *The Little Damozel* (1933)

outward stimuli. Her performance in a difficult part is as good as it well could be; it gives distinction to a film of which we should not otherwise be particularly proud.'[5] The score included Noël Coward's 'The Dream Is Over', and Anona Winn and Ray Noble's 'What More Can I Ask?' and 'Brighter Than The Sun'.

MARCH

'It let something loose in me that had been tied up before, I think. It may be that the secret of its wide appeal was the feeling of something coming loose.'[6] The film of J. B. Priestley's most famous novel, *The Good Companions*, was the first to receive a Royal Command performance, at the New Victoria cinema. A special screening was attended by the Marchioness of Londonderry to ensure that royal sensibility would not be offended. The film's director wondered if the moment when the eminently respectable Jess Oakroyd said 'Bloody awful' should be excised. Not at all. The Marchioness assured him, 'The king likes a bit of swearing.'[7]

Priestley's sprawling saga of a concert party's ups and downs had already reached the London stage in 1931, two years after the novel's publication and two years before Balcon's film. On that occasion, Priestley had himself collaborated on the adaptation, music provided by Richard Addinsell. An updated, Technicolor remake in 1957 directed by J. Lee-Thompson seemed out of time, even if the cast included Eric Portman's Jess Oakroyd and Celia Johnson's Miss Trant. With Joyce Grenfell's intrusion striking altogether the wrong note, and Janette Scott as Susie, the tone and playing in this later film had few of the qualities of the 1933 edition; its score was very much of its period but with none of the true 'pierrot' atmosphere, and the updating necessarily distanced the efficacy of Priestley's original. *Variety* was unimpressed with this second film version, describing 'a pedestrian musical ... It hardly stands comparison with a Hollywood musical', despite gallant efforts by choreographer Irving Davies in set-piece numbers. Then, there was 'the moderate quality of the score. There isn't a standout song.'[8] A 1974 London stage version with music by André Previn had the advantage of John Mills's Jess and Judi Dench's Miss Trant, but the spirit was missing. Most surprisingly, Yorkshire TV's prodigious 1980s adaptation by Alan Plater at last turned the book into a full-blown musical, with David Fanshawe's evocative and inventive score easily outstripping Previn.

Balcon's production of *The Good Companions* was one of the outstanding British films of the year, Saville's direction marking a pronounced improvement on much of the other product from British studios. Against the background of dullness and disappointment, accentuated by the grimy photography of mills, chimneys and industrial endeavour besmirching the English landscape – and thereby suggesting something of the socialist zest that Priestley expressed in the writing of his great *English Journey* – this adaptation, with scenario and dialogue by W. P. Lipscomb, is sure-footed. Essentially a bringing-together of disparate strands, the effectiveness of Priestley's story demands strong players. It has them here, in Mary Glynne's Miss Trant; Jessie Matthews's Susie Dean, the song-and-dance girl destined for stardom; John Gielgud's Inigo Jollifant[9] and, most touching of all, Edmund Gwenn's Jess. It's Priestley's literary generosity that opens the door to a superb supporting cast: Olive Sloane who has hysterics at losing her meek little lover; the blooming Margaret Yarde (a favourite of Tod Slaughter melodramas) as the outraged proprietor of a roadside caff; Wally Patch as a van driver scoundrel; Margery Binner's soubrette; a young Jack Hawkins as a perky lodger; dog-faced A. W. Baskcomb as the Dinky-Doos' comedian; Muriel Aked as the wife of Miss Trant's vicar; and Max Miller (more a special guest than an ensemble player) breezing in as a breathless Tin Pan Alley merchant.

Saville's film is also notable for its score, music by George Posford (*Goodnight, Vienna*) and lyrics by Douglas Furber, probably the cleverest in British sound pictures up to this time, with some fine underscoring, the work of Leighton Lucas, Bretton Byrd and/or Walter R. Collins. There's even a snatch of Vivian Ellis's 'The Flies Crawled Up The Window', from Balcon's Jack Hulbert vehicle *Jack's the Boy* of the previous year, played on a gramophone. The pastiche musical numbers are confined to the concert party context, arising naturally from that milieu.[10] Posford and Furber come up with a string of gems: 'Lucky For Me', sung first by Richard Dolman's juvenile; Baskcomb's policeman's song; Margery Binner's 'Under The Lilac Tree'; Dennis Hoey (the long-suffering Inspector Lestrade in the Hollywood Sherlock Holmes series) intoning 'Sailor Beware'; Matthews and company in the sprightly, silly 'I'm Gertie From Girton'. Beyond the pastiche, Posford and Furber are at their best in 'Three Wishes' (duetted by Matthews and Gielgud) and 'Let Me Give My Happiness To You', numbers that exemplify Matthews's appeal.

Even at a distance of eighty years, there's no denying her potency, her extraordinary brightness matched with an intensity that no other female star of the period could match. Her only competitor in the field was Gracie Fields, seemingly more natural and of the people than the over-elocuted Matthews, but Fields, although the better with a song (never Matthews's strongest asset), couldn't or wouldn't dance, and didn't respond to being glamourised on screen. It may be that *The Good Companions* marks not only the beginning of Matthews' ascendancy, but also its apex. All too quickly, throughout the decade the freshness began to fade, notably when Saville stopped directing her, and husband Sonnie Hale took control. But for now, Matthews's (or Susie Dean's?) urgent need to become a star struck a chord with British cinemagoers, hurrying to their local dream palaces to escape the general dreariness of 1930s Britain. As she tells Jollifant, 'It's not just for myself, Inigo – it's for my parents. To make up for their dreary journeys and hard work and rotten pay. Somehow I'd like them to know I'm having what they couldn't have.' It's at such moments that Priestley's sentiment strikes, or when Matthews goes into a dance when music, cinematography and lighting turn to magic, the effect so diaphanous, so ethereal, that one thinks the gods must be looking down on her.

Priestley had considered her unsuitable for the role, while Balcon remembered that 'for some reason she was generally regarded as a dead loss for films',[11] but after seeing her in rushes of *There Goes the Bride* he signed her for a two-year contract (£7,000 for the first, £9,000 for the second). She was already being overworked, making *The Midshipmaid* in the morning and *The Good Companions* in the afternoon, and already plagued by self-doubt. 'The camera scares me stiff,' she told Saville after watching one of her scenes. 'It tells the truth about me. It shows just what an ugly little bitch I am.'[12] He believed that 'Jessie was fully charged with sexual emotion, which she constantly attempted to stifle.'[13] The truth about Matthews will probably never be told, but for David Shipman 'her films do not survive as mere historical relics: many of them have a genuine gaiety – a rare quality in British films – and the impish charm of the star does not fade'.[14]

Meanwhile, C. A. Lejeune recognised that Priestley's book had been 'translated to the screen with sympathy and selection', presenting 'The first real example of the English picaresque on the screen'.[15] Of course, it was also a rare example of a notable British novel being transferred to the cinema and not being bastardised in the process. It rings with Priestley's conviction that 'perfection is not to be found, neither in man nor in the lot they're offered, to say nothing of the tales we tell of them, these hints and guesses, words in the air and gesticulating shadows, these stumbling chronicles of a dream of life'.[16]

The most commercially successful 1930s film that Cicely Courtneidge made without Jack Hulbert was Gainsborough's **Soldiers of the King,** produced by Michael Balcon, directed by Maurice Elvey (although Hulbert was reported as having directed much of Courtneidge's material), and scripted by W. P. Lipscomb, John Orton and Hulbert. Courtneidge recalled:

> I played a grandmother who sat in a box listening to her daughter sing 'There's Something About A Soldier That Is Fine, Fine, Fine'. I also played the daughter, proving that one of the advantages when making a film is that you can be in two places at once. Through a mixture of Jack's direction with Maurice Elvey, and a script that gave me the opportunity to give of my best, the result was a film which people saw more than once; in fact it was usually not so much a question of 'Have you seen *Soldiers of the King*'? but how many times?[17]

Another question was 'Who will be the new head of the Marvello Troupe?', an old established family of travelling players descended from Nell Gwyn. Their elderly matriarch star Jenny (Courtneidge) retires, passing the crown to her daughter Maisie (Courtneidge again, in a series of bewilderingly outlandish costumes). Their meetings involve some effective cinematic trickery. The affections and friction among the Marvellos is well portrayed by stalwarts Ivor McLaren, Olive Sloane and the Victorian barnstormer Bransby Williams. Soon enough, Maisie is centre stage in top hat and evening dress, male-impersonating her way through Noel Gay and lyricist Clifford Grey's 'The Moment I Saw You'. This, of course, is typical Courtneidge; as a swaggerer in military uniform she is the equal of Vesta Tilley, Ella Shields or Hetty King, and her femininity has a hectoring side to her that none of the others had. Her style may not be to everyone's taste, but who could question her superb technique? The adagio sequence, with no double in sight, reminds us that no one working in cinema today would even attempt it (Courtneidge was forty years old). A scratch of her leg, a turn of the eye … do not be deceived into thinking these are flashes of the moment. They are the carefully conceived nuances of a talent that knew its ability and limits, of an actress who was renowned for leaving nothing to chance. No beauty, but a sort of busy, no-nonsense friendliness and dependability that still fires off the screen, happy to sing 'Be At Home When Love Comes Knocking At The Door', or to get soaking wet in the roadside tea-stall scene, with little Ian Wilson (already by now a sort of mascot for British films) wordlessly pressing his face into the camera.

Unlike so many of its type, *Soldiers of the King* benefits from its two male leads. Hollywood star Edward Everett Horton lends his special qualities to his role of the Marvellos' manager. There's a bonus in Anthony Bushell's juvenile lieutenant, it being a mystery why the producers of British film musicals so often insisted on making romantic figures from the most visually unlikely material (Howes, Lupino, Gerrard, and a legion of others). The space between young and old, nicely pointed in this film, closes as the movie ends, with Jenny staring down at Maisie as she delivers the title song, before Jenny herself sings it as of old. As neatly wrapped a parcel of sentiment, comedy and romance and – not too far from the surface – sadness could scarcely have been conceived. The *Observer* considered that Courtneidge's performance was 'so much the best bit of individual showmanship that we have seen in a British film, that the weaknesses in the script take on microscopic proportions'.[18] Cicely Courtneidge might have been especially interested in Australia's reaction to her new movie, which – although it did not condemn her performance – had a dispiriting tone.

> Again and again, since the coming of talking films, the English studios have put forth flimsy stories of this character – stories which subside into horrific dullness when the actors do not exert themselves, and when the actors do put forth heroic efforts prove entertaining, but not commensurately so. If only the genius of English players could be backed by solider, more closely-knit thematic material, British films would reach brilliant heights of artistry. Perhaps the present migration of American actors and technical experts to London, counter-balancing a migration of English actors to Hollywood, will have an influence in this direction.[19]

Foreign product continued to be adapted to what film-makers considered British taste. Another off the Stanley Lupino assembly line, **King of the Ritz** was a Beaconsfield remake by Gaumont-British of the French *Le Roi des Palaces*, made the previous year with Jules Barry playing the hotel porter Claude who falls for a wealthy widow, played by Betty Stockfeld in both French and British versions. Claude comes to the rescue when her jewels are stolen and looks forward to a new life among high society, but, older and possibly wiser, goes back to portering at the Ritz and the comforting arms of his faithful girlfriend (Gina Malo). Carmine

Gallone directed the bilinguals, with Ivor Montagu and Clifford Grey translating Henri Kistemaeckers's play. Music was originally by Raoul Moretti, supplemented at Beaconsfield by Noel Gay and Clifford Grey's 'You'll Fall In Love' and 'Loving You Brings Me Gladness'. Among the cast list was Henry Kendall, who between 1933 and 1934 made nineteen films. He recalled that round about this time,

> An office boy had written to say I was a favourite of his, and could he have a photograph [...] because he could blow out his cheeks to an enormous size, all his friends said he ought to go on films. He added that, in his opinion, my pictures were all a terrible lot of tripe. I suddenly saw that he was right, and as I couldn't even blow out my cheeks beyond the normal, I decided to get out of films and back to the stage – fast.[20]

We may wonder if Kendall considered *King of the Ritz* 'tripe'. He would not have been alone in doing so.

APRIL

Had BIP learned nothing from their *Elstree Calling* in 1930, a film that delivered what many would have thought a death blow to revue? Three years later, BIP was still at it, now collecting a line-up of performers for **Radio Parade**, thrown together by directors Archie de Bear and Richard Beville, with an inept screenplay (hardly deserving of the name) by Claude Hulbert and Paul England. The most notable line of dialogue comes at the very end, when linking disc-jockey Christopher Stone, spluttering and stumbling through his introductions to the various items, at last seems to take pity on the film's audience. 'I hope you're not in a hurry to get home,' he tells them. 'I know I am.' Very sensibly, he puts his coat on and gets out of there. Extraordinarily, the following year Mr Stone, a star among BBC presenters, was filched by Radio Luxembourg for £5,000 a year, an achievement that may have originated the phrase 'money for old rope'.

Mercifully, he probably didn't have to sit through many of the acts (five minutes in the studio and he was done and dusted). These ranged from the dreary (the so-called comedy duo, Clapham and Dwyer, inexplicably top-liners of the period) to the sublime (Elsie Carlisle in a gorgeous medley). Elsewhere, it's an opportunity to see some major talents: impressionist Florence Desmond (late of *Sally in Our Alley*); flustered comedienne Jeanne de Casalis as Mrs Feather; character actress Mabel Constanduros; Elsie and Doris Waters's inventions Gert and Daisy, and Reginald Gardiner, best known for train impersonations but here impersonating motor cars.

Many such performers were far from their best when faced by a camera. Along the way, not only the sad state of British comedy but the deplorable state of British dentistry and the hideous state of male fashion are well to the fore. Only once does *Radio Parade* lift to another level, when Carlisle (introduced by Stone as 'a very favourite Saturday evening voice'), accompanied by some young musicians from Ambrose's Orchestra, effortlessly glides through her set, posing against a white piano for 'As Easy As ABC' and 'The Girl Next Door'. There is something so genuine, so unforced, about it, not least the exchanged glances between the young musicians. What happened to so many of these big band players when the bands went out of fashion, as soon enough they would? In the 1930s there was an industry for them; their faces crowd these films. Seeing so many of them in so many British musical films of this period reminds us of life's fragility.

MAY

Lilian Harvey's success in German cinema was never to be replicated in Britain. No matter how charmingly lithe she had been in *Ich und die Kaiserin*, the UFA original of **The Only Girl**, much got lost in translation in Robert Stevenson and John Heygate's version for the home market, worked up from the German of Walter Reisch, Robert Liebmann and Felix Salten. By the time of the British edition, Harvey had also lost her German leading man Conrad Veidt, replaced by Charles Boyer for the French and British filming. This alone helped unbalance things. Nevertheless, this is a captivating piece, with an interesting, quirky and (for its time) integrated score by its director Friedrich Hollaender, once a pupil of Engelbert Humperdinck and the composer for *The Blue Angel*. The historical romance of 1890 plot concerns a Marquis (Boyer) who, finding a lost garter, mistakenly identifies it as the garter of the Empress of France, when it is the garter of Juliet, the Empress's little hairdresser (Harvey). As the Empress, German star Mady Christians made a welcome second female lead, appearing alongside Harvey in all three language versions. *The Only Girl* turned out to be the last film Harvey made for UFA, which was increasingly open to political interference. Being of foreign descent, the film was not classified as British.

JUNE

Audiences exposing themselves to **Facing the Music** didn't realise they would be subjected to gobbets of Gounod and Wagner and a sprinkling of not so brilliant numbers from Noel Gay and the film's star-turn lyricist Stanley Lupino. A matronly Jose Collins, once the beating heart of the West End hit of the Great War *The Maid of the Mountains*, opens the proceedings on stage at the opera during the final moments of *Tristan and Isolde*. The film's shooting script describes her character Madam Calvinni as 'a prima donna type'. She has a niece who catches the eye of the as-usual susceptible Lupino, the most unlikely but tenacious of romantic hopefuls. A problem arises: Madam is losing her voice. This may be an in-joke from screenwriters Clifford Grey, Frank Launder and Lupino, recalling that on the very last night of the *Maid*'s run Collins had completely lost her voice but carried manfully on. Lupino thinks up a stunt to boost the diva's reputation – she will wear her priceless jewels for the Jewel Song in *Faust*, and he will stage a mock theft.

The opera scenes are shockingly badly done, including a rehearsal of the soldiers' chorus with the male ensemble marching around in trilby hats and bowlers. Director Harry Hughes can do nothing to disguise the lame, tiresome and seemingly endless feebleness of it all. 'I must have something for my throat,' insists Collins. Lupino: 'How about a razor?' *Facing the Music* does nothing to dissipate the feeling that Lupino's films never get near reflecting the lives of its intended consumers. The persistent theme of nightclub revelry, now with our seriously dishevelled hero madly declaring 'I've Found The Right Girl' (Gay-Lupino), strikes a completely false note among songs (including Lupino and juvenile starlet Nancy Burne as Nina Carson singing Gay and Lupino's 'Let Me Gaze') that choreography ignores. The ballet sequence in *Faust* seems to have strayed in from *Swan Lake*, before the final reels collapse into slapstick. The more seriously minded should be alerted to the casting of Doris Woodall as an operatic colleague to the statuesque Miss Collins. No great shakes as an actress, Woodall survived a successful career, having sung over 1,000 performances as Carmen, appearing with Carl Rosa Opera for twenty-five years.

Johann Strauss's *Die Fledermaus* would be offered with Technicolor luxuriousness in the Michael Powell-Emeric Pressburger *Oh Rosalinda!!* in 1955. Now, Shepherd's Bush hosted Gaumont's ***Waltz Time***, produced by Herman Fellner and directed by William Thiele, from A. P. Herbert's intelligent screenplay. Its heroine was Evelyn Laye, singing the 'Butterfly Song' and toasting life beside George Baker with 'A Glass Of Golden Bubbles'. The score also featured Baker singing 'Pretty One' and Frank Titterton urging 'Come Out, Vienna'. Laye's first talkie, it led to two more musical films the following year (*Princess Charming* and the sombre *Evensong*), neither of which propelled her to screen stardom. Reaction to the colourful (but black and white) *Waltz Time* was mixed. C. A. Lejeune considered it 'more fastidious than compelling, but it has a nice mannered ease that is more often associated with continental than with British studios', setting 'a new standard for British productions – technically nothing finer has ever been turned out from a British studio.'[21]

Maid Happy, filmed at Elstree and on location in Switzerland, followed the fortunes of schoolgirl Lena (Charlotte Ander) and her fondness for an older diplomat (Johannes Riemann). Garrett Graham's story was written up by Jack King, who also provided the music, and produced and directed by Mansfield Markham for Bendar Films (made up from Sir Albert Bennett and Major Darwin). Ander had made her name in Germany as Polly in Brecht's *Threepenny Opera* and had played opposite Joseph Schmidt in the German version of *My Song Goes Round the World, Ein Lied geht um die Welt.*

JULY

Following Courtneidge's solo success with *Soldiers of the King*, she and Jack Hulbert reunited for the Gaumont-British **Falling for You,** made at Islington and directed by Hulbert and Robert Stevenson. The formula is basically as David Shipman has described: 'to get Courtneidge into as many scrapes and disguises as possible, helped out of difficulties by an indifferent Hulbert [whose romantic interest was often fastened on a co-star more obviously glamorous than his wife] but getting him [as often as not] in the end'.[22] Some decent musical numbers helped, and *Falling for You* was lucky to have natty songs by Vivian Ellis and Douglas Furber, including Courtneidge's 'Why Has A Cow Got Four Legs?', presumably a descendant of Ellis's 'The Flies Crawled Up The Window' written for Hulbert in *Jack's the Boy*.

This romance of the ski slopes had a screenplay by Furber, Hulbert and Stevenson based on a story by Sidney Gilliat, with Hulbert also credited for additional dialogue. The Hulberts played competing press reporters Jack and Minnie, in quest of a fleeing heiress (Tamara Desni) with whom Jack is smitten, despite his insistent singing of 'You Don't Understand' which, since she replies in a foreign language, she probably doesn't. Along the way, Jack gets to sing 'Sweep' as one of the chimney variety, does ballet in plus fours and, almost Astaire-like, dances on a bar-top around a bottle. A hymn to the ultimate home-help, 'Mrs Bartholomew' is ideally fashioned to Courtneidge's very particular comedic gifts, which modern onlookers may think overworked, but the film remains highly watchable. One of *Picturegoer*'s correspondents was doubtful that the Hulberts would withstand over-exposure.

> In the next three years the Hulberts are to make eighteen films.[23] I wonder how much of their popularity they will have lost by then? In my opinion it will have waned immensely, unless they are careful in their choice of stories. Their type of comedy is not subtle and rather broad. And broad comedy is apt to turn to duplicated situations or gags. In *Falling for You* we actually had duplication in the film itself in addition to the familiar Hulbert material.[24]

The Monty Banks-type director played by Anthony Holles in **Britannia of Billingsgate** rightly worships his leading lady: 'What a woman,' he cries, 'the very spirit of this great country!' Unlikely as it seems, she's the wife of a fish and chip shop owner who becomes a glamorous film star.

As produced by Michael Balcon for Gaumont-British, Sinclair Hill directed the scenario by G. H. Moresby White and H. F. Maltby, based on a play by Christine

From fish and chip caff to film stardom: a true star, Violet Loraine, the *Britannia of Billingsgate* (1933)

Jope-Slade and Sewell Stokes, here and there, but by no means consistently, turned into something like cinematic gold-dust. Shots of the Thames, Whistler-like in the gloom, open out to busy scenes at Billingsgate fish-market, where Hill has clearly persuaded authentic workers to speak a few lines. Possibly in response to one of the attractive George Posford/Holt Marvell songs 'How Does A Fresh Fish Wish If The Fish Hasn't Got A Wishbone?', the action moves to the fish shop run by cockney Bert Bolton (Gordon Harker) and wife Bessie (Violet Loraine), parents to the dim and ridiculously pretentious Pearl (Kay Hammond) and speedway dirt-track enthusiast Fred (John Mills).

Outside in the street, a film is being made by the temperamental Italian director Guidobaldi. We can tell it's British because its two young lovers speak in absurdly over-elocuted tones, unlike those of the street characters we have already met. This is only one of the neat parodic touches in a picture that can be strikingly effective; it is the collision of the real world and the artificiality of the cinema world that energises it. If we look closely we can see the divide between reality and cinematic artificiality that distinguishes *Britannia of Billingsgate*, with Hill occasionally taking flight with an assurance that seems to affirm a new-found confidence in British musical film, with its opportunity to see behind the scenes at Gaumont's Shepherd's Bush studio. There's a John Baxter-like fondness for the ordinary man, the unsung, the forgotten. As Bessie washes up, she sings 'There'll Still Be Love' (surely one of the most entrancing songs of the decade) among her customers. These are no actors, but people pulled in from the streets around Shepherd's Bush, probably paid a pittance for a couple of hours' work on the studio floor: a father tending his child, two down-at-heel lovers about to kiss behind a newspaper, an ancient couple gnawing their food and drinking as they seem to respond unexpectedly to Bessie's words. These are among the film's most touching images; rawness is there.

Soon, Bessie is signed up to star in a musical picture, *Piccadilly Playground*, the presumably parodic title number of which sounds like some of those heard in other British musical films. The glimpse we get of the finished film is *definitely* parodic, with Bessie enthusiastically extolling London life against a decidedly wobbly Eros (almost certainly an 'in' joke by Alfred Junge), surrounded by grotesquely Toy-Town policemen with fantasised helmets and giant truncheons, surrounded by inappropriately dressed chorus girls. The delight Hill must have felt in orchestrating these scenes is obvious; they are all too brief. How much better if more time had been spent on the film within the film than on the protracted scenes at the speedway! Gaumont-British probably decided the audience would be more excited by these than by a subtle send-up of musical films.

The closing passage is one to treasure. Far from the ersatz glamour of the film studio, and the premiere she has just attended, Bessie is back to her life of fish and chips. But she is not. When Bert waves toodle-oo to Bessie, leaving her to get the work done, we see him walk not into the street but onto the studio floor, where the make-up man is ready with a set of false eyebrows. Guidobaldi and little Wilson excitedly arrive on set, instructing Bessie simply to be herself when the cameras roll. A few yards away, the orchestra strikes up. Surrounded by a little huddle of street people, Bessie sheds her usual self-consciousness and strikes up a reprise of 'There'll Still Be Love' as Bert and Guidobaldi look on from the floor. It is *Britannia*'s apotheosis, as Mutz Greenbaum pulls the camera away from Loraine, up, up and away, way above the studio floor, gradually revealing the sound technicians grappling with the British Acoustic Sound System recording equipment, the cameramen, the gantries, and then the orchestra itself, below the arc lights. It is this ultimate celebration of what film can do – and Loraine's wonderful playing – that, while never turning *Britannia of Billingsgate* into a masterpiece, beats at its heart. This is the most thrilling finale of the decade's musical films.

There are many incidental delights, not least Harker's sturdy Bert (note Harker's nervous tic of a cough and smacking of lips that carries through his many films), the delightful Drusilla Wills as a gossip-mongering crone, Holles's explosive Guidobaldi ('Good old Baldy' to Bert), the comfortingly lugubrious Gibb McLaughlin, and little Ian Wilson, still in place from the very beginning of British sound pictures, popping up here (uncredited) as Wilson, as if by now he was himself a mascot of British studios. Astonishingly, he was still around in 1962 for his night watchman cameo in *The Day of the Triffids* in perhaps its most memorable few moments in a Kew greenhouse, and lasted up until the *The Wicker Man* (1973).

Nevertheless, the occasion belongs to Violet Loraine as Bessie; without effort, she 'smacks the audience into hearty comradeship'.[25] When Bert interferes with the sound equipment of the film unit in the street, a microphone picks up her voice singing in the gaff, and inevitably Guidobaldi 'jumping around like a flea on a gridiron' has found a new singing star. Indeed he has: no less than Miss Loraine, one of the most forgotten (and rarely seen) British screen stars. If she was remembered in 1933, it was for having partnered George Robey in 'If You Were The Only Girl In The World' in the stage hit of the Great War, *The Bing Boys Are Here*. She is a revelation as this fish and chip Britannia, battering haddock with the casual ease of a fish-wife, dodging artifice through a rock-solid theatricality that somehow translates beautifully to the screen. Her stance, gestures, intonations may belong within the proscenium arch and even stretch back to silent melodrama, but Loraine has the soul of an artist, organic in her sway. The *Manchester Guardian* regretted that 'British companies are not yet so skilled as American in building a film up around a star'. It had no doubt that Loraine's 'personality triumphs […] but her art could well have been better served, both by scenarist and by cameraman'. Furthermore, 'It is perhaps also unfair to ask an actress to portray on her first screen appearance the uneasiness of a woman thrust into film fame'.[26] We may, of course, maintain that in this too Loraine triumphs.

Although filmed at Walton, a location not immediately associated with Ruritanian excess, the operetta **Prince of Arcadia** was strongly cast with ageing matinee idol Carl Brisson as the princely Peter opposite the Mirana of Margot Grahame. The director, Hanns Schwartz, was an Austrian Jew who had recently fled from the Nazis. Music, including the numbers 'A Crown Prince Of Arcadia' and 'If Only I Could Find Her', was by the prolific Robert Stolz, whose *The Song You Gave Me* was already in the pipeline. At this time, his musical play *Wild Violets* enjoyed success in London; he was also writing songs for the films of Jan Kiepura. The sternest of operetta critics, Gervase Hughes, accuses Stolz (along with his collaborator for the 1931 *White Horse Inn*, Ralph Benatzky) of dealing Viennese operetta 'its most crippling blow'. Mr Hughes argues that Stolz, in writing *White Horse Inn*, was a composer who had effectively abandoned true Viennese operetta.

> One gladly concedes that its uninhibited *bonhomie* was infinitely preferable to the sultry introversion of Stolz's *Peppina* or the sham glitter of Benatzky's *Cocktail* (both 1930). Artistic unity might count for little (slapstick jostled 'romance'), the tunes might be trivial and the intellectual appeal negligible, but none could deny that the décor was sumptuous. In an age of frustration, unease and much living-near-the-bone, *Im weissen Rössl* [*White Horse Inn*] was adjudged *kolossal*. The spectacular 'musical' had arrived; genuine Viennese operetta was now a thing of the past.[27]

The German original of 1932, *Der Prinz von Arkadien*, almost certainly had better stars in Willi Forst and Liane Haid. Perhaps Reginald Fogwell, co-producing with Archibald Nettlefold, had not the deft touch of Germany's Walter Reisch when it came to a toothsome screenplay, and the apparent youthfulness of Forst could not be equalled by Brisson. The plot broke no Ruritanian romance rules. Prince Peter abdicates and leaves his homeland (there was some location work in Switzerland), ending up in the arms of actress Mirana.

Meanwhile, Noël Coward's operetta **Bitter Sweet** reached cinemas retouched by the screenplay of British and Dominions' director Herbert Wilcox, Lydia Hayward and Monckton Hoffe. Wilcox's enthusiasm for the project was unbounded, asking the presumably rhetorical question 'Surely a better musical play has never been written?', perhaps overlooking the possibility that *Show Boat* and several other Jerome Kern musicals, as well as those of Friml and Romberg, might have the stronger claim. Nevertheless, this was the opportunity for Wilcox to follow up on his box office success with *Goodnight, Vienna*, and a seemingly perfect vehicle for that film's star Anna Neagle.

The sentimental piece, with Neagle playing old and young, was much liked by audiences but perhaps less by Coward, whose third act had been cut. In kindly mood, the *New York Times* welcomed 'an artistic production and its scenes are set forth with gratifying elegance and sober fluency'.[28] What was more, Neagle sang 'most agreeably', a description that did not always apply to her vocal efforts, although when seated at his piano while she performs one of his compositions Fernand Gravey has the look of a rabbit fixed in the headlights. It may be that this 'rather feeble filming [...] pleased a lot of people at the time'[29] but Wilcox later said it made no money, and its charms have faded with time. A good reason for revisiting it is little Ivy St Helier as cabaret singer Manon Le Crevette performing Coward's melancholic 'If Love Were All'. One of Coward's cleverest scores is well represented, with his winning waltz 'I'll See You Again' (he probably never wrote a better), 'The Call Of Life', 'Sweet Little Café', 'Kiss Me Before You Go Away' and Stuart Robertson's call for 'Tokay'. In 1940 Hollywood re-cooked the show with the starrier Jeanette MacDonald and Nelson Eddy, with gloriously schmaltzy results that nevertheless went in directions that Coward surely never intended.

Co-production between Germany's UFA studio at Babelsberg in Berlin and British studios more than once resulted in something interesting and captivating, as in *Early to Bed*, first made as *Ich bei Tag und du bei Nacht* ('I By Day, You By Night'). The idea may have sprung from *Cox and Box*, the Victorian farce by John Maddison Morton, used as the basis of the operetta by Gilbert and Sullivan, in which two workers unknowingly share the same room. Now, in Robert Stevenson, Robert Liebmann and Hans Székely's screenplay, its script and detail adjusted to British taste, Fernand Gravey (*Bitter Sweet*) was the waiter and Heather Angel, in a rare musical appearance, was the manicurist, taking over for British audiences from the original Willy Fritsch and Käthe von Nagy. Chris Whal notes that 'This quotidian love story is ironically counterpointed by the upper-class romance played out in a parody of an escapist film operetta, shown at the cinema next door.'[30]

Those shipped over to Germany for the occasion included several British character actors including Lady Tree (already delightfully present in *For the Love of Mike* and destined for *Heart's Desire*) as the devious landlady, bilingual-favourite Sonnie Hale as the cinema projectionist, Donald Calthrop (*Elstree Calling*), Edmund Gwenn, Athene Seyler (*Tell Me Tonight, Blossom Time, It's Love Again, The Lilac Domino, Sailing Along*) and Leslie Perrins, who went on, often as the moustachioed villain, to *Song at Eventide, Gay Love, Lily of Killarney, D'Ye Ken John Peel?, Rhythm in the Air, Southern Roses* and John Baxter's more modest *Sunshine Ahead*. *Early to Bed*'s original German edition had been directed by Ludwig Berger, but Stevenson supervised the British version. 'In The Talkies Every Sunday Night', 'If You Forget' and 'Free And Easy' had words by Rowland Leigh and music by Werner R. Heymann.

For Basil Dean, **This Week of Grace** had a typical *Peg's Paper* story ('from Factory to Castle') with a supporting cast of serious quality such as Helen Haye, leavening the music-hall humours of the working-class Milroy family (wonderfully played by Frank Pettingell and Minnie Rayner as parents, and Douglas Wakefield and Gracie Fields as their children). Social dislocation manifests when the Milroys are propelled into close proximity with the upper crust, with brilliant results that caused *The Times* to remark loftily on 'the uncomfortable humour being extracted from the awkwardness of the plebeian in high life.'[31] A Real Art production from Twickenham studios directed by Maurice Elvey, it was based on material by Nell Emerald and Maurice Braddell, adapted by H. Fowler Mear and Jack Marks.

In a park, out-of-work factory girl Grace (Fields) meets the Duchess of Swinford

Pre-war collaboration with the Germans: *Early to Bed* (1933)

(the original 'Peter Pan' Nina Boucicault in her first sound film) and agrees to become housekeeper for Lady Warmington (Helen Haye). In a situation that reverses that in Twickenham's uproarious adaptation of Ivor Novello's *I Lived with You* in which a Russian aristocrat moves in with a working-class family, Grace's parents and brother move into the Swinfords' baronial home. This is home territory for the glorious Miss Rayner, an actress for whom nature has never provided a replacement, and much of the film's merriment circles around her amiable bumbling. When lowly Grace falls for youngish Lord Clive Swinford (Henry Kendall), we are reminded again of *I Lived with You* in which lowly Ursula Jeans falls for Novello's Prince Felix. The restrictions imposed by the British class system, not for the last time in a Fields picture, must be dealt with, as it is here, with Grace marrying his lordship, leaving him when she becomes disillusioned, and reuniting with him before fade-out. Along the way, Eliza Doolittle-like, she acquires a posh accent, apparently sliding beyond her working-class background.

Grace has the advantage of a splendid score, partly co-written by Fields and her favoured, most regular, composer, Harry Parr Davies: 'Mary Rose', 'Melody At Dawn' and 'My Lucky Day', 'When Cupid Calls' and the signature 'Happy Ending', admirably written to Fields' particular skills, as was all Davies's work throughout her career. Fields whistles 'Happy Ending', almost guaranteeing its popularity; if Fields could whistle it, so could the barrow boy and the man on the Clapham omnibus. A comedy number by Bert Lee, Harris Weston and R. P. Weston, 'Heaven Will Protect An Honest Girl', became an enduring item in her repertoire. We should also be grateful for a British musical film with a witty title.

AUGUST

BIP should have considered itself lucky to host Hollywood's Bebe Daniels's debut in British talkies; at last, a genuine shot of American glamour. Daniels had been a favourite in Paramount silents, but when talkies arrived Paramount didn't even bother to test her, and Daniels bought out her contract. She went on to play *Rio Rita* for RKO in 1929, at which point Paramount complained, 'You didn't tell us you could sing.' Daniels replied, 'You never asked me.'

What original and exciting project did BIP offer Daniels? It didn't, opting instead for **The Song You Gave Me,** a remake of the 1930 *Das Lied ist Aus* that had starred Liane Haid and Willy Forst. Paul L. Stein's direction could do little to disguise the paucity of Clifford Grey's screenplay, based on Walter Reisch's original. Whatever qualities the picture had belonged to Daniels as the much-loved singer Mitzi Hansen, slighted when an audience member walks out during her impromptu performance at a celebration of her latest success. The walker-out is in fact the hero of the piece, Karl Linden (played with disarming quietness by Victor Varconi), whom Mitzi hires as her personal secretary. Predictably, they fall in love, dashing the pointless hopes of three admiring cavaliers Claude Hulbert, Lester Matthews and Frederick Lloyd. These musketeers carry the ineffective comedy.

Unfortunately, the script and camera too often step away from Daniels and Varconi. For some reason there's a protracted marionette sequence behind which lurks a pastiche of operatic conventions that must have gone way over the heads of cinema audiences. Later, a staunch singer in starched dicky and evening dress (Walter Widdop, who sang Tristan at Covent Garden that year) sings 'Don't Ask Me Why'. The Robert Stolz numbers are pleasant (notably the perky title song), and a refreshing break from the insipid dialogue and ridiculous plot, with the composer making maximum use of his 'Goodbye' number from *White Horse Inn*. Denounced as a 'very slight and obvious Viennese romance', *The Song You Gave Me* has been cited by Christian Cargnelli as 'Making no great impression at the time or hereafter [but] it nevertheless points forward to better, more successful Stein films in the same style and genre: Viennese pictures made in Great Britain.'[32] Perhaps thinking that things could only improve, Daniels remained in Britain for *A Southern Maid*. The prolific Stolz never seems to have been out of work, but who now remembers the theatre scores he wrote specifically for London – the light charm of the numbers in Lily Elsie's vehicle *The Blue Train* (1927), *Rise and Shine* (1936, with Fred Astaire) and the shortest-lived of these three flops, the 1960 *Joie de Vivre*?

SEPTEMBER

Originally filmed in France as *La Dame chez Maxim*, **The Girl from Maxim's** was directed and co-produced (with Ludovico Toeplitz) by Alexander Korda, the script reworked from the original Feydeau play by Harry Graham and Arthur Wimperis. Now, the girl was no less than the flagrantly seductive Frances Day, according to Low 'the young dizzy blonde […] whose brassy presence was somewhat out of tune with a lovely performance by Lady Tree, for example, and with the claustrophobic period atmosphere of Vincent Korda's design.'[33] Publicity stills for the movie reveal Day in a complex assortment of underwear. A great admirer of Miss Day, Eleanor Roosevelt assured her, 'I am quite unable to resist your extraordinary and tempestuous magnetism.' According to Michael Thornton: 'American-born and flagrantly bisexual, in an era that scarcely accommodated such things, [Day] had attracted men and women equally, becoming the mistress of four royal princes, and also of a future British Prime Minister.'[34] Other unlikely subjects who fell under her spell included the composer Vivian Ellis and George Bernard Shaw, both of whom wrote material for her.

Despite these recommendations, the film, having been made in France, did not qualify for British registration (in 1933 the same fate befell *The Only Girl* and *Early to Bed*), remaining on the shelf until after Korda's next, *The Private Life of*

Henry VIII. According to its publicity, *The Girl from Maxim's* was 'a cocktail of joyous merriment', a cocktail that seems not to have appealed to the public taste despite an impressive cast that involved Leslie Henson as Dr Petypon who, let loose in 1904 Paris, passes off the singing star at Maxim's, La Môme (Day), as his wife, in fact played by the too-seldom-used Lady Tree. Music was provided by the German Kurt Schröder, who also contributed to the Henry VIII epic, *Where Is This Lady?* and *The Song You Gave Me*.

Binnie Hale and Gordon Harker's professional partnership resulted in several interesting pictures through the decade, including the musical puzzler *Hyde Park Corner* (1935) and *The Phantom Light*. British Lion's **This is the Life**, produced by Herbert Smith and directed at Beaconsfield by Albert de Courville, had a screenplay by Clifford Grey worked up from his story, with dialogue by Bert Lee and Grey. Routine at the Tuttles' teashop run by Albert and Sarah (Harker and Hale) is thrown to the wind when they come into money, try clambering up the social ladder, and get involved (a particular hazard in British musical films) with American hoodlums, personified by Ben Welden as 'Two Gun Mullins'. When they return to their old lives, they are delighted to find Sarah's niece has transformed the shop into a splendid roadhouse, foreshadowing Harker's *Road House* (1934) in which he co-starred with Violet Loraine. Ray Milland and Betty Astell supported, with Percival Mackey and His Band. The pleasing songs were 'Give Her A Little Kiss' by Frank Steininger and lyricist Sonny Miller, and 'Two Hearts That Beat In Waltz Time', a typical Robert Stolz number with a lyric by Reginald Connelly.

At the end of **Going Gay**, Adelphi Film's attempt to come up with a winning partnership in Arthur Riscoe and Naunton Wayne, our heroes are in the air, bound for England, when they are informed they are en route to Venice. This seems to have been a promotion for their follow-up movie of the same year, *For Love of You*. For the moment, the first 'Jack (Riscoe) and Jim (Wayne)' film was directed by Carmine Gallone, produced (according to Low) by Frank A. Richardson, but according to the screen credits produced by Louis Whitman. If these are to be believed, the score was by that most neglected of composers, W. L. Trytel. The screenplay by Selwyn Jepson (based on his story), Jack Marks and K. R. G. Browne followed the carefree bachelors to Vienna, immediately whisking them off to a luxuriously appointed nightclub where sexual assignations may be made via tabled telephones. Nothing much happens, except a plot loosely built around Greta (Magda Schneider) who longs to be an opera singer but meanwhile seems content to perform Mr Trytel's uninspired musical doggerel, as in her duet with Jack, 'I Only Tell My Mother'. Mercifully, Wayne is not required for singing.

The fun might be described as innocent; it is certainly immature. In swimwear Jack serenades Greta with 'K-Kiss Me Goodbye', and his waterside pranks alongside

Jim have her (but not necessarily us) in stitches. 'You think I'm good?' asks Greta. 'Very good,' Jack replies, 'but you needn't always be.' It's little consolation that he tells her, 'Girls don't like to feel safe with a man.' Schneider looks pretty throughout but makes little impression here, despite her reputation for being Hitler's favourite actress. There is a fairly ludicrous musical finale at which Gallone and his team clearly throw everything: a musical extravaganza in the well of a huge apartment complex. Greta is hailed as a great opera discovery, and Riscoe (Wayne – and how thankful he must have been – was presumably safely back in his caravan) does some more embarrassing dancing around a fountain, dressed in a Grecian tunic and sock suspenders, while Thorold Dickinson's editing tries to whip up a storm of excitement. All that is left is for Greta to make a stunning success at her opera debut, although the production we see resembles more a village pantomime.

There was more style in ***That's a Good Girl***, not surprising as it was directed by and starred Jack Buchanan, who had made a substantial stage success of it in 1928. Herbert Wilcox, who had already produced Buchanan in *Goodnight, Vienna* and *Yes, Mr Brown*, produced at Elstree for British and Dominions, from a screenplay by Buchanan, Douglas Furber and Donovan Pedelty. The material was well suited to the star's casual air. He was joined for the occasion by Elsie Randolph in their second screen pairing, a partnership that remained solid but never threatened his superiority. *That's a Good Girl* struck a genuinely 1930s note. It benefited from a generous number of good songs, principally the central 'Fancy Our Meeting' by Joseph Meyer and Philip Charig with a Furber lyric, which Buchanan had sung with Jessie Matthews in the 1929 revue *Wake Up and Dream*, but also 'Now That I've Found You', the delightful 'Sweet So And So', 'The One I'm Looking For', 'Oo La La' and the frisky 'So Green'. The *Observer* thought the songs 'still remained static'.[35]

David Shipman describes Buchanan's picture as 'a minor triumph in that it successfully opened out a stage show which he had done (as star and producer) – a knockabout farce about a rich ne'er-do-well and his even richer aunts'.[36] Low considers that Randolph partnered Buchanan perfectly 'but rather overdid the mugging and cavorting, and left romance to the pretty stage actress Dorothy Hyson'. Low describes 'the basic plot, in which a debonair but penniless man about town can inherit a fortune only if he fulfils certain conditions' as 'a familiar standby ... and the film also conformed to a musical comedy convention whereby the second or third act transports everybody to a resort, the deck of a liner, a hotel or some other holiday setting – in this instance by moving the action to the Riviera'.[37] Wilcox had done location shooting in Antibes, Cap Ferrat and the Alps Maritimes, although his outside filming sometimes translated disastrously to the screen, as in his opening scenes of *King's Rhapsody* where the rocks of Spain bear an uncanny resemblance to elephant dung.

OCTOBER

The heart might not quicken at the prospect of yet another BIP vehicle for Stanley Lupino, but *You Made Me Love You* (no use of the 1913 Jimmy Monaco / Joseph McCarthy song) is one of the better, deserving to be remembered not only for its attempt at updating *The Taming of the Shrew* with its fair to middling score by Lupino, Noel Gay and Clifford Grey, but for its pairing of Lupino with by far his liveliest leading lady. Whatever termagant resided inside America's Thelma Todd was let loose here. This was an actress who had worked with Hollywood's comedy royalty, alongside the Marx Brothers, Laurel and Hardy, Jimmy Durante and Buster Keaton. Firing on all cylinders, and with a fiery sexuality that never interfered with the comic elements, Todd played petulant heiress Pamela Berne. Based on Lupino's storyline, Frank Launder's screenplay had Lupino as Tom Daley, son of a successful music publishing magnate, who spots Pamela in an adjacent car during a traffic-light halt, and is immediately obsessed with tracking down 'Miss Whatsername', rushing into a radio station to publicise his quest, destroying a microphone and melting his top hat in the process as his world-audience listens in. Todd is excused any singing, but proves uncooperative during Lupino's set-piece number 'Why Can't We?' in a farmyard.

Director Monty Banks doubles as a taxi driver in a sequence that might have come straight out of a silent, and instils the movie with a real sense of anarchy, letting Lupino and Todd propel the narrative with its violent eruptions, ending up with something approaching demolition of a house. It's difficult to take the emotional relationship between Lupino and his female star seriously in any of his other projects, but here the players spark each other; small wonder that Todd reputedly spoke of this as the film she most enjoyed making.

Todd charges through it with delight, slowly and convincingly becoming vulnerable. Unusually, the film includes a scene in which a reason for divorce is set up in a bedroom, a scene that not only underpins the film's 'seriousness' but exhibits some sort of bravado on the part of BIP's dealing with the censor, keeping one leg, as it were, on the floor of the bedroom. Todd died two years later in suspicious circumstances.

Following the unsatisfactory *The Song You Gave Me*, BIP set up Bebe Daniels in a screen adaptation of a 1920s operetta by Harold Fraser-Simson, ***A Southern Maid***. Another stab at making theatrical operetta work as cinema, this seemed a natural progression from BIP's filming of the better-known Fraser-Simson *The Maid of the Mountains*, which many agreed had not worked on screen. Rachael Low suggests that *A Southern Maid* is so awful that it might have been intended as a parody of the earlier film. That had been directed by the one-time Hollywood legend Lupino Lane, who appeared in *A Southern Maid* as Antonio Lopez, a characterisation in which 'his delicate and delightful mime revealed quite a different side of his talents'.[38] As mime never really caught on as vibrantly cinematic, this was not much of a recommendation.

Now, Daniels was cast as Dolores, a role originally played on stage in 1920 by the original Maid of those Mountains Jose Collins (recently the *grande dame* of Stanley Lupino's *Facing the Music*). The part did nothing for Daniels, further proof, if needed, that BIP was careless of treating her imaginatively. She was cast opposite Clifford Mollison, the two of them having to cope with dual roles as two sets of lovers. Mollison seemed an odd choice for a romantic lead, although he would be surprisingly charming in *Mister Cinders* (1934), in a film career that lasted until 1973 when he was reduced to the dire television-inspired *Love Your Neighbour*. BIP also found room for Australian Nancy Brown, who had somewhat inexplicably been BIP's Maid of those Mountains, when there had surely been more deserving candidates.

A Southern Maid was concocted by a little army of writers, with the 1920 libretto by Dion Clayton Calthrop and Harry Graham adapted by Austin Melford, Frank Miller, Arthur Woods and Harry Graham. Although the action allegedly took place in Santiago, location work was restricted to Elstree and Cheddar Gorge. The songs included 'Here's To Those We Love', 'Love's Cigarette', 'Southern Love' and 'Lonely Am I', but even Fraser-Simson's tuneful contributions (and one song, 'My Southern Maid', by George Posford and Holt Marvell) couldn't win it many admirers, and BIP was unable to get any American bookings. Nevertheless, the presence of its several distinguished players (Daniels, Lane and Harry Welchman) draws us in. Walter C. Mycroft produced and Harry Hughes directed.

NOVEMBER

More likely to be remembered for the first screen appearance of Errol Flynn than for its stars Harold French and Margot Grahame, *I Adore You* was a Warner Bros project produced for First National by Irving Asher. Paul England's screenplay from a storyline by W. Scott Darling was variously described as 'an amusing, if disjointed comedy, with a little leg-shaking and music',[39] as having 'an entirely novel theme',[40] and 'very light stuff, bright and amusing in spots', but lacking 'anything of novelty about it'.[41] It was a rare musical excursion for director George King, probably best remembered today for having filmed Tod Slaughter's melodramas, including *The Face at the Window*, praised by Graham Greene as 'one of the best English pictures I have seen' which 'leaves the American horror films far behind'.[42]

Kine Weekly summed up *I Adore You* as a 'bright, unassuming song and dance show [...] slight in story values, but bolstered up by spirited back-studio detail in which satire and showmanship play a prominent part'.[43] The film shared something with *Britannia of Billingsgate*, giving the audiences backstage glimpses of the Teddington studio. Choreographer Ralph Reader, sometimes referred to as a protégé of Busby Berkeley (although Reader's work is not of the same quality), devised routines for twenty-four West End chorus girls supplemented by six Cochran Young Ladies, backed by Carroll Gibbons and the Savoy Orpheans. Despite the necessary budgetary restrictions, there are moments when *I Adore You* gets close to extravagance in its telling of the romance between Norman Young (French) and film star (Grahame), unable to marry because of her contractual arrangements to the studio, solved when he buys it up. To what extent the movie had 'an entirely novel theme' remains debatable, but it seems to have distanced King from the conventional quota quickie.

Difficult as it is to believe, some of the British public may have been anxiously awaiting the cinematic return of 'Jack and Jim' in the pairing of Arthur Riscoe and Naunton Wayne. They got it in **For Love of You**, the follow-up to *Going Gay*, directed by Carmine Gallone and with a screenplay by Selwyn Jepson, filmed at Elstree and in Venice. Those eager for another escapade from Riscoe and Wayne (a sort of semi-musical version of the much more successful pairing of Wayne and Basil Radford) may conceivably have been satisfied with a plot involving American tenor Frank Forest, renamed Franco Foresta for the occasion, who would get to sing opposite Grace Moore in *I'll Take Romance*. Here, he plays Carlo Salvadore, married to a wife played by Diana Napier, and performs items from *The Pearl Fishers*, *Otello*, *Tales of Hoffman*, and the title song (words by Edward Pola, music by Franz Steininger). *For Love of You* was reissued in 1944 as *Carnival Time in Venice*, but eleven years after its debut it must have seemed somewhat out of time.

DECEMBER

Without Hulbert, Cicely Courtneidge was back at the Gaumont studios in Islington for her new Gainsborough vehicle *Aunt Sally*, devised and directed by Tim Whelan, with a screenplay by a well-practised triumvirate, Austin Melford, Guy Bolton and A. R. Rawlinson. Courtneidge played Sally, who takes on the personage of the French cabaret artiste Zaza, making a name for herself at the nightclub of Mike King Kelly (Sam Hardy). When the joint is targeted by gangsters, Sally/Zaza is kidnapped but safely returned. Jessie Matthews's *Gangway* depended heavily on just such a theme. Those involved along the way included the usually secondary lead Billy Milton, strolling through his big number, 'You Ought To See Sally On Sunday', supported by legions of over-dressed chorines. The Carlyle Cousins sang 'The Wind's In The West', reprised within Courtneidge's main (and almost signature) number 'We'll All Go Riding On A Rainbow', both these by the American composer Harry Woods who went on to write signature numbers for Jessie Matthews. Leslie Holmes ('The Smiling Vocalist') sang Woods's 'My Wild Oat'. The Busby Berkeley-like choreography was often caught in long aerial shots, but the geometric shapes lacked the symmetry of similar American product, not helped by the fact that the male dancers were appallingly costumed and much given to vaguely shuffling about. A dubious moment occurs during 'Rainbow' when Woods's lyric recalls Al Jolson ('O mammy mammy') and the image of Courtneidge turns into a negative. Otherwise, the star is on top form, quirky, angular, extraordinarily supple; we see a type of art that has died. The apache dance sequence is a fine example of her craft. As it was being shot, producer Michael Balcon visited the set. He reminded her that

> I saw you being brutally man-handled in an adagio act. Like a knight in white armour I came to rescue what I thought was a damsel in distress. 'You can't do this to her,' I protested to Tim Whelan, the director. 'Why not?' he said, unperturbed. 'She worked out the routine herself.' It was ever thus. There is nothing, bless your heart, literally nothing, you will not do to make us happy.[44]

1934

The microphones were left on as she dances around Junge's palatial floor; the squeaking of her shoes as she pirouettes across the floor can be clearly heard *Evergreen*

Lily of Killarney
Say It with Flowers
On the Air
Jack Ahoy!
Waltzes from Vienna
Happy
Boots! Boots!
The Queen's Affair
Love, Life and Laughter
The Unfinished Symphony
Two Hearts in Waltz Time
Princess Charming
Evergreen
Those Were the Days
The Broken Melody
How's Chances?
Over the Garden Wall
Music Hall
Danny Boy
Song at Eventide

Give Her a Ring
Chu Chin Chow
Blossom Time
My Song for You
Gay Love
There Goes Susie
Sing As We Go
Love-Mirth-Melody
Romance in Rhythm
My Song Goes Round the World
Mister Cinders
Evensong
The Broken Rosary
The Kentucky Minstrels
My Heart Is Calling
Road House
Spring in the Air
Radio Parade of 1935
Temptation

JANUARY

Julius Benedict's music for John Oxenford and Dion Boucicault's opera *The Lily of Killarney*, based on Boucicault's play *The Colleen Bawn*, was first heard at Covent Garden in 1862. Its success was immediate and recommended to film-makers in several silent versions beginning in 1922, when Eily O'Connor was its heroine. Eliot Stannard wrote the screenplay for the 1924 version directed by W. P. Kellino and starring Colette Brettel. BIP cast Pamela Parr in its 1929 adaptation directed by George Ridgwell. Five years on, the opera burst into sound in H. Fowler Mear's edition for producer Julius Hagen, now presented by Frederick White and Gilbert Church as ***Lily of Killarney***, 'A Musical and Dramatic Romance of the Emerald Isle'.

Here was a challenge for the cramped Twickenham studios; how could it effectively evoke the air, and airs, of Ireland? Before the opening credits rolled, the audience had a picturesque glimpse of Killarney's scenery, but it was then back to the studio, where a baronial hall filled with bulky furniture would have seemed familiar to those who had seen other of 'Uncle' Julius Hagen's productions.

There is much tally-ho-ing at the Hunt Supper enlivened by the dashing Sir Patrick Creegan (John Garrick), honest as the Irish day is long, in debt but in love with the unsophisticated lily of Killarney Eileen O'Connor (Gina Malo). She wins our hearts when she arrives on screen chewing sugar lumps. The arrival of a vicar might have dampened the festivities, but Stanley Holloway's Father O'Flynn ('What would old Ireland do without him?') is a lovable rogue, a dishevelled, hard-drinking reprobate from Donnegal, doing his party piece 'Father O'Flynn' by popular request. A villain appears in the shape of pencil-moustached Sir James Corrigan (played by regular no-gooder Leslie Perrins) who has other plans for Eileen, but it is the genial manner of Maurice Elvey's direction that makes this enjoyable, the Irishness never overdone but fond, with enough effective exterior scenes to break out of its Twickenham corset. Shreds of Benedict's music remain as when Garrick and D. J. Williams (a veteran of Tod Slaughter quota quickies) duet in 'The Moon Has Raised Her Lamp Above'. A scene in a country inn finds Percy Honri entertaining with one of his squeeze-boxes, the soft Irish voices lilting at his back as they hymn 'The Shamrock Of Ireland'. Excursions into the countryside provide an excuse for 'My Little Irish Jig', and – another incidental delight – a shepherd at a gate singing

>When the red sun is sinking over hilltops from afar
>In the stillness you'll hear it …
>The plaintive call of 'Bahhhhh' …
>Out in the heather
>We get them together
>Without any tether
>My sheep-dog and I

It may not be P. G. Wodehouse or Stephen Sondheim, but it's a delightful vignette, possibly written by Twickenham's resident, and much criticised, musical director W. L. Trytel. The oodles of sentiment are leavened by drama, notably when smuggler Miles-Na-Copaleen (beautifully played by Dennis Hoey) tries to rape Eileen, or when old Danny (Williams) dies after confessing to Father O'Flynn. Elvey's treatment ends with an endearing finale at Patrick and Eileen's wedding breakfast, with the leading players called on to make speeches in rhyme.

John Baxter began shooting *Doss House* at Twickenham in March 1933, and ***Say It with Flowers*** in November 1933. These set Baxter on a path that he assiduously followed throughout the 1930s and through World War II until his 1951 *Judgement*

Deferred. He effectively remade *Doss House* several times, reshaping, remodelling and cloning it into his seminal *Hearts of Humanity* (1936), *Love on the Dole* and *The Common Touch* (both 1941). It could also be claimed that he remade *Say It with Flowers* in various altered forms as *Music Hall* and *The Kentucky Minstrels* (both 1934), in films that invested in music-hall and variety, at their most blatant in such works as the Hazel Ascot vehicles *Talking Feet* (1937) and *Stepping Toes* (1938), but threading constantly through most of Baxter's productions. No other British director of his period can be said to have maintained so consistent a policy.

If *Say It with Flowers* is a musical film, as with all Baxter's work the musical content is interpolated, rarely shared with the characters running alongside the plot; the musical sequences do not usually emerge generally from the characters. The film has an almost documentary style beginning with a florid musical selection, courtesy of Trytel, including 'Won't You Buy My Pretty Flowers?', followed by Teresa del Riego's ballad 'Thank God For A Garden' accompanying shots of nursery gardeners tending flowers, crating them and sending them off to market, where Baxter inveigled some actual workers to play their part. This, and the extensive street market scenes that follow, provide fascinating glimpses of life as Baxter imagined it was lived on the streets of London. A few gems from H. Fowler Mear's joke book slip in: 'Rather short, aren't they?' enquires an attractive female shopper of some stockings. 'Oh,' replies the stallholder, 'they'll come up to your expectations.'

All is simplicity in Wallace Orton's scenario and Mear's streetwise dialogue. Kate Bishop (Mary Clare) is an ageing London flower-seller, a pensionable Eliza Doolittle with, in Clare's performance, more than a hint of the Royal Academy of Dramatic Art. Kate is happily married to gentle old stick Joe (Ben Field). The always watchable Clare makes a fair stab at binding her posies for the better-off passers-by, but looks as if she could eat Joe alive. She has a nasty cough, and feels weary. When a doctor prescribes complete rest, the Bishops' friends mount a concert for her benefit, raising funds for her and Joe to escape to the countryside.

In this, *Say It with Flowers* repudiates the contaminated air of the metropolis for the romanticized healthiness of wide-open spaces. Elderly stars of the music-hall are dragooned to appear at the concert. Baxter was fortunate in persuading some major music-hall performers into the studio. The greatest, in every sense, is Florrie Forde, truly the queen of the chorus-song, having introduced so many that persist to this day in some outreach of popular culture. Forde is splendidly static, monumentally encased in crushed velvet, belting out her famous choruses, among them 'Oh Oh Antonio' and 'Down At The Old Bull And Bush'. It is a perfect example of Baxter's insistence on social cohesion, on the integrity of the working class, and on the unbreakable link between the 'lower' classes and the phenomenon of music-hall, although by 1934 such entertainment was morphing into variety. The *Era* saw how 'the concert scenes converge into a perfect barrage on our emotions [...] It is difficult to imagine any audience not being moved to join in the old-time songs, even only sotto voce.'[1]

There are other rare glimpses of ageing favourites. 82-year-old Charles Coborn rattles through 'The Man That Broke The Bank At Monte Carlo' as if for the millionth time, but the real star of the occasion is Marie Kendall, vigorously feminist (and indicative of the physical violence that pervaded in many relationships) in 'Did Your First Wife Ever Do That?'. The highlight comes with Kendall's exquisite 'Just Like The Ivy (On The Old Garden Wall)', delivered with her particular use of vowels that give the number its unique emotional quality. As she sings, Baxter has the camera slowly track along the table where George Carney sits alongside his cronies. Each face is held in shot for just long enough for us to identify with every character. This is one of the most moving moments in a film that seems to have been made not only for, but of, the people. A decade later, social cohesion and the pride and taste of the common working man (in this case women) is expressed during the canteen concert scene in Frank Launder and Sidney Gilliat's *Millions Like Us*, when Bertha Willmott entertains the workers with 'Just Like The Ivy' and Vesta Victoria's 'Waiting At The Church'. You can almost sense the spirit of Baxter's work wishing the film to its spirited finale.

Say It with Flowers has an almost effortlessly authentic atmosphere, unashamedly sentimental, rightly announced in the opening credits as 'A Human Story'. Mear's dialogue manages to get in an occasional swipe at uncaring governments, and a nod and wink at sexual difference; as Kate observes, 'Boys will be girls and girls will be boys.' In the style of Dickens wandering the streets of London at night for copy, Baxter assiduously listened to cockneys and East Enders as he walked the London streets; *Say It with Flowers* exudes them. Later, he remembered this as 'In some respects […] my favourite film. It was the first one that I felt able to direct with some assurance, both in regard to story-telling and technical knowledge.'[2] The sometimes rudimentary production in no way hinders what still seems to be a heart-felt expression.

A poor excuse for not seeing a live variety show, **On the Air** perpetuated the idea that sound radio, not film, was the beating heart of British light entertainment. Made at Beaconsfield by British Lion, the various acts were marshalled by producer-director Herbert Smith, and dotted through Michael Barringer's loosely constructed scenario about radio stars performing at a charity event in a village hall. *Variety*, to whom most of the performers would have been unknown, wasn't fooled by the 'modicum of story' in a film about which there was 'very little to say'.[3] Nevertheless, there were some British top-liners in Max Wall, Egyptian sand-dancers Wilson, Keppel and Betty, and Davy Burnaby, late of *The Co-Optimists*. Leading ladies included Anona Winn, Betty Astell and Jane Carr, the latter recently of the White Coons Concert Party and one of the first performers to appear on British television in 1932. 'Black Coons' (or, as such acts were sometimes referred to, 'negro delineators') Harry Scott and Eddie Whaley, soon to be featured in John Baxter's *The Kentucky Minstrels* and sometimes billed as the 'Kolored Kings of Komedy', shared billing with Clapham and Dwyer, the Morecambe and Wise of their age. Over time, their ability to amuse may have diminished alarmingly.

FEBRUARY

In just such a way have the charms of jaunty Jack Hulbert perhaps slightly dimmed with time, but there is no denying his enormous popularity, on stage and on film, through the 1930s and beyond. One wonders if his appeal was predominantly intended for women or men, or both? To modern eyes, he may be the sort of man who, although he can't really dance or sing, jolly well gets up and has a go at both, with no hint of embarrassment and every suggestion of ease, but watching this through-and-through theatrical (he wrote and directed and choreographed as well as playing leads) amble through his routines can still be an invigorating experience. In *Jack Ahoy!* he presents as the jaunty British Jack Tar. While there is at least some vestige of sexual appeal in a handful of British leading men of the period, Hulbert seems almost devoid of it. Perhaps female audiences felt safe with Hulbert; they knew he was married to Cicely Courtneidge, who on screen didn't look like the sort of wife to stand any nonsense. Nevertheless, put against the Hollywood competition, Hulbert doesn't rise to greatness as actor, singer or dancer, but there is a pleasant, here for the moment and not be taken too seriously manner about him that is difficult to define.

He is perhaps not consistently at his best in *Jack Ahoy!*, a surprisingly damp effort from director Walter Forde, working well below his high water mark. It barely qualifies as a musical film, offering hornpipe dancing and the snappy 'My Hat's On The Side Of My Head' by Harry B. Woods and Claude Hulbert, and some badly cooked choreography. The best that may be said of Sidney Gilliat and John Orton's screenplay, with additional dialogue by Leslie Arliss, Gerard Fairlie, Austin Melford and Jack Hulbert himself, is that it might have brightened up if Mrs Hulbert had turned up for a couple of numbers. The supporting cast looks bored, as well it might since it is given almost nothing of interest to do. Stock Chinese villains about inscrutable business, a plummy leading lady and a sailor sidekick for the star tar who is weakly cast do nothing to help matters.

Alfred Hitchcock's *Waltzes from Vienna* did not enjoy a very enthusiastic press, dismissed by Leslie Halliwell who found 'very little music and very little Hitchcock in this extremely mild romantic comedy.'[4] Hitchcock admitted to feeling no sympathy for the material. He never directed another musical film, although music (who underestimates the impact of Bernard Herrmann's score for *Psycho*?) was an essential component of his work. Gene D. Phillips sees *Waltzes from Vienna* as boasting 'a felicitous integration of image and score that is exemplary for a musical of its time, since the numbers do grow out of situations in the story and are not merely tacked on to it, as was usually the case with the Hollywood backstage musicals of the period,[5] but it was the director himself who defined this time as the low point of his career. The reputation of *Waltzes from Vienna* may have suffered by being generally dismissed as of little importance in a genre historically and critically considered of little interest or relevance.

In the theatre, *Walzer aus Wien*'s libretto by A. M. Willner, Heinz Reichert and Ernst Marischka told the story of the two Johann Strausses – father (Edmund Gwenn) and son 'Schani' (Esmond Knight) – with music by both selected and organised by Erich Wolfgang Korngold and Julius Bittner. As it turned out, the show hadn't been much of a hit in Vienna in 1931, but ran for 607 performances in London later that year. It seemed ripe for film treatment, now entrusted to experienced Guy Bolton and Alma Reville, its music adapted by Hubert Bath and supervised by Louis Levy. It may be that filming at Shepherd's Bush proceeded without enthusiasm. There was little from leading lady Jessie Matthews, who recalled that '[Hitchcock] was then just an imperious young man who knew nothing about musicals. [This, of course, some may consider an advantage.] I felt unnerved when he tried to get me to adopt a mincing operetta style. He was out of his depth and he showed he knew it by ordering me about.'[6] One wonders what Hitchcock had to deal with.

It would have been interesting to know Matthews's reactions to her supporting cast of some of the finest actors of their generation, not least Gwenn and Knight and Fay Compton, elegant and touching as Countess Helga. Matthews's comments about Hitchcock can be measured against some of her later films, notably those directed by Sonnie Hale, whose talent did not touch Hitchcock's hem. It is unlikely, anyway, that she would have bothered to see the film more than once; revisiting it may have altered her opinion. Its qualities seem surer today. *Waltzes from Vienna* is infested with piquant touches: the madcap opening sequences; the 'Blue Danube' born among the rhythms of a bakery; the Countess's scarf caught up in a waistcoat; the elderly Strauss standing in the dimmed light of a bandstand. These are delicacies that evaded scores of British musical films of the period. There is mischievousness at work that pervades everything without impinging on the sentiment. *Waltzes from Vienna* is far from the lacklustre failure that its director and leading lady and many subsequent critics deemed it.

By the time **Happy** went into production at Elstree, it had already happened in Germany the previous year as *Es war einmal ein Musikus* and in France as *C'était un Musicien*. Frederic Zelnik produced and directed a movie that seemed ideally tuned to the talents of Stanley Lupino, now signed to Associated British Picture Corporation and responsible for adaptation, dialogue and scenario with Austin Melford, Frank Launder and Arthur Woods, based on the original screenplays by Jacques Bacharach, Alfred Hahm and Karl Noti. Lupino and his frequent on-stage partner Laddie Cliff live poverty-stricken in a garret landlorded by the veteran music-hall entertainer Will Fyffe (famously of 'I Belong To Glasgow'). Lupino has invented a siren device for alerting police to stolen vehicles; Cliff is a composer bandleader in search of a decent song. Unsurprisingly they come up with a lyric and Noel Gay melody for the skipping title number, as impromptu as Lupino's invention of the lyric for 'Steak And Kidney Pudding' in one of his cheapest but most effective pictures *Cheer Up!*. Soon enough, Lupino is doing some froggy-type dancing, and sparring with Cliff in some punishing physical comedy. The austere, faintly Germanic garret setting by Clarence Elder gives way to some superb high-society sets, luxuriously appointed nightclubs that bear little relationship to those frequented by the average cinemagoer, through which the moustache-manipulating Harry Tate revolves.

The boys blossom in this glamorous environment, with good luck turning on the arrival of a car insurance magnate and his daughter. Stars and moon rotate magically in a night sky as Lupino romances her, confirming 'There's So Much I'm Wanting To Tell You'. For a while, Lupino and the girl (Renee Gadd) become a sub-standard Astaire and Rogers, and Gadd has a nice moment in 'There Was A Poor Musician' as she bathes a little dog. The puppies pegged on a washing-line is one of several incidental niceties, not least Fyffe and the indestructibly statuesque Bertha Belmore duetting 'It's Wonderful'. Music credits, presumably accumulated along the multi-language route, are for Kurt Schwabach, Fred Raymond, Will Meisel, Ralph Stanley, Willy Rosen and Henrik N. Ege, with Fred Schwarz recognised for 'musical score'.

Basil Dean had long wondered where he might find another personality with the drawing power of Gracie Fields, when he was recommended a modest little picture that was currently wowing audiences in the north of England. Sitting alone, he viewed a copy of 'what proved to be a very crude affair – commonplace story, poor photography, with developer stains and scratched on the print. Yet, in spite of these infelicities, I thought to myself, here is another personality that seems to bounce off the screen.'[7]

Its star wrote of his first feature film *Boots! Boots!* that 'it was so dark in places you had to strike matches to see it. Courting couples liked it though.' This was no masterwork of British cinema. The star, George Formby (Junior), went further: the film was 'shocking ... It was hissed at, at its trade show'. It is difficult to define *Boots! Boots!*, for which Formby was paid £100 plus 10% of the profits, as much more than a Poverty Row production by the enterprising producer John E. Blakeley, working at the tiny Albany Studios, above a busy vehicle repair garage in London's Albany Street.

At least the title conveyed something of its below-stairs content. Formby played John Willie, boot boy at the Crestonia Hotel, where he fancies the maid Snooky (Formby's wife Beryl). When Snooky discovers she is heir to a fortune, it seems his love for her is slipping away, but they are reunited before fade-out. In part, this was a template for the bigger budgeted Formby films that followed. In these the star pretty much played the same character, partly inspired by his consumptive music-hall father George Formby (catchphrase 'Coughing well tonight'), also known as the Wigan Nightingale. The film seemed to know its place, having its premiere not in the West End but in Burslem, Stoke-on-Trent. Now, the predictable plot was punctuated by four numbers in the Formby manner: 'Sitting On The Ice In The Ice Rink', 'I Could Make A Good Living At That', 'Baby' and 'Why Don't Women Like Me?'. As his future career proved, they did. The shenanigans were directed by Bert Tracey. The credits claim a screenplay by Formby and Jack Cottrill, but should more accurately be ascribed to Formby and Arthur Mertz. Betty Driver is listed among the players but does not appear, abandoned on the cutting-room floor, possibly a victim of Beryl Formby's well-known jealousy of female competitors.

Dean was to write that 'George was a simple, uncomplicated person of limited talent, his principal means of expression a grin that seemed to spread right across the screen – and – of course! – his ukulele [...] But I soon discovered that he was a shrewd judge of his own capabilities and refused to step outside them. This was not a case of the comedian wanting to play Hamlet.'[8]

MARCH

Anna Neagle's next stepping-stone to movie stardom was Herbert Wilcox's ***The Queen's Affair***, another reshaped operetta, this time employing the music of Oscar Straus. Nadina, a simple shop assistant, makes the unlikeliest of social leaps by becoming queen of an eastern European country, but is rudely exiled when her fiefdom revolts. Two decades later, Wilcox and Neagle were still making nonsense of this type, exemplified by Wilcox's deadly *King's Rhapsody* (1955). Poor Nadina sets off on a Grand Tour, eventually bumping into the rebelling rogue Carl who had headed the revolt against her. As he is played by Fernand Gravey, warmed up from co-starring with Neagle the previous year in *Bitter Sweet*, Nadina of course falls in love with him, returning with him to her country where the besotted populace are thrilled to receive them. Made for British and Dominions at Elstree, *The Queen's Affair* had a screenplay by Samson Raphaelson, Monckton Hoffe and Miles Malleson (who also huffed and puffed as the Chancellor), based on the 1926 Berlin operetta *Die Königin* by Ernst Marischka and Bruno Granichstaedten. This had starred Fritzi Massary, who would make it to London in Coward's 1938 stage musical *Operette*. Neagle was buttressed by a solid cast including the squirrel-like Muriel Aked as Nadina's elderly handmaiden, Gibb McLaughlin, Hay Petrie, Michael Hogan and the Welsh tenor Trefor Jones. The sugary songs include 'I Love You So', 'Tonight', 'When I Hear Your Voice' and 'Fisherman's Waltz'.

In conceiving the storyline for **Love, Life and Laughter**, Gracie Fields's follow-up to *This Week of Grace*, actor-writers Joan Sterndale Bennett (for many years a performer at London's Players' Theatre) and Eric Dunstan (he appeared as himself the same year in *Death at Broadcasting House*) propelled Fields into Ruritania. Had Wilcox been its director and Neagle its star, the whole thing would have had the consistency of marshmallow, but between them Fields, director Maurice Elvey and screenplay writers Maurice Braddell and Gordon Wellesley avoided the worst excesses, lighting up the proceedings with anarchic exuberance.

We meet Fields parading on a float, dressed as Nell Gwyn and bowling oranges at passers-by to raise money for a children's hospital. This modern-day Nellie is the bright spark in a Britain suffering Depression. Where spirits need to be lifted, Fields sings 'Riding On A Cloud'. Arrested for breach of the peace, she charms the magistrate (Robb Wilton on good muddling form) into dismissing the case. 'C'mon,' she chirps, 'sing as we go!', dancing with a policeman (an unlikely occurrence in any decade) to demonstrate that we are all of common clay. Back in her bar where Percy Honri, patriarch of a notable accordion family, is entertaining the customers, she is spotted as a potential film star and invited to a grand ball given for King Boris. Nellie is rather more impressed by the King's son Prince Charles (John Loder), who has already wined and dined her. 'Fancy you knowing all the words on the menu card', she tells him, so we know she is artless. There seems little point in her falling for Charles as he is politically betrothed to a plain Jane, the Princess Grapfel (Norah Howard); cue for the film's tenderest musical moment with Fields mourning 'Cherie'. It's not long before she lets her hair down with a low-comedy number that was to become one of her best remembered, 'Out In The Cold, Cold Snow', done in what we might call the Rochdale manner, before her slapstick exit from the ball.

Surprisingly, Charles seems to have socialist principles, moving in with Nell's parents. Shades of Novello's genuinely funny non-musical comedy *I Lived with You* obtrude. This idyllic arrangement is upset when Charles's father dies, obliging him to return home and ascend the throne. It's Elvey's chance to throw caution to the wind, putting the film into top gear with the almost manic preparations for the coronation, with Ben Field as a bumbling mayor. Believing that Charles still wants her, Nell arrives, but soon appreciates the impossibility of the situation. She selflessly sets about beautifying plain Jane Princess Grapfel, admitting in song 'I'm A Failure, Dear, With You'. No other leading lady of the period could bring off so affecting a final sequence, ultimately bringing the story to its close with 'Love, Life And Laughter'.

David Shipman has written that Basil Dean, who produced for Associated Talking Pictures, 'saw [Fields] less as a heroine than as a clown, and she was normally lovelorn, only to lose the man to an ingénue in the end. Most of the humour was broad caricature.'[9] A tendency to surround her with supporting players who presented no challenge to her supremacy was probably unhelpful; that much is indicated in *Love, Life and Laughter*, in which it was pretty obvious that Ruritania was not Fields's home country. The star was being packaged in a manner that attempted to exploit the extremes of her talent (high and low and physical comedy and sentimental vocalising) without exploring the undeniable genius that ran through it. The on-screen credits make no reference to the composers of the so-so songs, contributed by Jimmy Harper, William (Will) E. Haines, Leo Towers and Victor Ford.

The life and music, and more especially the loves, of Schubert had commercial appeal to film-makers of the decade, finding an apogee in Richard Tauber's *Blossom Time* (August 1934) and in the now almost forgotten Cine-Allianz biopic bilingual *The Unfinished Symphony*. This was made in Austria, produced by Arnold Pressburger and originally directed by Willi Forst, when it was released as *Leise flehen meine Lieder*; the making of the English version was supervised by Anthony Asquith. It may have been denied a British certification, but its intelligent screenplay by Forst and Benn W. Levy, and its star performances from Hans Yaray as Schubert and Marta Eggerth as Caroline Esterhazy, were notable. The *New York Times* remarked that Eggerth 'helps the photoplay considerably with the warmth and skill of her interpretation of the Schubert songs' and that 'despite its mediocre and sometimes wretched photography' [a common complaint about British musical films of the decade] *The Unfinished Symphony* 'provides a politely winning background for the immortal lieder of the great composer'.[10]

In 1820 Vienna, a young Schubert is entranced by Emmie (Helen Chandler), an assistant in a pawn-shop, but eventually, thwarted in his love for the aristocratic Caroline, he destroys the final pages of his great symphony. This fulsome project involved the Vienna Philharmonic and State Opera chorus, as well as Gyula Howarth's Gypsy Band. Praising the recreation of the Austro-Hungarian milieu, the *MFB* curiously considered the film appropriate for children 'if not too immediately preceded by a good knockabout comedy'.[11] Rather more perceptively, Franz Marksteiner has suggested that Yaray's 'lovingly restrained performance [...] seemingly owes a lot to the kind of naïve respect and admiration Austrian grammar schools conveyed to their pupils. Yaray's way of speaking, owing to its musicality, was to become formative for the Viennese film'.[12]

APRIL

Although a native of Graz, Robert Stolz clung into old age to his reputation as 'Last of the Waltz Kings'. He was certainly one of the first Viennese composers to mine the possibilities presented by talking pictures in the 1930s, surviving professionally until the 1960s. Fecund as he was, his work is not particularly distinguishable. It included the German film operetta *Zwei Herzen im Dreivierteltakt*, directed by Géza von Bolváry. In Britain, this confection was reconstructed at the Nettlefold-Fogwell studios at Walton-on-the-Naze as *Two Hearts in Waltz Time*. The revised screenplay, based on Walter Reisch and Franz Schulz's original, was an in-house job by Reginald Fogwell and John McNally, but other personnel involved at least were adept in creating a continental sophistication – director Carmine Gallone, and stars Carl Brisson and Frances Day. The storyline had few surprises, with Brisson as composer Carl (looking too suave to pass for the real article) who is commissioned to write a new opera by impresario Greenbaum (Oscar Asche). Carl's mind turns to Helene Barry (Day) who, unknown to him, has been signed up as its star.

The plot was interrupted by several numbers including 'Two Hearts That Beat In Waltz Time In Old Vienna', 'Give Her A Little Kiss', 'Your Eyes Are So Tender' and 'Men, Oh How I Hate Them'. *MFB* saw 'a musical comedy of little distinction', but approved of 'the pleasant singing' of Brisson, and the performance of Asche. Danish matinee idol Brisson was nearing the end of his film career, moving to Hollywood for his last musical film, *All the King's Horses*, in which he co-starred with Mary Ellis. Asche, in his day a successful producer, writer and actor, having created the record-breaking *Chu Chin Chow* as well as playing its Abu Hasan (he found the long run 'terribly boring'), was bankrupt and difficult to work with by 1934. Hopefully his performance in *Two Hearts in Waltz Time* took his mind off his money troubles and accusations of domestic abuse. Leading lady Day somehow never quite became the star on film that she undeniably was on stage, but her starry days survived until 1944 with the diverting *Fiddlers Three*, before she slid into oblivion in the 1950s.

Michael Balcon made two attempts during the year to establish Evelyn Laye as a star of British musical film. The attempts were not particularly successful, despite Laye's competence. Part of the problem was the projects to which she was shackled. Maurice Elvey seemed as appropriate a director as any for the quirky *Princess Charming*, worked up from a 1930 stage play by F. Martos into a screenplay by L. du Garde Peach, with additional dialogue by Robert Edmunds. At face value, this is another dose of Ruritanian tosh. In fact, there is more on offer, not least Laye's spirited Princess Elaine, an unhappy royal promised (or condemned) as the bride of elderly King Charles of Aufland (the excellent George Grossmith). The arrangement is inconvenient because the king is happy with his mature mistress Countess Anna (Yvonne Arnaud). The people of Princess Elaine's country are in revolt. She escapes to Aufland only to find herself holed up in the embassy, where she is obliged for diplomatic reasons to marry a handsome stranger, the staunch Captain Launa (Harry [Henry] Wilcoxon). Matters are complicated by the arrival of a chuntering insurance agent Chuff (Max Miller) until a happy ending has the Captain restored from the asylum from which he has escaped.

Ludicrous and familiar as the situations are, the pleasures are considerable,

Evelyn Laye, almost a film star, as *Princess Charming* (1934)

provided by Laye but more especially and characterfully by Grossmith and Arnaud, the latter given the opportunity to play the piano at which she was adept. Their duet 'Too Many Women' offers the early hope that they will feature much more than they do. It's a witty example of the attractively inventive numbers by Ray Noble and lyricist Max Kester, against a background of the general score by Leighton Lucas. Laye's principal aria 'Love Is A Song' is memorable if trite but over too soon; indeed, most of the musical numbers begin well but tend to dribble away. A tailing-off after the parodic opening sequence of the Princess's awakening comes all too soon as the plot subsides into dullness, with Laye too often absent from the screen.

There is another problem in the casting of the famous stage comedian Max Miller. He made several films (mercifully, only a cameo that resembles an interruption in the otherwise excellent *The Good Companions*), but in *Princess Charming* his role has clearly been fashioned for him. Cinema constrains him. His brilliance on stage evaporates when faced with the camera. His inappropriate casting, the exhausting chatter he comes out with, and the dull doggedness that shrouds Wilcoxon are responsible for some of the charmlessness that overcomes *Princess Charming*. The central love affair is paler than pale. Patience is rewarded when Elvey wakes the film up in the closing sequences of absurd royal pomp, rather as he had in *Love, Life and Laughter*. It's not quite enough to bring the film into safe harbour, but this is nevertheless an interesting concept with its cleverly integrated musical numbers, among them 'The Princess Is Awakening', 'Near And Yet So Far', 'Brave Hearts', 'On The Wings Of A Dream' and 'When Gay Adventure Calls'. These may in themselves have been too parodic, and here and there too nuanced for general public consumption. *Princess Charming* lacks cohesion, and Laye has not the cinematic skill to draw us in. *Variety* considered it 'just below the peak of excellence for which Hollywood is noticed', but that [really?] Miller 'registers marvellously'.[13]

A theatre critic the like of whom would not be found today, James Agate made space in his elegant review of the Richard Rodgers and Lorenz Hart stage musical *Evergreen* to tell us that 'Miss Matthews, when she is not dancing exquisitely, shows how much of variety may enliven the seeming infantile, and once, for a passionate moment, rises above curds and whey.'[14] Alas, we have no idea at what 'passionate moment' she rose, or what her reaction was to Agate's words (if she ever read them, which seems unlikely). We do know that ***Evergreen*** was the consolidation of Matthews's place in British films, nurtured as she was under the supervision of Michael Balcon and director Victor Saville, aware that American musical comedy was 'unquestionably the best of the breed, both in the theatre and films'.

Playwright Benn W. Levy, librettist for the stage version, now adapted the play with new dialogue by Emlyn Williams from a scenario by Marjorie Gaffney, while some of the original Rodgers and Hart songs were joined by new numbers by Harry M. Woods. A definitive explanation of the facts around the possibility of co-starring Matthews with Fred Astaire seems unlikely, but he was tied into other commitments and she seemed to have no wish to work in Hollywood. The outcome was that Balcon and Saville chose Barry Mackay as Matthews's romantic interest. A stiff Britishness blows through the proceedings whenever he appears, while his movement to music isn't dancing – more like semaphore. A trick was missed here: why didn't they find an actor player who could look and move the part? Throughout her career, this question was never satisfactorily resolved.

Saville insisted on changes to Levy's play, as did the film's comic turn, Sonnie Hale. Their revisions worked well. After the movie premiered in America, Saville received a cable from Rodgers and Hart: 'Dear Victor, we wish we had thought of that story.' Saville's philosophy was simple enough. 'The screenplay had been written so that the musical numbers conformed to my belief that they must advance the story [...] This is the most satisfactory feature of musicals as we know them. Previously the story of a musical comedy stood still whilst the performers delivered their songs on cue.'[15] Thus, one of the best of Woods's songs sprang from Saville's idea that the impostor Harriet Green would reveal her true self at the end of the movie by a stage striptease.

There are moments when an enchantment pervades *Evergreen*, as in its beginning in the glow of an Edwardian music-hall, where the public's darling Harriet Green (Matthews) is giving – despite being in her salad days – a farewell performance, singing Vesta Victoria's 'Daddy Wouldn't Buy Me A Bow-Wow'. We see Harriet in long shot as if from a promenade bar at the back of the stalls, where ladies of the night discreetly ply their trade, until – magically – the camera hovers above her down-turned face as she lifts it to stare directly into its eye. In this, cinema-photographer Glen MacWilliams fixes Matthews's image. No one was ever to capture her qualities on screen as potently. At this moment, Harriet's farewell to her admirers seems the more prescient if we consider the vicissitudes of Matthews's subsequent career: 'I would rather leave you all at this moment, the moment when you love me most. I would never like to grow old before your eyes.'

Years later, Harriet's daughter (Matthews again) is persuaded to impersonate her dead mother, and becomes a great star until, hedged about with romantic and familial complications, she threatens to lose everything by exposing the deceit worked on her public. Luckily, they still love and forgive her. Matthews has excellent support from the surrounding cast, notably Ivor McLaren in a skilfully tuned performance as the elderly Marquis of Staines, Betty Balfour (by now diminished), and Hale as comic Leslie Benn. Gaumont-British's best was put to work: impressive settings by Alfred Junge, choreography by Buddy Bradley, and a fine score, with three numbers forever linked to its star: Woods's 'When You've Got A Little Springtime In Your Heart' with its extraordinary robotic dance sequence, as if some reels of Fritz Lang's *Metropolis* had got mixed up with it; Woods's 'Over My Shoulder'; and, most wonderfully, Rodgers and Hart's 'Dancing On The Ceiling'.

Matthews claimed that she devised this routine on the day of its shooting, with no assistance from Bradley. The microphones were left on as she dances around Junge's palatial floor; the squeaking of her shoes as she pirouettes across the floor can be clearly heard. The physicality of that sound seems to link us directly to the moment of its happening; it remains a wonderful few seconds of British cinema. The *MFB* felt let down by the 'Over My Shoulder' finale, deciding that the production 'everywhere rises above the material it is handling, but the last dance-ensemble is an anti-climax [it is indeed] which is apt to upset one's final impressions of the rest of the picture'.[16]

Evergreen was heartily welcomed by critics and public alike. For the *Observer*, Caroline Lejeune wrote of its star: 'Her movement and poise in this new picture [...] is enchanting: she has found just how to get the maximum effect from the minimum appearance of effort, and her best moments now have that emotional quality that comes from a perfect fitness of form and idea.'[17] Dan Navarro recalls 'the exquisitely talented Miss Matthews [...] a unique talent [...] a superb dancer who could disarm an audience' and who in *Evergreen* 'made a staggering impact on audiences around the world, and became established as an international star of the first magnitude'.[18] The cost to Matthews's well-being carried through subsequent productions. For now, she described her collapses during the filming of *Evergreen* as 'a nervous breakdown [...] Just a little one, hardly worth mentioning.'[19] Beyond these difficulties, Matthews has claim to be the Judy Garland and/or Ginger Rogers of British films – not so good a singer as Garland although going through similar traumas, but a better dancer than Rogers.

Arthur Wing Pinero's brilliantly constructed comedy *The Magistrate*, first seen in London in 1885, could want no better film version than BIP's **Those Were the Days**, skilfully adapted by Fred Thompson, Frank Launder and Frank Miller, and directed (one of his better efforts) by Thomas Bentley, fortunate to have gathered together so many gifted comic actors. Will Hay as the kindly befuddled magistrate Poskett may be the best known, but here he is matched by two superb cameos by George Graves as Colonel Lukyn and Claud Allister as his stiff-backed comrade-in-arms Captain Vale. In transposing the play's second act to a music-hall setting, the film makes a feature of some of the music-hall turns of the day (already re-dressing as variety). These are currants in the pudding, not integrated into any musical score but neatly inserted into this condensation of Pinero's non-musical original. They are home territory for Mr Bentley.

We have the incorrigible and bent-over Lily Morris, for some reason borrowing Marie Lloyd's 'Don't Dilly Dally', and sprightly Harry Bedford in one of his hit items, 'Carve A Little Bit Off The Top'. Some printed sources claim that it is an uncredited G. H. Elliott sloping his way through Leslie Stuart's cake-walkey 'Lily Of Laguna' (one of the most poignant songs of the halls), but it isn't; Elliott is known to have appeared only once on screen, in John Baxter's *Music Hall*. This 'coon' sequence in *Those Were the Days* is particularly interesting in that Bentley has the Elliott impersonator Frank Boston appeal directly to the cinema audience to 'sing up' with the chorus, just as he might have on stage. It's a naïve, slightly embarrassing touch, but fits the film's general air of friendliness, still hoping to capture the indefinable relationship between performer and spectator at the music-hall, in itself an art form that relies on the interplay between those on and off stage, probably more so than in any other art form. Away from the music-hall scenes, there is much to relish: a young (although not as young as the plot might suggest) John Mills as a sparky juvenile, Captain Vale abandoned on a crumbling balcony, and a priceless exchange between Mrs Poskett (Iris Hoey) and Colonel Lukyn concerning dates.

MAY

With Julius Hagen's production of **The Broken Melody**, Twickenham studios must have been punching above its weight. The term 'quota quickie' might have been invented for the product the industrious and apparently highly likeable Hagen ('Uncle' to his colleagues) churned out. As Geoff Brown has described, 'Working conditions at Twickenham were particularly gruelling. Shooting schedules were frequently no longer than ten days, and the studio boiled with activity, in different shifts, for 24 hours. Cameras were forced to pause, however, when trains rattled by outside – a watchman was positioned on the studio roof expressly to give the floor advance warning.'[20]

American-born Bernard Vorhaus made two musical films at Twickenham, *The Broken Melody* and in 1935 the less ambitious *Street Song*, understandably labelled by Geoff Brown 'an addle-pated musical'. Neither film is the best of Vorhaus, who had come to Britain on holiday and stayed until 1937 when he departed for Hollywood. Nevertheless, *The Broken Melody* needed a technician of considerable skill because its screenplay was a melodramatic melange cooked by Vera Allinson, Michael Hankinson and Twickenham's script editor H. Fowler Mear, who seems to have been ready for any challenge. Brown notes that Mear 'regularly provided lethal scripts peppered with stock gags culled from his own personal joke books'.[21] On this occasion, Vorhaus could hardly complain about the plot: he devised it. Another resident hurdle at Twickenham was musical director W. L. Trytel, known if only for mostly pedestrian, and rarely silent, musical soundtracks. For *The Broken Melody* he was expected to write passages of 'opera', while the studio became an opera house, a surprisingly spacious Parisian garret, a smart café, Devil's Island, and slave boat.

At least the Parisian garret was gloomy, with a piano on which struggling composer Paul Verlaine (John Garrick) composes his scores. His landlord's daughter Germaine (Merle Oberon) adores him. This is unreciprocated. Singing in a café,

Paul is eyed up by the glamorous opera star Simone St Cloud (Margot Grahame). Wearing a nightie made up from several dead ostriches, she seduces him, but soon enough Paul gets his opera 'The Broken Melody' staged, and for good measure gets to play the lead. As one of the first-night critics says, 'I can't remember a composer playing a lead in his own piece before', adding (perhaps having looked at the film script) 'The story's a little far-fetched'. Now on the up, Paul is surrounded by his music ('Where's my Symphony in F?').

Germaine encourages him to write popular tunes, but he loftily complains, 'I don't write for the man in the street.' Mistakenly, he abandons Germaine, planning to marry Simone ('the loveliest and most exciting woman!'). Germaine sings a tear-stained chorus of 'The Broken Melody'. Simone and Paul wed, and have a child, but happiness does not endure. Simone flirts with other men, notably caddish Pierre (Austin Trevor), but goes on to star in Paul's new opera 'Machine Fantasy'. Sadly, neither Twickenham's resources nor Trytel's musicianship or the screenwriters' imaginations stretch to giving us an excerpt from what sounds like a science fiction extravaganza that might have transformed opera for ever. The new work flops, and the relationship between Paul and Simone flounders. Paul attempts suicide but is rescued by a vagrant (Harry Terry). Paul kills Pierre, and leaves his son in the care of the still loving Germaine. Arrested for his crime, Paul is transported to Devil's Island, where he is reunited with the vagrant. Unseen and unmourned in Paris, Simone dies, and Paul escapes from Devil's Island. Time passes. At the opera, the ex-commandant of the prison (Charles Carson) – who would have guessed he was an opera buff? – recognises Paul as the prisoner he believed killed while attempting to escape. 'The story of your play is the story of Paul Verlaine', the ex-commandant tells him. He walks away, having decided not to expose Paul, giving way to a happy ending.

It's nonsense, but highly entertaining. James Carter's art direction works wonders in the recreation of the various locations, not least the gloriously artificial on-stage scenes of Paul's opera. You can sense how Vorhaus must have relished these. In the circumstances, the performances could not be bettered. For modern taste Garrick may resemble a clone of the suet-puddinged Nelson Eddy. He may not be much of an actor but he manages to make Paul a living entity, and the rest of the cast work with a will. Even Trytel has some success with the opera scenes, but for all we know they may be made up of odd bits and pieces of Donizetti or Meyerbeer. Perhaps, like Meyerbeer, Trytel wrote different variations for everything in different coloured inks. Vorhaus skilfully welds the many strands of this engaging little film together, using camera angles and gestures of the various locations to bring an almost impossibly melodramatic work home and dry.

JUNE

The odds of success for **How's Chances?**, filmed at Shepperton for Sound City, were limited. Director Anthony Kimmins, whose other works included George Formby's *Keep Fit*, *Trouble Brewing* and *Come On George!*, and who worked as a writer on Gracie Fields's *Queen of Hearts* and *The Show Goes On*, was challenged to produce the British version of the 1932 German movie *Der Frauendiplomat* as directed by E. W. Emo and starring Marta Eggerth. At Shepperton, Ivar Campbell and Harry Graham's adaptation of E. B. Leuthege and Kurt Braun's original screenplay had Tamara Desni as ballerina Helen, who proves helpful when dashing British ambassador Nottingham (Harold French) is romantically complicated by the wives of ministers whose agreement to a treaty is essential. Reissued in 1939 as *The Diplomatic Lover*, the music was by Hans May. Fleeing from Nazi oppression, 'By 1935 many of Germany's best singing birds, whether singers themselves, composers or musicians, had already flown the nest, to the supposed safety of Austria, or further afield',[22] in May's case to England where his first assignments included two remakes of films for which he had supplied scores in Germany, the Joseph Schmidt *My Song Goes Round the World* (October 1934) and the less-remembered *How's Chances?*.

Steve Chibnall in his celebration of the British quota quickie suggests that the continental allure of Desni was matched with the British solidarity of French 'probably in an attempt to improve the film's chances of playing as a first feature. The film's publicity described it as "one of the most lavish and scintillating entertainments which have yet been produced in this country", and the trade press reviews were enthusiastic, but in Leicester *How's Chances?* achieved only one booking and that as a supporting feature.'[23]

One of the pleasures of the year was BIP's next vehicle for Bobby Howes. **Over the Garden Wall** had a screenplay by H. F. Maltby and Gordon Wellesley, based on Maltby's play *The Youngest of Three*, and was directed by the Belgian John (properly Jean) Daumery, who died the same year aged 36. It is a happy memorial, with Howes on good form, partnered by a visitor from Hollywood, Marian Marsh. The tale of warring next-door neighbours had a first-class supporting cast including the ever-welcome Bertha Belmore as a sticky Edwardian spinster aunt to young Mary (Marsh), Margaret Bannerman as aunt to Howes's mischievous Bunny, and Syd Crossley, the archetypal crafty butler. David Rawnsley's excellent settings, contrasting the musty old-fashionedness of one establishment with the up-to-dateness of another, made the most of the studio's resources. The burgeoning romance between Howes and Marsh is convincing and sweetly told via shuttlecocks and finger puppetry at dead of night. There are pleasing songs by Vivian Ellis and lyricist Desmond Carter, with the brightest of openings in a bar of young men headed by a jubilant Howes singing the praises of 'Auntie'. The

Shadow play and neighbourly romance for Bobby Howes and Marian Marsh in *Over the Garden Wall* (1934)

eagle-eyed may note two uncredited appearances: a flash of Stewart Granger and – much rarer – Vivian Ellis at the piano. The soundtrack has Ellis playing in his effortlessly fluent manner. Marsh sits comfortably with her subordinate role which must have been a come-down after her work in America (fortunately, she had a distinguished future). There is a captivating little duet in 'Why Wasn't I Told?' and in 'Wrap Yourself In Cotton Wool' which opens out into an impressively choreographed fan dance devised by Ralph Reader along Hollywood lines, helped by aerial shots. *MFB* was justified in seeing this as 'one of BIP's best efforts' with Howes 'his usual witty self'.[24]

As rough and ready as a John Baxter production could be, ***Music Hall*** was to some extent a reiteration of themes threaded through the earlier *Say It with Flowers*; its working title had been *Say It with Song*. Hastily filmed (and it shows) in March 1934 at Twickenham, this particular 'Real Art' production of Julius Hagen had George Carney as Bill. Carney was Baxter's favoured leading man; the following year Baxter cast him in the title role of *A Real Bloke*, a description that perfectly sums up this actor's on-screen qualities. In *Music Hall* he's marshalling his Poverty Row cronies, among them Baxter regulars pudding-faced Mark Daly, tubby Edgar Driver and, fresh from *Say It with Flowers*, Ben Field, to save from closure the ailing Empire Music-Hall in 'Workhampton' (where work seems far from easy to come by). Audiences no longer like the modern fare presented there. Bill's answer is simple: bring back nice old-fashioned manager Mr Davis (Wilson Coleman) who will revive the artists and material that people like Bill imagine other people crave. The fact that at this point of the 1930s music-hall was in decline – indeed, some thought it had died a couple of decades earlier – is no impediment to the argument, with Bill insisting the people are not getting what they want.

Soon, Davis is planning a grand reopening of the revamped Empire, now spick and span (or as spick and span as anything ever looks in a Baxter film), which is rather more than can be said of the acts he has booked. A boy singer, Jimmy Bryant, tap dances; a Dutch Serenader does some ear-splitting yodelling; a dog act has a profoundly unsettling air about it; a pretty girl called Eve Chapman sings 'An Old-Fashioned Love Song' while chorines in synthetic wedding-cake crinolines float around her. Bill is moved by the dreary scraping of the Gershom Parkington Quintette ('Makes you think you've got a lot to be thankful for'). On this showing, it's a wonder that the newly revamped Empire didn't shut up for good that night, but Bill and his mates seem over the moon about the show. The only genuine topliner Baxter signed was the self-styled 'Chocolate Coloured Coon' G. H. Elliott, here singing 'Sue, Sue, Sue'. The closing sequence attempts a spectacular finale to Davis's gala, headed by Raymond Newell and a stage crammed with all sorts of Baxter's 'ordinary' people, leaving the audience 'With A Smile On Your Lips And A Song In Your Heart'. Twickenham's resident maestro W. L. Trytel contributed 'Brighter Days' and 'Cruising Jazz', both unmemorable. Similarly to *Say It with Flowers*, *Music Hall* exists in an almost entirely male-dominated world with male bonding and kinship forged and solidified by unquestioned moral values of social class, finding some sort of artistic expression through the dubious medium of light entertainment. Its performers are the workers' aristocracy.

JULY

The supposed attraction of using a popular song title for the title of a catchpenny feature probably threw up Panther Picture's ***Danny Boy***, produced at Cricklewood by Challis Sanderson and directed by Oswald Mitchell, who would go on to a catalogue of second- or third-drawer musical features including *Stars on Parade*, *Variety Parade*, *Shipmates o' Mine*, and two other 'song titled' productions, *Rose of Tralee* and *Lily of Laguna*. Dorothy Dickson, best known for her roles in Ivor Novello's stage operettas *Careless Rapture* and *Crest of the Wave*, made a rare screen appearance as Jane Kaye, estranged from husband Pat (Frank Forbes-Robertson) and son Danny (Ronnie Hepworth). The score included the title song, Denis O'Neil's 'The Mountains Of Mourne', 'Come Back To Erin' and the music-hall favourite 'Dear Old Pals'. Mitchell effectively remade the film for Butcher's in 1941 with Wilfrid Lawson as the lost husband and Ann Todd as Jane, and with a new screenplay by Vera Allinson and others.

The title ***Song at Eventide*** suggested an appointment with solemnity if not gloom, produced by John Argyle for Argyle Talking Pictures and directed at Cricklewood Stoll studios by Harry Hughes, whose *Facing the Music* and *A Southern Maid* had been seen the previous year. The new work, written by John Hastings Turner (author of the Boris Karloff horror *The Ghoul* for Gaumont-British in 1933), married a crime story to a song-heavy scenario. The film had the advantage of Fay Compton as cabaret singer Helen d'Alaste, whose past catches up with her. To prevent her secrets being revealed to her daughter (Nancy Burne) Helen pretends to commit suicide and retires to a convent. An attractive score offered Compton a rare singing role. The numbers included 'Wandering To Paradise', 'Gigolette', 'My Treasure', 'Dreaming' and 'Vienna City Of My Dreams' composed by Rudolph Sieczyński and lyricist Edward Lockton. The popular tenor Frank Titterton performed Ketèlbey's 'Sanctuary Of The Heart', and joined Compton in the duet 'For You Alone' (music by Henry Geehl, lyrics by P. J. O'Reilly).

Perhaps ***Give Her a Ring***, the story of a meddlesome, romantically inclined telephonist, reverberated two decades later in the plot of the Styne-Comden-Green musical *Bells Are Ringing*. Arthur B. Woods directed the English remake of the 1932 German original *Fräulein, falsch verbunden* that had starred Magda Schneider as Copenhagen's phone-happy Karen who eventually gets her boss as a husband. At Elstree, Clifford Mollison played boss Paul Hendrick and Wendy Barrie played Karen, supported by Zelma O'Neal as Trude Olsen. Based on a play by H. Rosenfeld, *Give Her a Ring*'s screenplay was by Marjorie Deans (whose subsequent musical films were *A Star Fell from Heaven* and *Kathleen Mavourneen*), lyricist Clifford Grey, and the German émigré Wolfgang Wilhelm.

Handsomely mounted, *Give Her a Ring* had impressive sets by Duncan

Sutherland and the sophisticated dash of Norman Hartnell's costumes. Woods, soon to direct the portmanteau *Radio Parade of 1935*, probably the most effective revue-like production of the decade to come from a British studio, had a flair for musical films. He went on to direct three of them, which were meant to make a British star of Keith Falkner, although Woods's masterwork was possibly the gripping *They Drive by Night* with Ernest Thesiger as a stocking murderer. By the time *Give Her a Ring* went into production at Elstree, its original composer Hans May, fresh from *How's Chances?*, had moved to England, and was on hand to supervise the remake's music. The songs included 'Giving Up The Stars', 'Come On And Love', 'The Lamp Of Love' and 'Let The Bells Ring' (another hint of what was to come with *Bells Are Ringing*). Ultimately, O'Neal's Trude is paired with singer Otto played by Erik Rhodes, who almost immediately moved to the US where his many 1930s pictures included *The Gay Divorcee* and *Top Hat*. More modestly, Mollison and O'Neal would team again for the Vivian Ellis *Mister Cinders*.

One of the greatest successes in London's West End during the Great War, alongside *The Maid of the Mountains*, the operetta *Chu Chin Chow* had opened in 1916, lasting a record-breaking 2,238 performances. Seven years on, the ever-enterprising Herbert Wilcox turned it into that most curious of objects, a silent musical film, persuading Berlin's UFA studios to facilitate a German production of Edward Knoblock and composer Frederick Norton's Arabian Nights extravaganza. In exchange, Wilcox agreed to act as distributor for Fritz Lang's epic *Die Nibelungen*, in effect trading off a masterpiece of cinema with an overblown costume melodrama whose massive sets and thousands of underpaid extras could not hold a candle to German filmmakers.

A sound version of **Chu Chin Chow** might have seemed a natural BIP project, but in 1934 Gaumont-British took it up, to be produced by Michael Balcon and directed by Walter Forde, the screenplay by Knoblock, L. du Garde Peach and Sidney Gilliat. Music-hall statesman George Robey is the top-billed Ali Baba, welcoming as a nice old uncle at a birthday party but thoroughly embarrassing in 'Anytime's Kissing Time', making comic hay of his inability to reach the high notes. In another sequence, there is an effort to duplicate his popular number 'I Stopped, I Looked, I Listened', but, like almost everything Robey does here, what might still have worked in front of a live audience dies the death in front of a camera. The spell-binder is Fritz Kortner as bloodthirsty brigand Abu Hasan, disguised as wealthy, respectable Chu Chin Chow. In support, John Garrick, set free from Twickenham studios, is an attractive romantic lead, making us wonder why he wasn't more often cast as such. Enriched, he can afford to wear drop-earrings, a luxury denied him at Twickenham. A more prominent attraction is Anna May Wong, satisfying the studio's need for oriental sexuality, but she makes a rather colourless Zahrat.

Despite the considerable efforts of designer Ernö Metzner to bring old Baghdad of popular imagination to the screen, the sense of painted backcloths locks the locale into the Islington studios. To describe Forde's direction of the frequently chaotic proceedings as busy would be an understatement, and at 100 minutes there is perhaps too much of a slender tale. One suspects that a tatty but colourful touring production of this theatrical antiquity would be more amusing; the painted backcloths could at least flutter in the breeze. Forde and his cast seem to take it all a little too seriously, going for the lush – always difficult in grainy black and white. *MFB* was not much impressed, finding the piece 'Rather wholeheartedly bloodthirsty for young girls, but grand for boys.'[25]

AUGUST

A 'romance to the music of Franz Schubert', **Blossom Time** became BIP's greatest commercial success to date, with a seven-week run in London and causing a sensation in Australia and America; one of its camera crew remembered it as *The Sound of Music* of its day. It established Richard Tauber as the studio's greatest, and possibly unlikeliest, star. Tauber had already bonded with the British public through his stage work, appearing at Drury Lane in 1931 in *The Land of Smiles*, and in 1933 playing Schubert in *Lilac Time*, on which *Blossom Time* was based. He had been a victim of Nazi repression, denounced as the 'Operetten-Rundfunkjude' (The Operetta-Radio-Jew) and vilified in Fritz Hippler's anti-Semitic film *Der ewige Jude* ('The Eternal Jew').

Blossom Time has a simplicity, a lushness, a clear sense of narrative drive and above all a tastefulness that can still have its effect today. The team was a strong one. The Austrian director Paul L. Stein had worked in German silents and since 1926 in Hollywood, before moving to Britain at the beginning of the decade, making *The Song You Gave Me* in 1933. He would go on to direct Tauber in the 1935 *Heart's Desire*, and in the 1940s the wonderfully sugar-feasting *Waltz Time* and *The Lisbon Story*. Screenplay, dialogue and lyrics for *Blossom Time* were by Franz Schulz, John Drinkwater and Roger Burford; the shooting script also credits Paul Perez as one of the writers. G. H. Clutsam's original score and adaptation of Schubert's material was under the musical supervision of BIP's musical director Idris Lewis.

Eighty years on, the piece wears well, if we accept that the plot, loosely based on Schubert's hapless love for Therese Grob (the character Vicki Wimpassinger in the film, played by Jane Baxter), might just as well have been pulled from a Barbara Cartland novel. In 1826 Vienna, Vicki is loved by impecunious schoolteacher Franz Schubert, but is in love with virile Count Rudi Von Hohenberg (Carl Esmond). A deluded Schubert thinks that Vicki wants to marry a penniless composer, but accepts her refusal of marriage, makes it up with Rudi, and sings with a boys' choir at the pair's lavish wedding. Alongside this Schubertian non-love affair runs the relationship between kindly Lafont (Charles Carson) and sparky Archduchess Maria Victoria (Athene Seyler). To accommodate Tauber's talents, the writers turn Schubert into a singer as well as composer, neatly interpolating several of his songs into the narrative.

Picturegoer Weekly complained of 'a story that is hackneyed and a development that is pedestrian. The singing of the star, however, compensates for a great deal and, despite its faults, the film has a certain gentle charm that has hitherto not often been achieved in British films [...] A story of artless simplicity is jumbled with a "Gay Vienna" atmosphere of sophistication and elaborate, if rather too obviously studio-made, spectacle and settings [by Clarence Elder and David Rawnsley]'.[26] While *The Times* concerned itself with the slow pace and the fact that it didn't stand comparison with Germany's somewhat similar *Congress Dances*, the *Jewish Chronicle* applauded Tauber but pointed to 'the utterly artificial and sugary little novelette story that forms the plot'.[27] In tune with this, *MFB* found it slow but praised Tauber, 'without whose singing [...] the film would have little attraction'. However, 'some may object to the sentimental religiosity of parts of it'.[28]

The public may not have been concerned with such niceties, for on its own level *Blossom Time* works superbly as a weepie, with Tauber as a tragic loner denied personal happiness. He is left alone at the film's close, adrift above Vicki's wedding ceremony. He sadly ruffles the hair of one of the choristers, before returning home alone to his garret, where the film magically falls into shadow, as if rays of dying daylight were playing around him. There are parallels to be drawn with Rodgers and Hammerstein's musicalisation of the von Trapp story: Schubert leading out his schoolboys over the Vienna hills, thrumming his guitar as they gaily sing (the film's 'Lonely Goatherd' moment?), and the saccharine level is as high as when Julie Andrews was on the march.

Adapted from a Cine-Alliance Joe May production, the 1933 *Ein Lied für dich*, the trilingual *My Song for You* was an engaging vehicle for Polish tenor Jan Kiepura, the Jonas Kaufmann of his day: good looks and a voice. What other male opera singer of the 1930s would have agreed to singing the title song in bathing shorts? The original German production was written by Ernst Marischka and Irma von Cube, reworked for the British version with a scenario by Richard Benson, dialogue by Austin Melford and additional comedy scenes by Robert Edmunds. It was handsomely designed by Alfred Junge. Kiepura gives a relaxed performance as tenor Ricardo Gatti, falling in love with Mary Newberg, played by the personable Aileen Marson, with the frequently multi-lingual Sonnie Hale as comic relief. The presence of Emlyn Williams and Gina Malo gives Kiepura support worthy of his talent.

The star is heard in Gounod's 'Ave Maria', Verdi's 'Celeste Aida' (involving some entertaining scenes of opera house rehearsals with elephants ready for a triumphal march) and in 'With All My Heart', composed by Mischa Spoliansky and lyricist

Frank Eyton. The *International Opera Collector* pointed out, 'The problems with films starring great singers is that, with few exceptions, they tend to be undistinguished as contributions to the cinematic art.'[29] This probably applies to *My Song for You*, which was a co-production between Gaumont-British and Cine-Allianz Tonfilm, capably directed at Shepherd's Bush by the busy Maurice Elvey. Its German connections denied it British classification.

Without Kiepura, the film is probably of little worth, for his 'good looks, personal charm, infectious zest in his job and wonderful singing certainly produce a most attractive entertainment: but he might almost as well sing his songs and his extracts from opera without the melodramatic background that beyond a few witty remarks and one or two bits of good fooling, contributes little to the entertainment'.[30]

Florence Desmond was probably at her best as an impressionist-comedienne, bridging a gap between musical comedy and drama, but never establishing herself as a major film actress. Was there an advantage in co-starring with the great American vaudevillian Sophie Tucker, on a visit to Britain, for British Lion's *Gay Love*, produced by Herbert Smith at Beaconsfield, and directed by Leslie S. Hiscott? The screenplay by Charles Bennett, Billie Bristow and John Paddy Carstairs was based on a play by Audrey and Waveney Carter. The story was of Gloria Fellowes (Desmond), a performer prone to breaking into impressions of Hollywood film stars – Mae West, Greta Garbo and, of course, Tucker – who clumsily falls for her sister's aristocratic suitor (Ivor McLaren). As so often in British musical films of the period, the supporting players are familiar and first-class, among them Leslie Perrins, Sydney Fairbrother and Enid Stamp-Taylor, but the accent inevitably falls on Tucker, who gets to sing 'Louisville Lady', 'My Extraordinary Man', 'Hotcha Joe' and (rich in innuendo) 'Imagine My Embarrassment'. Desmond makes her mark with 'Don't Blame Me', 'The Man For Me' and 'Mae Time', impersonating Mae West.

MFB was impressed by the 'splendidly even production in which swift action and captivating personality make an irresistible combination' in what was a 'brilliant entertainment', 'well above average.'[31] It was a minor miracle that British Lion managed to lure Tucker into a studio (why had none of the major companies done so?), but neither Tucker nor Desmond ever got the treatment they deserved in British musical films. Both slipped through the genre's fingers.

SEPTEMBER

Gene Gerrard, one of the least understandably matinee-idolised, late of *Out of the Blue* and *Lucky Girl*, was back for **There Goes Susie**, produced at Elstree for BIP by John Stafford, who also directed and co-wrote the screenplay from Charlie Roellinghoff and Hans Jacoby with W. Victor Hanbury. This lightest of confections, a British version of a 1933 German original, had Gerrard as struggling artist Andre Cochet. He uses pretty Madeleine Sarteaux (Wendy Barrie) as his model for a soap advertisement, not realising that she is the daughter of a rival company's magnate. The romantic complications that ensue are not noteworthy. The music was the last to be heard in films from Austrian Otto Stransky, who had died in 1932. His co-composer on the film, Niklos Schwalb, had been credited for the 1933 *The Girl from Maxim's*. The intended continental tone of *There Goes Susie* is unmistakable, despite the resolutely British supporting cast that includes Gibb McLaughlin, Gus McNaughton, Mark Daly (holidaying from John Baxter films) and the American Zelma O'Neal.

Gracie Fields's follow-up to *Love, Life and Laughter* was made at Ealing by Associated Talking Pictures and directed by Basil Dean. *The Times* decided that 'Gracie Fields presents a problem which English film studios have yet to solve.'[32] **Sing As We Go** happened at an interesting time; it might have been the coming-together of disparate elements in British society. Notably, it was written by J. B. Priestley. There is no doubt that Fields's resilient and increasingly iconic representation of a certain type of woman (a breed, if British musical films were to be believed, usually found only north of the border) with scant regard for glamour or social snobbery or authority chimed with Priestley. Dean was convinced that the playwright would be the perfect collaborator to spread the Fields's gospel, for Priestley's 'humour and strong characterisation would be well suited to the needs of the Lancashire star. He consented and quickly produced the outline of a story with excellent possibilities.'[33] The hope was that 'with Basil Dean's help [Priestley and Fields] might produce something better than the run-of-the-mill musicals which had dogged and, to some extent, damned Gracie's career.'[34]

The title was good; four words that summed up the philosophy that the film's star and author stood for – something cheery and tuneful torn from the various miseries of the Depression, laughing and chaffing with a stiff upper-lip. The sociological effects and causes of the Depression were uppermost in Priestley's mind at this time. By 1934 he was an established literary figure, as novelist (*The Good Companions* had been a turning-point in 1929), essayist, biographer (treatments of George Meredith and Thomas Love Peacock), and playwright (the first of his 'time' plays had begun with *Dangerous Corner* in 1932). In the autumn of 1933 the 39-year-old Priestley set off, a Hazlitt for a new age, on travels across the country that resulted in his *English Journey*, a 'rambling but truthful account of what one man saw and felt and thought', published in 1934. His intention was to describe and make sense of the lives of ordinary people.

Priestley was far from alone in this. This was a heyday of the British documentary film movement. Viewing these short features today, you are aware only of the two worlds, the divisions apparent in the scenes of coal-mining, voiced-over with the prissily posh voice of Donald Calthrop as he describes 'black countries of belching furnaces and humming machinery, industrial towns with grimy surroundings, and bewildering acres of streets'.[35] The documentary film recognised the problems of finding work, highlighted in Arthur Elton's 1935 *Workers and Jobs*, with its toll of men 'who have probably been on the dole for years'. Domestic deprivation is starkly revealed in Elton and Edgar Anstey's 1935 *Housing Problems*. The humanity tied up with these issues is accentuated by the absence of actors; there is something intensely moving in the life-battered men and worn-out housewives of *Housing Problems*, battling against filthy slums, no running water, bulging walls, crooked stairs, child mortality, and remaining valiant.

Listen to Mrs Hill. 'The upstairs is coming downstairs where it's sinking. Everything's filthy. Dirty filthy walls, and the vermin in the walls is wicked. Everything in the house is on the crook.' Hear how Mrs Grace woke to find 'a big rat' on her head. Hear Mr Berner, standing beside his wife and three children in their one-room shack. 'The cooking conditions is very hard, especially on the wife.' These were examples of dismal realities for the less fortunate living in British slums in the 1930s.

The apparent inability of British sound studios to use the medium of musical film to focus on, or even acknowledge, these real-life experiences of many of their customers is all too obvious. They were ready and willing to supply Ruritanian escapism, or to reflect life as luxuriously idled away in impossibly lush nightclubs from which Stanley Lupino's characters were sometimes expelled, or to suggest that life's ills might be remedied by a badly organised dance routine by the Sherman Fisher Girls. Is it possible that John Baxter was the only British film-maker of the period to embrace and incorporate social issues into his pictures such as *Doss House* and *Say It with Flowers*? What was more, his unceasing depictions of something vaguely resembling reality continued through the decade, reaching an apogee in 1941 with two sharply observed evocations of working-class life, *Love on the Dole* and *The Common Touch*. Both are remarkable documents.

We can suppose that Priestley's yearning for a fairer society may have endeared him to Baxter's film-making. In 1942 Baxter produced and directed a film version of Priestley's *Let the People Sing*. Priestley seems to have taken no part in its making, but in the climate of 1934 he was in a blessed position, a man whose passion and homely sympathy for the less privileged could be brought to bear on the British musical film. In Gracie Fields Priestley must have recognised an ideal messenger of his vision. In its way, *Sing As We Go* held promise; the pity is that the film turned out to be of little interest, a wasted opportunity, squandering what might have been achieved. Priestley's biographer considers *Sing As We Go* 'a quick piece of superficial work which Priestley preferred to forget as soon as it was written,'[36] and it's easy to agree. It doesn't reflect well on Priestley, who seems to have caved in to the film's commercialism, condemning the film to its obvious superficiality. Documentary film maker Paul Rotha lamented,

> I had hoped more from Priestley's *Sing As We Go*, more, that is, within the limits laid down for a vehicle for the vivacious Gracie Fields. Blackpool and Bolton are there in truth, but there through the eyes of the studio and not through the intimacy of an English journey. In these days of social unhappiness you cannot scratch the surface of an economic problem for the benefit of a gifted comedienne, nor can you employ comic effect to issues which are conditioning the very existence of countless persons. If this is to be the way of putting England on the screen, then stay in your studios, producers, and leave England to documentary.[37]

There is little to add to Rotha's pithy analysis. Now and again *Sing As We Go* scores as an historical record of what Blackpool was like in the mid-1930s, but on a human level it is of little account. Fields gets little support from co-stars John Loder and Stanley Holloway, and nobody else makes an impression. Trouble up t'mill makes a poor do of a film that deals so lightly with mass unemployment and social inequality. The songs, too, fail to convince. ATP presumably considered them of little importance as they failed to credit the composers. Fields's most favoured Harry Parr Davies wrote the two best numbers, the title song and 'Just A Catchy Little Tune'. Her comedic 'In My Little Bottom Drawer' was by Will E. Haines and Jimmy Harper. Most romantic of all is 'Love, Wonderful Love' by Leo Towers and Harry Leon, with a parodic version of Stephen Adams and Fred Weatherley's 'Thora' for good measure. But what a waste! No wonder Priestley (who must be held largely responsible for it) preferred to forget.

Philip Jenkinson gave warning that serves as well for Mancunian's ***Love-Mirth-Melody*** as for anything made by Butcher's Films:

> If you judge a Mancunian film for its surface value you're not going to get a hell of a lot out of it. I would be quite prepared to admit that you could get bored, pretty damned bored, if you were sitting through one after another. But if you were looking at them to find out about the social attitude, the expectations and the actual aspirations of most of the people who made them and the people who went to see them and the people who laughed at them and did get so much enjoyment out of them, then you're into a whole different area, because then you're into actually looking into real people. They cease to be celluloid characters […] How can this have happened?[38]

Jenkinson's words are as welcome as a sunburst on a foggy day. If you want undemanding amusement, wholesome but faintly anarchic fun, *Love-Mirth-Melody* is the right shop for it, although how many people got to see it is open to question.

Made at Mancunian's Albany Studios, produced by the unflagging John E. Blakeley and directed by Bert Tracey (he had written material for Laurel and Hardy), 'it is entirely possible that the film may have been screened without a classification for the trade before being withdrawn and never registered'.[39] This collection of variety turns interrupted by Arthur Mertz's slight showbiz story would scarcely have made it to the bottom of a half-decent music-hall bill, but a kindly domesticity creeps in, a sympathetic understanding that these people are doing their best; for how long is for others to decide. Nevertheless, we have South African boy alto Graham Payn (who two years previously had sung 'I Hear You Calling Me' and 'In An Old-Fashioned Town' for Pathé Pictorial), The Lionel Claff Band, 'Little Teddy Grey', The Royal Merry Four, Arthur Pond, Annie Rooney, 'Little Jean and Joan', and Duggie Ascot's Dancing Girls. The same year, Blakeley directed Mancunian's 25-minute *Musical Medley* featuring Graham Payn and Webster Booth.

Allied Film Productions' **Romance in Rhythm** was the sole product of Lawrence Huntington as writer, producer and director, filmed at Cricklewood as a quota quickie. Phyllis Clare, whose brief career in the 1930s had included *Aunt Sally*, played Ruth Lee, a London cabaret girl who breaks off her relationship with the musician Bob Mervyn (David Hutcheson). Bob is the main suspect when her new boyfriend is murdered, but the culprit is nightclub manager Mollari (David Burns). Carroll Gibbons's Savoy Orpheans are neatly worked into the cabaret floor sequences. When the film resurfaced in 1940 it was retitled *Night Club Murder*, and it is perhaps as a creator of mysteries rather than musical films that Huntington is remembered, notably for *Wanted for Murder* with its pianistic theme by Mischa Spoliansky.

OCTOBER

BIP hoped for a successful follow-up to *Blossom Time* in **My Song Goes Round the World**, the British remake of the 1933 German *Ein Lied geht um die Welt*, adapted from Ernst Neubach's original screenplay by Clifford Grey and Frank Miller, and produced and directed at Elstree by Richard Oswald. If Tauber seemed an unlikely figure for a cinema star, BIP's latest imported tenor was even more unlikely. Rachael Low mistakenly measures the Jewish Austro-Hungarian Romanian Joseph Schmidt at four feet tall (he was a little taller). On hearing him sing, the conductor Leo Blech remarked, 'Pity you aren't small.' 'But I am small,' said Schmidt. 'No,' replied Blech, 'you're *too* small.'

Schmidt was not accorded the respect to which he was due; the BIP screenwriters presented him as a curiosity. 'What does he want to sing?' asks an opera producer of Schmidt's character Riccardo, 'the "Song of the Flea"?' Riccardo admits 'People don't want to see me … You see, my figure!' The screenwriters and director presumably believe their customers would rather gaze at the film's love interest, John Longden, who was far from a great actor but was at least tall. After all, as someone else asks, 'Who would want to marry a freak like Riccardo?' It is the unpleasant shade of the circus booth that infiltrates this unappealing film. BIP's handling of their visiting star is extraordinarily insensitive, in marked contrast to his gentle voice and manner. Unlike the script, Schmidt behaves with dignity. His obvious lack of comfort with the English language suggests he may not even have been fully aware of the way in which he was being presented, although the same treatment may have been given him in the German original, from which some moments seem to have been dubbed. The sharp-eyed may notice an early example of product placement, with Schmidt's Parlophone gramophone record prominently displayed for the camera. As another character tactlessly remarks, 'Where do you find room for a big voice like that?' A more crass treatment of BIP's star could hardly be imagined.

The music is by Hans May, most attractively in 'One Life, One Love' and in the title song, in May's easily accessible Viennese manner. Other music includes 'The Linden Tree', 'Santa Lucia', 'O Paradise', 'Mourning', 'Osteria Lied', 'Frag Nacht', 'Launisches Glück', and 'Scenes That Are Brightest' from Wallace's *Maritana*. BIP subsequently starred Schmidt in the 1936 *A Star Fell from Heaven*.

If only BIP had signed Bobby Howes and Binnie Hale for the Elstree filming of Vivian Ellis's **Mister Cinders**. On stage in 1929, this delightfully silly musical comedy had enjoyed great success. It would be modestly revived in the unsympathetic West End of the 1980s, when a new audience discovered its lilt and charm. Howes and Hale may simply have been unavailable for the film, but it would have been worth the wait. For whatever reason, Clifford Mollison was now the male Cinderella or Mister Cinders or Jim Lancaster in what was effectively a rethink of the pantomime story. American Zelda O'Neal was a stodgy substitute for Hale, far from comfortable in her numbers; at least Mollison had a sort of angular friendliness about him. Produced by Walter C. Mycroft and directed with little sensibility by Fred Zelnik, the adaptation from the stage version was by Clifford Grey and Frank Miller, with additional (mostly unhelpful) dialogue from the Western Brothers who performed two numbers of their own, 'I Think Of You' and 'Aren't We All?', typical of their work but out of place here.

Things start promisingly with a snappy opener, 'Where's Jim?', and before long O'Neal is breaking into a number written by Ellis expressly for the film, 'Just A Blue Sky', a fair example of his quietly captivating style. His stage score had offered much more but little survived on screen. O'Neal's 'Spread A Little Happiness', an Ellis song that will perhaps achieve immortality, had been written in bed when he was seriously ill. It goes for nothing here. Listen to the original stage recordings by Howes and Hale and you will know you have been cheated.

Evensong, Gaumont's next attempt at establishing Evelyn Laye's film career, had mixed reviews. *Variety* praised her 'unsuspected talent' and 'compelling sincerity', deciding that 'As a picture it will rank in the very highest rank of British productions, if indeed, it isn't a strong candidate for the very top'.[40] A subsequent mention in *Variety* noted that Laye played 'with a force and artistry that is singularly important to the picture' in a production that was 'both competent and pretentious'.[41] *MFB* thought the production 'of a very high standard [...] the only weakness is in the scenario itself; although both the general theme, and each particular episode, maintain the interest, the picture seems to lack a unifying force'.[42] The project had a long genesis, beginning as a novel by Beverley Nichols before becoming a stage play by Nichols and Edward Knoblock that ran for 213 performances at the Queen's Theatre in 1932 before transferring to Broadway, where it managed only fifteen. Its non-singing star was Edith Evans. The idea of a musical version appealed to producer Michael Balcon and director Victor Saville. After the Ruritanian frivolity of *Princess Charming* what better than a melodramatic biopic about the rise and fall of a prima donna? The musical film was about to embrace a tragedy. Knoblock was responsible for its scenario and dialogue, in a 'screen adaptation' by Dorothy Farnum.

Maggie (Laye) has humble beginnings in the Emerald Isle, where friend George (Emlyn Williams) accompanies her at the piano, telling her she is one of the greatest singers in the world. The evidence, it has to be said, is scant. Transplanted to Paris, they cavort in a night-spot to Marie Lloyd's old favourite 'Tiddley-Om-Pom'. She is spotted by Svengali-like Kober (Fritz Kortner), who determines she will be a star. She auditions for the opera, singing from *La Bohème*. Maddened with jealousy, George attempts to kill her. Maggie, now famous as Irela, is courted by Archduke Theodore (Carl Esmond), who hopes to win her by hiding jewels inside her bouquets. Spoliansky and Knoblock's theme song 'I'll Wait For You' keeps the overshadowing melancholia alive, while Alfred Junge recreates a Venetian canal at Shepherd's Bush, where Irela is serenaded by a gondolier.

Irela means to marry the Archduke, much to the disapproval of Kober ('You are married to your voice'). Her lover follows her to Vienna where she sings *Traviata*, but (in the manner of British musical films) domestic politics dictate that he must marry a princess. Irela is expelled, and the Archduke put under arrest, although he intends to wed her 'whatever happens'. *War* happens, and an unhappy Irela does her bit for the troops, generously performing a medley of 'It's A Long Way To Tipperary', 'When You Come To The End Of A Perfect Day', Paul Rubens's 'I Love The Moon', Novello's 'Keep The Home Fires Burning', 'There's A Long, Long Trail A-Winding' and the parlour twilight comforter 'Love's Old Sweet Song'. Who should be in the throng listening to this but dear George. Meanwhile, the trenches explode and the slaughter continues.

Returned to England, a war-weary Irela ('This utter insanity must end') visits wounded George in hospital, attempting to rouse him by brokenly singing 'Tralee'.

Years pass, and times change as does Irela's character. Now a short-tempered, querulous and unhappy diva, she and her voice are no longer young. She endures the rise of a new star, Baba L'Etoile (Conchita Supervia), whose Musetta surpasses what Irela can achieve. Symbolically, Irela watches her new rival from the wings. The Archduke returns, older and recently widowed. 'I'm not quite what I was,' Irela tells him, but he agrees to marry her at last. Irela declines, preferring her career. Her donkey-faithful old dresser (Muriel Aked) departs for Margate, always a worrying event. Kober alone remains faithful, but it is her voice he has always loved. 'Those eyes,' he tells her, 'they don't want to fight the world any longer [...] The artist is dead.' Listening to one of her gramophone recordings, she plucks up the laurel wreath that as a great star adorned her head. She falls to the floor, the wreath dangling from her lifeless hand.

Evensong struck notes that most other British musical films of the period neglected. The 'serious' elements cannot disguise the fact that it is basically a romantic novel with music. Saville thought Laye especially good in the 'aged' scenes. She explained, 'I played my mother. I knew every one of her gestures, her walk and all her idiosyncrasies.'[43] It is a fine performance, but Laye's autobiography disregards not only *Evensong* but her entire film career. The other acting honours go to Kortner, playing with an intensity that cuts through the other performances. The brief appearance of the legendary Supervia has an added poignancy; she died in March 1936 after giving birth to a stillborn baby.

With the usual modesty of Butcher's Film Service, Wilfred Noy's production of **The Broken Rosary** was filmed at Isleworth, and lucky to have Harry Hughes as director. Loosely based by Adelaide Procter on her poem 'Legend of Provence', the plot concerned Italian singer, Giovanni (D'Oyly Carte tenor Derek Oldham), and Maria (Jean Adrienne), intended from childhood to be Giovanni's wife. Awkwardly, she is more attracted to his faithful pal Jack (Ronald Ward). Hoping to shake off his love for Maria, Jack becomes engaged to another girl, but Giovanni sees the predicament and gallantly steps aside so that Maria and Jack can marry. Along the way, Oldham breaks into 'Ave Maria'. The film is probably more noteworthy for featuring the veteran music-hall performer Vesta Victoria singing one of her biggest successes, 'Waiting At The Church'. Noy went on to direct Oldham in the 1936 musical film *Melody of My Heart*.

NOVEMBER

Produced by the ever-industrious Julius Hagen at Twickenham, with pierrot-on-the-sands sequences filmed on the front at Walton in August 1934, **The Kentucky Minstrels** was another John Baxter celebration of British music-hall in the wake of *Say It with Flowers* and *Music Hall*. Here, he turned to the 'blackface' minstrels, struggling to survive as the public's taste veered away from such diversion, in a screenplay by actor C. Denier Warren, John Watt and Harry S. Pepper (who had particularly appreciated Baxter's rustic homage *Song of the Plough* the previous year, and who now appeared with 'His White Coons'); additional dialogue was by Hagen's resident scribbler H. Fowler Mear, and Con West. The story moves along familiar Baxter lines. The minstrels are falling from favour when impresario Danny Goldman, played by Warren who was currently scripting the BBC's Kentucky Minstrels radio series, restores them to fame in a spectacular stage production, in which Debroy Somers's band, the Eight Black Streaks, and Nina Mae McKinney feature.

The American vaudevillians Scott and Whaley, who played Cuthbert and Pussyfoot in the radio series, are here transformed into Mott and Bayley, backed by the show's signature song 'Rastus On Parade'. Blackface minstrel shows were well established in the States before thriving in Victorian England. Several substantial careers were based on the idea of white men impersonating black: Eugene Stratton and G. H. Elliott ('The Chocolate Coloured Coon') and the eerie 'White Eyed Kaffir' G. H. Chirgwin were among the most popular. An all-white extravaganza *The Black and White Minstrel Show* ran in the West End for years, transferring to BBC TV when it became one of that institution's stellar productions before changing attitudes to racial matters prevailed. Gilbert and Sullivan included a pastiche of the blackface minstrel troupes in *Utopia Limited*. Another parodic manifestation occurs in the Wolf Mankowitz-Monty Norman stage musical *Belle*, as well as Peter Greenwell's operetta *The Three Caskets*. The *Daily Renter* recognised that Baxter 'handled the subject with something akin to reverence [...] with darky repartee creating chuckles, and here and there a tear-compelling situation leavening the mixture with humanity'.[44]

DECEMBER

The eventually trilingual German original of 1933 was *Mein Herz ruft nach dir*, another vehicle for the Polish tenor Jan Kiepura, reappearing in its British version as ***My Heart Is Calling***. A collaboration between Cine-Allianz and Gaumont-British, produced by Arnold Pressburger and directed by Carmine Gallone from a revised screenplay by Richard Benson, Sidney Gilliat and Robert Edmunds, the film was based on the original material of Ernst Marischka. Although made at Beaconsfield, the film was not classified as British. The score featured 'My Heart Is Always Calling You' and 'You, Me And Love', composed by Robert Stolz, with lyrics by Tommie Connor and Harry S. Pepper. Kiepura played Mario Delmonte, the star of a touring opera company. Stopping off at Monte Carlo, Mario falls in love with Carla (Marta Eggerth), hidden in his boat cabin. In defiance of opera managements, he stages an al fresco *Tosca*, and marries his stowaway. In fact, this is the film that brought Kiepura and Eggerth together to form one of the longest-lasting personal and professional partnerships in opera. The cast included the almost obligatory Sonnie Hale, Marie Löhr and Ernest Thesiger. *MFB* reported that 'The minor characters played by established theatrical stars have on this account a polish rarely to be found, and they provide at times a distinct relief. The direction is slow in the main, but very effective use is made of the crowd scenes that deserve particular attention. [It is] not good as a whole as the film thus regarded is spasmodic. There are, however, many individual points which stand out above the average.'[45]

The *MFB* was mildly enthusiastic about **Road House**. 'Violet Loraine plays the part of Belle convincingly, and the barman-turned-cabaret manager is always entertainingly depicted by Gordon Harker. The story switches rapidly from low comedy to melodrama, but holds the interest from first to last.'[46] Did the reviewer realise that this was effectively the follow-up to *Britannia of Billingsgate*, another co-starring project for Loraine and Harker? Produced by Michael Balcon for Gaumont-British at Shepherd's Bush and directed by Maurice Elvey (at one time Hitchcock was to have directed), *Road House* was adapted from a play by Walter Hackett, with scenario and dialogue by Leslie Arliss and Austin Melford. The components for success seemed to be in place: designs by Alfred Junge, songs by Harry M. Woods, and a strong cast that included Aileen Marson, Emlyn Williams, Hartley Power, Wylie Watson, Stanley Holloway and Marie Löhr.

Belle (Loraine) is back behind the bar of the Angel Inn, working alongside lip-smacking barman Sam (Harker). He wants to solidify their relationship by marrying her, but Belle is in love with aristocratic toff Archie Hamble. Sam helps Archie out, knowing it will please Belle, who finds success as a music-hall artiste, singing the novelty number 'There's No Green Grass Round The Old North Pole'. The Great War comes and goes. By New Year's Eve 1918 Belle has married Archie. They have a daughter Kitty but Archie dies and the child is given over to the care of Archie's mother. Sam breaks the news of her husband's death to Belle, who struggles on stage to sing 'Let The Great Big World Keep Turning' (the film's highlight). To escape, Belle embarks on a Grand Tour; she may never sing again.

Sam sells the Angel Inn to crooks who turn it into a road house, ostensibly respectable but in fact a cover for illegality. In search of Belle, Sam finds her working as a chambermaid in Nice. The reconciliation scene is infinitely touching, at the heart of the film, with Elvey coaxing superb performances from his stars. Sam brings Belle back to England where he features her in cabaret at the road house. Belle is reunited with Kitty, who is about to elope with one of the crooks. Belle persuades her not to go, encouraging her by 'Looking For A Little Bit Of Blue'. The film fizzles, although Loraine zips things up with 'What A Little Moonlight Can Do'. The dance floor becomes a swimming pool with girls disrobing for synchronised swimming, spectacular in its way but snatching the film from the control of its stars. *Road House* cannot, however, be overlooked. How could it when, apart from its many incidental delights, it offers a rare opportunity to see Loraine at work? When she consoles the music-hall patrons with 'Don't You Cry When We Say Goodbye' and Elvey swings the camera away to watch the faces of her customers, we know that this is a piece that still has the ability to move us.

In his *British Sound Films* David Quinlan has **Spring in the Air** as a 'below-average comedy with music'. It is one of many that has faded into obscurity. A John Stafford production, it was directed at Elstree by Victor Hanbury (*The Beggar Student, Where Is This Lady?, There Goes Susie, Ball At Savoy*) and Norman Lee, who also collaborated on the screenplay of a story that was clearly of foreign origin. In Budapest, Illona (Zelma O'Neal) works for her friends Vilma (Lydia Sherwood) and Max (Gus McNaughton) as a servant, but only to stay close to a frog-loving environmentalist Paul (German Theo Shall in his only British musical film). Meanwhile, Franz (Edmund Gwenn) is under the misapprehension that he is Ilona's father. To complicate the plot, Max makes a play for her, but at the film's end Ilona and Paul are brought together.

The ghost of BIP's *Elstree Calling* returned in Walter C. Mycroft's production of the variety revue **Radio Parade of 1935**, with Arthur Woods directing a host of talent of various competence. According to the credits, Reginald Purdell and John Watt provided a framework embellished by Woods, James Bunting, Jack Davies and Paul Perez. The plot is a thin veneer over a succession of acts. There is a welcome dash of music-hall in the presence of grotesques Nellie Wallace and Lily Morris, playing charladies at the 'National Broadcasting Group' (in lieu of the BBC). They have two duets, 'We Won't Say Good Morning' and 'We're Not Quite What We Used To Be'. The reliance on radio for its inspiration is obvious, but the casting is far from perfect, with Will Hay wasted as the Director General. The romance between Helen Chandler and Clifford Mollison just about links the segments, but it is the turns that matter.

Buddy Bradley's geometric choreography, spearheaded by commissionaire Billy Bennett, introduces us to those working at the NBG. Clarence Elder and David Rawnsley's sets are richly evocative of their period. Then, it's mostly variety turns: violin clowning from Ted Ray, impressions of Jimmy Durante and Mae West from toothy Beryl Orde, 'Wee' Georgie Harris, and the lounge-lizardly Ronald Frankau. Frankau's style now seems slightly repugnant, even though he's encouraging his audience to let its hair down ('Let's Go Wild'). More comedy comes from silly-ass piano-tuning Claude Dampier, a sort of pre-runner of Mike and Bernie Winters. Cross-talking Clapham and Dwyer, the mysteriously popular comic duo of the period, are as unfunny as ever: 'Have you got a fairy godmother?' 'No, I've got a cissy uncle.'

There is music by Hans May, Arthur Young, Benjamin Frankel, Bob Busby,

Lawrence Brewis, Carl Foulke and Jimmy Messini. A window cleaner (Jerry Fitzgerald) sings 'Let Me Go On Dreaming'; his pianist is composer Arthur Young. Most curious of all is the film's finale, proudly announced by a voice-over as 'for the first time in the history of radio, outdoor television in colour'. The burst of Dufaycolor proves a damp squib, grainy and ghost-ridden as black singer Alberta Hunter intones the mournful 'Black Shadows' backed by a lugubriously swaying chorus. It's a very strange – almost eerie – turn for the film to take, as she sings

> Black shadows, how they are haunting me
> All through the day and night.
> Lord, can't you make them white?
> [...] People regard me with hatred
> Like I was covered in sin.
> Must I appear to be fated
> All just because of my skin?

Where does this come from, at the end of a film remarkable for its insipidity? What on earth can its audience have made of this song, or the dance sequence with girls in leopard-skin bikinis dancing on giant drums? As if to revert to the mediocre, the colour sequence attempts a cheer-up dance routine but then – anti-climax upon anti-climax – a final reconciliation scene in black and white for the two lovers, in whom most of us long ago lost interest. Dufaycolor would be successfully used for British Movietone's filming of the May 1935 royal jubilee celebrations, but Claude Friese-Greene's colour recording of the final sequence of *Radio Parade of 1935* is a failure.

Few of the eager patrons sitting through *Temptation* in a British cinema would have realised that the film was shot in Paris at the Joinville Studios, the sanctuary to which producer Erich Pommer fled when the Nazis' stranglehold on German film-making became too strong to bear. Undefeated, and with a formidable catalogue of silents to his credit, Pommer went on to even greater glory, producing a string of musical films throughout the decade, including the seminal *Congress Dances*, *Monte Carlo Madness*, *A Blonde Dream*, *I By Day, You By Night*, *The Only Girl* and *Early to Bed*. *Temptation* is not without interest, having the frequently bilingual Frances Day as its seductive star opposite British veteran Stewart Rome. Day played Antonia, the wife of an unimaginative farmer (Rome) in a romantically complex scenario by Stafford Dickens, based on Melchior Lengyel's stage play *Antonia*. Reginald Connelly was lyricist for Paul Abrahám's music, involving 'What Is This Thing?' and 'Show Me The Way To Romance'. Despite, or perhaps because of, its inevitably Franco-German air, there was no absence of style under Max Neufeld's direction, but the film was inevitably denied British registration. Alfred Rodes's Tzigane Orchestra lent a continental flavour.

Frances Day, as usual offering what the title promised in *Temptation* (1934)

1935

It would be a hard heart that resisted its childish charm, or the sudden burst of ersatz Hollywood glamour when Balfour appears in a wedding gown of startling splendour, as her working-class neighbours release hundreds of balloons into a sky filled with some sort of hope
Squibs

His Majesty and Co.
Things Are Looking Up
In Town Tonight
Oh, Daddy!
Street Song
Radio Pirates
Variety
Off the Dole
Heat Wave
Hello Sweetheart
Squibs
The Divine Spark
Look Up and Laugh
Dance Band
Cock o' the North
Charing Cross Road
Me and Marlborough

The Student's Romance
Heart's Desire
Jimmy Boy
The Deputy Drummer
Car of Dreams
Honeymoon for Three
A Fire Has Been Arranged
Invitation to the Waltz
Music Hath Charms
No Limit
Father O'Flynn
First a Girl
I Give My Heart
Hyde Park Corner
Come Out of the Pantry
She Shall Have Music
Two Hearts in Harmony

JANUARY

The year begins interestingly with *His Majesty & Co.*, a modest piece directed by Anthony Kimmins for Fox Films, but 'a charming musical trifle, showing a delightful and typical English sense of humour.'[1] It was in sharp contrast to Kimmins's other 1935 project for Fox, *Once in a New Moon*, a sort of science fiction story set in middle England, with faint hints of things to come in R. C. Sherriff's fascinating 1939 novel *The Hopkins Manuscript* (why did a British studio never turn it into a movie?). Sally Sutherland's screenplay for *His Majesty & Co.* told the story of John (John Garrick), holidaying in the Ruritanian principality of Poldavia and falling for the oddly named Princess Sandra (Barbara Waring). Returning to Britain, he meets not only the princess but her parents (Morton Selten and Mary Grey). As the King is a wine expert and the Queen a decent cook, they get together to open a restaurant, where John can also sing at table. The by-now-ubiquitous Wally Patch as Bert Hicks represents the lower orders. The music is by Viennese Wilhelm Grosz, another émigré escaping from the Nazis, and probably best known as the composer of 'Red Sails In The Sunset'. Alfredo Campoli and His Tzigane Orchestra and speciality act Betty le Brocke were on hand to take the audience's mind off this unlikely tale.

Things Are Looking Up barely justifies inclusion, having only a title song, albeit a bright one by Noel Gay and lyricist Frank Eyton. Having Cicely Courtneidge as its star suggests that it might have been more digestible with more music to accompany her clowning, restricted here to playing very different twins. Michael Balcon produced for Gaumont-British at Shepherd's Bush. Albert de Courville directed the screenplay by C. Stafford Dickens and Con West, based on a story by Daisy Fisher and de Courville, with Vetchinsky as art director. In 1935 Courtneidge made a play for Hollywood success as the star of MGM's *The Perfect Gentleman* (aka *The Imperfect Lady*), incorrectly referred to by Courtneidge as *The Improper Gentleman*. She was introduced in a publicity promotional film by her co-star Frank Morgan as 'London's greatest contribution to the comedy screen'. Courtneidge was unimpressed with MGM, an organisation that apparently had no idea what she did. She described *The Perfect Gentleman* as 'rubbish. We remade the rubbish, twice with different directors. Finally Jack [Hulbert] tried to advise them, but it was just patching up a bad film.' Balcon clearly understood what Courtneidge could do. She does it to great satisfaction in *Things Are Looking Up*.

For many sitting at home, 7.30 on Saturday nights meant the BBC's popular radio programme ***In Town Tonight***, introduced by Eric Coates's 'Knightsbridge March' and the cry 'Violets, lovely sweet violets' of a Piccadilly Circus flower-seller, until a sudden quiet fell on all as the announcer explained, 'Once again we silence the mighty roar of London's traffic to bring to the microphone some of the interesting people who are in town tonight.' First broadcast in November 1933, the programme ran until 1960. Throughout its long run, it can hardly have overlooked any prominent British performers from the stage, variety and films.

Another example of radio's influence in British musical films, British Lion's *In Town Tonight* nevertheless couldn't present as a cinematic version of the BBC's product. Now, a record company is assembling artists, but the plot was of little significance to writer, producer and director Herbert Smith, who had assembled a catalogue of good to reasonable variety artistes. The best known of these were probably Stanley Holloway with the tale of 'Albert and the Lion'; sand-dancing Wilson, Keppel and Betty; the brilliant vent act Arthur Prince and Jim; and impressionist Beryl Orde. The coachloads of performers turning up at the British

Lion studios included The Seven Thunderbolts, Dave Apollon and His Romantic Serenaders, the Keller Hall Military Band, The Radio Rogues, The Carson Sisters, and sixteen high-kicking Tiller Girls. The general consensus was that Mr Smith's dialogue was undistinguished and the tempo sluggish.

FEBRUARY

While the English and French met to discuss the mounting rearmament of Nazi Germany, the rage began for a board game named Monopoly, Gracie Fields signed a record-breaking £150,000 deal to make three films, Mickey Mouse went into colour, Shirley Temple was given a midget-sized Oscar, contraceptives were made illegal in Ireland, and Gene Vincent – harbinger of a new and very different sort of entertainer – was born. Michael Balcon and Gaumont and the nodding bonneted head of Gainsborough Pictures continued to offer diversions that were unlikely to stir the emotions, but often involved considerable skills, as in the entertaining *Oh, Daddy!*.

Michael Powell was credited with the scenario for Austin Melford's play, based on a German work by Franz Arnold and Ernst Bach, that had enjoyed a moderate run at the Prince's Theatre in 1930. Co-directed by Melford and Graham Cutts, the film had a first-class cast headed by one of the principal sirens of the decade, Frances Day. The Dumhampton Purity League is headed by three farceurs, Leslie Henson, Alfred Drayton and little Robertson Hare. Dumhampton village had been in a sad state of sin before the League did its stuff. Now, 'the demon alcohol has been banished from our village, with them his confederates frivolity and worldliness.'

The moral collapse of the three crusaders is of course inevitable. When they are obliged to book into a London hotel, Lord Pye (Henson) is fascinated by cabaret singer Benita (Day), singing 'Now I Understand', displaying a feather fascinator to eclipse all others. Day's particular beauty is perfectly captured by Mutz Greenbaum's photography. Skimpily costumed in white fur, she encourages the attention of Pye, Rupert Body (Hare) and Uncle Samson (Drayton). 'Just like Tarzan you'll be my ape man/I'm getting so ferocious and you can't escape, man', she sings in 'You Bring Out The Savage In Me' surrounded by gyrating chorines. Barry Mackay seems incidental as Benita's beau. The catchiest of Sam Coslow's numbers, 'Hang On To Happiness' has Day by the Fountain of Youth, with Pye magically transformed into the son of the god Pan, cavorting shamelessly with Day and the chorus girls. Benita turns out to be Pye's stepdaughter, and he renames the League of Purity as the League of Happiness. Life has turned into a party, presumably attended by the *MFB* critic who found the film 'highly entertaining',[2] but not the *Observer*'s critic whose only comment was 'Oh Gaumont-British!'.[3]

MARCH

How are we to take Twickenham's 'Real Art Production' *Street Song*? It's that most fascinating of British studios at its most modest, more an exercise in sentimental naivety than anything else. If there is blame, director Bernard Vorhaus must share it, having co-written the original story with Paul Gangelin. *Street Song* is too evidently Poverty Row, and not much has been done to pay for decent songs.

John Garrick plays our hero, Tommy Tucker ('Possibly virile', comments Claud Allister when he hears Tommy sing 'Painting Pictures'). With a name like that, he can only be a decent chap, although he has got himself into a bit of bother. Lucy (non-singing Rene Ray) jogs along running a pet shop with her young brother Billy (Johnny Singer), but business is tough, which is not unexpected when one sees the curious and underpopulated menagerie Vorhaus has assembled for sale. She perks up after meeting street singer Tommy, and although the police suspect him of theft she takes him in as a lodger. Surprisingly, for so innocent a film, he obviously thinks she wants sex with him, but she makes it quite clear she does not. He helps her improve and make a success of the pet shop. Through Lucy, Tommy gets to sing on the radio, and inevitable success lies ahead, for Tommy's singing career and Lucy's business. The film's ambitions are pretty well summed up when Tommy sings, and Lucy and Billy cavort to, 'In Our Little Noah's Ark'. It's obvious that Twickenham didn't bother to get a choreographer in for a couple of hours. In its way, this is both the high and low point of the film, its music and lyrics, as here, presumably written by Twickenham's W. L. Trytel:

> While I'm painting the name upon the signboard
> You can sing and be happy as a lark,
> Then we'll start to get busy with the hammer and the nails
> In our little Noah's Ark.
> Happy and contented we can be, you see
> We will call the pets our fami*lee*
> Oh gee.
> Every cute little dog will have his biscuit
> They will tell us they're happy with a bark.
> We will give lots of cabbage to the rabbits every day
> In our little Noah's ark.

Eighty years on, it would be interesting to hear Vorhaus's take on this most innocent of little films. But eighty years on, the tired, worn-out animals in Ray and Garrick's 'little Noah's Ark' look far from happy as his actors trip gaily among them.

For different reasons, the behaviour of the humans involved in ***Radio Pirates*** also makes for uncomfortable viewing. When things are not going so well for songwriter Willie Brooks (Warren Jenkins), wireless shop owner Mary (Mary Lawson) and café proprietor Leslie (Leslie French) they decide to start broadcasting, setting themselves up as a rival to the BBC. For some reason, this involves them hiding in coffins and clambering about the clock face of Big Ben. Norman Loudon produced, and Donovan Pedelty expanded his original story into the screenplay, directed by Ivar Campbell for Sound City, with the music and lyrics of Mark Lubbock, although it might have been more sensible to disassociate themselves from the generally puerile material.

Some diversion is provided by Roy Fox and his Orchestra when the three rebel broadcasters take their microphones into London's nightclubs, where they also catch the amateur fooling of expert xylophonist Teddy Brown, and some inexpert dancing from Lawson. But it's the young men of Fox's band that catch the ear and eye in a selection of hillbilly songs. Elsewhere, a young Hughie Green is obliged to do impressions of Mae West and Chevalier; a more grisly encounter with the incipient host of television's *Opportunity Knocks* is difficult to imagine. Enid Stamp-Taylor gets to sing 'In A Place By Yourself', but Lubbock's songs fade away with a whimper. The only wonder is what inane things actors like French, Lawson and Stamp-Taylor were prepared to do at the behest of their director. For some reason, the film was reissued in a much-shortened version in 1940 as *Big Ben Calling*.

Variety can hardly have been helped by its title, despite its distinguished director Adrian Brunel; how many must have presumed this was just another rag-bag collection of acts that they'd probably seen dying the death on stage at the local Hippodrome? In fact, something a little different is attempted in a film that offers a panorama of a family's involvement with music-hall from 1890 to the present day. As *MFB* explained, 'a very decided effort has been made here to create a variety picture with a decided story, and also indirectly to provide topical fare for the jubilee year. The story is still rather on the weak side chiefly because too little emphasis is placed upon the climaxes and especially upon the final climax of the film.'[4]

Nevertheless, space is found for those regulars of many provincial bills Olsen's Sea Lions, singer Denis O'Neil, the great music-hall grotesques Nellie Wallace ('My Mother Said, Always Look Under The Bed') and Lily Morris ('Don't Have Any More, Mrs Moore'), songstress Tessa Deane, George Carney, the much exercised Sherman Fisher Girls, and even Billy Cotton's uproarious Band. Brunel and Oswald Mitchell's screenplay has an interesting conceit – the members of the music-hall Boyd family are played by members of the theatrical Livesey family: Barry, Jack, Sam, and Cassie, but not the best known of the dynasty, Roger. It is interesting that Brunel was associating with a project that harked back to *Elstree Calling*. *Variety* was produced by John Argyle for Argyle Talking Pictures at Cricklewood.

MAY

The Mancunian Film Corporation did not hold back in trumpeting the glories of *Off the Dole*, insisting that with this film George Formby 'definitely enters screen stardom'. It promised picture-goers 'all the ingredients that go to make a smashing hit', including 'Glorious Settings – Absorbing Interest – English Girlhood – The Apex of Beauty – Haunting and Rhythmic Melodies and the Highest Achievement of Comedy Ever Attained' in what was 'A Ripple – A Cascade – A Torrent of Laughter'.

The product was rather more prosaic, but the colourfully enthusiastic producer John E. Blakeley, who may have been as responsible for what was on screen as the named director Arthur Mertz, could not be suppressed. The future was to prove that Formby was indeed about to become a cinematic icon. As in *Boots! Boots!*, Formby played John Willie in this 'Musical Merry Burlesque', no longer working in a hotel but in his uncle's private detective agency. While unsuccessfully pursuing several criminals he breaks into various songs: the vaguely suggestive 'With My Little Ukulele In My Hand', 'I'm Going To Stick To My Mother', 'I Promise To Be Home By Nine-O'Clock' and, with its pungent understanding of market-trading psychology, 'If You Don't Want The Goods Don't Maul 'Em'.

'The inimitable dude comedian' Dan Young contributed to this 'Greatest Comedy Film Ever Offered in the History of the Screen' (Mr Blakeley going overboard again), as did Formby's formidable wife Beryl. *Off the Dole* seems to have had an obvious appeal to audiences north of the border, but with it Formby turned his head towards London. Along the way, Beryl fell to the wayside as his on-screen girlfriend, but remained in control of his career. As Philip Martin Williams has written, Formby's Mancunian films 'had proven Blakeley's instinct to be correct in that northern comedians could successfully be transposed to film. The same working-classes that attended the music-halls would also fill the cinemas to see their favourites on the screen.'[5]

Who now remembers Albert Burdon? Among the many forgotten names that crowd these pages, Burdon's comes back with a gentle friendliness that still communicates through the few films he made before his film career petered out in 1939 with *Jail Birds*. By 1935, Michael Balcon was looking to the little South Shields comedian to become a Gaumont-British star, co-producing **Heat Wave** at Islington with Jerome Jackson. Maurice Elvey directed the screenplay by Austin Melford (based on his original story), Jackson, and Leslie Arliss. Burdon was top-billed, above Cyril Maude and Les Allen, with Vera Pearce and Anna Lee in support. Now, the star was an innocent vegetable salesman, short and sweet. 'What are you?' asks the terrifying prima donna Gloria Spania (Pearce), 'a jockey?' She is a man-eater. After inspecting Albert Speed (Burdon) she commands, 'Take him away and bring me a menu.' In the manner of British musical films Albert thinks he is selling potatoes and cabbages to officials of a South American banana republic, but in reality they are revolutionaries planning to overthrow the President. Albert is mistaken for a gun-runner, but miraculously he is the conduit through which peace is restored.

Sadly, Burdon gets little chance to show what he can do, and is bereft of songs in the score by Maurice Sigler, Al Goodhart and Al Hoffman. Hired as male romantic lead, Les Allen with his crimped hair and unsmiling features fails to register; a clever saxophonist who became well known for his vocals with prominent dance bands, he had this one stab at cinema success, but his inability to project a personality cancels him out, despite getting the numbers 'San Felipe' and 'If Your Father Only Knew' (duetted with the patently non-singing Lee).

Although *MFB* thought it 'Fairly good entertainment [...] the crooner's songs last too long and leave one staring at a close-up of two faces which, however pleasant to look at, become wearisome when the view is prolonged.'[6] Most of the fun is generated when the glorious Pearce, in one of her fullest (in every sense) roles, fills the screen. Bending over, she recalls, 'My Boheme was one of the biggest things ever seen in New York.' Her practising of the scales has a devastating effect on a vase of flowers. 'Could you bring yourself to call me Fortescue?' asks the President. 'Why?' she asks. 'That is my name.' For those content with such nuggets there are other nuggets to be found. 'Senorita,' says the President as he studies Pearce's frame, 'you look enormous … enormously beautiful!'

Expectations are roused by the introduction of a cod opera sequence in which some of the principals participate, with our Albert, in the manner of Bobby Howes stepping into the women's operatic pageant in the 1937 *Please Teacher*, stepping in to a principal role without rehearsal. Sigler, Goodhart and Hoffman's operatic codding is nowhere near so witty as Waller and Tunbridge's attempt in *Please Teacher*, but Pearce and Burdon redeem it with a dazzlingly amusing toreador *pas de deux* that is undoubtedly the highlight of the film. In fact, *MFB* thought, 'The whole film smacks of comic opera, and indeed includes a burlesque of one, which is too sketchy to be amusing and is in the wrong place, as it delays the expected and desired denouement.'[7]

JUNE

Generally welcomed as an effective farce adapted from George S. Kaufman's play *The Butter and Egg Man*, Warner Bros' First National production of **Hello Sweetheart** at Teddington used an adaptation by Brock Williams to chart the story of British chinless (unlike his brother Jack) wonder Claude Hulbert playing Henry Pennyfeather, a poultry farmer who is persuaded by Americans to put up the money for a film. Try as he might, things go wrong and the film falls apart. Undeterred, plucky Henry turns it into a burlesque and success is guaranteed. The theme points towards Mel Brooks's *The Producers*. Irving Asher produced, and Monty Banks directed a company that included Gregory Ratoff and Jane Carr as Babs Beverley. The musical side of things is largely kept away from Hulbert in unintegrated sequences featuring the monologue specialist Marriott Edgar, Johnnie Nit, The Three Gins, and Carroll Gibbons providing musical diversion alongside the lyrics of James Dyrenforth. The choreography is by Ralph Reader.

Although she was once a star of silents, by the mid-1930s Betty Balfour's career in sound pictures was faltering. In *Evergreen* she was in a secondary role to Jessie Matthews, and despite its several pleasures the Albert Chevalier-inspired *My Old Dutch* (with its memorable vignette by Florrie Forde) did little to revive her. Balcon then co-starred her at Gaumont-British with John Mills in a Great War drama *Brown on Resolution*, but she was then sent off to Twickenham where she must have been overtaken with a feeling of *déjà vu*; this was her career come full circle. Much of her early success had been playing a flower-girl in a series of silents directed by George Pearson. Fourteen years on, she was back playing the same character, in what would be a final outing for ***Squibs***.

We can imagine what a welcome she must have had from producer 'Uncle' Julius Hagen and director Henry Edwards. Now, Squibs is living with her father Sam Hopkins (a perfectly cast Gordon Harker), still selling flowers down Piccadilly, catching the eye of dependable P. C. Charley Lee (Stanley Holloway, coasting his way through a part that allowed him the luxury of a Weston and Lee monologue). Times are hard, money is tight, but Squibs gets lucky when she wins a sweepstake (echoes of Pearson and Balfour's 1922 *Squibs Wins the Calcutta Sweep*).

In some ways much of the 1935 update comes over as one of Hagen's less well-resourced productions, but there remains something endearing about it. What matter that the crowd scenes are filled with the most extraordinary characters, some of whom seem to have little or no idea of what they are doing. They look as if they've been shipped in from a John Baxter picture, but the vigour of it all, the naivety, the curious little asides that creep in (costers dancing with baskets on their heads, fluffy toys set free in a street, a window of mannequins coming to life) win you over. The songs by Maurice Sigler, Al Goodhart and Al Hoffman may not be top-notch, but they catch the spirit of the piece admirably from the first, when a traffic jam erupts in 'One Way Street'. Balfour has a delightful soliloquy 'Have You Ever Had The Feeling?', sitting, it seems, at the feet of Eros. Ralph Reader was brought in to choreograph the big set piece 'The Londonola', a high-stepping ensemble celebration whipped up by Balfour and filmed with Bank Holiday relish.

Never mind that the costumes look newly arrived from Berman's theatrical costumiers – the vigour remains obvious. The cast is golden: a young Ronald Shiner, and a host of period character actresses including wispy Drusilla Wills as a nosy neighbour, and Olive Sloane. Magnificently prominent is Margaret Yarde, hilariously rhythmic as an egg-laying chicken when she watches the dancers doing 'The Londonola'.

Betty Balfour in her final portrayal of perky flower-seller *Squibs* (1935)

At the time, this final outing for Squibs was not notably successful. The *MFB* condescendingly noted it as 'somewhat mediocre, though it may well be enjoyable to many who are not too exacting in their standard [...] there is a lack of character and originality in the film as a whole'.[8] Perhaps, but the spirit of the film persists. It would be a hard heart that resisted its childish charm, or the sudden burst of ersatz Hollywood glamour when Balfour appears in a wedding gown of startling splendour, as her working-class neighbours release hundreds of balloons into a sky filled with some sort of hope. For those willing to give themselves over to its innocence, it's irresistible.

It may have starred a singer-actress who would enjoy acclaim and fame much longer than did Balfour, but the fact that Alleanza Cinematografica Italiana's ***The Divine Spark*** was a bilingual made at the Tirrenia Studios in Italy and refused a British certification suggests that we should overlook it. Its star was the German operatic Marta Eggerth, which makes overlooking difficult. Arnold Pressburger produced and Carmine Gallone directed the English version with its screenplay by Emlyn Williams and Richard Benson reworked from the original of Walter Reisch. It purported to be a biography of the composer Bellini (Phillips Holmes) who has a Neapolitan romance with Maddalena (Eggerth). She falls for him, but spurns him, thinking their relationship might affect his career. She dies. The effect on his music can only be imagined. *MFB* was having none of it, judging it 'generally second-rate, for the polish is all on the surface, and there is nothing underneath. Every element in the action is trite. Technique, sugar, and a musical background do not constitute a film. Most of the acting is not on a particularly high level.'[9] The supporting cast shipped to Italy for the pleasure included Benita Hume, Felix Aylmer, John Clements, Edward Chapman and Donald Calthrop. C. A. Lejeune thought it 'a pretty enough story of self-sacrifice, with nice settings, but the divine spark is hard to find'.[10]

David Quinlan is in no doubt that 'Gracie Fields just about overcomes a feeble plot about market-stallholders warding off the efforts of a chain-store to close them down by finding a Royal Charter, and beating off a siege at the Town Hall. Spirited enough, but the sort of tune played with more conviction by Michael Balcon at Ealing in the 1940s.'[11]

Alternatively, ***Look Up and Laugh*** may have been an inspiration for the regime of socially conscious productions that Balcon subsequently instigated. Once again, Fields was directed by Basil Dean in an 'original screenplay' from J. B. Priestley, with 'scenario supervision' by Gordon Wellesley. We may be reasonably confident that this was not one of Priestley's greatest achievements; his biographer Vincent Brome ignores it. Associated Talking Pictures doesn't credit the Harry Parr Davies songs. Despite the lack of interest from those who might have known better, *Look Up and Laugh* is an endearing work, preferable to the previous Priestley-Fields project *Sing As We Go*. The colourful cast provides excellent support, among it Huntley Wright, Douglas Wakefield, Tommy Fields and the once great music-hall comic Harry Tate who 'poor fellow, could not remember a single line for more than two minutes together. It was sad to compare this great comedian's state, now lapsed into senility, with his great days in those hilariously funny sketches – "Motoring", for instance – when vast music-hall audiences sat in their seats, rocking with laughter.'[12]

Fields plays Grace Pearson, a touring performer who returns home, where her father is the oldest stallholder at the local market. Grace's stammering brother Sidney (Tommy Fields) has lost his money on the dogs. The market is threatened with closure by the owner of Belfer's department store (Alfred Drayton), whose posh daughter (Vivien Leigh as a glamorous swan landed among a lot of squawking ducks) is sympathetic to the plight of the market traders, and is in love with Sidney. Although tempted by the offer of a West End show, Grace decides to stay and fight the eviction. The tussle involves good comedy business: Robb Wilton as a bumbling mayor; Grace and her cohorts disguising themselves as scouts; Grace hysterically standing in for a prima donna soprano; and a brilliant slapstick sequence in the piano department culminating in the almost total destruction of Belfer's stock. An interesting insight into characterisation has the stammering Sidney singing rather than speaking some of his lines (the rhythm of music overriding his speech impediment), and Tommy Fields makes the most of his role. Suggesting a plot twist that would later work for Ealing's *Passport to Pimlico*, the discovery of a royal charter safeguards the future of the market.

Despite singing one of Parr Davies's most lyrical ballads 'Love Is Everywhere', at the last Grace is left partner-less but happy in having rescued her friends and colleagues from oblivion. Snatches of 'Happy Ending', originally used in *This Week of Grace*, add to the enjoyment, as does a reprise of her signature 'Sally'. The relationship between star and audience is crucial. When Gracie winks, she winks at every one watching her: she embraces her admirers. Unlike almost all of her female contemporaries working in the industry during the 1930s, she turns the extraordinary trick of always seeming to be utterly and completely herself. She also performs Davies and Lawrence Wright's 'Look Up And Laugh', 'Anna From Anacapresi' (Davies-Fields), and Will E. Haines and Jimmy Harper's 'Shall I Be An Old Man's Darling?'.

JULY

BIP had a winner in the enjoyable **Dance Band**, with two attractive stars, a fascinating mime artist, two dancers, a good score and superb designs. Made at Elstree, the movie was produced by Walter C. Mycroft and directed by Marcel Varnel. The screenplay by Roger Burford, Jack Davies and Denis Waldock charts the love affair between bandleader Buddy Morgan, and a rival all-girl band headed by Pat Shelley. Buddy Rogers (as Morgan), with a genuine dash of transatlantic charm, has as competing bandleader the brightest and most appealing of American leading ladies, June Clyde. The mix around them works well, notably the young mime artist Leon Sherkot, and Manhattan speciality dancing duo Jack Holland and June Hart, swirling through 'The Valparaiso', composed by Mabel Wayne to Desmond Carter's lyric. Also featured is 'I Hate To Say Goodnight', Arthur Young's 'Lovey Dovey', 'Nagasaki' by Harry Warren and Mort Dixon, 'Chinatown, My Chinatown' by Jean Schwartz and William Jerome, and 'Sing Song Girl' by James F. Hanley and Joseph McCarthy.

At times the screen shimmers with the sets of David Rawnsley, not least in a finale that has colliding pianos and, at the end, both male and female instrumentalists atop giant mushrooms. *MFB* approved of this 'pipe dream which should have a wide appeal' in 'a straightforward, thoroughly competent piece of romanticism that is neither sentimental nor hyper-sophisticated [...] but the direction induces a light-hearted mood that makes one accept and enjoy every moment ...'.[13]

Oswald Mitchell, the champion of so many music-hall and variety performers, was the guiding light of the programme filler ***Cock o' the North***, producing for Panther Films at Cricklewood, writing the sentimental screenplay and co-directing with Challis Sanderson. George Carney, the 'real bloke' of British 1930s cinema, plays George Barton (note the frequently used trick of keeping a performer's Christian name for the character's name, thereby emphasising an audience's familiarity with the player), a locomotive driver who is to drive the new train 'Cock o' the North'. When he is hurt in a motor accident he is unable to work, but finds satisfaction in his young son Danny (fifteen-year-old Ronnie Hepworth who had been the Danny of Mitchell's *Danny Boy* the previous year). In the manner of John Baxter's *Say It with Flowers*, George's pals put on a benefit concert for him, somehow managing to persuade the West End cabaret favourite 'Hutch' (Leslie Hutchinson) to do his stuff, singing 'Two Tired Eyes' and 'Wake'. The comedians Naughton and Gold, and Horace Kenney, also appear. The statuesque Marie Löhr, coming down in the social scale from her normally *grande dame* roles, played George's wife. Mitchell and Sanderson reunited the following year for one of the best compendiums of music-hall acts, *Stars on Parade*.

Relentlessly bright, ***Charing Cross Road*** was the address inhabited by John Mills at his liveliest in a film that looked much older than its years. British Lion's producer Herbert Smith hired Albert de Courville to direct at Beaconsfield, but the results are little more than reasonable. The Con West and Clifford Grey script, based on a radio play by Gladys and Clay Keyes, fails to scintillate. Mills and co-star June Clyde burst with youthfulness, and it remains a fine example of Mills's talents as a song and dance man, but the atmosphere is stiffly artificial.

Showbusiness performers Tony (Mills) and Pam (Clyde) want to marry but will not make the commitment until they find theatrical success. Tony is catapulted to fame, leaves Pam standing, realises his error and ends up committing to Pam as we always knew he would. As so often before, our anxieties were unnecessary. Somehow, the emotions are never engaged. The film at least allows us to see the once-prominent American singer Belle Baker, giving something of her all here with 'The Roadway Of Romance Is Full Of Golden Dreams'. One of the characters remarks, 'She's got some of the finest songs in the world', but unfortunately this isn't one of them, despite Miss Baker's best efforts. The on-stage finale with Mills lost among hordes of galumphing West End dancing girls going through some dire movements looks like something from a keep-fit exercise in 1930, but by this time the distancing of the camerawork has long lost our interest, and the audience was probably heading for the exit, if only to escape before the statutory 'God Save the King'.

AUGUST

At Gainsborough they were coping with a duff title, a uniquely talented star comedienne in her second film of the year without her often co-starring husband, in a historical fantasy set in the reign of Queen Anne when the hapless men of England were being tricked into taking the king's shilling and being conscripted into the army. As in Courtneidge's *Things Are Looking Up*, **Me and Marlborough** sneaks by as a film musical in handing its star only one number (albeit one skilfully tailored for her male impersonating personae), Noel Gay and Clifford Grey's rollicking 'All For A Shilling A Day'.

Michael Balcon didn't count the picture as among his best, describing 'one dire flop […] my responsibility because I knew it was doomed to failure before we commenced shooting […] In deep despair, I tried my damnedest and every trick I could think of to cure something that was incurable'.[14] The fact that in her autobiography Courtneidge dismisses her British films in a few lines does little to encourage confidence. Matters are not helped by the absence of any possible on-screen female competition (the strong-minded Miss Courtneidge might not have appreciated it). It was said that she had eyes in the back of her head, ever aware on stage of what the most inconspicuous chorus girl was up to behind her back. Her hectoring, sergeant-major-type swagger dominates here, but there is more to the star's performance than pose and vigour; always when on screen she suggests a depth of feeling that would, late in life, have her acclaimed as a dramatic actress.

It is difficult to disentangle who wrote what. The title frame has 'by W. P. Lipscombe and Reginald Pound', but the scenario is credited to Lipscombe and Marjorie Gaffney, and the dialogue to Ian Hay, with Victor Saville directing.

Whoever is responsible, they make Courtneidge's Kit Ross, proprietress of 'The Duke's Head' inn, a fine heroine, first seen when she is hiding a young deserter, then getting herself into the army when her boyfriend Dick (Barry Mackay) is hijacked into military service. Her heady progress, constantly being promoted and reduced to the ranks and promoted again, withstands any number of near disasters, until she is reunited with Dick.

There may yet be a thesis on the relevance of *Me and Marlborough* as a feminist work. It is one in which the men play second fiddles, but they are well tuned in Alfred Drayton's Sgt Bull and Tom Walls's Duke of Marlborough, as well as in Ivor McLaren's French spy. Mackay, with the manner of a vent's giant dummy, is less effective; we wonder if a comic actor might have served better than a dull one. England in the 1730s is cleverly evoked in Alfred Junge's convincing designs, lending some historical flavour to what remains an entertaining film, with Courtneidge its one essential.

If your idea of a musical treat is a sub-Rombergian *Student Prince*, with gallons of imaginary beer being drunk out of empty mugs by elbow-lifting students in old Heidelberg, the concoction laced with alternately marching and anonymously pretty music, **The Student's Romance** may be the answer. It is dressed in BIP's finest style, produced by Walter C. Mycroft at Elstree, with luxuriously appointed sets by Cedric Dawe, supervised by Clarence Elder. There are moments that might belong in a better film than this, created by esteemed cinematographer and occasional director Otto Kanturek. This is basically an adaptation of Bruno Hardt-Warden and Fritz Löhner-Beda's *I Lost My Heart in Heidelberg*, based on a play by Löhner-Beda and Ernst Neumann. The operetta had music by Fredy (Fred) Raymond and lyrics by Ernst Neubach. Now, the credits awarded adaptation and scenario to Clifford Grey, Richard Hutter and Norman Watson, with new music by Hans May and lyrics by Clifford Grey. On the credit side, *The Student's Romance* has a handsome couple as its leads, Patric Knowles, eventually to be snaffled by Hollywood, and Austrian diva Grete Natzler who would soon (understandably) change her name to Della Lynd. Unfortunately, Miss Natzler seems to be reported missing for whole swathes of the picture, leaving it in much less appealing hands, but when let out of her caravan, and certainly when she is wandering through gorgeously artificial studio foliage singing May, Grey and Hutter's 'There's A Smile In The Skies Just For Me', her visits are worth waiting for.

Other musical items include 'I Lost My Heart In Heidelberg' by Raymond and Harry S. Pepper, 'Oh Lassie Come' (May/Grey), 'Marching Along Singing A Song', 'Put Down Your Swords' and 'The Busy Busy Police'. It seems unlikely that customers remembered any of them by the time they were out on the street. The story set in Austria in 1830 (there is some appalling stock footage to get a sense of place) doesn't much matter, but concerns the love between impecunious young composer Max (Knowles) and lovelorn Princess Helene (Natzler), daughter of the

Grand Duke and destined for an arranged marriage. The more lowly but kindly Veronika (Carol Goodner) supports Max, while veteran comic W. H. Berry lightens the mood. After various vicissitudes, Max and Helene rush into each other's arms watched by two camp policemen as the final frame dissolves.

C. A. Lejeune thought it 'pretty, conventional, and so slender that it's hardly there at all'.[15] *MFB* conceded that the original story may have been charming, but 'The direction is clumsy and full of stage tricks. The sets belong rather to the theatre. The dialogue is naïve and lacks sparkle. A great deal of the acting, too, belongs to the other medium.'[16] Remarkably, not one drop of beer was seen to slop from the Heidelberg mugs.

Christian Cargnelli sees **Heart's Desire** as

> at the heart of the Stein-Tauber collaboration. Though its director, unlike his star, has fallen into total oblivion, this great film is definitely his lasting achievement. *Heart's Desire* negotiates central aspects of exile: rootlessness, alienation, language loss. Unlike Tauber, Josef Steidler is not being expelled to England, but comes here voluntarily – and yet, his story evokes, if not in explicitly political terms, the fate of the exiled individual.[17]

At the time of writing, with the United Kingdom merely technically united to Europe, this treatment of a foreigner adrift in a foreign land takes on another level of meaning in a genre where other levels of meaning are seldom discernible.

How wrong can you be? Wealthy socialite Frances Wilson (Leonora Corbett) believes the arrogant tenor Van Straaten (Frank Vosper) to be the finest in the world. 'There isn't another tenor in Europe like you!' she tells him, but soon enough, at an old pleasure garden in Vienna on a spring night, she finds him: Josef Steidler (Richard Tauber), first seen scoffing his supper. 'The man is a peasant', someone comments. 'So was Caruso', answers another. It is time for Frances to make Josef famous in England. An enchanting farewell scene at the railway station as Steidler departs is made superbly cinematic by Stein. It is eclipsed by the railway carriage scene where we see Josef and his guiding-light friend Florian (Paul Graetz). Tauber sings 'Morgen muss ich fort von hier' ('Tomorrow I Must Leave') as he is torn from his homeland. Stein seems perfectly in tune with what is essentially natural to his star. Returning to Vienna after filming was completed, Tauber explained, 'I play a man whose nature and actions are essentially influenced by his love for his native Vienna and by his homesickness for this city. And it's this kind of emotion I have truly and deeply experienced.'[18]

Obvious as is his struggle with the English language, of which the film makes play, Tauber is touchingly effective throughout, even impressing dubious managers ('All tenors sing better tomorrow'). The musical content is, naturally, all Tauber. Happily, this includes three of his own compositions, the lovely 'My World Is Gold', 'Let Me Awake Your Heart' and 'All Hope Is Ended', as well as Schumann's

'Devotion' and 'A Message Sweet As Roses', and composer Rudolf Sieczyński and lyricist Edward Lockton's 'Vienna, City Of My Dreams'. No matter that Josef stars with Diana Sheraton (Diana Napier) in a hugely successful operetta *Venetian Moon*; home is where the heart is. He and Florian return to Vienna ('Vienna Mine') and Josef's true love Anna (Kathleen Kelly). Based on Lioni Pickard's story, Walter C. Mycroft's BIP production at Elstree had a screenplay by Bruno Frank, L. du Garde Peach, Roger Burford and Jack Davies, with additional dialogue and lyrics by Clifford Grey. As with *Blossom Time*, musical arrangements were by G. H. Clutsam, with the score conducted by Idris Lewis and Stanford Robinson.

Heart's Desire makes more claim to be a valuable work than *Blossom Time* because its theme of foreign transplantation and new promise has a resonance lacking in the other. The acknowledgement of Tauber's real-life situation is obvious. Like Stein, Tauber must to some extent have been emotionally and professionally adrift in Britain, despite so many of the colleagues he worked with in British studios also being émigrés. Both were artistically adrift, separated from the culture of their homeland. Two years later, Stein would tell a friend, 'There is no film industry here in England. Still, it remains a fact that some people are making pictures.'[19] It may be, as Cargnelli suggests, that Stein's name is all but forgotten. On hearing of his death, Arthur Dent, managing director of Wardour, the company that distributed both *Blossom Time* and *Heart's Desire*, remembered him as 'the man who did more in blending successfully art and industry in entertainment films than anyone I know', and that it had been 'a stroke of genius' to bring Tauber into British cinema.[20]

The diminutive Irish entertainer Jimmy O'Dea would have to wait a little longer before becoming a bigger name in the excellent *Penny Paradise* and *Let's Be Famous*. For the moment, he made do with Baxter and Barter Productions' **Jimmy Boy**. The trade press excitedly built expectation for Baxter's grandest project to date, involving a week's location shooting in Ireland, three weeks' shooting at the Stoll Studios in Cricklewood, a large cast of actors and an assortment of variety turns, as well as fifty ballet dancers choreographed by Wendy Toye. Harry O'Donovan and Con West's screenplay told the story of Jimmy, a poor Irish lad (O'Dea was thirty eight at the time) who gets work as a film extra and discovers that the movie's star (Enid Stamp-Taylor) is a spy. Graduating to lift-boy in a smart hotel, Jimmy unravels a dastardly plot to blow up London.

MFB found nothing to praise: 'Some fishing harbour scenes and two of the hotel cabaret turns, about ten minutes of the whole film, were worth putting on the screen.'[21] *Kinematograph Weekly* concurred, reviewing a film that was 'so disjointed and slipshod [that] its making appears to have been impromptu'.[22] Reporting this 'off-colour' Baxter production, *Era* agreed that O'Dea 'has possibilities as a film comedian, but his recent performance lacked spontaneity, while his personality did not always register'.[23]

Jimmy Boy seems to have been Kennedy Russell's first composing assignment for Baxter; he was to be one of the decade's busiest and least recognised composers writing for films. Here, Russell and lyricist Arthur Stanley contribute 'The Sky's The Limit' for O'Dea, and for Stamp-Taylor 'How Would You Like To Love Me?', as well as 'Love Life And Duty' and 'Hit The Spot'. Russell's subsequent work for Baxter's productions included *Sunshine Ahead*, *Men of Yesterday*, *Hearts of Humanity*, the Hazel Ascot vehicles *Talking Feet* and *Stepping Toes*, as well as scores for the *Old Mother Riley* series. As a stage composer he was not without significance, writing scores for the 1930 *Wild Rose*, the 1934 *By Appointment* in which Maggie Teyte sang the haunting 'White Roses', and in 1947 *The Nightingale*. His name is all but forgotten.

SEPTEMBER

Once a major star of silents, Lupino Lane struggled to establish himself in sound films. The self-directed non-musical *No Lady* (1931), a hen-pecked husband's vision of Blackpool life, didn't help. Two years later, his appearance in BIP's *A Southern Maid* did little to bring him back to mind. From here on, he self-directed, masquerading as Henry W. George, for St George's Pictures, in March 1935 with *Who's Your Father?* and in September *The Deputy Drummer*. A third effort, *Trust the Navy*, was released in December. Lane's brilliance as an acrobat was matched by a natural charm, evident in his very first silent reels as 'Nipper', the name by which he was still known in the 1950s. Made at the Fox studios at Wembley Park, **The Deputy Drummer** was based on the musical *Darling, I Love You*, which had enjoyed a moderate London run in 1930. The screenplay by thriller writer Peter Cheyney, Reginald Long, Frank Miller and actor-writer Arthur Rigby had Lane as Adolphus Miggs.

Once again, the hero of a British musical film is a struggling composer. In his shabby lodgings, on a broken-down piano, Miggs battles to complete his 'Rhapsody in Pink', composed for the film by Alec Templeton. He joins Bubbles O'Hara (Jean Denis) in singing 'Bread And Cheese And Kisses', nice enough but unmemorable. The clowning is below that seen in earlier Lupino works. The band that Bubbles is working with lacks a deputy drummer, and Miggs gets the job, passing himself off as aristocracy at the Sylvester's stately home. There is some intricate word-play involving Peggy Sylvester (Kathleen Kelly). Lane does a spectacular tumble down a steep staircase, and there is a fine plate-smashing scene with the ever-resplendent Margaret Yarde as Lady Sylvester. Sam Crossley, in his best lugubrious manner, is the crooked manservant involved in a jewel theft. At last, Lord Sylvester (screenplay writer Arthur Rigby) gets to conduct Miggs's Rhapsody, for which the orchestral parts seem magically to have materialised. A slapstick finale, with Lane prancing pan-like among diaphanously clad girls, and pursued by a tunic-wearing Crossley, redeems some of what has gone before, with the bonus of Yarde's involvement and a last great burst of Lane's physical stunts. Billy Mayerl and lyricist Frank Eyton wrote the songs. Best of all is Lane's solo pavement routine with the dog Brutus, 'Old Pal', deft and almost still. Something of the essence of Lane's talent resides here, unforced and still impressive.

One of the brightest offerings of the year was the British remake of the 1937 Hungarian *Meseautó* directed by Béla Gaál, translated as **Car of Dreams**. A sense of enjoyment infuses much of this Gaumont-British production, filmed at Shepherd's Bush. It has good things going for it – essentially the adaptation from Miklós Vitéz and Vadnay László's original by C. Stafford Dickens, and Richard Benson and Austin Melford's agile screenplay – but all components are strong. John Mills is the most agreeable of juveniles as Robert Miller, son of a wealthy father whose business is making brass musical instruments. Robert's happy disposition breaks into his march through the instrument-making factory as he bids 'Goodbye Trouble'. Lower on the financial scale is Vera Hart (Grete Mosheim), daughter of a struggling antique shop owner (the excellent Paul Graetz). Vera is a shopaholic window-shopper with extravagant tastes but no money. When she window-shops a Rolls Royce, she is spotted by Robert, who has just bought it. Convincing her that she is being given the car free as a publicity stunt, Robert makes her a present of it and appoints himself her chauffeur. Still in the showroom, he takes her for an imagined spin as they duet 'Car Of Dreams', written by Sigler, Goodhart and Hoffman.

Vera applies for and gets a job at the factory, but is unaware that Robert is the boss's son. Their romance is both helped and hindered by instrument-tester Henry Butterworth (Robertson Hare, especially funny as he instructs Vera on her secretarial duties: 'Breathe on the stamp – alternate blows!') and the boss's secretary Anne Fisher (Norah Howard, getting the chance to sing 'Do A Little Good To Someone'). Misunderstandings arise when Robert offers Vera a future in 'two rooms over a garage', and there never seems much future in the alternative affection for Robert's colleague (not much competition as played by Jack Hobbs), but confusions are sorted and the expected happy ending is reached.

In her one British film, Mosheim makes for a pleasing heroine, light of voice and melancholic of appearance. Her name was unknown to the British public, but Balcon knew her work, and must have used the opportunity of her appearance in the West End play *Two Share a Dwelling* to sign her. She brings a particular quality that was probably unique (imagine the role done by almost any of the then fashionably cast British actresses and the point is made). Mills's breezy confidence, and the sense that he utterly believes in what he is doing on camera, never tires. The score, shared between Mischa Spoliansky, lyricist Frank Eyton, and the Sigler-Goodhart-Hoffman team, is nicely crafted. *MFB* pronounced it 'high entertainment value' and suitable for children over ten.[24] Conversely, for C. A. Lejeune it was 'quite, quite undistinguished […] a kind of derivative *Sunshine Susie* without the infectious flow of the earlier picture […] I am afraid *Car of Dreams* is not one of our best British models by any way.'[25]

As Lupino Lane's film career slipped its moorings, that of his cousin Stanley Lupino thrived. He produced and starred in his next two pictures, **Honeymoon for Three** and the less splashy but genuinely enjoyable *Cheer Up!*, seeing out the decade with four more that included two of his neatest efforts, *Over She Goes* (1937) and *Hold My Hand* (1938). He supplied the storyline for *Honeymoon for Three*'s 'scenarist' Frank Miller, enlivened by a handful of songs by Billy Mayerl and Frank Eyton. Throughout his career, Lupino was luckier in his co-stars than many others of the period; here, Aileen Marson makes for a personable sparring partner, playing wealthy Yvonne Daumery. The glittering nightclub world that seems to haunt Lupino's films is there at the start, complete with a moving platform on which the orchestra accompanies his paean to hedonistic enjoyment, 'Make Hay While The Moon Shines'.

As usual in Lupino films, our hero, playing Jack Denver, has to work hard at getting the girl, although it is obvious from the beginning that Yvonne's fiancé Raymond (Jack Melford) isn't much competition. Being a decent sort of chap, Jack agrees to marry Yvonne when they are caught in what was known as a 'compromising position'. Jack accompanies his wife and Raymond on board ship to America, where they plan to get a quickie divorce but inevitably – Yvonne has already sung 'I'll Build A Fence Around You' – Raymond loses out to Jack.

A set-piece dance routine at sea catches the spirit of so much of Lupino's work with the idiosyncratic frog-stepping and sudden balletic explosions that are as endearing as they are home-made. It remains the film's closest shot at Hollywood, while remaining utterly British, its choreography by Carl Hyson and Leslie Roberts. At one moment, Lupino describes himself to a small girl as 'Short, dark and ordinary' but the very persistence of his screen appearances suggests his friendly presence had what was needed to ensure his continued success through the decade. The Stanley Lupino phenomenon may well have relied on a whole bag of tricks, to which he perfectly knew how to add a smattering of brightly agreeable but forgettable musical numbers, but it is difficult not to side with him. 'The youthful spirit of the film would make it a delightful one for boys and girls, but the divorce motif takes it out of this class,' reported the *MFB*, but it remained 'a thoroughly good evening's entertainment for the light-hearted.'[26]

OCTOBER

A Fire Has Been Arranged, an 'arsonic' comedy, is one of Twickenham's most ambitious and diverting comedies of the early 1930s, produced by Julius Hagen and directed by Leslie S. Hiscott. It follows the efforts of Bud (Flanagan) and Chesney (Allen) to retrieve a horde of jewels they had stolen ten years earlier and hidden at a location subsequently taken by a big department store where the female staff wear extraordinary uniforms. The shop faces collapse under the crooked management of swindling Shuffle (C. Denier Warren) and Cutte (Alastair Sim), who devise a plan to burn the place down. Employee Oswald Blenkinsop (Robb Wilton, as befuddled as ever) is mainly concerned with the efficiency of the store's fire-fighters, played by the tapping Buddy Bradley Girls. Bradley's quasi-Hollywood choreography enlivens the impromptu fashion parade as introduced by Wilton, Harold French and Mary Lawson in Maurice Sigler, Al Goodhart and Al Hoffman's nifty 'It Doesn't Cost A Thing To Smile', and the practice fire-drill number for Wilton and the Girls, 'We're The Latest Members Of The Fire Brigade'. Ultimately, Flanagan and Allen join up for one of their casual duets, the gently rolling 'They're Building Flats Where The Arches Used To Be' by Flanagan and Horatio Nichols. These provide slight musical interludes, but delightfully period.

The picture could hardly be more 'Twickenham', emanating from an original story by the studio's resident scripter H. Fowler Mear (who has clearly had a field day selecting some very stale witticisms from his infamous joke book) and James A. Carter, also responsible for art direction. Equally indispensable at Twickenham is the studio's resident musical supervisor W. L. Trytel, contributing a stream-of-consciousness, wall-to-wall background score that chunters along meaninglessly without detracting from our enjoyment.

The precariously fragile Lilian Harvey left her mark on cinema without ever being heartily adopted by the British public. She moves through her pictures with the ghost-like grace of a balletic changeling. *Invitation to the Waltz* was to be her only British film, according to the *MFB* 'remarkable for its director's (Paul Merzbach) handling of different masses (such as the bands of soldiers) and his skilful interweaving of currents of movement across the screen'.[27] Her long sojourns in Hollywood and Germany distanced her appeal to British audiences, but her quality is worthy of celebration. Merzbach and his cinematographers serve her well, even if Harvey looks older than her twenty-nine years, now and then reminding us of the fearsome cook Fanny Cradock. At Elstree, Walter C. Mycroft marshalled BIP's highest production values, with brilliantly designed '1803' sets by Clarence Elder and John Mead.

The piece originated with a radio play by Eric Maschwitz (as Holt Marvell) and composer George Posford, the rights bought by BIP as a vehicle for the British-born

Harvey, whom Maschwitz describes as 'the cockney film star'.[28] The screenplay was by Merzbach, Clifford Grey and Roger Burford, with shreds of Posford's original score adapted by G. Walter Goehr in what was an only intermittently musical film. Its set-piece highlight is the title song, in Elder's sumptuous theatrical milieu, with Harvey partnered by Anton Dolin, doubling as choreographer. The rest of the film is on a more modest but tasteful scale.

In London, 1803, the little dancer Jenny Peachey (Harvey) is fancied by the Duke of Wirtemberg [sic], but flirts with handsome lieutenant Carl (Carl Esmond), feeds elephants at the zoo, and is confused between the identities of the Duke and his much more appealing attendant. The composer Weber (Richard Bird) is her rehearsal pianist. She is taken up in Venice by dance teacher Lombardi (Charles Carson): 'You will dance in every great capital.' Complications ensue when the Duke travels to Venice, and England is threatened by Bonaparte (second-billed Esme Percy). A gondolier sings 'Dear Love, Come Soon', but Weber gets the idea of a waltz from peasant dancing and Harvey shows Lombardi how it is done before making her debut with it at the Stuttgart Opera.

The story is not especially cohesive, and its characters with few exceptions (Hay Petrie as a petulant French dancing master, and the always excellent Carson) do not convince. This leaves Harvey as the film's reason for being. There are moments, as when she takes off with cat-like leaps, a thin, frail creature, beautifully captured by Dolin (or did Harvey herself devise it?) and the crystal clarity of Ronald Neame and Claude Friese-Greene's cinematography. Harvey's childlike frame contains the seeds of tragedy, and even so unlikely a project as *Invitation to the Waltz* cannot disguise it.

What is it about **Music Hath Charms** that seems slightly forced in its jollity and enthusiasm? Its real star is the bandleader Henry Hall with his BBC Dance Band in a showcase of his music and admirable musicians. Music (as Congreve told us) may indeed have its charms, but it has all sorts of effects on all sorts of people, of which we have copious examples here, as Hall's music invades and alters people's lives. As Hall himself realises, 'All kinds of people listen to us, from the North Pole to the Equator.' We meet plenty of them during the course of this compendium movie. 'We've got a lot to thank Henry Hall for', say a smiling couple in a crofter's cottage, and it is hard to believe that the charming Mr Hall could upset anyone. There is a great deal of his music in the film, interrupted by scenes involving different characters, prancing through a dental surgery, charming lazing police officers in a park, setting the judge and jury and lawyers in a dreary courtroom swaying.

Hall comes over as a kindly soul. There is exuberance as he takes deprived children on a jolly, glimpses of his domestic arrangements as he leaves his smiling children on the doorstep, and when he waves goodbye with his signature farewell 'Here's To The Next Time' we know another meeting will be a joyride of British band music. Perhaps the film is best when it lets us see and hear his band players, the young men like vocalist Dan Donovan. His instrumentalist colleagues may be anonymous for most of the audience, but they are after all the backbone of Hall's empire, and there is something affecting in seeing them enjoy their moment in the spotlight, even when their dialogue borders on the embarrassing.

Thomas Bentley, one of the decade's greatest advocates of music-hall and variety, is credited as supervising director, with other segments directed by Alexander Esway, Walter Summers and Arthur Woods. Produced at Elstree for BIP by Walter C. Mycroft, the screenplay was assembled by L. du Garde Peach and Jack Davies Jnr; the latter's other writing credits of the decade included *Mister Cinders*, *Heart's Desire* and *A Star Fell from Heaven*. The actors filling in the gaps between Hall's music include W. H. Berry, Arthur Margetson and Billy Milton, but none are more than incidental. Even cabaret-famous Hildegarde is not over-exposed, singing Mabel Wayne and Desmond Carter's charmer 'Honey-Coloured Moon'; they also contribute 'Big Ship'.

Pieced together from its four directors, with four cinematographers filming its segments, *Music Hath Charms* kept BIP designer Duncan Sutherland and his supervising art director Clarence Elder busy, while Benjamin Frankel oversaw the musical arrangements. Several of Hall's compositions are heard: the title song, 'Many Happy Returns Of The Day', 'I'm Feeling Happy', 'There's No Time Like The Present', 'Ju-Ju', 'East Wind', 'Just Little Bits And Pieces' and (written with Margery Laurence) his thematic 'Here's To The Next Time'. Also featured are R. S. Hooper and Roger Eckersley's 'It's Just The Time For Dancing', and Collie Knox and Norah Purton's 'In My Heart Of Hearts'.

NOVEMBER

The ascent of George Formby from the almost Poverty Row productions of early Mancunian comedies to a contract for a major feature with Associated Talking Pictures was marked by *No Limit*, produced by Basil Dean and directed by Monty Banks from the screenplay of Tom Geraghty, Fred Thompson and Gordon Wellesley (also scenario editor), based on a story by Walter Greenwood. A Bank Holiday air prevails in a jolly piece that more or less establishes a template of the many Formby vehicles to follow.

Clarity was imperative; situations that involved a specific fascination, preferably topical. George, apparently inept, mind-muddled, accident-prone, romantically gauche, alarmingly innocent, but ever ready to make the best of things by picking out a melody on a ukulele – there was always one about somewhere – to accompany cheeky lyrics (even, occasionally, merely charming lyrics), rises from modesty to satisfactory attainment, winning not only the admiration of others and self-confidence but the girl of his choice, often of a type that some may have considered out of his league. With skilful writers and capable directors at his back, these characteristics make up the Formby brand, a franchise that effectively kept his film career buoyant until the end of the war.

The *MFB* pondered the qualities of his first major picture, thinking Banks's direction 'very "stagey" and probably George Formby would be happier in that medium'. As for the female companions that accompanied him in each of the series (one hesitates to call any of his leading ladies co-stars; the studios and Beryl Formby forbade such aspiration), they are barely distinguishable, dutifully following one another, as if at a safe distance from the male star. In fact, *No Limit* is a rare example of a Formby girlfriend allowed to take a little of the limelight off our George, and how refreshing (no matter how highly we value him) it is. Florence Desmond, a considerable talent that British studios failed to exploit, is a delight here; it was regretted that 'Miss Desmond has only to look pretty – a great waste of material'.[29] She nevertheless manages to be delightful in two duets with Formby, perching on a bar to explain 'I'm Riding Around On A Rainbow' (written by Formby and Fred E. Cliffe), or musing through Harry Parr Davies's 'Your Way Is My Way'. As happy as she looks, Desmond was unenamoured of her leading man, and only reluctantly agreed to return to play second fiddle all over again in his next, *Keep Your Seats, Please*. She was lucky at least to take her turn in a film, set among the TT races on the Isle of Man, that remains one of the star's most immediate and enjoyable.

A romance of the shamrock, Butcher's **Father O'Flynn** was ideal fodder for devotees of the Hibernian. Subtlety need not detain us. Produced at Shepperton by Wilfred Noy, and co-written by Noy and Walter Tennyson, this 'programmer' essentially provided opportunities for bursts of Irish song, having enrolled two excellent songsters, Tom Burke (the eponymous hero) and Denis O'Neil. Kindly Father O'Flynn (Burke) has brought up pretty Macushlah Westmacott (Jean Adrienne) from childhood, after her father (dastardly Henry Oscar) left her homeless. He now means to get his hands on money she has inherited, for nefarious purposes. Interrupted by well-known ballads, he finds his plan thwarted by the valiant O'Flynn and Macushlah's boyfriend Nigel (Robert Chisholm). Cosmopolitan relief is offered by Ethel Revnell and Gracie West, and the much-used Sherman Fisher Girls, between numbers such as 'Father O'Flynn', 'Ave Maria', 'Macushlah', 'Let's Fall In Love' and 'I Know Of Two Bright Eyes'.

In the afterglow of *Evergreen*, in June 1935 Jessie Matthews informed *Picturegoer*, 'The situation is that I am on contract to Gaumont-British for the next three years at least, and I shall probably go to Hollywood under the "star-exchanging" system for one picture a year.' 'I arrange nearly all my own dances', she told readers, and she had no intention of moving to America.[30] Her domestic life with husband Sonnie Hale drew much attention. In March 1934 Matthews had asked why there was such interest 'in Mrs Hale's home affairs and home life? Why cannot she be allowed to work out her own destiny, in whatever way she desires?' She vigorously defended her right to privacy in an article 'Hands Off My Private Life', subheaded 'Hollywood stars may favour party orgies, but Jessie Matthews and Sonnie Hale seem to be happy with a couple of cycles and a good read.'[31]

At Gaumont-British she had the continued confidence of producer Michael Balcon, the director Victor Saville under whose supervision she would do the best of her work, and the most sympathetic of cinematographers Glen MacWilliams. The new work, **First a Girl**, had German antecedents, based on Reinhold Schünzel's play *Viktor und Viktoria* and the subsequent Alfred Zeisler film, newly screenplayed by Marjorie Gaffney. *MFB* was not persuaded, finding the story 'preposterous', complaining of over-long dance routines, unfunny comedy, and expressing 'misgivings' as to the film's propriety, although 'there are a number of good songs'.[32] Victorian and Edwardian propriety had seldom been upset by the appearances of the male impersonators of the time, the sometimes eerie American Ella Shields ('Burlington Bertie From Bow'), nimble Vesta Tilley ('Jolly Good Luck To The Girl Who Loves A Soldier'), or Hetty King ('Ship Ahoy').

Matthews's impersonation did not impress all. C. A. Lejeune, confessing that she found cross-dressing distasteful, wrote that 'It distressed me to see Jessie Matthews and Sonnie Hale, both of whom I admire enormously, reduced to this sort of undergraduate antic.'[33] This treatment of cross-dressing avoided any challenges to gender issues; here, it is merely a peg on which to pin a plot little more ludicrous than others. As in *Evergreen*, it pursues a story about impersonation. Why this should have been thought necessary to promote Matthews's image remains a mystery, this time suspending belief in the fact that the star plays a girl who takes over from a voiceless drag artist (Hale). As a man pretending to be a woman she becomes a sensation. This naturally complicates her love life involving Griffith Jones. As in *Evergreen*, a satisfactory denouement depends on her exposing her true self, but the allure of *Evergreen* is not recaptured.

Variety's take was that the movie's 'lethargic tempo' concealed 'certain appeal, several tuneful songs and nice backgrounds, but doesn't ring the bell', with songs by Maurice Sigler, Al Goodhart and Al Hoffman that were 'rhythmic and fetching but cannot overcome the retarded movement of the book.'[34] The numbers included 'Half And Half', 'Say The Word And It's Yours', 'Written All Over My Face' and Matthews's best item 'Everything's In Rhythm With My Heart', as well as Donald Stewart singing 'Little Silkworm' and 'I Can Wiggle My Ears'.

As Michael Thornton exuberantly informs us, Matthews was riding the crest of her popularity, her fan mail accounting for 70% of letters sent to the studio. Moreover, 'At the Ideal Home exhibition that winter it was noticed that she was ambidextrous. She signed more than 3,500 autograph books in an hour and a half using both hands alternately.'[35] It is not clear how this astonishing fact was established.

Saville was aware of his star's precarious temperament:

Deep inside her there was a war going on. She was, emotionally and professionally, a very passionate woman. But at heart she was a prude. The prudery fought to suppress the passion and produced breakdowns and other nervous symptoms which brought out rashes all over her body.[36]

It was time for BIP to indulge in more light operatic hokum. *I Give My Heart* went about it with some flair and taste. As nobody seems to have considered making a film of any British operetta (Gilbert and Sullivan, for two, were left on the shelf apart from a 1939 *Mikado*), BIP looked to foreign parts, coming up with *Die* [The] *Dubarry*. It had first played on stage in 1931 Berlin, a reworking of the 1879 *Gräfin Dubarry*, now with a libretto by Paul Knepler and J. M. Welleminsky, but more importantly with the music of Carl Millöcker, arranged for BIP by Theo Mackeben. Walter C. Mycroft's screen version was directed at Elstree by Marcel Varnel in an adaptation and scenario by Frank Launder, Roger Burford and Kurt Siodmak. Luxurious settings were designed by David Rawnsley under the supervision of Clarence Elder; the results were distinctively magnificent. Desmond Carter and Rowland Leigh wrote new lyrics.

In 1769, flirtatious seamstress Jeanne (Gitta Alpár) falls for young cove René (Patrick Waddington), romancing him on exterior shooting in a park as they duet 'Before We Met'. In fact, Alpár has already charmed her way to the front of the film with 'Good Luck Today Will Come My Way', and tops this when, in black camiknickers, she performs the glorious title song, singing alongside a nightingale in Rawnsley's delightful Arcadian fantasy. She makes for a spirited heroine, clearing a table in spectacular fashion at an incipient orgy, and taking centre stage in a wonderfully atmospheric exterior sequence as hot air balloons ascend. Her social conquest is complete when she is named Madame de Pompadour. At last, Alpár gets a chance to play a trouser sequence when she commands the crowds in the revolutionary square, proving to the lovesick René that she is indeed the Dubarry.

The otherwise mainly male characters are neatly played by decent actors, among them Owen Nares and Arthur Margetson, but this is Alpár's film. The cleanliness of Claude Friese-Greene's photography and the striking black and white costumes looking to the effect that Cecil Beaton would subsequently create for *My Fair Lady*'s 'Ascot Gavotte' are notably stylish. This is a film that is frequently ravishing, and its charms, with the singing of Alpár as its centre, have not dimmed. Up to the final frame, she is still matching the nightingale in notes only audible to dogs, and just to prove it one of the little blighters runs towards the cinema audience as the image fades into black.

Bordering on the curious, at times **Hyde Park Corner** seems more like a London address than a British musical film, and a musical that anyway only breaks into song twice, both times involving a leading lady of the lighter stage, Binnie Hale. We have the Adam brothers to blame for having built this apparently elegant house, which we first visit in 1780, when Gordon Harker, in charge of a contingent of Bow Street Runners, leads a raid on a gambling session. The good and bad are easily identified. Gibb McLaughlin is the sneering, cheating villain Sir Arthur Garnett, and the owner of the house is poor tortured Chester (moody Eric Portman). Chester's loss at cards loses him his house, but Garnett is exposed as a cheat. They fight a somewhat tame duel. Chester is mortally injured, only coming round to claim he stabbed himself. Before dying, he curses Garnett: 'Sooner or later this house will bring ruin and death to you and yours.' As one of the characters remarks, 'I wouldn't want a curse on my house.' However, this does propel the plot onwards for another long hour.

It is now that *Hyde Park Corner* turns into a sort of time play, the complexities of which seem impenetrable. Now, the action updated to 1935, another Chester (obviously the same one as in 1780, since he is played by an even moodier Portman) is equally addicted to gambling. Sir Arthur Garnett (presumably a descendant of the 1780 Garnett) is murdered, and Chester accused of his death. Old Bow Street runner Harker (in best lip-smacking form, and having a heyday with malapropisms) is reincarnated as cockney P. C. Cheatle. He is matched by the natty petty thief and pickpocket Sophie (Hale, now reincarnated), whose ancestor Sophie arrived in the gambling den of 1780 wearing a preposterously voluminous dress that looked like a reject from Gitta Alpár's wardrobe, but was by Schiaparelli. The 1780 Sophie has already sung one of the two songs by Sigler, Goodhart and Hoffman, 'You Don't Know The Half Of It', and gets another in 1935, 'Did You Get That Out Of A Book?'. As these are sung by Binnie Hale, the top-billed Sophie, we should at least be grateful for a glimpse of a clever artist at work.

The relationship between Harker's funny little Cheatle and Hale's perky Sophie dominates the 1935 scenes as the film flips between comedy and incipient tragedy. At the same time, the Cheatle-Sophie relationship meanders between cheeky friendship and flurries of sexual frisson. Here, as with much of *Hyde Park Corner*, it's best not to doze off if one wants to penetrate the developments. Ultimately, a dead body is found behind a curtain, and the butler (who has an uncanny resemblance to the 1780 Garnett) is also played by the understandably glum McLaughlin. The absurdities abound but there are compensations, although *MFB* found the plot confusing, the direction uneven, the first part dragged, the police court didn't convince and the acting was generally 'colourless', bar Hale and Harker who nevertheless lacked subtlety. *Hyde Park Corner* was produced by Harcourt Templeman for Grosvenor Films at the Regent Studios, Welwyn, and directed by Sinclair Hill. The screenplay was based on the 1934 Walter Hackett play, its adaptation and additional dialogue credited to Selwyn Jepson, although the contribution of D. B. Wyndham-Lewis (who had written Hitchcock's *The Man Who Knew Too Much* the previous year) went uncredited.

DECEMBER

One of several Jack Buchanan pictures long vanished into the mist, **Come Out of the Pantry** squeaked across the bridge that divided comedy film from musical film, being, according to the *MFB*, 'really a musical comedy with the music cut to the minimum. Jack Buchanan sings and dances for perhaps ten minutes and the rest is straight comedy.' Furthermore, the 'musical comedy' dialogue was weak.[37] Rachael Low was no more impressed, describing 'A determinedly mid-Atlantic film about an English aristocrat in America [...] a disappointing film directed with uninspired flatness by Jack Raymond.'[38] Graham Greene's verdict was even more damning, deeming it 'quite meaningless to any but an English audience.'[39]

Buchanan's reputation has so faded that it is difficult to revive its significance, or to suggest his predominance in British stage and film history. Three decades on, Herbert Wilcox, with whom Buchanan often worked, wrote, 'There is no one like Jack Buchanan in the film world today. Charming, handsome beyond description, and masculinely [*sic*] virile to a degree, I doubt if we shall see his like again. For elegance and charm he stood alone [...] I doubt if any member of the theatrical profession ever did as much for the down-and-out troupers as Jack. They would line up on Saturday night and seldom go away without something for a meal and a drink.'[40]

As British and Dominions' producer, Wilcox was at the helm of *Come Out of the Pantry*, directed by Raymond whose early work on *Splinters* had sounded the British musical film its starting pistol. Austin Parker and Douglas Furber adapted Alice Duer Miller's novel *Come Out of the Kitchen*, which had already turned up as a Broadway play and as a 1919 American silent. A firm believer in cinematic recycling, Wilcox made a sort of remake for Anna Neagle in 1948, renaming it *Spring in Park Lane*. That version with its impossibly smart impersonation of British post-war dullness has retained some of its post-war romantic appeal while the Buchanan original has withered, perhaps leaving in its wake memories of the two Sigler, Goodhart and Hoffman numbers 'Everything Stops For Tea' and 'From One Minute To Another', delivered in the star's usual delicately brushing manner.

Wilcox's intention was to beguile the American market (changing from 'kitchen' to 'pantry' tells the lie). The aristocratic Robert Brent (Buchanan), made unexpectedly penniless by a bank collapse, is in New York. In Central Park he runs into Eccles (Ronald Squire), ex-butler to the millionaire Beach-Howard family. Brent gets taken on as a footman, and successfully romances Hilda Beach-Howard (visiting American Fay Wray). Paramount had anyway turned it into a Hollywood musical in 1930. As *Honey*, it was a success for two leading ladies, Nancy Carroll and the inimitable Lillian Roth, with songs by W. Franke Harling and Sam Coslow. In Wilcox's hands, the 1935 film version was made less welcome.

The all-male dance bands of the 1930s were the precursors of the boy bands of a much later day, enjoying a popularity perhaps at its zenith in the inter-war years. British studios made hay while the bands shone. What might at first have seemed nothing more than an easy option, an excuse to build a film around an existent musical entity with some sort of narrative, could in the right hands become something as, or more, inventive and entertaining than a musical film built around other components. Of course, production values varied tremendously; we see the results of such disparate treatment in picture after picture.

The personalities of the different bandleaders matched that of many of the musical performers of the decade. There was the integrity of meeting Henry Hall or Ambrose or, as in the excellent ***She Shall Have Music***, Jack Hylton, in a semblance of how they were in real life and when backed by their 'boys'. The film was a family affair for Twickenham, directed by a major shareholder of the studio Leslie S. Hiscott, and employing Victor Trytel (W. L. Trytel was already the permanent supervisor of the studio's music) as assistant director.

Hagen's in-house writer H. Fowler Mear**,** joke book at hand, concocted a screenplay with Arthur Macrae, who would go on to write light comedies and material for London revues; their script was worked up from a storyline by Paul England and the busy actor-writer C. Denier Warren. The plot was built loosely around Hylton's plan to take his band broadcasting on a world cruise. The jigsaw motif at the top of the film neatly suggests the way the film has been put together. 'I've always wanted my own theatre', says Hylton.

He would become one of the major impresarios in the West End, his name synonymous with some of the greatest names in showbusiness. In 'Sailing Along On A Carpet Of Clouds', he has the advantage not only of his superb musicians that include Brian Lawrence (who in 1937 would appear in *Variety Hour* and *Sing As You Swing*), but of the always welcome June Clyde as perky songstress Dorothy Drew. Silly ass Claude Dampier is on board for some of his odd-ball comedy, apparently in demand during the 1930s. It may be untrue that he developed his hesitant, muddle-headed style as a means of being kept by studios for longer than he had been contracted. Dampier's dialogue is no worse than most of the rest, with Fowler Mear's witticisms up to standard: 'You've had a wire from the Kennel Club – Bow Wow!'

The story fades as the ship travels the world, Venice, Spain, Vienna, and on, each location appropriately suggested in James A. Carter's clever sets. It is in the acts that join the travels of 'The Band That Jack Built' that the film excels: the soprano-voiced blind performer Alec Templeton in 'Merry Month Of May'; Australian singer Magda Neeld; exotic dancer Mathea Merryfield (her gravestone remembered her as 'a Beauty and the Toast of Europe'); the cruelly choreographed Dalmora Can-Can Dancers; a touch of the classical in the Leon Woizikowski Ballet, and some terrifyingly precocious examples of Terry's Juveniles, with two scarily masked nightmare-inducing infants, at the close. The bewildering selection of turns was knocked into shape by choreographer Howard Deighton. The numbers include 'Don't Ask Me Any Questions', 'May All Your Troubles Be Little Ones', 'My First Thrill', 'Nothing On Earth', 'The Runaround', 'The Hylton Stomp', 'Why Did She Fall For The Leader Of The Band?' and Diana Ward singing 'Moaning Minnie'.

Producer John Clein's Time Pictures seems not to have survived beyond its one and only 1930s entry, **Two Hearts in Harmony**. The frequently indifferent *MFB* suggested the picture might be worth seeing, having 'flashes of real interest' in 'a pleasingly contrived film with some deeper value'.[41] Directed by the prolific William Beaudine, whose achievements would include some of the best of the Will Hay comedies, this second-drawer effort was filmed at Shepperton with the top-billed Californian Bernice Claire as yet another example of that stock character, the nightclub cabaret singer. The American press had welcomed her in First National's 1930 film of the Oscar Hammerstein-Herbert Stothart-George Gershwin operetta *The Song of the Flame*; she was 'not the Hollywood type of beauty, but she has a great deal of charm and her singing is most beguiling'.[42] In that film, her character had sparked a Russian revolution, but nothing revolutionary came out of the more sedate *Two Hearts in Harmony*.

Adapted by Robert Edmunds and A. R. Rawlinson from a story by Samuel Gibson Browne, it followed the fortunes of chanteuse Micky (Claire) who wants to better herself, getting a job as governess to young Bobby (Paul Hartley), the son of wealthy hedonist Lord Sheldon (played by highly born George Curzon). Micky has a chastening influence on the pleasure-craving life of her employer, resulting in the expected marital outcome. Some puppetry attracts notice, as well as the songs 'Just In Between' by Chick Endor and Charlie Farrell, 'Long Live Love' by Eddie Pola and Franz Vienna (otherwise known as Franz Steininger), and 'Don't Go On A Diet'. American bandleader Jack Harris and his boys enliven the nightclub scenes, which include a song *intended* as tasteless. This was too much for Mr J. Stevens of Liverpool, who wrote to *Picturegoer* protesting against 'the cheap vulgarity so evident in many of the British-made films on view at present'.[43]

The charming cover belies a correspondent's complaint that *Two Hearts in Harmony* (1935) was guilty of 'cheap vulgarity'

1936

Gay and Carter's title song is pure joy; the sense of absolute enjoyment suffuses the picture *Cheer Up!*

Stars on Parade
Ball at Savoy
Limelight
Sunshine Ahead
Cheer Up!
Queen of Hearts
When Knights Were Bold
Soft Lights and Sweet Music
Jack of All Trades
Public Nuisance No. 1
Beloved Impostor
Faithful
King of Hearts
Happy Days Are Here Again
Forget-Me-Not
Melody of My Heart
It's Love Again
Shipmates o' Mine
Men of Yesterday
Everything Is Rhythm
She Knew What She Wanted
A Star Fell from Heaven

The Robber Symphony
Dodging the Dole
Annie Laurie
Calling the Tune
Guilty Melody
Keep Your Seats, Please
Rhythm in the Air
Song of Freedom
Gypsy Melody
The Beloved Vagabond
Southern Roses
Land Without Music
Everybody Dance
Live Again
The Last Waltz
Dreams Come True
This'll Make You Whistle
Everything in Life
Variety Parade
Sporting Love
Pagliacci
Murder at the Cabaret

JANUARY

It is unlikely that Oswald Mitchell is much mentioned in scholarly discussions of British film directors, but we owe him a debt. Mitchell's interest in the slightly tatty world of music hall and variety is a cornerstone of his work. It could not be more obvious than in his third picture, Butcher's Film Services' *Stars on Parade*, following on from his 1934 *Danny Boy* and the 1935 *Cock o' the North*. What makes *Stars on Parade* so appealing is that Mitchell and his co-director and editor Challis Sanderson make no attempt at a credible threading story. The turns that turned up to be filmed at Cricklewood are a fascinating collection that includes performers whose reputations have endured, and lesser immortals for whom Mitchell's little film provides a resting place. Some, indeed, qualify as 'wines and spirits', the theatrical term reserved for those performers whose names (like the details of available alcoholic beverages) were printed in the smallest type at the bottom of a variety bill.

Among the less remembered are 'Radio's Schoolgirl Sweetheart Pat Hyde', accompanying herself on the accordion in 'Only A Shanty In Old Shanty Town'; laid-back brothers Syd and Max Harrison with their acrobatic dancing; and the soprano street singer Pat O'Brien singing the Irish favourite 'Old Fashioned Mother Of Mine'. 'Go on, Pat O'Brien', urges music-hall veteran Albert Whelan (he of the signature music for 'The Three Bears') to 'make us cry', and – decades later – he still may. The Australian vocal impersonator Navarre does some sophisticated imitations of Tauber and Chevalier and – with Mitchell seemingly intent on giving his audience a dose of 'serious' music – Debroy Somers's band hammers out some Wagner and the popular bits of Rossini's overture to *William Tell*. Here and there, matters are interrupted by the expert drunkenness of Jimmy James, renowned for his inebriated comedy in an era when drunkenness was played on stage and film for easy laughs.

Mitchell has greater treats in store. Here is the illusionist Horace Goldini in an act of glacial precision, pulling rabbits and birds from thin air, and disappearing his female assistant. Goldini is reputed to be the man who invented the illusion of sawing a woman in half, advertising for volunteers and offering $10,000 per victim if the experiment should prove fatal. Then, there is the *tableau vivant* of 'The Superb Act', two human figures, two dogs and a compliant horse, all powdered white, posing stock still and silent in a series of attitudes, among them 'Retrieving', 'The Rose of No Man's Land' and 'Tranquillity'. In an age when attitudes to animal training are very different from those in the 1930s, these make for difficult viewing.

It is however in its comedy that *Stars on Parade* excels in two particulars, the first being Robb Wilton's ageless policeman sketch, and secondly in a 'complete' filming of the stage sketch 'Bridget's Night Out', with Arthur Lucan as firebrand Mrs O'Flynn (he would not adopt the name of 'Old Mother Riley' until after filming *Kathleen Mavourneen* in 1937) waiting up late at night for the return of her socially ambitious daughter Kitty, played by Lucan's wife, the notoriously tough Kitty McShane. This is the centrepiece of Mitchell's film, an invaluable record of Lucan's superlative clowning in a type of female impersonation that has long vanished. A protracted study of verbal and acrobatic nonsense, it reaches its apogee in a savage pot-breaking sequence and the old woman's emotional breakdown. At this point, McShane's ineptitude threatens to ruin the illusion, so uncomfortably does she begin crooning a lullaby, 'Goodnight Mother'. But the mastery of what has gone before, witness to Lucan's genius, cannot be denied. His brilliance was inevitably diminished in the long series of 'Old Mother Riley' comedies that Lucan went on to make until as late as 1952.

Operetta aficionados may have welcomed **Ball at Savoy**, the British remake of the German *Ball im Savoy* directed by Steve Sekely and starring Gitta Alpár and Hans Jaray. The original theatre work by Hungarian composer Paul Abrahám had played successfully in Berlin in 1932. By the time of Stafford Films' production at Elstree, Abrahám, in common with many others, had been hounded from Germany. Never establishing himself so solidly as Lehár or Kálmán, Abrahám nevertheless provided 'a bit of foreign colour, a profusion of catchy 1920s dance tunes not necessarily reflecting the time or the place of the action, and languorous "pop" love songs – generally with a "sophisticated" foreign phrase as the title'.[1] The operetta, renamed *Ball at the Savoy*, played in London at Drury Lane in September 1933.

The screenplay by Akos Tolnay and Reginald Long based on the original version by Alfred Grünwald and Fritz Löhner-Beda was directed at Elstree by W. Victor Hanbury, with the imported glamour of Marta Labarr and Conrad Nagel in leading roles. Cannes is agog at the arrival of prima donna Anita Stella (Labarr) who is to appear at a charity concert. British diplomat John Egan (Nagel) attends, passing himself off as a Baron Dupont. With the intervention of waiter George (Fred Conyngham), the scene is set for the not unusual mix of romantic complication and mistaken identity, with the almost obligatory theft of some jewellery thrown in. Labarr's singing, the acting of Nagel, and the hoofing of Conyngham and his dancing partner Lu Anne Meredith drew praise, but otherwise the film was 'slow, tortuous, and almost entirely lacking in even superficial logic'. As much, of course, could be said of a great number of other entries of the period. *MFB* also sniffed at the 'odds and ends of "naughty" by-play' as being 'pointless'.[2] Labarr sang 'C'est Vous', 'King Of My Heart' and 'Wake Smiling'. Elsewhere, Nagel sang 'I Can't Do Without You', and Conyngham and Meredith essayed the 'Rio De Janeiro'.

There was not much better reception for **Limelight**, another item in producer Herbert Wilcox's determination to make a star of Anna Neagle; now, the film was vaguely based on an incident in her own career, written up by Laura Whetter. David Shipman describes this as one of the director's 'ratty' musicals.[3] The other intention of *Limelight* was to make a film star of Neagle's co-star Arthur Tracy, according to the publicity department a 'Musical Sensation', known to the public as 'The Street Singer', with his predilection for the most sentimental and trite of ditties such as 'In A Little Gypsy Tea Room' and 'It's My Mother's Birthday Today'. When the film reached America as *Backstage*, *Variety* suggested that 'as a romantic actor he leaves much to be desired'.[4] Tracy had proved popular at the London Palladium; Wilcox seemed unbothered that his stiffness on screen was almost catatonic. By the time he got around to his autobiography, Wilcox had either forgotten or ignored the film.

Whetter's script, such as it was, concerns showgirl Marjorie Kaye (a little close to real life, as Neagle's name had been Marjorie Robertson until Wilcox reinvented her) who brings street-singing busker Bob Grant (Tracy) into the company when the leading man drops out. This goes to Bob's head (and possibly to Tracy's), and confusion abounds. The situation recalled Wilcox's backstage visit to Jack Buchanan when Wilcox was looking for a new leading lady, and Buchanan recommended chorus girl Marjorie Robertson. Buchanan's brief appearance as himself acknowledges that link. *Limelight* has not enjoyed the continuing affection of the British public in the way that other of Neagle's films have, while Tracy is all but forgotten. The following year, he made *The Street Singer* with Margaret Lockwood.

Meanwhile, those on set for *Limelight* included the legendary ballerina Tilly Losch in a Javanese dance, theatrical historian W. MacQueen-Pope, Geraldo and his Sweet Music, the Hippodrome Girls, and choreographer Ralph Reader who partnered Neagle in her routines. Tracy probably needed little encouragement to deliver his theme song, 'Marta – Rambling Rose Of The Wild Wood'. Also included was Arthur Wood's 'The Sandman's Serenade' and two numbers that *Variety* thought standouts, Tracy's torch song 'Stranded' and the 'Whistling Waltz' around which was mounted a lavish sequence. Tracy 'also has a drunk scene and about six lines to speak, which would make his performance, I suppose, what is known as acting'.[5]

Only fit for 'the unsophisticated, industrial and provincial patron',[6] John Baxter and John Barter's **Sunshine Ahead** was Wallace Orton's only directorial credit, working to a screenplay by Con West and Geoffrey Orme loosely constructed around the efforts of a programme organiser (Eddie Pola) to produce a variety show at 'UK Radio'. Once again, a British film studio in the mid-1930s centres itself on radio; had nothing really changed since *Elstree Calling*? The producer's ambitions are thwarted by a journalist critic, played by that most typecast of pencil-moustached villains Leslie Perrins, but the day is saved when the radio company films at the various locations where the acts are working. Those acts are, it has to be said, of the modest kind, although headed by Jack Payne and His Band, on this occasion dressed up as pirates and singing 'All Jolly Pirates' to prove it. Whiffs of concert party circle around 'The Two Leslies' (Sarony and Holmes), and husband and wife Harry S. Pepper and pianist Doris Arnold, culminating in a spectacular 'Six Piano Jazz Symphony'.

Other treats include the Harmonica Band, the continental flavour of Pasqual Troise and His Mandoliers and Banjoliers, and a burst of classical music with an operatic sequence from Gounod's *Faust*, performed by Ruth Naylor, George Baker and Webster Booth. The original music, agreeable but forgettable, is by Kennedy Russell and lyricist Reg Connelly. Filmed at Cricklewood in fifteen days, *Sunshine Ahead* did not bode well for Orton's future, with *Kinematograph Weekly* complaining that 'There may be sunshine ahead, but this amateurish conception of a jolly radio programme never catches up with it. No ingenuity whatever is displayed in the banding together of the turns; even the items expected to shine are dimmed by cramped staging and raucous sound.'[7] Built on the site of a former aeroplane factory, the Cricklewood studio in Camden was founded by the theatre impresario Oswald Stoll in 1920, when it claimed to be the largest in Britain. By the mid-1930s the studio was best known for turning out quota quickies, and was a favourite location for Butcher's films, including several in the Old Mother Riley series. Although the decade was a productive period at Cricklewood, and a new sound stage was added the year after *Sunshine Ahead*, the studio closed in 1938.

FEBRUARY

The sunny but cold and wet February of 1936 was undoubtedly brightened by the reappearance of Stanley Lupino in a Stanley Lupino Productions' production. *Cheer Up!* declared its intention and seemed intent on achieving it. Lupino's storyline was absurd, naïve and unoriginal, and there was little that Michael Barringer's screenplay could do to disguise it, and nothing to disguise the frequently shambolic choreography organised by Carl Hyson and Leslie Roberts. It did, however, have one of the nicest scores of the decade, with music by Billy Mayerl, Noel Gay and Val Guest, with Lupino, Frank Eyton and Desmond Carter as lyricists, the music arranged by Percival Mackey and His Orchestra.

Lupino plays musical show writer Tom Denham who, with his writing partner Dick Dirk (jocular Roddy Hughes) has written a show, 'London Town'. Short of funds in a café, they compose an off-the-cuff (and quite possibly off the menu) song 'Steak And Kidney Pudding', a typically slight but pleasing Mayerl-Eyton number. Failing to get work as an actress, showgirl Sally (Sally Gray) gets a job as a maid to a failed financier and his wife. After misadventures, Tom gets his show, and Sally. Whatever we may think of the extract we see, 'London Town' is a great success.

The comedy is unlikely to have patrons rolling in the aisles, but *Cheer Up!* is highly enjoyable. It takes place in that social hinterland that is Lupino's natural home. Strapped for cash, Tom and Dick begin in abject poverty, involving scenes in which they most unappealingly appear in their underwear, before experiencing the ersatz glamour of those exorbitantly expensive nightclubs beloved of 1930s British film studios. The social transition is apparently necessary if they are to achieve their ambition: theatrical triumph. The social devices in use throughout *Cheer Up!* would have been scarcely recognisable, and almost certainly not available, to the majority of its cinema-going audience. The only success to be esteemed here is metropolitan, and precariously appointed to take place within a proscenium arch that its director Leo Mittler can hardly be expected to disguise.

Despite its utter artificiality and absurdities, or perhaps because of them, *Cheer Up!* doesn't outlive its welcome as many other British theatrical backstage pictures of the period do. This is in no small way due to the generous peppering of musical numbers. Mayerl and Eyton go on to contribute Gray's solo 'There's A Star In The

Stanley Lupino forgetting the nation's troubles in *Cheer Up!* (1936)

Sky', imaginatively photographed by Curt Courant in a hall of mirrors where other voices sing back at Gray, and female models present a West End dress parade of chic evening gowns. One can almost sense the intended titillation of this, as if Lupino's working- and middle-class audiences were being shown something so sophisticated as to be unattainable. It's one of the film's cleverest tricks, as the supremely plummy singing voice of Gray (if not dubbed) inhabits the fantasy.

Gay and Carter's title song is pure joy; the sense of absolute enjoyment suffuses the picture. Somehow, Mittler, the décor of J. Elder Wills, the sound engineering of A. D. Valentine, photography and choreography, shine on screen. The clarity and precision of Roddy Hughes's introduction to the song at the piano have a lifelike quality. When Lupino starts his frog-like dancing, Hughes plays along. Outside in the garden, a crowd of passers-by dance in the rain under their umbrellas in another of Hyson and Roberts's makeshift routines. There is rather more precision when Tom and Sally dine in a classy hotel. For some reason, a wedding cake sits on the table. When they celebrate their 'Pleasant Meeting' the confection comes to life in an Arcadian ballet that may be said to be the icing on the cake. At last, we get to see what appears to be the closing number of Tom and Dick's smash-hit musical, 'London Town', credited to Val Guest. It would be easy to criticise the finale's choreography, just as slapdash as what has gone before, but the cavorting of lawyers, Chelsea Pensioners, scouts and guides, street-hawkers, policemen, and the coming to life of a waxworks, zip along to a conclusion that has Lupino and Gray in an Astaire-Rogers moment, slipping and looping across the rooftops of London. This film has a marvellously friendly exuberance, exemplified in Carter's simple lyric for the title song:

> I've got a philosophy to share with you:
> Clouds that are dull and dreary
> Cover a sky of blue.
> You've only to wait until the clouds roll past
> Don't let your heart grow weary
> Nothing that's bad can last.
>
> Cheer up!
> The skies are gonna clear up
> So everybody cheer up, it's gonna be fine.
> Wake up!
> The skies are gonna break up
> So give yourself a shake-up
> It's gonna be fine.
>
> All the animals in the ark
> Said although it looks wet and dark
> When we reach the high-water mark
> The sun will shine
>
> So, cheer up!
> Give every kind of fear up
> The skies are gonna clear up
> It's gonna be fine.

Whatever happens to Gracie Fields, even when she is catapulted from being a humble seamstress entertaining people at a tea-stall to a West End musical star decked out in crinolines big enough to conceal several families, she is still undeniably 'our Gracie'. She is our Gracie throughout Associated Talking Pictures' ***Queen of Hearts***. The emotions she conveys as she sings eclipse artifice or directorial advice; she delivers complete emotional disclosure, in which nothing is allowed to come between artist and onlooker. If we are talking *souls*, the most 'ordinary' of people can identify with her, relate to the fanciful goings-on on screen, because Fields exposes her own. Rachael Low notes that Fields 'was given an adoring suitor [John Loder as a star of West End musicals!] and a romantic ending [with more than a passing resemblance to Toytown]. In view of her very broad slapstick in a wild car ride and a grotesque apache dance this adoration is rather difficult to believe, despite apparent effort to make her look softer and more appealing.'[8]

Once again, Fields was produced by Basil Dean, now working alongside director Monty Banks (his first Fields film; he would marry her). Their professional pairing bore great results in a piece that never stops moving, although *MFB* was not over-enthusiastic, conceding that his direction 'is straightforward and workmanlike', and 'while not outstanding' resulted in a thoroughly entertaining film of its kind.[9] Banks turns up as a pugnacious passer-by in the street and as a flagrantly melodramatic actor of the Victorian school in a cod-theatrical scene. Dean and Banks bring together a superb team of comedy actors who know how this material needs to be performed – a parade that offers little Tom Payne as the stage-door keeper, lugubrious Syd Crossley as a much-put-about policeman, a thoroughly flustered Hal Gordon and – always welcome as she majestically fills the screen – the slightly sinister Margaret Yarde.

The 'original screenplay' is by Clifford Grey and H. F. Maltby (briefly seen as a spluttering solicitor). Anthony Kimmins is credited with dialogue, and Douglas Furber with additional dialogue, with Gordon Wellesley as 'scenario editor'. The score by Fields's most associated composer Harry Parr Davies, and Will E. Haines and Jimmy Harper, includes the finale title number, a typically Lancastrian comedy item in 'Orphans Of The Storm', and Fields's ballads 'Why Did I Have To Meet You?' and 'Do You Remember My First Love Song?' During one of Fields's impromptu performances in the street, we have the rare chance to see Davies at the piano. *The Times* remarked that 'It is a far cry from *Modern Times* to *Queen of Hearts*, yet Miss Gracie Fields and Mr Chaplin have much in common.'[10] When *Queen of Hearts* was launched at the New Paramount Theatre in Tottenham Court Road, a 'typical Lancashire lunch' was laid on – a spread of kippers, tripe and jam, shrimps, winkles and onions. It was perhaps appropriate for the premiere of a movie that would 'place Miss Fields among the custard-pie immortals.'[11]

Freed from his contractual agreement with Herbert Wilcox, Jack Buchanan had one of his greatest successes with ***When Knights Were Bold***, produced by Max

Schach and directed by Jack Raymond (*Splinters*) for Capitol Films. The 1906 play by Harriet Jay (writing as Charles Marlowe) had already been used for two British silents, in 1916 when Maurice Elvey directed James Welch as the hero, and in 1929 when Wilcox cast Nelson Keys. Now, the screenplay by Austin Parker and Douglas Furber reunited Buchanan with Fay Wray, who had played opposite him in the 1935 *Come Out of the Pantry*. Buchanan glides through these proceedings with consummate ease.

He plays Sir Guy De Vere, ex-Indian army, returning to England on his inheritance of the family's estate at Little Twittering, where he faces a stuffy bunch of relatives. Hoping to liven life up a little, he throws a party at which he is concussed by a suit of medieval armour. His dreams of the chivalric life of the fifteenth century come true when he is transported through time, which happily allows him to romance his attractive cousin Rowena (Wray). Some madcap, surreal scenes involving an assault on the family castle by soldiers on fantastical bicycles add to the fun, but Buchanan remains its *raison d'être*, ambling rather than dancing his way through it all. 'I'm Still Dreaming', he sings, reprising the melody in an apparently effortless shuffle, and goes on to sing 'Let's Put The People To Work' and, with a chorus of soldiers, 'Onward We Go'. Two teams were responsible for the score: Harry Perritt and George Windeatt, and the better-known Sigler, Goodhart and Hoffman.

There was a mixed critical reaction. Showering praise on Buchanan, the *Manchester Guardian* reported that the 'direction often seems ponderous and the jokes as subtle as a blow with a knuckle-duster, but it is hard to describe as clumsy a production which succeeds so fully in its object'.[12] Low recalled that 'A dream sequence of the days of chivalry and a relaxed performance from Buchanan pleased his fans but the film was slow and full of comedy clichés and in future Schach was to steer clear of middling British directors like Jack Raymond'.[13] There was a muted response to its reissue in 1942, when the *Daily Express* reported that 'the film script is a rare triumph of unimaginativeness'.[14] The *New York Times* considered it 'a pointless trifle, a minor vaudeville skit […] Why expose a blunder which had better be forgot?'[15] For the *Observer*, 'a lot of the time it is distinctly funny'.[16]

British Lion's ***Soft Lights and Sweet Music***, directed by Herbert Smith, remains a valuable social document. Yet again, the British musical film looked to radio for its material. Austen Croom-Johnson had first presented the BBC radio programme *Soft Lights and Sweet Music* in 1934. In the *Radio Times* schedules it stood out as up-to-the-moment in popular music against what else was available to the listening British public, as a glance at an August day's broadcasting indicates.

12.00	The Whitby Municipal Orchestra
1.00	Organ Recital

1936 157

1.45	Midland Studio Orchestra
3.00	Torquay Municipal Orchestra
4.30	Chelsea String Quartet
6.30	Gershom Parkington Quartet
8.00	Promenade Concert

Finally at 10.30, Sydney Kyte and His Band direct from the Piccadilly Hotel. Cinemagoers had already had a dose of Gershom Parkington, when that stoic band of musicians rubbed shoulders with variety turns in *Music Hall*, and at 6.30 in the evening must have had a decidedly soporific effect on anyone tuning in. It was much more appropriate that Kyte's Piccadilly Hotel band should polish the day off, as various other of the popular and less well-known dance bands did before broadcasting shut down for the night. One of the best-loved bands was Ambrose – *Bert* Ambrose –who was at the heart of the film *Soft Lights and Sweet Music*. Vocalist Jack Cooper summed it up by singing 'We're Tops On Saturday Night'.

The splendid assortment of acts is loosely compered at 'Cowbridge Hall', an institution for very mature students presided over by Harry Tate, who subsequently appears in one of his 'motoring' sketches. Among the Cowbridge students are the Western Brothers posing as two of the unlikeliest TV engineers you could imagine, and performing two of their topical numbers, 'After All That' and 'Don't Be A Cad' as they 'televise' the various turns around London. Evelyn Dall fires on all cylinders in 'Lost My Rhythm, Lost My Music, Lost My Man' and 'I'm All In'; Elisabeth Welch, fresh from her triumphant contributions to Ivor Novello's *Glamorous Night* at Drury Lane, sings 'Yesterday's Thrill'; the classy Turner Layton sings at the piano 'My SOS To You'; Wilson, Keppel and Betty sand-dance; 'Hollywood Beauties' parade, direct from the Dorchester Hotel. We also have the Five Charladies; young Jimmy Fletcher in a cover version of Arthur Tracy's oleaginous 'It's My Mother's Birthday Today (I'm On My Way With A Lovely Bouquet'); the Four Flash Devils in 'Nola'; Donald Stewart singing 'South American Joe'; and Max Bacon discovered at his studio stall down the Mile End Road after some stock footage of the real thing, performing 'Cohen The Crooner'. The most extraordinary of all is the bewilderingly elastic Karina in an apache dance.

The British public's affection for Jack Hulbert was strong enough to attract it to the series of films whose titles traded on the friendly reaction to the star's name; as the first in 1932 had declared, *Jack's the Boy*. When the action was all at sea, it had been *Jack Ahoy*. In 1934 he was *another* Jack (Campbell) in *The Camels Are Coming*. By 1935 he was *Bulldog Jack*, before graduating to **Jack of All Trades** (alias Jack Warrender) for Michael Balcon at Gainsborough, filmed at Islington and at the Welwyn Shredded Wheat Factory. As with many of his theatrical and film projects, this had Hulbert's fingerprints all over it, as co-director with Robert Stevenson, and co-author of dialogue with Austin Melford. The screenplay by J.

O. C. (John) Orton based on Paul Vulpius's play *Youth at the Helm* was helpfully littered with numbers by Sigler, Goodhart and Hoffman, 'You're Sweeter Than You Thought You Were', 'Where There's You There's Me' and the deliciously period 'Tap Your Tootsies', an open invitation for Jack to do just that, taking the song over from Bruce Seton and Betty Astell at a nightclub in a looping, lanky dance that may partly have been arranged by Philip Buchel but was possibly done on the hoof by Hulbert.

The plot is of little interest, with Jack a beguiling con man who bluffs his way into working with banker Lionel Fitch (Robertson Hare). Jack's schemes enrich the bank, but when he is exposed as a fraud his affairs are taken over by Frances Wilson (Gina Malo). Matters are resolved after a splendidly madcap sequence with Jack as a fireman battling with a hose (accompanied by 'Pop Goes The Weasel') and a moving walkway (to a Post Horn Gallop). The last of Jack's solo films was entertaining enough, but for some the absence of Cicely Courtneidge would have meant disappointment; the couple would be reunited the following year for one of their best efforts, *Take My Tip*.

On stage two years earlier, Frances Day and Arthur Riscoe had been a winning combination in the Vivian Ellis musical *Jill Darling* at the Saville Theatre. Ellis wrote music and lyrics for **Public Nuisance No. 1**, with Day and Riscoe now presented as Frances Travers and Arthur Rawlings. Produced at Beaconsfield by Herman Fellner and presented by C. M. Wolf for the Cecil Film Corporation, this self-styled 'musical extravaganza' was directed by Marcel Varnel. It's not a wholly satisfactory experience.

Riscoe's appeal hasn't aged well, especially when saddled with schoolboy humour. 'Hold up your right hand', commands a policeman; 'Why?' demands Riscoe. 'I don't want to go anywhere!' As a romantic lead, he is a non-runner. Whatever magic happened on stage when he and Day met isn't much in evidence in a film that hasn't much of a plot but plenty of 'unsatisfactory material',[17] built around a silly story about Riscoe working as a waiter at his rich uncle's swanky hotel in Nice. Before leaving England, he has fallen for Day, for whom he arranges to win a holiday … in Nice. At least this gives her the excuse to arrive at the 'Blue Mediterranean Sea' wearing a stunning all-white creation.

The most enjoyable moments of the film show off Ellis's happy score, with an extended musical sequence for Day's arrival in Nice, as well as her lost-in-the-fog 'Me And My Dog', a song Ellis had written specifically for her. C. A. Lejeune agreed that Day's career was indeed stuck in a fog. The film opens in an epitome of those London nightclubs so familiar to fans of Stanley Lupino that one expects his pop-eyes to stare out at you at any moment. Instead, we have a disgracefully inebriated Riscoe rolling about singing 'Hotsy Totsy' as chaos breaks out around him. As usual, the audience is invited to roar with laughter at ungovernable drunkenness, there being little wit to be found elsewhere outside of Ellis's 'Between You And Me

And The Carpet', 'Swing' and 'Give Me A Place In the Sun'. Val Guest's scenario and dialogue was based on an idea by Franz Arnold. C. A. Lejeune regretted that Day 'goes from one bad farce to another bad farce, with little direction and less opportunity'.[18] Day may not have been at her happiest, having been suspended from her Gaumont-British contract; working for Cecil Films at Beaconsfield must have seemed like a professional demotion. Ultimately, she was obliged to pay damages to her old studio for having worked for Fellner. He ran into financial difficulties and killed himself shortly after the release of *Public Nuisance No. 1*.

MARCH

Stafford Films' quota quickie **Beloved Impostor**, based on Ethel Mannin's *Dancing Boy*, was produced by John Stafford and directed at Welwyn by Victor Hanbury. Ambitious waiter George (Fred Conyngham) hopes to make his way as a cabaret star in London, where he is taken in by kindly Mary (Rene Ray). Like so many young ambitious males in British musical films of the period, he prefers the allure of a sultry cabaret star, in this case 'La Lumiere' (played by French import Germaine Aussey), to the more homely Mary. When La Lumiere's light begins to fade for him, George fights her and is haunted by the certainty that she is dead. The sympathetic Mary stands by him. In fact, La Lumiere is alive and probably kicking, and George is able to return to Mary and his career in cabaret. Ray is equally at home in *Please Teacher* and *Street Song* as when playing the tweeny in *The Passing of the Third Floor Back* in which she gave one of her finest performances. When Hollywood turned her down for *Rebecca* she wrote novels, including the science fiction *The Strange World of Planet X*, made into an early Hammer horror. Conyngham's personality is not vivid but he's a pleasing presence, and he and Ray make an attractive team. Space is made for appearances by Gwen Farrar (her only other British films were *She Shall Have Music* and the 1937 *Take a Chance*), Leslie (Hutch) Hutchinson singing 'Nothing But Dreams', the acrobatic Calgary Brothers, and Bombardier Billy Wells.

In Britain, director Paul L. Stein's reputation was enhanced by the highly successful *Blossom Time* and *Heart's Desire*. It seemed good sense for producer Irving Asher to hire him for Warner Bros' first musical film to be made outside of America, at the Teddington studios. Those directors so often responsible for domestic product sometimes lacked Stein's natural aptitude for continental sensibility. As Christian Cargnelli has written, Stein was

> just what a real Viennese, in a way, is all about. Charm alone, however, will not get you anywhere if you are a director; experience, especially in working with actors, meticulous casting, organisational skills – in one word, craftsmanship – certainly will. In

his British films Paul Stein continued to do what he had previously, and successfully, done in Germany and Hollywood: he tried to bring out the best in his actors.[19]

The reception for *Faithful* suggests that on this occasion Stein's charm may not have pulled off the trick. Brock Williams's screenplay is almost a mirror image of the plot of *Beloved Impostor*. The Viennese singer Carl Koster (the distinguished German Hans Sonker) marries musical student Marilyn (the Scots-American Jean Muir). He embarks on an ambitious career in London's nightclubs. Alas, just like dissatisfied George in *Beloved Impostor*, he is distracted by the siren attractions of a glamorous woman, played by Chili Bouchier, no longer Herbert Wilcox's preferred leading lady. Kindly impresario Danny Reeves (a straight role for matinee idol Gene Gerrard) persuades Carl to see the light despite being in love with Marilyn himself. Pierre Neuville's score includes a number for Sonker, 'For You, Madonna', with a lyric by Percy Edgar. *Picturegoer* noted 'a slight romantic comedy […] cut to a pattern',[20] while *MFB* thought the story 'extremely obvious' and found Bouchier's vamp 'weak', sniffily commenting that a few things about the film 'rescue it from absolute mediocrity'.[21]

Based on Matthew Boulton's play *The Corduroy Diplomat*, **King of Hearts**, produced by Butcher's at Cricklewood, was primarily the work of director Oswald Mitchell, co-writing with Walter Tennyson. Beyond the fact that it had one of the most respected of music-hall artists as its star, it is of little interest today. Will Fyffe was one of the busiest of his generation, as successful in films as on stage and on gramophone records. In its modest way, *King of Hearts* has some significance as social document, dealing with British class prejudices. Lowly waitress May Saunders (Gwenllian Gill) is in love with middle-class Jack Ponsonby (Richard Dolman), much to the dismay of his socially superior parents (Amy Veness and O. B. Clarence at their snootiest). They do their utmost to break the couple up, but May's wily old docker father Bill (Fyffe) is determined to keep them together. Relief from this sociological turmoil comes from the Spanish performer José Frakson, known for his table trick magic with cigarettes and for the 'Vanishing Birdcage' illusion, along with exhibition dancers Constance, Lilyan and Mayo, and Java's Tzigane Band. Heartily made in Butcher's friendliest manner, *King of Hearts*, with its naïve but well-meaning shot at tackling social divisions leavened by variety turns, must have found a ready response from certain types of audience. Horace Sheldon, a regular at Butcher's, was responsible for the music.

Happy Days Are Here Again, variously known as *Stage Folk*, *Variety Follies* and *Happy Days Revue*, was yet another backstage ups-and-downs story of failure and success, at least with a grain of authenticity as its stars were the genuine variety article The Houston Sisters: Renee, Shirley and Billie, now playing Kitty, Nita and Mickey. The sisters may not be well remembered, but two performers – Ida Barr and Marie Kendall – who featured in Dan Birt, F. H. Bickerton and Alan Rennie's screenplay rank with the music-hall greats, and were rarely lured into British studios. It is a particular pleasure to find Ida Barr, sometimes-billed 'Britain's Premier Singer of Rag-Time Melodies', who had introduced 'Everybody's Doin' It' and 'Oh, You Beautiful Doll' to domestic audiences. Somewhat oddly, director Norman Lee has her singing 'Fall In And Follow Me' and a male impersonator number 'Put Me Among The Girls'. Also featured is Marie Kendall whose 'Just Like The Ivy' had been a highlight of John Baxter's *Say It with Flowers*; she reprises it here. Others include speciality act Bert and Michael Kidd, and Syd Seymour and His Mad Hatters. The film was produced by John Argyle for Argyle Talking Pictures, and Guy Jones was responsible for the music, although the best-known item was the popular title song, joining 'The Toy Drum Major', the 'Topsy Turvy Blues', 'A Bench Beneath The Tree', 'Hey There, Circus Clown', 'If You Haven't Got A Train' and 'Rhythm'.

British studios of the 1930s were eager to sign up internationally renowned male singers, among them Richard Tauber (*Blossom Time*, *Heart's Desire*, *Land Without Music*, *Pagliacci*), Joseph Schmidt (*My Song Goes Round the World*, *A Star Fell from Heaven*) and Jan Kiepura (*City of Song*, *My Heart Is Calling*). One of the greatest, Beniamino Gigli, made only one British film, a remake of the 1935 German *Vergiss mein nicht*. **Forget-Me-Not** was produced by Alexander Korda and Alberto Giacalone and directed by Zoltan Korda for London Film Productions. The German screenplay by Ernst Marischka was reworked by Hugh Gray and Arthur Wimperis, but although this British version of the bilingual was filmed at the Worton Hall studios in Isleworth, it was not registered as British. The film has considerable charm. Inevitably, it is the voice of Gigli that wins attention as he delivers items from Verdi's *Rigoletto*, Meyerbeer's *L'Africaine* and Donizetti's *L'elisir d'amore* – as well as 'Say You Will Not Forget Me', 'Lullaby', 'Venetian Serenade' and 'Come Back To Me', the original music by Mischa Spoliansky – but outside of these moments *Forget-Me-Not* is worth sitting through.

Opera star Enzo Curti (Gigli), widowed and caring for his young son, meets British secretary Helen Carlton (excellent Joan Gardner) who has begun a shipboard romance with naval officer Hugh Anderson (Ivan Brandt). They make convincing lovers, but when Helen hears Enzo sing she is infatuated. At their first meeting, Helen tells Enzo that she is returning to England the next day. Not wanting her to go, but struggling with expressing himself in English, he tells her, 'Tomorrow, I speak English perfectly'. This leads to one of the most endearing sequences, when a dictionary helps him communicate his feelings. He and Helen marry. Enzo embarks on a world tour, and so on to Covent Garden for *L'elisir d'amore*. Hugh returns to see Helen, begging her to leave with him for Australia. Meanwhile, Hugh's jealous lover Irene (Jeanne Stuart) tells Enzo that Helen is planning to leave him. Desolate, Enzo has to go on stage, but Helen is in the audience, alone in a box. As he is singing the title song, he sees her leaving. Returning home, Enzo lullabies his son to sleep. Helen returns. Gigli may not be the most natural of actors, and clearly struggles with a foreign language and his dictionary, but, supported by a splendid company that includes Charles Carson, Hugh Wakefield and Hay Petrie, he is the beating heart of *Forget-Me-Not*.

APRIL

Incorporated Talking Films' **Melody of My Heart** is basically a rethink of Bizet's *Carmen*, an opera that easily came to mind when a British film studio needed an operatic subject that its audience might just have heard of. Four years earlier, Marguerite Namara had played Carmen in BIP's version of the opera, *Gipsy Blood*. Now Lorraine la Fosse, whose only other British movie was the 1930 *London Melody*, played the oddly renamed heroine Carmel, still (as in Bizet) working at the local cigarette factory, and still torn between two lovers, Joe (Derek Oldham) and Jim (Bruce Seton). Happily, in this update by Brandon Fleming, based on a storyline by Vladimir Shovitch, Carmen (alias Carmel) survives to a happy ending. The film was produced at Cricklewood's Stoll studios by Fleming and George Barclay, and directed by Wilfred Noy. Considerable musical resources were involved, including the London Philharmonic Orchestra, the Covent Garden Opera Chorus and Horace Sheldon's Orchestra, but *Melody of My Heart* did not prove much of a critical or commercial success, despite Oldham's 'Whisper In Your Dreams' and 'I Give You My Love', or Wensley Russell's 'Butcher's Love Song'. In 1954 Hollywood updated Bizet's opera more successfully in *Carmen Jones*, when Dorothy Dandridge played the tragic heroine, singing Oscar Hammerstein II's lyrics.

MAY

According to Victor Saville, **It's Love Again** was 'the best Matthews that I directed, most decidedly due to the original screenplay of Lesser [Samuels] and his American co-author, Marion Dix [Saville overlooked the additional dialogue of Austin Melford], plus a first-class score, words and music by Sam Coslow [and, perhaps Saville forgot, Harry Woods]. It was a gay provocative piece of frivolity and provided Jessie with the opportunity to give the performance of her career.'[22] 'For once', wrote Graham Greene, 'it is possible to praise an English musical above an American. Nor has the long tubular form of Miss Jessie Matthews, the curious charm of her ungainly adolescent carriage, ever been better exploited.'[23] For Low, this was 'gay and tuneful and with outstanding comedy sequences seemed even more successful than the previous film [*First a Girl*]'.[24]

The construct was skilful, beautifully designed by Junge, boosted by the publicity department's excitement at having Robert Young imported from Hollywood to play opposite Matthews, but it meant that Matthews's only authentic dancing partner for the movie was the all but uncredited Cyril Wells. Nevertheless, Young executes a few steps as if preparing himself for a dance competition. To compensate, he brings an assured Hollywood dash that is notably missing from the proceedings.

To get herself noticed, chorus hopeful Elaine Bradford (Matthews) impersonates a character invented by Peter Carlton (Young), Mrs Smythe-Smythe, the sort of woman who bags a tiger or two before breakfast. Making her first public appearance, the glamorous Mrs Smythe-Smythe fascinates the clientele at the Imperial Hotel, one of Junge's most spectacular settings, in a sinuous routine with Wells's gigolo. Carlton is amazed when his invention is reported by the press as a real person. This mystery woman is invited to an Indian-themed soirée given by Mrs Durand (Athene Seyler), to which an authority on the Far East is also invited. Freddie (Sonnie Hale) impersonates an ex-India colonel to prevent Elaine being exposed as an impostor; the party is full of elderly men looking like replicas of Freddie. 'Tony's In Town' features a magnificent giant clockwork elephant. Mrs Durand asks Elaine, aka Mrs Smythe-Smythe, to 'demonstrate the rare temple dances of the East in which she is as you know a renowned expert'. Memories are evoked of Anna May Wong, but the Eastern sounds turn to jazz. Elaine thinks the genuine colonel (nicely cameoed by Robert Hale) is Freddie in disguise. The party culminates in a shoot-out.

One of the most outstanding sequences in a London park is the 'Gotta Dance' number. At last Elaine gets a star part in a musical, but as Mrs Smythe-Smythe. The theme of impersonation that pervades Matthews's *Evergreen* and *First a Girl* provides yet another storyline, one that Matthews's writers and producers seemed fixated on. The impersonation persists up to the opening night of Mrs Smythe-Smythe's London musical. Junge's fantastical tropical stage set for 'I Nearly Let Love Go Slipping Through My Fingers' showcases Matthews in a skin-tight silver cat suit that must have had provincial audiences gaping. C. A. Lejeune thought this 'a piece of utter incompetence laced with the plain vulgar'.[25] Young is sidelined when Wells once again stands in as Matthews's dancing partner. The press is about to expose the deception that has been played on the public. Not surprisingly, Elaine has had enough, and Mrs Smythe-Smythe walks out of the opening night, only to return as Elaine, claiming the stage for a lonely reprise of 'I Nearly Let Love' before going into a frenzied 'Gotta Dance'.

What can have lured prospective customers to sit through ***Shipmates o' Mine***? Not its main players John Garrick and Jean Adrienne, about whom most of the audience knew nothing and cared less; perhaps those of a nautical turn? Produced by Butcher-Empire and concocted by director Oswald Mitchell and George Pearson, this homely offering, based on a story by Ivor Bellas, opened with some tired stock footage of British merchant shipping before taking refuge in the Cricklewood studios. Sailors sing 'Rolling Home', introducing a plot around the fortunes of an ex-Merchant Navy crew. 'I shall be in command at home,' quaffs Lorna (Adrienne), newly married to Jack Denton (Garrick). As for a sailor's wife: 'Yes,' we are told, 'they're wonderful women,' presumably because they have to put up with so much. After a mini-Titanic upset, Jack's ship, the *Neptune*, is abandoned. Momentarily, Mitchell's film lapses into a mini *A Night to Remember* movie, but with rather more limited resources, and a lot of slanting cinematography.

Jack, of course, only abandons ship when there is no alternative: 'Goodbye, old girl.' Back on land, he is arraigned for wrecking his vessel and asked to resign. Disgraced, he seeks his fortune in Australia, where he hears that Lorna, left in England, is dangerously ill. In a drinking den (cue for 'Old Ship Of Mine') he learns of her death. For the next eight years, he works on a farm, bringing up his and Lorna's son Tony (Derek Blomfield) who wants to be (you've guessed) a sailor. At the 'Neptune' reunion dinner at a supposedly sophisticated nightclub, the often-sighted Sherman Fisher Girls appear in skimpy nautical wear, waving mops as they dance. Male sailors pop up in the cabaret to sing 'Ship o' Mine'. The *Neptune* is to be repaired and brought back into commission, and his comrades want Jack as captain. All ends happily when Tony reveals where his father is. Jack is restored to his old ship. He and Tony salute the camera at fade-out.

'The film is slow and drags,' reported the *MFB*, and 'one is constantly conscious of the screen. Especially is this true of the dinner, at which a revue featuring, among others, the Sherman Fisher girls is staged; the dancing is badly photographed, and the whole sentiment of the dancing and singing rings false.'[26] Accurate appraisal as this may be, it is undeniable that *Shipmates o' Mine* is a warm-hearted innocent. Polly Ward, the Horace Sheldon Orchestra, the Radio Male Voice Choir and the superb singing impressionist Navarre with 'The Old Sow – Susan Is A Funniful Man' provide interpolated diversions. *MFB*'s review ended with a sting in the tail, noting that 'The fun supplied by Wallace Lupino, Mark Daly and Frank Atkinson is the one bright spot in the film. Some of the jokes are antiquated besides being crude.'[27]

With reason, John Baxter's working title for his next production was Grimaldi's old pantomime cry *Here We Are Again*, retitled **Men of Yesterday**. Baxter's musical films were not of the integrated type, but dramatic pieces mixed with music-hall and variety. The discarded title would have reminded audiences that Baxter had indeed been here before, with its story about social cohesion, and the decency of humankind, subjects that held this director in thrall throughout his career. The qualities that imbue *Men of Yesterday* were rare in British studios of the time. For this project, he had three stars to relay that message, to help promote what this most workmanlike director could do with a simple film: make of it a political statement against greed, poverty, class distinction, lack of education and the machinations of bad government. It is highly doubtful if the three stars themselves had any inkling of Baxter's intention. In Baxter's film the imported theatrical turns are never allowed to usurp the central purpose. As *MFB* reported, it was not the stars that shone but 'it is on the scores of men appearing as, presumably, themselves, that the film depends so successfully for its broad effects; for detail it depends on genuine people with genuine feelings'.[28]

The very title suggests the retrospective nature of *Men of Yesterday*; as so often with Baxter, there is this sense of things not being as good as they once were, and for a great number of the population living through the depression of the 1930s it was an understandable reading. *Men of Yesterday* belongs with some of Baxter's finest early work such as *Doss House*, the non-musical *A Real Bloke* (perfectly cast in George Carney) and *Say It with Flowers*, but is directly linked to his first feature of 1932 *Reunion*, and the 1934 *Lest We Forget*. The review of that picture in *The Times* might as well apply to *Men of Yesterday* and *Lest We Forget* and much else of Baxter's output when it comments on *Reunion*'s 'utter disregard for all the laws of selection and construction. Both the director and Mr Rome cheerfully accept the pamphleteering form of sentiment, and the result is curiously and disturbingly impressive.'[29]

Baxter cast Stewart Rome, the distinguished star of a great number of silents and sound films, to play the lead in all three. In *Men of Yesterday* he plays Major Radford, a soldier of the Great War, inspired by a mission to ensure a peaceful world by bringing together French, German and British soldiers from past conflicts. When a dispirited Radford falls on hard times, his faithful army orderly (Sam Livesey) from the Great War days pulls him through, and the longed-for reunion of old soldiers goes ahead.

On hand to lighten the load are Baxter's music-hall stars, who by 1936 might be said to have lived through its golden age. The American male impersonator Ella Shields sings her most famous number, 'Burlington Bertie From Bow'. Baxter knew his audience would know the song. Its very appearance in the film is an open invitation for the audience to join in; Baxter was at the very centre of cinema of and for the community, and possibly the father of musical film sing-a-longs. No matter that Shields looks and sounds and acts as if from another, troubled world; she brings a strange smack of reality to bear on the commonplace. Then, there is George Robey, one of the busiest of that earlier generation in British studios, making few concessions to screen acting. He made five films in 1936, four the following year, and sustained a movie career until after the war. Meanwhile,

> In the main scenes when the ex-servicemen of all countries appeared, I decided to get Will Fyffe to represent Scotland. I could write at length about this artist. When he sang 'Glasgow Belongs To Me', it was as if a dream had come true – and his timing! ... We discussed producing a film in which he was to have played a Scottish doctor resident in the countryside ... I feel it would have been a classic of laughter and tears.[30]

JUNE

Even the best-known boy bands of today don't get to be film stars. The best-known bandleaders of the 1930s were luckier: think Henry Hall in *Music Hath Charms*, or Jack Payne in *Say It with Music*. The turn of 'Harry Roy and His Famous Band' came in **Everything Is Rhythm**, and as much is true of what's best in the picture. It was a Joe Rock production made at Elstree, and Rock also 'supervised' Alfred Goulding's direction of the screenplay by Syd Courtenay and Jack Byrd based on a storyline by Tom Geraghty that vaguely suggested events in its bandleader's life, now relived in the character of Harry Wade. At first, Harry's band struggles, and is said to lack novelty, until on their beam ends they get a date at the swanky Grosvenor Club, when they appear dressed in saucepan lids, washboards, aprons and scrubbing-brush epaulettes, in 'The Last Word In Love'. An instant success, they are booked for the even swankier Regal Hotel, where George Provis and A. L. Mazzei's Germanic designs momentarily lift the film to another level.

Chorus girls make vague dancing moves organised by Joan Davis as the legendary Mabel Mercer delivers 'Black Minnie's Got The Blues'. There is some artful trick camerawork when miniature chorines dance on Roy's piano as he sings 'Make Some Music', before Princess Paula ('Mrs Harry Roy', otherwise known as Princess Pearl or Pearl Vyner Brooke, in real life the daughter of the Rajah of Sarawak) describes the 'Man Of My Dreams'. He, of course, is her real-life husband Mr Harry Roy (alias Mr Harry Wade), but the Princess Paula has already been committed to an arranged diplomatic marriage in her principality of Monrovia, to which she is recalled. This reveals an appallingly acted and directed scene between her ghastly bore of a prospective husband Rudolph (Gerald Barry) and the Duke (Robert English), both of whom go in for apocalyptic acting. Princess Paula returns home to do her duty, leaving Harry with his, a cue for some sticky sentimental scenes at the domestic hearth. To forget his troubles, Harry and band embark on a world tour, a cue for some grainy stock footage. Inevitably, the band is booked for Monrovia, and Princess Paula is in the audience, to hear the man from whom she has forcibly been separated sing 'Life Is Empty Without Love'. Soon enough, Mr and Mrs Harry Roy are off on their 'Sky High Honeymoon', white-clad in an aeroplane topped with the boys of his band.

It's a cheery and almost Hollywood-inspired ending to a jolly occasion. Mrs Roy is no actress but more solid in singing 'Without Love' in a recording studio scene. Harry makes up for this, bringing natural warmth to what he does, and the songs are first-class.

Perhaps the most refreshing thing about **She Knew What She Wanted** is its amoral heroine. The Rialto production has a screenplay by Thomas J. Geraghty and Frank Miller based on the George and Ira Gershwin musical *Funny Face*, for which Paul Girard Smith and Fred Thompson had written the book. Fred and Adele

Astaire played London for its 1928 run at the Princes' Theatre. Four of the original numbers remain: ''S Wonderful', 'Let's Kiss And Make Up', 'My One And Only' and the title song. Thomas Bentley produced and directed at Welwyn. The rule-breaking heroine is Frankie (Betty Ann Davies), thrown out of finishing school and growing up a bad lot. On the credit side, she helps catch a band of thieves, and ends up with handsome bandleader Peter Thurston (Fred Conyngham). Others involved include Googie Withers as Dora, and comedian W. H. Berry.

This was a rare starring role for Davies, often cast as careworn women (as in *It Always Rains on Sunday*, *The History of Mr Polly* and the 'Fumed Oak' segment of *Tell Me Tonight*). The brightest thing about Bentley's film is Albert Burdon. Reviewing it, *MFB* sighed, 'The plot of a musical comedy is not required to be consistent or probable, but some novelty is expected. Situations, dialogue and dances are equally lacking in originality. There is a great deal of drinking, and much of the humour is dependent on the intoxication of the characters. The juvenile leads work hard but are obviously inexperienced. Claude Dampier [as Jimmy Reeves] overacts in the part of the guardian – but is amusing in his way; and Albert Burdon is genuinely funny. The settings are lavish, and the photography [Curt Courant] and lighting good.'[31]

If the follow-up vehicle for Joseph Schmidt after his 1934 *My Song Goes Round the World* had been just another backstage romance spiced with 'classical' music BIP's ***A Star Fell from Heaven*** might have been indistinguishable from many others of the ilk. In fact, it's an unexpected delight. In its modest way, it anticipates *Singin' in the Rain*. Director Paul Merzbach, fresh from Lilian Harvey's stylish *Invitation to the Waltz*, brings an incisive treatment to the screenplay of Dudley Leslie, Marjorie Deans, Val Guest, Jack Davies and Geoffrey Kerr, and additional dialogue of Gerald Elliott. At least this is one of those occasions when the British film industry seems to be holding up a mirror to itself and not taking the reflection too seriously. The owner of Miracle Films, Fischer (George Graves), describes one of his proposed scenes to Douglas Lincoln (Harry Milton):

> '… with beautiful hula-hula girls floating along in a gondola on a coral-bound shore – it's never been done before – eating grapes from a gold saliva [*sic*] and a man playing the violin.'
>
> Milton: 'Couldn't we get Fritz Kreisler?'
>
> Groves: 'Fritz Kreisler … Is he good?'
>
> Milton: 'Good? Huh! He's a virtuoso.'
>
> Groves: 'Well, I don't care about his morals so long as he can play the violin.'

Fischer never lets up. 'Did you like my theme song?' asks Milton. 'I always like *that* theme song,' replies Fischer, ever ready with a pungent criticism: 'In two words, he's mediocre.' As the owner of Miracle Films, he also gets the best line of the script: 'If it's a good film, it's a Miracle.' During filming, the film's comics, Graves and W. H. Berry, gave Schmidt a hard time, as Milton recalled. 'He was so small that in certain scenes, he had to walk on soap-boxes laid end to end out of camera, so as to appear of normal height.'[32]

Hans May contributed new music in his usual competent manner, setting Ruth Feiner's lyrics, as in the charming 'I'll Sing A Song Of Love To You' sung by Schmidt to Anne Heinmeyer (Florine McKinney). Other numbers include the title song, 'I'm Happy When It's Raining', 'La Coeur De La Vie' and 'Wine And Waltz'. *MFB* was enthusiastic, reporting a 'refreshing musical with a new plot' and that Merzbach had 'nearly produced a parody of the average musical film' that was 'well above the average'. It suggested that 'many will be interested in the exposure of the technique of faking'.[33] The temperature drops when Schmidt stops singing and begins acting, but *A Star Fell from Heaven* to some degree justifies its title, enjoyably enabled by the star's obvious humility. C. A. Lejeune saw 'Another tale, with tenor solo, of life in the film studios, that seems to me quite, quite sad.'[34]

Caviar to the general, the bilingual **The Robber Symphony** perhaps elevated the British musical film to art-house status. It owed its existence to Friedrich Feher, a distinguished actor better known for playing in the 1920 German silent *The Cabinet of Dr Caligari*. Feher attempted a new sort of musical film, one that had a narrative thread but radically altered the balance between speech and music. By the time filming began, Feher, composer, producer and director, had also co-written its screenplay with Jack Trendall, and its score.

For its length of 136 minutes, the story was of the simplest. Musical street-urchin Giannino (Feher's son Hans Feher), his dog, his mother (Feher's wife Magda Sonja) and his donkey trek across the Tyrol. Thieves have hidden a stash of stolen gold coins in Giannino's piano-organ. They follow him, hoping to retrieve their horde, but are caught. Produced for Concordia by BIP, this sometimes almost surreal fairy-tale, interestingly photographed and with many stunning sequences, was produced by Robert Wiene and Jack Trendall. No expense was spared in its year-long filming, at Shepperton, in Nice, Switzerland and at Mont Blanc. Dialogue was kept to the minimum, throwing the responsibility back onto the screen picture and the music, its importance established by an overture, played by the London Symphony Orchestra.

The *MFB*'s critic doubted that the threads of the story had been drawn together, but 'the music is pleasing to the ears; and in so far as the film is an endeavour to produce by straightforward means, a closer unity between music and picture than hitherto, it may be said, within its own limits, largely to have succeeded.'[35] A. Vesselo (probably the *MFB* critic) agreed that 'The intimate alliance of music and fantasy is in principle wholly commendable. But, whatever the form of the music in itself, the combination is not symphonic, but, rather, operatic.' That argument owes something to Webster Booth's unexpected presence, contributing a

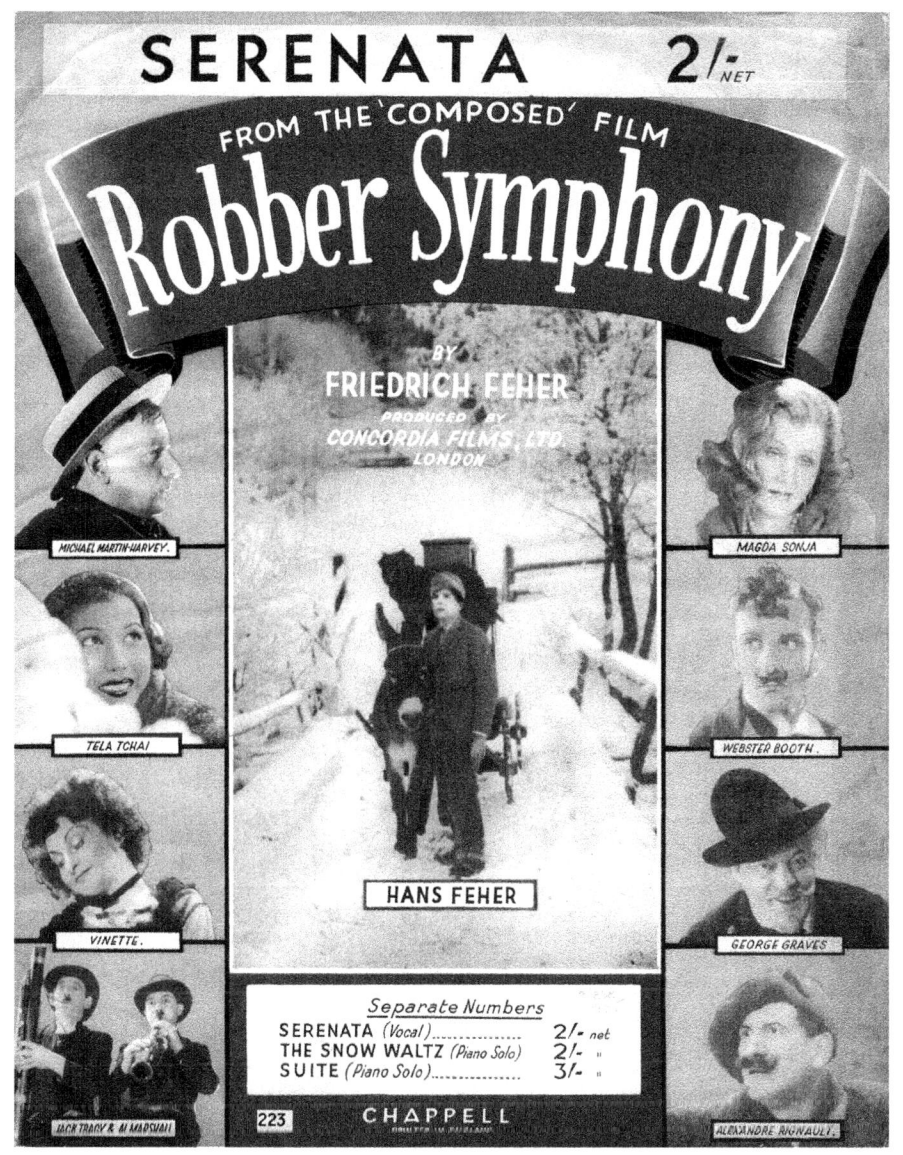

Offering the unexpected; not much talking in *The Robber Symphony* (1936)

ravishing 'Romance' and 'Serenata'; there was, too, the 'Snow Waltz'. Vesselo goes on to suggest 'Here perhaps may even be opera's legitimate successor – the transmutation of that hitherto over-synthetic medium into something more complete and closely-knit.'[36] However, the luxury lavished on *The Robber Symphony* could not be other than an exception to the rule. Vesselo continues his argument that the film is a sound appreciation of the screen-value of fantasy, made strong and assisted towards atmospheric unity by an exhilarating lightness of touch, by the pervading presence of a series of attractive musical motifs, and by a tempo as revealing as it is deliberate. The fairy-tale plot, which concerns itself with the pursuit through Alpine country of a small boy belonging to a band of street-performers, by a company of robbers who have hidden a stocking full of gold coins inside his piano-organ, is rightly simple in idea, and allows full scope for ingenious development. The importance of the music is unmistakably stressed in the opening, where an overture is played through at length by a complete orchestra, a brief shot of which appears once more at the close. Dialogue is not absent, but has been reduced to a minimum: it is interesting to observe that after the long musical beginning the entry of the human voice is actually a trifle disturbing.[37]

It is, however, doubtful that Vesselo's voice was heard by any of the studios producing British musical films.

JULY

The apparently lost *Dodging the Dole*, made at the Highbury studios by Mancunian's producer and director John E. Blakeley, followed up on the previous year's *Off the Dole*. That had the advantage of George Formby as its star, but by now he had deserted small-fry Mancunian Film Productions for the big time with *Keep Your Seats, Please*. It's unlikely that *Dodging the Dole* was shown anywhere south of Rotherham. In the mid-1930s it was a prime example of product intended principally for the eyes and ears and wallets of the industrial north, in the same year that Arthur Lucan was embarking on a screen career aimed at just such a clientele, before his Old Mother Riley character propelled him into the mainstream of popular cinema.

Dodging the Dole may have been more interesting and unusual than its dingy title suggests. Allegedly written by the author of *Off the Dole*, Arthur Mertz, 'The story really does nothing, other than providing a link between a mannequin parade, cabaret show and Lancashire sing-song.'[38] The action centres on the evasive tactics of two work-shy unemployed, frustrating the efforts of the dole officer supervisor. Various variety turns unknown to the West End appear with some neat bill-matter. This includes the work-shy pair, Fred Walmsley ('The Lancashire Favourite') and, in his first film role, Barry K. Barnes ('The Dole Dodger'); Bertha Ricardo ('Dainty and Demure'); the 'Little Bundle of Fun' Tot Sloan; ventriloquist Roy Barbour ('The Simplicity of Genius') and Dan Young ('The Charming Fool') as the office boss. Tantalisingly, there is also 'The Generator of Electric Radiance' Jenny Howard (real name Daisy Blowes), sometimes called 'the poor man's Gracie Fields', who seems to have had more success when she moved to Australia. If *Dodging the Dole* remains lost, we may never have the pleasure of seeing Howard performing

'Waiting At Table'. Other musical delights come from Bertini and the Tower Blackpool Band, and Arturo Steffani and His Silver Songsters, who would again appear on screen in the 1945 *What Do We Do Now?*.

Annie Laurie: its very title suggests a tuneful, sentimental encounter. Mondover Film Productions brought together Wilfred Noy and co-producer and director Walter Tennyson with writer Frank Miller, but would make only one more feature, the following year's *Little Miss Somebody* (hoping to make a star out of Binkie Stuart), before shutting up shop. A romance of barge life, *Annie Laurie* follows the fortunes of talented Annie (Polly Ward) whose singing talent leads her and her kindly father Will (Will Fyffe) out of disappointment. Will's way of life – he's master of the horse-drawn barge – is threatened by modern innovation, but his luck changes when he and Annie take up with a travelling showman.

Miller already had an impressive catalogue of screenplays for musical films at his back, including the 1933 *Letting in the Sunshine* for Albert Burdon, co-writing the Vivian Ellis *Mister Cinders* (1934), and 1935's *Honeymoon for Three* for Stanley Lupino. Ward was a pleasant addition to anything she played in, in at the birth of British musical films with *Elstree Calling*, taking in *His Lordship* (1932), *Shipmates o' Mine* (1936), Formby's *Feather Your Nest* (1937), Lupino's *Hold My Hand* (1938), and others. Fyffe brought solidity to all he did. Producers clearly relied on him, providing him with one of the most successful film careers that any of the 'golden age' music-hall stars enjoyed, and he worked from *Elstree Calling* until his death in 1947. *Annie Laurie* also features the orchestra of Horace Sheldon, a long-serving musical director for Butcher's Film Services, the Rodney Hudson Girls and – most wonderfully – Doris and Her Zebra.

A brief 'overture in the dark' alerts audiences to the arrival of ***Calling the Tune***, filmed at Ealing by Phoenix Films, made up of producer Hugh Perceval, director Reginald Denham and writer Basil Mason, here credited with 'scenario and dialogue'. Rachael Low considered that Phoenix Films 'were meant to be rather sophisticated', suggesting that this company had higher, possibly (a word seldom applied to British musical films) intellectual, aims than any others. Critics found Phoenix 'rather highbrow' and redolent of 'BBC flavour'.[39] Denham warns the viewer in the opening credits that *Calling the Tune* is 'concerned with the development of the gramophone industry but is entirely fictitious in character'. A suspicion dawns that what follows may be laudatory but tedious. The film is certainly a strange, unevenly formed beast, at first featuring meek and mild Eliot Makeham in one of the many meek and mild roles he undertook, as the inventor of 'durable records', whose patent is about to be stolen. Charles Penrose comes to the studio to record 'The Laughing Policeman', once considered hilarious. Those who survive Mr Penrose's ageless anthem have even less to laugh at as the film proceeds. For the classically minded we have Dame Nellie Melba (at least, the back view of someone pretending to be her) warbling 'Oh, For The Wings Of A Dove' into a microphone.

Somewhere along the line, matters are complicated by the skipping of years and bringing the (supposed) action up to date. Now, electric has replaced acoustic recording, but the best Phoenix can do for our amusement is George Robey in a patter-song, and singing 'Safety First'. As we look at Mr Robey, our attention wanders from the words to wondering at the state of dentistry in the mid-1930s. Nevertheless, the recording engineer is beside himself. 'It was all I could do to keep from laughing,' he tells Robey, a line for which Mr Robey may have slipped him a five pound note. *Calling the Tune* lurches clumsily from one thing to the seemingly unconnected other: bits of *Peer Gynt*; Sir Cedric Hardwicke intoning; a string quartet mournfully reviving Tosti's 'Good Bye'; Sir Henry Wood recording some Percy Grainger.

As if all this were not enough, we are introduced to 'a sort of visual telephone' known as television, and informed, 'It will be a sensation when it's perfected.' The plot climaxes when villainous Dick Finlay (Donald Wolfit) attempts to blow up his rival's record-making factory, at which late moment (too late to make a difference) the film seems about to take off. For *MFB*, *Calling the Tune* induced mixed feelings; it was 'unpretentious and adequate', and 'naïve and melodramatic'.[40] Phoenix Films' idea of 'good' music or worthwhile culture may strike the modern viewer as simplistic, while the inclusion of Robey and Penrose's concert-party contributions suggests that those responsible for *Calling the Tune* (and there are precious few decent tunes in it) were, much less forgivably, humourless.

AUGUST

David Quinlan marks **Guilty Melody** as a 'rather slow and strange mixture in which spy and musical plots get in each other's way',[41] as its title suggests. A bilingual directed by Richard Potter for Franco-London Films (the alliance was short-lived) at Ealing, it was written by G. F. Salmony from a novel by Hans Rehfisch, and produced by Friedrich Deutschmeister. Nils Asther played the impresario Galloni, married to diva Marguerite Salvini (Gitta Alpár). Unfortunately, British intelligence officer Richard Carter (John Loder) falls for her exotic charms. Unknown to her, Galloni is a spy, apparently infiltrating her recordings for the gramophone (she might have had a role in *Calling the Tune*) with coded messages for the enemy. The derring-do culminates in Marguerite being arrested as a spy, but Carter proves her innocence. This melodrama, peppered with Nicholas Brodszky's music, was Alpár's penultimate British film, soon followed by *Everything in Life* released in November 1936.

SEPTEMBER

> Anything starring the lad from Wigan could be revived again and again in the town centre, for all the staff had to do was open the doors and stand well back, even on the third or fourth run.[42]

Leslie Halliwell's recollection leaves us in no doubt about the efficacy of the George Formby films. But one evening at the Lido in Bolton's Bradshawgate, at a showing of George Formby's ***Keep Your Seats, Please***, the star unexpectedly walked on stage. When the startled audience cheered him, the man in the light grey suit explained that he and his wife Beryl were passing through Bolton and had seen the film was showing at the Lido. Beryl – supervising her husband's actions as she was used to doing – was out of sight in the wings; George told them she wouldn't come on stage because she wasn't dressed up. Would he give them a song? He couldn't. It was a pity, but he'd left his ukulele in the car. For young Halliwell, sitting in the audience with his mother,

> Suddenly he was gone, the lights were down, the curtains were parting and the film beginning. We watched in a gentle daze. It was the nearest we had ever been to a real film star, though Mum remembered once standing at the back for a personal appearance by the then well-known Guy Newall and Ivy Duke, the stars of a silent melodrama which she thought was called *The Sound of Running Water* [a close call, but it was *The Lure of Crooning Water*].[43]

It's good to know that Formby may not have lost contact with his roots, or the sort of northern audiences who had tolerated *Boots! Boots!* and *Off the Dole*, having been catapulted from Mancunian Films to major British studios. *Keep Your Seats, Please*, made for Associated Talking Pictures at Ealing, had him reunited with producer Basil Dean and director Monty Banks as for *No Limit*. If a template for a Formby film was emerging, the new project made some effort to dilute it. Based on Elie Ilf and Eugene Petrov's Russian play *Twelve Chairs*, the screenplay was concocted by Tom Geraghty, Ian Hay and Anthony Kimmins. Its origins may have been Russian, but were manicured into material that accommodated one of its star's most popular songs, 'When I'm Cleaning Windows'. Formby's almost childlike persona helped get the occasional *double entendre* past the censor. As with Fields (but without her fragility), Formby's relationship with a cinema audience was elemental. He exuded a genuine fascination and enjoyment with whatever world he found himself in. This was enough to secure him an unassailable position. Nevertheless, Low reminds us that 'Unlike Gracie Fields, his screen personality did not reflect his real character. Dean and others have described him as mean and selfish, and commented on the endless rows with his jealous and ambitious wife.'[44]

Child performer Binkie Stuart, commemorated in one of the songs of Harry

Parr Davies, Harry Gifford and Fred E. Cliffe, 'Good Night Binkie', made her film debut. Effectively, in a Formby film nobody else much mattered beyond the star, but Florence Desmond took on the role of girlfriend, briefly doing her Gracie Fields's impression in 'You've Got Me Standing On The Tip Of My Toes', reprised by four-year-old Binkie. As other actresses cast as George's love interest would discover, they were of little significance, and had to put up with Beryl's zealous protection of her husband. As for Desmond, Dean had 'the utmost difficulty in persuading her to work with him again, especially when she discovered that her part consisted mainly of rushing after George, carrying a child of three in her arms. But, as she frankly admits, she needed the money.' Dean recognised that Formby's success was based on his personality. 'He didn't act gormless as many successful Lancashire comedians have done, he *was* gormless, at least as far as the audience was concerned, and they took him to their hearts accordingly.'[45]

If you needed a tutorial on how to go from working as a riveter on a construction site to being a brilliant dancer, Fox British's ***Rhythm in the Air*** told you all you needed to know in 72 minutes. Its director Arthur B. Woods seems to have been particularly fascinated with musical films, turning out some of the more interesting examples and attempting to make a star out of Keith Falkner. *Rhythm in the Air* was both dance musical and biopic, with American Jack Donohoe playing himself (thinly disguised as Jack Donovan) opposite his real-life wife Tutta Rolf in a screenplay co-written by Donohoe and Vina de Vesci. Donohoe had begun as a New York hoofer in *Ziegfeld Follies*. He went on to work on choreography for several British pictures including *Paradise for Two* (1937) and in 1938 *Everything Happens To Me*, *Keep Smiling* and Falkner's *The Singing Cop*. *Rhythm in the Air* had an attractive score, to which Kenneth Leslie-Smith, James Dyrenforth, Bruce Sievier (who also worked as lyricist on the 1932 *Where Is This Lady?* and the 1936 *Gypsy Melody*) and Peggy Cochrane contributed. The numbers include 'You're On My Mind All Day', 'Walking The Beam', 'Spring All The Year Round', 'Well I'll Be Darned It's Love' and 'Man I Saved Up For A Rainy Day'.

If uncluttered sincerity were all, ***Song of Freedom*** might be the film of the year. Eighty years on, it is ever-present in a picture that balances its simplicity with its strength of purpose. Its star, Paul Robeson, was already known to British audiences for his West End *Show Boat* of 1928, and his notable 1930 *Othello*. Based on a story by Major Claude Wallace and Dorothy Holloway, with 'screen adaptation and scenario' by Fenn Sherie and Ingram D'Abbes, Exclusive Films' *Song of Freedom* was produced by H. Fraser Passmore at the British Lion studios in Beaconsfield. Low has written that Robeson

> wished to redeem his reputation after being criticised for playing Bosambo in *Sanders of the River*. *Song of Freedom* shows him as a black British docker who becomes

famous as an opera singer and seeks to bring the benefits of Western civilisation to the land of his forefathers. This misguided attempt to re-establish the left-wing Robeson as an intelligent and concerned person mixed his singing and some fairly realistic scenes of racial harmony in dockland with an egregious caricature of African life which was unintentionally far from flattering. It was certainly unusual, and was treated with cautious respect by some critics, not knowing quite what to make of it.[46]

On the west coast of Africa in 1700, the primitive island of Casanga, where pagan rites prevail, is ruled by the cruelly tyrannous Queen Zinga. Her son (Robeson) escapes. Years pass, and the story moves to England, where opera impresario Gabriel Donozetti (Esme Percy) overhears 'a coloured man' singing: it is John Zinga. 'To hear a voice like that and lose it, it is a crime.' John feels out of place in England, despite his devoted wife Ruth (Elisabeth Welch at her most sedentary); together they dream of a 'Sleepy River'. In a local bar, John exhibits a gloomy mood in 'Lonely Road', but under Donozetti's teaching he becomes a famous opera singer. The significance of this achievement is underscored by the fact that he is a black man. At the height of his British success, he appears in opera as 'The Black Emperor' (a fascinating set-piece), brilliantly designed and directed. In place of his curtain speech, John breaks into the 'Song Of Freedom'. An anthropologist in the audience recognises this as being the national anthem of Casanga. John turns his back on his career and returns to his homeland with its 'backward, impoverished' populace. 'I am your king,' he tells them, but the witch-doctors want none of it, and his people reject him. At last, he persuades them by singing 'The King's Song'. He returns to England and continued stardom, but will return to Casanga, where he will presumably westernise the witch-doctors.

John's almost religious zeal may be understandable. As a native of the island and their true ruler, he has the right to lead them into the light, but the missionary enlightening is given the twist that it will be undertaken by a black man. This hardly seems significant in a film that remains charming and highly watchable, even moving. Robeson's status as performer and man carries all. *Film Weekly* quoted his conviction that

> I believe this is the first film to give a true picture of many aspects of the life of the coloured man in the west. Hitherto on the screen, he has been caricatured or presented only as a comedy character. This film shows him as a real man, with problems to be solved, difficulties to overcome. I am sure the audience will appreciate the picture as much for its unusual honesty of characterisation as for the dramatic intensity of the story.[47]

He is sympathetically directed by J. Elder Wills, more widely known as an art director. Almost immediately, Wills turned to directing another Robeson project, *Big Fella*. A valuable feature of both projects is the memorable music by Eric Spear, with lyrics by Henrik Ege. The *Manchester Guardian* considered, 'certain weaknesses in this story neither Paul Robeson nor Elisabeth Welch is able to overcome, and *Song of Freedom* is at times more naïve than simple, though the early European scenes depict negro life with a naturalness which is refreshing.'[48]

The year was brightened by the arrival of the 'Mexican Spitfire' Lupe Velez in *Gypsy Melody*. When RKO ended her American contract in 1934, she moved to Britain for Julius Hagen's *The Morals of Marcus* (1935) – the change from Hollywood to Twickenham must have been traumatic – before being signed by Anglo-French director Edmond T. Gréville, who in 1935 had begun his own film company, British Artistic. As it happened, *Gypsy Melody* would be British Artistic's *only* film; the debt-laden company collapsed in 1937. Did its only film matter much? The title suggests that audiences might expect yet another dose of Romany escapism, with the not inconsiderable advantage of the fiery Velez and her leading man Alfred Rode, also seen in *The Blue Danube* (1932) and *Temptation* (1934).

Emil Reinert produced at Elstree from a storyline by Rode, worked into a screenplay by Irving Leroy and Dan Weldon, itself adapted from René Pujol's original screenplay for the French film *Juanita*, which Rode had produced and starred in the previous year. It says something for the popularity of Rode's gypsy band, the Tzigane Orchestra, that this, rather than Velez, seems to have been the main draw, and it was the band, not Rode ('very unconvincing') or Velez ('musical comedyish'), that most impressed.[49] *Kine Weekly* noted that some scenes visibly suffered from 'drastic economy. Editing has also been drastic, with scenes obviously omitted, leaving bad gaps [and] the whole thing gives the impression of having been somewhat laboriously translated from a foreign language.'[50] Apart from the supporting Margaret Yarde as a duchess and Fred Duprez as an American impresario, the praise was mainly for *Gypsy Melody*'s musical moments, principally the Tzigane Orchestra's version of Liszt's Second Hungarian Rhapsody, and Velez sang 'Song of the Guitar' (lyric by Bruce Sievier, music by Rode) accompanied by Rode and his musicians.

Nevertheless, at its heart this is a pertinent film. At a time when the dominance of Nazism was gripping the country, in its far from vivid manner *Gypsy Melody* threw a not very bright light on racial prejudice, even ethnic cleansing, although the idea was heavily buried in what was intended as the lightest of musical confections. In the Grand Duchy of Seeburg, Captain Eric Danilo (Rode) is imprisoned after being involved in a duel, but escapes with 'comic' milliner Madam Beatrice (Jerry Verno) and meets up with the wild gypsy dancer Mila (Velez). In Seeburg, the Romany way of life is not approved of, but Danilo and Mila overcome prejudice and achieve great success with their musical entertainments. Their success spreads across the globe, until an aeroplane in which they are travelling crashes in Seeburg. Changes of attitude to the gypsy culture leads on to the happy conclusion, when Danilo is made Lord Chancellor and marries Mila. Meanwhile, Hitler's persecution of gypsies lurked beyond cinema's door.

A mixed critical reaction awaited *The Beloved Vagabond*. Its publicity announced Maurice Chevalier in 'His Gayest Role', although British posters had his co-star Margaret Lockwood above the title and Chevalier very much diminished below it. Customers were promised 'Just the right popular mixture of adventure and romance', but that, of course, was not for the publicity department but for the public to decide. Low describes it as 'highly regarded despite the elaborate and unlikely story',[51] but *MFB* disagreed, noting the creaking plot and remarking that 'To make affection and innocence real on the screen is a hard task, and here there is little success', in a picture that was 'tedious and disappointing'.[52] Ludovico Toeplitz produced the Toeplitz Productions' bilingual, directed at Ealing by Kurt (Curtis) Bernhardt. Several writers shared responsibility: Wells Root, and scenario and dialogue by Arthur Wimperis, Hugh Mills and Walter Creighton, based on a novel by W. J. Locke.

The moustachioed Chevalier played happy-go-lucky young architect Gaston de Nerac, romancing Joanna Rushworth (imperturbable Betty Stockfeld). Joanna is also desired by rich Count de Verneuil (Austin Trevor), who blackmails Joanna's father (Charles Carson) into forsaking Gaston, now with a young boy, Asticot – a promising artist – as his only companion. Bereft, Gaston and Asticot move to France where they meet Blanquette (Lockwood), a poor musician, singing a British music-hall favourite 'Daisy Bell'. Soon, the three of them are strolling players entertaining the villages they pass through, forming the 'Orchestre Paragot'. Meanwhile, Joanna marries the Count, but is left a widow and, still in her weeds, visits a drunk Gaston at the Café Delphine. Blanquette, who loves Gaston, generously assures her that Gaston still has need of her, and Joanna returns to England reunited with Gaston. Once there, however, Joanna realises he and Blanquette and Asticot belong together, and stands aside. Curiously, Chevalier gets to sing 'Loch Lomond', but the soundtrack was conceived by Darius Milhaud. Other music was composed by Mireille and Heimann (Werner R. Heymann). Diverting and charming as *The Beloved Vagabond* now and then is, it could not save Toeplitz Productions, which, crippled by debt, became one of many short-lived film companies of the decade.

The self-styled 'Prime Minister of Mirth', George Robey scarcely deserved top billing for Capitol-Grafton's *Southern Roses*, produced by Isidore Goldschmidt and Max Schach, and directed at Denham by Fred Zelnik. Neil Gow's screenplay from a play by Rudolph Bernauer is at least bright and breezy, as well as unremarkable, with music by Johann Strauss and Hans May. This was 'inoffensive' although marred by 'inefficient and under-rehearsed chorus work'.[53] On the credit side, it has two decent leading ladies in Gina Malo as (sweet) Mary Rowland and Chili Bouchier as (to-be-avoided) Estella Estrello. Bouchier flings herself into the film with abandon, as if she has just realised she is no longer a movie star. There is a pleasurable glimpse of Vera Pearce as substantial 'Carrie The Cannon Ball Queen'.

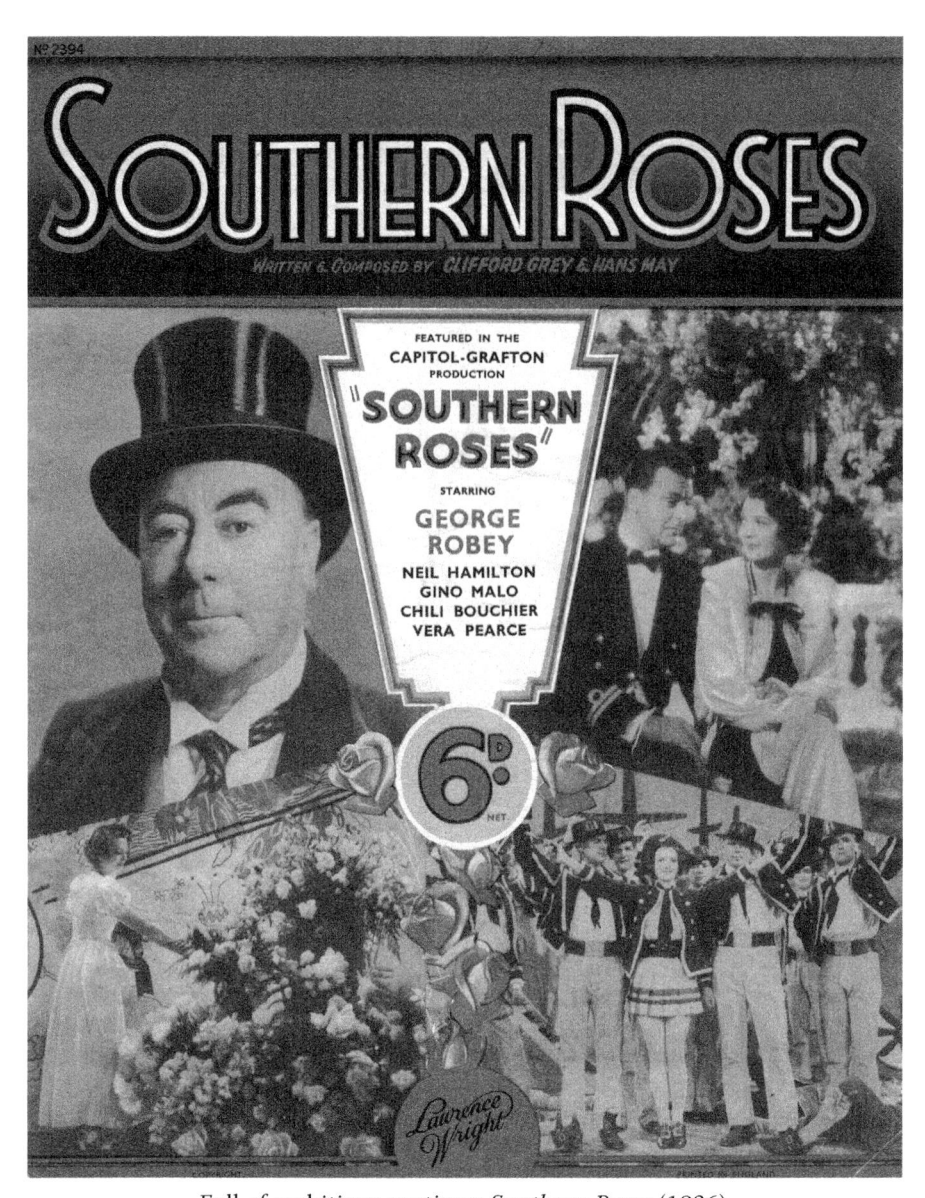

Full of ambitious routines: *Southern Roses* (1936)

In fact, the musical moments of *Southern Roses* are the best reason for sitting through it, quirky as that experience is. Malo does a turn at the Trocadero nightclub, charming a boys' night out of British upper-crust naval officers who look as if they've never swabbed a deck. She beguiles them by singing 'Southern Roses'. Viewing Mary from a discreet distance is Leslie Perrins, the personification of the British supporting feature villain; you can tell by his eyes being too close together and his pencilled moustache. Perrins soon vanishes, leaving the floor free for romance between Mary and the most voluble of the caped naval officers, Reggie (Neil Hamilton). Mary consolidates her place in his affections by performing a ridiculous piratical number in the Trocadero's programme; like the other musical sequences in *Southern Roses*, it has to be seen to be believed. Ridiculous does not mean unenjoyable.

Formulaic misunderstandings and muddled identities bulk out the plot. Paint magnate Higgins (Robey) is described as a 'profiteering barbarian' by his combatant in business Miss Rowland (Athene Seyler). Matters are resolved when the highly temperamental Estella (Bouchier 'putting on her parts again') marries her toy boy, Higgins's son Bill (Richard Dolman). The comedy is pretty standard 1930s British musical film. When Higgins pontificates about going into politics he asks, 'Why should we have foreign relations? Some of ours are bad enough.' No doubt audiences in the dark tittered at this observation in 1936, but what can they have thought of Malo's great production number made around May's lively 'Carissima', with choreography that can only be described as mincing, or the extraordinary birthday celebration for Robey when his typists arrive through a very unlikely row of windows? Absurd as it is, *Southern Roses* survives as an entertaining curiosity.

OCTOBER

It was Oscar Adolf Hermann Schmitz who in 1904 christened England 'Das Land ohne Musik', recalling Heinrich Heine's opinion of the 1840s that 'Nothing is more terrible than English music, except English painting'. Of course, by 1936 anyone called Adolf could hardly expect to be taken seriously in England. One wonders if those responsible for giving **Land Without Music** its title were aware of Adolf and Heinrich's slurs? Could the film they were making be satirical? Surely not? (It wasn't.) Some prints of the film forewarn the audience in the opening credits that they are about to sit through 'an original satirical operetta written for the screen'. This may have sent some rushing for the exit. They would have missed a treat, one of Richard Tauber's most entertaining films, full of enchanting Oscar Straus melodies, with lyrics by Clifford Grey.

This is no more than a musical fantasy. In the Grand Duchy of Lucco the ruling Princess Regent (Diana Napier) has outlawed music, blaming her kingdom's bankruptcy on her people's passion for making it. Her edict is challenged when one of Lucco's most distinguished sons, the famous singer Mario Carlini (Tauber), comes home. ('What? No music?') He agrees to break the law by appearing in a secret concert in the forest's Robbers Cave. Unknown to him, he has already met and serenaded the princess with 'Smile For Me', but at their second meeting she is rather less impressed with him, and he is arrested. At last, perhaps not only for political reasons, the Princess relents and music floods Lucco again. Although the final frame does not find her in Carlini's arms, we have the impression that they will be spending musical evenings together.

As a side-dish to the main plot, mild comedy is supplied by Jimmy ('Schnozzle') Durante as a newspaperman, and pert June Clyde as his daughter Sadie. When shown in the States, Durante had top billing; bringing him into the frame was done to widen the film's appeal to the foreign market. Leslie Halliwell thought the film 'artless but attractively played operetta with the star in excellent form',[54] and Tauber seems more relaxed than in previous films. Napier may not be a great actress, more beneficent schoolmistress than Ruritanian princess, but it's a nicely controlled performance. A disappointed *Observer* described 'not a very subtle work'; 'It is nice enough music, and good enough fooling to make you overlook its occasional amateur moments.'[55]

A considerable number of heads had been knocked together in the film's compilation, working from a story by Fritz Koselka and Armin Robinson, an adaptation by Rudolph Bernauer, a screenplay by Marian Dix and L. du Garde Peach, and additional dialogue by Eric Maschwitz and Ernest Betts. Made at Denham and produced by Capitol's Max Schach (*Southern Roses*, *The Lilac Domino*), *Land of Music* was directed by Walter Forde.

Yet another picture that Cicely Courtneidge fails to discuss in her autobiography, **Everybody Dance** was a Gainsborough film produced at Islington by Michael Balcon and directed by American Charles Reisner (his only British credit). Looking beyond the domestic market, Balcon and Gaumont-British wanted to push product in the States. Courtneidge's co-star Ernest Truex was imported from Hollywood. American screenwriter Ralph Spence teamed with Leslie Arliss (whose other work included Formby's *Come On George!* in 1939 and – long after Courtneidge's golden years – *Miss Tulip Stays the Night*) and Stafford Dickens who had scripted *Things Are Looking Up* the previous year. The stumbling block was that Courtneidge's idiosyncratic comedic skills were unlikely to appeal to foreign audiences. Balcon commissioned an American team of songwriters, Mack Gordon and Harry Revel, providing a bright title song, 'What Does It Get Me?', and 'My! What A Different Night'. C. A. Lejeune notes that 'the film, as a whole, is a combination of all the less distinguished qualities of American and British picture making.'[56]

G. B. Morgan Productions' **Live Again** (aka *I Live Again*) had the one-time villain of Hollywood silents Noah Beery as faded opera singer Morton Meredith, 'living again' by putting his belief in a younger singer and living by courtesy of the reflected glory. In John Quin's screenplay, the up-and-coming songbird, played by the utilitarian John Garrick, was called John Wayne. It seemed an odd choice of name for a fictional character. Didn't Quin watch films? In 1936 the real John Wayne (birth name Marion Morrison, which wouldn't at all have done for his image) had already

With or without the great Jack Hulbert, the indomitable Cicely Courtneidge insists that *Everybody Dance* (1936)

made nine movies and just turned his back on a different career as the recording artist 'Singing Sam'. In fact, Garrick was incapable of an unattractive performance, providing an all-purpose leading man who could sing and act reasonably. Domestic studios had never tried to establish a British Nelson Eddy leading man, despite several attempts to discover a domestic Jeanette MacDonald. Nevertheless, Garrick was in steady demand by producers from the 1933 *Lily of Killarney* onwards, along the way playing a composer condemned to transportation in *The Broken Melody*, the title role in *D'Ye Ken John Peel?*, a rhapsodising pet shop decorator in the sublimely silly *Street Song*, a nautical widower in *Shipmates o' Mine* and a Chinese toy boy with a penchant for drop earrings in *Chu Chin Chow*.

At Elstree Rock, Arthur Maude had secured the notable American star Bessie Love to play Kathleen Vernon; she had been one of D. W. Griffith's stars in the 1915 *Birth of a Nation* and *Intolerance* (1916). Another fledgling company doomed to failure, G. B. Morgan Productions made only one other musical film in the decade, *Mad About Money*, that gave British audiences the chance to gaze at Lupe Velez.

The transition of operetta from stage to screen showed little sign of slowing down. There must have been those who hoped that **The Last Waltz** was a none too subtle title marking the genre's final curtain call. (No chance; it would still be alive and sometimes kicking at the end of World War II.) Meanwhile, how many of its customers realised to what extent these stage works had been mauled in the process? *The Last Waltz*, a bilingual filmed in Paris at the Billancourt Studios, was based on Oscar Straus's hugely successful 1920 *Der letzte Walzer* that had played London in 1922, starring the original 'Maid of the Mountains' Jose Collins. On that occasion, *The Times* considered it a 'rather heavy light opera', in contrast to the *New York Times* opinion that there had been 'no equal in light opera in this city in the last ten years'.[57]

Produced by Gina Carlton for Warwick Films, *The Last Waltz* was written by Reginald Arkell (*Street Singer*) and directed by Leo Mittler (*Cheer Up!*). The Czech singer Jarmila Novotná played Countess Vera Lizavetta in both the French version (*La Dernière Valse*) and the English, with British stalwart Harry Welchman taking over the role of Count Dimitri from his French predecessor. Co-director Gerald Barry played Prince Paul, politically obliged to find a wife. His choice is Countess Vera, who has fixed on Dimitri. Another applicant for the prince's wife arrives and marries him, solving Vera and Dimitri's dilemma. The numbers included 'Believe Me, I'm Quite Sincere' and 'The Magic Waltz'.

A generous dollop of romantic escapism arrived with the hand-me-down **Dreams Come True** made by London and Continental at Ealing. It was the sort of film that Frances Day seemed doomed to attend: bastardised operetta. Lehár's *Clo-Clo*, adapted from a 1914 comedy, premiered in Vienna in 1924, opening in London the following year. Richard Traubner describes it as 'a return to the Lehár of old pre-war days, gay, light-hearted, uninterested in the tragic, unrequited love stories that distinguished his last works'.[58] The 1935 Austrian film version *Die Ganze Welt dreht sich um Liebe* had starred the great Marta Eggerth; London and Continental's remake, produced by Ilya Salkind and John Gossage, had a screenplay by Donald Bull and dialogue by Bruce Sievier, directed by *Calling the Tune*'s Reginald Denham.

In Vienna, the charms of seductive performer Ilona Ratkay (Frances Day) work their magic on rich farmer Albert von Waldenau (Hugh Wakefield) and his son Peter (Frederick Bradshaw). Albert suspects Ilona may be his illegitimate daughter. The moral/sexual implications of the storyline may have unnerved some of its British audience; some would have considered it typically continental. One wonders why its British version did not make the effort to change the location and characters to home territory; its obvious 'foreignness' made it seem fake. Not much of Lehár's score survives, but there is the consolation of having Day sing 'Love's Memory' and 'So Must Our Love Remain'. *MFB* found London and Continental's depiction of Vienna somewhat Home Counties, but praised Day's overcoming of 'thin sentimental' material, remarking that, unusually, she was a performer who looked beautiful when singing.[59]

For a time, British audiences had the opportunity to see a film of a stage musical that was still running in the West End. *This'll Make You Whistle* closed in February 1937, long after Herbert Wilcox and General Film Distributors had let loose their picture. Its star, Jack Buchanan, along with several other principals including Elsie Randolph, Jean Gillie, William Kendall, David Hutcheson and Maidie Hope, filmed during the day and returned to the stage show for another live performance. The piece ran along the usual Buchanan lines, with the astonishingly laid-back star as fancy-free Bill Hopping, for some reason finding himself engaged to two women, Laura (Marjorie Brooks) and Joan (Gillie). The wit is in line with most other British musical films ('You're the bigamist fool in London'). The last thing Bob needs is to bump into model Bobbie Rivers (Randolph – somehow never a star in her own right). There is a change of locale to northern France's playground of Le Touquet to bring a touch of continental glamour to the staginess. The play was adapted for the screen by its original authors Guy Bolton and Fred Thompson. Songs are by the American team of Maurice Sigler, Al Goodhart and Al Hoffman, and include 'Crazy With Love', 'There Isn't Any Limit To My Love', 'I'm In A Dancing Mood', 'The Wrong Rhumba', 'My Red Letter Day' and the title song. The film was made at Elstree, its designers L. P. Williams and Hylton R. Oxley making the most of the studio's spaciousness, but the air of artificiality is hard to shake off. Buddy Bradley choreographed.

Of the many production companies of the decade that came and went, Tudor Films, created by George Loftus (otherwise the Marquess of Ely) and the aviator

Tom Campbell Black, is one of the least remembered. Tudor was fortunate to get Gitta Alpár as their star for *Everything in Life*, and Hans May as its composer. American Courtney Terrett and James E. Lewis provided a screenplay charting the conquest of young composer hopeful Geoffrey Loring (American import Neil Hamilton) by glamorous diva Rita Boya (Alpár). Directed at Highbury by J. Elder Wills (Paul Robeson's *Song of Freedom* and *Big Fella* were two of his most successful assignments), *Everything in Life* was, despite its title, found wanting by *MFB*'s verdict that its 'weak incoherent story is only redeemed from yawning tedium by Gitta Alpár's singing. But neither camera, clothes, nor make-up are kind to her, nor do the melodies give her much scope.'[60]

Alpár's extraordinary get-ups, and almost gruesome cosmetic decoration, were no worse than anything visited on Jessie Matthews who, despite every humiliation her studio's costume department could inflict on her, managed to preserve some sort of identity of her own. The undeniably impressive Alpár sometimes seems to have been devoured by the image supplanted on her. It's a relief that May's score sounds more alluring to us now than it did to contemporary critics: the title song, 'My First Thought Is You', 'In The Spring', 'Take My Hands', 'Everybody's Dancing', 'To Everything In Life' and 'In The Morning' are pleasant if not noteworthy. The following year, Alpár would make her last British feature *Mr Stringfellow Says 'No'*, once more working opposite her *Everything in Life* co-star Hamilton. When she departed the British studios, a substantial amount of the continental glamour that had infused British musical films went with her.

Oswald Mitchell was in his element as writer and director of Malcolm Picture Productions' *Variety Parade*, produced at Cricklewood by Ian Sutherland and Reginald Long, and based on the loosest of storylines by Con West. The least pretentious of British directors, Mitchell assembled an interesting number of the sort of acts that audiences wouldn't be much bothered about after the coming war. There was the novelty of 'Mrs Jack Hylton and Her Boys', obese Teddy Brown who had spent four years in the New York Philharmonic Orchestra and appeared in many British features, and the moustache-twirling Harry Tate. One of the strangest items was G. S. Melvin's routine as a totem-pole of a girls' scout-mistress. There was clowning from the distinguished 'Noni and Partner' (the partner is probably his son Horace). Feeling sorry for the childlike Noni, Queen Mary had handed him a bloom from her bouquet at the 1928 Royal Variety performance, after which he was known as 'The Clown to Whom the Queen Gave a Flower'. Keeping things going were comical brothers Dave and Joe O'Gorman, the ubiquitous Sherman Fisher Girls, the Corona Kids and Nat Gonella and His Georgians. *Variety Parade* also gave a hiding place to the midget Wee Georgie Wood, whose final years were inexplicably spent writing indigestible gossip about the lower levels of showbiz for the *Stage* newspaper.

DECEMBER

Bouncing Stanley Lupino was back on screen for Christmas 1936 with a horse-racing musical farce, **Sporting Love**, made for Hammer Productions and British Lion at Beaconsfield. An emasculated adaptation of the stage musical that had played at the Gaiety Theatre in London, closing in January 1935 after 302 performances, it had the patented Lupino brightness. *MFB* decided that 'In no respect is the film polished, but its rollicking good humour and pace are sufficient compensation in a farce of this kind.'[61] Lupino and his most regular stage partner, Laddie Cliff, played Brace brothers Percy and Peter. Their efforts to win the Derby are unsuccessful, but romantic fulfilment awaits them through the intervention of a kindly aunt who insists that they both produce wives for her scrutiny. Lupino's original theatre piece was adapted by Fenn Sherie and Ingram D'Abbes. Hammer again teamed producer H. Fraser Passmore with director J. Elder Wills, bringing in composer Eric Ansell to work on the score alongside Billy Mayerl. The songs included 'In The Spring Time', 'It's Derby Day', Charles Harris's old favourite 'After The Ball', and Cliff singing his composition 'Coal Black Mammy', co-written with Ivy St Helier.

Pagliacci must have been a dream project for Richard Tauber, who had long wanted to put an opera on screen. When Trafalgar Film Productions' picture reached the USA it was retitled *A Clown Must Laugh*, but Tauber, who had put his own money into the project, had little to laugh about. 'On with the motley' may have been the battle cry of Leoncavallo's one-act masterpiece, but in its transition from opera house to cinema things went awry. Otto Kanturek was a distinguished cinematographer, and yet his work here was all but ruined by part of the production being filmed in British Chemicolor, based on a system of colourisation used by UFA. Many operettas had been transferred to the screen with debatable degrees of success, but *Pagliacci* fell flat. There was praise for Tauber's singing, sharing the screen with wife Diana Napier, and Steffi Duna (her voice dubbed by Angela Parselles). Despite their efforts, producer Max Schach and director Karl Grune could not create an organic work. A small army of writers had put together a screenplay, among them Monckton Hoffe, Roger Burford, actor Fritz Kortner and Bertolt Brecht. Low considered the result

> slow and confused, padded with obviously studio-made sequences of the touring company on the move in the mountains, perfunctory acting and an uneasy combination of operatic convention and realism. Tauber, who dominated the film to such an extent that he was even given an aria transposed from another character, sang magnificently, but the production was unworthy of him.[62]

The year's entries end not only with a bang but a whimper. The bang is courtesy of a deadly bullet instead of a blank, fired during **Murder at the Cabaret**, M. B. Productions' only production of the decade. Reginald Fogwell directed, co-produced with Nell Emerald, and co-wrote with Percy Robinson. The commixture of murder and music is not unique to *Murder at the Cabaret* but the result was desultory. Fogwell, at one time Twentieth Century Fox's publicity manager before making silents and moving into sound pictures, went unappreciated. In 1932, his quickie *The Temperance Fete*, despite the presence of George Robey, fell foul of *Kinematograph Weekly*'s announcement that 'The conception, treatment and presentation bear the stamp of the amateur, and at no period does the film rise above the low level of mediocrity.'[63] This serves as well for *Murder at the Cabaret*, in which the *MFB* discerned no saving grace, explaining that 'The production is weak throughout, with no proper sustaining of film sequence; cutting is bad and the settings are mediocre. Whether or not the scenario is to blame, none of the artists give good performances.'[64] Regular cinemagoers would have sought in vain for a recognisable name on the marquee, but Phyllis Robins sang 'Powder Blues' and 'Forgotten Women', among whose number she would all too soon be counted. The murderous side of things concerns a jealous girlfriend who arranges the death of an unwanted male. The cabaret sequences involved several names unknown to the sophisticated, among them Alvis and Capla, Chick Farr and Farland, and Holland's Magyar Band. By the time the reviews appeared, Fogwell had already moved along the quota quickie production line for his blissfully titled *Terror on Tiptoe*, the cast including the once headlining leading lady of British silents, Mabel Poulton.

1937

Its producers perhaps thought the film would sink very nicely of its own accord without having to finance the shipwreck
Glamorous Night

Café Colette
Wake Up Famous
London Melody
Please Teacher
Head Over Heels
Moonlight Sonata
Kathleen Mavourneen
Feather Your Nest
Mayfair Melody
Variety Hour
Calling All Stars
The Show Goes On
The Street Singer
The Gang Show
Rose of Tralee
O-Kay for Sound
Glamorous Night
Song of the Forge
Take My Tip
Sunset in Vienna
Big Fella

The Penny Pool
Let's Make a Night of It
Talking Feet
Sing As You Swing
The Lilac Domino
Keep Fit
The Girl in the Taxi
Gangway
Command Performance
Over She Goes
The Minstrel Boy
The Last Rose of Summer
Rhythm Racketeer
Shooting Stars
Saturday Night Revue
Paradise for Two
The Sky's the Limit
Intimate Relations
Melody and Romance
Mad About Money

JANUARY

Café Colette began life on radio, first broadcast by the BBC in 1933; stage success at the London Palladium with George Robey followed in 1934. For the film, theatrical polymath Eric Maschwitz turned to his radio original, basically a programme of foreign dance music played by the orchestra of Walford Hyden and His Café Colette Orchestra, transmitted as if from a Parisian café. Compered by Dino Galvani, the programme lulled radio listeners into believing it was indeed coming direct from a French café. Hyden was qualified for the job; his other manifestations included Walford Hyden and His Ciganskies and, seen in a Pathé short, Walford Hyden and His Magyar Orchestra.

The short-lived Garrick Film Company's version, produced by W. Devenport Hackney and directed at Wembley Studios by Paul L. Stein, had a screenplay by Maschwitz, Val Valentine and Katherine Strueby, based on an idea by Val Gielgud. Vanda Muroff (the Norwegian Greta Nissen in her last film role) is an aristocratic Russian spy. Romantic lothario Ryan (Paul Cavanagh) resists her charm, but he too is a spy. The plot developed along conventional lines well known to Maschwitz. The Parisian atmosphere, perhaps easier to get away with on radio, was not wholly convincing, but the music of George Posford (a regular collaborator with Maschwitz) helped to lighten the load. Among others involved were Sally Gray, Donald Calthrop, dancers Cleo Nordi and Ronnie Boyer, the always watchable Olive Sloane, Charles Carson, and, in their only film, the Tzigansky Choir.

The dashingly continental flavour of the wireless programme was so realistic that Maschwitz claimed 'an international hoax had been played on the audience, particularly as many listeners had written letters to the imaginary establishment in Paris, which were forwarded to the BBC by the French Postal Service'.[1]

So far as its leading man was concerned, Premier-Stafford's *Wake Up Famous* might better have been titled *Wake Up Less Famous*. Gene Gerrard's film career as director and star was drawing to a close. There would be one more feature, the 1938 comedy *Glamour Girl* directed by Arthur B. Woods for Warner Bros First National. There remained only the eight-minute short, *Dumb Dora Discovers Tobacco* of 1945, reissued two years later as the even less appealingly titled *Fag End*. Gerrard, devastatingly described by Low as 'shorter and less well known than Jack Buchanan',[2] suffered from the near-collapse of the British studio system as the mid-1930s were left behind. If Chamberlain had persuaded Hitler to arrange 'peace in our time', the futures of leading men in British movies may have been different. They might even have prospered, but the likes of Gerrard essentially belong to the decade, their voices, the too-often ungainly or crimped hairstyles, the over-posh elocution, the unflattering make-up, and the confusion that clearly existed between professional choreography and the amateur lolloping-about that runs through so many 1930s British musicals (and Gerrard lollops with the best).

Gerrard cannot seriously be considered a romantic figure, although the cinemagoer of 1937 was asked to believe it. Leading British male actors of the 1930s? There is not a Brad Pitt or Hugh Jackman among them. What, indeed, were the necessary qualifications? For modern tastes, the talents of Jack Hulbert, billed above the title for a string of films built specifically around him and culminating in the 1938 *Kate Plus Ten*, seem vague. The comedy is liable to veer to the terrible, the singing is loose, the dancing slopes and swerves, and turns frog-like whenever Stanley Lupino hoves into view. Meanwhile, Barry Mackay's efforts at partnering Jessie Matthews resemble a keep-fit exercise for incipient arthritics. With Hulbert, it's as if only the sudden Cheshire cat-like grin retains a potency. As a romantic lead, we can't be expected to take Hulbert or Mackay seriously. Nevertheless,

Mackay deserves a posthumous award for persistence, and was possibly in awe of the possibility that he might be replaced by Fred Astaire. Mackay ploughed on, through the Matthews vehicles *Evergreen*, *Gangway* and *Sailing Along*, matching Frances Day in *Oh, Daddy!* and Mary Ellis in the most boring *Glamorous Night*, and teaming up with Courtneidge in the already over-heavy *Me and Marlborough*. The catalogue is long considering that Mackay could neither sing nor dance (perhaps not even act); at least Gerrard attempts all three.

Premier-Stafford's producer John Stafford hired Basil Mason to provide *Wake Up Famous* with a screenplay involving hotel clerk Alfred Dimbleden (Nelson Keys), film director Fink (Gerrard), a gang of jewel thieves (how audiences must have yawned when this all too familiar collection of bad'uns invaded the screen), and a well-tried sequence of misunderstandings, assumed identities and romantic foolishnesses, removing the action to France. Fink mistakenly (who can blame him in such scripts?) thinks Dimbleden is a songwriter. He isn't, but writes a song that hits the spot. An injection of continental glamour is attempted in the casting of Bela Mila (who had already played in British studios for *Ball at Savoy* and *Beloved Impostor*) as Agatha Dimbleden. Josephine Huntley Wright as a wannabe film star and the nimble Fred Conyngham (rightly described by Denis Gifford as 'Britain's B-picture Fred Astaire') inject some life. Perhaps Balcon signed Mackay as Matthews's leading man because he didn't have Conyngham's telephone number.

Ultimately, the responsibility for *Wake Up Famous* resides with Gerrard as star and director. The *MFB* noted a curate's egg of an affair, played too slowly, suggesting that 'diverse activities have been unfortunate for the film. The story is of the loose and casual kind frequent in farces, and needing strong direction to pull it together. This it has not had.'[3]

FEBRUARY

The modesty of the Windmill's antics in three shorts, *Song in Soho*, *Windmill Revels* and *Carry On London*, survives as evidence as to why this London entertainment with its proud legend 'We Never Closed', basically recreating items from that theatre's repertoire of nudity and comedy, could scarcely be compared to the splendours of yet another Herbert Wilcox musical phantasmagoria. His publicity department was busy proclaiming that 'The story of a girl who played her hand-organ and made monkeys out of two diplomats is a picture that will make monkeys of all previous box-office records'. It is doubtful that this prophecy was fulfilled. *MFB* welcomed a 'screen novelette' with his star Anna Neagle in a 'rather inane' part of a street Arab who becomes a famous dancer.[4] There is no doubt that Wilcox, Neagle's Svengali, saw Neagle's own background within. Based on a story by Ray Lewis (possibly written on a matchbox), the screenplay was by Florence Tranter and Monckton Hoffe. Neagle was about to burst into a dramatic actress winning countless admirers for her impersonations of strong women. Her success in Wilcox's *Victoria the Great* (September 1937) was such that he immediately remade it in colour as *Sixty Glorious Years*. Meanwhile he turned to *London Melody*, in which the street-dancing Jacqueline is 'discovered' by Italian diplomat Marius Andreani. This role, following the trend of importing foreign leading men to play opposite Neagle in *Bitter Sweet* and the *Victoria* biopics, went to Tullio Carminati, who had already played opposite Neagle in Wilcox's 1936 *The Three Maxims*.

For **London Melody** (not to be confused with the 59-minute 1930 film of the same name), songs were provided by Sigler, Goodhart and Hoffman, among them 'The Eyes Of The World Are On You' and 'Jingle Of The Jungle', with appropriate dance breaks organised by Ralph Reader. A fire at the British and Dominions studios in February 1936 had the shooting moved from Elstree to Pinewood. After Neagle's screen performance as Charles II's favourite Peg of Old Drury in 1935, Wilcox decided that audiences would see her dance again, and Wilcox, according to Shipman, 'shoved her into three ratty musicals, *Limelight* (1935), *The Three Maxims* and *London Melody*'.[5] By the time Neagle returned to post-war films, Wilcox had mated her professionally to Michael Wilding.

What a relief, after a Neagle-Wilcox potboiler, to welcome **Please Teacher**. They may not be the Rodgers and Hammerstein of British musicals, but Jack Waller and Joseph Tunbridge, almost totally forgotten by present-day filmgoers, wrote some of the most delightful and evocative stage musicals of the period, among them *Virginia* (from which came the spiritual-like 'Roll Away Clouds'), *Tell Her the Truth*, *He Wanted Adventure*, *Mr Whittington*, *Big Business* and *Bobby Get Your Gun*. The 'Bobby' was diminutive stage comic Bobby Howes, around whom Waller and Tunbridge, and lyricists R. P. (Bob) Weston and Bert Lee, structured three musicals, all of which reached the screen with their male star in place: *For the Love of Mike*, *Yes, Madam?* and *Please Teacher*. Credited on screen as by K. R. G. Browne, R. P. Weston and Bert Lee, BIP's Elstree production was directed by Stafford Dickens, who also wrote the screenplay. Although he contributed screenplays to other musical films including *Command Performance* and Courtneidge's *Things Are Looking Up*, *Please Teacher* was his only directing credit.

Tommy Deacon (Howes) arrives in England from India, and is mistaken for a gym master at Miss Trundle's Academy for Young Ladies run by sisters Agatha (Bertha Belmore) and Petunia (Vera Pearce). He is introduced as a gentleman 'in knickers and a funny hat' (it's a pith helmet). Howes and the gloriously built Pearce waste no time in getting into some intricate comedy play, and before long Pearce is in the gym at 'Exercise'. Her performance, as anyone who has seen her will attest, is something out of the ordinary. The dialogue is sparky and fleet. 'You'll find a good man hard to find,' Agatha warns Petunia. Petunia replies, 'I have.' Anyway, 'Mr Tommy has just returned from India where trousers are not essential.' When the Chinese villain of the piece (Lynn Harding) meets the formidable Agatha, he relates an old Chinese proverb, 'The man shall command from the house-tops and the woman shall kneel and obey.' Agatha replies (and what a way Belmore has with her lines), 'Indeed. You know, we have an old proverb here that says "The bull bellows but the cow delivereth the milk".' A sleepwalking scene is a highlight.

The comedy is beautifully played, while the (thankfully few) romantic moments are soon done with. There is, however, the wooing by Deacon of pretty pupil Ann Trent (Rene Ray) in 'You Give Me Ideas' with its brilliant lyric: 'I don't know classical languages, nor why four slices of bread are two sandwiches when there's no ham but, you give me ideas.' Then, 'I don't know why a horse whinnies or why housemaids always wear short pinnies, don't know a thing about love but, you give me ideas.'

In 'Mind How You Go Across The Road' Howes instructs Ray in the Highway Code. For 1937 audiences this was contemporary stuff, Leslie Hore-Belisha having just introduced the Belisha Beacon. The lyric is a delight:

>Mind how you go across the road
>When you cross the road be very careful
>Be very careful, whatever you do.
>Mind how you go across the road
>When you cross the road
>Or else a chauffeur may knock you over
>Then I shall lose you.
>Don't ever lose your head
>Stop when you see the red
>And at the yellow go slow
>Then when you see the green
>You'll know it's all serene
>Pick up your tootsies and go
>
>So, mind how you go across the road
>When you cross the road
>Although you're agile
>You are so fragile
>So light and airy
>You're like a fairy
>You're too seraphic
>For city traffic
>So mind how you go across the road

Please Teacher has no shortage of musical gems. 'Hail Women Of History' is a hilariously ridiculous pastiche of choral exultation with the commanding Belmore proclaiming man as 'that crawling worm' in a tribute to her sex worthy of any modern-day feminist, concluding with a Howes-Pearce *pas de deux*. In the manner of Amy Woodforde-Finden, Wylie Watson (a regular member of the Waller-Tunbridge shows) joins Howes and Pearce in the Indian trio 'Temple Bells'. The material works beautifully, not least because its principals were an established stage team.

In some ways ***Head Over Heels*** may have marked the beginning of Jessie Matthews's decline. The *MFB* criticised 'a definite lack of the sparkle and gaiety which this class of picture needs' in a film that was 'strongly British in characterisation' but 'treated too heavily for its type'.[6] Victor Saville had directed her previous, *It's Love Again*, but left this project to Matthews's husband and sometime co-star Sonnie Hale. Now, she was matched with the French Louis Borell and the gentlemanly Robert Flemyng, neither of whom ignited the screen.

Based on Francis de Croisset's play *Pierre ou Jack*, the adaptation by Fred Thompson and Dwight Taylor had a scenario by Marjorie Gaffney and dialogue by Taylor, but its attraction as the basis of a musical film is difficult to understand. The opportunity to break away from the conventional format of a backstage novelette about a heroine wanting stardom was not grasped. *Head Over Heels* is pretty dull stuff, enlivened now and again by some half-decent songs by the American team of Mack Gordon and Harry Revel. At least the film is song-rich, with 'pleasant tunes and occasionally ingenious lyrics':[7] 'Head Over Heels In Love', 'Through The Courtesy Of Love', 'Looking Around Corners', 'There's That Look In Your Eyes Again' and 'Don't Give A Good Dash Darn' (the last perhaps a sop to the American market; did anyone in Britain use such language?). Matthews even gets to sing some advertising jingles. Most successful is the Buddy Bradley-choreographed 'May I Have The Next Romance With You?'. It captures Matthews's strangely phantom presence.

Once again, no one at Gaumont-British had bothered to find her a dancing partner (Matthews, anyway, might not have welcomed the competition). In fact, this is to the number's advantage, as Matthews is accompanied by male dancers who make the eeriest of partners. Despite their intensely dark sexuality (rare in British musical films, and rarer still when Matthews was in the frame), she comes across as a superb dancer and remote personality.

The pervading greyness that clouds too much of *Head Over Heels* is not helped by some uncharacteristically dreary sets from Alfred Junge, some half-hearted attempts at a continental atmosphere (perhaps acceptable to audiences unaccustomed to foreign travel), and an abundance of talk. On the floor at Shepherd's Bush, shooting had to be closed down in August 1936 when Matthews had a breakdown. In September, Michael Balcon closed down filming again, with only nine days' work remaining. Matthews had her appendix removed, and shooting resumed in December.

The result pleased many, but cracks were showing. Graham Greene thought Matthews 'ill-served' by the film. Writing in *Film Weekly*, Stephanie Le Cocq was one of several to express doubts about the clothes she wore. 'I do not think a small-town milliner would be proud of them. In my opinion the average London business girl dresses better than the screen Jessie Matthews. It says a great deal for this star's acting ability and charm of personality that she is so popular abroad.'[8] In *Picturegoer*, Yvonne Thomas considered Matthews's head 'neat and pretty' (she overlooked the awful hairstyling), 'but her hats seem specially designed to disguise the fact, for in films she appears either wearing something like a huge cabbage leaf on her head or, alternatively, an imitation of an antiquated coal-scuttle'.[9]

Responding to this criticism, the fashion house of Worth offered to reinvent Matthews's look. Hale rejected the offer, apparently content to allow her to appear in wardrobes of ridiculously piecemeal get-ups, as if a street market had been plundered for remnants, and wastepaper-baskets. Superficial as this minor furore seems, it was an indication that Matthews was, in more ways than one, sliding out of fashion.

Reviewing *Moonlight Sonata*, *MFB* wistfully considered that 'In years to come musicians will be grateful for this sympathetic material. But cinemagoers of today may be disappointed with a film that lacks the usual ingredients.'[10] That, of course, depended on what cinemagoers considered the usual ingredients of a British musical film to be – often enough joke-book comedy, listless emotional frissons and absurd storylines set in ritzy nightclubs or Ruritanian principalities not found on any map. Of these, at least, *Moonlight Sonata* is reasonably devoid, being a filmic celebration of the pianist Ignace Jan Paderewski, playing not only the piano but himself. Made by Pall Mall Productions at the Denham Studios, it had a screenplay by Edward Knoblock and dialogue by E. M. Delafield, based on a story by Hans Rameau and directed by its producer Lothar Mendes.

The writers locked Paderewski into an unlikely scenario in which an aeroplane carrying the famous musician makes an emergency landing, making him the unscheduled guest of the Swedish Baroness Lindenborg (a rare film appearance by the theatrical Dame Marie Tempest). The Baroness's daughter Ingrid (soulful Barbara Greene), supposedly affianced to the boy-like lumberjack Eric (American Charles Farrell), is infatuated by Paderewski's fellow passenger, the suave and lustful playboy Mario de la Costa (Eric Portman). Mario is exposed as a stage hypnotist, while Ingrid and Eric are reunited courtesy of the spiritual pull of Beethoven. As Paderewski explains, 'I will try to make the Moonlight Sonata speak to you.' The great pianist dominates the first twenty minutes of the film, playing at a magnificently staged concert. Its audience contains an enraptured child (Binkie Stuart), tousled and curly-headed in a party frock with puffed sleeves, and fortified by a bag of sweeties. Ingrid recalls her mother playing the Moonlight to her ('It means everything sacred to me').

The sight of the pianistic maestro hammering away may not be cinematically compelling, but he and Tempest, her quiet unobtrusive style bringing a dignified air to the proceedings, help the film rise above curiosity or documentary. Eric is roused when Ingrid threatens to leave him for caddish Mario, threatening 'I'm going to put you across my knee and spank you'. Amidst much else along similar lines, some of it set in unconvincing forestry, Paderewski finds time to go through Chopin's Heroic Polonaise, Liszt's Hungarian Rhapsody, his own Minuet in G, and, at last, the first movement of the Moonlight.

John Argyle's **Kathleen Mavourneen** was an Argyle-British Production made at Welwyn. Argyle had first used a song title, *Love's Old Sweet Song*, for a film in 1933. *Kathleen Mavourneen* is one of the best 'Irish' musical films of the decade, based – the credits tell us – 'on the world famous song'. Its success is in no small measure due to the direction of Norman Lee, perhaps helped by 'Irish adviser' W. G. Fay, and safely delivered in its excellent performances. In a well-populated Liverpool inn among the docks, there is plenty of Irish stew on the menu. Avuncular Dan Milligan (Talbot O'Farrell) adds to the gaiety by relating 'The Day That Old Rafferty's Daughter Got Wed'. Fine-voiced Mike Rooney (robust Tom Burke) wants to marry Kathleen O'Moore (American Sally O'Neil), serenading her with the title song.

When Burke sings, we know the grey dawn is breaking, and the listening customers are understandably enraptured. Dan hands out presents to a family about to leave for America. It's a touching sequence in Marjorie Deans's intelligent screenplay, based on a story by John Glen and (possibly) a novel by Clara Mulholland. Kathleen's father has died. The kindly Mike pays for Kathleen and her young brother and sister Pat and Sheila to move to Ireland, to live with her aunt, Mary Ellen O'Dwyer (Sara Allgood). Kathleen falls for a handsome landowner, Dennis O'Dwyer (Jack Daly), and has to deal with his unpleasant mother Hannah O'Dwyer (the formidable Ethel Griffies). It's a neatly turned-out picture, with a genuine air of care around the family disagreements that haunt it, and O'Neil is worthy of its title role; she had already played the character in America for Tiffany Films' 1930 *Kathleen Mavourneen*, and she owns the part again here. Although the piece is strong enough to hold its own, we have the bonus of the Tara Troupe of Irish Dancers, the young champion Irish step-dancer Rory O'Connor, piper Sean Dempsey, Frank Lee's Tara Ceilidh Band, and the Classic Symphony Orchestra conducted by Guy Jones. Most beguilingly, we have Burke serenading his love for Kathleen with 'Eileen Alannah'.

As if these were not riches enough, we have music-hall double act, husband and wife Arthur Lucan and Kitty McShane, playing mother and daughter. At the time of filming *Kathleen Mavourneen* Lucan's character was Mrs O'Flynn, subsequently becoming Mrs Riley. Robert V. Kenny suggests that Lucan and McShane were brought into the picture 'to enhance the film's appeal to Irish-American audiences [and presumably to the Irish population at home] when it was released in the States in 1938'.[11]

Mrs O'Flynn bursts into the film at a village fair, expostulating and gesticulating, distraught that her daughter Bridget Mary Josephine O'Flynn is missing (a recurring reason for the old mother's fits of exasperation). Bridget is entered for a dancing competition. The comedy is thin and the effect disappointing; it is a wonder then that, despite the evidence of *Kathleen Mavourneen*, Butcher's signed them for *Old Mother Riley*, a feature of their own, made at Cricklewood and released in August 1937. Its commercial success was such that it began the string of 'Old Mother Riley' films that ran through until *Mother Riley Meets the Vampire*, by which time (1952) the title had dropped the 'Old', and in which an exhausted Lucan, now parted from Kitty, was teamed with an equally exhausted Bela Lugosi. Along the way, Kennedy Russell remained a faithful contributor to the scores. A more detailed account of the series is included in the 1940 *Old Mother Riley in Society*.

We should not forget that *Kathleen Mavourneen* has a thoroughly affecting final scene, a moment of intense regret followed by the delight of children tucking into the wedding feast.

MARCH

William Beaudine, one of the most prolific of American directors, had started in silents in 1922, and worked consistently through to 1966, culminating in two kitsch horror-western quickies, *Billy the Kid Versus Dracula* and *Jesse James Meets Frankenstein's Daughter*. By the time he got to direct George Formby in Associated Talking Pictures' **Feather Your Nest** he had already directed features for several British comedy performers: Monty Banks in *So You Won't Talk* (1935); *Dandy Dick* (1935), *Boys Will Be Boys* (1935) and *Where There's a Will* (1936) for Will Hay, and *Educated Evans* (1936) for Max Miller. Formby could have wished for no more qualified director. Based on a story by Ivar and Sheila Campbell, *Feather Your Nest* has a screenplay by Val Valentine and Austin Melford, with contributions by Anthony Kimmins and Robert Edmunds. Melford's robust career in British musical films included scripts for many other Formbys including *Keep Fit*, *I See Ice*, *Let George Do It*, *Spare a Copper*, *Turned Out Nice Again* and *South American George*. Melford, along with a close-knit team of songwriters particularly tuned to the Formby phenomenon, kept their star's career on course for a decade.

Now, Formby is Willie Piper, an accident-prone assistant at the Monarch Gramophone Company, anxious for a salary rise, but more likely to be sacked for clumsiness. He plans to marry Mary (Polly Ward), daughter of the waspish landlady at the Fox and Hare, where he has rooms. The company has signed a pretentious singer, Randall, who is about to record a number. Willie and Mary are planning to buy their own house, and settle on 'The Nest', but it's a rubbish new-build. This may be a comment on the state of British housing two years before

World War II. The lovers happily look to the future with Harry Gifford, Fred E. Cliffe and Formby's 'When We Feather Our Nest'.

Randall makes his recording, singing a staid, embryonic version of what would become one of Formby's most iconic songs. Willie drops the master recording of 'Waiting By The Lamp On The Avenue', rendering it useless. Mary sees what must be done. Willie will record the song himself, accompanying himself on the ukulele, while she surprises us by skilfully accompanying him on the piano. For this, Noel Gay tweaked 'Waiting By The Lamp' into the much more immediate 'Leaning On A Lamp-Post'. The record, of course, is a hit (and became one of the songs with which Formby was inextricably associated). Willie and Mary move into 'The Nest', and Mrs Taylor gives her blessing. At a house-warming party, Willie confesses 'I'm As Happy As A Sandboy', written by the 'The Two Leslies', Leslie Holmes and Leslie Sarony. During the ensuing jollity, thieves remove all the furniture. This is one of the film's funniest scenes, stressing the utter domesticity and gentleness at the heart of the story. It seems that Willie is doomed to ever be a failure when he ends up in jail, but he is freed and acclaimed as the singer. There was fulsome praise for Formby in the *MFB*, which only lamented, 'The rest of the cast give him good support, though they are not up to his own standard.'[12]

British baritone Keith Falkner was already well known for his performances on the concert platform, on radio and on recordings when Warner Bros mounted a campaign to make a star of him. *Mayfair Melody* was the first of three films to showcase Falkner's talents, all three masterminded and directed by Arthur Woods, and made at Teddington. Warner Bros' and, more importantly, Woods's belief in Falkner is obvious. Indeed, the Falkner phenomenon is almost unique in British musical films. A cohesive team joined Woods in the enterprise, including composer Kenneth Leslie-Smith and lyricist James Dyrenforth, who also provided the story for *Mayfair Melody*. The music included 'San Diego Betty', 'Without The Moon', 'Wings' and 'A Song Doesn't Care'.

The *Era* welcomed Falkner, 'owner of a pleasing but not exactly electrifying singing voice and about whose acting the less said the better […] The story given Mr Falkner is not unduly impressive, and it is Joyce Kirby who actually walks away with the honours […] in a role which could have been both irritating and preposterous.'[13] In 1933 Kirby's appearance in *Waltz Time* had inspired the *Observer* to name her 'the most likely of the Gainsborough "baby stars"; she has the face and the spirit for success, and you will be hearing from her again'.[14] *MFB* commented that 'with faultless speech' Falkner 'never suggests the faintest impression of a mechanic; but his voice – probably the best baritone in England – records gloriously'.[15]

Inevitably, mechanical Mark (Falkner) turns his back on the garage to become a singing star, encouraged by the admiring Brenda (Kirby) although for a time bedazzled by the worryingly named Carmen (Chili Bouchier in another firebrand subsidiary role). Choreographer Jack Donohue was another essential of Woods's team, mounting effective musical sequences. *MFB* shrugged the film off as 'a silly story around which is woven plenty of broad comedy',[16] but *Kine Weekly* liked its 'shy, disarming reticence' [something quite distinct in contemporary musical films], noting 'The show lacks nothing in stagecraft, the musical ensembles that decorate the ending are artistically and ingeniously contrived, nor is bright repartee absent from the dialogue.'[17] No copies of *Mayfair Melody* seem to have survived, a tragedy compounded by the fact that the subsequent Falkner movies, *The Singing Cop* and *Thistledown*, are also lost. Perhaps it doesn't matter. The *Observer* critic asked, 'Is the British public really so silly as Messrs Warner Brothers seem to believe?'[18]

Mayfair Melody was deemed good enough to be booked for the Empire, Leicester Square, a distinction denied Fox's knocked-up concoction **Variety Hour**, directed at Wembley by the Canadian Redd Davis, busy making quota quickies throughout the decade; the same year he made the Flanagan and Allen *Underneath the Arches* and the dismal *Sing As You Swing*. Little more than a string of acts, *Variety Hour* was linked by Clapham and Dwyer as two wannabe performers passing themselves off as American radio comperes. There are compensations for sitting through the bill. There is a splash of the close harmony-dancing Wiere Brothers, the 'One Direction' of their day (British Pathé had already filmed their frolics with a pantomime horse), and of the American country music balladeer Carson Robison and His Pioneers. Raymond Newell, the incisive leading man of several West End musicals, also seen in Pathé Pictorials, leads the company in what the *MFB* considered a 'rather heavily patriotic finale'.[19] Jack Donohue, choreographer for the Falkner pictures, dances. Others appearing include Helen Howard, the Norwich Trio, and Kay, Katya and Kay.

Another film lacking plot or cohesion, British Lion's **Calling All Stars** begged the question, 'How many stars responded?' to producer-director Herbert Smith's request. Lazy as these compilations of disparate theatre and nightclub turns may seem, they did serve a function at the time, offering audiences the sort of stuff they would expect if they stayed at home to listen to the wireless or visited the local variety theatre. What other reason (or excuse) was there? Today, the films serve another purpose, not only through their preservation of defunct art forms but as evidence of how domestic audiences were beguiled in the 1930s. It is undemanding fare. Among those on show is Evelyn Dall singing 'The Organ Grinder's Song' (with a chained monkey) and, removed to a nightclub setting, 'I Don't Wanna Get Hot', with Ambrose and His Orchestra. The musical items have worn better than the film's comedy sequences in the hands of old-timers such as Davy Burnaby (notably of The Co-Optimists concert party), Flotsam and Jetsam (it's like a Masonic evening with songs), and, rather more welcome but never as effective as he was on stage, Billy Bennett. The female comedians can barely be recommended. Ethel Revnell and Gracie West were popular on the halls but achieve nothing in a ramshackle cockney item. Elisabeth Welch, too often saddled with undistinguished songs, sings 'Nightfall'.

There are plums in the pudding. The peerless Carroll Gibbons and the Savoy Orpheans back the close-harmony Three Canadian Bachelors singing 'Painting Rainbows'; there is brilliant dancing from the Nicholas Brothers; Buck and Bubbles strut 'The Rhythm's OK In Harlem', and Sam Browne, Ambrose's vocalist, performs 'Serenade In The Night' and 'The Peanut Vendor'. The Twelve Aristocrats, at first as sedate as a factory's formation dance team, goes acrobatic. Impressive as this is, it pales beside the scary choreography of the Bega Four's Hungarian Apache Dance, accompanied by Eugene Pini and His Orchestra.

APRIL

An air of despondency hangs over Gracie Fields's last film for Associated Talking Pictures, *The Show Goes On*. It certainly did. Here was an attempt by its producer-director Basil Dean, with scenario and dialogue by Anthony Kimmins, Austin Melford, and E. G. Valentine, based on a story by Dean and Kimmins, to break from the northern confines that threatened to restrain her. The problem was that whatever role Fields played on screen, audiences expected to recognise Fields inside it. Dean's attitude to his star was different to that of Monty Banks; Dean wanted to utilise her dramatic potential.

Nevertheless, the new film started Up North, at the last night of a Lancastrian pantomime at Hindlebury's Theatre Royal. A drunk Dick Whittington, unable to make it on stage for the walk-down, is replaced by chorus-girl Sally Scowcroft (Fields). Determined to resist her parents' pressure to keep her working at the local mill, she wants to succeed as a performer. Her stolid boyfriend Mack (John Stuart) is unimpressed, insisting 'I don't want you to be an actress'. The weak-chested composer Martin Fraser (Owen Nares) spots her in a pierrot show at Colwyn Bay and invites her to dinner. Inevitably he begins writing songs for her; the good news is that these are mostly the work of Field's much underrated composer Harry Parr Davies (the credits hyphenate him). Martin is clearly a thinking man, expressing the opinion that 'I believe people want melody. They're getting tired of noise.' He has a cough.

Sally Scowcroft becomes Sally Lee, but her fortunes are mixed. Her father loses his job, Mack asks her to go to Canada with him (not likely). She gets a job in a touring show singing Martin's songs but audiences are bored by their sentimentality, wanting the comedy they expect of her. She turns one of Martin's compositions 'In A Little Lancashire Town' (by Will E. Haines and Jimmy Harper) into a comic turn. In her home town, audiences shout 'Give us something comic!'. Obligingly, she sings 'I Never Cried So Much In All My Life' (by Harry Castling, Will E. Haines and Jimmy Harper). There is more comedy in 'The Co-Op Shop' (by Bert Lee, Harris Weston and R. P. Weston), and reassurance in Davies, Will E. Haines and Jimmy Harper's 'We're All Pals Together'. Fields continues with Martin's (i.e. Parr Davies and Eddie Pola's) 'My Love For You'. Martin's cough worsens. Mack leaves the scene. Ma and Pa seem, rather inexplicably, to grow rich. Learning that Martin has been paying her an inflated salary out of his own pocket to help her career, she goes to see him, and insists that he accompany her on a holiday in California.

About to leave England, she sings Davies's 'You've Got To Smile When You Say Goodbye' to a shipload of departing sailors, in the most satisfactory and moving sequence of the film. Martin manufactures a quarrel with her, knowing that he has no future and wishing her to succeed. She is offered a leading role at Drury Lane. Martin knows that 'She was born for laughter'. Now, Sally is transformed into a glamorous star, ruling her career with complete confidence. Martin dies. Sally makes a great success of her Drury Lane engagement in an extravagantly choreographed finale (designed by Cathleen Mann and choreographed by American dancer Carl Randall), singing 'A Song In Your Heart' (by Davies and Eddie Pola) as Mack gazes lovingly on from a box.

There is little flesh on the bones of Dean's concept. The relationships between Fields and the male leads never quite take fire. The scenes of Sally's home life don't convince. At moments the film seems to be about the conflicting elements in Sally's talent – should she make us laugh or cry? The sumptuous finale negates the argument, for we see that Sally is required to do neither. Dean provides plenty of theatrical atmosphere in backstage sequences and in the girls' dressing room at the pierrot show. Frank Atkinson, uncredited as a boozy old thespian, is an asset, but Fields looks less comfortable than in her earlier work.

MFB's reviewer seems to have been bored with a film that 'becomes inconsequent and uninteresting', complaining of 'an astonishing lack of comedy' in 'the least satisfactory film that Gracie Fields has made'.[20] More recently, Jeffrey Richards, recognising that *The Show Goes On* ends with 'the inevitable glamorization of Gracie', deduces that 'She has become part of the Establishment, her role now to minimize class differences, stress social mobility by talent and channel all energies into national consensus'.[21] This may or may not have been music to Miss Fields's ears.

Sounding the sort of title Herbert Wilcox might have dreamed up, British National's **The Street Singer** was produced at Pinewood by Dora Nirva, previously production manager for the Chevalier-Lockwood curiosity *The Beloved Vagabond*. Reginald Arkell scripted a storyline by Paul Schiller and the film's French director Jean de Marguenat in his only visit to British studios. The al fresco warbler is the Russian-born American balladeer Arthur Tracy, who modestly compared himself to Caruso. After success in the USA, he moved to Britain in the mid-1930s, top-lining at the Palladium. His bravura renditions of 'Marta, Rambling Rose Of The

Wild Wood' and the frankly laughable 'It's My Mother's Birthday Today' followed him throughout his career. Richard King (Tracy) gives up a successful stage career to busk in the streets with Jenny Green (Margaret Lockwood) and her father Sam (Arthur Riscoe). Richard is 'discovered' in his guise as the street singer, and Jenny becomes his leading lady in the West End. It was generally agreed that Tracy sang better than he acted. Music is provided by piano duettists Rawicz and Landauer, and Lew Stone and His Band, and included 'Halfway To Heaven', 'Street Serenade' and 'Haroun El Rachid'. Lockwood recalled that during filming Tracy 'would sit in his dressing-room listening to his own recordings with tears in his eyes'.[22]

Ralph Reader deserves more than to be remembered as the man who taught a generation of boy scouts how to get into musicals. His work in theatre and film has long been overlooked, but the mere mention of his best-known composition 'Riding Along On The Crest Of A Wave' (for which he wrote words and music), inevitably featured in **The Gang Show**, brings his name into focus. Herbert Wilcox was the most obvious choice of producers to bring Reader's famous organisation to the screen, directed at Pinewood by Alfred Goulding, but patrons expecting wall-to-wall songs and sketches were faced with Marjorie Gaffney's screenplay with the Gang Show's *éminence grise* playing 'Skipper', a humble clerk who dreams of putting on a big show filled with singing boys. He is encouraged by secretary Marie (Gina Malo), who nurses 'hopes'. 'He called me darling!' she cries just before the big finish. The romantic element is pootling compared to what those scouts have to offer – not only an enthusiastic burst of amateur theatricals and youthful spirits, but a sense of incipient male solidarity. It's a generous dose of guaranteed optimism, two years before World War II, with the Nazi shadow already looming. Were audiences confused that Reader, already known throughout the world for The Gang Show, was now playing a man who dreamed of putting such a show on? What tortuous uncertainty awaited the British cinemagoer!

   The crest of the wave was already at its height this year, during which The Gang appeared at the Royal Variety Performance. Musical items in the film version included 'Children Of The New Regime', 'I've Got A Rainbow In My Heart', 'Birds Of A Feather', 'With A Twinkle In Your Eye' and (the most appropriate and inevitable of finales) 'Crest Of A Wave'. 'Danny Boy' and 'Mother Macrae' are performed by the Welsh wonder-boy Dillwyn Thomas, immortalised in short trousers in a Pathé short of the same year, when he sang 'Vienna, City Of My Dreams'. Stewart Robinson sang 'That Song In My Heart'. Does the present-day scout movement offer a badge in musicals? Whatever, Reader was content, explaining, 'I've got the biggest family in the world, even though all my "sons" have different fathers.' No doubt this caused much chortling across the worldwide scout movement.

The American distributors of Butcher's **Rose of Tralee** informed cinemagoers that the film was 'Approved and endorsed by the Legion of Decency and Irish Societies' and that they were about to see 'The Shirley Temple of Ireland'. It's a wonder Temple didn't sue. What satisfaction could its writer and director Oswald Mitchell have derived from this project? His achievements included five Old Mother Riley pictures, the 1935 *Stars on Parade* in which Arthur Lucan and Kitty McShane made their screen debut, and at the end of his career he was directing a tired Tod Slaughter in the gruesome melodrama *The Greed of William Hart*.

For *Rose of Tralee*, Mitchell assembled a cast that spanned the ages, satellites circling its four-year-old star. Binkie Stuart's short-lived celebrity began when she played in the Formby *Keep Your Seats, Please* the previous year. As one of the characters comments, 'That child's got talent. She might be good for the films', and later, 'I think there might be a fortune in her.' Sadly, there is little talent visible in Stuart's performance, her singing and dancing hesitant. Her rendition of 'Come Back To Ireland' can have done nothing for the tourist trade.

In later life, she recalled that her talents 'made me perfect for motion pictures',[23] but beyond having some physical resemblance to Hollywood's much more famous curly-headed moppet – curly blonde hair – Stuart was in no way exceptional. One can sympathise with the reviewer for *MFB* who found her 'rather an anxious looking little star'.[24] Looking back, she described a childhood of mental abuse, with her father forcing her into films. On one occasion, a scene involved her in being locked inside a suitcase. Terrified, Stuart refused to comply. Her father was called, and she capitulated. She subsequently discovered that her father had spent the money she had earned; nothing was left. He told her, 'Who would pay you to do anything?' He continued to control her until she finally broke away, leaving home at the age of twenty-one. Her film career had ended by the time she was seven.

The simple plot of *Rose of Tralee* involves a singer husband (Fred Conyngham) and wife (Kathleen O'Regan) who have drifted apart but still long for one another. They are eventually brought together through the auspices of their daughter Rose (of Tralee, naturally). The bulk of the songs (Irish melodies including Percy French's 'The Mountains Of Mourne', 'Did Your Mother Come From Ireland?' and 'Believe Me, If All Those Endearing Young Charms') fall to the pleasant Conyngham. As wife Mary, O'Regan must have wondered what had happened to her career after playing leads in Sean O'Casey's *Juno and the Paycock* and *The Plough and the Stars*. The other wasted opportunity was of veteran entertainer Talbot O'Farrell, in his glory days billed as 'The Greatest Irish Entertainer of All Time', bringing bags of charm to his theatre audiences with such ballads as 'The Lisp Of A Baby's Prayer'. Alas, he is song-less here, reduced to playing a sort of benign uncle figure to the diminutive star, and joined by Sydney Fairbrother as a kindly landlady who takes in Mary and Rose when they have nowhere to go. O'Farrell and Fairbother can't have been too discouraged by *Rose of Tralee*: the following year they appeared again with Stuart in *My Irish Molly*.

MFB's verdict was that *Rose of Tralee* 'cannot be described as a good picture, but humorous warm-heartedness, backed up by Irish melodies, gives it entertainment value.'[25] Perhaps, but it sets its sights way too low. Frank Gilman's art direction emphasises the grim, and the women's fashions are deplorable, although Conyngham gets to wear an amazingly speckled overcoat. Ultimately, watching the four-year-old leading lady go through her moves is an unsettling experience, not helped by O'Farrell referring to her in one scene as 'the biggest midget in the world'.

Gainsborough's *O-Kay for Sound*, written by Marriott Edgar and Val Guest, produced by Edward Black and directed at Islington by Marcel Varnel, offered a feast for fans of The Crazy Gang, based on George Black's London Palladium success by Bert Lee and R. P. Weston. Michael Carr and Jimmy Kennedy contributed the title song, 'Free' (captivatingly sung in the street by Flanagan and Allen), and 'There's A Big Day Coming' performed by a blacked-up Flanagan and exhilarating black dancers. Weston and Lee's 'Ta Ta! Ta Ta!' segued into the naval parade finale with popular baritone Peter Dawson explaining 'The Fleet's Not In Port Very Long'. The film has many witty elements in the choosing of a film title, a cleverly devised ballet designed by Vetchinsky, and the cow grazing on pasture sequence. The clowning is fast, accurate and endearing, with guest appearances from apache dancers Lucienne and Ashour, dancer Patricia Bowman, The (female) Radio Three, the ever-ready Sherman Fisher Girls and Can-Can troupe The Robenis.

Ivor Novello is best remembered for the extravagant musicals he wrote for the Theatre Royal, Drury Lane. Three of these, *Glamorous Night*, *The Dancing Years* and *King's Rhapsody*, reached the screen. The only advantage that the latter two had over the first was that they were made in colour; all three failed to retain the appeal of their stage originals. With what excited anticipation must Novello fans have flocked to their local cinema to see what film had done for **Glamorous Night**, his first success at the Lane in 1935. The Associated British Picture Corporation and BIP's production was overseen by Walter C. Mycroft and directed at Elstree by Brian Desmond Hurst. The screenplay by Dudley Leslie, Hugh Brooke and William Freshman seemed written down to the meanest intelligence, reducing Novello's work (book and music; the lyrics were by Christopher Hassall) to absurdity. It had of course been just as absurd on stage, but better done. Now, apart from feeble settings for what, in all seriousness, was called 'Gypsy Land' (the gypsies lived there; we know they are gypsies because they run about with flaming torches and dance with their hands on their hips), a host of other problems damned it.

 The most essential lack was of a male star. Novello's film career had ended three years earlier with *Autumn Crocus*, in which he played a Swiss bed and breakfast proprietor, difficult as it was to imagine him cooking up a full Swiss breakfast. There is no evidence that he was approached about recreating his original role of Anthony Allen for *Glamorous Night*; the cinema audience had to make do with Barry Mackay. Mary Ellis repeated her stage role of Melitza Hjos, singer, and the mistress of a king despite being a gypsy (from Gypsy Land). Ellis's theatrical allure and thrilling voice are less effective on screen. There is a lack of warmth and naturalness, a hauteur, that distances us from her, and a less likely gypsy (unless it were one who went to Roedean) is difficult to imagine. BIP presumably meant to beef up the film with its Hollywood imports, Otto Kruger as a brooding wimp of a king, and Victor Jory as the Gestapo-type Baron Lyadeff, flapping in and out of scenes like a bad-tempered bat. Olive Gilbert, without whom a Novello musical in the theatre would be unthinkable, merely walks on, while Phoebe, Melitza's dresser, is played by Maire O'Neill (not a patch on the stage Phoebe, lovable Minnie Rayner). Elisabeth Welch, the black singer given two numbers in the stage show ('Shanty Town' and 'The Girl I Knew'), is nowhere to be seen.

The story of rebellion and the usurping of monarchy (there is a vast amount of scraping and curtseying) overthrew much of Novello's original plot in which Anthony Allen is the inventor of television. The film makes vaguely suggested allusions to Hitler, and to abdication – something of a hot topic, for Edward VIII had surrendered the throne a few months earlier – although Novello originally had in mind the furore around the romance of King Carol of Rumania and Mme Lupescu. Everything now, including the emotional dimension, is removed to Ruritania, and therefore nothing lifelike is available, even with Melitza as the trilling power behind the throne. Slabs of song are tossed in, some of which Ellis sings almost condescendingly. Keith Lister's choreography is appropriately tasteless.

Sandy Wilson, a Novello enthusiast, condemned the film as 'creakingly directed' and 'shoddily produced with inadequate resources; in fact one would estimate that the theatre company probably outnumbered that employed on the screen. Without the presence of Mary Ellis, it would be just another second-grade melodrama with music.'[26] Graham Greene agreed that it 'has the advantage of Mary Ellis's daemonic good looks' but was 'about as bogus as a film could be'.[27] Most lazy of all, it ignores the set-piece shipwreck that had stunned audiences at Drury Lane, so messy that it had to be cleared away in the interval. This was an extraordinary omission – a film missing the great filmic opportunity of its source material. Its producers perhaps thought the film would sink very nicely of its own accord without having to finance the shipwreck. In America, *Variety* considered the film's chances of success negligible, scoffing at the notion that Miss Ellis might be mistaken for an inhabitant of Gypsy Land.

MAY

A one-time leading man of British silents, Henry Edwards directed Butcher's *Song of the Forge*, produced by Wilfred Noy and Norman Hope-Bell at Cricklewood. Based on a story by J. D. Lewin, H. Fowler Mear's screenplay followed the adventures of dependable village blacksmith Joe Barrett and his son William, intended to follow in father's footsteps. However, William wants to be an engineer, and falls out with his father. They part in 1906 and do not meet for twenty-one years. William returns, successful, wealthy and knighted. He sees that his father's smithy has closed down, and builds grand new almshouses for the pauper locals.

Stanley Holloway, in the dual roles of father and son, had been busy in British musical films from their beginnings in 1930 with *The Co-Optimists*, and was now firmly established as a character actor of distinction via *Lily of Killarney*, *Sing As We Go*, *Road House*, *D'Ye Ken John Peel?* and *Squibs*, as well as for his humorous monologues. Musical items include 'The Poacher' and 'Why Can't We?'. A splendid supporting cast includes Lawrence Grossmith, Davy Burnaby, C. Denier Warren, 'mascot' Ian Wilson, Mervyn Johns, and a display by the Rodney Hudson Dancing Girls. Almost half an hour of material was cut when the film was reissued in 1939 as *The Village Blacksmith*.

Consistently popular on screen throughout the decade, Jack Hulbert and Cicely Courtneidge had a success with *Take My Tip*. Produced by Michael Balcon for Gaumont-British and directed by Herbert Mason at the Lime Grove Studios in Shepherd's Bush, the screenplay by Hulbert, Sidney Gilliat and Michael Hogan was loosely based on Francis de Croisset's play *La Livrée de Monsieur le Comte*. The judicious mix of high comedy and music has songs by Samuel Lerner, Al Goodhart and Al Hoffman, expertly tailored for the stars, as in 'Birdie Out Of A Cage' and the typically nonchalant 'I Was Anything But Sentimental'. The zestful choreography is by Philip Buchel (on this occasion assisted by Scott Courtney), who had already arranged the dances for Hulbert's *Jack's the Boy* and *Jack of All Trades*, and would do the same for Anna Neagle's musical films. The plot exists to provide plentiful opportunity for misunderstandings and impersonations, with Hulbert and Courtneidge as Lord and Lady Pilkington, swindled out of their money by con man Buchan (Harold Huth) and determined to get it back. The situation has echoes of the Hulberts' own financial misfortunes.

C. A. Lejeune saw the film for what it was: 'the whole show is bright and able in the polite West End manner', wound about 'a non-existent oil well – an apt subject, it would seem, for a practically non-existent film'.[28] *Sight and Sound* was impressed: 'Jack Hulbert and Cicely Courtneidge have a grand time [...] impersonating head waiters, Brazilian countesses and Anglo-Indians. This is the best film they have made together. They are given the right sort of situations, there is a merciful absence of youthful lovers and neat direction by Herbert Mason.'[29] *Take My*

Tip was their last film of the decade, followed by a final hurrah in British musical films in the excellent *Under Your Hat* in 1940. It would be twenty years before they went back to the studios, appearing together in the Diana Dors B-movie *Miss Tulip Stays the Night* and in a sedentary but Technicolor Danziger Brothers version of Agatha Christie's *Spider's Web*.

JUNE

Directed by Norman Walker, **Sunset in Vienna** had a surprisingly interesting screenplay by Marjorie Gaffney and Harrison Owens, based on a story by Florence Tranter. Although set around the First World War, it anxiously looked forward to what effects on personal relationships any future war would bring. Its barely concealed message could hardly have been clearer to British audiences, even though, under the banner of producer Herbert Wilcox, it presented as a staple melodrama of novelettish proportions.

On the eve of hostilities, Austrian Gelda Sponek (Lilli Palmer) marries the Italian officer Captain Antonio 'Toni' Baretti (Tullio Carminati, fresh from Wilcox's *London Melody*). Gelda's brother Adolphe is a spy, and is shot by Toni. This, and the pressures brought on the marriage caused by Gelda and Toni's countries being on opposite sides, proves too much, and they part. Without one another, their lives are bleak, and Gelda becomes the lover of a playboy, while Toni has lost everything. After much suffering bravely borne, they reunite.

Barbara Ziereis considers *Sunset in Vienna* as

> A typical melodrama; the settings are not realistic, the characters are rarely more than stereotypes. The film draws heavily on markers of national identity. Foreignness is represented as exotic, and expressed through set design and costume as much as through the behaviour of the characters [...] The film addresses overtly problems of mixed marriages in wartime [and] deals with divided loyalties. In terms of overall message the film suggests that the boundaries of national identity impede the lovers in their pursuit of happiness.[30]

Songwriters Lerner, Goodhart and Hoffman contributed a title song and the reassurance that 'We'll Never Run Short Of Love'.

Big Fella, Paul Robeson's follow-up to *Song of Freedom*, is unworthy of him, a hotch-potch of crude comedy, second-rate musical numbers, coarse acting and poor sets (especially surprising since its designer, credited here as Buntie Wills, is in effect the film's director and accomplished designer J. Elder Wills). Robeson rises above it all, dominating his surroundings not only in stature but with that innate charm that overcomes the film's drawbacks.

In Marseilles, Joe (Robeson) is 'Lazin' (one of the better musical items by

Safely guarded by Paul Robeson, Elisabeth Welch dreams of doing nothing very much in British Lion's *Big Fella* (1937)

composer Eric Ansell and lyricist Henrik Ege) on the studio-bound quayside where he scrapes a living. An English boy, Gerald Oliphant, is missing, presumed kidnapped. When Joe finds him, Gerald explains that he has run away from his parents. Unconcerned about a visit from Social Services, Joe takes the fifteen-year-old (Eldon Gorst) home, where he is looked after by Joe and Amanda (Elisabeth Welch). 'I wanted to enjoy myself like other boys,' Gerald tells Joe. Since leaving home, larking and playing, he's had a 'faine taime'. Gerald is so upper-crust confident and cut-glass voiced that we suppose the film must be about the stark differences between his culture and that of Joe, but nothing quite so intriguing emerges. Gerald clings to Joe, enjoining Joe and Amanda into his 'Buntie' club (is this some sort of in-joke of Wills's?).

Gendarmes with artificial French accents search for the boy, while customers at the café where Amanda sings seem to be from the East End. Gerald eventually disappears from Joe's, too. Spike (played by Roy Emerton, frequently cast as a baddie) kidnaps him and, hoping for a reward, returns the sickly boy to his parents. Gerald wants only to be with Joe, and his parents decide that Joe may visit him. Impressed by Joe, they invite him to return to England with them so that Joe and he can be together. Joe agrees, but at the dock he decides to stay with Amanda and, in probably the only truly moving moment of the film, walks back to his old happy life with her.

Based on Claude McKay's novel *Banjo*, Fenn Sherie and Ingram D'Abbes's screenplay is lightweight material for what the film's posters called 'The World's Greatest Singing and Dramatic Star'. The parental scenes are frankly ridiculous, and any sense of 'black' issues is ignored, with Welch consigned to the background despite two so-so numbers, 'One Kiss' and 'Harlem In My Heart'. At least we hear Robeson sing, in 'Roll Up, Sailor Man', 'All God's Chillun Got A Robe', 'Ma Curly-Headed Baby', 'River Steals My Folk From Me', and James Dyrenforth and Eric Ansell's 'You Didn't Ought To Do Such Things'. Additional numbers are by Hugh Williams and G. H. Clutsam. Eslanda Robeson, the star's wife, is uncredited as the owner of the café.

The film is mostly ignored in biographies of Robeson. Despite its obvious weaknesses, it is testament that at this early stage of his career he was already passionately intent to continue 'the human struggle – the common struggle of all oppressed peoples including the working masses, specifically the labouring people of all the world – and that is my philosophy'.[31]

No philosophical argument troubles Mancunian's easy-going ***The Penny Pool***, produced by John E. Blakeley at Highbury Studios and directed by George Black. Blakeley had been considering a film about football pools (then a national obsession) for the Yorkshire comedian Douglas Wakefield, when on a train between Manchester and London he met playwright Ronald Gow. By the end of the journey Gow outlined a story. This may not have been quite so impromptu as it seems; the same year Gow provided a storyline about football pools for the film *Lancashire Luck*. Back in Manchester, Blakeley had Arthur Mertz work up a screenplay that has Renee Harland (Luanne Shaw) dismissed for filling in her pools form at work. Her boyfriend Tommy (Tommy Fields) gets her as job as manager of a café. Her pools coupon turns out to be a winner claimed by somebody else, but all is settled by the closing credits.

The plot leaves space for comedy and music concerning Macari and His Dutch Serenaders, the Marie Louise Sisters, Mascot and Morice, Jack Lewis's Singing Scholars and the Twenty Gordon Ray Girls. The songs 'How Sorry I Am For Old People' and 'Lancashire' have lyrics by Mertz and Albert Stanbury. Wakefield, Billy Nelson, Chuck O'Neill and Jack Butler join forces for Billy Mayhew's 'It's A Sin To Tell A Lie'. Slapstick being no stranger to Mancunian, Wakefield and his gang's antics involve the comedian's 'garage' sketch culminating in an exploding tyre. He also has time to perform 'Break The News To Mother' and 'Julie And Myrtle'.

JULY

British musical films built around the then fashionable domestic big bands are invaluable records of a culture that would be jolted by war. It was inevitable that bandleaders might not be the best of actors. *Let's Make a Night of It* overcomes the problem by casting personable Charles 'Buddy' Rogers as waiter/bandleader Jack Kent, romancing Peggy Boydell (June Clyde, an agreeable leading lady who avoided pertness). They had been successfully paired two years earlier for *Dance Band*. Based on Henrik Ege's radio play *The Silver Spoon*, F. McGrew's adaptation was screen-played by Hugh Brooke and directed by Graham Cutts.

Peggy's parents, grumpy but pussy-cat Henry Boydell (Fred Emney on glorious form) and scatty Laura (perfectly cast Iris Hoey), run nightclubs, Henry 'The Silver Spoon' and Laura, duped by gangsters, the 'Coconut Beach'. The plot holds together a generous selection of variety acts, allowing nightclub siren Viola Vanders (Claire Luce) to sing her new 'sensation' 'The Spider And The Fly', supported by Jack Harris and His Band in a gossamer setting by Clarence Elder and Cedric Dawe. There is much more: Mrs Bradley's Formation Dancers, who soon turn acrobatic; Oliver Wakefield's verbal gymnastics; workmen in the street breaking out into 'You Gotta Take Your Pick And Sing'; the apache-dancing Percy Athos Follies; Afrique doing impressions of Tauber, Wallace Beery and Arthur Tracy; Irene Prador singing Ray Noble and Allan Murray's 'For Only You'; chubby-cheeked Zelma O'Neal singing 'Honey Bunch'; a street-singer bursting into 'My Irish Song'; and the phenomenally frenetic tap-dancing of The Four Franks. The composers include Michael Carr and Jimmy Kennedy, and the songs, although not distinguished, are pleasant. 'Let It Rain, Let It Pour' and 'If My Heart Says Sing, I Sing' are sung by Clyde, 'Something In My Eye' and 'Why Don't You Come Down To Earth?' by Rogers. Walter C. Mycroft produced for Associated British Picture Corporation.

The farcical complications of Mr and Mrs Boydell trying to keep their ownership of their nightclubs a secret from one another are nicely handled. Matters come to a splendid head when both joints are raided by idiotically disguised plain-clothed police (beautifully played by farceurs Bertha Belmore and Syd Walker), before a neat finale featuring guest appearances from some of the best current bands – Jack Jackson, Jack Harris, Sydney Lipton, Eddie Carroll, Joe Loss, Harry Acres, and Rudy Starita's Marimba Band – gathered together in a monumental setting. There is much to enjoy in *Let's Make a Night of It*.

An unmissable example of the decade's musical films has Jack Barty, as 'common' a man as the great George Carney (for whom the speech may well have been written), welcoming those from the wealthier classes ('nobs') to a charity music-hall show:

> I've no doubt that some of you haven't travelled so far east as this before. I dare say that some of you people from the west think that we down here are a queer lot of people – but I want to say this for you – you're the grandest lot of mixers I ever met in my life and if you lived down here with us you'd realise that's the greatest compliment we ever pay anybody. Good luck to you, and God bless you all.

The words are probably from Twickenham's resident scripter H. Fowler Mear – the jokes are almost certainly from his joke book of long dried-up chestnuts ('May I call you Anthony?' 'No thank you. I already have an alarm clock'). The storyline is credited to Geoffrey Orme and Jack Francis, but the sentiment is John Baxter, the creator and director of UK Films' *Talking Feet*. The *MFB* might justifiably complain about the film's utter naivety, but naivety is part of its charm. This is Baxter propaganda, the proposed closure of a local hospital stopped by a working-class community that gets up a concert to raise funds for its survival. Youth is at the helm. The campaign is fired by seven-year-old tap-dancing Hazel Barker, played by seven-year-old Hazel Ascot. Surely this would be Britain's Shirley Temple? The film was certainly 'British to the core […] The sentiment is honest, the parade of turns, most of which are new, is handled with real showmanship, while the small star, Hazel Ascot, is refused any attempt at precocity'.[32]

Ascot's father had a dancing school in Charing Cross Road and it was here that Baxter, planning a music-hall film, saw the young girl performing. He decided to reshape the project and build a new production around her. The plot is of the slightest but has ample opportunities for Baxter to get his message over. Proving that nothing has changed since 1937, the story has the government criticised for being down on the working man ('They're capable of everything!'), who must instead look to his own for support – and, in a Baxter film, will not find them wanting ('Many a warm heart beats beneath a dirty shirt'). Nevertheless, the workers – the splendid Joe (Barty) and a rich selection of Baxter's repertoire of street people and market traders – have to turn to the upper class to fund the campaign ('Go for those who've got the money'). The scene in which Joe and Hazel brave the aristocrats of the district in their palatial home may seem excruciating, but the over-emphasised referencing of social distinction sits at the heart of the piece.

Conversely, we may see *Talking Feet* simply as yet another excuse for Baxter to film some extraordinary turns. Hazel holds juveniles' auditions for the show, sitting through a blacked-up 'coon' singer John Lockwood doing his G. H. Elliott impersonation, a short-trousered xylophonist, a young girl doing an appalling Sophie Tucker impression, a male impersonator doing 'Following In Father's Footsteps', and a boy doing an impression of music-hall veteran Albert Whelan. This may seem curious to those unfamiliar with Mr Whelan's act, but the taking off of his evening dress and the putting on again of them to the strains of 'The Three Bears' (along with which he whistled) was Whelan's trademark entrance and exit. The acts are more interesting than the performances of Miss Ascot's co-stars Enid Stamp-Taylor and John Stuart.

We have generous dollops of the show that Hazel organises. The Dagenham Girl Pipers and the Military Pipers present 'The Gathering of the Clans' in a pantomime Highlands setting, followed by the 'famous international bass' William Heughan, as the adolescent Scotch Kilties watch on from the orchestra pit. Most curious of all is the pyramid of child pianists (credited as 'The Minipiano Ensemble of Fourteen Juveniles') knocking out the *William Tell* overture. At the pyramid's summit (how did he get up there?) the pianist Mark Hambourg renders (perhaps not as Max Wall said, 'like rendering fat in a frying pan') Chopin's A major Polonaise. Hambourg declared himself 'frightened to death', as well he might. He is the icing on this musical pyramid of Kafkaesque proportions, the boys in Eton collars and the girls with enormous white bows in their hair. One wonders what enduring psychological effect the making of this nightmarish scene left them with; did any of them ever want to see a piano again?

The film ends with the stirring revelation of the Band of the Royal Marines, joined by rows of under-rehearsed sailors backing Hazel in a battleship finale ('Jack's Ashore') and a lovely burst of 'Rule Britannia' as Hazel's dog runs on stage for a final close-up. It's an endearing end to a film that defies us to direct criticism at it. It bears Baxter's unmistakable stamp, promulgating his belief that

> Conditions in the country were not good, and comedy and music seemed the best ingredients to offer, and by doing so I could keep my film unit busy […] Hazel Ascot became a firm favourite […] a quite remarkable dancer – quite unequalled in this country. So popular were these films that they were selected to launch some of the Odeon cinemas that Oscar Deutsch was regularly opening at the time.[33]

In later life, Ascot claimed her dances had mostly been done in one take, and that 'as a dancer, I was better [than Temple]. I was a bit shy, and I was British and all my talent was from the knee down.'

Rough-hewn and artificial as Baxter's *Talking Feet* may be, it retains an innate naturalness. It at least seems to exist for a reason. ***Sing As You Swing*** is the antithesis, an empty, meaningless bunch of variety bits and pieces with some of the most depressing suppliers of entertainment of the decade. It was produced by Joe Rock and directed at Elstree's Rock Studios, and the credits claim a story by Clifford Grey and a screenplay by Syd Courtenay. There seems to have been no effort to make the thing watchable. Not only do we have to suffer the deadly cross-talk of Clapham and Dwyer, but the irritation of Claude Dampier. For the rest, we have mostly to put up with second- or third-drawer performers, as with impressionist Beryl Orde: 'She can imitate everything', we are promised, but may be disappointed. Evelyn Dall sings 'Let's Dance' and 'That's As Far As It Goes', and Lu Anne Meredith sings the title song, credited to Grey and Cyril Ray. The Four Mills Brothers sing 'Solitude' and 'Nagasaki', and Brian Lawrence sings 'The Mountains Of Mourne'. Big band music comes over better, represented by Mantovani and His Tipica Orchestra, and Nat Gonella and His Georgians.

European operetta, strained through a British sieve, returned with the Grafton Films-Capitol-Cecil production at Welwyn of composer Charles Cuvillier's 1911 ***The Lilac Domino***. On stage, it had been especially well received in London in 1918, surviving in the British repertoire until a 1944 London production. As screenplayed for Grafton by Basil Mason, Neil Gow, R. Hutter and Derek Neame, the action was switched from Nice and Monte Carlo to Budapest. Fred Zelnik directed, with additional music provided by Hans May and lyrics by Clifford Grey. Low thought it 'prettily staged and pleasantly sung by June Knight [as the domino Shari de Gonda] and American tenor Michael Bartlett [as Count Anatole]. All the usual ingredients were there – dancing peasants, brother officers, a masked ball, a lost fan, lovers' misunderstandings. The sets of Oscar Werndorff were ornate and the film, with many crowd scenes, was another expensive one.'[34]

Described by the concise David Quinlan as a 'musical caper whose time has long passed', Rudolf Bernauer, E. Gatti and B. Jenbach's old stage play was adapted for Cuvillier by Gatti and Jenbach, the plot revolving around Knight as the daughter of a Hungarian baron. Infatuated with Bartlett's Hussar Count, but alarmed at his gambling addiction, she disguises herself as the Lilac Domino and turns him back to her. Unimpressed by the undistinguished acting, *MFB* thought it 'in every detail a rubber-stamp film: it is hardly possible to criticise its individual merits or demerits. The artificial singing and dancing sequences, the "gay Hungarian" atmosphere, the interspersed comedy elements – all are exactly according to the book, and all devoid of the slightest pretence at realism.'[35] C. A. Lejeune's briefest of reviews simply quoted various characters asking 'Have you seen the Lilac Domino?' – 'Dear me, yes.'[36] Harry Acres was musical director for a score that included Knight singing the title waltz and 'My Heart Will Be Dancing'.

AUGUST

Ealing's next project for George Formby was a rare example of the British musical film responding to a contemporary issue. This is not to say that **Keep Fit** was a deeply thoughtful sociological treatment of a current problem, even if Ealing subsequently claimed the territory, more humbly begun by John Baxter, of offering its audience examples of cohesive neighbourliness. But in 1937 it was a poor popular newspaper or magazine that did not have an advertisement showing a skinny wretch of a young man on some beach (more likely Blackpool than the Costa del Sol) having sand kicked in his face by a muscular Adonis of a bully, especially humiliating as the weakling's love interest was usually there to witness it. As a well-tried music-hall gag has it: 'I saw this advertisement. It said "Become a strong man today. Send for our free booklet. Tear along the dotted line" … I hadn't the strength.'

The British public's physical fitness was of considerable concern to the government. The Women's League of Fitness and the Women's League of Health and Beauty were doing sterling work, and by 1937 had become international organisations. Disappointing results at the 1936 Olympics raised an alarm, as did concerns over malnutrition. Hiking, sunbathing, jumping, somersaulting, running and rowing – anything that stood the faintest chance of making the country more healthy – was suddenly desirable. The public was also increasingly bombarded with issues of sleek Nazi youth, with the Germanic exultation of male beauty manifesting as a viable threat to the enemy. Perhaps it was no longer enough for ladies to float diaphanously in circles of gossamer around fountains. The example of Vera Pearce undergoing strenuous exercise in *Please Teacher!* suddenly seemed invaluable. Breathing in God's air and dancing at the same time was no longer enough. Fitness was all. As a cinematic emblem of the effort needed, George Formby was almost God-sent (more 'before' than 'after' sending for the booklet). Anthony Kimmins directed his screenplay co-written with Austin Melford, produced by Basil Dean and Jack Kitchin.

As a barber in a department store, friendly but apparently gormless George Green (Formby) is fingers and thumbs, although able to pull a ukulele out of the air without warning. His feelings for manicurist Joan Allen (Kay Walsh) seem doomed to failure when she is desired by the well-set-up salesman Horace Kent (Guy Middleton). Both men sign up to a keep-fit competition, in which Horace inevitably triumphs until the boxing match confrontation, at which George proves to be a knockout. Harry Gifford and Fred E . Cliffe contribute 'Biceps, Muscle And Brawn', 'I Don't Like' and a title song for their toothy star. In its way, *Keep Fit* is one of the neatest of Formby's plots. The fact that he presents at the beginning of his films as lacking in confidence, physically and often emotionally inadequate, makes him the ideal stand-in for the weakling on the beach with sand in his eyes. We know that George will conquer all, teach the bad guys a lesson, and get the girl. Somehow, he got enough strength up to tear along the dotted line.

Doing his bit to keep Britain moving: our George in *Keep Fit* (1937)

Another operetta adaptation that seemed slightly out of time, **The Girl in the Taxi**, a major bilingual production made by Unity Films under the Ealing banner, made such scant use of the work's original score that it scarcely seemed worthwhile. A bewildering array of credits informed audiences that the screenplay was by Austin Melford (elsewhere Val Valentine is also listed) and Fritz Gottfurcht 'from his screen story', based on Jean Gilbert's 1910 operetta *Die Keusche Susanne*, its original libretto by Georg Okonkowski translated by Arthur Wimperis and F. Fenn, with lyrics by Arthur Wimperis and Frank Eyton. Produced by Kurt Bernhardt and Eugène Tucherer, and directed by André Berthomieu, it had a plot that bore resemblance to Pinero's farce *The Magistrate*, filmed with musical sequences as *Those Were the Days*, in which Will Hay and his inaccurately dated son John Mills throw caution to the winds by visiting a music-hall.

Much the same happens in *The Girl in the Taxi*, when the highly respectable founder of the 'Society for the Reward of Virtue' Baron des Aubrais (Lawrence Grossmith) frequents the Moulin Rouge. He is intrigued by its Can-Can dancers and the seductive Suzanne Pommarel (Frances Day). *Variety* thought Day 'adequate' but 'not important' in the role that on the London stage had made a star of Yvonne Arnaud, although 'the music is as tuneful as ever, but curtailed, and the words altered to conform to the changed settings called for on the screen.'[37]

Secondary principals Henri Garat and Jean Gillie sing 'The Sun Will Shine', Garat and Day have an undistinguished waltz song, and there is a brief version of 'The Young Dog And The Old Dog'. In its way, the film is a typical example of the films Day too often fell into, but her cool sexuality comes through. John Deverell is amusing as Suzanne's unlikely husband, but the sparkling entertainment suggested by the opening credits never quite materialises.

Jessie Matthews returned in **Gangway**. The title itself might have been a gift to an imaginative director: perhaps a production number for the star of the show along a never-ending gangway? Sailors dancing to her rescue? The setting of the number cries out for more imaginative choreography. Even Stanley Lupino's cut-price choreography in *Honeymoon for Three* had a stab at a protracted dance routine travelling over a ship. *Gangway* has barely begun when we already fear disappointment, awaiting the reappearance of the heroine in another cauliflower-leaf hat, another ensemble of frills and fragments of furbelows. Low considered that its production values were high, 'with elegant sets, but the songs [by Lerner, Goodhart and Hoffman] were not memorable, the complicated plot was shapeless and unsatisfactory and Sonnie Hale's direction lacked the emotional involvement of Saville.'[38] A title song, 'When You Gotta Sing', 'Moon Or No Moon', 'Lady Whozis' and Buddy Bradley's choreography puncture the uninteresting dialogue, with special orchestrations by Bretton Byrd whose work in British musical films often went uncredited.

The lack of a decent dancing partner cannot have helped, although Matthews subsequently repudiated the idea of ever working with Astaire, suggesting that 'Fred works best with lesser dancers. I could never just be a partner. When he danced with Eleanor Powell, who was his technical equal, that came off rather weakly.'[39] Rumours that Gaumont had signed Hollywood's Ray Milland were unfounded, and standby Barry Mackay was again brought into service. He is a soggy presence, his robotic movements to music resembling a keep-fit exercise that might more effectively have featured in Formby's most recent film. Ironically, at one point Mackay says of film stars, 'No one expects anything of them, except bad acting.' There is a wealth of it here, not least in his portrayal of a top-hatted Scotland Yard inspector, although here, of course, he's a 'dick'. *Gangway* gave itself another problem by being set in New York, but Dwight Taylor's original story and the screenplay by Lesser Samuels and (most unwisely) Hale were from the start lumbered by its basic artificiality. There was a thumbs down from Graham Greene in the *Spectator*:

> Miss Jessie Matthews has only once been properly directed – by Mr Victor Saville. Mr Sonnie Hale, whatever his qualities as a comedian, is a pitiably amateurish director and as a writer hardly distinguished. As for Miss Matthews, she isn't given a chance. Her figure like an exaggerated and Voguish advertisement is oddly asexual. Coquetry – and much less love – should never be demanded of her. When she dances – attractive and ungainly – it should be by herself; no dance of hers should end in the sentimental lyric and the labial embrace.[40]

For C. A. Lejeune, *Gangway* was 'the sort of refined romp that England obviously supposes that America thinks that English films should be'.[41] Another critic described 'a grand burlesque of gangster warfare' with 'a well-contrived suspense to lend the whole affair an air of authenticity despite its edge of caricature'.[42] *MFB* brushed the film off as a 'crook comedy with songs and dancing [...] There is less, and less elaborate singing and dancing than in previous Jessie Matthews' films.'[43] *Variety* was equally unimpressed, counting it 'a disappointment' with its star 'overwhelmed by a badly prepared script and far from adroit direction and production [...] Miss Matthews has five opportunities to display her Grade AA tootsie-trotting abilities, but they're incidental and no production backgrounds are built up to set them off.' More tellingly, it suggested that 'Perhaps it would be best all round to stop making the Matthews films a family affair'.[44] At times, *Gangway* looks like nothing more than a cheap gangster movie, with its star as an unconvincing moll who got dressed in the dark. Something had clearly gone wrong with the Matthews franchise.

We first see 'street singer' Arthur Tracy in Grosvenor Films' grandiloquently titled **Command Performance** in the midst of swirling Romany gipsies against a painted backcloth. He wears tight trousers and has startling drop ear-rings. With some relief, we discover that this is a scene from the film he is shooting. He is a busy performer, mobbed by theatregoers anxious to touch the hem of his trews. We are hardly surprised to learn that his voice is tired. No sooner does he arrive at a theatre than he's pushed on stage to deliver his signature aria 'Marta, Rambling Rose Of The Wild Wood'. This is such a success that he asks the audience, 'May I sing you that undying melody, "Trees"?' An usherette swoons in anticipation before the audience agrees to his suggestion. Having worked himself up into a dangerous overexcitement, he embarks on 'Danny Boy', but his voice cracks. The plucky audience joins in to cover the gaps. His voice momentarily recovers, but there is the worrying aspect of a nervous breakdown. This is especially bad timing as he is up for a 'command performance' at the end of the month. The pressure building, he escapes to the country, very reminiscent of the Gypsy Land in *Glamorous Night*. Having spent thirty minutes with Mr Tracy, it is with some relief that we meet gipsy Lilli Palmer.

Of course, the street singer is a great hit with the Romany people, singing 'The Whistling Gypsy's Lullaby', a peculiarly eerie composition, to a sickly child. Not content with this, he essays 'My Gypsy Dream Girl, Meet Me At The Gate To Dreamland'. At the command performance we are given the Toreador's Song from *Carmen* and then (with gracious permission from the monarchy) he sends a sung message via microphone to the sickly child. He leaves for Gypsy Land. The child awakens to his reprise of 'The Whistling Gypsy's Lullaby' as the camera at Pinewood respectfully pulls away, a rare effective stroke of Sinclair Hill's direction.

Hill's screenplay, co-written with the veteran George Pearson and Michael Hankinson, is peppered with musical items, among them 'Dance, Gypsy, Dance', 'The Old Oaten Bucket', 'Daisy Bell', 'Genevieve' and 'Jolly Great Lumps Of Duff', of which Mr Tracy's film seems a fair example. Produced by Harcourt Templeman, the film is sometimes identified as being based on a play of the same name by Stafford Dickens (used for the 1931 American movie of the same name starring Una Merkel and Neil Hamilton), but it bears no discernible resemblance to Dickens's work.

As for Tracy's film being a command performance, the *MFB* had its doubts:

> The gipsy scenes strike a false note. Many of the scenes, intended to be pathetic, fall into bathos and become absurd. The final sequence of the child's illness is funny in its silliness, a supposedly unconscious child constantly being awakened in order to be sung to sleep or given a toy elephant. The story is stickily sentimental, the acting is mediocre, the dialogue often strained and jerky, and the direction slow and inclined to drag.[45]

The year was immeasurably cheered by one of the best musicals built by and around Stanley Lupino, ***Over She Goes***; it is also one of the cleverest of the decade, and certainly one of its most stylish. He wasted no time in getting the stage show into the cinema. It had opened at the Saville Theatre in September 1936 and closed May 1937, almost immediately going into production at Elstree with Walter C.

Mycroft producing for the Associated British Picture Corporation. It had the luxury – denied far too often to shows transferred from stage to film – of retaining important members of its original cast, and it is superb. Elizabeth Meehan and Hugh Brooke's screenplay, adapted from the stage original, is wholly successfully directed by Graham Cutts, with swift playing that never flags.

A musical tantivity around the romances of three sets of lovers, Tommy Teacher (Lupino) and Dolly Jordan (Gina Malo), Billy Bowler (Laddie Cliff) and Kitty (Sally Gray), and Harry Drewsden (John Wood) and Pamela (Claire Luce), *Over She Goes* is quintessentially 1930s in its manner, no more so than when Pamela and Harry discuss their bad habits in a lighthouse. Pamela confesses,

> I will not complain
> If you have a theory that I'm just a bit insane
> It's a normal query – People think I'm mad
> I attract attention
> Here's one bad habit I could mention.
> I breathe on windows for I like to trace a heart
> And keep writing your name
> I chalk on pavements tender words when we're apart
> It's my favourite game.
> On bathroom mirrors, there I hope you'll see
> The words 'I love you' done in soap, you'll see.
> I breathe on windows and while I've the breath to start
> I'll keep doing the same
> I'll keep writing your name.

Billy Mayerl's easy melody is an exact response to Desmond Carter and Frank Eyton's lyric as the lovers climb the apparently endless steps of the lighthouse. Luce's sinuous ascent is pure 1930s glamour, totally at ease with itself, and when the song is finished and the top of the lighthouse reached, her final gossamer movements into the arms of Wood personify the period – it is a gem of British film-making, one in which all of its participants (designer, composer, lyricists, actors, cameramen, costume designers et al.) have their part. Throughout, Otto Kanturek's photography is outstanding.

The sense of everything being right persists, not least in the score. Only in the finale built around Michael Carr and Jimmy Kennedy's title song – the only one not by the Mayerl-Carter-Eyton team – does the precision slightly falter, largely because the blatantly black and white effect doesn't work too well. Otherwise, the songs are a delight, with 'A County Wedding' prophesying 'There will be a triple wedding'. Lupino, Cliff and Wood have a film-stopper of a number in 'Side By Side', with its brilliant lyric that takes them on a Grand Tour of the studio's floor, depositing them at last on a travelling rug. Welcome latecomers to the picture are Bertha Belmore's understandably bewildered Lady Drewsden, and the police officers summoned to sort out the muddles, the marvellously pompous Inspector Giffnock (Syd Walker) and his highly educated assistant Sgt Oliver (Richard Murdoch). The pride they take in their work is expressed (along with some exquisitely staged policeman-dancing) in 'We Policemen Think We Police Are Grand'.

Perhaps *Over She Goes* finds the British musical film in its ideal place. It retains its ability to entertain with skill, verbal and musical wit.

SEPTEMBER

Were audiences lured into cinemas by recognising the title of a film as a song they already knew? It was a trick often used. **The Minstrel Boy** at least sounds vaguely historical, most appropriately when we consider its creators. This was the last film to be produced and directed by the prolific Sidney Morgan, a major figure of early British cinema responsible for making films at Shoreham and beyond. Primitive as much of this work now seems, Morgan's achievement was extraordinary. The screenplay is by Sidney's daughter Joan, a leading actress of silents and subsequently novelist and playwright, here credited as Joan Wentworth Wood.

Made at Elstree, this was the only production of Dreadnought Films. The minstrel boy of the title is Irish bandleader Mike (capable Fred Conyngham), working alongside band singer Dee Dawn (Chili Bouchier). We hear her performing 'Love's A Racketeer' and 'The Best Things In Life', and dancers Xenia and Boyder perform 'Tango Town'. Mike's wife Angela (Lucille Lisle) thinks him unfaithful and leaves him. They are reunited when Mike attempts to kill himself. However, Conyngham manages to sing 'When Loves Are So Many', Paul Rubens's Edwardian favourite 'I Love The Moon', and the title song. He is joined by Pat Kavanagh and Basil Langton for 'McDougall, McNab and McKay'. Percival Mackey and His Band play 'My Moonlight Madonna' by William Scotti and Paul Francis Webster, and 'Sweet Muchacha' by Milton Ager, Alan Cameron and Al Hoffman. Inoffensive and mildly entertaining, *The Minstrel Boy* was a tepid attempt to establish Lisle as a romantic leading lady.

Producer and director James A. Fitzpatrick made a series of quota quickies in the 1930s inclining to the artistic, some designed to be immediately recognisable to the audience as in the 1937 *Auld Lang Syne*, some built around the lives of composers, as in the 1938 *Georges Bizet* and *The Life of Chopin*. For **The Last Rose of Summer**, W. K. Williamson wrote a screenplay based on Thomas Moore's poem. A 1920 silent of the same name had starred Owen Nares and Daisy Burrell; Fitzpatrick's version had John Garrick as Moore, Kathleen Gibson as his sweetheart, and Malcolm Graham as Lord Byron, against an Irish background. South African composer Gideon Fagan was responsible for the music, a string of traditional airs ('The Last Rose Of Summer', 'The Minstrel Boy', 'Those Endearing Young Charms' and 'Oft In The Stilly Night') making up the quota time. Garrick and Gibson went directly into the next Fitzpatrick short, *Bells of St Mary's*.

OCTOBER

Ancient stock footage of London introduces another feature intended to make a star of a bandleader, Harry Roy. In **Rhythm Racketeer**, Roy has the added responsibility of playing dual roles, as some sort of impression of himself (now called Harry Grand) but also as American crook Nap Connors. Mrs Roy, professionally known as Princess Pearl, co-stars as Karen Vosper. John Byrd developed the screenplay from Betty Laidlaw and Robert Lively's story 'What Next', turning on the lifelike resemblance of the doppelgängers, allowing Connors to pass himself off as the bandleader. Connors and his associates (including Johnnie Schofield, heard in a reprise of one of the best songs, 'You Struck The Right Note') pull off a big jewel theft, putting Grand (the real Roy) in the frame. Lerner, Goodhart and Hoffman's other numbers, the title song and 'Seven Different Sweeties A Week', are effective, as is Cyril Ray and Eddie Pola's 'I Fell In Love With A Poster'. Roy is an appealing companion, and the voice is distinctive. The plot moves along conventional lines, interrupted by an extraordinary sequence in which Roy's musicians assume grotesque female masks; it makes for an unsettling moment. Memories of Little Tich are evoked with a long boot dance. Made at Elstree by Rock Productions, the film was produced by Joe Rock and directed by James Seymour. The production values are not notable, and there is an awkward discrepancy between location and studio-bound shots, but as an archival document of Roy's work the film has worth.

Compared to *Rhythm Racketeer*, **Shooting Stars**, made by Viking Films at Cricklewood, seems to belong to an earlier age. Shockingly bad stock footage of an audience enraptured by what the cinema audience is being offered is hardly justified by the variety turns presented by the uninvigorating Fred Duprez. He over-eggs the pudding, promising 'a galaxy of stars unparalleled … giants of the entertainment world', claims that don't strike home when we see our old friends the Sherman Fisher Girls in top hats and gauntlets, tapping on the lids of several pianos, and doing a belly dance. Debroy Somers and His Band turn up with singer Phyllis Robins (from the 1936 *Murder at the Cabaret*) performing 'The Meanest Thing You Ever Did Was Kiss Me' and the plaintive 'I Saw A Ship A-Sailing'.

Scott and Whaley, the transatlantic 'coon' double act and the subjects of John Baxter's *The Kentucky Minstrels* (1934), are vigorously showcased in a neatly scripted sketch closing with 'My Shadow's Where My Sweetheart Used To Be', ending with the shadow itself being given a two-fingered salute. The comedians had first appeared on stage in Britain in 1909, and were never to return to America. Most remarkable is the apache act Karina, Vadio and Hertz. The skills and dexterity of Karina are astonishing to behold in what is basically an acrobatic dance routine devoted to the subjugation of the female. It is she and her fellow acrobats, and Scott and Whaley, performing acts that would be politically impossible to replicate, who provide the reason for *Shooting Stars*.

Time had not weakened British studios' penchant for the variety vaudeville disguised beneath the veneer of a thin plot: witness the self-styled 'Big Musical Revue of 1937', Warwick Ward's production of *Saturday Night Revue*, directed by Ward at Welwyn. Vernon Clancey's scenario was all but submerged by the interruption of music-hall turns, with a fashionable sprinkling of bands, represented by Sydney Kyte and His Orchestra with vocalists Dinah Millar and Gerald Fitzgerald, the Royal Kiltie Juniors, and Billy Reid's Accordion Band. Wee Georgie Harris sings 'Come Along With Me' as part of the floor show at the Mayfair Moons Club, where romancing Mary Dorland (Sally Gray) and Jimmy Hanson (loping Billy Milton) do their cabaret act, singing Michael Carr and Hamilton Kennedy's 'Gorgeous Night'. Another club, also known as Moon's, is to be found in less auspicious environs frequented by a more cosmopolitan, mixed-race audience. The plot revolves around the confusion and misunderstandings of having two clubs with similar names, but it's a plot that idles among the variety turns.

Along the way, Webster Booth sings Paul Rubens's 'I Love The Moon', and gangly Lancastrian comic Reg Bolton does his well-known (Up North) boxing sketch, the items compered by ex-BBC John Watt, a well-known name in 1937, and once the director of radio's *Workers' Playtime*. Beguiled by these delights, it's difficult to take the hero's difficulties seriously, even when he's temporarily blinded in a car accident. A nurse (presumably trained at RADA) is at his elbow, but it seems that the love between Mary and Jimmy is doomed. Happily, he appears as 'The Unknown Lover', unmasked and with his eyesight restored, at the piano. The lovers are reunited, singing 'Together' by Michael Carr and Wilhelm Grosz. It's all pleasant enough but nothing very distinctive emerges.

NOVEMBER

The long run of film successes that Jack Hulbert enjoyed throughout the decade had not yet run out of steam. There was a general welcome for Alexander Korda's London Film Productions' *Paradise for Two*, sometimes recognised by its American release title *The Gaiety Girls*. The lightness of touch is surprising considering its co-producer, Günther Stapenhorst, had been the commander of a German U-boat. Its director, American Thornton Freeland, would go on to one of the most enjoyable of Stanley Lupino's movies, the 1938 *Hold My Hand*.

The screenplay is credited to the German Robert Liebmann, based on his story, and to Arthur Macrae, author of much intimate revue material. In Paris, a chorus girl, Jeannette (American Patricia Ellis), is mistaken for the partner of millionaire Rene Martin (Hulbert), in what was essentially a remake of the 1933 German film ... *und wer küsst mich?* (*And Who Is Kissing Me?*) directed by E. W. Emo. Mischa Spoliansky's score, with lyrics by W. Kernel, includes 'In A Paradise For Two' and 'When You Hear Music', enhanced by the choreography of Jack Donohue and Philip Buchel. David Quinlan praises the film as 'refreshing, capably directed [and] nicely done in all departments',[46] and *Variety* approved: 'The astute formula of making soluble the British talents of Jack Hulbert and the American savor of Patricia Ellis has resulted in one of Britain's better musicals. Direction, acting and dancing blend splendidly in the Hollywood manner.'[47] The proceedings were greatly helped by a strong supporting cast.

The first Jack Buchanan musical made under his own aegis, ***The Sky's the Limit***, paired him with an actress new to British films, the Russian Mara Loseff, who had notably played opposite Richard Tauber in the 1930 *The Land of Smiles*. Buchanan and Douglas Furber fashioned a screenplay from Ralph Spence's story about an aeronautic designer romantically entangled with opera singer Isobella (Loseff). Buchanan and Lee Garmes directed. For the first time it seemed the star had complete control of what he was doing on screen, but the *Era*, recognising he was 'debonair as ever', suggested that 'the screen has yet to discover how to use this light-footed dancing-lead to the best advantage'. Loseff's singing was praised, although her acting was 'a little immature'.[48]

Space was made for a series of musical items, and the piano duetting of Marjan Rawicz and Walter Landauer, who also wrote with lyricist Desmond Carter 'Without You', 'Venice In The Moonlight', and 'Too Lovely To Be True'. American songwriters Abner Silver and Al Sherman wrote 'My Beloved', 'Swing, Madam' and 'Just Whisper I Love You'. This was Loseff's only British film. Personal difficulties contributed to her decline; she was last seen at Bournemouth Winter Gardens in 1950.

Depressing as it is that the British musical film so often made no apparent effort to shake itself free of unimaginative screenplays, ludicrously unlikely situations, feeble comedy and romantic clap-trap, now and again half-decent work broke through. On the face of it, ***Intimate Relations*** was more of the same, tosh with songs. Its suggestive title may have sparked interest in some patrons, but innocuous fun lurked within. Based on a 1932 play by Stafford Dickens, Tudor Films' adaptation by Frank Atkinson (although Dickens has the on-screen credit) was produced by Herbert Wynne and directed by Clayton Hutton.

Musical comedy star Molly Morrell (June Clyde), accompanied by '50 Lovelies', sings 'Building A Castle In The Air' from her West End show 'Encore for Maisie'. Businessman George Gommery (Garry Marsh) would like to have an affair with her, while Gommery's highly strung assistant Freddie Hall (Jack Hobbs) has to brush off the unwanted attentions of Gommery's wife (Vera Bogetti). The unfolding farce is played at speed, even by the usually stolid Marsh, but the surprising star of the occasion is Hobbs, an actor whose voice, mouth, teeth, cadences and style tie him utterly to the decade; you simply can't imagine how he would have got work beyond December 31st 1939. It's one of the neatest comic performances in the canon. He may be a non-starter in the romantic stakes, but what he does with a hat is masterly. There is excellent comedy from Moore Marriott as Molly's scrounging father.

There is just enough music not to stall the pace. Lew Stone (no actor) and His Band get involved with 'speciality numbers' by Bernard Francis, and dance ensembles by Alfred Esdaile and John Hepburn. Clyde joins Stone for the spectacularly staged 'I Love You So' that has her tapping on a giant xylophone. Her 'Ordinary' duet with Hobbs suggests that even as the decade wound down, the British musical film's attitude to musical numbers had not much altered from its earliest productions. The song recalls a musical play trick of the 1920s, a prolonged mime of domestic married bliss. Sandy Wilson used the technique for the song 'A Room In Bloomsbury' in his 1950s pastiche of 1920s musical comedies, *The Boy Friend*.

DECEMBER

Many followers of the television talent show *Opportunity Knocks* were probably unaware of its compere's film career. Hughie Green was the star of British Lion's **Melody and Romance**, directed at Beaconsfield by the busy Maurice Elvey. He and L. du Garde Peach wrote the screenplay from Elvey and Leslie Howard Gordon's storyline. Excitement is kept at bay in a plot about a Wapping boy, Hughie Hawkins (Green). His friend Margaret Williams (Margaret Lockwood) wants to be just as famous as he does. Success must be theirs by the closing credits, and is achieved by Hughie roping in his gang of young pals, and rescuing Margaret from a great fire. A strong cast agreed to be involved, among them Alastair Sim, Jane Carr, Charles Hawtrey reciting 'To be or not to be', and Garry Marsh.

One can only imagine what they made of Mr Green's antics, but his talents did not go unappreciated. By now, provincial audiences must have been inured to spectacles of this kind, but the *Whitstable Times and Herne Bay Herald* confessed that 'it is difficult to choose the highlight of his performance. Many picturegoers will undoubtedly applaud his impersonations of Charles Laughton and Lionel Barrymore, whilst others may prefer his comedy.'[49]

Those who occasionally glimpsed Mr Green doing his stuff on *Opportunity Knocks* and the quiz show *Double Your Money* might not easily have equated the man they saw with the dashing, lively, romantically inclined young spark sweeping through *Melody and Romance*, or in his earlier incarnation as 'Britain's 14-year-old Wonder', who had become famous in 1933 through the BBC's radio programme

In Town Tonight. Michael Kilgarriff, the fearless biographer of theatrical curiosities, has Green as 'a compulsive talker, a tiresome, difficult man of rolling-eyed insincerity and paranoid disposition'.[50] By 1937, of course, Green had probably not achieved complete metamorphosis. Adding verisimilitude to an otherwise bald and unconvincing narrative, footage of the Crystal Palace's destruction by fire took the place of excitement.

The final film of the year hinted at cosmic explosion. It came in the shape of the 'Mexican Spitfire' Lupe Velez's vehicle ***Mad About Money***, variously known as *Stardust* and *He Loved an Actress*. Made at Elstree Rock studios by William Rowland, this was the last movie directed by the American Melville Brown. He had recently moved to Britain, returning to Hollywood at the end of the year, and dying in 1938. Based on a story by John F. Harding, *Mad About Money* had a screenplay by the American John Meehan Jnr, who would provide the story for the Keith Falkner *Thistledown* the following year. Morgan Productions had grand plans for *Stardust*, originally intending to make it in colour, but technical problems turned it black and white.

Perhaps Velez was colour enough. She played Carla de Huleva (possibly a hell of a woman and certainly a coup for the studio), ever-ready for a rhumba, poor as a church mouse but passing herself off as wealthy and thereby attracting the attention of crafty Peter Jackson (Wallace Ford) who is collaborating on a projected movie with playboy Roy Harley (Ben Lyon). The songs by composer Kenneth Leslie-Smith and his regular lyricist James Dyrenforth (together they wrote scores for all three Keith Falkner films) included Velez's appropriately titled 'Perpetual Motion', Lyon's 'Oh So Beautiful', and Jean Colin as Diana West singing 'Little Lost Tune' and 'Dustin' The Stars'. *Today's Cinema* reported a 'cut-to-pattern story', a 'bemusing plot' and musical set-pieces that had 'aural and ocular appeal'.[51] These had choreography by the prolific Hollywood dance director Larry Ceballos, who had just done service in *Rhythm Racketeer*.

1938

Humble origins and lowly professions provide the starting point from which the star must rise, preferably and almost inevitably, to show-business heights of acclamation *Follow Your Star*

Lily of Laguna
The Singing Cop
Sweet Devil
Sailing Along
I See Ice
Thistledown
Chips
On Velvet
Around the Town
We're Going to Be Rich
Mountains o' Mourne
Little Dolly Daydream
Kicking the Moon Around

Break the News
Stepping Toes
Follow Your Star
Hold My Hand
Lassie from Lancashire
Calling All Crooks
Penny Paradise
Save a Little Sunshine
Yes, Madam?
It's in the Air
Keep Smiling
My Irish Molly

JANUARY

The habit of borrowing a famous song title for a new British musical film died hard, never having weakened at Butcher's Film Services. The creators of *Lily of Laguna* had long histories. Sidney Morgan produced. His daughter Joan, the one-time silent screen star of Shoreham and beyond, provided the story as Joan Wentworth Wood. Oswald Mitchell directed the screenplay written by Ian Walker (*Rose of Tralee* and *My Irish Molly*). In November 1934 the *Era* had reported that production was soon to begin at Shepherd's Bush on a Gaumont-British *Lily of Laguna*, to be directed by Jack Raymond. It was hoped that Robert Donat would star. It is doubtful that Butcher's version bore any relationship to the Gaumont-British project, which seems not to have materialised; even so, it is unlikely that Butcher's would ever have lured Donat into their studios. Four years later, in November 1937, the *Era* assured its readers that 'important and dramatic scenes' involving leading lady Nora Swinburne were that week being shot by Butcher's at Walton-on-Thames.

The star of the musical show 'Lily of Laguna', Gloria Grey (Swinburne), leaves the profession to marry an Edinburgh scientist. Wedded bliss fades and Gloria goes back to the boards. Years pass. Her daughter falls in love with a Scotsman. Gloria also is drawn to him, but realises her daughter has prior claim. A displeased suitor shoots Gloria, a misadventure that reunites Gloria with her ex-husband.

In the circumstances, Swinburne emerges with dignity. The *MFB* sighed that it was 'inclined to be tedious and could have been shortened', complaining that 'the character of the scientist is a caricature of an intelligent person – the Professor as imagined by the ignorant'.[1] The *Era* was grateful for Swinburne's 'restraint, intelligence and subtlety' and found the film 'moderately interesting and moderately entertaining', although Mitchell's handling of the material 'lacks conviction on the whole'.[2]

Leslie Stuart's title song had given music-hall performer Eugene Stratton his greatest success in 1898, and subsequently it became one of the numbers most associated with G. H. Elliott who performed as 'The Chocolate Coloured Coon'. In an age when such titles were not deemed offensive, Stratton was also known for the unfortunately titled 'All Coons Look Alike To Me'. Now, the whiskered title song was performed by Talbot O'Farrell, along with 'When Flanagan Went To Spain', 'The Banshee', 'Mighty Like A Rose' and 'Charmaine'.

Second of the Warner Bros-First National attempts at Teddington to make a Nelson Eddy out of British baritone Keith Falkner, the idea of **The Singing Cop**, directed by Arthur Woods, lay in its working title of *Music and Mystery*. Brock Williams and Tom Phipps's screenplay, from a story by the film's songwriters James Dyrenforth and Kenneth Leslie-Smith, was no more successful than previous efforts in other films. Now, continental operatic diva Maria Santona (visiting Marta Labarr) is suspected by Scotland Yard of espionage; it's therefore time to call in undercover policeman Jack Richards (Falkner). Naturally (or as naturally as could be managed) Jack turns out to have a splendid singing voice, and ends up playing a surprisingly handsome Mephistopheles, joined by the chorus of Covent Garden opera in excerpts from Gounod's *Faust*. Contemporary reviews suggest that Falkner's acting had not much improved, but his singing was much appreciated. Matters were enlivened by the presence of Chili Bouchier (who had also played in *Mayfair Melody*) as Kit Fitzwillow, and Ivy St Helier as Sonia Kassona. The choreographer was Jack Donohue. The *MFB* thought that 'Direction and acting are adequate, but the film will be entertaining chiefly to music lovers.'[3]

Jack Buchanan is credited with having discovered one of the liveliest, most personable, and neglected British actresses of the 1930s, Jean Gillie. Having already made appearances in *His Majesty and Co.*, with Buchanan in *This'll Make You Whistle*, and *The Girl in the Taxi*, she was now the leading lady of Jack Buchanan Productions' **Sweet Devil**, adapted by Ralph Spence and Geoffrey Kerr from the 1935 French film *Quelle drôle de gosse!*. On that occasion, loopy secretary Lucie was played by the glamorous Danielle Darrieux; now, renamed Jill Turner for British audiences, Gillie was Buchanan's and director René Guissart's choice for the girl who has a crush on her starchy boss Edward Bane (the clue is in the name), played by William Kendall. When Bane's business partner Tony Brent (Bobby Howes) arrives, Jill's emotions go haywire. Tony rescues her from a fake drowning stunt, taking her to his home where his engagement party is in full swing. The ensuing antics include Howes doing a passable imitation of a ventriloquist's dummy, and Gillie in an entertaining drunk scene. American composer Pem Davenport was credited with the songs 'You Should Be Set To Music' and 'What's Going To Happen To Me?'.

The *Surrey Mirror* thought this 'one of the most uproariously funny comedies ever made',[4] endorsed with restraint by the *MFB* as a 'lively and light-hearted piece of nonsense'.[5] Less warmly, C. A. Lejeune found it 'coy' and

> a little like a French farce with Danielle Darrieux called *Mad Girl*, we once saw, except that Miss Jean Gillie is by no means a Darrieux. It is even more like every English house-party film we have seen since our studios broke into society, with jorums of champagne, lots of dull décolleté, and more ill-mannered people to the square yard than one can meet in any other locale of the films.[6]

FEBRUARY

Jessie Matthews's abundant talents were well used by Gaumont-British in her last musical film of the decade ***Sailing Along***, with its agreeable screenplay by Lesser Samuels based on Selwyn Jepson's storyline. It marked a return to form after *Gangway*. With decent dialogue that avoided the strained attempt to Americanise, superb sets by Junge, attractive songs from Arthur Johnston and Maurice Sigler, and a supporting cast stronger than in any other of Matthews's films, it was the best of those directed by Sonnie Hale, even if some regretted the lack of Victor Saville who had steered her film career from *The Good Companions* (1932) through to the 1936 *It's Love Again.*

Sailing Along has the refreshment of its *plein air* atmosphere with riverside and barge settings, even if its story plays out along well-trodden lines, the heroine beginning as one sort of person but wanting to be another (a showbusiness star, basically). At least Matthews would have had sympathy with such creatures, for despite her subsequent protestations that she never wanted to be a star, she had worked assiduously to become one. Here, the heroine is lively river-girl Kay Martin, eternally squabbling with hero waterman Steve Barnes (Barry Mackay returning for service as a Matthews hero after *Evergreen* and *Gangway*). The tomboy antics of Kay and the rough jocularity of Steve leave no doubt that they will be putting up the banns by final frame. Kay's longing is of course to achieve musical stardom, presumably in the sort of impossibly opulent stage productions imagined in films

Britain's 'Dancing Divinity' Jessie Matthews in the bracing *Sailing Along* (1938)

like *Sailing Along*. Her ambitions are emboldened by Hollywood imports Roland Young and Jack Whiting, with Athene Seyler and Alastair Sim in high comedy manner, doing what they can with so-so material.

At this crucial moment of Matthews's career, and as war threatened, she (or Hale) may have thought that in Whiting they had at last found the ideal musical partner she conspicuously lacked. It's a convincing performance. The *MFB* agreed that Matthews 'sings adequately and dances superbly' but Whiting 'matches her in dancing ability and outshines her in singing and acting', while others in the cast had to do with crumbs from the table.[7] This might have been the perfect match, with Whiting standing in for the absent Astaire. The pipe dream of a Matthews-Astaire partnership can never have seemed likely. Astaire was wise to steer clear of it. Meanwhile, Whiting was both an asset and a threat to his co-star, effortlessly bringing off a brilliant routine, presumably worked by himself and choreographer Buddy Bradley, in 'Souvenir Of Love', reprised by Matthews. Here is one of the few moments in Matthews's films when a male dancer takes the attention. The experiment would not be repeated.

R. B. Marriott, who had criticised the star's previous films as lacking 'spontaneity, really effective dialogue, and original story material', now applauded Hale's direction as 'swift, gay and witty'. What was more, *Sailing Along* was 'certainly the most polished romantic comedy with music ever made in our studios: and for vitality, deftness and general entertainment value it equals any, and is superior to many that have come from that over-rated motion picture making town across the Atlantic Ocean'.[8]

The songs are modest but captivating: 'Trusting My Luck' (Matthews recklessly tap-dancing on deck), 'My Heart Skips A Beat', and the emblematic 'My River', a vague shadow of Kern and Hammerstein's 'Ol' Man River' and at times almost a spiritual – it's one of the best numbers in any of her films. In fact, it's the components of *Sailing Along* that for once succeed, Junge's sumptuous sets putting on a brave face just as the sun is setting on Matthews's career and the industry around British musical films. For a blessed moment, it seemed that if productions of such quality might still be possible, hope was high, even on rivers apparently populated only by pensionable old sea-dog extras. Where on earth were all the *young* men in British musical films? The lack of virility at a time when the male population yet had to be called up to save the country from Nazism is astonishing, and surrounding Matthews with a lot of old men did nothing for her image.

A crowning glory comes with the finale, an extended routine for the star, weirdly costumed (she looks like a Parisian apache dancer waiting for a partner to throw her across the room) as she and Whiting stroll the patently artificial riverside. It's a strange narrative. The balleted choreography is sub-Frederick Ashton. With mathematical precision, Michael Thornton has estimated that 'Jessie and Whiting danced about twenty miles to get it on film. It must have been agony for a woman with impaired circulation in one leg'.[9] At the end of this sequence, the two stars glide into an absurdly Arcadian landscape of topiary and painted backcloth, with elegantly posed extras standing to attention as if appearing in a mid-European operetta. It's a final conquest of vulgarity over intelligence, unworthy of some of what has gone before. In its efforts to keep the public entertained, the best the studio could come up with was – yet again – an impossibly unreal vision. Impossibly unreal visions are perfectly in place when they have the ability to move those who behold them, but where were those for whom such a patently silly arrangement nudged the sensibilities?

The sight of Matthews drifting into this Arcadian landscape is one of the most vividly memorable images of her films, perhaps because hindsight allows us to see it as a receding into the past. Hale was expected to direct her next film, somewhat worryingly titled *Asking for Trouble*, but consistent criticism of his role in his wife's career may have played its part in the project being scrapped. Instead, Gaumont-British, with considerable lack of imagination, put her into the non-musical *Climbing High* directed by Carol Reed. Saville directed her brief contribution to the Hollywood compendium *Forever and a Day*, released in London in 1943. Her declining popularity was merely confirmed the following year by British National's *Candles at Nine*, a weird mix of terror (unfrightening) and Matthews singing 'I'd Like To Share With You' (music by Harry Parr Davies, lyric by Harold Purcell). The dancing, shared once again with a male who, for all we know, may have wished to remain as anonymous as his non-credit suggests (it is Guy Fielding), features high kicks, twirling and stretching in the usual Matthews manner. A final film hurrah came in 1958 with a supporting role in MGM's *Tom Thumb*. In long overdue colour, she had one number, for which she was dubbed.

After partnering George Formby in *Keep Fit*, Kay Walsh returned to duty as George Formby's girlfriend in Associated Talking Pictures' *I See Ice*, another Basil Dean production, with Anthony Kimmins as director and co-writer with Austin Melford. The milieu is the world of ice shows that were currently popular. These persisted into the 1950s at such venues as Wembley Park, Harringay Arena, Earl's Court and the Empress Hall. Such skating extravaganzas usually had vast casts with exhibition speciality dancers, and often original scores, as in the 1951 *London Melody* with its fifteen numbers by Robert Farnon and one by cast member Norman Wisdom. In *I See Ice*, Judith Gaye (Walsh) and Paul Martine (Cyril Ritchard in a selection of extraordinary costumes) are professionally partnered; he, of course, wants more, but we see from the beginning that clumsy innocent Formby (playing George Bright) will be the winner. Ritchard, perhaps symbolically, is ice cold. We wonder if Ritchard looked in the mirror before agreeing to appear in his outfits?

George has invented a miniature camera that takes images furtively. He describes what might be seen 'In My Little Snapshot Album' (Jimmy Harper, Will E. Haines and Harry Parr Davies). He is taken on by Martine as a props man, but causes chaos on stage and is fired. A ferocious landlady turns him out. George takes Judith to The Lotus Club where his lack of sophistication is exposed when he orders jam roly-poly pudding. He serenades her with Roma Campbell-Hunter and Parr Davies's 'Noughts And Crosses'. His antics land him in prison, where he ponders 'Mother, What'll I Do Now?' (Formby-Fred E. Cliffe). The film's final set-piece is an ice hockey match, but here the pace and centre of the story falls away. Kimmins's dependence on stock footage, and the obvious substitution of Walsh for Judith's skating sequences, as well as footage of a rapturous audience seen in more than one other British musical film, put us at more of a remove from the action. A return to form for Kimmins and Formby would be just around the corner with November's much more entertaining *It's in the Air*.

MARCH

Modelled by director Arthur Woods, Keith Falkner's career in British musical films was certainly unusual. The last of his three films, **Thistledown**, produced by Irving Asher at Teddington for Warner Bros and First National, had a screenplay by Brock Williams based on a story by John Meehan Junior and J. O. C. Orton. The Woods-Falkner team remained in place from the earlier pictures, with a musical score by Kenneth Leslie-Smith and James Dyrenforth, and choreography by Jack Donohue.

Thistledown has a different atmosphere to Falkner's *Mayfair Melody* and *The Singing Cop*. Here is a heather-sweet love story set in Scotland, taking the opportunity to feature 'a complete pictorial record of the development of the Highland costume', a first (the studio claimed) on screen.[10] Falkner plays a wealthy Scots laird, Sir Ian Glenloch, scion of an old family long feuding with a rival clan. Glenloch's problems are accentuated when he marries ex-opera diva Therese (Aino Bergö). Tiring of roaming in the heather, she goes to Vienna and revives her career. Years pass. Glenloch has travelled widely in an effort to forget Therese, but on returning to his bankrupted castle he finds her, and the son he didn't know he had. The notice in *MFB* suggests that the disappearance of *Thistledown* is a loss, an 'unsophisticated story most attractively played'. Bergö's 'outstanding' voice can no longer be heard. As for Falkner, he 'steals the picture. He has an engaging personality and an exquisite voice'.[11] To be heard, on film, no more.

No-nonsense baritone balladeer Peter Dawson could have found no better refuge for 'The Sea Is The Life For Me' than British Fine Arts Pictures' *Chips*, produced and directed at Cricklewood by Edward Godal. This adventure story for boys, made with the assistance of the Boy Scouts Association, was in the shadow of Ralph Reader's *The Gang Show* of the previous year. Vivian Tidmarsh's screenplay ensures its characters will ride that crest of a wave, with some scenes filmed at Poole Harbour. Chips (Tony Wyckham), a decent lad in a spot of bother, is on probation, but longs for salvation by joining the sea scouts. Enrolled, he takes a boat out to sea, and gets into even more trouble when smugglers kidnap him. This improbable adventure for impressionable juveniles features much incipient talent, including Twenty Tiny Tappers and Terry's Juveniles, besides the singing of Dawson's sea-girt Salty Sam. The best reason for sitting through *Chips* is its supporting artists, among them Robb Wilton, comedian Billy Merson (who had first appeared silently on screen with *Billy's Spanish Love Spasm* in 1915), and Davy Burnaby, veteran of *The Co-Optimists*.

Spring might be returning with hopes of new life and sunny disclosures, but British studios seemed resistant to original thought. Too often, the suspicion that anything would pass muster for presentation to the public persisted. In its continuing, and by now pretty well exhausted, preoccupation with serving up cold scraps of variety turns, laughably plotted operettas warmed up from foreign sources, remakes of films that even as originals were of little note, and musicals with much of their scores emasculated, torn from their West End roots, British cinema was excluding itself from serious consideration as an art form.

Working at the coal face of the quota quickie, with little hope of ever being considered relevant or important, Widgey Raphael Newman tread a solitary path in provincial film-making. His passion, however – with its echoes of John Baxter – was undeniable. He was a man of considerable charm and persuasion, but his efforts were not consistently appreciated. Steve Chibnall pays tribute to Newman as 'the Crown Prince of the Quota', responsible in 1932 for *The Merry Men of Sherwood* and in 1935 for an oddball entertainment about Shakespeare, *The Immortal Gentleman*, shamelessly promoted by Newman as having 'The Greatest Cast of British Stars Ever Assembled in One Picture'. So grandiose a claim could hardly be made of *On Velvet*, whose leads are the ubiquitous but ever-welcome Wally Patch as cockney bookie Harry Higgs, and Joe Hayman as Jewish bookmaker Sam Cohen. Together, they start a commercial television advertising company. Harry and Joe quarrel with their wives and see their offspring fall for one another. It is innocent fare all too hastily assembled.

The theme of advancement in mass communication, although handled casually, has echoes of *Elstree Calling* and a queue of lesser works that had played around the idea of radio as a sort of talking television. In no case had the theme been subject to the writer's intelligence; the very idea that such a theme in such a film might deal in any depth with interesting ideas was out of the question, and in its way *On Velvet* made no advance on *Elstree Calling*. As Chibnall points out, 'Occasionally the quota quickie was so up to the minute that it got ahead of itself', and *On Velvet* 'anticipated the arrival of commercial television by almost two decades. But Newman's gags, delivered by Wally Patch and Joe Hayman, were "antique" rather than futuristic.'[12]

John Quin's screenplay makes way for a catalogue of turns including the apparently humourless comic duo Collinson and Dean, Eric Barker, the Columbia Choir (Columbia distributed the film), Bellings' Dogs, and Rex Burrows and His Orchestra, with singers Nina Mae McKinney and Julie Suedo. The *MFB* dismissed Newman's offering as 'tedious, maudlin and lacking in good taste'.[13]

JUNE

If one of the purposes of the British musical film was to hire variety turns who happened to be free for a couple of hours during the few days set aside for shooting, *Around the Town* was another example. Fenn Sherie and Ingram D'Abbes spun its basically non-existent plot around the personality of Vic Oliver, who audiences were expected to believe was down-at-heel theatrical agent Ollie Rose. Adding insult to injury, they also had to swallow Finlay Currie as brash American producer Sam Wyngold. This was a prelude to sixty-eight minutes of juggled tosh, as Ollie sought out acts and songwriters for Wyngold's approval, before getting hitched to his daughter Norma played by American Irene Ware, the Miss United States of 1926.

Of Austrian origin, Oliver was a prodigiously talented artist and composer, had starred at the London Palladium and studied under Mahler, and married Churchill's daughter. Michael Kilgarriff recalls, 'The only occasion upon which we saw Mr Oliver was [on stage] at the Brighton Hippodrome; he told some breath-takingly vile jokes and then sat down to accompany a soprano in the Bach-Gounod 'Ave Maria'.'[14]

Around the Town secured the presence of the songwriting team of Jimmy Kennedy and Michael Carr on screen, as well as the Two Charladies, the Tin Pan Alley Trio, the Rhythm Sisters, and Al and Bob Harvey. Maurice Winnick and His Band represented the then inescapable big band. Herbert Smith produced and directed for British Lion, earning *MFB*'s censure that 'No attempt is made to put these acts over with any skill, nor to weave out of them a coherent whole'.[15]

During the decade, flirtations between female stars of British musical films and Hollywood studios seldom had happy endings. Now, Tinsel Town wanted to turn Gracie Fields into a Jeanette MacDonald with comic spasms in ***We're Going to Be Rich***, produced for 20th Century Productions by Robert T. Kane and Samuel G. Engel, and directed at Denham by Fields's husband Monty Banks. Following *The Show Goes On*, Darryl F. Zanuck signed Fields for $200,000, claimed to be the highest figure yet paid to any film performer. The siren call of Hollywood had not been avoided, but Fields kept her distance, insisting that the picture was made in Britain. With a screenplay by prolific Sam Hellman and Engel (his first and only), based on a story by James Edward Grant, the film hovered somewhere between Puccini's *The Girl of the Golden West*, a Western, and Lancashire hotpot, matching Fields with American leads Victor McLaglen and Brian Donlevy. A stony-faced *MFB* complained of a plot that was 'the crudest routine stuff that jerks along in patches of uninspired dialogue' with Fields and McLaglen 'competent and no more; they play their parts in sections rather than as a preconceived whole'.[16]

Variety decided, 'Will do well in England. In the States, will slide into the duals.'[17] The *New York Times* disagreed, thinking it 'vigorous, lusty, and amusing

'Our Gracie': optimistic as ever for *We're Going to Be Rich* (1938)

comedy, excellently backgrounded and graced with a strong supporting cast', in which Fields 'not only brought the house down but had the ruins chuckling'.[18] In November 1938 the *Manchester Guardian* recalled how

> A year ago a New York journal, with a tolerant shake of the head, put down the popularity of Gracie Fields to the quaint old-world appetite of Britons for 'vulgar

grimaces' and humour of the 'flea-scratching' order. Three months ago New York, having seen *We're Going to Be Rich*, took Gracie to its heart, and declared through the same irreverent organ that 'in failing to recognise her long ago Hollywood has been guilty of a serious nonfeasance.'

What was more, 'British film producers cast her as she was, in "romantic leads", and only blind devotees liked the results; Hollywood (disguised as Denham) has given her a cosmopolitan appeal and translated it into the language of film.'[19]

In Melbourne, Kit Robson (Fields) is a singer married to ne'er-do-well Dobbie (McLaglen). He sinks her money into the purchase of a Johannesburg gold mine. Complications ensue, interspersed with a generous array of songs delivered by the star in 'her own knock-me-down way'.[20] Interpolated titbits of British music-hall pay little attention to historical accuracy. In a story set in 1880, we hear two numbers originally performed by Charles Coborn, 'The Man That Broke The Bank At Monte Carlo' (1891) and 'Two Lovely Black Eyes' (1886), as well as Jose and Lottie Collins's 1891 'Ta-Ra-Ra-Boom-De-Ay'. R. P. Weston and Bert Lee ensure a dash of genuine Fields with 'Will You Love Me When I'm Mutton?' (one wonders what the American producers made of that one), while Harry Parr Davies was retained to provide the two central numbers, the 'Trek Song' and 'The Sweetest Song In The World'. These provide the most effective moments of the film, alongside the typically optimistic 'Ee, By Gum!' by Ralph Butler and Howard Flynn.

Despite contemporary complaints, *We're Going to Be Rich* deserves reassessment. As Low notes, it may be that Fields's humour and ability to switch instantly from comedy to remorse 'was strictly for local consumption, and teaming her with American stars in an unfamiliar format dismayed her British fans without attracting an American following.'[21] A return to Britishness seemed certain when her next film was announced as *Piccadilly Circus*.

Romantic blarney flourished in ***Mountains o' Mourne***, under the guise of another popular parlour song, Percy French's composition of 1896. Surely this must be a Butcher's Film Services production? – and so it was, made in conjunction with the more intellectually named Rembrandt Film Productions, directed at Walton by Harry Hughes. R. B. Marriott described it as 'unpretentious and often very naïve', praising Niall MacGinnis's performance as Paddy Kelly for bringing 'reality and conviction into a story which otherwise fails to exist'.[22] The non-existent story by Daisy L. Fielding was reworked in Gerald Brosnan's screenplay, following the progress of young Paddy from his humble beginnings in Ireland to cosmopolitan success after his voice is discovered by a BBC talent scout. Alas, success leads Paddy into a liaison with selfish socialite Violet Mayfair (Betty Ann Davies) before, to the audience's satisfaction, he reverts to homely Mary Macree (Rene Ray).

MacGinnis sang 'Ireland In Spring' and 'With My Shillelagh Under My Arm', but seems never again to have burst into song on screen, and is now best remembered for being satanic in the cult horror *Night of the Demon*. There could be little doubt about a supporting cast that includes Jerry Verno, fearsome Freda Jackson, the authentically Irish Maire O'Neill, and Eve Lynd, composer of the 1948 stage musical *Cage Me a Peacock*. Cornelia and Eddie, Andre and Curtis, and Percival Mackey's Band add to the jollity.

After scene-stealing in *Rose of Tralee*, Britain's tiniest star Binkie Stuart was placed under contract by Butcher's Films. Her popularity was sufficient for her to be mobbed by fans when making a personal appearance at Brighton Odeon in 1938. Would Butcher's *never* give up its habit of poaching the title (and sentiment) of old songs? Now, the ideal candidate was **Little Dolly Daydream**, and who was littler than four-year-old Stuart, in her way a living embodiment of the song Leslie Stuart had composed in 1897, inspired by his daughter Dolly. Oswald Mitchell co-wrote the screenplay with Ian Walker, and directed a film that is inevitably held up by the extreme delicacy of its star. Old hands were hired to appear alongside, unfolding a plot about curly-headed Dolly running away from home, meeting a grizzled old organ-grinder and getting mixed up with a bunch of crooks before being put to bed early with a nourishing mug of hot milk. Today, someone might already be on the telephone to social services, but quaintness prevails, and Talbot O'Farrell sings the title song and the faintly nauseous 'The Lisp Of A Baby's Prayer'. Guy Jones and His Band give musical support. John Argyle produced for Argyle-British.

A British musical film starring Ambrose threatened to become an annual event, in the wake of the 1936 *Soft Lights and Sweet Music* and 1937 *Calling All Stars*. Big bands were rarely more popular than the one run by Ambrose, around whom Vogue Film Productions constructed **Kicking the Moon Around**. Many hands were needed for light work, with a screenplay shared between Angus Macphail, actor Michael Hogan, playwright Roland Pertwee and Twickenham's quick-on-the-typewriter Harry Fowler Mear, based on a story by Tom Geraghty.

Blonde songster Evelyn Dall is music shop assistant Pepper. Hal Thompson plays millionaire Bobbie Hawkes, whose fiancée Flo (Florence Desmond) is exposed as money-grabbing when he tricks her into believing he has lost his fortune. Happily, Hal meets Pepper, and before Mear can extract a couple of gags from his infamous joke book she is vocalizing for Ambrose (signature tune 'When Day Is Done'). Dall is no more or less interesting here than in any other of her film appearances, Desmond as under-used as in hers. A vengeful Flo gets Pepper drunk before her act in the hope of ruining her career. This being impossible in a British musical film, all is resolved to Flo's dissatisfaction. Produced at Pinewood by Herbert Wynne, *Kicking the Moon Around* was directed by Walter Forde, with a score by Jimmy Kennedy and Michael Carr. The supporting cast has echoes of John Baxter, including writer-actor C. Denier Warren, Davy Burnaby (ex-Co-Optimist), Edward Rigby, and 'real bloke' George Carney. Maureen O'Hara appears as a secretary. Along the way, Desmond gives impressions of Katharine Hepburn and Garbo, and Dall sings 'It's The Rhythm In Me' and 'No Song About Love'. Also heard are 'Mayfair Merry Go Round' and 'Two Bouquets'.

It may have been news to British audiences that Jack Buchanan Productions' **Break the News** had already debuted as the French movie *Le Mort en fuite*. The British version, directed at Pinewood by René Clair, teamed Buchanan with Maurice Chevalier in a screenplay by Geoffrey Kerr based originally on Loïc Le Gouriadec's novel. The result is disappointing. The *MFB* applauded a 'thoroughly cheerful show' but 'considering the array of talent engaged, this seems rather small beer, but a refreshing draught nevertheless'.[23] The *Era* found it 'all thoroughly amusing entertainment, directed with skill',[24] but for Bosley Crowther in the *New York Times* 'the performances are uninspired. [Buchanan and Chevalier] go about their merry-making with little cheer, and the one song ['It All Belongs To You'] that Cole Porter has written for them to sing lacks the spark. And June Knight [late of the unlamented *The Lilac Domino*] as a revue star, is mostly flat.'[25]

Yet, the basic concept seems promising, with the male stars as ageing chorus-boys in a show dominated by Grace Gatwick (Knight). Weary of being overlooked, ambitious Teddy (Buchanan) and retiring Francois (Chevalier) devise a publicity stunt whereby Teddy will vanish, presumed murdered by Francois. With Francois awaiting execution, Teddy is delayed by a foreign revolution. The strong company features a host of dependables, among them Robb Wilton, Felix Aylmer, Garry Marsh, Guy Middleton, Wally Patch and, fresh from providing love interest in *The Singing Cop*, Marta Labarr. As well as Porter's number, the male stars duetted in 'We're Old Buddies' by Buchanan and Van Phillips.

Hazel Ascot's film career with UK National, begun with *Talking Feet*, ended with **Stepping Toes**. It was in effect very much the same film, a reunion for some of the previous film's cast and evidence of director John Baxter's penchant for remaking the same picture in different forms, as in his *Doss House* 'series'.

Little Hazel Ascot's Hazel Barker of *Talking Feet* has metamorphosed into little Hazel Warrington, and Enid Stamp-Taylor, her mother in *Talking Feet*, into a different mother. Other of Baxter's repertory store of players are enrolled, including Edgar Driver, Jack Barty, Ernest Butcher, along with the usual Baxter line-up of variety turns. Several would almost certainly never have made it on screen with any other director: The Cone School Girls, The Three Dots, and the Sanders Twins. The strangely aloof Wee Georgie Wood guested, and Baxter's obsession with the therapeutic effect of classical music on the working class manifests in the violinist Campoli. During the three-week shoot at Sound City the studio was also invaded by 150 pupils from Dover's Duke of York's School performing the 'Parade Of The Tin Soldiers' against a backdrop of Dover Castle.

Based on a storyline by Jack Francis and Barbara K. Emary, H. Fowler Mear's screenplay broke no new ground, vaguely charting Hazel's progress from talent show hopeful to star status, simultaneously bringing together her mother and estranged grandfather and saving their showbusiness reputation. The sometimes easy-to-please *Kinematograph Weekly* warmly welcomed it. 'The evening is Hazel's. No great shakes as a singer, she yet manages to put songs over effectively; but her dancing is phenomenal, and her personality winning [...] a lively tempo is maintained throughout, and the whole concern is bathed in a refreshing atmosphere of good humour'.[26] For *Era* this was 'one of John Baxter's best efforts, a variety film with real ideas behind it [...] Very cleverly, too, John has catered for the young picture-goer by including a mass of juvenile performers, among whom Hazel Ascot stands out as definitely a future star.'[27] With the coming of war, this was not to be. Plans for a third film, with a circus setting, were discarded.

There would have been few regrets felt by 'H. M.' of the *Observer*, who gave *Stepping Toes* a roasting, declaring it would 'hardly be worth mentioning if it did not glaringly reveal why so many British pictures are drearily unsuccessful'. He sat through 'the worst dialogue that I can remember hearing for a long time' (e.g. 'What's your name?' 'Hazel!' 'I bet you're a nut!'), among 'sickly sentimentalities'. Listing the supposed inadequacies of Baxter's work, he asked 'Could amateurishness go further?' and suggested that domestic producers should work towards a particularly British school of film, otherwise 'they will go on making films that are as clumsy and ineffective as *Stepping Toes*'.[28]

JULY

No doubt the cockles of many hearts were warmed at the prospect of 'street singer' Arthur Tracy singing 'It's My Mother's Birthday Today' in a film that (doubtful though it is that anyone was particularly interested) 'brings to the screen for the first time the actual facts concerning Arthur Tracy's rise to fame'.[29] This information was divulged via Belgrave Films' **Follow Your Star**, produced at Pinewood by Harcourt Templeman and directed by Sinclair Hill on one of his less-inspired days. Hill and Tracy handed the storyline to screenplay writers George Pearson and Stafford Dickens, with Mr Tracy no doubt taking a moment off from crooning over-sweet ballads to peer over their shoulders to make sure the 'actual facts' of his progress to stardom were correct. Working lad Arthur Tee is doomed to life in a factory. Here, surely, as so very often before, the British musical film made a miscalculation by having a hero who aspires to be better than he is, and – naturally – succeeds handsomely, usually romantically as well as financially, enjoying great commercial success and regarded as a highly privileged and notable person. Surely, filmmakers needed to stare from the screen at their audiences? Menial jobs often marked the start of these film characters' careers; it's easy enough to find examples. The audience for such films were made up of a great many of such people.

From the days of *Boots! Boots!*, with Formby as boot-boy Willie, the pattern is set. Humble origins and lowly professions provide the starting point from which the star must rise, preferably and almost inevitably, to showbusiness heights of acclamation. But what message was this for the average working-class patron of the British musical film? Watching these pictures, the message is clearly spelled: Albert Burdon in *Letting in the Sunshine* is *only* a window-cleaner; John Garrick in *Street Song* is *only* a street busker; Jessie Matthews in *Sailing Along* is *only* a barge-hand; Keith Falkner in *Mayfair Melody* is *only* a garage mechanic. They begin as ordinary people and end up personages; it is the measure of their success that is applauded. The list is endless. At least, as the year turned, one of the first titles to emerge from British studios made no pretence of what is was about: *Let's Be Famous*. There is no law against such a philosophy, but one of the spurious effects of British musical films was to suggest, and clearly demonstrate, that anything less than stardom, anything menial or of practical use to society, is undesirable, and needs to be escaped from. The other thing was that while Hollywood excess might get away with such attitudes, British studios could provide only ersatz impressions, at the end giving in to the fact that whatever success did, it did not necessarily eradicate the humble origins from which success had been clawed. Attainment is reached by sitting at a table in a highly unconvincing nightclub.

And so with Tracy, exulting in his rise from the gutters of street-singing to the showbiz heights for which the humdrum longed. So it is with Mr Tee, doomed to life in a factory until he joins a travelling circus and begins to clamber up the slippery ladder to wealth and fame, this time by warbling over-emotional ballads and, *Pagliacci*-like, singing 'Laugh, Clown, Laugh', hinting at some far-off depth of feeling that seems, in Mr Tee's case, to remain some way away. Reduced to singing in the street (back again, as it were, to the level of much of his audience), he climbs back up the greasy pole, becoming a West End star. *MFB* obliquely concluded it was 'put over with no attempt to make it seem other than it is'.[30] The songs are by Jimmy Kennedy and Michael Carr. The score includes the spiritualised 'De Lawd Loves His People To Sing', 'Waltz For Those In Love', 'Misty Islands Of The Highlands' and 'Goldilocks'. Tracy's efforts were supported by Belle Chrystal as girlfriend Mary.

AUGUST

If the *Era* was to be believed, the new Stanley Lupino offering was 'on the whole, a fine piece of real, good, hearty fun. Unfortunately it loses some of its slickness by unnecessary trimmings.'[31] This should not stop the curious from exploring **Hold My Hand**, one of the more palatable British musical films of the decade. Lupino had co-written and starred with Jessie Matthews in its stage version at the Gaiety Theatre seven years earlier. Associated British Picture Corporation's film version, made at Elstree, had a stronger cast than its theatrical original. Now, Lupino was comedy-paired with the superb Fred Emney as Lord Milchester, married to a ladyship in the forbidding shape of Bertha Belmore. Those who think the Marx Brothers' Margaret Dumont the epitome of middle-aged women need to meet Miss Belmore, one of the true *grandes dames* of British cinema; nobody since has dared replace her.

Hold My Hand succeeds at almost every turn. It has three appealing female leads: singers Sally Gray and Polly Ward (real name Byno Poluski) and American import, not too well served here, Barbara Blair. The comedy is fast and intricate, as might be expected in the hands of experienced farceurs: look at what Lupino and Emney do with some glasses and a decanter and a folding document, or the 'baby diddums' in which they converse. If those 'unnecessary trimmings' include sour-faced Gibb McLaughlin and Charles Penrose ('The Laughing Policeman' of recording fame) as two disinterested bank managers, and at the tail end of the piece, the gloriously pompous and almost stationary police inspector of Syd Walker, so be it.

Produced by Walter C. Mycroft, the screenplay by Clifford Grey, Bert Lee and William Freshman was based on Lupino's original stage work. The film's songs neatly slot into the action. Romantic support John Wood duets Polly Ward in the title song by Noel Gay, Maurice Elwin and Harry Graham, and in 'As Long As I Can Look At You', an artless attempt at flirtation by Grey, Weston and Lee, sung in a railway station refreshment room. Particularly charming and artificially contrived is Gay and Desmond Carter's quartet 'Spring', with Philip Buchel's (and probably Lupino's) pretty choreography, incorporating a moment of Lupino's frog-dancing across a garden pond. Another deft period touch is evident in Sigler, Goodhart and Hoffman's 'Turn On The Lovelight' duet for Lupino and Grey. Lupino comes over as one of the easiest-going and charming comedians of the decade. After much restrained activity, there is a Busby Berkeley-type finale set in a fantastically oversized Greta Green smithy, with giant anvils and cavorting dancing girls adding a dash of not-quite-Hollywood-standard glitz. Thornton Freeland directs with a sure understanding of the breezy goings-on.

One of Florrie Forde's many 'chorus' numbers (they often gained lasting popularity devoid of their verses) was 'She's A Lassie From Lancashire', written by Lipton, Murphy and Neat, and a great hit in 1907 provincial pantomimes. Its title was revived to draw customers to a film that otherwise offered little inducement to attend. ***Lassie from Lancashire***, concocted by Doreen Montgomery and Ernest Dudley and directed by John Paddy Carstairs, was produced at Welwyn by John Corfield. Showbusiness hopefuls Jenny (Marjorie Browne, billed in variety as 'Red-Headed and Ruthless') and Tom (Hal Thompson, late of *Kicking the Moon Around*) find stardom, although the 'charming little love story is merely the excuse for a number of catchy songs and jokes which are not only funny but clean'.[32] Set on the Isle of Wight, the film is interspersed with such turns as Rio and Santos, the Three Music-Hall Boys, Ronnie Munro, and the double act Billy Caryl and Hilda Mundy.

Kinematograph Weekly thoughtfully reported **Calling All Crooks** as 'good fun for those who did not take their pleasure too seriously'.[33] In plainer speech, *MFB* decided that 'The completely irresponsible story is of no consequence whatever', with dialogue that was 'facetious and ribald. It is a pity that better material could not have been provided for a clever and popular team.'[34] That team of Billy Nelson, Chuck O'Neill and Jack Butler supported comic Douglas Wakefield, well known enough to potential audiences to play 'Dougie'. Arthur Mertz contrived a screenplay for Mancunian Films, loosely built around a fraudster (typecast nasty Leslie Perrins) trying to extort money from a dentist. This unlikely material was advertised by producer John E. Blakeley as a 'Merry Musical Burlesque' and sometimes more extremely as 'Another Screaming Musical Comedy Burlesque'. It was directed at Cricklewood by George Black Jnr.

The enterprise was squarely aimed at northern patrons in 'lesser' halls, for whom the slapstick sequences of whitewashing were considered ideal entertainment. The general crudity of invention was to a degree sidelined by Hal Wright and His Circus, the noise of Thirty Gypsy Revellers, the Master Singers, vent act Raymond Smith, Velda and Vann, the Seven Royal Hindustans of circus fame, and the ever-kicking Sherman Fisher Girls. There was a song, 'Daphne'.

OCTOBER

After recent disappointment, what a pleasure to find a charmer in **Penny Paradise**, the idea conceived by Basil Dean who also produced for Associated Talking Pictures at Ealing. An above-average screenplay is credited to Thomas Thompson, W. L. Meade and Thomas Browne, with Carol Reed directing a film of many qualities, satisfyingly bringing together its disparate elements. From its opening, *Penny Paradise* seems cared for, remarkably sunny, told with gentle wit and an army of little touches that distinguish it.

In Liverpool, Joe Higgins (Edmund Gwenn) is the much-loved captain of an old tug, assisted by his kindly, unsophisticated and accident-prone mate Pat O'Leary (Jimmy O'Dea), who fancies Joe's bar-maiden daughter Betty (Betty Driver). Their jog-along working-class lives are altered when Joe comes into a fortune on the football pools, but Pat has forgotten to post the coupon. Unable to break the truth to Joe, Pat looks on as Joe excitedly embarks on a new life of spend, spend, spend – but truth will out.

Somehow, the writers and performers convince us beyond doubt, when the truth emerges, that all is for the best; the fortune is better lost. The acting is very fine, not least the beaming kindliness of Gwenn, deeply affecting throughout, and the gentle O'Dea in a naturalistic performance that suggests he might have gone further as a film performer. He gets to sing Davies's 'Mrs Mulligan's One Of The Quality Now'. Betty Driver, too, stands apart in the canon of British musical films in her seemingly organic ordinariness. It's too bad that she is doomed to be labelled as a sub-Gracie Fields when her talents are so unlike. Driver never moves into comedy, only perfecting a sort of domestic intensity, convincing through the plucky 'Stick Out Your Chin' and the stoic 'You Can't Have Your Cake And A Penny Too', a theory that must have struck a chord with pound-shy cinema audiences of 1938. With no recourse to sentimentality, Driver treats her dramatic scenes head-on, with the slightest of touches. In Harry Parr Davies's standout torch number 'Learn How To Sing A Love Song', she is quite the equal of Fields.

There is excellent support from all, and a gem of a performance by that most Irish of actresses Maire O'Neill as the wily fish and chip shop owner Widow Clegg. With Reed's help, she never misses a nuance. Her reticent entanglement with Joe is a delight, he – in competition with the alarming photograph of the late departed Mr Clegg above the widow's mantelpiece – nervously trying to plight a troth while she informs him that her late husband always 'got all his dues and demands'. Reed also draws wonderful performances from a money-grabbing Aunt Agatha (Ethel Coleridge) and her dried-up husband (Syd Crossley on top miserable form).

For once, the trifling story seems enough, firmly rooted and built on with its strong sense of place and character. Rare enough for any British musical film, you are aware of its having been directed, of care having been extended. The horror of Pat's forgetting to post the winning coupon is brilliantly and simply emphasised by Reed concentrating on the gaping maw of the letterbox, accusingly staring back at Pat. Irishness is never far away. Even when Pat at first realises the implications of his inaction, he finds solace in the fact that 'There's no music in the world like the songs of Ireland'. For once it is true, as he distractedly sings 'Bridget Mulligan'.

The stars of *Save a Little Sunshine* had competition from a supporting cast that included two comics, Max Wall and Tommy Trinder, who would go on to do much finer work than this. The Welwyn Studios' production by Warwick Ward had a screenplay by Vernon Clancey and Victor Kendall, with additional dialogue by Gilbert Gunn, adapted from W. Armitage Owen's play *Lights Out at Eleven*. Director Norman Lee had to deal with the picture's star, Scots comedian Dave Willis – presumably in the hope that he would become a Scots version of Formby – and singing actress Patricia (Pat) Kirkwood. 'The screams of the demon director' left her in fear of filming for the rest of her career; 'the feeling that I could do nothing right damaged my confidence and I stiffened up like a robot whenever he called "action".'[35]

Era complained of a weak plot and loosely constructed scenario, with the *MFB* agreeing that it was all 'limp and patchy'; 'the dialogue (except for one line) is dull, the slapstick hesitating and the variety turns more than semi-detached'.[36] The simple plot involves jobless Dave Smalley (Willis) turning a run-down boarding house into a nightclub with the help of girlfriend Pat (Kirkwood). The screenplay gives better opportunities to the supporting players, principally Peggy Novak as a dragon of a landlady, and old opera singer Mrs Melworthy (Annie Esmond). The eagle-eyed will spot an uncredited Charles Penrose ('The Laughing Policeman', unlaughing here) in the cabaret finale. Musical numbers include 'Nothing Can Worry Me Now', 'Everything In France Is Hunky-Dory' and 'Down In The Deep Blue Sea'. They may sound like sub-standard Noel Gay, but Willis and Kirkwood duetting the title song, and its unexpectedly sumptuous reprise with tap-dancing bellboys and waitresses, are a delight, even if the choreography is ill-coordinated. In hope of something similar but better, Willis and Kirkwood reunited the following year for *Me and My Pal*.

NOVEMBER

Admirers of Waller-Tunbridge musicals will need no urging towards *Yes, Madam?*, an enjoyable if not completely satisfying reworking of the 1934 London Hippodrome stage show. We must be grateful that Bobby Howes, Bertha Belmore, Vera Pearce and Wylie Watson repeated their stage roles here (who else could have impersonated such actors?). The pity is that, again, the historically acclaimed stage partnership of Howes with Binnie Hale, one of the happiest matchings of the 1930s, was not happening on film. Neither Howes nor Hale had repeated their stage roles in the film of *Mister Cinders* (the disappointing results of this are apparent when we see the picture), and now Hale's stage role in *Yes, Madam?* went to Diana Churchill.

Made at Elstree by Associated British Picture Corporation, the film was produced by Walter C. Mycroft and directed by 'screaming' Norman Lee (lately of *Save a Little Sunshine*) in a reworking of the stage original by Clifford Grey, Bert Lee and William Freshman, based on K. R. G. Browne's novel. Amusing as it is, *Yes, Madam?* isn't as felicitous as *Please Teacher*. Much of the comedy is laboured, waiting to be interrupted by apposite songs and (perhaps just as well) unwilling to attempt set-piece numbers. A will declares that Bill Quinton (Howes) and his cousin whom he has never met, Sally Gault (Churchill), will each inherit £80,000, but only if after being in service for a month they have not been dismissed. This ridiculous situation throws up all sorts of stock misunderstandings. There is the meekest of villains in the ever-dapper Tony Tulliver (Billy Milton), trying to grab the cousins' bequests, but the film's best moments almost always involve the incomparable Belmore, and Pearce as substantial cabaret artiste Pansy Beresford ('No true heart ever beat beneath a pair of tights!').

The film's treatment of the songs is not especially sympathetic. The musical numbers are by Weston, Lee and Grey, and Waller and Tunbridge. Churchill helps Howes with the duet 'What Are You Going To Do If Love Comes?', trying to catch the spirit of Hale's inimitable playfulness, but makes little impression. The other duet from the stage show, 'Sittin' Beside O' You', is missing. A title song and 'Something Will Happen Today' are not especially interesting, but the insertion of the 'Cat's Duet', courtesy of Rossini via Waller and Tunbridge, remains effective. Hanging over all is the feeling that these sorts of musicals were reaching their final destination. Pearce takes to the dance floor for 'Czechoslovakian Love'. Her strenuous routine with Howes is such heavy work (after which Miss Pearce must surely have retired to her dressing-room for a lie-down) that one wonders for how many years such nonsense could continue.

Formby was seldom better than in the wonderfully entertaining *It's in the Air*, masterminded for Associated Talking Pictures by producer Basil Dean and writer and director Anthony Kimmins. George Brown doesn't know his left hand from his right – a problem that persistently gets him into scrapes – not least when he longs to be an Air Raid Warden. Others would be wrong to think this disqualifies him from success as he sings 'They Can't Fool Me' (by Formby, Harry Gifford and Fred E. Cliffe, brilliantly styled to the star's needs). When he tries on his sister's fiancé's RAF uniform, he begins a misadventure that ultimately lands him in prison. He's mistaken for a despatch rider, and infiltrates the service, too often the victim of practical joker Corporal Craig (Jack Hobbs) but ready to entertain everyone with his uke, describing 'Our Sergeant Major' (Formby-Gifford-Cliffe). Craig tricks George into settling down for a bath and the night in the Sergeant Major's quarters. This is beautifully directed, with fine playing from Formby and the superb Julien Mitchell's Sergeant Major, forever secretly learning to play the ukulele.

Mayhem of various sorts breaks out at intervals, choreographed to perfection by Kimmins. Harry Parr Davies's 'It's In The Air' consolidates George's relationship with his fellow men, backed by Ernest Irving's almost celestial orchestration. It reminds us that some of the very best Formby numbers are those that involve others; they accentuate George's essential gift for companionship. Through it all, George maintains his dignity and, thanks to the support of the Sergeant Major's daughter Peggy (Polly Ward), we are never in doubt of a happy outcome, even when he takes up a plane in the hilariously eventful finale, before bringing it safely down. He is rewarded by being accepted into the service. The musical finale tops everything, a sort of mock-Hollywood number at a camp concert, with George supposedly piloting a plane. It makes for the happiest of landings.

DECEMBER

Following 20th Century Productions' spatial expansion of the Gracie Fields franchise in *We're Going to Be Rich*, there was a return to the more familiar domestic with 20th Century's **Keep Smiling**, originally titled *Piccadilly Corner*, and renamed *Smiling Along* in America. Fields plays disillusioned entertainer Gracie Gray, who turns her back on a cheating management and with some of her theatrical colleagues moves to her uncle's farm. With the help of Bert Wattle (Roger Livesey) they work their way to success. Here, just before the outbreak of war, are shades of the pierrot concert parties, with a hint of *The Good Companions* in the nimble screenplay of William Conselman, and scenario by Val Valentine and dialogue by the playwright Rodney Ackland, the whole based on Sandor Frago and Alexander Kemedi's story 'The Boy, the Girl and the Dog'. The dog is Skippy, already a canine star from playing Asta in the 'Thin Man' films. Monty Banks directs a splendid company that includes Gracie's brother Tommy as Bola, American Jack Donohue (doubling as choreographer) as Denis Wilson, and Peter Coke (BBC radio's 'Paul Temple') as the concert party's pianist Rene Sigani.

Harry Parr Davies contributes 'Giddy Up' and the casual jazz of 'Swing Your Way To Happiness'. Also heard are 'The Holy City', 'You've Got To Be Smart In The Army' by Leslie Elliott and Robert Rutherford, 'Parade Of The Matadors' by Peter Yorke, 'Peace Of Mind' by Gerald Paul, and a standout comedy number for Fields, 'Mrs Binns's Twins', by Jimmy Harper and Will E. Haines.

As Jeffrey Richards points out, Fields's films transmitted 'a message of courage and cheerfulness, delivered not by a politician or statesman but by one of their own, who knew what they were enduring and whose advice could be trusted'.[37] Of all performers in British musical films of the decade, it is Fields who catches perfectly the spirit of the moment, hopeful, resilient, displaying forbearance when contemplating what might come. This is a quality denied every other leading lady who worked in the British musical film genre, and the camera caught it. No wonder the *MFB* lauded her 'intense vitality', no matter 'whether she is dancing in a sinking houseboat, knocking people over the head in a funfair or singing – with an unexpected beauty and dignity – the anthem in a little country church, she is always "Our Gracie", the darling of the North'.[38] The *Observer* cautioned against such enthusiasm, describing a minor romp and comedy 'of the rough and ready sort'.[39]

The year ended with a decisive whimper when Argyle-British Productions served up *My Irish Molly*, produced at Welwyn by John Argyle and based on his story. Director Alex Bryce had to deal not only with a dire screenplay (he wrote it with Ian Walker) and additional dialogue by W. G. Fay that seems not to have improved matters, but with car-crash editing, slack performances, clumsily interpolated songs, and a star who had to be in bed by six o'clock. The *People* warned readers of 'a feeble story with practically nothing to recommend it'.[40] Of most interest are two of its performers, virile balladeer Tom Burke and brilliant Maire O'Neill. As Eileen, another Irish performer Maureen Fitzsimmons (soon to be Maureen O'Hara) gets entangled in an insipid romance with good-looking American Bob (Phillip Reed). *MFB* was unencouraging, complaining that O'Hara 'has everything to learn about acting' and that her movements were 'awkward, and she lacks poise'.[41]

For a moment, it seems as if we're in for yet another passable cockles-of-the-heart-warmer, until the arrival of curly-headed (blatantly à la Shirley Temple) tot Molly Martin (Binkie Stuart). To pull the heart-strings tighter, she is an orphan. From this moment, the film is scuppered. It's an uncomfortable experience watching her plod through her scenes. Even as she serenades farmyard animals, bidding them 'How Do You Do?', great dollops of artificial innocence enshroud her.

The story, anyway, is ludicrous. Molly is sent to live with a miserable aunt and uncle (he wants to drown her little dog Skippy, which gives a clue as to the sort of uncle he is). Not surprisingly, Molly prefers to live with another aunt (O'Neill). Meanwhile, good sort Danny Gallagher (Burke), tired of being one of the great British unemployed, goes to America where he becomes one of the great American unemployed, although despair can apparently be swept away by breaking into an Irish aria. 'What about a song before you go?" ask his comrades just as he's about to leave for the States, and he obligingly goes straight into 'Off To Philadelphia'. Tramping the unfriendly streets of America, he sings 'Ireland, Mother Ireland' as the screen fills with scenic glimpses of far-off Killarney. The lure is too much for Molly and Eileen who have followed him to the States and they return with him to Ireland. There is no doubt that, as O'Neill tells Burke, he is 'the great boyo for the Irish tune'. Back home, Molly becomes famous on radio's 'Shamrock Baby Food Hour', and dressed in national costume sings 'With Me Shillelagh Under Me Arm' to rapturous acclaim. Someone insists 'She's the most colossal thing you've ever seen'.

1939

What must those devoted, underpaid, overworked performers slogging away at Gilbert and Sullivan every night of the year up and down the length of the country have made of this?

The Mikado

The Mikado
Me and My Pal
Let's Be Famous
Trouble Brewing
The Lambeth Walk

Music Hall Parade
Shipyard Sally
Discoveries
Come On George!
Lucky to Me

JANUARY

The operas of Gilbert and Sullivan, with their strange amalgam of period wit, tunefulness, absurdity and unquestionable respectability, continue to be played throughout the land, although without the authenticity and strict manner of the D'Oyly Carte Opera Company, which lived through surely the longest tour ever, from 1875 to 1982, with various necessary changes of personnel along the way. Leslie Baily prophesied that 'Stage and screen are likely to present Gilbert jazzed and Sullivan streamlined in productions boosted with sex and speed to fit the temper of the age we live in.' He looked forward to 'directors who will give us freshly charming interpretations of these Old Masters'.[1] So far as cinema is concerned, he has perhaps looked in vain.

Under the mantle of G and S Productions, the American composer-conductor Victor Schertzinger was the first to attempt a British filmic Gilbert and Sullivan. *The Mikado* was adapted for the screen by Geoffrey Toye, D'Oyly Carte's musical director between 1919 and 1924, when he had had the temerity to rewrite Sullivan's overture to the troublesome *Ruddigore*. Toye co-produced with Josef Somio, and conducted the film's score, but his cinematic revision of the original stage work was not especially happy. A muddled prologue doesn't help matters, while six numbers are cut and other music curtailed, along with some dialogue.

What must those devoted, underpaid, overworked performers slogging away at Gilbert and Sullivan every night of the year up and down the length of the country have made of this? D'Oyly Carte's chorus got itself into the picture, but at Pinewood only a couple of principals in the current stage production made the transition to screen. The current stage Nanki-Poo, John Dudley, was replaced by the pleasant-enough American singer Kenny Baker. Ivy Sanders and Margery Abbott, the two contemporaneous Yum-Yums, were usurped by British starlet Jean Colin. The almost legendary Mikado of Darrell Fancourt was replaced by the almost unknown John Barclay. Such changes probably filled G & S aficionados with horror, as would its musical cuts ('I've Got A Little List' and 'There Is Beauty In The Bellow Of The Blast' fell victim). The company's principal comedian Martyn Green is in place as the miserable worm of a tailor Ko-Ko, and Sydney Granville repeats his famous turn as Pooh-Bah. He should have known what he was doing; he had joined the company in 1908. Katisha, Gilbert's obligatory plain, middle-aged contralto (beloved of all his operas), was now played by the non-D'Oyly Carte Constance Willis, standing in for Ella Halman, the company's regular Katisha. Prettified by the designs of Vertes (not those used in the stage production), and boosted by the London Symphony Orchestra, the film premiered at the Leicester Square Theatre on 12 January.

'Sullivan has never been better sung,' pronounced the *MFB*, but 'Can the Gilbertian humour be reproduced in another medium? Will a generation brought up on superficial verbal wisecracks appreciate the subtlety and penetrating barbs of satire?' Nevertheless, 'Technically the film is as near perfection as may be in an imperfect world' and the acting was 'thoroughly competent, conscientious and careful'.[2] A die-hard G & S specialist regretted, 'With the best will in the world it is difficult to regard the film of *The Mikado* with other than modified rapture.'[3] As the *Manchester Guardian* realised, the G & S works were 'the most conventional thing in our modern theatre, and their intense conventionality is the cinema's great obstacle'.[4] C. A. Lejeune thought it 'an odd film that pulls this way and that and never quite gets anywhere'.[5]

Indeed, performers were so strait-jacketed into the D'Oyly Carte stage productions that taking a different step to the right or left, unless sanctioned by the director, was a punishable offence. Perhaps the film was 'surely an occasion when your cinematic purist must lock his principles away and be ruled by the genial tyranny of D'Oyly Carte'.[6] Perhaps the Americans had the better idea; they seemed to enjoy their own more daring reworkings, *The Swing Mikado* and *The Hot Mikado*. Any locked-away plans for G and S Productions to film other of the Savoy operas were shelved, and subsequent efforts to make them work on film have disappointed.

Frankie Howerd played Ko-Ko in the dire 1963 *The Cool Mikado*, directed after a fashion by Michael Winner; Howerd thought it 'absolutely incomprehensible gibberish'.[7] It is. D'Oyly Carte got a second shot at filming the opera in 1966, without involving outside performers; the result is uncinematic and dreary. Although on stage the operas have been tweaked and brought back to a semblance of life in various energised versions, the works of Gilbert and Sullivan have proved resistant to serious rethinking. D'Oyly Carte, understandably worn down by years of toil and predictability, shut up shop in 1982. While directors endlessly juggle with new concepts of Verdi and Wagner and Puccini, directors faced with G & S must scratch their heads. Nevertheless, Schertzinger's film is a visual treat. Frank S. Nugent in the *New York Times* recommended 'one of the most luscious productions of the operetta in history. Never were there such costumes or sets, never such colours – mother of pearl, dun, peach, orchid, all the pastel range'.[8] It's just the rest that's colourless.

FEBRUARY

Me and My Pal was the second attempt to make north of the border comedian Dave Willis a cinema favourite, following his 1938 *Save a Little Sunshine*. A change of director came with Thomas Bentley replacing 'screaming' Norman Lee. Warwick Ward produced for Welwyn Studios, with Vernon Clancey and Gilbert Gunn's screenplay that no doubt had Willis filling the gaps with bits and pieces of his old stage routines, punctuated by his strange passion for sausage rolls. The 'My Pal' of the title is his fellow removal man, easy-going Hal (George Moon). The pair are first seen driving their obviously unmoving van, singing Gunn's 'Keep On Moving Along'. It seems we might be in for some mild musical items, but the song is over before they hit the first traffic lights in a film that is musically emaciated.

That allows even more time for Willis's comedy, not helped by his toothbrush moustache that reminds us of Charlie Chaplin (no comparison) and Adolf Hitler. A vague plot about a gang of car insurance fraudsters materialises under the leadership of Andrews, played by Arthur Margetson; once a leading man of London musicals, in his heyday he had played opposite Lily Elsie. The spoof mock-American gangsterism scenes are badly done, and why do gansters like Andrews always refer to their middle-aged colleagues as 'boys'? There is what the writers must have considered coruscating wit, as when after a car accident Willis is asked, 'Where were you hurt?' – 'On the arterial bypass.'

Left over from *Save a Little Sunshine*, Pat Kirkwood is a negligible presence as Peggy. She first saw the film accompanied by her mother, at the Haymarket in Newcastle (she was playing Dandini in the city) on 8 February 1939. Her reaction is unrecorded. Once or twice the picture jerks into life: Moon models some remarkably hideous male underwear of the period; location scenes at a funfair momentarily take our minds off the rest (little Eliot Makeham is on the dodgems); and at a prison concert (somewhat lush considering the venue) Kirkwood sings 'Dinah' and 'You're Nobody's Sweetheart Now', before a crazy revolving stage bedroom-type finale. Sophistication is not in the air. If we are to believe the ecstatic enjoyment of the on-screen audience, hilarity is at its height. Be warned: these shots are frequently used stock footage.

MARCH

Lively as it is, the Jimmy O'Dea vehicle *Let's Be Famous* (what *other* hope, after all, was there for the mass of the audiences that would see such films?) is a disappointment after the excellent *Penny Paradise*. That had boasted a fine supporting company, denied to *Let's Be Famous*. Roger Macdougall and Allan MacKinnon's screenplay has its top-billed Irish star as Jimmy, well-loved proprietor of a local

Let's Be Famous provided refuge for Noel Gay and Frank Eyton's melancholic number for the undervalued Betty Driver (1939)

shop and post office in a rural outpost of Ireland, so remote that the arrival of a motor car is an event. Its occupant is a BBC talent scout (Garry Marsh) who arranges for Jimmy to be on the panel of a spelling bee broadcast from London; mistakenly, Jimmy thinks he has been chosen for his singing talent (he hasn't any).

From here, the story develops along well-trodden lines, with Betty Pinbright (Betty Driver) also singing at the BBC after she wins a local crooning championship competition, although forbidden by her strict father and ex-music hall mother (Lena Brown in her only feature film, giving a spirited rendition of 'Fall In And Follow Me' and 'Whistle If You Want Me'). Driver's scenes, her authenticity, wake the film up. She has the advantage of Noel Gay's breezy songs, and knows how to put them across convincingly: 'I Ran Into Love', 'I've Got A Hunch' and the melancholic 'The Moon Remembered But You Forgot' with its Frank Eyton lyric.

Produced at Ealing for Associated Talking Pictures by Michael Balcon, the film was directed by Walter Forde. With his 'sprightly direction, Noel Gay's music, and the feeling that the actors are enjoying it all even more than the audience, this unpretentious film provides laughs from beginning to end'.[9] According to Charles Barr, the only recommendation for this 'tedious experience' was its depiction of how the BBC worked immediately before the outbreak of war, 'the vulgarity of the advertising world, and the Northern genuineness of the heroine', along with 'the generation conflict, akin to so many Ealing films of the time'.[10]

Formby fans could look forward to a regular supply of fun in a series that would keep him at the forefront of British cinema until his bowing out in 1946 with the appropriately titled *George in Civvy Street*. What saucy songs he would be getting away with! Anthony Kimmins, director of **Trouble Brewing**, decided against the lyric 'Will he kiss her under the nose/or underneath the archway where her Sweet William grows?/If he's fresh and gets too free/I hope a bulldog bites him in the place it bit me', but there was still room for one of George's sauciest titles 'Fanlight Fanny', along with 'Hitting The High Spots Now' and 'I Can Tell By My Horoscope', written to order by Fred E. Cliffe and Harry Giffford, and infiltrated by Formby.

This time, George is George Gullip (it sounds rather as George looked, a fish fighting for air), compositor at a newspaper's printing works. He has a win at the races but discovers that the money he's given is counterfeit, and turns wrestler and waiter to get his winnings back and get the girl, in this case Googie Withers as Mary Brown. Could a more commonplace name have been found for the voluptuous Withers? It's as if the writers and Mrs Formby conspired to make George's love interest sound as uninteresting as possible.

There is efficient manipulation of the Formby formula in the screenplay by Kimmins, Angus Macphail and Michael Hogan, but C. A. Lejeune remarked that in his best work 'he has simply been the fool of a violent situation' and that now he 'manages to be less individual than I ever remember him. The sharp buzz-saw voice, the gormless charm, have their effective moments, but the film as a whole is a disappointing Formby.'[11] Adam Wilson considered Formby as 'a physical caricature of himself, like a Picasso sculpture leering through a gym window', shoehorned into a picture where the 'Formby tunes are crowbarred in, often with unapologetic ham-fistedness'. The slapstick finale in a brewery might be fun, but 'Most of the film drags along as if someone has taken Formby's end of pier act and used it to conjure up a film – a film that is procedural, episodic, and unfortunately a little boring.'[12]

APRIL

It's a particular sadness that Lupino Lane's extraordinary talents should have been so squandered after returning from Hollywood. The prophetic wailing of *Variety*'s review of his earlier *No Lady* rings in the ears: 'It is doubtful whether even the record of recent British productions can point to a more dire piece of work'; 'a few more like this and they'll have to rescind the Quota'; 'If this is Lupino Lane's idea of making pictures, something ought to be done about it.'[13]

Theatrical compensation came with the stage show *Me and My Girl*, the piece for which Lane is, if at all, remembered. Its success on stage was staggering. It originally played in London from December 1937 for 1,646 performances, followed by several successful revivals (1941, 1945 and 1949) in all of which Lane played cockney Bill Snibson. At the time of the film version, **The Lambeth Walk**, Lane was still appearing in the London production. Low's comment that it 'seems to have been corny and overplayed, trading on the popularity of the original' remains the impression, zest having been removed.[14] Nevertheless, the *MFB* applauded it as excellent: 'While following closely the original play, its original cockney verve is enhanced by brisk direction [by the surely unsuitable for the occasion Albert de Courville] and delightful musical settings.'[15] Sadly, those delightful settings didn't extend to most of Noel Gay's theatre score, only using the duet 'Me And My Girl' for Lane and leading lady Sally Gray, and 'The Lambeth Walk', not so much a dance as a never-ending amble, here worked up into an on-screen frenzy. The tune will never leave you. Apart from this, what comes across is the suspicion that Lane has been through its motions a great many times before. Produced by Anthony Havelock-Allan at Pinewood, the screenplay was by Clifford Grey, Robert Edmunds and John Paddy Carstairs.

JUNE

One of the unsung directors of British cinema, Oswald Mitchell sustained his career through the 1934 *Danny Boy* until, in the year of his death, the 1949 *The Temptress*. By 1939 he had already directed the original *Old Mother Riley* in 1937, and *Old Mother Riley in Paris* in 1938, followed in 1939 by *Old Mother Riley M.P.* – enough to test anyone's endurance. Mitchell had also been 'on parade' before, with *Stars on Parade* (1935) and *Variety Parade* (1936); now, it was time for a **Music Hall Parade**, a Butcher's Film Services production made at the Walton Studios.

Mitchell co-wrote with another foot soldier of British cinema, the prolific Con West, who deserved a medal for writing Lucan and McShane's films and a host of other, often low-budget, features. The plot follows Jean Parker (Glen Raynham), who takes on her father's music-hall after he dies. The dashing Dick Smart (Richard Norris) helps her succeed, staging a nationwide hunt for talent.

It has to be said that by the time Hitler was about to wage war on the world, British music-hall was already starting on turning up its toes. The cream of performers – those who in future years would be remembered in histories of music-hall – had already done their best, leaving Mitchell with a line-up of artists, many of whom are now forgotten. *Music Hall Parade*'s company includes northern comic Frank E. Franks, The Three Jokers, The Australian Air Aces, an act called 'Bird Courtship' by the astonishing Arnaut Brothers, and singer Eve Becke performing 'Stop the Clock' and 'Angelino Piccolino'. Top of the bill is Billy Cotton and His Band, but audiences also had to put up with impressionist Hughie Green.

JULY

According to Gracie Fields's brother Tommy, 'I don't think she ever really made what I call a good film.' She seemed to agree, regretting that after her first, *Sally in Our Alley* ('written properly. You had something to play with'), those that followed were 'stitched up around five or six songs. They weren't real stories to start off with; the stories were not good. They'd say "Get six songs ready, Gracie, because you're going to make a film."' The end of her genuinely British film career, before Hollywood claimed her, came with one of her most significant works, 20th Century's **Shipyard Sally**. Produced by Robert T. Kane, written by Karl Tunberg and Don Ettlinger, it was the last of her pictures to be directed by Monty Banks.

Nothing much seems to have changed since her last screen outing. Once more she is the plucky, unattached, indomitable champion of her working class, a none-too-successful stage performer, Sally Fitzgerald, encumbered with a card-sharp old rogue of a father, the Major, played by that most idiosyncratic of British comic actors Sydney Howard in a rich flow of namby-pamby outrageousness. He is one of the unusual joys of the occasion, without necessarily fitting in well with what is happening around him. We must also be grateful that in this case Gracie has no hint of a love interest, almost always the weakest component of her earlier pictures; men, anyway, always paled in comparison. Instead, the film satisfies itself with the father-daughter relationship. Sally's father buys her a run-down Irish pub. Making the best of a bad job, she wins over the rough-hewn clientele with the rollicking 'Grandfather's Bagpipes', before going straight into a stirring 'Annie Laurie'.

Any happiness is short-lived, for the Depression looms over the film, just as it was looming over those watching it in cinemas all over Britain. The shipyard's order books are empty; shipbuilding on Clydeside is in its death throes. This is not to be tolerated by Sally, or Gracie. 'You boys are the greatest shipbuilders in the world,' she tells the unemployed. Determined to bring work back to the yards, she leaves for London to persuade those in power to support the workers, cueing one of Harry Parr Davies's most remembered anthems, 'Wish Me Luck As You Wave Me Goodbye'. It's a little masterpiece of bespoke composition for its star; a lifetime later, it's almost impossible to think of anyone other than Fields singing it with such effortless soul.

In London, she hopes to turn the head of elderly Lord Randall (gentle Morton Selten), bumping into all the expected social barriers, at one point impersonating a young toff and meeting verbal gymnast and general nitwit Oliver Wakefield, throwing inhibitions to the wind with 'I've Got The Jitterbugs' and even managing a sort of striptease. Ultimately, of course, she succeeds in changing the government's position; new ships will once again be made at Clydeside. In celebration, we have a prolonged close-up of her singing 'There'll Always Be An England'. It's a fitting, stirring, deeply affecting envoi, a validation of the extraordinarily personal relationship she had built up with the British public, a direct transmission of Fields's being.

Despite the fact that the plot more or less stalls when Sally reaches London, the *Manchester Guardian* thought 'the cloak of chivalry suits her well, although it has not in the past sufficed to hide the inadequacy of her films' material'.[16] The *Observer* praised 'a story that has just enough serious background to lift it above the level of ordinary comedy'.[17]

SEPTEMBER

British Grand National's **Discoveries**, produced and directed at Highbury by Redd Davis, survives as a memento of talent-spotter Carroll Levis, the Hughie Green or Simon Cowell of his day. In common with those subsequent manifestations, there was little actual talent discernible in Mr Levis, who probably only had himself to blame, having suggested the storyline for *Discoveries* and cooked up a screenplay with Cyril Campion and Anatole de Grünwald, who should probably have known better. Levis (admirably placed to do so) played himself. Michael

Kilgarriff reminds us that Levis began life as 'The Great Richelieu, Magician, Eminent Hypnotist and Necromancer'. He inaugurated a hugely successful tour of his amateur night out show and its popularity 'kept the show on the road until the 1950s, proving if proof were needed the limitless self-delusion of the amateur artiste'.[18] Levis went on bravely insisting that 'Every Discovery is a Star of Tomorrow', a discernible error of judgement. The delusion upheld by the film seemed particularly mistimed, although one genuine star performer, Ronald Shiner, was dragged into it.

Those seeking professionalism are rewarded here and there by a cast that includes Kathleen Harrison as a maid, Bertha Belmore as a WPC, Doris Hare and Barbara Everest. Attempts to brighten things up include The Three Rascals, Lew Stone and His Band, comedian Issy Bonn, Afrique, and boy soprano Glyn Davies inspiring the nation by singing 'There'll Always Be An England', but too often the emphasis wanders back to Levis, 'a distinctly camera conscious compere who has to struggle with unpromising material'.[19]

NOVEMBER

A regular supply of George Formby was an essential of cinemagoing throughout the war. In this, Formby probably suffered more than Fields by being obliged to fit into a mould he had sculpted for himself. As David Shipman explained, 'His scriptwriters knew how to exploit him – from these same talents came most of the best post-war comedies – but once the war came, circumstances changed and Formby was no longer the cornerstone of Ealing comedies'.[20] Indeed, 'With the outbreak of war, George's persona required almost no alteration for use in the war effort. His "little man" became a symbol of democracy, keeping up everyone's spirits with a smile and a song and fighting spies and saboteurs instead of peacetime crooks'.[21]

Come On George! was the last Formby to be directed by Anthony Kimmins, who compiled the screenplay with Leslie Arliss and Val Valentine, produced at Ealing for Associated Talking Pictures by Jack Kitchin. This time, George is an ice-cream seller at a racecourse. A tale of the turf, concerning an ungovernably wild horse called Maneater, unfolds. The minor miracle is that the ice-cream man turns out to be the only man who can ride him effectively and, of course, gets to the winning post by the end of the picture. Seventeen-year-old Pat Kirkwood, late of *Save a Little Sunshine* and *Me and My Pal*, plays Formby's love interest, Ann, but is not allowed to sing, and a stolen on-screen kiss apparently had to be filmed when Formby's wife was off-set.

The *Manchester Guardian* noted that 'Compared to the Marx Brothers it is all rather like a cheerful evening in words of one syllable; George Formby's warm vulgarity ensures that it is in fact cheerful'.[22] As for the songs by Formby, Harry Gifford, Fred E. Cliffe and Allan Nicholson – 'I Couldn't Let The Stable Down', 'I'm Making

Headway Now', 'Goodnight Little Fellow' and 'Pardon Me' – they are 'perhaps, not as catchy as usual, but otherwise this is Formby fun at its best'.[23] In fact, the songs interrupt the narrative unexpectedly and disjointedly, and are musically and lyrically third-rate, at times testing the water for suggestiveness, as in 'She made my spare parts twice the size'. Antics in a railway yard, when window-cleaning, and at a flea circus pass the time, and George gets to disguise himself as a maid and as a circus performer, 'The Golden Phantom', for some sawdust slapstick. The support is generally weak, except for George Carney as Ann's policeman father, and Gibb McLaughlin as a dotty brain specialist. Emboldened by such treatment, George becomes fearless, overcoming every obstacle except the faint feeling that this is getting to be tired stuff, and ending with the philosophical contentment of 'Eee! What a to-do!'.

The Stanley Lupino catalogue creaked to a conclusion with the lamely titled **Lucky to Me**, a warmed-up adaptation of Lupino's 1928 stage musical *So This is Love*. Provincial newspapers hoped to whip up enthusiasm by promoting the film as 'A timely tonic for a weary world. Very acceptable popular entertainment',[24] promising 'No Rationing Here! Laughter Uncontrolled! Lashings of Laughter, Music and Girls'.[25] On screen, exhaustion seems to have been reached, with the Old Mother Riley-weary Thomas Bentley as director, insipid songs, chronic choreography, and jokes so old that one can almost hear the responding groans. There is also the silly plot, at once convoluted and uninteresting, about a couple getting married and boxing and stocks and shares and lovers hiding their relationship, all of it tackled by a hard-working comedian at the end of a long tether after years of service.

Walter C. Mycroft produced Clifford Grey's screenplay for Associated British Picture Corporation, based on the story by Lupino and Arthur Rigby. Lupino plays opposite two American female leads, Barbara Blair as wife Minnie and top-billed Phyllis Brooks as Pamela. Neither makes much of their roles, such as they are in a script laden with fruitless sexual innuendo. Noel Gay's songs are below par. David Hutcheson and Brooks duet the title song on a studio beach, but the few location shots sit uncomfortably with studio filming. Inane dialogue pauses for Gene Sheldon's 'Fish Song'. Lupino is confined to apparently endless verses of 'Let's Be Grateful For What We Haven't Got' – an understandable lyric in the circumstances. This is interrupted by a hastily inserted sequence in which he sings an up-to-the-moment lyric – so up-to-date that Lupino has to read the words. It's the one moment of the film, thrown together as it seems to be, that might have seemed relevant to those obliged to sit through it.

> Sing a song of England, give a rousing cheer
> It's nasty to be Nazi, so thank the Lord we're here.
> We've got no Gestapo, we've no swasti*ka*
> But all the same we're very pleased to be just what we are.

It's not Ira Gershwin, Noel Gay, Oscar Hammerstein II or Waller and Tunbridge, but it at least references – however ineffectively – world events, as if a flag has, ever so limply, been waved. It is made even more meaningless by the vapid events into which it has been stuffed. It seems odd that one of the most absurd scenes involves Lupino and one of his leading ladies madly destroying books, at a time when the Nazis were burning them.

It would hardly be a Lupino film if the action didn't move to a glitzy nightclub where customers assume rictus smiles when anybody breaks into song. This time it's called 'The Golden Ring', all modernity and tubular chairs, where a band of black musicians, 'The Knuckledusters', is looking particularly despondent. The entry of dancing girls wearing boxing gloves and performing a routine that delivers knockout blows to their colleagues suggests that at this moment in British musical films desperation has set in, just as a boxing ring descends on to the club's floor, and – for some unexplained reason – girls in Edwardian bathing dress prance around insisting 'I Do Like To Be Beside The Seaside'. By the time Lupino drags up as one of the female bathers it's all over, the audience having endured an avalanche of mildly suggestive dialogue about the lack of wedded consummation. At this gloomy point, the by no means unappealing Mr Lupino, who has done so much to cheer up the nation, slips unobtrusively out of its back door into its undisturbed footnotes. He died in 1942.

1940

Robeson, whom we can define as being officially 'outside' British culture, is the central spirit, the defining cog of the film, providing a totally authentic spiritual strength that borders religiosity

The Proud Valley

The Proud Valley
Laugh It Off
Band Waggon
Let George Do It!
Pack Up Your Troubles
Old Mother Riley in Society
Garrison Follies

Somewhere in England
Crook's Tour
Under Your Hat
Sailors Three
Spare a Copper
Cavalcade of Variety

JANUARY

Director Pen Tennyson began studio shooting of Ealing's *The Proud Valley* on 23 August 1939, the day the Molotov-Ribbentrop Pact locked the Russians and Germans into their war-footing. Eleven days later, Neville Chamberlain's declaration of war with Germany was broadcast from Downing Street. The King's message to the nation warned of 'dark days ahead', urging the public to 'fervently commit our cause to God'. Throughout the 1930s, British cinema, and indubitably the British musical film, had observed an unwritten mandate not only to entertain but divert attention from the country's Depression. Once people were inside the doors of the local Norvic or Odeon, film offered the possibility of shuffling off everyday care. As the 1930s progressed the threat of war increased, and when war broke out (although it was considered 'phoney' between September 1939 and May 1940) the situation had a radical effect on British film production. Nevertheless, between 1940 and the end of war in 1945, British studios produced musical films that attempted to respond to the times. Creatively and artistically, the attempt was by no means consistently successful. Some studios blithely continued churning out stuff as if nothing had changed, during a period when cinema – even the froth of the least ambitious of musical films – might be expected to serve more purpose than in peacetime.

The BBC approved of *The Proud Valley*. A month after its release, it broadcast a shortened version of the soundtrack on radio. This signal honour said something about the film's potency, the screenplay by Tennyson, Jack Jones and Louis

Golding, based on a story by Herbert Marshall and Alfredda Brilliant. Charles Barr identifies the film as 'the first in the Ealing cycle of war-effort films which dramatize the contribution that a section of the nation, military or civilian, can make to the whole'.[11]

It is most likely the film would be forgotten today were it not for its star Paul Robeson, playing black American drifter David Goliath. We are offered parable as much as film. It is tempting to see *The Proud Valley* as fictional counterpart to the Strand Film Company's documentary *Eastern Valley* (1937), director Donald Alexander's utopian vision of how unemployed colliery workers of the South Wales valleys might regain their respect and nobility by working the land in co-operative harmony, a concept initiated by Quakers. Alberto Cavalcanti's montage of miners' lives in the 1935 *Coal Face*, with its score by Benjamin Britten, provides another powerful record of the Welsh miners in what the commentary describes as 'the basic industry of Britain'. In retrospect, both *Coal Face* and *Eastern Valley*, underpinned by Welsh choral singing, stand as laments for toilers of an abandoned industry.

One of the problems of Tennyson's film is its very fiction. The lives we can see taken from life in the documentaries put any dramatic imitation in shadow. Welsh mining was at the heart of John Ford's 1942 *How Green Was My Valley*, its landscape almost absurdly romanticised by Hollywood. Dilys Powell complained that despite its many beauties, 'something of the salt and wildness of the people has gone'. In filming Richard Llewellyn's novel, America had permitted excess: 'The rooms in which they live are too spacious and smooth; the line of slatey grey houses by the pithead is too cosy…'.[2] No fear of such exaggeration in Tennyson's film, where economy prevailed.

Phil Morris considers *The Proud Valley* as 'not a classic film. It is not even a very good one. It is, however, a powerful document evidencing the deep spiritual bond forged between one of the most extraordinary cultural figures of the 20th century and the Welsh working-class'.[3] For the *MFB* here was 'a moving and enthrallingly interesting story of courage, endurance and self-sacrifice […] the hazards of the miner's life, wonderfully reproduced, are breath-taking, while the tragedy of unemployment is poignantly revealed'.[4]

Black 'outsider' Goliath is heard singing 'Lord God Of Abraham' in the street by choirmaster Dick Parry (Edward Chapman). Recognising the quality of the voice, Parry brings Goliath into choir practice. There is some racial prejudice, some doubt, but those who get to know Goliath are won over; as Parry tells his choir, 'Aren't we all black down that pit?' Morris suggests that the 'firmly-drawn equivalence between white and black working class men does seem quite radical even for the era of the Popular Front'.[5]

The simplicity running through the film contributes to its effectiveness, but inevitably it is Robeson's powerful but unassuming presence that dominates this portrait of the Welsh miners and their families. It presents its audience with a sub-culture, outside the London or Ruritanian settings on which so much of the film industry fixed. In Robeson, man and actor combine in promulgating social progress when its directors decide to close the mine and decimate the lives of its employees. Robeson's purpose is to pursue a humanitarian philosophy; his association with the project, in its quiet insistence on human rights and equality, is crucial. An early draft of the script had the abandoned workers themselves re-opening and running the shut-down pits; in the film, the miners led by Goliath march on London to demand they be saved. The war sits at the back of the film, another burden of oppression (we hear the cry of 'To hell with Hitler!') borne by the men as Goliath marches the disadvantaged disenfranchised to London. Robeson, whom we can define as being officially 'outside' British culture, is the central spirit, the defining cog of the film, providing a totally authentic spiritual strength that borders religiosity.

The film is replete with Welsh sound breaking through as in Mai Jones and Lyn Joshua's 'You Can't Stop Us Singing', Ernest Irving's arrangements of 'Slag Heap' and 'Ar Hyd y Nos', Mendelssohn's 'Thanks Be To God' and 'Saint Anne's', and Harry Burleigh's arrangement of 'Deep River', sung at the funeral of Parry. At the close, Robeson cements his affinity with the men he has worked with when he hymns 'Land Of My Fathers'. Men can become one in the search for what is fair and just.

It isn't as if Robeson turned up for filming, took the pay and departed for greater projects; he was a different sort of film star. In the 1930s he made several visits to Welsh coal mines. In 1949 he returned to Wales, visiting Woolmet Colliery and lunching with the workers in their canteen. The occasion was filmed for Pathé News. He sang 'I Dreamed I Saw Joe Hill Last Night' to them. It is doubtful that they ever forgot it.

The title of John Baxter's ***Laugh It Off*** suggests that in a period of national emergency it should have been available on prescription. Produced by John Corfield and directed by Baxter and Wallace Orton for British National at the Nettlefold Studios, Walton-on-Thames, Bridget Boland and Austin Melford's screenplay may not have anticipated the 'Baxterisms' to which it might be exposed. After making the 1939 Syd Walker comedy *What Would You Do, Chums?*, British National and Baxter had several projects lined up including a sequel to the Walker picture. That project didn't materialise, but in a difficult climate British National grasped the moment, becoming one of the most consistently productive production companies of the war. Their policy seems clear: 'The public require "escape" and amusement – we will provide them.'[6]

Laugh It Off qualifies by its light-heartedness and determination to cheer, but in Baxter's hands the film becomes another opportunity to broadcast his philosophy of social integration, evident throughout his work since the seminal *Doss House*. Of Baxter's contribution to that work the documentary film writer Ralph Bond wrote that 'it almost marks a revolution in British film production [...] What is important is that a British film company has dared to dramatize the lives of people for whom the last word in luxury is a bed to sleep in at night.'[7] All this is only a segment of Baxter's bigger portrait of the British working class, sustained by its abiding association with and regard for the theatre in general and music-hall in particular. The uncharitable might suggest the appearance in a Baxter movie of variety turns (by no means all of them first-class, and some barely competent) is a necessary plugging of gaps to make up a decent running time, but this is not what Baxter is about.

The wartime privations at the heart of *Laugh It Off* – theatrical lodgings and military quarters – are trifling beside those of *Doss House*. The shadow of war nevertheless hangs over the 'Blackpool Super Follies' concert party as it winds up its summer season. A chill wind blows across the town when Chamberlain is heard declaring war on the wireless; the pierrots are all at sea. The Follies' chirpy comic Tommy Towers (Tommy Trinder) signs up for the army, organising a camp concert. It's the excuse Baxter needs to bring in his turns, among whom – and surely it's to Baxter's credit – there is not one star name. Trinder, on the brink of bigger success in British films, is anyway enough, but what a selection British National has collected for our amusement: Geraldo and His Orchestra; the Georgian Singers, Darvelle and Shires and the Three Maxwells together in 'Anybody Can Dance', and the Julias Ladies Choir. The songs by Kennedy Russell, Ronnie Munro and Marr Mackie include 'There'll Always Be Time For A Song' sung by Jean Colin, 'S'Afternoon', 'Growing Old Together' (with its lyric by Reginald Reisie, also responsible for the title song), and the ladies' choir praying 'God Send You Back To Me'.

For the finale, Sidney Burchell's rousing 'What Do They Say Of England?' unleashes Baxter's proper patriotism in a manner Geoff Brown has called 'bizarre', as stock footage of war preparation fuses with a mass invasion of the stage. It is ultimately the natural connectivity of its star that makes the film's point. Brown has it right: Trinder 'leaps through the film, cheeky, friendly, and chirpy, giving his audience his catchphrase "You lucky people!", a conniving wink, and a direct invitation to sing along with the characters on screen. It's the film's most touching moment ...'[8] A somewhat less impressed *MFB* found it 'a simple happy-go-lucky kind of story which will please the unsophisticated and those who like Tommy Trinder,'[9] while for *Kinematograph Weekly* it was 'just the show to give the troops'.[10]

There is much to enjoy here, including a rare opportunity to see the veteran music-hall artiste Ida Barr as army canteen manageress Mrs McNab. In her heyday it was said of Miss Barr, 'Ida Barr? She could 'ide a bleedin' pub'. For some reason, the 'Hall of Memory' sequence of music-hall lollipops does not include the ragtime numbers for which Barr was well known – Irving Berlin's 'Everybody's Doin' It Now' and Nat D. Ayer's 'Oh, You Beautiful Doll'. An excellent supporting cast involves Wally Patch, Peter Gawthorne and Baxter regular Edgar Driver.

As was the case with other musical films produced during the year, **Band Waggon** seems perfectly pitched for its time. The pairing of Arthur ('Big Hearted') Askey and Richard ('Stinker') Murdoch in the BBC's 1938 radio series – 'Radio's Greatest Success' according to the film's credits – carried through to Jack Hylton's stage tour in 1940, and so on to Gaumont-British's film, produced at Shepherd's Bush by Edward Black for Gainsborough, and directed by Marcel Varnel. A host of writers – John Watt, Harry Pepper, Gordon Crier, Vernon Harris, J. O. C. Orton, Val Guest, Marriott Edgar and Bob Edwards – concocted this gallimaufry built around Askey and Murdoch's setting up home on top of Broadcasting House.

With his welcoming cry of 'Hello, playmates!' Askey is a pint-sized Everyman, shuffling off every wartime inconvenience and, unlike Formby, never particularly bothered by romance. Askey's very smallness seems suitably puny beside the threat of Hitler, who almost finds his domestic equivalent at the BBC in pompous supremo Claude Pilkington (Peter Gawthorne). Askey and Murdoch discover a supposedly haunted castle haunted by a supposedly haunting ghost (Moore Marriott). The castle is being used by foreign agents – Nazis, of course – transmitting secret information via a secret radio station.

Their scheme is routed with swift, inventive comedy and excellent musical numbers. Jack Hylton and His Band and a more relaxed than usual Pat Kirkwood and Bruce Trent perform Noel Gay and Frank Eyton's 'The Melody Maker' on a pirate ship. Gay and Elton also contribute 'The Only One Who's Difficult Is You' and (Gay alone) 'After Dark'. Kirkwood's 'Heaven Will Be Heavenly' by Harry Parr Davies and Roma Campbell-Hunter is beautifully staged. Askey is most prominent in Kenneth Blane's 'A Pretty Bird', Robert Rutherford and Frank Wilcock's 'Big Hearted Arthur', and the amusing cod oratorio à la Waller and Tunbridge, 'Old King Cole'.

The curious relationship between radio and television that had haunted British musical films from *Elstree Calling* onwards takes over the final segments of *Band Waggon*. Despite the obvious problems of wartime, television was slowly growing in popularity, and in 1938 had transmitted its first ever Sunday night drama (adventurously, Pirandello's *Henry IV*). By the start of 1939 there were around 11,000 television sets in use, but on 1 September 1939 the government closed television transmissions from the BBC. Business was resumed in June 1946.

So it is that the television sequence that makes up the finale of *Band Waggon* accentuates the relevance of the new medium, not then available to the British public. The variety show that Askey and Murdoch organise has Hylton and his boys in the band arriving by horse-drawn cart. Askey works his way through some pretty tired fooling, as the band boys look on, understandably bemused. At last, we see Askey for what he superbly is, the epitome of that long-dead uncle of light entertainment, the concert party. The *MFB* approved 'a thoroughly enjoyable crazy entertainment' in which the two leads 'will not disappoint their many radio admirers […] Askey works tirelessly and puts over an exuberantly and riotously funny performance'.[11]

One of the several radio series destined for British studios, and yet another Noel Gay winner in *Band Waggon* (1940)

An interminable song and dance to 'Bumps-a-Daisy' serves as a background to the film's summing up. Watching the broadcast, a BBC official says, 'At last, somebody's thought of an original end.' It isn't quite that, although finishing a picture by exploding a goat was probably a first.

MARCH

The atmosphere of war was equally essential to Ealing's ***Let George Do It!*** with its scenes of blacked-out confusion – ideal conditions for a plot that thrives on misunderstanding. The latest Formby had an agile screenplay by John Dighton, Austin Melford, Angus Macphail and Basil Dearden, tailored to its wartime setting and directed by Marcel Varnel. Andy Goulding has recognised that 'The arrival of war sparked the most fertile run of brilliance in Formby's career', citing *Let George Do It!* for 'the superior quality of the music'[12] which may not be apparent to all viewers.

This George is effectively the same George, late of Mancunian's *Boots! Boots!* and everything that came afterwards. He is now known as George Hepplewhite, ukulele-playing member of the Dinky-Doos concert party, mistaken (that black-out again) for special British agent Bill Norman. An innocent in an untrustworthy world, Hepplewhite is soon entangled with an organisation of foreign agents (Nazis by any other name) transmitting military information via musical codes played by a nightclub band run by Mendez (Garry Marsh). This is not altogether fanciful; the British government was concerned that national secrets might be communicated to an enemy in such a way, or that lyrics in a foreign language might be used nefariously. Fortunately, our George has the assistance of ultra-cool British agent-cum-hotel-receptionist Mary Wilson (Phyllis Calvert), looking as if she wouldn't be out of place at Bletchley Park.

The expected quota of bright songs by Formby, Fred E. Cliffe, Harry Gifford and Eddie Latta – 'Grandad's Flannelette Nightshirt', 'Oh, Don't The Wind Blow Cold', 'Mr Wu's A Window Cleaner Now' and the cheering-up 'Count Your Blessings And Smile' – spill out with the usual assortment of references to ladies' knickers, silk stockings and looking through bathroom windows. The most inspired moments include a slapstick sequence in a bakery and a memorably daft dream sequence involving swastika-decorated underpants. George also knocks Hitler's block off. One can imagine the audience thoroughly approving of such an unprovoked assault.

Butcher's industrial efforts to gladden the war-troubled population continued with ***Pack Up Your Troubles***, featuring the World World I favourite 'Pack Up Your Troubles In Your Old Kit-Bag' written by George Asaf in 1915. One of the few chorus songs of its period to be well-remembered, it was memorably sung by Florrie Forde in *Say It with Flowers* (1934). *Kinematograph Weekly* praised *Pack Up Your Troubles* as a 'richly humorous picture of the Army today', although S. P. Mackenzie suggests that the picture 'clearly fitted the tendency to situate the new war in the context of the old'.[13]

Produced by F. W. Baker, the film was directed at the Nettlefold Studios in Walton-on-Thames by veteran journeyman Oswald Mitchell, with a screenplay by

Milton Hayward and Reginald Purdell, based on an original (but not very) story by Con West. Purdell doubled as one of the film's leads, garage-owner Tommy Perkins who teams up with his pal Eric Sampson (Wylie Watson), an ex-ventriloquist, to travel to France. Once there, they are captured by the Germans but escape with the help of Eric's ventriloquism skills, bringing valuable information home with them. Patricia Roc played Tommy's ATS girlfriend Sally, rewarded by marriage at the film's conclusion. It is a happy opportunity to air some old songs, and the *MFB* seemed satisfied. 'The title expresses the whole spirit of this film, which is cheerful, light-hearted nonsense. The somewhat ordinary story is redeemed by excellent acting and [Purdell and Watson] are extremely funny.'[14]

APRIL

Old Mother Riley in Society belongs as much to its director John Baxter as to its clown, Arthur Lucan. It could not be the work of any other. Even if we take Lucan out, as it were, of the picture, it remains essentially Baxter. Surprisingly (we may ponder on its Freudian significance) the storyline is by Lucan's wife and (on stage and screen) daughter Kitty McShane. The screenplay is by Austin Melford, Barbara K. Emary and Mary Cathcart Borer, their efforts possibly heartened by the (mistaken) rumour that the picture would get a major London showing. It was made for British National, and filming commenced at Nettlefold on 12 February 1940.

Although one of the least known of the Old Mother Riley series, *'in Society'* is one of the most interesting. Consider the plot alongside Lucan and McShane's real-life relationship. Kitty Riley is in the chorus of a provincial *Aladdin*, and gets pushed on stage to sing Kennedy Russell's 'I Think Of You No Matter Where You Are'; remember this sentiment, the merest suggestion of the torrent of sentimentality to come. Mother takes a fish and chip supper back to the humblest of abodes, but Kitty is already seduced by theatrical glamour, wined in smart restaurants by her beau, Tony. She is promoted to the role of Aladdin, passing her mother off as her dresser. When Kitty marries, mother is merely one of their servants. Turned away at the front door by a snooty manservant, she explains, 'I never use the back door, even when I'm going to the pawn-shop.' Kitty's love for her mother is never doubted, but in high society she can't bring herself to admit their relationship.

At a reception where Kitty's social acceptability is tested (essential if Tony is to rise in his ministerial career), one of the staff learn that Kitty had once been a chorus girl. During the floor show arranged by Kitty, one of the girls sings Kennedy Russell's 'It Isn't The Clothes That Make The Girl' (the lyric at least points at the film's message), a statement emphasised when the dancers shed most of theirs. Tony gets a job at the ministry but thinks Kitty's dresser does not fit in with their social status. Mother vanishes into the night, getting a job at the Sunlight Laundry and listening to radio music as she works. At last, Kitty tells Tony that she is Mother Riley's daughter. He is determined to reunite them, but the old woman has been fired from the laundry for giving rich people's clothes to the poor. She gets a job in a mean household that shelters seven little children. As they sit ready for bed in the glow of a roaring fire, Mother Riley relates the parable of the old hen that lost her chick. Reduced to sleeping in a rooming-house ('Women: Beds 6d.'), she banters with the other female down-and-outs. After long searching, Kitty and Tony rescue her. She recuperates at Kitty's luxurious home, while Tony's sympathetic parents convince the old mother that she has no need to be ashamed of her humble background; they themselves made their name 'in sausages'.

There can be no doubt that *Old Mother Riley in Society* is cut to Baxter's cloth. As Mother Riley slides inexorably into the dregs of existence there are obvious echoes of almost everything Baxter has obsessed about in *Doss House* and *Hearts of Humanity*, and his unflagging celebration of the goodness of society, as in *Say It with Flowers*. However, the prospect of directing Lucan and McShane was not something that Baxter necessarily welcomed. He confessed that the idea was perhaps 'pretty terrible' but realised that the old washerwoman had her uses as 'a great character for propaganda purposes'. *Old Mother Riley in Society* is evidence enough, although the propaganda is social rather than political; we might name it Baxterism.

He was, anyway, following on the cinematic path already set by Lucan and McShane. Arthur and Kitty had made their screen debut in *Stars on Parade* (1936), performing their well-established stage act 'Bridget's Night Out'. They returned the following year in *Kathleen Mavourneen*. It was not until Mrs O'Flynn was rechristened for *Old Mother Riley* (1937) that the series began under the stewardship of Oswald Mitchell who followed up with *Old Mother Riley in Paris* (1938) and *Old Mother Riley M. P.* (1939). Musical responsibility for those films had been passed from Horace Sheldon (*Stars on Parade*, *Old Mother Riley*) to Guy Jones (*Kathleen Mavourneen*), to Percival Mackey (*Old Mother Riley in Paris*, *Old Mother Riley M. P.*). Director Maclean Rogers had music by Ronnie Munro for the 1939 *Old Mother Riley Joins Up*.

Alongside Baxter's appointment as director for *Old Mother Riley in Society*, Kennedy Russell was credited for its music. His contribution is not particularly significant but is an example of the many minor composers whose work threaded the cinema of the period, often going uncredited and certainly un-applauded. Baxter and Kennedy remained in place for *Old Mother Riley in Business* (1940), in which 'The variety trimmings, represented by a clever juvenile act and a neat and versatile concert party, are a box-office tit-bit',[15] and for *Old Mother Riley's Ghosts* (1941), after which Baxter resigned from the series. Russell stayed on for *Old Mother Riley's Circus*, directed by Thomas Bentley in 1941, and *Old Mother Riley Detective*, directed by Lance Comfort in 1943.

Russell's main concern with '*in Business*' and '*Ghosts*' is its underscoring, when the music competently accompanies or emphasises what is happening on screen. Experienced Old Mother Riley specialists were put to work for *Old Mother Riley's*

Circus, its story by Con West and Geoffrey Orme, with Barbara K. Emary providing additional dialogue. Desmond O'Connor was Russell's lyricist for 'A Tear, A Smile, A Sigh', sung by Kitty at a birthday party for her old mother who blows a man's toupee off as she blows out the candles on a birthday cake. O'Connor's lyric bears an uncanny resemblance to the epitaph that Kitty was to have engraved on Lucan's tombstone a decade later.[16] Also heard was Leo Friedman and Beth Slater Whitson's 'Meet Me Tonight In Dreamland'.

Made at Rock Studios, the film once again uses the mother-daughter estrangement theme so effectively used by Baxter in *Old Mother Riley in Society*, but barely disguises its shoddiness. Diversion is provided by glimpses of circus acts of the time: the (actually, famous) Hindustans, The Balatons, The Carsons, Reading and Grant, Isabel and Emma, Eve and John Banyard, Marlock and Marlow, Speedy, Harry Koady, and Jean Black. Such turns were meat and vegetables to director Oswald Mitchell, whose career was dominated by his passion for variety performers, preferably (or so it seems from his films) those on the lower rungs. Russell's song for Kitty in *Old Mother Riley's Circus* turns out to shine a light on McShane's character, as explained in a letter written by Ken Behrens in September 1988. Behrens had worked on Will Hay films, and on two of the Riley series 'which I can only describe as pandemonium. There was hardly a peaceful moment during the six weeks' filming.' In 1956, Behrens was working as an editor at the film department of ATV, where some of the Riley films were being shown on Sunday afternoons. Cuts had to be made to make way for the commercials.

> On one occasion I had to cut five minutes from *Old Mother Riley at the Circus* [sic]. In this film Kitty sang one of her ghastly songs which ran for four minutes. This was the ideal scene to cut and it ended up on my cutting-room floor. After it had gone on the air, my phone rang at home and it was Kitty calling me all the names she could lay her tongue to, telling me that I had cut her best scene. I felt like telling her that she never had a best scene.

In fact, there were few opportunities for the vicarious enjoyment created by Kitty's singing in what remained of the series. Russell was still on hand for *Old Mother Riley Detective* (1943), but the last of the wartime entries – *Old Mother Riley Overseas* and *Old Mother Riley at Home* – saw the return of veteran Riley director Oswald Mitchell, with Percival Mackey in charge of music. Then, the series went dormant until 1949 when Renown promised a wider audience with better production values. Despite such treatment, Lucan's manic disorganisation seemed to overcome all, and the absurd concept of the Old Mother taking over a sophisticated London hotel at least offered up the possibility of Kitty and Willer Neal as a cabaret act, with a now visibly ageing Kitty in the most girlishly Irish of costumes performing 'Galway Bay' and being serenaded by a throaty Neal promising 'I'll Take You Home Again, Kathleen'. It has to be seen to be relished. Kitty also joins the Old Mother in a snatch of 'Oh Patrick, Mind The Baby'.

Their new director, John Harlow, was also in charge of *Old Mother Riley Headmistress*, which may or may not have been some sort of pastiche of Ronald Searle's St Trinian's cartoons or one of the hit films of that year, *The Happiest Days of Your Life*, or both. Now, Kitty conducts the choir (the Luton Girls) at St Mildred's School for Young Ladies in 'Count Your Blessings', and joins them, white-frocked and puff-sleeved, in Johann Martini's 'Till All Our Dreams Come True' to an English lyric by Desmond O'Connor. It has been suggested that by the time of the 1951 *Old Mother Riley's Jungle Treasure*, directed by Maclean Rogers, Lucan and McShane refused to work together, making separate visits to the studio to film their scenes. The publicity machine for *Old Mother Riley's Jungle Treasure* poured out ideas for promotion. After all, 'The title of the film obviously lends itself to stunts based on the word *Treasure*.' One imagines hordes of eager youngsters clogging up the countryside in their response to one idea from a publicity leaflet from the film:

> Contact the secretary of your local Cycling Club and get him to organise a 'Treasure Hunt'[...] Choose a suitable location in the country, not too far from your town, and arrange for a number of tickets to be hidden in the locality. The cyclists participating in the hunt should be told to look for certain clues *en route*. These clues would guide them to the locality where the 'Treasure' is hidden. The hidden tickets or 'Treasure' will, of course, admit the finders free of charge to a showing of *Old Mother Riley's Jungle Treasure* at your theatre.

The ninepennies had one more opportunity to enjoy Lucan, now without McShane, in *Mother Riley Meets the Vampire*; possibly in recognition of the advancing years, the 'Old' was dropped. The couple's marriage and working partnership had collapsed after years of turbulence. In the theatre, Lucan toured as Old Mother Riley with a new daughter, while Kitty toured with a new Old Mother Riley. It was said that they criss-crossed the country with their disparate companies. In his screen swansong, Lucan is paired by the washed-up Hollywood Dracula Bela Lugosi, in a ramshackle tale of blood-drinking comedy horror involving robots. John Gilling's direction is of the desperate variety. Of all the series, this remains the most curious. It also yields the most amusing musical moment, when in her falling-down corner shop Mother Riley breaks into Leslie Sarony's 'I Lift Up My Finger And I Say Tweet Tweet'. There being no Kitty to accompany her, she is backed by Hattie Jacques and Dandy Nichols as two nosy customers who have popped in for a bag of sugar but momentarily bloom into chorus girls. Close observation of Jacques and Nichols is required. There was clearly no question of another take. Blessedly not, or we would not have this lovely chaos going on behind one of Britain's greatest clowns. Once more, we can give thanks for the many schools of joy given to us by British musical films (or even, as here, films with a bit of music in them). In the final frame, we can only sympathise with Lucan's last cry as the film exhausts both our patience and his career with the words, 'This is the end!'

JULY

Yet another 'putting-on-a-show' film, but one of the first to paint enforced military life as a fun-packed adventure, Butcher's **Garrison Follies** has the RAF camp at Rastminster Aerodrome as its playground, with Barry Lupino as Alf Shufflebottom, in civvy street a plumber but in uniform a cornet-player. Confusion erupts with the arrival of ex-Indian Army Major Hall-Vett, played by veteran actor-screenwriter H. F. Maltby, also responsible for the screenplay with director Maclean Rogers and assistant director Kathleen Butler. The *MFB* thought Maltby's 'dug-out major has to be seen to be believed' in a 'cheerful, tuneful, light-hearted spectacle guaranteed to cure the worst case of blues. Everything is delightfully exaggerated, from the apoplectic major to the trumpet player who apparently plumbs in his spare time.'[17]

Maclean Rogers, long confined to second and third division projects, had been persistently busy through the 1930s but only now began dabbling in musical film. Vocalist Anne Lenner, and the Six Rose Petals, are among the supporting turns, but the film belongs to Maltby. His credits remind us of the substantial contribution he made to the genre. As a screenplay writer, alongside his slyly witty dialogue for several Tod Slaughter melodramas, he wrote for *Britannia of Billingsgate, Over the Garden Wall, For the Love of Mike, Queen of Hearts, Rose of Tralee, Weddings Are Wonderful, Gert and Daisy's Weekend* and others. As an actor he can be seen, splendidly emphatic, in *Those Were the Days, Falling in Love, Queen of Hearts, Calling the Tune, Jack of All Trades, Wake Up Famous, O-Kay for Sound, Take My Tip, Sing As You Swing, Facing the Music* and, inevitably, the Old Mother Riley series.

In his *Funny Way to be a Hero*, John Fisher writes of Frank Randle: 'Had he been born twenty, even ten years previously, [he] may well have achieved the Hollywood eminence of Laurel or Chaplin.'[18] Gracie Fields called Randle 'the greatest character comedian that ever lived.'[19]

John Montgomery reminds us that Randle sometimes proved bigger box-office than pinned-up Errol Flynn or siren Marlene Dietrich, both of whom at least kept their teeth in. As soon as he reached manhood, Randle had his extracted, the better to ripen his characterisation of old men. This knowledge could not be made more public than in his films, where he is seen, toothless, to put them back in place. So disorganised is Randle's screen persona that we wonder if they are not his own but a set of dentures knocking about the studio doing nothing in particular. It may be, as Jeffrey Richards suggests, that Randle's depiction of 'the scrofulous old satyr, frothing with ale and senile lust […] made too narrow and specific an appeal to achieve that universal symbolic status that George [Formby] attained.'[20]

But we should not underestimate Randle's place in British comedy films. He is possibly its most original creative genius, an elemental personification of consistent restlessness – something, obviously, that Formby and the lesser comics who worked through this period were not. Fisher gives a sublime definition of the man, describing 'a body comprising an assortment of independent, self-functioning units [...] his loose-limbed body had the floppy dignity of a seal'. He had a 'slaphappy disregard for the brushes he underwent with both authoritarians and flirts'.[21]

Would Randle's flame have burned the brighter had he been contracted to one of the major studios? No point in wondering, as no major studio would have taken him on. Instead, he seems to have been perfectly happy working for peanuts and John E. Blakeley's Mancunian Films. We must be grateful to Blakeley for capturing this insanely polite but totally anarchic creature for posterity. Had he worked only on the music-halls and in variety, his reputation would by now surely have dwindled into that oblivion that awaits eccentric notoriety. We only have to wait for his appearance on screen for chaos to erupt. No actor could more swiftly and recklessly induce pandemonium than this wizened, destructive Puck, bent on the annihilation of every social nicety, in denial of sophistication, casting off social pretence, delivering an object lesson in political incorrectness and proving himself the rarest of the rare. Watching this man at work is pure joy.

Mancunian's ***Somewhere in England*** was shot at Nettlefold Studios, Walton-on-Thames, to a screenplay (this, at least, was the bare bones, although who knows what happened when Randle walked on set) by Blakeley (credited as Anthony Toner) and Arthur Mertz, credited as Roney Parsons. The plot of any Randle picture is of little importance, but this one is built around the troubles of Lance-Corporal Kenyon (Harry Kemble), wrongly accused of misconduct at a northern army camp. His reputation is restored by his fellow recruits. *Somewhere in England* proved such a success that it became the first of several 'Somewhere' titles to star Randle, teamed here for the first time with the much more sedentary Harry Korris, long an established favourite in Blackpool and noted for the radio series *Happidrome*. The comedy team is completed by two other clowns, little squeaking Robbie Vincent ('Let me tell you!') and the nobby gentleman of Dan Young. Both are expert foils to Randle, who manages to work in his famous stage impersonation of the grisliest of ancient happy hikers. Musically, *Somewhere in England* was directed by the ever-busy Percival Mackey, with composer Albert W. Stanbury and lyricist Mertz collaborating on the title song, 'Beat Of The Drum' and 'What Is Love?'. Formby, Fred E. Cliffe and Harry Gifford contributed 'Our Sergeant Major'.

AUGUST

John Baxter's considerable contribution to the British musical and non-musical film during World War II mark him as a major figure in the decade's cultural landscape. *Crook's Tour*, produced by John Corfield for the thriving British National at Rock Studios, may not be his greatest achievement, but it is consistently amusing. This was a third film outing for Charters (Basil Radford) and Caldicott (Naunton Wayne) as two imperturbable cricket-obsessed friends, first seen in 1938 in Hitchcock's *The Lady Vanishes* and subsequently Carol Reed's *Night Train to Munich* in 1940. Frank Launder and Sidney Gilliat created the characters for a BBC radio series, now adapted for the screen by Barbara K. Emary.

Crook's Tour takes the insouciant couple to the Middle East and on to Istanbul and Budapest. Lured by the siren-song gesticulations of nightclub singer La Palermo (Greta Gynt), they unwittingly acquire state secrets useful to foreign governments. La Palermo turns out to be as British as afternoon tea, although she seems anything but when performing Kennedy Russell's songs, 'Every Time You Look At Me', 'One Night Of Heaven With You' and, working herself into a continental frenzy with two male gypsies, 'Gone, Gypsy Lover, Gone From Me'. As so often before, the songs are presented as part of a featured cabaret, playing no part in the story's development.

Kinematograph Weekly considered that 'the atmosphere, although colourful, lacks authenticity, and the absence of contrast makes it difficult to distinguish between the gags and the thrills'.[22] For *MFB*, Radford and Wayne were 'in their best and most benignly idiotic mood throughout this light-hearted nonsense, yet manage to convey subtly that there may be something in this old school tie business after all'.[23] Charters and Caldicott survived until 1943 when Launder and Gilliat brought them back for *Millions Like Us*. Carol Reed considered reviving them in 1949 for his *The Third Man*, but decided against it. They appeared in similar guise in Ealing's 1949 *Passport to Pimlico*.

SEPTEMBER

Jack Hulbert and Cicely Courtneidge may have had their best moment in the 1937 *Take My Tip*, but by the beginning of war they were turning to theatre work. **Under Your Hat**, directed for Grand National by Maurice Elvey at Worton Hall Studios, Isleworth, suggested that their very particular brand of comedy might be succeeded by other talents. As a successful stage show, *Under Your Hat* had closed in April 1940. As a film, it seemed to be at a remove from the world that most cinemagoers were living in. Perhaps it was enough that, as its posters proclaimed, the film brought the 'King and Queen of Comedy Together for the Best Time Ever!'. Royalty, however, may be dethroned.

Despite its competent screenplay by playwright Rodney Ackland, Anthony Kimmins, L. Green and revue writer Arthur Macrae, this adventure centred on husband and wife Jack and Kay Millett, but the atmosphere belonged as much to the previous decade as to 1940. The atmosphere was theatrical, the well-hewn stylistic playing a little out of place in a circumstance of war. Courtneidge's comedy had always been centred in technique (it's still there in 1962 when as an elderly music hall artiste she did her well-known soldier impersonation in *The L-Shaped Room*), especially evident in *Under Your Hat* when she performs Vivian Ellis's 'The Empire Depends On You'. There probably isn't a British actress alive today who could do what Courtneidge does here; the technical achievement of the routine is wondrous. But this is middle-class – surely upper middle-class West End – territory, and *Under Your Hat*, despite its many jollities and moments to savour, smacks of the drawing-room when it might somehow have reminded us of the Anderson shelter.

Whatever the circumstances, Hulbert and Courtneidge could not fail to amuse, popping up in the most unconvincing of disguises. 'I Won't Do The Conga' gives her the chance to do some of her most exaggerated moves. It would be fifteen years before she and Hulbert went back into studios, in the cheaply turned-out 1955 *Miss Tulip Stays the Night* when they were billed below Diana Dors. Times were changing. *Under Your Hat* was one of the last twists of the Hulbert-Courtneidge cocktail shaker.

OCTOBER

Noel Gay and Frank Eyton's splendid 'All Over The Place' and the mere presence of its star Tommy Trinder entitle the inclusion of Ealing's **Sailors Three**, otherwise a patently non-musical film. *MFB* reported, 'A couple of catchy songs [the other being little more than a snatch of Harry Parr Davies's 'Sing A Happy-Go-Lucky Song'] add yet more to the joyous mixture, which is guaranteed to chase the worst dose of blues away.'[24] It is perhaps with *Sailors Three* that Trinder consolidates his pre-eminence among the principal film comedians of the war. Neither Formby nor Askey brought what Trinder could bring to the screen. They never escaped being performers; Trinder *was*. Up there, staring out at the cinemagoing public, he could be the person you wanted to see in the mirror. He might be said to be the male equivalent of Gracie Fields, except that Trinder didn't really sing – even his singing seemed real, his singing, like the man, *was*. His remarkable qualities, his name, have all but faded from the pages of cinema history, despite the pictures he made during the war effort: as actor in *The Foreman Went to France* (1941), the 1942 *The Bells Go Down*, and, in 1944, *Champagne Charlie* (one of the few masterpieces in these pages) and *Fiddlers Three*.

Before the three fiddlers, *Sailors Three* had a clever screenplay by Angus

Macphail, Austin Melford and John Dighton, chronicling the seafaring careers of Tommy Taylor (Trinder), Admiral (Claude Hulbert) and Johnny (a cockney Michael Wilding, before Anna Neagle introduced him to Herbert Wilcox's Mayfair). Trouble begins when they mistakenly board a German boat. Walter Forde's direction never falters in a piece that, far from helping audiences forget the war, brings it centre stage in a sort of theatre of absurdity, dotting it with witty touches (the Hitler tattoo is one) until it reaches its cleverly constructed conclusion. In the final frame, Trinder gets the girl and winks at the audience as the studio orchestra strikes up a refrain of 'All Over The Place'. He had previously asked, 'Do you want any bananas?' His profound skills as a performer gave audiences the reassurance that all would be well. If we had been there, we would surely have been whistling Gay's care-less tune on the homeward bus.

DECEMBER

Spare a Copper was Ealing's latest Formby, produced by Michael Balcon and Basil Dearden, and directed by John Paddy Carstairs. Dearden and Austin Melford wrote the screenplay with Roger Macdougall; Macdougall also wrote music and lyrics for Formby's songs 'On The Beat', 'Ukulele Man' and 'I Wish I Was Back On The Farm'. Formby, Fred E. Cliffe and Harry Gifford wrote the tailor-made 'I'm Shy', for which the star was accompanied by Arthur Young on the Novachord. *Spare a Copper* serves its war-effort purpose by casting Formby as reserve policeman George Carter, whose driving (or flying) ambition is to join the Flying Squad. It is Merseyside in 1939, and saboteurs (popular as villains in musical films at this time) are intent on destroying a new ship, the *HMS Hercules*. We realise how devious these people are when we learn that that most inoffensive of clean elderly gentlemen, Eliot Makeham, is one of the dastardly gang, hand-in-hand with saboteurs (read Nazis). As usual, George has the support of a girlfriend, played here by Dorothy Hyson, her pearly diction suggesting she might not be George's usual type. The *MFB* marked this as 'a good George Formby Film, and has a better story than most'.[25] Carstairs skilfully sustains the action, helped by Louis Levy's incidental music, through to its impressive Wheel of Death sequence and slapstick finale.

Butcher's *Cavalcade of Variety* properly has no place in this book. Supposedly produced by F. W. Baker and supposedly directed by Thomas Bentley, it is made up of a series of variety turns snatched from earlier pictures of Oswald Mitchell's, *Stars on Parade* (1936), *Variety Parade* (1936) and *Music Hall Parade* (1939). The only intervention is from ventriloquist Peter Brough with his dummy Jimmy (Archie Andrews did not arrive until 1944) introducing the acts with some hastily prepared dialogue. Despite this, *Cavalcade of Variety*'s rag-bag makes irresistible viewing, with no irrelevant plot to confuse us.

1940

In order of appearance, we see some extraordinary performers interspersed with some lesser. The Billy Cotton Band opens with 'The Danube Swing', featuring a black dancer, followed by the Sherman Fisher Girls hoofing a sub-Busby Berkeley routine. Eve Becke sings 'Angelino Piccolini'. The madly dangerous motor-cycling troupe the Australian Four Air Aces must have had theatre audiences cowering under their seats before the days of Health and Safety. Bobby Henshaw lowers the temperature with clowning around a ukulele.

'These Foolish Things' is delivered with an artificial whiff of Mayfair by the female Radio Three. Comedy returns with northern favourite Frank E. Franks in a sketch involving much domestic abuse (woman on man) so violent that it might be useful in any sociological study. Baby-voiced Phyllis Robins explains what will happen 'When I Grow Up', making way for the Arnaut brothers in a music-hall act the likes of which will never be seen again, as they whistle-speak an ornithological romance. The cheeky all-girl Corona Kids back angular female impersonator G. S. Melvin in his girl-guide lecture 'You Can't Beat The Old Fleecy-Lined [Knickers]'. Rarer still is a sketch, 'The Solicitor', for Tom Gamble, a long-forgotten comedian who comes over as a watered-down Robb Wilton.

The flamboyantly attired Macari and His Dutch Serenaders make a blessedly brief appearance, yodelling and evoking the atmosphere of *Miss Hook of Holland*. By this time, possibly sated at the treats spread before us, the best acts have closed down for the day, leaving us with impressionist Ernest Shannon, some eccentric dancing, the eerie Noni and his partner having fun with a piano, the most sedate Can-Can you could imagine (from the New Empire Dancing Girls), and the slightly terrifying Mrs Jack Hylton whipping up a storm from 'Her Boys' before leading them into 'Taking A Stroll Around The Park'. The suddenly military tone of 'Let's All Go Up In The Sky' inhabits a finale.

1941

In character, their conversations give the impression of being unscripted, a particular skill of theirs, and at their happiest in the least pretentious of settings, which Butcher's would have been more than happy to provide   *Gert and Daisy's Weekend*

Danny Boy
Turned Out Nice Again
Facing the Music
He Found a Star
I Thank You

Gert and Daisy's Weekend
Bob's Your Uncle
Hi Gang!
South American George

MAY

So attached was director Oswald Mitchell to his 1934 version that he remade *Danny Boy* for Butcher's seven years later, when its original screenplay was replaced by one from Vera Allinson, to which he and A. Barr-Carson contributed. Back then, it had starred musical comedy star Dorothy Dickson and Frank Forbes-Robertson; the remake had Ann Todd as Jane Kaye, returning from the States to Britain in search of ex-husband Nick (John Warwick) and son Danny (Grant Taylor). Mitchell's new company had the advantage of Wilfrid Lawson and David Farrar in supporting roles, as well as Wylie Watson and music-hall veteran survivor Albert Whelan. Produced by Hugh Perceval and made at Ealing, it attracted mixed reviews. For some, it was 'sentimental nonsense' with Todd 'woefully mis-cast' and 'The popular songs might have raised wartime morale, but things must have been at a pretty low ebb for anyone to have emerged from watching this slipshod entertainment with a spring in their step.'[1] In more kindly mood, the *MFB* thought that 'the simple story is developed sincerely and humanly [sic] by the players' and that 'scenes of London in the blitz are well photographed and almost too realistic'.[2] A trawl of highly sweetened old songs yielded mildly mournful items such as Percy French's evocative 'Mountains o' Mourne', 'Love's Old Sweet Song [Just A Song At Twilight]', Frederick Weatherly's brilliant lyric for the 'Londonderry Air' title song sung by Todd, 'Abide With Me', and 'If Tears Could Bring You Back'. This was an emotional territory in which Butcher's felt at home.

JUNE

The last of George Formby's Ealing series, **Turned Out Nice Again**, eschews the war altogether; rather, we have a domestic comedy based on Hugh Mills and Wells Root's stage play *As You Are*, which had played at the Aldwych Theatre in January 1940 for a modest seventy-five performances. On stage, Edward Chapman played Fred Pearson, Formby's role in the film (renamed George Pearson). Perhaps as a goodwill gesture, Balcon gave Chapman the supporting role of Uncle Arnold, but Diana Churchill as Lydia was replaced in the film by Peggy Bacon, one of the more characterful of Formby's female co-stars. Sensibly, formidable Elliott Mason was retained as George's smothering mother ('The day you were born I was four and a half hours under chloroform').

Austin Melford's adaptation of the stage play inevitably opens up the original, with ample opportunities for displays of ladies' lingerie and skimpies (probably beyond the dreams of most female cinemagoers in 1941) in a saga of two competing underwear companies. Formby is as ever the innocent at large, aghast at the least reveal of flesh. Watching chorines in a well-choreographed nightclub routine, he is appalled by 'cheeky fast-cats dancing in their knickers'. His ukulele is brought into play as he sings the praises of his company's stays and woolly pants in 'You Can't Go Wrong In These' – as Roger Macdougall's lyric insists with its finetuned *double entendre*, sung to the accompaniment of a lingerie fashion parade.

Our George and his Lydia are convincingly at odds when George's mother is making a profession of trying to break them up. Lydia wants to be the new sort of female ('Modern women don't want reliable brassieres,' she tells him) while mother is feigning heart attacks. Surprisingly, there is no attempt to turn mother into a sympathetic old dear before fade-out, with much invested in George and Lydia's relationship. As in *Spare a Copper*, Macdougall is responsible for most of the musical content: 'You're Everything To Me' and the excellent 'Emperor Of Lancashire'. Indeed, Macdougall's songs emanate from the plot more naturally than in many other Formbys. On more traditional lines, Eddie Latta and Formby's 'Auntie Maggie's Remedy', with its catalogue of winks and nudges, is just what audiences paying to see the star had ordered. We can only guess how much a part was played by *Turned Out Nice Again* in the British public's relationship with female underwear. George, at least, takes obvious pleasure in 'panties or scanties'.

JULY

For director Maclean Rogers, at work since the 1928 silent *God's Clay*, the war seems to have sparked an involvement with musical films, with *Weddings Are Wonderful* in 1938, *Garrison Follies* in 1940, and in 1941 the first of two pictures with Elsie and Doris Waters, *Gert and Daisy's Weekend*. His **Facing the Music** of the same year was produced for Butcher's by F. W. Baker. Kathleen Butler, her name synonymous for having turned out so many sentimental scripts, wrote the screenplay with Rogers. The little-remembered Bunny Doyle played hapless hero Wilfred Hollebone who gets a job in a munition factory, promises to be a disaster but instead prevents one, saving the nation from the nefarious activities of foreign spies. Mitchell's cast was sturdy, with Betty Driver as Wilfred's girlfriend Mary, the splenetic H. F. Maltby as Mr Bulger, Chili Bouchier, Eliot Makeham, Wally Patch, and 'Gaiety Girl' Ruby Miller, whose autobiography perpetuated the legend that adoring men drank champagne from her slipper. *Facing the Music* won few such plaudits, the *MFB* announcing that Rogers's direction 'lacks that speed and sureness which is necessary in a film of this kind if it is not to be allowed to dwell on its improbabilities'.[3] Driver's 'You Don't Have To Tell Me, I Know' was written by Art Noel and Don Pelosi. Percival Mackey supervised the music.

SEPTEMBER

The main purpose of John Corfield's production of **He Found a Star** may have been to cash in on the current popularity of its own star Vic Oliver, now married (and thus even more in the public eye) to Winston Churchill's daughter Sarah. Bridget Boland's screenplay, adapted with additional dialogue by Austin Melford from Monica Ewer's novel *Ring o' Roses*, had the gossip-column couple as Lucky Lyndon and Ruth Cavour, who build up a theatrical agency, thus opening the door to whatever variety acts Corfield managed to engage. Oliver gives the dominant performance, with Churchill less comfortable. In contrast, Evelyn Dall is brightness itself as Suzanne, singing 'Salome' and 'Rhumba'. A few of the musical items make the film just about worth sitting through. There is Uriel Porter singing 'I Got A Robe', 'Nobody Knows The Trouble I've Seen', and Manning Sherwin and Harold Purcell's 'Waitin''. We hear Robert Atkins sing 'Widdecombe Fair' and 'Invictus' and the revue artist Gabrielle Brune in 'Loch Lomond'. Expert hands are at the tiller, with direction by John Paddy Carstairs, sets by Alfred Junge, choreography by Philip Buchel, and musical direction by Benjamin Frankel. *MFB* seemed unbothered by the 'pleasing story, well told without unnecessary sentimentality, and with a good balance of light comedy'.[4]

Those weary of George Formby, and wary of his desertion from Ealing to Columbia-British, could at least turn to Arthur Askey, riding a wave after his 1940 *Band Waggon* and 1941 *The Ghost Train*. **I Thank You** (an Askey catchphrase) showed Gaumont-British's determination to make him one of Gainsborough's major stars, and was produced by Edward Black and directed by farce-happy Marcel Varnel. Watching the film almost eighty years on, it's difficult to accept the *MFB*'s verdict that Varnel's contribution is 'indifferent' or that 'by and large the film

One of the many songs for British musical films, composed by Manning Sherwin, heard in *He Found a Star* (1941)

gives an impression of a number of people using a medium to which they are not accustomed, and even Arthur Askey and 'Stinker' [Richard] Murdoch cannot compensate for this even to their fans'.[5] In fact, it's Askey that takes most of the frames, with Murdoch overshadowed if not overlooked.

The domestic atmosphere of war on London could hardly be more pronounced than at the start, set deep in Aldwych Tube Station where locals settle down for the night, safe from German bombs. It's an early rise for nippy Arthur, facing the day with Noel Gay and Frank Eyton's joyful 'Hello To The Sun' with its catalogue of things to be done, let the bombs drop where they may.

> I'm up with the lark
> I'm out in the blue
> I'm Gone with the Wind
> I'm down with the 'flu

The story by Howard Irving Young is built into the Askey-friendly screenplay by Marriott Edgar and Val Guest, fluctuating around a far from original plot about putting on a show and becoming a star (two stars, if you count Murdoch). It barely matters in a film with long, enjoyable lapses into comedy and song, as when the male stars assure one another in another Gay-Eyton number 'Half Of Everything Is Yours'. It may be that this was a late addition to the shoot, with Askey and Murdoch reading its lyrics. Topically, Gay and Eyton also contribute 'Let's Get Hold Of Hitler' ('How high shall we hang him? High, high, high!'), sung by Charles Henry Forsythe. He was accompanied for the film by Addie Seaman and Eleanor Farrell, forming the popular American vaudeville trio who worked in Britain during this time. These rumbustious entertainers also perform Gay and Eyton's 'Oh, Johnny, Teach Me To Dance', and Seaman's gawkily eccentric dancing is one of the unexpected treats.

The spectre of a receding music-hall hovers in the presence of rugged Lily Morris, aristocratically cast as ex-music-hall star Lady Randall. Little is made of her, but she has her moment, entertaining the crowds in the Underground with one of her chorus numbers, as if she was still top turn at the Chiswick Empire. For some reason, she doesn't get to sing one of her own numbers, but Vesta Victoria's 'Waiting At The Church'. One wonders why Morris agreed to the substitution, and who was brave enough to suggest it.

OCTOBER

For Butcher's Film Services, Maclean Rogers returned along with co-writer Kathleen Butler and H. F. Maltby for the roll-up-your-sleeves friendliness of **Gert and Daisy's Weekend**. Sister act Elsie and Doris Waters were variety stalwarts of the 1940s, most at home on stage or on the BBC's *Workers' Playtime* broadcast from factory canteens. Their humour was homely and unpolished. Glamour was absent, although it was said that in real life they favoured *haute couture* and probably had an account with Norman Hartnell. In character, their conversations give the impression of being unscripted, a particular skill of theirs, and at their happiest in the least pretentious of settings, which Butcher's would have been more than happy to provide. Their weekend is taken up with unwittingly finding themselves in charge of some evacuated children. They cope with the minimum of fuss, even when things are complicated by some stolen jewels.

Whatever the troubles, Gert and Daisy roll up their sleeves and get on with it, an example to every cinemagoer. Among a generous selection of old favourites they sing 'She's A Lily But Only In Name' under the disapproving gaze of O. B. Clarence, an actor born to play shockable vicars. These are women of the world, vital to the war effort, holding up a mirror to the work-weary housewives looking on. Especially welcome is a rare film appearance by The Aspidistras, parodic duettists hilariously played by Elsie French and John Mott. The *MFB* remarked on the authenticity of the British settings compared to the design excesses of Hollywood, although this was probably to do with Butcher's meagre budget rather than artistic integrity. The following year, the Waters made *Gert and Daisy Clean Up*, and in 1944 *It's in the Bag*.

NOVEMBER

Butcher's was at its roughest and readiest for the Albert Modley entertainment ***Bob's Your Uncle***. Director Oswald Mitchell teamed with Vera Allinson for the screenplay, produced by F. W. Baker at Welwyn Studios. Railway station porter Albert Smith (Modley) is a part-time Home Guard member under orders from Sgt Brownfoot (Wally Patch) and blustering Major Diehard (H. F. Maltby), of whose daughter Dorothy (Jean Colin) Albert lives in hope. Modley, billed in the variety halls of the North – his natural home – as 'Lancashire's Favourite Yorkshireman', had found success in the BBC radio series *Variety Bandbox*. He just about holds *Bob's Your Uncle* together alongside fellow comic George Bolton. The musical sequences are among its weaker elements, with Modley and Colin duetting for 'Hey, Little Hen' and Colin crooning 'My Curly-Headed Baby'. The 'V For Victory' finale is extraordinarily effortless, as if Mitchell has finally thrown up his hands in despair. It says something for the film that it is all but stolen by a startlingly talented baby.

DECEMBER

Ben Lyon and Bebe Daniels were established stars in America before becoming British favourites. Texas-born Daniels had already scaled the heights of Hollywood, beginning in her father's stock production of *Richard III* as 'The World's Youngest Shakespearean Actress'. She made Westerns, and at thirteen signed with Pathé for some Harold Lloyd silent two-reelers. Cecil B. DeMille put her under contract, then Paramount. Her leading men included Rudolph Valentino, John Barrymore and Douglas Fairbanks. In Britain, she was in two musical films of 1933, *The Song You Gave Me* and *A Southern Maid*, but her very presence suggested her glory days in Hollywood were by then over. In 1936 she and Lyon had a major success at the London Palladium, and stayed. Their nationwide popularity soared with a radio series for the BBC, *Hi Gang!*, with a year-long run from May 1940, just as Britain's 'phoney war' ended. With their vivid links to America's stars, they included wireless contributions from Judy Garland and Tyrone Power.

The British public took to 'the Lyons' as it took to few other transatlantic cuckoos in the nest. Gainsborough was quick to exploit their stage and radio success, although **Hi Gang!**, produced by Edward Black and directed by Marcel Varnel, bore little resemblance to the radio series. Marriott Edgar, Val Guest and J. O. C. Orton's screenplay, with additional dialogue by Howard Irving Young, had the stars as American broadcasters working for competing radio stations. Both adopt British boys. Daniels's boy turns out to be Will Hay's colleague Graham Moffatt, accompanied by his ancient Uncle Jerry (another Hay compatriot, Moore Marriott). The treatment is not without style, billing Daniels as 'The Liberty Girl', Lyon as 'Her Other Half' and Vic Oliver as 'The Nuisance with the Ideas'.

Manning Sherwin and lyricist Val Guest, at this time regularly supplying scores for Gainsborough, wrote the songs: 'We Chose The Air Force' (of which Lyon had been a distinguished member), 'My Son', 'I Am Singing To A Million', 'They Call Me Sal', and the title song. Also heard were George Posford and Harold Purcell's 'It's A Small World' sung by Lyon, and 'The Down And Out Blues', written by that most idiosyncratic of music-hall performers, gloomy Sam Mayo. The film may be a shadow of Daniels's best work. She and Ben made two more visits to British studios, in 1953 for *Life with the Lyons*, based on another successful radio series that featured the Lyons' children Barbara and Richard, and *The Lyons in Paris* (1955).

George Formby's move from Ealing to Columbia-British registered with **South American George**, made at Elstree's Rock Studios. Scripted by Leslie Arliss and Norman Lee, with additional dialogue by Austin Melford, and produced and directed by Marcel Varnel, it cast its star in the dual roles of stumbling nincompoop George Butters and Italian opera singer Gilli Vannetti (wrongly printed as Vassetti in a newspaper article shown on screen). Audiences settling down for a

Formby treat may have been puzzled by its opening scene, portraying the dying moments of Violetta in *La Traviata*. This dalliance with high culture is soon cut short; we have been watching an opera on stage, another feather in the cap of the temperamental Vannetti.

We are in familiar territory, with the George we know and love roaming the streets and popping into the local snug to sing 'The Barmaid At The Rose And Crown', one of Roger Macdougall's apposite compositions. George is taken on at the opera as an extra but creates uproar and is sacked. Vannetti, a diva of the first water, puts on his parts and walks out, to the dismay of his personal secretary Carole Dean (Linden Travers), who spots the physical similarities between Vannetti and the ever-bumbling George. She persuades him to impersonate the absconded tenor. In his new persona George entertains at an old performers' home where his aunt (Muriel George) resides. This is one of the most touching scenes in Formby's pictures, as he encourages the elderly residents to 'Swing Mama' (another Macdougall success).

Some attempt is made to introduce the star's numbers more intelligently into the script, but there is little doubt that the pictures he made from here on 'continued the decline though the plots were more amorphous, less constraining'.[6] This is probably true of *South American George*, although few of his fans would have recognised a sea change brought on by a switching of studios. In fact, there are moments in this picture that show Formby at his most professional. More, it suggests his potential, and how his career might have moved into areas beyond the formulaic structure that confined him. Nevertheless, the quirky sequences where he talks with himself don't sit too happily with the rest; then, suddenly, his face and voice fill the screen and we see the familiar potency.

The supporting cast is particularly enlivened by Jacques Brown as a frantic agent, and Ronald Shiner and Alf Goddard's double-act as lovable rogues. There is a bonus in Muriel George (everybody's ideal auntie) at her old dears' concert, singing a snatch of 'I Can't Forget The Days When I Was Young'. The film perhaps outstays its welcome and is unable to resist giving George yet another straight-to-camera number, J. Lyons's 'My Spanish Guitar'. This follows the theatrically chaotic finale, suggesting that Columbia-British was still fine-tuning the formula that had so long kept Formby at the top of the game.

1942

The very glimpse of a passing woman stirs him: 'Ooh, I'll warm yee.' The woman that ignores such refined attention is quickly identified as 'Frozen Fanny' *Somewhere in Camp*

Somewhere in Camp
Let the People Sing
Gert and Daisy Clean Up
Much Too Shy
Rose of Tralee

We'll Smile Again
Somewhere on Leave
We'll Meet Again
King Arthur Was a Gentleman
The Balloon Goes Up

FEBRUARY

The second in Mancunian's 'Somewhere' series, **Somewhere in Camp** reunited much of the team assembled for the 1940 *Somewhere in England*, with producer F. W. Baker, and director John E. Blakeley co-writing the screenplay with Arthur Mertz. Frank Randle and Harry Korris headlined, supported by the spiffingly gentlemanly Dan Young and the adenoidal Enoch of Robbie Vincent. Beyond these, the performances must be endured. Without Randle and his cohorts the result would be unbearable; with them, it's a delight. When they leave the screen, leave the room.

Randle, the toothless, manic Puck, literally crashes into the film, initiating a series of chaotic set-pieces that probably eclipse similar attempts during the decade to bring vibrant idiocy to the screen. 'Eee,' he tells his audience, 'I'm full o' gas.' The destruction of a billiard table, and the gang's reactions at a medical examination (followed by Randle's contortions in a dentist's chair), provide low comedy at its most raw. Beside Randle's futile attempts to display the usual social graces – try as he does, with emphatic politeness – his sexual prowess knows no bounds. The very glimpse of a passing woman stirs him: 'Ooh, I'll warm yee.' The woman who ignores such refined attention is quickly identified as 'Frozen Fanny'.

One can almost (but not quite) hear Max Miller daring as much, except that Miller's genius belonged to the stage, not to film, where his presence is irritating. Randle, on the other hand, makes no concessions for the camera. This, he seems to be informing the audience, is what I am; take me as you please. His is an elemental talent.

Alongside the comedy, a romance of young love is played out at its most theatrically ridiculous by fresh-faced John Singer, only recently a boy actor playing

Tobias in Tod Slaughter's *Sweeney Todd*, and Charm School hopeful Antoinette Lupino, billed as Tonie Lupino. Their stilted, plummy exchanges provide a comedy all of its own. The domestic scenes with the heroine's parents are beyond parody. The unremarkable numbers by composer A. W. Stanbury and lyricist Mertz are mercifully brief: 'Make Up My Mind', 'Regimental Pets', 'All Aboard For Victory', and the title song.

APRIL

Kinematograph Weekly suggested that 'For a man with [John] Baxter's experience and long list of successes, it seems strange to say that **Let the People Sing** will give him his big chance, but in a way he looks upon this as his big break.'[1] The *MFB* explained that 'This story has been devised to present a moral concerning the virtues of democracy, and the importance of public alertness: the example shown is local, but opportunity is not lost to suggest the national implications.' Furthermore, 'the whole thing is conceived in terms of theatre.'[2]

The genesis of *Let the People Sing* begins with J. B. Priestley's 1939 novel, 'deliberately designed to be read [naturally, by the author, who was a skilled broadcaster] over the radio'. Describing the book as a 'pot-boiling novel and watered down ingredients from *The Good Companions*', his biographer suggests that 'The novel uncannily anticipated the mood of the people and provided an inspiring catch-phrase which re-echoed when the attack on London finally began.'[3] The British National picture, made at Borehamwood Rock Studios, used a Noel Gay and Frank Eyton song first heard in the 1940 London revue *Lights Up!*. Subsequently, Barbara K. Emary and director Baxter's screenplay does not make room for much else musically, although Baxter's regular composer Kennedy Russell and lyricist Desmond O'Connor hit the mark with the jolly 'I Love A Roly-Poly Like The Missus Always Bakes For Me' and 'You Can't Give Father Any Cockles', with a pleasing if slight ballad for ingenue Patricia Roc in 'Send For Me'.

This is an affectionately made film, full of incidental surprises and with some touching performances. A cousin to Priestley's novels *The Good Companions* and *Lost Empires* it may be, but the cinematic version of *Let the People Sing* benefits from Baxter's involvement as writer, producer and director, and it is his voice, as much as (probably more than) Priestley's, that rings through it. Vincent Brome suggests that 'the emotional climate of the book fitted the moment', 'inspired, like H. G. Wells' novel *Mr Britling Sees It Through*, by a nation closing its ranks against the threat of war.'[4]

The symphonic fanfare that accompanies the opening credits, presumably the work of Russell, promises a film of rather more grandeur than we might expect of Baxter, but the piece ranges from sentimental homeliness to the sort of proselytising so evident in another Priestley film, *They Came to a City*. The central thrust of *Let the People Sing* springs from the same principle that inspires that Ealing experiment in minimalism: the meeting of strangers. Now, it is little second-rate comic Timmy Tiverton (Edward Rigby), late of the 'Warmer and Merrier' concert party, wrongly suspected of being a bomb-planting anarchist, and the intellectual Czech refugee professor Ernst Kronak (Alastair Sim), whose permit to stay in Britain has expired. 'In essence', Kronak explains, 'the comic is spiritual', a quality he shares with Tiverton. When they are taken on by Hassock's Concert Party, they join forces as champions against Dunbury's local council's campaign to forbid public entertainment being staged in the Town Hall. The local worthies want it turned into a museum.

An unlikely figure in the struggle to 'let the people sing' is the querulous and permanently plastered Sir George Denberry-Baxter, played at his fruitiest by Fred Emney. The casting throughout is superb. Oliver Wakefield, too often cast as silly-ass, is a revelation as under-his-mother's-thumb Sir Reginald. With the all too obvious lack of handsome young men in British musical films, Wakefield has much more potential than his usual screen roles suggest. Olive Sloane (and how we cheer whenever she comes in view) is exactly right as ex-music-hall performer Daisy Barley; her reunion with Tiverton is especially touching. Any blinking will miss the briefest of appearances by Ida Barr, the artiste reputed to have brought American ragtime to Britain; her presence here can only be an act of charity by Baxter.

It is to Sim's Professor Kronak that the film turns for what passes as intellectual argument, as the wise old scholar warns that if they are not careful the British people will lose 'what we will not trouble to keep'. In an impassioned speech to the tribunal deciding the fate of the Town Hall, Kronak insists on 'the liberty of the individual', expressed in 'a very deep love, a poetical love, rooted deep down in the unconscious, of England and the English way of life which we find everywhere among the common people – humour, and irony – and along with these, a profound depth of sentiment'. He is, of course, the mouthpiece of Baxter as well as Priestley. There is no doubting the profound sentimentality of Baxter's message, the more passionate when voiced by a refugee about to be deported from the country he is extolling, telling us that 'as a foreigner, I love these traditions very much, and England would be much poorer without them'. Those who appreciate the genuineness of Baxter's (via Priestley's) commitment will sympathise with the naivety of expression.

The tribunal is chaired by the pro-enjoyment Sir George, at his most blunt and rude (and most plastered). His hilariously drunken rebuttal of the anti-enjoyment pro-museum lobby headed by snooty Lady Foxfield (Annie Esmond) is a highlight of the film. His manservant has earlier warned us that 'He's barmy when he's bottled'. The tribunal ends triumphantly with his finding for the Hall's future as he announces straight to camera, 'You can't stop the people!' This is the cue for Baxter's propaganda to gather its skirts. As crowds of extras march on the Town Hall, he superimposes images of Britain's war workers, laundry girls, typists, sailors, factory hands, airmen – all the toilers against Hitler's oppression – in a cumulative crescendo that puts the stamp on Reginald's insistence that the people must win and that the Hall shall be for 'the making and enjoyment of music in all its forms until such time as the people themselves feel that they no longer require the Hall'.

The resolving of Priestley's story reinforces Baxter's belief in the vital necessity for entertainment – even if it's only a tribute to roly-poly pudding. Those crowds storming the Hall in search of song and dance as they chorus 'Let The People Sing!' hand the film back from its principal actors to the watching cinema audience. Thus, Baxter marries the disparate elements that inhabit so many of his films, sentimental, childlike, but essentially and not altogether subliminally, political. As Geoff Brown has noted, 'A similar technique was used at the end of [Baxter's] *Laugh It Off*, but the result here has much greater impact, vividly expressing in music and images the same ideas that can seem so dead when baldly expressed in dialogue.'[5]

Success is confirmed in the final frame of a plaque: 'The Hall is presented for all time to the people of Dunbury for the making of music and the promotion of good fellowship among all men'. In 1942, this may have been taken as another small victory over Hitler and all those who would forbid the possibilities of enjoyment.

JULY

The sense of ambition evident in *Let the People Sing* could hardly be expected of a Butcher's film, and in this **Gert and Daisy Clean Up** does not disappoint. The ladies were the invention of Elsie and Doris Waters, redoubtable siblings and sisters to actor Jack Warner; their particular stamping-ground in British studios was World War II. They clung to the lower rungs of cinema history through a series of quickly turned-out pictures tied into the war effort. As John Fisher describes, 'Daisy's torn raincoat, Gert's yellow jumper, the dangling string bag, became to a vast public symbols of people they really knew.'[6] Make do and mend was the order of their day.

The film was produced for Butcher's by F. W. Baker at the Riverside Studios in Hammersmith and directed by Maclean Rogers. Kathleen Butler, H. F. Maltby and Harry Gibbs's screenplay was no doubt supplemented by Elsie and Doris's own material. The plot is of its time, emphasising the need for salvage (no old saucepan or iron railing is safe) and the sisters' hatred of black marketing (tinned pineapple chunks a speciality). Concerned for the common good, they set up a neighbourhood restaurant (the government's official management of 'British Restaurants', originally unappetizingly called Community Feeding Centres, had been introduced at the time of food rationing). For good measure, Gert and Daisy also help a merchant seaman.

The easy domesticity of the film is to some extent counter-balanced by the slightly more cerebral presence of Jamaican gospel-singer Uriel Porter playing Snow White and singing 'Coaling' as if in the shadow of Paul Robeson. The Waters sisters came up with songs of their own making: 'We'll Shout Hooray Again', 'Home Sweet Home Again', 'Little Gypsy Of The Seven Seas' and 'Salvage'. As examples of female emancipation at a time of national strife, the sisters probably deserve a thesis of their own.

There are moments during *Much Too Shy* when its star looks distinctly uncomfortable, perhaps wondering if his move to Columbia-British was a bad idea. And reading the screenplay can hardly have inspired Formby. The risqué comedian Ronald Frankau was responsible for the 'original story', adapted for public consumption by Walter Greenwood, assisted by Michael Vaughan, John L. Arthur and Jack Marks, directed by Marcel Varnel and filmed at the Rock Studios. No doubt the adaptation hoped to steer clear of Frankau's somewhat off-colour, not to say very silly, idea. As the percipient Michael Kilgarriff has remarked, Frankau was notable for 'the prolificity of his material for concert-party, cabaret and revue, much of it highly sophisticated, i.e. filthy'.[7] The *MFB* brushed *Much Too Shy* aside as 'a good enough example of a Formby film'.[8]

Handyman George Andy is a none-too-bright odd-job man. We know this because Formby sings Eddie Latta's 'Handy Andy'. He has a talent for painting faces, but nothing below the neck and never (perish the thought) a woman's body, because as the title has already told us, he is much too shy, although Latta's lyric and our George's knowing grin suggest otherwise.

> I gave a girl a gold watch
> She said 'It's rather light.
> It's got no works inside it
> Now surely that's not right.'
> I said 'Now, don't you worry,
> I'll give you the works tonight.'
> Oh, it comes in handy being a handyman.

Of course, the challenge of putting the female form on canvas must be faced, with George visiting various artistic establishments (curiously unconvincing) where he meets artists looking and behaving exactly as one would expect artists to be presented in a Formby film. The easy fun to be got from guffawing at 'modern', even 'surrealist', art cannot be avoided, running alongside George's horror of naked females. On more than one occasion, a ukulele (yes, there is even one lying about in the art school) rescues us from the plot for a few minutes, so that George can perform 'They Laughed When I Started To Play', co-written by the star and Fred E. Cliffe. The hitherto ethereal art students are instantly transformed into mindlessly grinning fans, while George's rictus smile as he plucks away is not always convincing.

A crisis is reached when George paints naked local ladies. Their blushes are spared by his having partially obscured their nakedness by obliging bits of forestry. This work of art ends up being used on advertisement hoardings. At this point the film loses whatever credibility it has, with deranged housewives organising a lynching party and setting fire to his dwelling, citing a 'criminal breach of decency'. Meanwhile, George has at least got through Dorothy Day's 'Talking To The Moon About You', and 'Delivering The Morning Milk' by himself, Cliffe and Harry Gifford.

Jimmy Clitheroe makes for a friendly companion to Handy Andy, but later generations of cinemagoers may question the casting of a 26-year-old midget as a young boy. Robert Murphy suggests that the appeal of Formby's essential naivety is inevitably spoilt by having Clitheroe alongside, and that consequently 'George comes across as merely a fool'.[9] There is some compensation in the presence of two fine character actresses, but neither Kathleen Harrison nor Hilda Bayley is given anything worthwhile to do. The constant whiffs of prudery that fog the script and screen, broken up by the star's suggestive lyrics, make for a strange mixture.

AUGUST

It is unclear why Butcher's invested in ***Rose of Tralee***, a remake of their 1937 original. That 'rather naïve parable'[10] had been written and directed by Oswald Mitchell. For the new version, producer F. W. Baker brought in Germain Burger as director, with the screenplay now credited to Mitchell, Kathleen Tyrone and Ian Walker. A selling-point of the original had been little Binkie Stuart as Rose O'Brien, now played (to much less press interest) by Angela Glynne.

John Longden was cast as Paddy O'Brien [1937: Fred Conyngham] and Lesley Brook as Mary O'Brien [1937: Kathleen O'Regan], with Talbot O'Farrell retaining his role of Tim Kelly. The advent of war (only a threat in 1937) seems to have been the company's reason for returning to the story, which the *MFB* found 'rather slight, and there is far more sentiment than is necessary'. What was more, 'the acting is rather forced'. Happily, it reported that Longden 'sings a number of Irish songs quite well',[11] under the baton of Percival Mackey, one of the most prolific musical directors of the period in British musical films.

OCTOBER

John Baxter's contribution to the war's musical films continued with his production and direction of British National's *We'll Smile Again*, written by Barbara K. Emary, Austin Melford and one of the film's stars, Bud Flanagan. Less gloomy shades of Baxter's *Doss House* swirl around a picture that helped cement the screen partnership of Flanagan and the more sophisticated Chesney Allen. Allen plays film star Gordon Maxwell who takes down-and-out Bob Parker (Flanagan) off the streets. Topically, they meet when Maxwell is opening one of the government's 'British Restaurants'. Together, they will untangle the dastardly efforts of Nazi agents who have infiltrated British film studios, transmitting valuable information to the Nazis via film dialogue. Baxter explained,

> I have always looked upon my association with Flanagan and Allen as putting the seal on my professional work, for if I could be accepted by them I felt I too could consider myself a 'pro'. Our association was a happy and successful one and meant much to me. The first picture was aptly titled *We'll Smile Again* [its working title had been *Three's a Crowd*], and the effect was just what audiences needed.[12]

Kinematograph Weekly gave a guarded reaction, complaining that the story had 'very little substance or form' but that 'sandwiched between its crowded backstage kaleidoscope scenes are delightful songs by Gwen Catley and crisp cracks by Bud Flanagan. The two give the entertainment a good leg-up in the popular crazy category'.[13] Perhaps comparing Baxter's leading ladies to their Hollywood counterparts, *Variety* was disappointed by Phyllis Stanley ('poor singing voice, cannot dance, and is sadly lacking in the required glamor') and by Peggy Dexter who 'acts much too much like an extra suddenly shoved into a part worthy of a Barbara Stanwyck'.[14] *MFB* thought Baxter's direction 'admirable in a type of film with which he is not usually concerned'.[15] Kennedy Russell and lyricist Desmond O'Connor brightened the proceedings with 'Tonight You're Mine', 'Waltz Of Delight', and a title song.

NOVEMBER

The Lord of Misrule, Frank Randle, followed February's *Somewhere in Camp* with Mancunian's *Somewhere on Leave*, backed by usual suspects Harry Korris, Dan Young and Robbie Vincent. Efforts to constrain Randle within the screenplay by Roney Parsons (Arthur Mertz) and Anthony Toner (producer John E. Blakeley) were doomed to failure when he walked on set. The film is a feast of low comedy, with no pretence of sophistication. Randle's explosive behaviour is not merely bad. It is, rather, inevitable. This is the only way this character knows how to behave; never for a moment does he consider it might be incorrect or socially

Flanagan and Allen looking delighted to be singing Kennedy Russell's amiable title song for John Baxter's *We'll Smile Again* (1942)

unacceptable. For Randle, any challenge has devastating possibilities. It is not that he cocks a snook at society: he refuses to take it on any other than his own terms, although he literally may fall over himself in efforts to placate and please those he meets. It is partly this that makes him a unique force in British cinema, an antithesis of the ever-subservient Formby. Formby puts it on; Randle doesn't intend to.

Unlike Formby, he is classless, for the simple reason that no class would want to claim him. His comedy travels the straight line, along paths that he alone can take.

In *Somewhere on Leave* Randle's destruction of a grand piano is a superb example of his work, done with what he believes to be professional, unblinking zeal. We imagine Mancunian's cameraman hiding from the missiles that Randle would inevitably launch. Irreligious, disrespectful, nihilistic as he may seem, he is in fact none of these, but living his own ramshackle, chaotic existence, laying it bare before us, with no hint of artifice.

His stage routine 'Putting Up the Banns' is a highlight, with Korris as the accepted parody of a vicar, Vincent as his pig-tailed female assistant, Young as the prospective bride (the vicar calls her 'a spinster who's never been spinsed'), and Randle as the sex-hungry old lecher eager to get on with it, romancing his bride-to-be with 'I'll soon knock that silly giggle off thy dial!'. The obligatory romantic side-dish involves boyfriend Pat McGrath and girlfriend Antoinette Lupino, now billed as Toni Lupino, in some jaw-clenching dialogue (the *MFB* described their scenes as 'ludicrous'), but they provide unintended amusement. Blakeley opens up the film when the hero's wealthy mother welcomes visitors to her home. Toni Edgar Bruce gallantly plays the high society card in constrained circumstances. Randle repays her hospitality by destroying a bathroom. There is a sequence of pure kitsch in A. W. Stanbury and Mertz's pierrot number 'Boy Meets Girl' duetted by McGrath and Lupino.

Randle-watchers will observe that at the close of this scene he puts his teeth in, possibly to mark the film's imminent conclusion. Before the picture fades, we see the great, dangerous star jitterbugging. 'I'm a great Jitterbugger,' he coos, probably intending to cause as much disruption on the dance floor as elsewhere.

Hughie Charles and Ross Parker's 'We'll Meet Again' had been recorded in 1939 by Vera Lynn. The song was to be inextricably linked to British morale in World War II; it was inevitable that British studios would exploit Lynn's popularity. Columbia-British signed her for three projects, the first with the heaven-sent title already known to its potential audience, **We'll Meet Again**. The result was encouraging. Although the *MFB* considered that 'the varied situations lack originality', it decided that the star's 'charming voice and extensive repertoire of songs more than atone'.[16] Based on a story by Derek Sheils, the screenplay by James Seymour, with contributions from Howard Thomas and John L. Arthur, followed novelettish conventions, but good production values and sympathetic direction by Phil Brandon meant that sentimentality was kept reasonably under control.

Peggy (Lynn), a not especially talented dancer in a West End show during the blitz, fills in on stage when an audience is invited to stay until the All-Clear. She is, of course, noticed. Her success tells us to expect a romance with the usual trimmings. Peggy's 'Be Like The Kettle And Sing', by Tommie Connor, Desmond O'Connor and Walter Ridley, borders on Gracie Fields territory, but the other numbers in a pleasing score are ideally fashioned to Lynn: Ridley and O'Connor's 'I'm Yours Sincerely'; Bert Reisfeld and Jack Popplewell's sultry 'After The Rain'; Harry Parr Davies, Barbara Gordon and Basil Thomas's 'All The World Sings A Lullaby'; and the title song. Space is made for Geraldo's band to introduce 'You Never Knew'.

Much is made of Lynn's association with the BBC, represented here by the mildly comedic Betty Jardine as Miss Bohn, secretary to Mr Hastropp (Frederick Leister). They give the best performances. Peggy's romantic interests, represented by Ronald Ward and Donald Gray, are little more than ciphers. Making no claims as an actress, Lynn behaves well in a role that bridges the gap between herself and characterisation. She is almost convincing when she beseeches her composer boyfriend to share his music 'with the people on the ground … people would hum it!'. This at least reminds us of Lynn's war effort, enhanced here by the scenes in a children's home, and in her efforts to reunite Ruth (Patricia Roc) with husband Bruce.

The film's final moments have Lynn at a massed gathering of servicemen, but it is probably in a more domestic setting that she is best remembered today. Lionel Bart's 1962 musical *Blitz!* includes 'The Day After Tomorrow' – effectively a pastiche of Lynn's wartime songs – which Lynn recorded. It was played at the Adelphi Theatre every night of the long run, with Lynn's voice heard on the radio as Londoners gathered around it, finding comfort in its promise of reunion. In 1942, *We'll Meet Again* (the song and the film) spoke for all those separated by war.

DECEMBER

A less agreeable experience than *We'll Meet Again* suggested that Arthur Askey ('Hello, playmates!') had cinematically peaked with *I Thank You*. Within two years all hope was lost with *Bees in Paradise*, but for now the public was offered a battledress comedy with a title that promised something fantastical, or at least mythological. What it got instead was the decidedly dull **King Arthur Was a Gentleman**, a Gainsborough picture for Gaumont-British, produced at Lime Grove by Edward Black and directed by Marcel Varnel. Scripted by Marriott Edgar and Val Guest (no doubt with Askey interpolations), it had songs by Manning Sherwin and Guest, orchestrations by Bob Busby and choreography by Buddy Bradley. The atmosphere of the barracks predominates, the ill-fitting uniforms redolent of square-bashing making ugly visuals. And where, oh where, is King Arthur? The action took place far away from any Camelot.

'I'm going to be the biggest little man in the British army,' chirps Arthur, but the piece offers him insubstantial material and expects him to deliver it while bored extras look on. His leading ladies, songstress Anne Shelton (British and homey) and Evelyn Dall (transatlantic and bubbly), occasionally provide brighter moments,

Arthur Askey and co-stars doing their bit for morale during wartime in *King Arthur Was a Gentleman* (1942)

with Dall insisting (despite there being no evidence) that 'You'll Love The Army', dispensing the theory that 'Actions Speak Louder Than Words' and confessing 'Got A Bee In My Bonnet'. Shelton, never comfortable on camera, joins the stiffly unappealing male love interest Peter Graves, impersonator Jack Train and Askey to sing 'Why Can't It Happen To Me?', and Askey makes the most of 'You Know What King Arthur Said' as he rubs down a tank. In familiar style, he sings the buzzing 'Honey On My Mind' in the manner of his well-known 'Bee' song. There is a good deal of music from Sherwin and Guest, rather more inventively written than in most other British films of the period, but still commonplace. On the male side, Graves, Train (doing his impressions direct to camera) and Max Bacon leave a depressing impression of the quality of male talent available to British studios during World War II. Nimble and natty as Askey is, he cannot overcome the tedium in which he is encased.

A female double-act from the music-halls to rival that of Elsie and Doris Waters, lanky Ethel Revnell and diminutive Gracie West made two features for New Realm, the first of them *The Balloon Goes Up*, written by Val Valentine and directed, after a fashion, by Redd Davis. The stars were variously billed in theatres as 'The Long and Short of It' and 'The Two Oddments', but New Realm ignores the coupling, giving Ethel an above-the-title billing, with Gracie reduced to the ranks. What Gracie thought of this is not recorded. Producer E. J. Fancey seems to have been parsimonious when it came to production values, while Ethel and Gracie make do with some supporting players of meagre talent. Comedy at its broadest and least subtle dominates as the girls apply to join the Women's Artillery Air Force, forestalling acceptance by putting on the uniforms. Despite persistent mayhem and high larks, they survive a medical examination – Gracie: 'I'm as strong as a horse.' Ethel: 'He's not asking what you look like' – eventually running down black marketeers (they're foreigners, of course, and inevitably Nazis), and knuckling down to their WAAF duties by messing about with barrage balloons.

The entertainment's assemblage is undoubtedly crude, but remains a valuable social document, and a rare example of two almost forgotten performers, best when they are on screen together; in those sections where Gracie is not wanted on voyage we begin to worry. Ronald Shiner adds a professionalism but is rarely seen. There is far too much of popular songster Donald Peers singing 'You've Gotta Smile' and 'I'll Soon Be Coming Home' by Sam Kern (almost certainly no relation to Jerome), best known for writing Max Miller's signature 'Mary From The Dairy'. Optimistically, Peers also sings 'Keep Looking For The Rainbow', while Ethel solos with Kern's 'Winnie The Wench On The Winch', and joins Gracie for Henry Talbot's jolly 'We Do See Life'. It seems extraordinary that within a few years Donald ('By A Babbling Brook') Peers had teenagers screaming with admiration whenever he appeared. A barrage balloon almost takes over the last scenes of the film, but Ethel and Gracie (hopefully still on speaking terms) nudge their way back on screen with Will E. Haines's title song, and a cheery thumbs-up to the war-weary audience.

1943

This may not be the work of a perfectionist, but is nevertheless a work of purpose
Theatre Royal

It's That Man Again
Variety Jubilee
Get Cracking
The Dummy Talks
Happidrome
I'll Walk Beside You
Miss London Ltd
Theatre Royal

Rhythm Serenade
Somewhere in Civvies
Up with the Lark
Down Melody Lane
It's in the Bag
Battle for Music
Bell-Bottom George

JANUARY

Gaumont-British's film of 'The Radio Sensation with Twenty Million Listeners', *It's That Man Again*, is testament to its star Tommy Handley. Denis Gifford claims the wireless version was 'the most famous and popular radio comedy series ever'.[1] Although Ted Kavanagh and Howard Irving Young's screenplay necessarily involves Handley's Mayor of Foaming at the Mouth in a plot, it fails to altogether submerge the star's effectiveness in dealing with 'crazy, inconsequential material'.[2] In a film produced by Edward Black and filmed at Shepherd's Bush, director Walter Forde manages the incorporation of several of the radio series' characters and catchphrases: Dorothy Summers as ever-obliging Mrs Mopp ('Can I do you now, sir?'), the excessive politeness of Claude and Cecil, and the Lord Haw-Haw-like broadcasting of Funf (impressionist Jack Train). The Mayor takes over the bombed-out Olympian Theatre, along with its drama school. Efforts to make a success of it are interrupted by the programme's characters, allowing Mrs Mopp to do a cod ballet and the mildest of striptease. The songs of Hans May and his lyricist Alan Stranks are not distinguished. They include 'Oh Mr Crosby' sung by a female trio that includes Jean Kent, Greta Gynt's 'Don Valentino', Handley's 'Tenderfoot Song', 'Just For Tonight' for a dubbed Kent, 'No, Not Now' and 'Dear Old Glory'. The comedy depends heavily on Handley's quick-fire technique and apparently spontaneous verbal by-play, culminating in his direct farewell to camera, 'Ta-ta for now'.

MARCH

The *MFB* had no complaint of Butcher's ***Variety Jubilee***, reporting that 'Direction and production as a whole are as simple as this story, content to present the variety turns which are the main reason for this film.'³ The film knows its place. Fair enough, but *Variety Jubilee* is rather more; despite its obvious naivety, it has the air of a *spectacle demandé*, skilfully concocted by the prolific sentimentalist Kathleen Butler providing story and screenplay, with Mabel Constanduros chipping in with dialogue. Maclean Rogers is an appropriate director for a neatly packaged mini-saga that, no matter how used we may have become to its components, strikes home.

This story of a modest theatrical dynasty follows three friends parted only in death: Joe Swan (Reginald Purdell), Kit Burns (Ellis Irving) and Evelyn Vincent (Lesley Brook). The steadfastness of their relationship is briskly told alongside rolling vignettes of social and political change set against the changing fortunes of music-hall. An affection for the genre is immediately apparent, almost as if Butler and Mitchell are suggesting that film exists principally to bring music-hall back to life. A theatrically dishevelled George Robey strolls into view as an exemplar of what was once great ('He's one of the best! You're still top of the bill, George, after fifty years!'). Another ancient, Charles Coborn ('Isn't he wonderful? He's over 90!'), arrives, rattling through his classic 'The Man That Broke The Bank At Monte Carlo', a number he had sung in 1891. What we see of 'modern-day' Kit singing 'Comrades' suggests he isn't in the same class as those old-stagers, but there is no lack of sincerity in Irving's performance. Joe remembers Kit on stage as 'one of the greatest stars. He wasn't a riot – he was a panic!'

Joe and Evelyn, duettists, sing 'After The Ball' with convincing affection, but it is Kit who marries Evelyn. Disappointed as Joe is, the friendship remains, and the music-hall lives on. Tom E. Finglass blacks up, impersonating Eugene Stratton in Leslie Stuart's 'Lily Of Laguna'. The daughter of Marie Lloyd, Marie Lloyd Junior (but elderly) goes through the motions of one of her mother's biggest hits, 'One Of The Ruins That Cromwell Knocked About A Bit', with not a whisper of mother's charisma. John Rourke impersonates Gus Elen for "Alf A Pint Of Ale". The resplendently proportioned Betty Warren, complete with Directoire stick, plays Florrie Forde for the chorus songs 'In The Twi-Twi-Twi-Light' and 'Has Anybody Here Seen Kelly?'. Warren's best role was just around the corner in the 1944 *Champagne Charlie*.

Time passes. Joe returns wounded and emotionally damaged from the Boer War. Kit and Evelyn rehabilitate him. A blacked-up minstrel troupe presents a Southern scene around 'Waiting For The Robert E. Lee', and suddenly suffragettes are protesting in music-halls, and the Great War explodes. Soprano Tessa Deane does the most obvious thing by singing Ivor Novello's 'Keep The Home Fires Burning'. At the end of war, Ella Retford rouses the customers with 'Take Me Back

To Dear Old Blighty' and, inevitably, the vaguely sinister 'Pack Up Your Troubles'. Tragedy intervenes: Kit's son Chris is killed in action. Back on stage, Wilson and Keppel perform their sand dancing without Betty, whose name is erroneously included in the credits.

It is time for the General Strike and the music-halls are doing badly, although 'The people will come back to variety'. As usual, the distinction between music-hall and variety is never satisfactorily explained. Kit dies. Evelyn dies. It is now for Joe to live out his friendship with them by caring for their grandson. Hope springs: it is 1936 and music-hall has become, through some strange transmogrification, 'high-speed variety'. Odd, then, that the first example of this is Robey performing 'I Stopped, I Looked And I Listened', which he had sung on the London stage in the 1916 *The Bing Boys Are Here.*

The shadow of the Nazis darkens Britain. Begone dull care, for we have Slim Rhyder, the lanky, emaciated genius bicycling technician. What need is there to worry about the prospect of international conflict when we see his crazy, inexplicable act, forever circling the stage in ever-more ridiculous positions? Joan Winters recalls a gentler age with 'Richmond Hill', followed by what is indisputably *Variety Jubilee*'s top-of-the-bill, the remarkable Ganjou Brothers and Juanita; their stunning acrobatic brilliance has not dimmed after eighty years. It is fitting that the musical finale should have Kit and Evelyn's grandson, now in battledress for the new war, proudly leading 'The Song Of The Marching Men' as the Band of the Coldstream Guards parade. Like everything that has preceded it, this speaks of the best sort of patriotism.

John Fisher has identified Formby's films as 'a simple, undemanding concoction of sincere naivety, open-eyed innocence, stunning vitality, and, of course, his songs'.[4] By the time of the Columbia-British ***Get Cracking*** there were indications that the star's screen career was past its peak. This did not depress the *MFB*'s applauding verdict that 'Thanks to a reasonable script, this is a better comedy than [he] has ever made before. It has many good lines, a number of clever and amusing situations and a certain air of crazy possibility.'[5] The jury may be out. Dick Fiddy describes 'a somewhat substandard story [...] pleasant enough, but it's hardly vintage Formby',[6] while Halliwell rates it as 'average'.[7]

The screenplay by L. du Garde Peach, Edward Dryhurst and Michael Vaughan, based on du Garde Peach's own story, was produced and directed at Denham by Marcel Varnel. Highlighting the activities of the Home Guard, it follows the adventures of George Singleton (Formby) as a parallel 'war' breaks out between the rival defence units in the villages of Major and Minor Wallop. George triumphs when he builds his own secret weapon, a home-made tank. Dinah Sheridan took her turn as Formby's romantic interest, fulfilling another necessary commitment of the Formby formula (no chance of any musical actress being cast: she might want to sing!). A narration by E. V. H. Emmett added a new touch, but as ever the action stopped for Formby's songs, the prescribed currants in the pudding. Considering he was purported to have 400 in his repertoire, he is to be commended for only performing three of his own, the title song co-written with Eddie Latta, and (with Fred E. Cliffe) 'Under The Blasted Oak' and 'Home Guard Blues'.

The best thing about *The Dummy Talks* is its promisingly off-beat title. Unfortunately, it's a poor mélange of crime and musical diversion. John Clifford and Con West's original story was screenplayed by Michael Barringer, produced by Wallace Orton and directed by Oswald Mitchell, for whom the variety setting seemed ideal. The *MFB* described how 'a rather flimsy story has been contrived as a peg on which to hang a number of well-known music-hall turns [...] and this rather upsets the film's continuity'.[8]

The seediness of backstage life on the halls is well caught, but the plot becomes increasingly muddled by interruptions. The thing has barely taken off when Jack 'Blue Pencil' Warner reads one of the absurd letters that formed part of his stage act. Claude Hulbert is to the fore as special reserve officer Victor Harbord ('I'm not an ordinary policeman – as a matter of fact, I'm on the Stock Exchange'). In either capacity, he is the standard silly-ass of British light comedy. On stage, the Lai Founs are concerned with the much more serious business of plate-spinning. There is something vaguely sinister in the mind-reading act of Marvello (Charles Carson) and Maya (Hy Hazell, billed here as Derna Hazell). Confusing the issue, we have impressionist Beryl Orde, displaying little reason for being on screen; her attempts at impersonation fall flat. The mystery is interestingly worked up, but the thread is tenuous.

For some, Mitchell's fascination with music-hall acts will be compensation enough (the acrobatic act with a tiny gymnast is one of the oddest). The Skating Avalons whizz, and Warner performs his 'Funny Occupations' and 'That's A Nice 'Ats 'At That Is'. It is forty-five minutes into the film before a truculent ventriloquist is found dead. The substitution of a midget for the vent's doll is genuinely eerie. Ivy Benson, in a speaking role, entertains with her 'All Ladies Orchestra', accompanying Evelyn Darvell's 'The World Belongs To Me' by J. Lester-Smith, Alf Ritter and Horatio Nicholls. Ivy's girls perform Gaby Rogers and Harry Phillips's 'The Roundabout Goes Round'. Orde ploughs on, singing 'Oh, Johnny, Oh' in the manner of an American comedienne, and demonstrating how Nellie Wallace might sing 'Excelsior'. Even more peculiarly, she leads a male chorus in Edwardian dress in 'Teasing', written by F. W. Lee and C. H. Taylor. In common with much else in this picture it seems to have nothing much to do with anything. Hidden within, uncredited, are Ian Wilson, Patricia Hayes and Olive Sloane.

APRIL

The somewhat incoherent *Happidrome* had sound beginnings, debuting on BBC radio in February 1941. The insistence that 'We're all happy at the Happidrome' would carry through until the end of 1947, but this was a format that radio, rather than film, owned. The transformation from wireless to screen put the picture alongside *Café Colette*, *Band Waggon*, *ITMA* and *Hi Gang!*, proving how tricky the necessary adjustments were. *Happidrome* depended on the comedy team of Harry Korris as Mr Lovejoy, Robbie Vincent's Enoch, and Cecil Frederick's Ramsbottom. Aldwych Films, under the aegis of impresario Tom Arnold and Jack Buchanan, commissioned the screenplay by Arnold and James Seymour, produced by Harold Boxall and directed by Philip Brandon. No matter that 'Not to have heard the radio version would leave film audiences completely bewildered',[9] the fast-moving result is surprisingly happy, its musical numbers well-choreographed by Joan Davis.

Something like a plot about a company turning a theatrical production of a tragedy into a successful musical meanders through the scenes. The attractive songs include Harry Parr Davies and Phil Park's 'Take The World Exactly As You Find It' and 'You Are My Love Song', both sung by Leslie A. Hutchinson ('Hutch'); Stefan Vokes and Ian Grant's 'Nobody Discovers Me' sung by bright spark Bunty Meadows; Korris and Ross Parker's 'Let Me Tell You' (Vincent's catchphrase); Korris and Robertson Cogan's signature 'We Three', and Ernest Longstaffe's 'Come To The Happidrome'.

Another of Butcher's productions built around a famous song, **I'll Walk Beside You**, produced by F. W. Baker and directed by Maclean Rogers, had a screenplay by *éminence grise* Kathleen Butler, with dialogue by Mabel Constanduros exploiting the atmosphere of Alan Murray and Edward Lockton's parlour favourite. The film's cinematographer Geoffrey Faithfull went on to direct the 1945 *For You Alone*, effectively a sort of remake of *I'll Walk Beside You*. The relationship between music lovers John Brent (Richard Bird) and Ann Jackson (Lesley Brook) is shaken by the war. John is reported as missing by the Navy. Ann, working in a children's hospital, becomes engaged to a doctor. John, his memory gone, is reunited with Ann, and the message of the title song is observed. The strong supporting cast includes Hilda Bayley, Irene Handl and Beatrice Varley. The musical content is carefully handled, with tenor John McHugh singing the title ballad. No less than the London Symphony Orchestra was persuaded to appear, with the Welsh choir of St David's Singers. The score also featured Warren Hastings and Herberte [*sic*] Jordan's 'Goodnight Little Man'.

MAY

Arthur Askey's *Miss London Ltd* is a happier experience than his 1942 *King Arthur Was a Gentleman*. It has the most promising of starts, with Anne Shelton as railway station announcer Gail Martin introducing 'The 8.50 Choo-Choo From Waterloo-choo', its lyric suggesting that railway stations are principally used for lovers' meetings ('It's bringing your boy in, so start ship-ahoying'). Besides alerting us to the shocking quality of wartime baggage, it opens up Manning Sherwin and Val Guest's song in a manner rarely seen in British musical films. The score is inventive without being remarkable.

When blonde Terry Arden (Evelyn Dall) arrives in London from the USA to see how the company she co-owns is doing, she is horrified to find her escort business on its knees, and that 'Miss London' is Arthur Bowman (Askey). The girls on his books, offered up as escorts to lonely servicemen on leave from the war, seem to have posed for Victorian semi-pornographic daguerreotypes ('They're a bit long in the tooth!' 'Have they still *got* teeth?'). A bright song helps Terry and Arthur and secretary Joe Nelson (Jack Train) clear the cobwebs ('A Fine How Do You Do'). Terry and Arthur arrange for Gail to escort man-about-town Captain Rory O'Moore (Peter Graves on excellently relaxed form) but at his hotel, in an amusing scene interrupted by Askey and waiter Romero (Max Bacon), Gail makes it clear that her escorting stops at the bedroom door. Her friendly, mature girl-next-door appeal distinguishes her from the heavily made-up, more professionally astute 'escorts' that now get onto the 'Miss London' books. The *MFB* sniffed, 'The girls, headed by crooners Evelyn Dall and Anne Shelton, have the hard glamour and comely bodies wanted by "escort girls" and the general situations lend themselves to some smut, and occasionally a little wit in the dialogue.'[10]

Dall's performance never palls, even as she advises us to 'Keep Cool, Calm And Collect'. As her more reticent British counterpart, Shelton is well served in 'You Too Can Have A Lovely Romance', which she shares with Askey and encyclopedic salesgirl Jean Kent, and the teasing 'If You Could Only Cook', shared with Graves and Bacon. Askey works tirelessly, whether briefly flitting dangerously through Kenneth Blain's 'Moth' song ('Just had a nibble of a lady's nightie'), an obvious cousin to the star's famous 'Bee' number, or delivering his cabaret act at a piano straight to camera. Train's skill as an impressionist is unimpressive (he does a rotten Robb Wilton) but he is joined by Askey and Dall in a neat parody of the Marx Brothers. More curiously, Dall does a devastatingly accurate Jessie Matthews. Richard Hearne makes a superfluous-to-requirements late appearance that would have been better left on the cutting-room floor.

The whole thing is breathlessly paced, and with its particularly agile score (how interesting it would be if Sherwin and Guest had got their hands on a Formby film) Gainsborough's *Miss London Ltd* remains highly watchable. Produced at the Lime Grove studios at Shepherd's Bush by Edward Black, it was directed by Val Guest who co-wrote the screenplay with Marriott Edgar and co-wrote the songs with Sherwin. Guest went on to direct Askey's next, *Bees in Paradise*, reassembling much of the *Miss London Ltd* company.

From his beginnings in film, John Baxter's fascination with music and light entertainment was an essential, there in his very first assignment as assistant director of the 1932 *Reunion*, the story of a down-on-his-luck army major, peppered with songs from the Great War. Baxter's debut as director, the 1933 *Taking Ways*, was a vehicle for comedian Leonard Morris that incorporated music-hall turns including The Rigoletto Brothers and dancer Johnnie Nit. Baxter's next, *Doss House*, established Baxter's manifesto, a documentary-like depiction of poverty against a backcloth of music (this time, classical). A decade on, his work remained true to what had gone before, the amalgam – seemingly organic – of his commitment to social togetherness with the support and relief of both 'light' and 'serious' music.

In 1942, Baxter's *Let the People Sing* had chimed with J. B. Priestley's hopeful anticipation of social cohesion, arguing that having a public hall available for the singing of songs about roly-poly puddings was more vital to the community than if the hall were turned into a museum. Baxter's *We'll Smile Again* (1942) began his long association with Bud Flanagan and Chesney Allen. Such was its success that British National wasted no time signing them for **Theatre Royal**, a sort of sequel in the sense that they played the same characters. Now, theatre owner Gordon Maxwell (Allen) and props man Bob Parker (Flanagan) join forces to save the Theatre Royal from redundancy by staging a revue that will bring back the people. Producing and directing, Baxter was on home ground with a plot that recalled much else of his work, working from a screenplay by Flanagan, Austin Melford and Geoffrey Orme, complete with a choreographed ballet by Wendy Toye. Supporting artists retained from *We'll Smile Again* were Peggy Dexter, Horace Kenney, and popular soprano Gwen Catley singing 'Tell Me Truly' and 'I Know I Must Be Dreaming'. The other numbers by Kennedy Russell and his lyricist Desmond O'Connor were 'Roll On Tomorrow', 'Here's To You', 'I'll Always Have Time For You' and 'One Of The Boys In Town'.

The *MFB* criticised the 'slight, somewhat disconnected and unoriginal plot'.[11] When we watch the film today, Baxter's distinctive touch alerts us to his lifelong intrigue with cinema. Here, he brings in boy drummer Victor Feldman – one of the many young performers he featured throughout his career, along with references to the Regency clown Joseph Grimaldi's professional struggles. The fondness with which Baxter infuses his work is there when the camera pans along a line of the Theatre Royal's staff, just as the camera has passed across the faces of the music-hall audience in *Say It with Flowers*; it is one of *Theatre Royal*'s most touching moments.

This may not be the work of a perfectionist, but is nevertheless a work of purpose and, as Geoff Brown has expressed, 'the important features for audiences

– now as much as then – are the warmth and good fun of Flanagan and Allen, the atmosphere of theatre camaraderie, the fun poked at high-brow drama, and the jokes about common ills like income tax.'[12] The diversity of Baxter's work continued throughout the year with *Old Mother Riley Detective* and a lively adaptation of Priestley's *When We Are Married* (both directed by Lance Comfort), and producing and directing Clive Brook in *The Shipbuilders,* his final association with British National.

JUNE

A significantly different creative team from that responsible for Vera Lynn's screen debut *We'll Meet Again* was in place at Columbia-British for **Rhythm Serenade**, produced by Ben Henry and associate producer George Formby and directed by Gordon Wellesley. The screenplay by Basil Woon and Marjorie Deans was based on Deans's story, with contributions from Margaret Kennedy and Edward Dryhurst.

From the moment we see Ann Martin (Lynn) tending wounded servicemen in a battle-scarred landscape (beautifully evoked in George Provis's set) as they sing Annette Mills's 'When We're Home Sweet Home Again', we believe in this character. It is Lynn's very ordinariness that inspires confidence; we know she is doing her best, and are prepared to accept the result. Her natural way with the evacuated children under her care personifies her quality, as much as her relationship with the war-altered men ('Sing us another song, miss!'). She obliges with 'Bye And Bye (we'll laugh at all the tears we have shed)' by Jimmy Wakely, Fred Rose and Johnny Marvin. Wellesley tastefully sets the bar high, but it isn't long before Ann's comic-cuts spoil-sport brothers Jimmy Jewel and Ben Warriss arrive home on leave. Insisting that Ann's place is in the home, they gobble up much of the footage with their stage routines. Ann wants to enlist ('They need women in the services'). Thinking of her late mother, she consoles her father with 'The Sunshine Of Your Smile'.

Ann longs to join the Wrens, but she is wanted in her community for factory work, and for looking after the childrens' nursery. A romance with a mentally troubled serviceman John Drover (Peter Murray-Hill) intervenes. She imagines him to be subsisting in the grounds of an impressive house, unaware that he is its owner. Without disclosing his involvement, he arranges for the nursery to move into his property, and Ann guides him back to health. Glamourised, she sings Michael Carr's 'It Doesn't Cost A Dime'. At a gala concert, Jewel and Warriss do another routine, and Jimmy Clitheroe plays the accordion. Ann performs the Reginald King-Jack Popplewell 'With All My Heart' before leading factory workers into a reprise of 'I Love To Sing', but still wants to be in uniform, against the wishes of her factory boss. 'You're glory struck,' he tells her. 'You never think of the army behind the limelight. I need you here, Ann, I need you here badly. Everyone of us must do the job he's fitted for.'

Drover, now healthy and fighting at sea, hears Ann's voice on the radio singing 'So It Goes On' in a broadcast from a factory in the Midlands. She knows now that her future with him is secure, and is content to be a cog in the great un-conscripted machinery of women workers, as she voice-overs the film's final images of wheel-turning industry, as if Columbia-British had hired a poet from the documentary film movement.

> See those wheels turning
> Furnaces burning
> Chimneys black against the sky
> Guns fashioned out of steel
> Shells to feed their relentless hunger
> Tanks, planes, ships!
> Eager hands toiling to one glorious end – Freedom!
> And so it goes on from dawn 'til dusk
> From dusk 'til dawn
> Never failing, never halting
> And so it goes on and on and on

AUGUST

Butcher's took on Mancunian's chaotic star Frank Randle for *Somewhere in Civvies* under the aegis of ever-busy director Maclean Rogers. The ensuing chaos that broke out at the Riverside Studios in Hammersmith skittered around Con West's screenplay, to which Randle had contributed. Randle's previous 'Somewhere' pictures, *Somewhere in England*, *Somewhere in Camp* and *Somewhere on Leave*, had been made for Mancunian by John E. Blakeley, to whom Randle returned for the 1949 *Somewhere in Politics*. Meanwhile, *Somewhere in Civvies* had its star as a private who escapes army life only to find that life in Civvy Street is quite as difficult, especially when the fortune he is left can only be claimed if he is proved to be sane. Unsurprisingly, in Randle's case this proves far from easy. Nancy O'Neil sings Sonny Miller and Tod Stevens's 'Somebody's Kisses', and Ernest Dale performs Ernest Longstaffe's 'When The Sergeant Major's On Parade'.

DECEMBER

Lupino Lane greatly admired the comedy double-act Revnell and West, warning 'Woe betide any comedian who has to follow them in any programme without an interval between.'[13] Watching the two, mercifully brief, films they made to boost the war effort, we must presume they worked better on stage. Following on their 1942 *The Balloon Goes Up*, New Realm mounted ***Up with the Lark***, produced by

E. J. Fancey and directed by Philip Brandon. The result has been described as 'Broad comedy with musical interludes: pretty unbearable, even in wartime'.[14] This chimes with the *MFB*'s comment that 'Those who do not find [Revnell and West] funny will be inclined to agree with Ethel when she says "Things might be worse, but I don't see how".'[15]

Based on a story presumably written on a matchbox, the early scenes are at least better directed than those in *The Balloon Goes Up*, but things get worse. Disguised as men, they embark on exposing a gang of black marketeers; the local clergyman is one. The girls land in a comfortable, hospitable prison but are released so that they may track down the criminals. In the countryside, Ethel (with Gracie very much in the background) sings Will E. Haines's 'Let's Go Cuckoo!' ('If you can't go cuckoo, go cock-cock-cock-a-doodle-do'). They reach Sunnyside Farm, and sleep in a tree. Now posing as Land Girls, they are put to work milking cows and harnessing a horse.

A supposedly spooky graveyard scene marks a low point amidst the general inanity, but things improve when Ethel (once again *sans* Gracie) extols the virtues of being 'Up With The Lark'. The action is spun out at a celebratory dance, until second-fiddle Gracie and bizarre Ethel rout the gang. Ethel is understandably terrified when a ghost appears, leaving his top hat on her bottom and informing the cinema audience, 'That's the end.' Van Straten's Piccadilly Orchestra represents the almost obligatory dance band expected in films of the period. We are left wondering what poor Gracie thought of being made subordinate to her face-contorting partner, and how embarrassed scriptwriter James Seymour and original story writer Val Valentine must have felt when they saw how things had turned out.

Having dispatched Revnell and West, New Realm got busy with a laboratory-produced concoction of footage from previous variety-based features. Their **Down Melody Lane** drew on *Cock o' the North* and *Variety* (both 1935), *Variety Parade* (1936), *Lily of Laguna* (1938), and *Music Hall Parade* (1939). The selection includes Dudley Rolph singing Leslie Stuart's 'Lily Of Laguna', Hutch singing 'Wake', girl-guider G. S. Melvin recommending underwear for chilly weather, Eve Becke singing 'Angelino Piccolino', Anita Lowe singing 'She's A Lassie From Lancashire', Billy Cotton and Band with 'Fall In And Fly' and the 'Danube Swing', and Arnley and Gloria performing 'It's Rhythm'. The ubiquitous Sherman Fisher Girls are seen with Ennis Parkes in 'Let's All Go Up In The Sky'. Others featured include Phyllis Robins, the Australian Air Aces, Naughton and Gold, and the Houston Sisters. The producer of this unexciting assortment was E. J. Fancey.

Elsie and Doris Waters returned for Butcher's highly successful romp *It's in the Bag*, produced by F. W. Baker and directed by Herbert Mason. Con West's screenplay resulted in what the company's press-book proclaimed as 'one of the Best Slapstick Productions from a British Studio we have had for a long time', a recommendation taken from *Daily Film Renter*. Based on the story of the Twelve Chairs in the 1928 Russian novel by Ilf and Petrov, already redeployed by Formby's *Keep Your Seats, Please*, West's version has sisters Gert and Daisy vying with their landlady's son in search of £2,000 tied into the hem of an old dress. Their adventures include impersonating a leading lady and child in a theatrical production. Butcher's assembled a magnificently characterful cast that includes Ernest Butcher, Reginald Purdell, Irene Handl, Megs Jenkins and little firebrand Esma Cannon. The sibling stars wrote the film's blindly hopeful 'Put A Penny Underneath Your Pillow', admirably suited for keeping the public pecker up. The *MFB* reported that 'Gert and Daisy are well up to their usual form, fooling and back-chatting' in a film that 'moves with immense speed from one fantastic episode to another'.[16]

Battle for Music, a semi-documentary from Strand Productions, can claim to be one of the *most* musical of British films, telling of the London Philharmonic Orchestra's struggle to continue during wartime. Its documentary film producer-director Donald Taylor must be held responsible for *Battle for Music*'s shortcomings, not uncommon in documentary productions: non-actors expected to cope with scripted, stilted, dialogue; poor editing and bad dubbing; too much library footage; actors sharing the screen with non-actors. All this is true of *Battle for Music*, but Taylor has good reason, as we too have good reason to be grateful for this remarkable documentation.

For some, its stars may be the cast list of British conductors pictured in lollipop segments of classical pieces: Constant Lambert conducting Tchaikovsky's *Romeo and Juliet* and Moiseiwitsch playing Rachmaninov's Piano Concerto No 2; Warwick Braithwaite conducting Saint-Saëns's *La Princesse Jaune* and Mozart's Symphony No. 40; Eileen Joyce playing Grieg's Piano Concerto; Adrian Boult conducting Elgar's 'Cockaigne' Overture, and Malcolm Sargent conducting Beethoven's Symphony No. 5 after informing the concert hall (and cinema) audience that a nearby building is on fire.

> Hitler may blow this hall sky-high – you, me, everybody – but there's one thing he cannot touch: Beethoven's 5th Symphony. This music will live long after Hitler and his regime is completely forgotten, so I think perhaps there's nothing better we can do than continue to play it, nothing better you can do than to remain and hear it.

Running alongside these luminaries are the three 'real bloke' players of the LPO orchestra who decided to take its future into their own hands: gentle Charles Gregory, Francis Steed and, most prominently, Thomas Russell, who would become the orchestra's secretary and figurehead. These are the real stars of the picture. Russell persuaded J. B. Priestley to lend his support to the saving of the LPO, making a speech (re-enacted for the film) at the Queen's Hall in July 1940. The LPO surmounts a torrent of vicissitudes: it faces liquidation; when the players want to play in France, the country is about to fall to the Nazis; when they plan a concert in Brighton, there is an air-raid; when they find a home at the Queen's Hall, the building is destroyed by enemy action.

It remains a wonder that *Battle for Music* was ever made. After a faltering start, with Priestley agreeing to write the script (ultimately written by St John Legh Clowes), the project was abandoned, until the Ministry of Information revived it in 1941, only to pull it again a few hours before shooting was due to begin. But Russell and Taylor's persistence eventually got the film made.

The message could not be clearer. As Charles Gregory says, 'It's rotten to go down the drain', and always there is the need for the orchestra to reach people beyond the privileged class – its message, really, is not dissimilar to that drummed out by John Baxter, for 'If it breaks up, orchestral music is finished in this country'. The glimpse we get of concert-goers at the opera leaves us in no doubt that this is a pursuit available only to the highly privileged. Unexpectedly, Jack Hylton arrives to book the orchestra into variety theatres, hoping to introduce classical music to a wider public. As the film tells us, 'The curtain is falling on a world threatened and menaced by Nazi aggression. But the audience forgets the tragedy of Europe in the magic of great music.'

'For those who like Formby getting into scrapes and singing three or four songs, direction, production and supporting cast do not greatly matter – which in this case is just as well.'[17] Perhaps **Bell-Bottom George** is one of director Marcel Varnel's less successful assignments, but by now Columbia-British's Formby franchise was reaching a sell-by date. It took five writers – Edward Dryhurst, Peter Fraser, John L. Arthur, Richard Fisher and Peter Creswell – to manufacture a screenplay that offered little originality. George is a waiter who finds himself unofficially in the Navy. All sorts of larks ensue, but things turn out nice again when he rounds up a gang of Nazi spies. The well-trodden plot, the lack of pace and sense of spontaneity, the songs stuffed into the dialogue, the endlessly grinning faces of extras forced to listen to yet another number from the star (perhaps a second or third take!), and the feeble comedy with hammocks and bird impressions; how much more could the public stand? The songs perk things up here and there, with Harry Parr Davies and Phil Parks's tailor-made 'If I Had A Girl Like You' (it was Anne Firth, with no hope, as usual, of a song), 'Swim Little Fish' (sung to a glass bowl), and the title song. George also performs Elton Box and Desmond Cox's 'It Serves You Right'.

1944

It is unequivocally a masterpiece; the summation of everything
British musical films owed to the honourable art of music-hall
Champagne Charlie

Demobbed
Bees in Paradise
Heaven is Round the Corner
Candles at Nine
One Exciting Night
Champagne Charlie

Give Me the Stars
Fiddlers Three
My Ain Folk
Dreaming
He Snoops to Conquer

MARCH

An appreciation of Mancunian Films may be an acquired taste; admiration may be difficult to justify – appreciation may follow. The gloriously enjoyable *Demobbed*, produced and directed by the unflagging John E. Blakeley, collected some giants of northern comedy under the pretence of a screenplay by Blakeley (credited as Anthony Toner) and Roney Parsons (in fact, Arthur Mertz), loosely based on a story by Julius Carter and Max Zorlini. Costing just over £30,000, *Demobbed* was 'trade shown in February 1944 and by 1946 had been screened in half the country's cinemas with estimations that it would earn three times its production costs'.[1]

Its quartet of rustic clowns is worth every penny spent by Blakeley and his expectant patrons: Norman Evans, the 'Over the Garden Wall' ample-bosomed neighbour 'Fanny Fairbottom'; rubbery Nat Jackley; wannabe upper-crust Dan Young of the frenzied squawk; and rarely filmed Betty Jumel, one of the zaniest and least remembered female exponents of music-hall. They take to the floor in a Hawaiian routine, assisted by Felix Mendelssohn's Hawaiian Serenaders. The comedians clear the floor for two artistes who, according to their introduction, 'are known throughout the English-speaking world, idolised in millions of homes' and are to appear in 'a glorious song scena' 'The Garden of Romance', its décor bearing a remarkable resemblance to many a tea-cosy. Extras enter, dressed most unsuitably for a trip around the garden, as the film switches from high comedy to kitsch, with Anne Ziegler and Webster Booth performing 'Until' and 'Just A Song At Twilight', and Booth singing 'I Hear You Calling Me' and 'Two Little Words [Good Bye]'. A sort of plot is of even less interest than usual, only occasionally getting in the way of the comical and musical antics, as in the sketch with Young as a ventriloquist with rubber-limbed Jackley on his knee.

People arriving late at **Bees in Paradise**, at least if they were acquainted with the operas of Gilbert and Sullivan, may have wondered if they had mistakenly walked into a lamentably amateur production of their *Princess Ida*. Anyone watching *Bees in Paradise* after 1956 may wonder if it was the inspiration for the British sci-fi *Fire Maidens from Outer Space*. Whatever enthusiasm had been stirred during the early days of war by Arthur Askey's earlier pictures such as *Band Waggon* and *I Thank You* was squandered, despite several of those who had helped Askey to cinema success being involved, including Edward Black as producer, Val Guest as director and Marriott Edgar as his screenplay co-writer.

Of particular disappointment is the Manning Sherwin and Val Guest score; their songs for *Miss London Ltd* had been its brightest component. Still, the songs pour out: Jean Kent explaining 'I'm A Wolf On My Mother's Side'; chummy Anne Shelton encouraging us to 'Keep A Sunbeam In Your Pocket' and mooning 'Don't Ever Leave Me'; she and Askey sharing 'It Happens'; Kent joining Askey for 'Are You Naturally Romantic?', and a child performer at the Turkish baths insisting that 'Melody Is The Swing'.

When Askey, Max Bacon, Peter Graves and Ronald Shiner wash up on Paradise Island, they soon learn (via song) that 'Women Are The Greatest Ones'. Men are used purely for breeding purposes, and by decree of the all-female government are killed when their usefulness ends. Jean Kent's Minister of Propaganda, dressed like all her compatriots as if she's just stepped out of a Flash Gordon Saturday morning serial, announces, 'The female is paramount at all times.' Guest's fondness for shots of pin-up girls squatting on the rocks; an embarrassing love scene between Kent and Graves (he behaves like an officer and mostly a gentleman); the appearance of a crocodile; the leaden comedy of Bacon and Askey; the ill-conceived songs (try Askey and Shelton ping-ponging through 'I'm A Hither And A Dither') – all help to scupper this Gaumont-British attempt at musical farce.

The *MFB* found it 'Weak in construction and dialogue and the finale comes quite inconclusively and without tying up a number of loose ends. The continual jest of the male-hunting females soon palls and Paradise Island quickly belies its name. Arthur Askey has to carry too much of the fun with insufficient material to work on and is not too well supported by the cast.'[2] The film's absurdities cut across what might have been an interesting, even thought-provoking, piece around female emancipation. Badly stung by *Bees in Paradise*, it would be a decade before Askey returned to British studios.

American girl singer Leni Lynn had signed up with Hollywood for MGM's 1939 *Babes in Arms*. Her 1944 move into British studios was less happy, with British National's attempt to build her as a star for the domestic market. Produced by Frederic Zelnik and directed by Maclean Rogers, **Heaven is Round the Corner** has a screenplay by Austin Melford, A. Hilarius and Paul Knepler, but the best they could come up with is an utterly conventional account of applause and romance in Paris. Losing her lover amidst the chaos of war, Joan Sedley (Lynn) returns to Britain, where they are eventually reunited. The *MFB* agreed that 'Leni Lynn has a voice, but that is about all', as well as complaining that 'its continuity and the performances of the chief characters is poor'. Without the casting of Glaswegian music-hall veteran Will Fyffe, 'the film would have no merits'.[3] It did, however, have a charming title song written by Kennedy Russell and lyricist Desmond O'Connor.

MAY

Jessie Matthews's involvement with British National's thriller **Candles at Nine** effectively brought the curtain down on her British film career. The fragile quality of her personality had withered. Neither Wallace Orton's production nor John Harlow's direction (he co-wrote the screenplay with Basil Mason, based on a novel by Anthony Gilbert) could rediscover it. When elderly Everard Hope (Eliot Makeham) is murdered, his money goes to actress Dorothea (Matthews) who becomes the murderer's target. The murderer is the old man's housekeeper, hood-eyed Beatrix Lehmann.

Matthews has one number, 'I'd Like To Share With You', in which she is joined by dancer Guy Fielding (for his pains, uncredited). Harry Parr Davies and Harold Purcell's song is pleasant enough to accompany Matthews's familiar twists and trademark kicks but is nothing like as good as the better songs of past years. One can scarcely imagine it having been filmed more uninterestingly.

JULY

As Vera Lynn's third picture proceeds, it may occur to us that her film career is unlikely to last. She belongs up there because of the times. With a screenplay by Harry Irving Young and Peter Fraser, and additional dialogue by Margaret Kennedy and Emery Bennett worked up from Fraser's original story, the film's title **One Exciting Night** may not have been the reaction of those who watched it. This is not to say that the production by Ben Henry and Culley Forde or the direction of Walter Forde are to blame. Lynn's sincerity, and her pleasing ordinariness that remains intact on screen, shine through this story of mild thrills and spills amidst gangsters.

The film spends a good deal of time finding reasons for its star to break into song. She does so attractively, beginning with a promise in Michael Carr and Jimmy Kennedy's 'There's A New World Over The Skyline' (presumably, when the war is won) as she and her pals cycle through the countryside. Better times can be looked forward to, but she inspires community singing by telling a multi-national collection of servicemen that it's just as good to look back, in Dave Franklin's 'It's Like Old Times'.

The plot can't break out of its hackneyed corset in which too many musical films are confined: our Vera (this time she's called Vera Baker) wants nothing so much as to be a star. Muddles over a lost wallet, a painting by Rembrandt (really?), and a relationship with impresario Michael Thorne (Donald Stewart) resolve themselves in the expected way. How else, when she has sung Jack Popplewell's 'One Love' at him? Broadcasting from a salvage van, she sings Walter Ridley and Tommie Connor's 'You Can't Do Without Love' to a stunned public. At a rehearsal for a charity concert, she sings 'It's So Easy To Say Good Morning'. As she gets ready to do some sleuthing, she sings George Boulanger's 'My Prayer' with its English lyric by Jimmy Kennedy, by which time the film has pretty well run out of excuses for her to sing. It's all harmless enough, and Lynn copes admirably. Ultimately, neither she nor the picture is distinctive enough to overcome the reason why Lynn remains so highly regarded in British popular culture: she sang when Britain needed to hear her singing.

Despite British studios' many attempts to recreate music-hall, dating back to Britain's first sound films, it took a Brazilian director to capture its essence. Michael Balcon was responsible for bringing to Britain director Alberto Cavalcanti, with his reputation as the founder of the French 'realist' school, in order to inject new vigour into the documentary film movement. Cavalcanti headed the GPO Film Unit, and from 1939 the Crown Film Unit, and in 1942 Balcon entrusted him with a feature film, Ealing's *Went The Day Well?*.

Critical reaction to this retelling of a Graham Greene story about Nazis invading an English village was mixed. Its powerfulness has not diminished. It may seem remarkable that a Brazilian director should become so subsumed in British culture, for, if we see *Went The Day Well?* as a 'war' film, its personification of wartime Britain is startlingly brilliant – and how much more British could it be, taking place in 'Bramley End'? You can almost smell the apples.

Ian Aitken has written of Cavalcanti's second feature for Ealing, ***Champagne Charlie***, as extolling 'the pursuit of guileless pleasurable gratification, rather than social standing and self-sacrifice, which appears to bond this particular community together, and such a celebration of hedonist intemperance clearly distinguishes *Champagne Charlie* from most other Ealing films of the period'. Furthermore, 'the humanist orientation […] is far from insipid or bland. *Champagne Charlie* mobilises a vigorous humanism, shot through with sardonic irony, which nevertheless indirectly allows issues of class and gender differences to be voiced.'[4] It is unequivocally a masterpiece – the summation of everything British musical films owed to the honourable art of British music-hall that they had plundered from the beginning of sound pictures.

Cavalcanti's feeling for Victorian music-hall may have been stimulated by his membership of the Players' Theatre under the arches of Charing Cross, where Evans's Supper Club, rechristened 'Late Joys', offered an ever-changing diet of Victorian music-hall songs. It was here that he met James Robertson Justice, perfectly bearded as a member of the Players' audience; uncredited, Justice and John Hewer (another Players' performer) can be briefly seen among the music-hall patrons. Players' favourite Vida Hope plays a barmaid, and the ballets are devised by Charlotte Bidmead, the Players' choreographer of pastiche Victorian ballet. Who knows how many other refugees from the Players' Theatre were inveigled to appear?

Designer Michael Relph's recreation of the Victorian music-hall and Eric Stern's glorious costumes (with Warren sumptuously gowned) are fascinatingly attractive, although some have questioned the period accuracy. The lushly decorated numbers we see on stage are almost certainly in excess of what contemporary audiences would have got for their money, but we never feel that the authentic atmosphere of music-hall has been in any way modernised, unlike the obvious restyling in the 1945 *I'll Be Your Sweetheart*. The quality of lighting, the naphtha flames illuminating the performers, the crude mechanical trickery of 'Hit Him On The Boko' and 'Hunting After Dark', the superb puff and swagger of the screenplay by Austin Melford, John Dighton and Angus Macphail, the way the artistes tuck into a steak and kidney pie – all seem authentic, relished. On stage or in the wings, Cavalcanti's camera has a fluidity that keeps the film's pulse throbbing.

The irresistible pull of Cavalcanti's film is in its affection for its three central characters, genuine *lions comiques* of the Victorian music-hall in George Leybourne ('Champagne Charlie') played by Tommy Trinder, and Albert Vance ('The Great Vance') played by Stanley Holloway. They are joined by Bessie Bellwood, 'beloved of uncouth audiences',[5] a riotous Valkyrie who could knock a cabman out cold (the comic Arthur Roberts once described her as 'Surely a veritable Jekyll and Hyde among comediennes'), played by Betty Warren. Each made the most of their short, hectic lives. Bellwood died aged thirty-nine in 1896, Vance (in fact Alfred Peck Stevens) died aged forty-nine in 1888, and Leybourne aged forty-two in 1884. Maurice Willson Disher characterises these idols of the halls as 'strictly moral in principle, however they might be in practice. Judged by the virtues that are the heart's test, they were as good as bread.'[6] Their performances and those of the supporting cast are exemplary; it is perhaps best to overlook the uninteresting puppy-love of Jean Kent and Peter De Greef.

The plot concentrates on the rivalry between Joe Saunders (renamed George Leybourne because he has walked from Leybourne to London to seek fame as a singer) and 'The Great Vance', famous, conceited and faintly ridiculous. Leybourne's unexpected success on the halls, where he is promoted by Bessie Bellwood, awakes Vance's jealousy. Ultimately, the three join forces to prevent the closing down of the music-halls. Challenging Leybourne to a duel, Vance is astounded when Leybourne accepts. The outcome, of course, is comical, but an even greater duel is begun – a duel of songs, in which Leybourne and Vance try to outdo one

Eric Fraser's drawing of Tommy Trinder in Cavalcanti's superb paean to Victorian music-hall *Champagne Charlie* (1944)

another in a seemingly never-ending assortment of 'drinking' numbers. These are central to the film's wealth of music in a picture that can justifiably claim to be one of the most musical ever made by a British studio. The 'song duel' between Leybourne and Vance involves items 9–15 in the running order of musical numbers:

1. Overture [arranged by Ernest Irving]
2. Arf of Arf and Arf [Una Bart]; Trinder
3. Don't Bring Shame On The Old Folks [Irving/Frank Eyton]; Trinder
4. Come On, Algernon [Lord Berners/Diana Morgan/T. E. B. Clarke]; Warren
5. Don't Bring Shame On The Old Folks: reprise [Irving/Eyton]; Trinder
6. Ballet [Irving]; Jean Kent and Dancers
7. Hit Him On The Boko [Irving/Eyton]; Trinder
8. Strolling In The Park [Billy Mayerl/Eyton]; Holloway
9. Ale, Old Ale [Irving/Eyton]; Trinder
10. I Do Like A Little Drop Of Gin [Mayerl/Eyton]; Holloway
11. Burgundy, Claret And Port [Mayerl/Eyton]; Trinder
12. Rum, Rum, Rum [Irving/Eyton]; Holloway
13. The Brandy And Seltzer Boys [Mayerl/Eyton]; Trinder
14. A Glass Of Sherry Wine [Mayerl/Eyton]; Holloway
15. Champagne Charlie [Alfred Lee/George Leybourne]; Trinder and Ensemble
16. Ballet: Polka [Berners]; Jean Kent and Dancers
17. The Man On The Flying Trapeze [Leybourne/Lee]; Trinder
18. Not In Front Of Baby [Irving/Eyton]; Warren
19. By And By [Noel Gay/Eyton]; Trinder and Men
20. Hunting After Dark [Mayerl/Morgan/Clarke]; Trinder, Holloway, Warren
21. Finale: Champagne Charlie [Lee/Leybourne]; Trinder and Ensemble

In reality, Leybourne's repertoire included a good number of songs celebrating drink, among them 'Come Fill Me A Tankard', 'Cool Burgundy Ben', 'Lemonade And Sherry', 'Moët And Chandon', 'Sparkling Piper Heidsieck' and 'Woman And Wine'. His 'Rolling Home In The Morning' tells its own tale, as does his open invitation, 'Who's Coming Out For A Spree Tonight?'. Vance's ripostes included 'Cliquot! Cliquot!', 'Our Glorious English Beer', 'Soda And B' [sic], and 'Sparkling Moselle'. Bellwood's most popular number was 'What Cheer, 'Ria!', possibly eclipsed by the notoriously suggestive 'She Sits Among The Cabbages And Peas'.

The Victorian songs sung by Leybourne, Vance and Bellwood (each had plenty of them) might have been used in the film. Any retelling of the story of Champagne Charlie without use of Leybourne's most famous song (although he and Lee also wrote 'The Daring Young Man On The Flying Trapeze' in celebration of Leotard) would be inexcusable. But what we have is a minor miracle in British musical films: perhaps the finest, most inventive, score, indeed, an abundance of score under the musical supervision of Ernest Irving. From the brilliantly compiled overture to the spanking orchestrations of the songs, we should relish the quality of this work, and the contributions from a collection of composers providing what are essentially pastiche Victorian music-hall songs: Una Bart, T. E. B. Clarke, Diana Morgan, Lord Berners (he provided not only the music for Warren's enchantingly suggestive 'Come On, Algernon' but, as a piano piece which Irving orchestrated, the 'Polka'), two of the finest composers of light music in Noel

Gay and Billy Mayerl, and lyricist Frank Eyton. Their contribution to *Champagne Charlie* is immeasurable.

Drink is mother's milk to the population of *Champagne Charlie*. It pours through the film, cascades out from behind the bars of the Mogador, has sailors rollicking unsteadily down a gap in the street, has songwriters in a frenzy to write songs about it; drink and song become synonyms for unadulterated pleasure. Cavalcanti's achievement, however, is so much more. The opening scenes, when George and his young miner brother Fred (Leslie Clarke) arrive in London, strike out in their intensity; the parting of the brothers is encapsulated in Cavalcanti's camera following Fred as he walks away. It is one of the friendly delights of the film that, without a word, we see Fred back sitting beside the seasoned old boxer Tom Sayers (Eddie Phillips). They are together again in the glorious montage that closes the film; we know, and perhaps Cavalcanti wants us to know, that Fred has found a friend.

The final montage is one of the happiest events of the period in British musical films. The music-halls are saved: time for a drink! The happiness is shared by all the film's main protagonists in a series of tiny vignettes. The most catching moment may be when Jean Kent and Peter De Greef are sitting at a table drinking wine, and cheeky lad Harry Fowler (the epitome of a boy actor in the 1940s) takes a glass and gulps it down. We know that he, too, will grow up into that world of sheer pleasure and uncluttered enjoyment; so it goes on. Naturally, it is left to Tommy Trinder to offer the final toast in champagne which he does directly to the cinema audience. It is highly likely that many of them had never so much as seen a bottle of the stuff, but the refreshment of spirit that Trinder offers the cinema audience is a gift beyond price.

British National scarcely paused for breath after mounting *Heaven is Round the Corner*, and its next project for its lightly operatic ex-Hollywood starlet Leni Lynn was *Give Me the Stars*. To what extent it gave its audience stars is questionable, but it teamed young Lynn with one of music-hall's most amiable old codgers, Will Fyffe. Producer Frederic Zelnik and director Maclean Rogers reunited, with a screenplay by Rogers and Austin Melford based on a story by A. Hilarius and Rudolph Bernauer. Orphaned American song-thrush Toni Martin (Lynn) moves to Britain to be with her hard-drinking, faded music-hall performer uncle Hector MacTavish (Fyffe). Her talents are recognised when she stands in for her 'indisposed' uncle. She finds love with the steadying influence of engineer Jack Ross (Emrys Jones), and sings Kennedy Russell's evocative 'Throughout The Years'. British National reused Lynn for the 1946 operetta *Spring Song*, where she was third-billed below Carol Raye and Peter Graves.

OCTOBER

Various delights await in Ealing's *Fiddlers Three*, a sort of follow-up to Tommy Trinder's naval adventure of 1940 *Sailors Three*. It's a highly enjoyable event, with its frequently witty, even subtle, screenplay by Diana Morgan and Angus Macphail (exampled by the running joke of messengers bringing unwanted news to Nero, delivering it in florid Shakespearean verse before being thrown to the lions), excellent décor by Duncan Sutherland, appealing score by several hands (Mischa Spoliansky, Harry Jacobson and Geoffrey Wright, and lyricists Morgan, Robert Hamer and Roland Blackburn), superb incidental music by Spike Hughes, and the film's three stars – Trinder, Francis L. Sullivan and Frances Day – at their best.

On leave from the Navy, Tommy (Trinder) and 'Professor' (Sonnie Hale) are cycling through the countryside, dreaming of 'Sweet Fanny Adams' (Wright-Blackburn) when they rescue Wren Lydia (Diana Decker) from a marauding motorist. Stopping off at Stonehenge ('Another government housing scheme gone wrong!'), they recall a legend about Midsummer's Night, when a lightning strike will send those struck by it back to the past. They find themselves in AD 43, facing a group of Roman soldiers. 'Funny how you can't get away from ENSA,' says Tommy. Transported to Rome, he and Professor are readied for human sacrifice, while Lydia is to be sold as a slave. The grossly pleasure-loving Nero delights in every excess, and has just had his mother drowned ('Poison's getting so vulgar!'). 'We shall disembowel you the slow way,' he informs them.

Morgan and Macphail stuff the script with sexual innuendo delivered with aplomb by Sullivan and by Day's sultry Poppaea, described by Professor as 'the first glamour girl'. When Professor drags up, Nero thinks he has seen him before. Professor suggests they must have met at a horse race. 'Ah, yes,' replies Nero, 'we did you both ways.' Titus (Ernest Milton), direct from Roman camp, eyes up the soldiers. Every moment in Poppaea's company throws up another innuendo, and her murderous progress through history is beautifully described in 'Caesar's Wife' (Jacobson-Morgan-Hamer). Trinder's impersonation of a glamorous Brazilian Carmen Miranda-type is another highlight, written by Wright. Nero is impressed: 'We create you a Dame of the Roman Empire.'

He watches Poppaea bathing in ass's milk ('You've got more than five inches of milk in that bath, my love'), and she admits 'I'm A Fool About Love' (Spoliansky-Morgan-Hamer). Her handmaiden Thora (Elisabeth Welch) sings 'Drums In My Heart' (Spoliansky), which is perfectly suited to Welch's dark music voice, and redolent of the sort of cabaret numbers Novello wrote for her in his stage musicals. 'Oh,' she pleads in Morgan's yearning lyric, 'send me a lover as tall as a tree.'

Matters, as they must, come to a head with Nero's orgy, doomed to end in the burning of Rome, but not before Tommy has sung the delicious 'You Never Can Tell' (Jacobson-Morgan-Hamer), a number with the breeze of a Noel Gay, blissfully perfect for Trinder. The spectacular firework display arranged by Nero will of course get out of control, even as he plays 'Keep The Home Fires Burning' on his fiddle, while the Britons are got ready for throwing to the lions. Another Midsummer's Night lightning strike sends the 'fiddlers three' back home to wartime Britain, cycling as fast as they can from Stonehenge as the orchestra swells with 'Sweet Fanny Adams'.

The components that make up *Fiddlers Three* are some of the most successfully integrated of the time, in a piece whose optimism never flags. Its constantly wry observations on Britain at war make their mark. The responsibility at last resides with Trinder, surely one of the most underrated comedy performers of British cinema. His natural charm, and an ability to apparently look the camera in the eye, is never in doubt. More importantly, he is as much a romantic as comedic figure (play down the idea though he may). His film career speaks for itself: an actor, a man who seemed not much different from many of the young men who watched him on screen, all those he called 'You lucky people'. He is perhaps unique in British musical films of the period, bringing an instantly recognisable humanity and easy brilliance to whatever he touches. Through the medium of film, he belonged to the people, as he belongs to us now.

NOVEMBER

In the succession of romantic features built around a song that almost every cinemagoer would recognise, Butcher's *My Ain Folk*, produced at Merton Park studios by F. W. Baker, was the creation of that most expert of writers for such sentimental material, Kathleen Butler. Jean Mackenzie (Moira Lister) leaves her idyllic home in the Highlands (her mother is Mabel Constanduros) to take up war work in a Glasgow factory. Her boyfriend Malcolm Keir, in the Merchant Navy, is reported 'missing, believed lost'. Clinging to her belief that he is alive, she manages to stop a strike at the factory, and organises a concert for the workers. Malcolm returns. Some brightness was added by Nicolette Roeg as Betty Stewart.

A bundle of Scottish songs presided over by the well-known tenor Walter Midgley are incorporated: 'Annie Laurie', 'Mary', 'The Road To The Isles', 'Loch Lomond', 'Comin' Thro' The Rye' and, inevitably, the title number, while Lorna Martin chimes in with 'Mountain Lovers' and 'Will Ye No Come Back Again?'. The *MFB* thought it 'rather over-loaded' with such items.[7] Directed by Germain Burger, *My Ain Folk* was successful enough to be reissued in 1946 and 1949.

Breaking from British National with whom he'd worked consistently since 1939, John Baxter was professionally at sea.

> I felt the desire to continue film production but as an independent free from the policies and intrigues of a large organisation. But what would I use for money on the

scale required? I went to visit Flanagan and Allen at the Palace Theatre, where they were playing in the successful revue *Hi-De-Hi*. After I had explained my position Bud said 'Let's make a film!' That's what we did.[8]

If **Dreaming** is not in the front rank of Baxter's work, it has his characteristics. Reginald Purdell's screenplay for this Flanagan-Allen vehicle opens questioningly: 'What, if anything, is a dream?' Here, it's a series of unlikely, subconsciously induced comedic sequences, involving darkest Africa, horse-racing, and the setting up of a British Stage Door Canteen. Flanagan, concussed and taken to hospital, does the dreaming, rather in the manner of a number he shares with Allen, 'Flying Thro' The Rain'.

It would not be a Baxter film without the imprimatur of his philosophy. The War Office is wary of what a Stage Door Canteen might lead on to, preferring a 'refining influence'. 'Sounds a bit poofy to me,' says Flanagan. There is no stopping Baxter inserting a variety programme, with violinist Alfredo Campoli whizzing through a segment of Mendelssohn's Violin Concerto, the Band of the Coldstream Guards, Reginald Foort (placed within Duncan Sutherland's celestial set) pounding his organ with Rossini's overture to *William Tell*, and 'Let's Have Another One' to accompany a tap-dancer. Over-sized Teddy Brown ('Two men for the price of one') does his stuff up and down the xylophone.

The *MFB* appreciated the 'reasonably good crazy comedy', although Flanagan's jokes were 'not very funny and sometimes puerilely vulgar'.[9] The climactic scenes have the stamp of Baxter, as dream fuses with reality when Flanagan and Allen meet themselves on screen. 'You know, I understand they don't speak off-stage,' says Allen, but we know that's ridiculous; their relationship is organically perfect. A visiting officer from the States speaks not only for himself but for Baxter when he tells the watching servicemen, 'You owe a great debt of gratitude to the men and women of the vaudeville stage – which you folks over here call the music-hall.' The echo of George Carney's comment on music-hall performers in *Say It with Flowers* could not be clearer: 'They've always looked after our class.' Baxter ties us to the idea of inarguable camaraderie as Britain's favourite double-act sways through 'Underneath The Arches' and 'Home Town'.

Edgar Anstey wrote that Baxter 'has always been outstanding in his ability to obtain sincere impersonations from professional actors'. He was 'a film-maker of long experience, who combines a strong and proved sense of what the public wants with a social conscience'.[10] The inclusiveness of the cinema audience is at the film's core. Standing at Allen's side, Bud is speaking to the people in the dark:

> So we, ladies and gentlemen, wish to thank you sincerely for your kind listening to our humble efforts to entertain you with a song and a smile now and always. Goodbye, and God bless you!

Formby's association with Columbia-British continued with *He Snoops to Conquer*, directed at the Gainsborough studios by Marcel Varnel. The screenplay by Stephen Black, Howard Irving Young, Norman Lee, Michael Vaughan and Langford Reed seems to be a concerted attempt to underpin the star with some social relevance, the *MFB* describing it as 'a strange mixture of extravagant, not very funny farce and quite effective denunciation of bad housing and corrupt town councils.'[11] One begins to see why the original title, *Asking for Trouble*, was rethought. Here, George is George Gribble, general dogsbody for a dodgy local council. Via various misadventures, our George exposes the council and gets his girl, in this case (still pulling above his weight) Elizabeth Allan. The songs are efficient: Eddie Latta's 'If You Want To Get Your Photo In The Press'; Harry Gifford, Fred E. Cliffe and Formby's 'Hill Billy Willie'; and 'Unconditional Surrender' by Cunningham and Leo Towers.

1945

Flight from Folly
For You Alone
I'll Be Your Sweetheart

I Didn't Do It
Waltz Time
Home Sweet Home

FEBRUARY

After being cast as Dave Willis's companion in *Save a Little Sunshine* (1938) and *Me and My Pal* (1939) and, obliged not to sing, as Formby's girl in the 1939 *Come On George!*, Pat Kirkwood had gone on to *Band Waggon* (1940). Theatre work occupied the rest of the war until her first leading film role in **Flight from Folly**. Kirkwood gives it a passing mention in her autobiography, recalling only that its producer-director Herbert Mason was one of the few directors who didn't end up screaming at her.

The Warner Bros/First National production was written by Basil Woon, Lesley Storm and Katherine Strueby from a story by Edward Goulding. Sue Brown (Kirkwood), a stage performer but working as a nurse, takes on the charge of neurotic composer-cum-playboy Clinton (Hugh Sinclair), joining him in Majorca ('The Majorca' was the film's big number) where he attempts reconciliation with his first wife, before deciding Sue is the better option. Edmundo Ros and His Band, the speciality act Halamar and Konarski, and the idiosyncratic comedy of Sydney Howard in his last screen role provide diversion.

The *Daily Mail* critic offered up the film as 'a tremulous but definite step towards a school of British musicals', on what grounds we can only guess, with the film now believed lost. At the same time, it criticised the designs, exploring 'new regions of banal ugliness', among which the star danced a rhumba that 'evoked Haringay rather more than Havana'. The *Manchester Guardian* voted the picture 'unworthy' of Kirkwood's 'limited but genuine talent', while Halliwell found it a 'leadenly titled and played variation on *Random Harvest* with dreary musical numbers'.[1]

Kirkwood's stage career skidded through several musicals, all commercially unsuccessful: *Chrysanthemum*, Noël Coward's *Ace of Clubs*, *Roundabout* and *Wonderful Town*. Her film career ended in 1956 with a biopic of male impersonator Vesta Tilley, *After the Ball*.

MARCH

Butcher's *For You Alone* remains one of the year's most interesting entries, commended by *Today's Cinema*: 'The passage of time deals kindly with a picture of this pattern – an expertly confected blend of wholesome sentiment, light-hearted comedy, moving pathos and well-loved music.'[2] So successful was this remake of the 1943 *I'll Walk Beside You*, directed by Maclean Rogers and starring the same actress, Lesley Brook, that it was reissued in 1948 and 1949. Butcher's expertise at this sort of thing was unarguable; indeed, *Today's Cinema*'s description may be accepted as the definitive description of Butcher's purpose, steadfastly maintained throughout the war. There may be good reason to claim that Butcher's was, perhaps eminently among the British studios, doing essential war work, a campaign that extended well beyond the end of war. A history of Butcher's contribution to British film history is notably missing from the shelves.

For You Alone was produced by F. W. Baker and directed by Geoffrey Faithfull, the cinematographer of *I'll Walk Beside You*. His only other directorial credit is for the 1946 *I'll Turn To You*. *For You Alone* had an effective screenplay by Montgomery Tully, worked up from a story by the indispensable (at least, to Butcher's) Kathleen Butler. Butcher's and Butler's old trick of titling a film after an old song was in play, this time the work of H. E. Geehl and P. J. O'Reilly, and sung on screen by no less than Heddle Nash. This 'cross-over' between popular parlour music and drama naturally links Butler and Butcher's with the work of John Baxter. This amalgam of classical and 'light' music not only with sentimental drama but with low comedy can of course be found in the work of other studios, not least Mancunian. It establishes a sort of No-Man's-Land of sub-culture that most major studios largely eschewed. For Butcher's, it was home.

The carefully assembled doings of *For You Alone* had Brook as vicar's daughter Katherine, whose brother (Jimmy Hanley) is missing on active service. Found, he returns home with a blinded comrade-in-arms (Manning Whiley) who falls for Katherine. When he ultimately realises she is in love with another (Robert Griffith) he gracefully retires from the scene. Possibly not in sentimental mood, the *MFB* found 'welcome comedy relief' in Hanley, Irene Handl and Dinah Sheridan, 'but the film [at 105 minutes] is much too long, and many scenes of wartime village life, though mildly entertaining, might, with advantage, have been omitted.'[3] The film, not least because of Brook's melancholic gentleness, remains a feather in Butcher's cap.

JUNE

Why as war ended did the British musical film look back on itself, at the history on which it had depended since the beginning of sound, as if suddenly conscious of a debt owed? The 1944 *Champagne Charlie*, and now, at the very end of war, the remarkable *I'll Be Your Sweetheart*; who could resist its brio, its bustling players, its heart-tearing lapses into sentimentality, its score both newly minted (by director Val Guest and composer Manning Sherwin) and old, at its centre a forgotten master-writer of music-hall songs, George Le Brunn. The credentials of Le Brunn, a composer-lyricist who usually worked in collaboration with another, are simply verified by the fact that he wrote over thirty songs for Marie Lloyd, and a host of others for her compatriots. His work survives in a catalogue of numbers in different styles fashioned for the disparate characters of Victorian music-hall, including Gus Elen's 'It's A Great Big Shame' and 'If It Wasn't For The 'Ouses In Between', Dan Leno's 'Young Men Taken In And Done For', and 'Oh! Mr Porter'. This last is sung at the beginning of Gainsborough's film by Margaret Lockwood's music-hall star Edie Story, around whom the screenplay by Guest and Val Valentine, with additional dialogue by Edward Percy, revolves.

Bob Fielding (Michael Rennie) means to be a music publisher, and asks Le Brunn (Moore Marriott) to write a song for him. Another songwriting pair, Kahn and Kelly (Vic Oliver and Jonathan Field), struggle to get their new number 'I'll Be Your Sweetheart' accepted. Their profession is threatened by 'pirates' who are stealing their livelihood by printing their songs cheaply and selling them cheaply in back alleys; soon, an industry of musical piracy threatens to ruin the careers of the music-hall's songwriters.

Edie is trying a new number, 'What Is The Use Of Loving A Girl If The Girl Don't Love You?', when pushy Jim Knight (Peter Graves) tries to persuade her to sing one of his own, 'I'm Banking Everything On You'. Knight's future is as much at risk as that of the others, and they join forces to beat the pirates. Fielding buys 'I'll Be Your Sweetheart' (in fact, written by Harry Dacre). On stage, Edie performs W. H. Penn and A. H. Fitz's 'The Honeysuckle And The Bee', wittily choreographed by Wendy Toye, if a long way from the more authentic music-hall staging of numbers in *Champagne Charlie*. Victorian music-hall never had such complex or enchanting production numbers of this sort – in this, *I'll Be Your Sweetheart* looks to Hollywood. Throughout, Maudie Edwards (playing Mrs Jones) obligingly dubs Lockwood's songs.

Genuine music-hall obtrudes here and there. We see Eugene Stratton and hear him off-camera singing one of the songs Le Brunn wrote for him, 'The Dandy Coloured Coon'. The title number is given a spectacular airing with Lockwood accompanied by natty schoolboys. Songs, so often pushed into the sidings of British musical films, have full play here, no matter that they are sometimes dismissed as unimportant ('Oh, that vulgar tune'); Fielding believes that 'These songs

British musical film with conscience: *I'll Be Your Sweetheart* (1945)

are the life-blood of the public'. Edie and Kahn get to sing Tom Mellor and Charles Collins's 'I Wouldn't Leave My Little Wooden Hut For You'. Kahn and Kelly write 'Mary Anna'. The struggles with copyright continue as Le Brunn lies on his death bed, attended by his devoted wife Liz (perfectly, Muriel George). Poverty-stricken, he dies as his 'Oh, Mr Porter' is played in the street. His eyes fail him at last, as he urges Liz, 'Put another penny in the gas.' The ballet around Edie's 'Sooner Or Later' is another delightful sequence, a precursor of Cecil Beaton's 'Ascot Gavotte' design. Edie tells the music-hall audience of Le Brunn's death, and that he had only £1.07 pence to leave to his wife. Surely, she begs them, they will no longer buy songs from the music publishing pirates? Clutching the manuscript, she sings 'his last song, from his death bed', the uproarious 'Liza Johnson'.

At last, Parliament passes the copyright law, one of its supporters responding, 'Call it gutter music if you choose. I say the time will come when countries will rise and fall by such gutter music, music men may march to, music that may make or break an empire – gutter music.' A happy ending ensues when the pirates are routed and Edie accepts Fielding's proposal of marriage. 'We've won this fight because we were all united,' says Edie, 'songwriters, publishers and artists.' The fight is won not least because of the performances of the purposeful cast, Robert Nesbitt's generous devising of the musical numbers, Toye's inventive choreography and dancing, the orchestrations by Benjamin Frankel and Bob Busby, and the musical direction by Louis Levy. Everything about the British musical film is celebrated here, in a picture that stands alongside *Champagne Charlie* as an example of what it could achieve.

'I'm getting used to his face now,' cries Mrs Tubbs (Hilda Mundy) of her new theatrical lodger, the apparently gormless George Trotter (George Formby). Not surprising, since the face had been a staple of British cinema for a decade. Columbia-British's *I Didn't Do It* had its star accused of the murder of an Australian trapeze artiste. Surely not our George! Of course not: it is a fellow trapeze artiste in 'The Flying Devils'. Howard Irving Young, Stephen Black and Norman Lee's screenplay, with contributions from Peter Fraser and Michael Vaughan, keeps the film, produced and directed at Shepherd's Bush by Marcel Varnel, on its toes. Formby steams through it with supreme professionalism, introducing three songs along well-tried lines: Formby and Fred E. Cliffe's 'I'd Like A Dream Like That When I'm Awake' and 'He Was Such A Daring Young Man', and Cunningham and Leo Towers's 'She's Got Two Of Everything'. Harmless enough, but Varnel might have saved audiences the spectacle of the extras, as ever, mindlessly grinning as soon as a ukulele comes into focus.

There is some arduous comedy wrenched from the permanently inebriated Mr Tubbs (Billy Caryl), but pleasing support from skivvy Merle Tottenham, Wally Patch as Scotland Yard's puzzled Sergeant Carp, and Carl Jaffé as cunning criminal Vance. Our George ogles the blonde Boswell Twins ('Two for the price of one') who get to sing 'Try Try Try Again', but his girlfriend Betty (Marjorie Browne) is weakly drawn. Attempts by a deranged psychiatrist to prove George of unsound mind prove useless. As a vent's dummy informs us, 'It's turned out nice again' (as if we didn't know it would), with the murderer in custody and George a musical star.

JULY

The opening legend of *Waltz Time* defines the territory: 'Once upon a time, in old Vienna, the Waltz was considered a naughty and immoral dance.' This last huzzah for the British musical film operettas of the war could not be more cooked through, wrapped in ribbons and covered with the thickest layer of Royal icing. Its composer, Hans May, revel as he may in the syrupy essence of his by no means unattractive score, was a persistent toiler of his craft, sadly left out of Richard Traubner's masterly history of operetta, perhaps for good reason. That genre, precariously balanced between opera and musical comedy, had persisted throughout British and American film history since the beginning of sound pictures. In *Waltz Time*, obligingly placed at the end of our era, it may well have reached its apogee. Lionel Collier's review for *Picturegoer* enthused:

> This delightful British film takes us back to the days when stage musical comedies provided so much lilting and tuneful music. It is not only excellent entertainment but a positive relief from the ever-prevalent swing.[4]

Webster Booth, the most elegant of British tenors, hooks us from the start. He is a troubadour strolling the streets of the romantic old city as his soprano companion Anne Ziegler (Mrs Booth), soon to begin her own warbling, hands out publicity leaflets for their next gig. May's unmissable musical accent is firmly placed in Alan Stranks's lyric, 'You *Will* Return To Vienna', as if there is no choice but to submit to the place, where

> Still, I hear the thrill of her music
> Still, within my lonely soul I know
> You *will* return to Vienna.
> Sparkle of wine
> Music divine
> Starlight above
> Laughter and love.
> Though you may sigh in Vienna
> Dreams never die in Vienna.
> Hope lights the gloom
> And the lilacs will bloom
> 'Til you return to Vienna.

Considered by the authorities a threat to public morals, the waltz has much to answer for, its absence from court lamented by the royal ladies-in-waiting. 'The waltz at court?' demands Princess Maria (Carol Raye). 'Have you lost all decency? The very idea!' A more likely threat to decency is dashing Count Franz von Hofer (dashing Peter Graves), 'the biggest gad-about in the country'. Maria inherits the crown on her father's death, but her counsellors object to her getting married to von Hofer, although in no doubt about his ability to fill the palace nursery. ('You will carry out the duties of a husband to the best of your ability … which we understand is remarkable!') This dubious endorsement is the closest Montgomery Tully, Henry James and Jack Whittingham's screenplay, based on an idea by Karl Rossier and original story by James, comes to tastelessness. They agree to the marriage only on certain restricting conditions, which von Hofer rejects.

Maria, unable to resist the lure of the waltz, visits a local hot-spot, the Golden Lantern, where romantic intrigue unfolds amidst the whirling dancers. The inn is hosted by George Robey, bluffing his way through a few lines, and interrupted by the strangest of numbers, 'Little White Horse' sung by Kurt Wagener, assisted by a pantomime cow. Booth and Ziegler return in cabaret mode, Booth performing 'Land Of Mine' ('Though I go from Pole to Pole, I hear music deep in my soul') before Ziegler goes into 'The Song That Will Never Die' accompanied by violinist Albert Sandler. Romantic entanglements conclude with the unsurprising marriage of Maria and von Hofer, but not before the film shrugs off its plot for a guest appearance by Richard Tauber's shepherd, sitting at his open window to welcome 'Break Of Day' before stepping out to greet his sheep. Tauber returns for the closing frames, standing in the church balcony among choirboys, reprising his 'Break Of Day' as the lovers tie the knot. We have already been assured of the immortality of a certain dance as Raye and Graves execute 'The Heavenly Waltz'. May's music may lack brilliance and get left at the cinema's door, and the coldness of print suggests that Stranks's lyrics are pretty basic, but the score effectively sustains this lightest of entertainments that (as with much else of its specialised genre) seems almost beyond parody. Geoff Brown suggests that

> Overall, May's mature scores of the mid-1940s are an uneven jumble: often mediocre when the melodic material is straightforwardly lyrical; often imaginative and effective when he aims for expressionist tonal colours […] perhaps deep down May never stopped being the silent cinema veteran of the 1920s who loosely stitched mood music together in chameleonic compilations.[5]

Waltz Time was directed by one of the major émigré directors of the period, Paul L. Stein. Unlikely as it seems, four years later he directed a stage version that meandered around provincial British theatres, despite having written in September 1945 that 'In my opinion the film stinks, but the public is always right.'[6]

AUGUST

It might be unwise to expect Frank Randle to be the one to give the farewell salute to the wartime British musical film; the sort of salute that this seriously mischievous elder statesman of comedy would offer might not get past the censor. But the official ending of hostilities on 2 September 1945 gives us pause to contemplate one final tribute to the British studios' attempt at cheering up the people, and to remember the important contribution of one of the least acknowledged, certainly one of the least praised – Mancunian – made to British social history.

In the Butcher-Mancunian *Home Sweet Home* we can couple this with a recognition of Randle, the socially irresponsible Puck, the wrecker of order, the dismantler of conventional nicety. As the war ends, we do not look to Mancunian, or to any other of the many British studios, for an intellectual response to ever-changing society. We do not need a pronouncement about what has been or what better is to come, although one of the younger characters points out that 'Class distinction didn't count in the war and it mustn't count now'.

Nevertheless, in *Home Sweet Home*, producer-director John E. Blakeley and Arthur Mertz provide a screenplay through which their frequently toothless star may rampage. In this judicious, vibrant, innocent mêlée of low, lower and lowest comedy and high jinks, everything seems to be as it has been before. The casting is impeccable. How could it be otherwise, with the splendid performances of Hilda Bayley and H. F. Maltby as its socially embattled senior citizens, the double-act of Donovan and Bryl, eccentric dancers Arnley and Gloria, and, quite as dapper and no more or less convincing than the other male heroes of British films of the period, the upstanding Tony Pendrell? His heroine is the vivid Nicolette Roeg. Too soon lost to films, Roeg went on to become a notable leading lady of London musicals in the 1960s, including the original productions of *Oliver!*, *Belle*, *Fiorello!* and *Two Cities*. Here, she kicks up her nightclub heels with 'Sally's Not Going Back To The Alley'.

Mancunian, even as the sounds of war shift and quiet, prises open the door of what many of its audience considered 'serious' music, in a schmaltzy garden scena fronted by 'The World's Greatest Duo-Pianists' Rawicz and Landauer, dispensing Liszt's Hungarian Rhapsody No. 2. Before we know it, curtains part to reveal a spectacle of extraordinarily cramped kitsch, in which Helen Hill (backed by a lady harpist, lady violinist and lady cellist, all neatly ringleted) warbles 'The Blue Danube', and the title song. Listening to this, we may hear echoes of George Carney's emotional response to the scrapings of the Gershom Parkington Quintette in John Baxter's 1934 *Music Hall*: 'Makes you think you've got a lot to be thankful for.'

It would be convenient for our purposes if Randle's film career neatly reached its end with *Home Sweet Home* but Randle carried on with *When You Come Home* and *Holidays with Pay* (both 1947), *Somewhere in Politics* (1948), *School for Randle*

(1949) and *It's a Grand Life* (1953) when he bumped into the country's current glamour queen Diana Dors ('Eee, you're a hot'un!). He died in 1957, by which time British musical films had reduced to a trickle, and a feeble trickle at that: a brave remake of *The Good Companions* that tried to ape Hollywood, the semi-American *Let's Be Happy*, the ridiculously 'hip' *Rock You Sinners*, the dull semi-operatic semi-vehicle for Harry Secombe, *Davy*, and the worn-out music-hall biopic *After the Ball*.

The British musical film stood naked before the public, bereft of many of the talents and vivacity that had sustained it from 1929 on. There was no place for the likes of Randle, Lupino, Howes, Matthews, Buchanan. Insurrection, and the unassuming potency of enjoyment, had vanished. 1958 was equally depressing, with Butcher's sporting their own beyond-parody 'hip' 'musical' *The Golden Disc*, Anglo-Amalgamated's 'hip' musical *Six-Five Special* (based on the TV pop series), Tommy Steele's 'hip' musical *The Duke Wore Jeans*, and a lacklustre compendium called *Hello London* through which Sonja Henie skated in Eastman Colour. What British studios had once assiduously produced, for good or ill, was no longer being made.

At such a late moment, is it wise to consider the relationship between the origins of British musical films and the films themselves? In his superb book about Frank Randle, *King Twist*, Jeff Nuttall settles on something so fundamental that I should have recognised it for myself. Thinking of Blakeley's Mancunian films, he writes,

> There were perpetual attempts at scripting, direction, introduction of outside talent, at pretending that the films were, in fact, film. Basically, as idiom went, they were not film. They were music hall.[7]

Although he is writing about Randle's last 'cinematic' assignment, *It's a Grand Life*, Nuttall's observations might apply to anything Randle ever did in the presence of a camera:

> Finally Blakeley sticks his camera in front of a burning car, a gymnasium rub-down table, a boxing ring which, in true music-hall manner, has a curtain rather than an audience behind it. Into these situations Randle and his gang of lunatic urchins, released from the frames of *Film Fun*, scramble about like gobbling insects, striking their poses, pulling their faces, tripping over, falling down, double-taking and smiting one another until the cinema actually begins to smell of sawdust and lions.[8]

The words engraved on Randle's gravestone were taken from a paper he kept always in his wallet.

> I got nothing that I asked for
> But everything I had hoped for.

> Despite myself my prayers were answered.
> I was among all men richly blessed.

Who will remember?

Reg Stone telling us he'll be getting along in *Splinters*; Jessie Matthews's feet squeaking as she dances on the ceiling in *Evergreen*; Lilian Harvey breaking into elfin leaps in *Invitation to the Waltz*; Frances Day entreating us, despite the Depression and unemployment and the state of British slums and the rise of the Nazis, to hang on to happiness in *Oh, Daddy!*; John Garrick and Rene Ray wishing they'd had dancing lessons before filming in the pet shop for *Street Song*; Richard Tauber shepherding sheep in *Waltz Time*; the classic sketches of Arthur Lucan, Robb Wilton, G. S. Melvin, and all the other British comic actors of the day; Vera Pearce exercising in the school gymnasium for *Please Teacher*, or explaining the benefits of Czechoslovakian love in *Yes, Madam?*; Jack Hulbert with or without Cicely Courtneidge and Cicely Courtneidge with or without Jack Hulbert; the closing scene of *Britannia of Billingsgate* and every and any bit of film that has Violet Loraine in it; Stanley Lupino frog-stepping in his valiant attempts to cheer us up; Marie Kendall strangling her vowels and clinging to the ivy, and Mary Clare and Ben Field going off to the seaside on a donkey-shay in *Say It with Flowers*; Jack Whiting giving Jessie Matthews a run for her money in *Sailing Along;* plastered Fred Emney defying the cinema audience to 'Let the people sing!'; Margaret Yarde's chicken impersonation during 'The Londonola' in *Squibs*; Our Gracie waving goodbye; Jack Buchanan constantly bumping into Elsie Randolph; Tom Burke, heartbreak singer, dreaming of Kathleen Mavourneen; Mary Ellis playing Novello's gypsy Melitza so unconvincingly, and Olive Gilbert reduced to walking across the screen in *Glamorous Night*; Bobby Howes celebrating the invention of the Belisha Beacon, doing a cat duet with Wylie Watson and giving ideas to Rene Ray about ham sandwiches; the Sherman Fisher Girls probably not aware of what film they were appearing in; Tommy Trinder saluting the wartime audience with a toast in champagne and young scamp Harry Fowler downing his in one; John Wood and Claire Luce climbing the steps of the lighthouse and breathing on windows in *Over She Goes,* these accompanied by some of the most deft British and American composers of their time, their work lighter and freer than air.

We catch those airs still, breathing on windows and wondering what became of it all.

Notes to the Text

1929 notes
1. Sandy Wilson, *Ivor* (London: Michael Joseph, 1975), p. 53.
2. *Variety*, 18 October 1923.
3. *Variety*, 25 February 1925.
4. Rachael Low, *Film Making in 1930s Britain* (London: George Allen and Unwin, 1985), p. 77.
5. Pamela Hutchinson, *Guardian*, 21 September 2015.
6. *Bioscope*, 20 November 1929, p. 30.
7. *Variety*, 26 February 1930.
8. *Manchester Guardian*, 24 November 1929, p. 20.

1930 notes
1. *Bioscope*, 24 October 1928, p. 60.
2. *Variety*, 26 February 1930.
3. *Bioscope*, 12 February 1930.
4. *Variety*, 9 July 1930.
5. *Variety*, 10 September 1930.
6. *Bioscope*, 5 March 1930, p. 30.
7. *Bioscope*, 19 March 1930, p. 39.
8. Leslie Halliwell, *Halliwell's Film Guide*, 6th edn (London: Paladin, 1988), p. 809.
9. Tim Bergfelder and Christian Cargnelli (editors), *Destination London: German-speaking Emigrés and British Cinema, 1925–1950* (New York and Oxford: Berghahn Books, 2008), p. 205.
10. *Bioscope*, 12 March 1930, p. 43.
11. *Bioscope*, 12 March 1930.
12. *Bioscope*, 5 February 1930, p. 25.
13. Rachael Low, *Film Making in 1930s Britain* (London: George Allen and Unwin, 1985), p. 175.
14. *Bioscope*, 28 May 1930, p. 35.
15. *Bioscope*, 4 June 1930, p. 39.
16. Low, *Film Making in 1930s Britain*, p. 174.
17. David Quinlan, *British Sound Films: The Studio Years 1928–1959* (London: B. T. Batsford, 1984), p. 39.

1931 notes
1. *Bioscope*, 14 January 1931, p. 34.
2. Bennett's novel was subsequently made into the 1968 Broadway musical *Darling of the Day*, with music by Jule Styne.
3. Basil Dean, *Mind's Eye* (London: Hutchinson, 1973), p. 157.
4. *Bioscope*, 15 July 1931, p. 27.
5. *Manchester Guardian*, 10 July 1931, p. 8.
6. *Bioscope*, 4 November 1931, p. 19.

7 Ibid.
8 *Manchester Guardian*, 31 October 1931.
9 'Catch a Fallen Star', BBC1 documentary, 1987.
10 *Bioscope*, 11 November 1931
11 Rachael Low, *Film Making in 1930s Britain* (London: George Allen and Unwin, 1985), p. 134.
12 Mordaunt Hall, *New York Times*, 27 June 1932.
13 *Bioscope*, 1 July 1931, p. 31.
14 *Observer*, 6 December 1931.
15 Low, *Film Making in 1930s Britain*, p. 87.

1932 notes
1 Chili Bouchier, *Shooting Star: The Last of the Silent Film Stars* (London: Atlantis, 1995), p. 74.
2 *Bioscope*, 13 January 1932, p. 14.
3 Frank Nugent, *New York Times*, 6 November 1934.
4 Leslie Halliwell, *Halliwell's Film Guide*, 6th edn (London: Paladin, 1988), p. 566.
5 Vivian Ellis, *I'm on a See-Saw* (London: Michael Joseph, 1953), p. 129.
6 Ibid., p. 130.
7 *Bioscope*, quoted in Allen Eyles and David Meeker (editors), *Missing Believed Lost* (BFI, 1992), p. 42.
8 *Kinematograph Weekly*, quoted in Eyles and Meeker, *Missing Believed Lost*, p. 42.
9 malcolmgsw, *www.imdb.com*.
10 Lord Gibson of the *Financial Times*, quoted in Maude's obituary in the *Independent*, 21 October 1988.
11 *New York Times*, 13 March 1935.
12 Eric Maschwitz, *No Chip on My Shoulder* (London: Herbert Jenkins, 1957), p. 56.
13 *Bioscope*, 30 March 1932.
14 David Shipman, *The Great Movie Stars: The Golden Years* (London: Hamlyn, 1970), p. 409.
15 David Quinlan, *British Sound Films: The Studio Years 1928–1959* (London: B. T. Batsford, 1984), p. 69.
16 *Film Pictorial*, 3 December 1932, p. 19.
17 Steve Chibnall, *Quota Quickies: The Birth of the British 'B' Film* (London: BFI, 2007), p. 216.
18 *Kinematograph Weekly*, 9 June 1932, p. 43.
19 *Lucky Girl* opened at the Shaftesbury Theatre, 14 November 1928, playing for 150 performances.
20 Ellis, *I'm On a See-Saw*, p. 129.
21 Rachael Low, *Film Making in 1930s Britain* (London: George Allen and Unwin, 1985), p. 132.
22 Ibid., p. 118.
23 *Manchester Guardian*, 30 September 1932.
24 Basil Dean, *Mind's Eye* (London: Hutchinson, 1973), p. 166.
25 It should not be forgotten that the memories of those working in show business are not infallible. In her autobiography, Courtneidge mentions *Please Teacher* as one of the films she appeared in during the decade. She didn't.
26 Tim Bergfelder and Christian Cargnelli (editors), *Destination London: German-speaking Emigrés and British Cinema, 1925–50* (New York and Oxford: Berghahn Books, 2008), p. 54.

Notes to Pages 49–71 331

27 Ibid., p. 55.
28 Ibid., p. 50.
29 *New York Times*, 14 April 1933.
30 Juliet Gardiner, *The Thirties: An Intimate History* (London: Harper Press, 2011), p. 666.
31 Michael Thornton, *Jessie Matthews* (London: Hart-Davis, MacGibbon, 1974), p. 98.
32 *Kinematograph Weekly*, quoted in Allen Eyles and David Meeker (editors), *Missing Believed Lost: The Great British Film Search* (London: BFI, 1992), p. 44.
33 Chibnall, *Quota Quickies*, pp. 216–17.

1933 notes

1 *Variety*.
2 *Picturegoer*.
3 *West Australian* (Perth), 8 September 1933.
4 Rachael Low, *Film Making in 1930s Britain* (London: George Allen and Unwin, 1985), p. 146.
5 *Observer*, 19 February 1933, p. 12.
6 J. B. Priestley in conversation with Alan Plater in Yorkshire TV's 1980 documentary *On the Road*.
7 Roy Moseley, *Evergreen: Victor Saville in his Own Words* (Carbondale, IL: Southern Illinois University Press, 2000), p. 66.
8 *Variety*, 3 April 1957.
9 Replacing the originally cast Henry Ainley, subsequently reduced to voicing the introduction.
10 As distinct from the Alan Plater-David Fanshawe television adaptation which broadens the score into a non-concert party context.
11 Michael Balcon, *Michael Balcon Presents … A Lifetime of Films* (London: Hutchinson, 1969), p. 63.
12 Jessie Matthews and Muriel Burgess, *Over My Shoulder* (London: W. H. Allen, 1974), p. 134.
13 Moseley, *Evergreen*, p. 73.
14 David Shipman, *The Great Movie Stars: The Golden Years* (London: Hamlyn, 1970), p. 383.
15 *Sight and Sound*, spring 1933, vol. 2, no. 5, p. 22.
16 The closing words of Priestley's novel.
17 Cicely Courtneidge, *Cicely* (London: Hutchinson, 1953), p. 119.
18 *Observer*, 19 March 1933, p. 14.
19 *Sydney Morning Herald*, 14 August 1933.
20 Henry Kendall, *I Remember Romano's* (London: Macdonald, 1960), pp. 134–5.
21 *Sight and Sound*, summer 1933, p. 59.
22 Shipman, *The Great Movie Stars*, p. 125.
23 I can find no trace of this fact.
24 Letter to *Picturegoer* from Edith Race of Sheffield, 3 March 1934.
25 *Manchester Guardian*, 4 July 1933, p. 9.
26 Ibid.
27 Gervase Hughes, *Composers of Operetta* (London: Macmillan, 1962), p. 152.
28 Mordaunt Hall, *New York Times*, 24 August 1933.
29 Leslie Halliwell, *Leslie Halliwell's Film Guide*, 6th edn (London: Paladin, 1988), p. 107.

30. Bergfelder, Tim, and Cargnelli, Christian (editors), *Destination London: German-speaking Emigrés and British Cinema, 1925–1950* (New York and Oxford: Berghahn Books, 2008), p. 55.
31. Basil Dean, *Mind's Eye* (London: Hutchinson, 1973), p. 203.
32. Bergfelder and Cargnelli, *Destination London*, pp.126–7.
33. Low, *Film Making in 1930s Britain*, p. 167.
34. Michael Thornton, *Daily Mail*, 28 March 2008.
35. *Observer*, 1 October 1933, p. 16.
36. Shipman, *The Great Movie Stars*, p. 84.
37. Low, *Film Making in 1930s Britain*, p. 147.
38. Ibid., p. 119.
39. *Capitol* (Australia), 18 June 1934.
40. *Mirror* (Perth), 30 June 1934.
41. *Australasian*, 23 June 1934.
42. Leslie Halliwell, *Leslie Halliwell's Film Guide*, 6th edn (London: Paladin, 1988), p. 325.
43. Quoted in Allen Eyles and David Meeker (editors), *Missing Believed Lost: The Great British Film Search* (London: BFI, 1992), p. 49.
44. Courtneidge, *Cicely*, p. 214.

1934 notes
1. *Era*, 17 January 1934.
2. Geoff Brown and Tony Aldgate, *The Common Touch: The Films of John Baxter* (London: BFI, 1989), p. 37.
3. *Variety*, 13 February 1934.
4. Leslie Halliwell, *Leslie Halliwell's Film Guide*, 6th edn (London: Paladin, 1988), p. 1115.
5. Gene D. Phillips, *Alfred Hitchcock* (London: Columbus Books, 1984), p. 61.
6. Michael Thornton, *Jessie Matthews* (London: Hart-Davis, MacGibbon, 1974), p. 108.
7. Basil Dean, *Mind's Eye* (London: Hutchinson, 1973), p. 211.
8. Ibid., p. 212.
9. David Shipman, *The Great Movie Stars: The Golden Years* (London: Hamlyn, 1970), p. 191.
10. *New York Times*, 14 January 1935.
11. *Monthly Film Bulletin* (*MFB*), 1934, p. 60.
12. Tim Bergfelder and Christian Cargnelli (editors), *Destination London: German-speaking Emigrés and British Cinema, 1925–1950* (New York and Oxford: Berghahn Books, 2008), p.130.
13. *Variety*, 15 May 1934.
14. James Agate, *Immonent Toys* (London: Jonathan Cape, 1945), p.80.
15. Moseley, Roy, *Evergreen: Victor Saville in his Own Words* (Carbondale, IL: Southern Illinois University Press, 2000), p. 74.
16. *MFB*, 1934, p. 29.
17. *Observer*, 10 June 1934.
18. Dan Navarro, 'The Matthews' Musicals: Enduring Young Charms', *American Classic Screen: Features*, vol. 2, no. 1 (September/October 1977), pp. 37–8.
19. Jessie Matthews and Muriel Burgess, *Over My Shoulder* (London: W. H. Allen, 1974), p. 115.

20. Geoff Brown, 'Vorhaus: A Director Remembered', *Sight and Sound*, winter 1986/87, p. 41.
21. Ibid.
22. Bergfelder and Cargnelli, *Destination London*, p. 204.
23. Steve Chibnall, *Quota Quickies: The Birth of the British 'B' Film* (London: BFI, 2007), pp. 39–40.
24. *MFB*, 1934, p. 42.
25. *MFB*, 1934, p. 48.
26. *Picturegoer Weekly*, 28 July 1934, p. 16.
27. *Jewish Chronicle*, 24 August 1934, p. 34.
28. *MFB*, 1934, p. 79.
29. *International Opera Collector*, vol. 3, p. 105.
30. *MFB*, 1934, p. 60.
31. *MFB*, 1934, p. 57.
32. Dean, *Mind's Eye*, p. 206.
33. Ibid., pp. 204–6.
34. Vincent Brome, *J. B. Priestley* (London: Hamish Hamilton, 1988), p. 157.
35. *Industrial Britain*, directed by Robert Flaherty, Empire Marketing Board Film Unit, 1931.
36. Brome, *J. B. Priestley*, p. 157.
37. Paul Rotha, *Sight and Sound*, autumn 1934.
38. *Mancunian Presents*, documentary film, part I.
39. Craig Lapper, quoted in Philip Martin Williams and David L. Williams, *Hooray for Jollywood: The Life of John E. Blakeley and the Mancunian Film Corporation* (Ashton-under-Lyne: History on your Doorstep, 2001), p. 28.
40. *Variety*, 25 September 1934.
41. *Variety*, 20 November 1934.
42. *MFB*, 1934, p. 67.
43. Roy Moseley,*Evergreen: Victor Saville in his Own Words* (Carbondale, IL: Southern Illinois University Press, 2000), p. 81.
44. *Daily Renter*, 15 November 1934.
45. *MFB*, 1934, p. 117.
46. *MFB*, 1934, p. 103.

1935 notes
1. *MFB*, 1935, p. 23.
2. *MFB*, 1935, p. 11.
3. *Observer*, 17 March 1935, p. 16.
4. *MFB*, 1935, p. 40.
5. Philip Martin Williams and David L. Williams, *Hooray for Jollywood: The Life of John E. Blakeley and the Mancunian Film Corporation* (Ashton-under-Lyne: History on your Doorstep, 2001), pp. 31–2.
6. *MFB*, 1935, p. 53.
7. Ibid.
8. *MFB*, 1935, p. 73.
9. *MFB*, 1935, p. 85.
10. *Observer*, 6 June 1935, p. 14.
11. David Quinlan, *British Sound Films: The Studio Years 1928–1959* (London: Batsford, 1984), p. 102.

12 Basil Dean, *Mind's Eye* (London: Hutchinson, 1973), p. 207.
13 *MFB*, 1935, p. 69.
14 Moseley, Roy, *Evergreen: Victor Saville in his Own Words* (Carbondale, IL: Southern Illinois University Press, 2000), p. 84.
15 *Observer*, 2 February 1936, p. 14.
16 *MFB*, 1935, p. 91.
17 Tim Bergfelder and Christian Cargnelli (editors), *Destination London: German-speaking Emigrés and British Cinema, 1925–1950* (New York and Oxford: Berghahn Books, 2008), p. 132.
18 Ibid., p. 133.
19 Letter from Paul L. Stein to Paul Kohner, 21 May 1937.
20 Letter from Arthur Dent in *The Cinema*, 9 May 1951, p. 27.
21 *MFB*, 1935, p. 104.
22 *Kinematograph Weekly*, 22 August 1935, p. 24.
23 *Era*, 21 August 1935, p. 16.
24 *MFB*, 1935, p. 122.
25 *Observer*, 6 October 1935.
26 *MFB*, 1935, p. 125.
27 *MFB*, 1935, p. 158.
28 Eric Maschwitz, *No Chip on My Shoulder* (London: Herbert Jenkins, 1957), p. 142.
29 *MFB*, 1935, p. 174.
30 *Picturegoer*, 'My Come-Back', 14 June 1935.
31 *Picturegoer*, 10 March 1934.
32 *MFB*, 1935, p. 169.
33 *Observer*, 10 November 1935, p. 14.
34 *Variety*, 27 November 1935.
35 According to Michael Thornton's *Jessie Matthews* (London: Hart-Davis, MacGibbon, 1974), p. 12.
36 Ibid.
37 *MFB*, 1935, p. 192.
38 Rachael Low, *Film Making in 1930s Britain* (London: George Allen and Unwin, 1985), p. 149.
39 *Spectator*, 6 December 1935.
40 Herbert Wilcox, *Twenty-Five Thousand Sunsets* (London, Bodley Head, 1967), p. 92.
41 *MFB*, 1935, p. 178.
42 Mordaunt Hall, *New York Times*, 7 May 1930.
43 Letter from J. Stevens to *Picturegoer*, 4 July 1936.

1936 notes
1 Richard Traubner, *Operetta: A Theatrical History* (London: Victor Gollancz, 1984), p. 336.
2 *MFB*, 1936, p. 7.
3 David Shipman, *The Great Movie Stars: The Golden Years* (London: Hamlyn, 1970), p. 407
4 *Variety*, 7 July 1937.
5 C. A. Lejeune, *Observer*, 31 May 1936, p. 12.
6 *Kinematograph Weekly*, 23 January 1936, p. 31.
7 Ibid.

8. Rachael Low, *Film Making in 1930s Britain* (London: George Allen and Unwin, 1985), p. 164.
9. *MFB*, 1936, p. 82.
10. Basil Dean, *Mind's Eye* (London: Hutchinson, 1973), p. 208.
11. *Manchester Guardian*, 6 March 1936, p. 22.
12. *Manchester Guardian*, 2 June 1936, p.11.
13. Low, *Film Making in 1930s Britain*, p. 200.
14. *Daily Express*, 30 March 1942.
15. *New York Times*, 31 March 1942.
16. *Observer*, 23 February 1936, p. 14.
17. *MFB*, 1936, p. 43.
18. *Observer*, 1 March 1936, p. 14.
19. Tim Bergfelder and Christian Cargnelli (editors), *Destination London: German-speaking Emigrés and British Cinema, 1925–1950* (New York and Oxford: Berghahn Books, 2008), p. 138.
20. *Picturegoer*, 23 May 1936.
21. *MFB*, 1936, p. 41.
22. Moseley, Roy, *Evergreen: Victor Saville in his Own Words* (Carbondale, IL: Southern Illinois University Press, 2000), p. 78.
23. Michael Thornton, *Jessie Matthews* (London: Hart-Davis, MacGibbon, 1974), p. 133.
24. Low, *Film Making in 1930s Britain*, p. 137.
25. *Observer*, 30 August 1936, p. 12.
26. *MFB*, 1936, p. 83.
27. Ibid.
28. *MFB*, 1936, p. 82.
29. *The Times*, 29 December 1932.
30. John Baxter, autobiography, quoted in Geoff Brown and Tony Aldgate, *The Common Touch: The Films of John Baxter* (London: BFI, 1989), p. 54.
31. *MFB*, 1936, p. 83.
32. Billy Milton, *Milton's Paradise Mislaid* (London: Jupiter Books, 1976), p. 130.
33. *MFB*, 1936, p. 100.
34. C. A. Lejeune, *Observer*, 29 November 1936, p. 16.
35. *MFB*, 1936, p. 100.
36. *Sight and Sound*, summer 1936, p. 27.
37. Ibid.
38. Philip Martin Williams and David L. Williams, *Hooray for Jollywood: The Life of John F. Blakeley and the Mancunian Film Corporation* (Ashton-under-Lyne: History on your Doorstep, 2001), p. 32.
39. Low, *Film Making in 1930s Britain*, p.161.
40. *MFB*, 1936, p. 113.
41. David Quinlan, *British Sound Films 1928–1959* (London: B. T. Batsford, 1984), p. 78.
42. Leslie Halliwell, *Seats in All Parts* (London: Granada, 1985), p. 57.
43. Ibid.
44. Low, *Film Making in 1930s Britain*, p. 163.
45. Dean, *Mind's Eye* p. 213.
46. Low, *Film Making in 1930s Britain*, p. 257.
47. Marie Seton, *Paul Robeson* (London: Dennis Dobson, 1958), p. 107.
48. *Manchester Guardian*, 18 September 1936, p. 20.

49 *MFB*, 1936, p. 129.
50 *Kine Weekly*, quoted in Allen Eyles and David Meeker (editors), *Missing Believed Lost* (London: BFI, 1992), p. 69.
51 Low, *Film Making in 1930s Britain*, p. 161.
52 *MFB*, 1936, p. 128.
53 *MFB*, 1936, p. 171.
54 Halliwell, *Halliwell's Film Guide,* 6th edn (London: Paladin, 1988), p. 581.
55 *Observer*, 6 December 1936, p. 14.
56 *Observer*, 4 October 1936, p. 18.
57 Traubner, *Operetta*, p. 282.
58 Ibid., p. 256.
59 *MFB*, 1936, p. 212.
60 *MFB*, 1936, p. 191.
61 *MFB*, 1936, p. 193.
62 Low, *Film Making in 1930s Britain*, pp. 203–4.
63 *Kinematograph Weekly*, 28 January 1932, p. 29.
64 *MFB*, 1936, p. 213.

1937 notes
1 Martin Dibbs, *Radio Fun and the BBC Variety Department, 1922–67* (London: Palgrave Macmillan, 2019), p. 69.
2 Rachael Low, *Film Making in 1930s Britain* (London: George Allen and Unwin, 1985), p. 118.
3 *MFB*, 1937, p. 11.
4 *MFB*, 1937, p. 30.
5 Shipman, *The Great Movie Stars: The Golden Years* (London: Hamlyn, 1970), p. 407.
6 *MFB*, 1937, p. 53.
7 *Manchester Guardian*, 13 April 1937.
8 Quoted in Michael Thornton, *Jessie Matthews* (London: Hart-Davis, MacGibbon, 1974), p. 141.
9 Ibid.
10 *MFB*, 1937, p. 97.
11 Robert V. Kenny, *The Man Who Was Old Mother Riley* (Albany, GA: BearManor Media, 2014), p. 161.
12 *MFB*, 1937, p. 123.
13 *Era*, 10 March, 1937.
14 *Observer*, 18 June 1933.
15 *MFB*, 1937, p. 54.
16 Ibid.
17 Quoted in Allen Eyles and David Meeker (editors), *Missing Believed Lost: The Great British Film Search* (London: BFI, 1992), p. 75.
18 *Observer*, 15 August 1937, p. 11.
19 *MFB*, 1937, p. 56.
20 *MFB*, 1937, p. 77.
21 Jeffrey Richards, *The Age of the Dream Palace: Cinema and Society in 1930s Britain* (London: Tauris, 2010), p. 186.
22 Michael Kilgarriff, *Grace, Beauty and Banjos: Peculiar Lives and Strange Times of Music Hall and Variety Artistes* (London: Oberon Books, 1998), p. 259.

23 *Daily Telegraph* obituary, 11 February 2014.
24 *MFB*, 1937, p. 76.
25 Ibid.
26 Sandy Wilson, *Ivor* (London: Michael Joseph, 1975), p. 203.
27 *Spectator*, quoted in Wilson, *Ivor*, p. 203.
28 *Observer*, 6 June 1937, p. 16.
29 *Sight and Sound*, summer 1937.
30 Barbara Ziereis, 'From "Alien Person" to "Darling Lilli": Lilli Palmer's Roles in British Cinema' in Tim Bergfelder and Christian Cargnelli (editors), *Destination London: German-speaking Emigrés and British Cinema, 1925–1950* (New York and Oxford: Berghahn Books, 2008), p. 174.
31 Radio interview with Robeson.
32 *Kinematograph Weekly*, 8 July, 1937, p. 21.
33 Baxter's unpublished autobiography, *Stepping Stones*.
34 Low, *Film Making in 1930s Britain*, p. 203.
35 *MFB*, 1937, p. 142.
36 *Observer*, 18 July 1937, p. 14.
37 *Variety*, 15 September 1937.
38 Low, *Film Making in 1930s Britain*, p. 244.
39 Matthews talking to an audience in Toronto in 1972.
40 Quoted in Thornton, *Jessie Matthews*, p. 142.
41 *Observer*, 3 October 1937, p. 16.
42 Michael Orme, *Illustrated London News*, 16 October 1937, p. 19.
43 *MFB*, 1937, p. 166.
44 *Variety*, 18 August 1937.
45 *MFB*, 1937, p. 165.
46 David Quinlan, *British Sound Films: The Studio Years 1928–1959* (London: B. T. Batsford, 1984), p. 128.
47 *Variety*, 2 March 1938, p. 25.
48 *Era*, 4 November 1937, p. 16.
49 *Whitstable Times and Herne Bay Herald*, 22 October 1938, p. 2.
50 Kilgarriff, *Grace, Beauty and Banjos*, p. 119.
51 *Today's Cinema*, 30 November 1938.

1938 notes
1 *MFB*, 1938, p. 9.
2 R. B. Marriott, *Era*, 13 January 1938.
3 *MFB*, 1938, p. 37.
4 *Surrey Mirror*, 5 August 1938, p.7.
5 *MFB*, 1938, p. 12.
6 *Observer*, 6 March 1938, p. 14.
7 *MFB*, 1938, p. 11.
8 *Era*, 27 January 1938.
9 Michael Thornton, *Jessie Matthews* (London: Hart-Davis, MacGibbon, 1974), p. 143.
10 *Era*, 11 November 1937, p. 17.
11 *MFB*, 1938, p. 98.
12 Steve Chibnall, *Quota Quickies: The Birth of the British 'B' Film* (London: BFI, 2007), p. 106, quoting *Kinematograph Weekly*, 17 March 1938, p. 34.

13 *MFB*, 1938, p. 76.
14 Michael Kilgarriff, *Grace, Beauty and Banjos: Peculiar Lives and Strange Times of Music Hall and Variety Artistes* (London: Oberon Books, 1998), p. 207.
15 *MFB*, 1938, p. 131.
16 *MFB*, 1938, p. 132.
17 *Variety, Leslie Halliwell's Film Guide*, 5th ed., p. 1125.
18 *New York Times*, 5 July 1938.
19 *Manchester Guardian*, 1 November 1938, p. 13.
20 Rachael Low, *Film Making in 1930s Britain* (London: George Allen and Unwin, 1985), p. 261.
21 Ibid.
22 *Era*, 14 April 1938, p. 4.
23 *MFB*, 1938, p. 65.
24 *Era*, 17 March 1938.
25 *New York Times*, 2 January 1941.
26 *Kinematograph Weekly*, 7 April 1938, p. 28.
27 *Era*, 8 July 1938, p. 16.
28 *Observer*, 21 August 1938, p. 11.
29 *Era*, 30 December 1937, p. 51.
30 *MFB*, 1938, p. 154.
31 *Era*, 21 July 1938, p. 11.
32 *MFB*, 1938, p. 197.
33 *Kinematograph Weekly*, quoted in Philip Martin Williams and David L. Williams, *Hooray for Jollywood: The Life of John E. Blakeley and the Mancunian Film Corporation* (Ashton-under-Lyne: History on your Doorstep, 2001), p. 36.
34 *MFB*, 1938, p. 183.
35 Patricia Kirkwood, *The Time of My Life* (London: Robert Hale, 1999), p. 60.
36 *MFB*, 1938, p. 219.
37 Jeffrey Richards, *The Age of the Dream Palace: Cinema and Society in 1930s Britain* (London: Tauris, 2010), p. 172.
38 *MFB*, 1938, p. 236.
39 C. A. Lejeune, *Observer*, 12 February 1939, p. 12.
40 *People*, 25 June 1939, p. 6.
41 *MFB*, 1938, p. 277.

1939 notes
1 Leslie Baily, *The Gilbert and Sullivan Book* (London: Spring Books, 1966), p. 1.
2 *MFB*, 1939, p. 1.
3 D. Graham Davis, *Gilbert and Sullivan Journal*, quoted in Baily, *The Gilbert and Sullivan Book*, p. 446.
4 *Manchester Guardian*, 12 January 1939, p. 11.
5 *Observer*, 15 January 1939, p. 10.
6 *Manchester Guardian*, 12 January 1939, p. 11.
7 Robert Ross, *The Complete Frankie Howerd* (London: Reynolds and Hearn, 2001), p. 114.
8 *New York Times*, 2 June 1939.
9 *MFB*, 1939, p. 40.
10 Charles Barr, *Ealing Studios* (Oakland, CA: University of California Press, 1998), p. 189.

11 *Observer*, 18 June 1939, p. 12.
12 Adam Wilson, http://www.cineoutsider.com/reviews/dvd/t/trouble_brewing.html.
13 *Variety*, 20 May 1931.
14 Rachael Low, *Film Making in 1930s Britain* (London: George Allen and Unwin, 1985), p. 268.
15 *MFB*, 1939, p. 93.
16 *Manchester Guardian*, 3 August 1939, p. 11.
17 *Observer*, 6 August 1939, p. 7.
18 Michael Kilgarriff, *Grace, Beauty and Banjos: Peculiar Lives and Strange Times of Music Hall and Variety Artistes* (London: Oberon Books, 1998), p. 157.
19 *MFB*, 1939, p. 185.
20 David Shipman, *The Great Movie Stars: The Golden Years* (London: Hamlyn, 1970), p. 209.
21 Jeffrey Richards, *The Age of the Dream Palace: Cinema and Society in 1930s Britain* (London: I. B. Tauris, 2010), p. 203.
22 *Manchester Guardian*, 7 December 1939, p. 12.
23 *MFB*, 1939, p. 200.
24 *Shepton Mallet Journal*, 13 September 1940, p. 2.
25 *St Andrews Citizen*, 1 June 1940.

1940 notes

1 Charles Barr, *Ealing Studios* (Oakland, CA: University of California Press, 1998), p. 20.
2 Dilys Powell, *The Golden Screen* (London: Headline, 1990), p. 31.
3 Phil Morris, *Wales Arts Review*, 12 February 2013.
4 *MFB*, 1940, p. 2.
5 Morris, *Wales Arts Review*, 12 February 2013.
6 *Kinematograph Weekly*, 21 September 1939, p. 10.
7 Ralph Bond, *Close-Up*, September 1933.
8 Geoff Brown and Tony Aldgate, *The Common Touch: The Films of John Baxter* (London: BFI, 1989), p. 71.
9 *MFB*, 1940, p. 2.
10 *Kinematograph Weekly*, 4 January 1940, p. 10.
11 *MFB*, 1940, p. 1.
12 Andy Goulding, blueprintreview.co.uk, 3 July 2012.
13 S. P. Mackenzie, *British War Films 1939–45* (London: Continuum, 2001), p. 196.
14 *MFB*, 1940, p. 54.
15 *Kinematograph Weekly*, 26 September 1940, p. 14.
16 Kitty's instruction was that Arthur's tombstone should read: 'Arthur Lucan, better known and loved by millions of children as Old Mother Riley. Don't cry as you pass by but say a little prayer'. Their son subsequently described 'those vulgar little lines'.
17 *MFB*, 1940, p. 109.
18 John Fisher, *Funny Way to be a Hero* (London: Frederick Muller, 1973), pp. 174–6.
19 Ibid., p. 177.
20 Jeffrey Richards, *The Age of the Dream Palace: Cinema and Society in 1930s Britain* (London: I. B. Tauris, 2010), pp. 192–3.
21 Fisher, *Funny Way to be a Hero*, pp. 167–8.
22 *Kinematograph Weekly*, 29 September 1940, p. 12.
23 *MFB*, 1940, p. 127.

24 *MFB*, 1940, p. 159.
25 *MFB*, 1940, p. 182.

1941 notes
1 David Parkinson, https://www.radiotimes.com/film/ftz5rc/danny-boy/.
2 *MFB*, 1941, p. 55.
3 *MFB*, 1941, p. 81.
4 *MFB*, 1941, p. 113.
5 *MFB*, 1941, p. 130.
6 Shipman, *The Great Movie Stars*, p. 209.

1942 notes
1 Quoted in Geoff Brown and Tony Aldgate, *The Common Touch: The Films of John Baxter* (London: BFI, 1989), p. 86.
2 *MFB*, 1942, p. 29.
3 Vincent Brome, *J. B. Priestley* (London: Hamish Hamilton, 1988), p. 242.
4 Ibid.
5 Brown and Aldgate, *The Common Touch*, p. 88.
6 John Fisher, *Funny Way to be a Hero* (London: Frederick Muller, 1973), p. 198.
7 Michael Kilgarriff, *Grace, Beauty and Banjos: Peculiar Lives and Strange Times of Music Hall and Variety Artistes* (London: Oberon Books, 1998), p. 113.
8 *MFB*, 1942, p. 83.
9 Robert Murphy, *Realism and Tinsel: Cinema and Society in Britain 1939–49* (London: Routledge, 1989), p. 195.
10 David Quinlan, *British Sound Films: The Studio Years 1928–1959* (London: B. T. Batsford, 1984), p. 139.
11 *MFB*, 1942, p. 97.
12 From *Stepping Stones*, quoted in Brown and Aldgate, *The Common Touch*, p. 90.
13 *Kinematograph Weekly*, 8 October 1942, p. 27.
14 *Variety*, 3 December 1941.
15 *MFB*, 1942, p. 126.
16 *MFB*, 1943, p. 1.

1943 notes
1 Denis Gifford, *The Golden Age of Radio: An Illustrated Companion* (London: B. T. Batsford, 1985), p. 133.
2 *MFB*, 1943, p. 13.
3 *MFB*, 1943, p. 26.
4 John Fisher, *Funny Way to be a Hero* (London: Frederick Muller, 1973), p. 105.
5 *MFB*, 1943, p. 38.
6 Dick Fiddy, https://www.radiotimes.com/film/g6gfrk/get-cracking/.
7 Leslie Halliwell, *Leslie Halliwell's Film Guide*, 6th edn (London: Paladin, 1988), p. 395.
8 *MFB*, 1943, p. 25.
9 Ibid.
10 *MFB*, 1943, p. 49.
11 *MFB*, 1943, p. 62.
12 Geoff Brown and Tony Aldgate, *The Common Touch: The Films of John Baxter* (London: BFI, 1989), p. 95.

13 Michael Kilgarriff, *Grace, Beauty and Banjos: Peculiar Lives and Strange Times of Music Hall and Variety Artistes* (London: Oberon Books, 1998), p. 226.
14 Quinlan, *British Sound Films: The Studio Years 1928–1959* (London: B. T. Batsford, 1984), p. 257.
15 *MFB*, 1943, p. 134.
16 *MFB*, 1943, p. 133.
17 *MFB*, 1944, p. 1.

1944 notes

1 Philip Martin Williams and David L. Williams, *Hooray for Jollywood: The Life of John E. Blakeley and the Mancunian Film Corporation* (Ashton-under-Lyne: History on your Doorstep, 2001), p. 51.
2 *MFB*, 1944, p. 27.
3 *MFB*, 1944, p. 13.
4 Ian Aitken, *Alberto Cavalcanti: Realism, Surrealism and National Cinemas* (Trowbridge: Flicks Books, 2000), pp. 142–3.
5 Colin MacInnes, *Sweet Saturday Night* (London: MacGibbon and Kee, 1967), p. 136.
6 M. Willson Disher, *Winkles and Champagne*, p. 19.
7 *MFB*, 1944, p. 127.
8 Quoted in Geoff Brown and Tony Aldgate, *The Common Touch: The Films of John Baxter* (London: BFI, 1989), p. 100.
9 *MFB*, 1944, p. 139.
10 *Spectator*, 17 March 1944.
11 *MFB*, 1945, p. 139.

1945 notes

1 Leslie Halliwell, *Leslie Halliwell's Film Guide*, 6th edn (London: Paladin, 1988), p. 353.
2 *Today's Cinema*, 23 March 1948.
3 *MFB*, 1945, p. 29.
4 *Picturegoer*, 4 August 1945, p. 13.
5 Geoff Brown, 'Music for the People: Escapism and Social Comment in the Work of Hans May and Ernst Meyer', in Tim Bergfelder and Christian Cargnelli (editors), *Destination London: German-speaking Emigrés and British Cinema, 1925–1950* (New York and Oxford: Berghahn Books, 2008), p. 210.
6 Letter from Stein to Paul Kohner of 15 September 1945, quoted in Bergfelder and Cargnelli, *Destination London*, p. 136.
7 Jeff Nuttall, *King Twist* (London: Routledge and Kegan Paul, 1978), p. 52.
8 Ibid., pp. 56–7.

Select Bibliography

Aitken, Ian, *Alberto Cavalcanti: Realism, Surrealism and National Cinemas* (Trowbridge: Flicks Books, 2000)
Aitken, Ian (editor), *The Documentary Film Movement: An Anthology* (Edinburgh: Edinburgh University Press, 1998)
Balcon, Michael, *Michael Balcon Presents … A Lifetime of Films* (London: Hutchinson, 1969)
Barr, Charles (editor), *All Our Yesterdays: 90 Years of British Cinema* (London: BFI, 1986)
Barr, Charles, *Ealing Studios* (Oakland, CA: University of California Press, 1998)
Bergfelder, Tim, and Cargnelli, Christian (editors), *Destination London: German-speaking Emigrés and British Cinema, 1925–1950* (New York and Oxford: Berghahn Books, 2008)
Brome, Vincent, *J. B. Priestley* (London: Hamish Hamilton, 1988)
Brown, Geoff, and Aldgate, Tony, *The Common Touch: The Films of John Baxter* (London: BFI, 1989)
Chapman, James, *The British at War: Cinema, State and Propaganda 1939–45* (London: I. B. Tauris, 2000)
Chibnall, Steve, *Quota Quickies: The Birth of the British 'B' Film* (London: BFI, 2007)
Dean, Basil, *Mind's Eye* (London: Hutchinson, 1973)
Ellis, Vivian, *I'm on a See-Saw* (London: Michael Joseph, 1953)
Eyles, Allen, and Meeker, David (editors), *Missing Believed Lost: The Great British Film Search* (London: BFI, 1992)
Fisher, John, *Funny Way to be a Hero* (London: Frederick Muller, 1973)
Gardiner, Juliet, *The Thirties: An Intimate History* (London: Harper Press, 2011)
Gardiner, Juliet, *Wartime: Britain 1939-45* (London: Review, 2005)
Gifford, Denis, *Entertainers in British Films: A Century of Showbiz in the Cinema* (Westport, CT: Greenwood Press, 1998)
Gifford, Denis, *The British Film Catalogue 1895–1985* (London: David and Charles, 1986)
Gifford, Denis, *The Golden Age of Radio: An Illustrated Companion* (London: B. T. Batsford, 1985)
Gifford, Denis, *The Illustrated Who's Who in British Films* (London: B. T. Batsford, 1979)
Halliwell, Leslie, *Leslie Halliwell's Film Guide*, 6th edn (London: Paladin, 1988)
Halliwell, Leslie, *Seats in All Parts* (London: Granada, 1985)
Kilgarriff, Michael, *Grace, Beauty and Banjos: Peculiar Lives and Strange Times of Music Hall and Variety Artistes* (London: Oberon Books, 1998)

SELECT BIBLIOGRAPHY

Kilgarriff, Michael, *Sing Us One of the Old Songs: A Guide to Popular Song 1860–1920* (Oxford: Oxford University Press, 1998)

Kobal, John, *Gotta Sing, Gotta Dance: A Pictorial History of Film Musicals* (London: Hamlyn, 1971)

Low, Rachael, *Film Making in 1930s Britain* (London: George Allen and Unwin, 1985)

Mackenzie, S. P., *British War Films 1939–45* (London: Continuum, 2001)

Milton, Billy, *Milton's Paradise Mislaid* (London: Jupiter, 1976)

Montgomery, John, *Comedy Films 1894–1954* (London: George Allen and Unwin, 1968)

Moseley, Roy, *Evergreen: Victor Saville in his Own Words* (Carbondale, IL: Southern Illinois University Press, 2000)

Murphy, Robert, *Realism and Tinsel: Cinema and Society in Britain 1939–49* (London: Routledge, 1989)

Overy, Richard, *The Morbid Age: Britain and the Crisis of Civilization* (London: Penguin Books, 2010)

Palmer, Scott, *British Film Actors' Credits, 1895–1987* (North Carolina and London: McFarland, 1988)

Perry, George, *The Great British Picture Show* (London: Hart-Davis, MacGibbon, 1974)

Quinlan, David, *British Sound Films: The Studio Years 1928–1959* (London: B. T. Batsford, 1984)

Richards, Jeffrey, *The Age of the Dream Palace: Cinema and Society in 1930s Britain* (London: I. B. Tauris, 2010)

Richards, Jeffrey (editor), *The Unknown 1930s: An Alternative History of the British Cinema, 1929–1939* (London: I. B. Tauris, 2000)

Shipman, David, *The Great Movie Stars: The Golden Years* (London: Hamlyn, 1970)

Swynnoe, Jan, *The Best Years of British Film Music 1936–1958* (Woodbridge: The Boydell Press, 2002)

Thornton, Michael, *Jessie Matthews* (London: Hart-Davis, MacGibbon, 1974)

Traubner, Richard, *Operetta: A Theatrical History* (London: Victor Gollancz, 1984)

Warren, Patricia, *British Film Studios: An Illustrated History* (London: B. T. Batsford, 1995)

Warren, Patricia, *The British Film Collection 1896–1984: A History of the British Cinema in Pictures* (London: Elm Tree Books, 1984)

Williams, Philip Martin, and Williams, David L., *Hooray for Jollywood: The Life of John E. Blakeley and the Mancunian Film Corporation* (Ashton-under-Lyne: History on your Doorstep, 2001)

Wood, Linda, *British Films 1927–39* (London: BFI, 1986)

Index of Film Titles

Annie Laurie   171
Around the Town   232
Auld Lang Syne   **3–4**, 218
Aunt Sally (film)   45, **79–80**, 109

Ball at Savoy   32, 34, 115, **150**, 189
Balloon Goes Up, The   **293**, 302, 303
Band Waggon   **261–2**, 276, 298, 307, 318
Battle for Music   304–5
Bees in Paradise   291, 300, **307**
Beggar Student, The   **33–4**, 115
Bell-Bottom George   **305**
Beloved Impostor   **159**, 160, 189, 242, 254
Beloved Vagabond, The   31, **177**
Big Business   **23–4**, 190
Big Fella   184, **205–7**
Bitter Sweet   **70–1**, 88, 190
Blossom Time   32, 71, 90, **103–4**, 109, 133, 159, 161
Blue Danube, The   **35–6**, 176
Bob's Your Uncle   279
Boots! Boots!   **87–8**, 123, 173, 238, 263
Born Lucky   **53–5**
Brat, The   **20–1**
Break the News   236
Britannia of Billingsgate   17, **66–9**, 78, 114, 268, 327
Broken Melody, The   19, 38, **96–7**, 182
Broken Rosary, The   112

Café Colette   **187–8**, 298
Calling All Crooks   240
Calling All Stars   **197–8**, 235
Calling the Tune   **171–2**, 183, 268
Candles at Nine   229, **308**
Car of Dreams   44, **135–6**
Cavalcade of Variety   272–3
Champagne Charlie   5, 11, 271, 295, **309–13**, 320, 322

Charing Cross Road   129–30
Cheer Up!   4, 33, 51, 87, 136, **152–4**, 182
Chips   230–1
Chu Chin Chow   2, 91, **102–3**, 182
City of Song   2, **26–7**, 28, 161
Cock o' the North   **129**, 148, 303
Come On George!   98, 180, **254–5**, 318
Come Out of the Pantry   51, **144**, 156
Comets   9–10
Command Performance   190, **215–6**
Congress Dances   **34**, 44, 49, 104, 116
Co-Optimists, The   2, **5–6**, 84, 197, 204, 321
Crook's Tour   270

Dance Band   **128–9**, 208
Danny Boy (1934)   **101**, 129, 148, 252
Danny Boy (1941)   274
Dark Red Roses   **5**, 17
Demobbed   306
Deputy Drummer, The   134–5
Discoveries   253–4
Divine Spark, The   52, **127**
Dodging the Dole   170–1
Down Melody Lane   303
Dreaming   315–6
Dreams Come True   182–3
Dummy Talks, The   297

Early to Bed   71, 74, 116
Elstree Calling   **10–11**, 16, 27, 32, 43, 63, 71, 115, 122, 151, 171, 231, 261
Evensong   65, **111–2**
Evergreen   21, 31, **93–5**, 125, 140, 141, 163, 189, 226, 327
Everybody Dance   180
Everything in Life   172, **184**
Everything Is Rhythm   166

INDEX OF FILM TITLES

Facing the Music (1933)   46, **64–5**, 78, 101, 268
Facing the Music (1941)   275–6
Faithful   159–60
Falling for You   66
Father O'Flynn   140
Feather Your Nest   171, **195–6**
Fiddlers Three   91, 271, **314–5**
Fire Has Been Arranged, A   137
First a Girl   **140–2**, 162, 163
First Mrs Fraser, The   39
Flame of Love, The   14, **15–16**
Flight from Folly   318
Follow Your Star   237–8
For Love of You   75, **79**
For the Love of Mike   **53**, 71, 190, 268
For You Alone   298, **319**
Forget-Me-Not   161–2

Gang Show, The   **200**, 230
Gangway   79, 189, **214–15**, 226
Garrison Follies   **268**, 275
Gay Love   71, **105**
Gert and Daisy Clean Up   **285–6**, 279
Gert and Daisy's Weekend   268, 275, **279**
Get Cracking   296–7
Gipsy Blood   **29–30**, 34, 40, 162
Girl from Maxim's   **74–5**, 106
Girl in the Taxi   **214**, 225
Give Her a Ring   101–2
Give Me the Stars   313
Glamorous Night   **202–3**, 216
Going Gay   **75–6**, 79
Good Companions, The   52, **59–61**, 93, 106, 226, 244, 283, 326
Goodnight, Vienna   **38–9**, 57, 60, 70
Greek Street   17–19
Guilty Melody   172
Gypsy Melody   174, **176**

Happidrome   269, **298**
Happy   86–7
Happy Days Are Here Again   160–1
Happy Ever After   47–9
Harmony Heaven   **13–14**, 25, 27, 50
He Found a Star   276

He Snoops to Conquer   317
Head Over Heels   192–3
Heart's Desire   71, 103, **132–3**, 139, 159, 161
Heat Wave   123–4
Heaven is Round the Corner   307–8
Hello Sweetheart   124–5
Hi Gang!   280, **298**
His Lordship   **40–2**, 55, 171
His Majesty and Co   **118–19**, 225
Hold My Hand   14, 33, 51, 136, 171, 220, **238–9**
Home Sweet Home   325
Honeymoon for Three   **136**, 171, 214
How's Chances?   **98**, 102
Hyde Park Corner   75, **142–3**

I Adore You   78–9
I Didn't Do It   322–3
I Give My Heart   142
I See Ice   195, **229–30**
I Thank You   **276–8**, 291, 307
I'll Be Your Sweetheart   3, 310, **320–2**
I'll Walk Beside You   **298**, 319
In a Monastery Garden   37–8
In Town Tonight   **119–20**, 223
Indiscretions of Eve   40
Intimate Relations   221–2
Invitation to the Waltz   34, **137–8**, 167, 327
It's in the Air   230, **243**
It's in the Bag   279, **303–4**
It's Love Again   71, **162–3**, 192, 226
It's That Man Again   **294**, 298

Jack Ahoy!   42, **85**, 157
Jack of All Trades   42, **157–8**, 204, 268
Jack's the Boy   36, **42–4**, 45, 60, 66, 157, 204
Jimmy Boy   133–4
Just for a Song   17

Kathleen Mavourneen   101, 149, **194–5**, 265, 327
Keep Fit   98, 195, **212**, 229
Keep Smiling   174, **244**

Keep Your Seats, Please   140, 170, **173–4**, 201, 304
Kentucky Minstrels, The   14, 83, 84, **112–13**, 219
Kicking the Moon Around   **235–6**, 239
King Arthur Was a Gentleman   **291–3**, 299
King of Hearts   160
King of the Ritz   62–3

Lambeth Walk, The   251
Land Without Music   161, **179–80**
Lassie from Lancashire   239–40
Last Rose of Summer, The   218–19
Last Waltz, The   182
Laugh It Off   **259–60**, 285
Let George Do It!   195, **263**
Let the People Sing   107, **283–5**, 300
Let's Be Famous   133, 238, **249–50**
Let's Make a Night of It   208–9
Lilac Domino, The   71, 180, **211**, 236
Lily of Killarney, The   19, 38, 71, **81–2**, 182, 204
Lily of Laguna   101, **224–5**, 303
Limelight   **150–1**, 190
Little Damozel, The   57–8
Little Dolly Daydream   235
Live Again   180–1
London Melody   **189–90**, 205
Look Up and Laugh   127–8
Looking on the Bright Side   44, **46**–7
Lord Babs   37
Love Life and Laughter (Fields film)   **89–90**, 93, 106
Love on the Spot   44
Love on Wheels   32, **45**
Love-Mirth-Melody   108–9
Love Race, The   33
Loves of Robert Burns, The   16–17
Lucky Girl   **42**, 106
Lucky to Me   255–6

Mad About Money   182, **223**
Maid Happy   65–6
Maid of the Mountains, The   **45–6**, 64, 77, 102, 182

Marry Me   32, 33, 45, **47**
May Fair Melody   **196–7**, 225, 230, 238
Me and Marlborough   **130–1**, 189
Me and My Pal   242, **248**, 254, 318
Melody and Romance   222–3
Melody of My Heart   112, **162**
Men of Yesterday   134, **164–5**
Midshipmaid, The   52, 61
Mikado, The   **246–8**, 142
Minstrel Boy, The   218
Miss London Ltd.   **299–30**, 307
Mister Cinders   78, 102, **110**, 139, 171, 242
Monte Carlo Madness   **44–5**, 116
Moonlight Sonata   193–4
Mountains o'Mourne   234–5
Much Too Shy   286–7
Murder at the Cabaret   **185–6**, 219
Music Hall   38, 83, 95, **100**, 112, 157, 325
Music Hall Parade   **252**, 272, 303
Music Hath Charms   **138–9,** 166
My Ain Folk   3, **315**
My Heart Is Calling   27, 52, **113–14**, 161
My Irish Molly   201, 224, **224–5**
My Song for You   27, 28, **104–5**
My Song Goes Round the World   66, 98, 114, **109–10**, 161, 167

No Limit   **139–40**, 173

Off the Dole   **123**, 170, 173
Oh, Daddy!   24, 44, **120**, 189, 327
O-Kay for Sound   **202**, 268
Old Mother Riley in Society   195, **264–6**
On the Air   84–5
On Velvet   231
One Exciting Night   308–9
Only Girl, The   **64**, 74, 116
Out of the Blue   **31**, 106
Over She Goes   33, 44, 136, **216–18**, 327
Over the Garden Wall   **98–100**, 268

Pack Up Your Troubles   263–4
Pagliacci   2, 40, 161, **185**, 238
Paradise for Two   174, **220–1**
Penny Paradise   133, **240–1**, 249

INDEX OF FILM TITLES

Penny Pool, The   207–8
Piccadilly Nights   19
Please Teacher   53, 124, 159, **190–2**, 212, 242, 327
Prince of Arcadia   13, **69–70**
Princess Charming   28, 65, **91–3**, 111
Proud Valley, The   257–9
Public Nuisance No 1   158–9

Queen of Hearts   98, **155**, 268
Queen's Affair, The   88

Radio Parade   63–4
Radio Parade of 1935   102, **115–16**
Radio Pirates   121–2
Raise the Roof   12–13
Rhythm in the Air   71, **174**
Rhythm Racketeer   **219**, 223
Rhythm Serenade   301–2
Road House   28, 75, **114–15**, 204
Robber Symphony, The   168–70
Romance in Rhythm   109
Rose of Tralee (1937)   101, **200–2**, 224, 235, 268
Rose of Tralee (1942)   287

Sailing Along   71, 189, **226–9**, 238, 327
Sailors Three   **271–2**, 314
Sally in our Alley   **27–9**, 63, 252
Saturday Night Revue   220
Save a Little Sunshine   **241–2**, 248, 254, 318
Say It with Flowers   38, **82–4**, 265
Say It with Music   **51**, 166
She Knew What She Wanted   166–7
She Shall Have Music   **145–6**, 159
Shipmates o' Mine   14, 101, **163–4**, 171, 182
Shipyard Sally   45, **252–3**
Shooting Stars   219–20
Show Goes On, The   98, **198–9**, 232
Sing as We Go   **106–8**, 128, 204
Sing as You Swing   145, **210–11**, 268
Singing Cop, The   174, 197, **225**, 230, 236
Sky's the Limit, The   221
Sleepless Nights   33, **50–1**

Soft Lights and Sweet Music   **156–7**, 235
Soldiers of the King   28, 45, **61–2**, 66
Somewhere in Camp   **282–3**, 288, 302
Somewhere in Civvies   302
Somewhere in England   **268–9**, 282, 302
Somewhere on Leave   **288–90**, 302
Song at Eventide   71, **101**
Song of Freedom   **174–6**, 184, 205
Song of Soho   13
Song of the Forge   204
Song You Gave Me, The   69, **73–4**, 75, 77, 103, 280
South American George   195, **280–1**
Southern Maid, A   46, 74, **77–8**, 101, 134, 280
Southern Roses   71, **177–9**, 180
Spanish Eyes   23
Spare a Copper   195, **272**, 275
Splinters   **6–8**, 51, 52, 144, 156, 327
Sporting Love   185
Spring in the Air   115
Squibs (series)   12, 19–21, 38, 55, **125–7**, 204, 327
Star Fell from Heaven, A   101, 139, 161, **167–8**
Stars on Parade   101, 129, **148–9**, 201, 252, 265, 272
Stepping Toes   38, 134, **236–7**
Street Singer, The   151, 182, **199–200**, 208
Street Song   19, 96, **121**, 159, 182, 238, 327
Student's Romance, The   131–2
Sunset in Vienna   205
Sunshine Ahead   51, 71, 134, **151–2**
Sunshine Susie   **31–3**, 43, 45, 47, 136
Sweet Devil   225–6

Take My Tip   158, **204–5**, 268, 270
Talking Feet   83, 134, **209–10**, 236
Tell Me Tonight   27, **49–50**, 71, 167
Temptation   **116**, 176
That's a Good Girl   76
Theatre Royal   300–1
There Goes Susie   34, **106**, 115
Things Are Looking Up   **119**, 130, 180, 190
This is the Life   75

This Week of Grace   **71–3**, 89, 128
This'll Make You Whistle   183, 225
Thistledown   197, 223, **230**
Those Were the Days   **95–6**, 214, 268
Trouble Brewing   98, **250–1**
Turned Out Nice Again   195, **275**
Two Hearts in Harmony   146
Two Hearts in Waltz Time   13, 32, **91**

Under the Greenwood Tree   4–5
Under Your Hat   205, **270–1**
Unfinished Symphony, The   52, **90**
Up with the Lark   302–3

Variety   **122**, 303
Variety Hour   145, **197**
Variety Jubilee   295–6
Variety Parade   101, **184**, 252, 272, 303

Wake Up Famous   **188–9**, 268
Waltz Time (1933)   **65**, 196
Waltz Time (1945)   103, **323–4**, 327
Waltzes from Vienna   85–6
We'll Meet Again   301
We'll Smile Again   **288**, 300
We're Going to Be Rich   **232–4**, 244
When Knights Were Bold   51, **155–6**
Where Is This Lady?   34, **51–2**, 75, 115, 174
Why Sailors Leave Home   24–5

Yellow Mask, The   21–3
Yes, Madam?   190, **242–3**, 327
Yes, Mr Brown   **56–7**, 76
You Made Me Love You   77

General Index

Abbott, Margery   246, 263
Abrahám, Paul   32, 56, 116, 150
Ace of Clubs (musical)   318
Ackland, Rodney   244, 271
Acremont, A.   21
Acres, Harry   209, 211
Adams, Stephen   108
Addinsell, Richard   40, 59
Adrienne, Jean   112, 140, 163
Afrique   208, 254
After the Ball (film)   318, 326
Agate, James   93
Ager, Milton   218
Ainley, Henry   39
Aitken, Ian   309
Aked, Muriel   60, 88, 112
Albers, Hans   44, 45
Alexander, Donald   258
All the King's Horses (film)   91
Allan, Elizabeth   317
Allan, Marguerite   4
Allen, Les   123, 124
Allgood, Sara   194
Allinson, Vera   96, 101, 274, 279
Allister, Claud   95, 121
Alpár, Gitta   142, 143, 150, 172, 184
Alvis and Capla   186
Ambrose, Bert   64, 145, 157, 197, 198, 235
Ames, Rosemary   44
Ancelin, Robert   15
And Who is Kissing Me? (film)   221
Ander, Charlotte   45, 65
Andre and Curtis   235
Andrews, Julie   104
Angel, Ernst   45
Angel, Heather   71
Ansell, Eric   185, 206, 207
Anstey, Edgar   107, 316

Apollon, Dave, and His Romantic Serenaders   120
Arabian Night, An (film)   3
Arcadians, The (musical)   2, 9
Arch, Albert H.   19
Argyle, John   101, 122, 161, 194, 235, 244
Arkell, Reginald   182, 199
Arliss, Leslie   85, 114, 123, 180, 254, 280
Arnaud, Yvonne   91, 93, 214
Arnaut Brothers   252, 273
Arnley and Gloria   303, 325
Arnold, Doris   151
Arnold, Franz   120, 159
Arnold, Tom   298
Arthur, John L.   286, 290, 305
Arthurs, George   21
As You Are (play)   275
Asaf, George   263
Asche, Oscar   91
Ascot, Duggie   109
Ascot, Hazel   83, 134, 209–10, 236–7
Asher, Irving   78, 124, 159, 230
Ashton, Frederick   228
Askey, Arthur   6, 261, 271, 276–8, 291–3, 299–300, 307
Asking for Trouble (proposed film title)   229
Aspidistras, The   279
Asquith, Anthony   90
Astaire, Fred   13, 51, 53, 66, 74, 87, 94, 154, 166, 167, 189, 215, 228
Astell, Betty   75, 84, 158
Asther, Nils   172
Atkins, Robert   276
Atkinson, Frank   164, 199, 221
Atlantic (film)   16
Aumonier, Stacy   5
Aussey, Germaine   159
Australian Air Aces   252, 273, 303

Autumn Crocus (film)   202
Ayer, Nat D.   260
Aylmer, Felix   127, 236

Babes in Arms (film)   307
Bach, Ernest   120
Bach, Johann Sebastian   232
Bacharach, Jacques   86
Backstage (film)   150
Bacon, Max   157, 293, 299, 307
Bacon, Peggy   275
Baecker, Otto   15
Baily, Leslie   246
Baker, Belle   130
Baker, F. W.   263, 272, 276, 279, 282, 285, 287, 298, 303, 315, 319
Baker, George   65, 151
Baker, Kenny   246
Balalaika Choral Orchestra   16
Balanchine, George   5
Balatons, The   266
Balcon, Michael   17, 32, 33, 37, 43, 45, 52, 60, 61, 66, 80, 91, 93, 94, 102, 111, 114, 119, 120,123, 125, 127, 130, 135, 141, 157, 180, 189, 192, 204, 250, 272, 275, 309
Balfour, Betty   11, 20–1, 55, 94, 125–7
Ballets Russe   5
Banjo (novel)   207
Banks, Monty   24, 53, 66, 77, 125, 139, 155, 173, 195, 198, 232, 244, 252
Bannerman, Margaret   98
Barbour, Roy   170
Barclay, George   162
Barclay, John   247
Bard, Ben   2
Barker, Eric   231
Barnes, Barry K.   170
Barr-Carson, A.   274
Barr, Charles   250, 258
Barr, Ida   160–1, 260, 284
Barrie, Wendy   52, 101, 106
Barringer, Michael   38, 84, 152, 297
Barry, Gerald   166, 182
Barry, Joan   39
Barry, Jules   62

Barry, T.,   5
Barrymore, John   280
Barrymore, Lionel   222
Bart, Lionel   291
Bart, Una   312
Barter, John   133, 151
Bartlett, Michael   211
Barty, Jack   209, 236
Baskcomb, A. W.   52, 60
Bath, Hubert   4, 86
Baxter, Jane   103
Baxter, John   19, 38, 51, 68, 71, 82, 84, 95, 100, 106, 107, 112, 113, 125, 129, 133, 151, 161, 164, 209–10, 219, 231, 235–7, 259, 264–6, 270, 283, 288, 300–1, 305, 315, 316, 319, 325
Bayley, Hilda   287, 298, 325
Be Mine Tonight (film)   49
Beaton, Cecil   142, 322
Beaudine, William   146, 195
Becke, Eve   252, 273, 303
Bedford, Harry   95
Beery, Noah   180
Beery, Wallace   208
Beethoven, Ludwig van   193, 304
Bega Four, The   198
Behrens, Ken   266
Bellas, Ivor   163
Belle (musical)   113, 325
Bellings' Dogs,   231
Bellini, Vincenzo   127
Bells Are Ringing (musical)   101, 102
Bells Go Down, The (film)   271
Bells of St Mary's, The (film)   219
Bellwood, Bessie   310, 312
Belmore, Bertha   87, 98, 190, 191, 208, 217, 239, 242, 254
Benatzky, Ralph   45, 70
Benedict, Julius   2, 81, 82
Bennett, Albert   65
Bennett, Arnold   27
Bennett, Billy   115, 197
Bennett, Charles   105
Bennett, Emery   308
Bennett, Joan Sterndale   89
Benson, Ivy   297

GENERAL INDEX

Benson, Richard   104, 113, 127, 135
Bentley, Thomas   13, 50, 95, 139, 167, 248, 255, 265, 272
Beresford, Maurice   46
Bergen, Paul   40
Berger, Ludwig   71
Bergö, Aino   230
Berkeley, Busby   14, 79, 239, 273
Berkeley, Reginald   16, 20, 42
Berlin, Irving   31, 51, 260
Bernard, Peter   25
Bernauer, Rudolph   177, 180, 211, 313
Berners, Lord   312
Bernhardt, Kurt (Curtis)   177, 214
Berry, W. H.   132, 139, 167, 168
Berthomieu, André   214
Bertini and the Tower Blackpool Band   171
Bettinson, Ralph Gilbert   19
Betts, Ernest,   180
Beville, Richard   63
Bickerton, F. H.   161
Bidmead, Charlotte   310
Big Ben Calling (film)   122
Big Broadcast (film)   50
Billy Reid's Accordion Band   220
Billy the Kid Versus Dracula (film)   195
Billy's Spanish Love Spasm (film)   231
Bing Boys Are Here, The (revue)   69, 296
Binner, Margery   60
Bird, Richard   138, 298
Birt, Dan   161
Birth of a Nation (film)   182
Bittner, Julius   86
Bizet, Georges   29, 30, 162, 218
Black and White Minstrel Show, The (stage and TV revue)   113
Black, Edward   202, 261, 276, 280, 291, 294, 299, 307
Black, George   202, 207, 240
Black, Jean   266
Black, Stephen   317, 322
Black, Tom Campbell   184
Blackburn, Roland   314
Blackmail (film)   3, 39
Blain, Kenneth   299
Blair, Barbara   239, 255

Blakeley, John E.   2, 29, 87, 109, 123, 170, 207, 240, 269, 282, 288, 290, 302, 306, 325–6
Blane, Kenneth   261
Blech, Leo   109
Blitz! (musical)   291
Blomfield, Derek   164
Blonde Dream, A (film)   116
Blondie of the Follies (film)   50
Blow, Sydney   52
Blowes, Daisy *see* Howard, Jenny
Blue Angel, The (film)   44, 64
Blue Train, The (musical)   74
Blum, Roger   45
Bobby Get Your Gun (musical)   190
Bogetti, Vera   222
Bohème, La (opera)   111
Bohemian Girl, The   1–2
Boland, Bridget   259, 276
Bolton, George   279
Bolton, Guy   79, 86, 183
Bolton, Reg   220
Bolváry, Géza von   91
Bond, Ralph   259
Bonn, Issy   254
Booth, Webster   109, 151, 168–9, 220, 306, 323
Borell, Louis   192
Borer, Mary Cathcart   264
Boston, Frank   96
Boswell Twins   322
Bouchier, Chili   35, 36, 57, 160, 177, 179, 196, 218, 225, 276
Boucicault, Dion   81
Boucicault, Nina   71
Boulanger, George   309
Boult, Adrian   304
Boulton, Matthew   160
Bowman, Patricia   202
Box, Elton   305
Boxall, Harold   298
Boy Friend, The (musical)   222
Boyd, Dorothy   2
Boyer, Charles   64
Boyer, Ronnie   188
Boys Will Be Boys (film)   195

Boys Will Be Girls (film)   25
Braddell, Maurice   71, 89
Bradley, Buddy   94, 95, 115, 137, 183, 192, 214, 228, 291
Bradshaw, Frederick   183
Braham, Philip   5, 39
Braithwaite, Warwick   304
Brandon, Philip   290, 298, 303
Brandt, Edward   14
Brandt, Ivan   161
Braun, Kurt   98
Brecht, Bertolt   65, 185
Brettel, Colette   81
Brewis, Lawrence   116
Bright Eyes (film)   12
Brilliant, Alfredda   258
Brisson, Carl   3, 13, 69–70, 91
Bristow, Billie   105
Britten, Benjamin   258
Brodszky, Nicholas   172
Brome, Vincent   127, 283
Brook, Clive   301
Brook, Lesley   287, 295, 298, 319
Brooke, Hugh   202, 208, 217
Brooks, Marjorie   183
Brooks, Mel   124
Brooks, Phyllis   255
Brosnan, Gerald   234
Brough, Peter   272
Brown on Resolution (film)   125
Brown, Geoff   15, 96, 112, 260, 285, 300, 324
Brown, Jacques   281
Brown, Lena   250
Brown, Melville   223
Brown, Nancy   46, 78
Brown, Teddy   10, 11, 40, 122, 184, 316
Browne, K. R. G.   75, 190, 242
Browne, Marjorie   239, 323
Browne, Sam   198
Browne, Samuel Gibson   146
Browne, Thomas   240
Bruce, Toni Edgar   290
Brune, Gabrielle   276
Brunel, Adrian   10, 122
Bryant, Jimmy   100

Bryce, Alex   244
Buchanan, Jack   39, 56–7, 76, 144, 151, 155–6, 183, 188, 221, 225–6, 236, 298, 326, 327
Buchel, Philip   43, 158, 204, 221, 276, 239
Buck and Bubbles   198
Bull, Donald   183
Bulldog Jack (film)   42, 157
Bunn, Alfred   2
Bunting, James   115
Burchell, Sidney   260
Burdon, Albert   123, 124, 167, 171, 238
Burford, Roger   103, 128, 133, 138, 142, 185
Burger, Germain   287, 315
Buried Alive (novel)   27
Burke, Thomas (Tom)   29, 140, 194, 245, 327
Burleigh, Harry   259
Burnaby, Dave   5, 84, 197, 204, 231, 235, 245, 327
Burne, Nancy   65, 101
Burnell, Helen   10
Burns, David   109
Burns, Robert   16–17
Burrell, Daisy   218
Burrows, Rex   231
Busby, Bob   115, 291, 322
Bushell, Anthony   52, 62
Bushman, Francis X   1
Butcher, Ernest   236, 304
Butler, Jack   208, 240
Butler, Kathleen   268, 276, 279, 285, 295, 298, 315, 319
Butler, Ralph   234
Butter and Egg Man, The (play)   124
By Appointment (operetta)   134
Byrd, Bretton   60, 214
Byrd, Jack   166
Byrd, John   219

Cage Me a Peacock (musical)   235
Calgary Brothers   159
Calthrop, Dion Clayton   78
Calthrop, Donald   10, 23, 71, 107, 127, 188

GENERAL INDEX

Calvert, Phyllis   263
Camelot (film)   4
Camels Are Coming, The (film)   42, 157
Cameron, Alan   218
Campbell-Hunter, Roma   229, 261
Campbell, Ivar   98, 122, 195
Campbell, Sheila   195
Campion, Cyril   253
Campoli, Alfredo   119, 236, 316
Cannon, Esma   304
Cantor, Eddie   50
Careless Rapture (operetta)   101
Cargnelli, Christian   74, 132, 133, 159
Carissima (stage musical)   15
Carl Rosa Opera Company   65
Carlisle, Elsie   63
Carlton, Gina   182
Carlton, Harry   12, 13, 17
Carlyle Cousins   53, 79
Carmen (operetta and film)   29, 162, 216
Carmen Jones (film)   162
Carminati, Tullio   190, 205
Carney, George   84, 100, 122, 129, 165, 209, 235, 255, 316, 325
Carnival (film)   36
Carnival Time in Venice (film)   79
Carol, King of Romania   203
Carpenter, Constance   17
Carr, Jane   84, 125, 222
Carr, Michael   202, 208, 217, 220, 232, 235, 238, 301, 308
Carré, Michael   20
Carroll, Eddie   209
Carroll, Nancy   144
Carry on London (film)   189
Carson Sisters   120
Carson, Charles   97, 104, 138, 162, 177, 188, 297
Carsons, The   266
Carstairs, John Paddy   44, 105, 239, 251, 272, 276
Carter, Audrey   105
Carter, Desmond   17, 21, 32, 33, 47, 98, 129, 139, 142, 152, 217, 221, 239
Carter, James A.   97, 137, 145
Carter, Julius   306

Carter, Waveney   105
Cartland, Barbara   103
Caruso, Enrico   199, 132
Caryl, Billy   240, 322
Casanova (operetta)   45
Castle, Hugh   15
Castling, Harry   198
Catley, Gwen   288, 300
Cavalcade (play)   57
Cavalcanti, Alberto   11, 258, 309–13
Cavanagh, Paul   188
Ceballos, Larry   223
Chamberlain, Neville   188, 257, 260
Champagne (film)   12
Chandler, Helen   90, 115
Chaplin, Charles   155, 248, 268
Chapman, Edward   127, 258, 275
Chapman, Eve   100
Charell, Erik   32
Charig, Phil   42, 76
Charles, Hughie   290
Charlot Girls   10, 11
Chelsea Nights (film)   3
Chester, Betty   2
Chevalier, Albert   125
Chevalier, Maurice   50, 122, 149, 177, 199, 236
Cheyney, Peter   134
Chibnall, Steve   40, 42, 55, 98, 231
Chick Farr and Farland   186
Chinese Bungalow, The (film)   39
Chirgwin, G. H.   113
Chisholm, Robert   140
Chopin, Frédéric   37, 194, 210, 218
Christians, Mady   64
Chrysanthemum (musical)   318
Chrystal, Belle   238
Church, Gilbert   81
Churchill, Diana   242, 243, 275
Churchill, Sarah   276
Claff, Lionel   109
Clair, René   32, 236
Claire, Bernice   146
Clancey, Vernon   220, 241, 248
Clapham and Dwyer   63, 85, 115, 197, 211
Clare, Mary   83, 327

Clare, Phyllis   109
Clarence, O. B.   160, 279
Clarke, Jack   33
Clarke, Leslie   313
Clarke, T. E. B.   312
Clarke, Trilby   14
Clein, John   146
Clements, John   127
Cliff, Laddie   5, 6, 33, 87, 185, 217
Cliffe, Frank E.   140, 174, 196, 212, 229, 243, 250, 254, 263, 269, 272, 286, 287, 297, 317, 322
Clifford, John   297
Climbing High (film)   229
Clinton-Baddeley, V. C.   40
Clitheroe, Jimmy   287, 301
Clo-Clo (operetta)   182
Clowes, St John Legh   305
Clown Must Laugh, A (film)   185
Clutsam, G. H.   103, 133, 207
Clyde, June   129, 145, 180, 208, 221
Coal Face (film)   258
Coates, Eric   119
Coborn, Charles   84, 234, 295
Cochran Young Ladies   79
Cochrane, Peggy   174
Cocktail (film)   70
Cogan, Robertson   298
Coke, Peter   244
Coldstream Guards   296, 316
Coleman, Wilson   100
Coleridge, Ethel   240
Colin, Jean   223, 247, 260, 279
Colleen Bawn, The (play)   81
Collier, Lionel   323
Collins, Charles   322
Collins, Jose   46, 64, 78, 182, 234
Collins, Lottie   234
Collins, Walter R.   60
Collins, Winnie   22
Collinson and Dean   231
Collinson, Francis M.   22
Columbia Choir   231
Comden, Betty   101
Come Out of the Kitchen (novel)   144
Comer, Dave   23

Comfort, Lance   265, 301
Common Touch, The (film)   83, 107
Compton, Fay   86, 101
Cone School Girls   236
Connelly, Reginald   75, 116, 151
Connor, Tommie   113, 290, 309
Conrad, Barbara   57
Conselman, William   244
Constance, Lilyan and Mayo   160
Constanduros, Mabel   63, 295, 298, 315
Conyngham, Fred   40, 150, 159, 167, 189, 201, 202, 218, 287
Cool Mikado, The (film)   247
Cooper, Jack   157
Corbett, Leonora   45, 132
Corduroy Diplomat, The (play)   160
Corfield, John   239, 259, 270, 276
Cornelia and Eddie   235
Corona Kids   184, 273
Coslow, Sam   120, 144, 162
Cotton, Billy   39, 122, 252, 273, 303
Cottrill, Jack   88
Courant, Curt   26, 153, 167
Courtenay, Syd   24, 166, 211
Courtneidge, Cicely   28, 42–3, 49, 61–2, 66, 79–80, 85, 119, 130–1, 158, 180, 189, 190, 204–5, 270–1, 327
Courtney, Scott   204
Coward, Noël   31, 40, 57, 58, 70–1, 88, 318
Cowell, Simon   253
Cox and Box (operetta)   71
Cox, Desmond   305
Cradock, Fanny   137
Crawford, Mimi   3
Crazy Gang, The   202
Creighton, Walter   177
Crest of the Wave (musical)   101
Creswell, Peter   305
Crier, Gordon   261
Croom-Johnson, Austen   156
Crosby, Bing   50
Crossley, Syd   17, 98, 155, 241
Crowther, Bosley   236
Currie, Finlay   232
Curzon, George   146

GENERAL INDEX

Cutts, Graham   44, 46, 120, 208, 217
Cuvillier, Charles   211

D'Abbes, Ingram   174, 185, 207, 232
D'Oyly Carte Opera Company   112, 246–7
D'Ye Ken John Peel? (film)   38, 71, 182, 204
Dacre, Harry   3, 320
Dagenham Girl Pipers   210
Dale, Ernest   302
Dale, Shirley   34
Dall, Evelyn   157, 197, 211, 235, 236, 276, 291, 299
Dalmora Can-Can Dancers   145
Daly, Jack   194
Daly, Mark   100, 106, 164
Dampier, Claude   115, 145, 167, 211
Dancing Boy (novel)   159
Dancing Years, The (musical)   202
Dand, C. H.   26
Dandridge, Dorothy   162
Dandy Dick (film)   195
Dangerous Corner (play)   106
Daniels, Bebe   73, 77, 280
Darewski, Herman   23
Darling, I Love You (musical)   134
Darling, W. Scott   78
Darrieux, Danielle   225, 226
Darvell, Evelyn   297
Darvelle and Shires   260
Daumery, John (Jean)   98
Dave Apollon and His Romantic Serenaders   120
Davenport, Pem   226
David, H. W.   23
David, Worton   21
Davies, Betty Ann   167, 234
Davies, Edna   13, 23
Davies, Glyn   254
Davies, Irving   59
Davies, Jack   115, 128, 133, 139, 167 (and Junior, 139)
Davies, Marion   50
Davis, Joan   166, 298
Davis, Redd   197, 253, 293

Davy (film)   326
Dawe, Cedric   131, 208
Dawson, Peter   202, 230
Day of the Triffids, The (film)   69
Day, Dorothy   287
Day, Frances   24, 31, 39, 74, 91, 116, 120, 158, 182, 183, 189, 214, 314, 327
de Bear, Archie   63
de Casalis, Jeanne   10, 63
de Courville, Albert   52, 75, 119, 129, 251
De Croisset, Francis   192, 204
de Forest, Lee   2
De Greef, Peter   310, 313
de Grünwald, Anatole   150, 253
de Létraz, Jean   45
De Marguenat, Jean   199
de Vesci, Vina   174
Dean, Basil   29, 44, 46, 47, 71, 87 –9, 106, 127, 139, 155, 173, 198, 212, 229, 240, 243
Deane, Tessa   122, 295
Deans, Marjorie   101, 167, 194, 301
Dearden, Basil   263, 272
Death at Broadcasting House (film)   89
Decker, Diana   314
Deighton, Howard   146
del Riego, Teresa   83
Delafield, E. M.   193
DeMille, Cecil B.   280
Dempsey, Sean   194
Dench, Judi   59
Denham, Reginald   171, 183
Denis, Jean   134
Dent, Arthur   133
Desert Song, The (operetta)   46
Desmond, Florence   28, 29, 63, 105, 140, 174, 235, 236
Desni, Tamara   66, 98
Deutsch, Oscar   210
Deutschmeister, Friedrich   172
Deverell, John   214
Dexter, Peggy   288, 300
Dickens, Charles   47, 50, 84
Dickens, Stafford   52, 116, 119, 135, 180, 190, 216, 221, 237
Dickinson, Thorold   39, 76

GENERAL INDEX

Dickson, Dorothy   101, 274
Dietrich, Marlene   268
Dighton, John   263, 272, 310
Diplomatic Lover, The (film)   98
Disher, Maurice Willson   310
Disney, Walt   19
Dix, Dorothy   39
Dix, Marion   180
Dixon, Mort   129
Doble, Frances   5
Dolin, Anton   5, 138
Dolman, Richard   44, 46, 60, 160, 179
Donat, Robert   224
Donizetti, Gaetano   161
Donleavy, Brian   232
Donohue, Jack   174, 197, 221, 225, 230, 237, 241, 244
Donovan and Bryl   325
Donovan, Dan   138
Doris and Her Zebra   171
Dors, Diana   205, 271, 326
Doss House (film)   82, 83, 107, 165, 236, 259, 260, 265, 288, 300
Double Your Money (TV series)   222
Dover's Duke of York School   236
Doyle, Bunny   276
Drake, Charlie   44
Drayton, Alfred   37, 120, 128, 131
Drinkwater, John   103
Driver, Betty   88, 240, 241, 250, 276
Driver, Edgar   100, 236, 260
Dryhurst, Edward   296, 301, 305
du Garde Peach, L.   91, 102, 133, 139, 180, 222, 296
Dubarry, Die (operetta)   142
Dudley, Ernest   239
Dudley, John   246
Duke Wore Jeans, The (film)   326
Duke, Ivy   173
Duke, Vernon   21
Dumb Dora Discovers Tobacco (film)   188
Dumont, Margaret   239
Duna, Steffi   40, 185
Dunstan, Eric   89
Dupont, Ewald André   15
Duprez, Fred   176, 219

Durante, Jimmy   77, 115, 180
Dyrenforth, James   125, 174, 196, 207, 223, 225, 230

Eastern Valley (film)   258
Eckersley, Roger   139
Eddy, Nelson   71, 97, 182, 225
Edgar, Marriott   125, 202, 261, 278, 280, 291, 300, 307
Edgar, Percy   160
Edmunds, Robert   91, 104, 113, 146, 195, 251
Educated Evans (film)   195
Edward VIII   203
Edwards, Bob   261
Edwards, Henry   125, 204
Edwards, Maudie   320
Ege, Henrik N.   87, 175, 206, 208
Eggerth, Marta   51, 52, 90, 98, 113, 127, 183
Eichberg, Richard   15
Eight Black Streaks   113
Elder, Clarence   15, 87, 104, 115, 131, 137, 139, 142, 208
Elen, Gus   295, 320
Elgar, Edward   304
Elliott, G. H.   95, 100, 113, 210, 225
Elliott, Gerald   167
Elliott, Leslie   244
Ellis, Mary   91, 189, 203, 327
Ellis, Patricia   221
Ellis, Peter   39
Ellis, Vivian   31, 36–7, 43, 60, 66, 74, 98, 99, 102, 110, 158, 171, 271
Elsie, Lily   74, 248
Elton, Arthur   107
Elvey, Maurice   28, 37, 61, 71, 82, 89, 91, 105, 114, 123, 156, 222, 270
Elwin, Maurice   239
Emary, Barbara K.   236, 264, 266, 270, 283, 288
Emerald, Nell   71, 186
Emerton, Roy   207
Emmett, E. V. H.   296
Emney, Fred   208, 239, 284, 327
Emo, E. W.   98, 221

GENERAL INDEX

Endor, Chick   146
Engel, Samuel E.   232
England, Paul   2, 3, 63, 78, 145
English Journey (J. B. Priestley)   59, 106
English, Robert   166
Ervine, St John Greer   39
Esdaile, Alfred   222
Esmond, Annie   242, 284
Esmond, Carl   103, 111, 138
Esway, Alexander   139
Ettlinger, Don   252
Evans, Edith   111
Evans, Maurice   12
Evans, Norman   306
Evans, Rex   9
Everest, Barbara   254
Everything Happens to Me (film)   174
Ewer, Monica   276
Eyton, Frank   47, 50, 105, 119, 135, 136, 152, 214, 217, 250, 261, 271, 278, 283, 312, 313

Face at the Window, The (film)   78
Fag End (film)   188
Fagan, Gideon   218
Fairbanks, Douglas   280
Fairbrother, Sydney   105, 201
Fairfax, Lance   30, 34
Fairlie, Gerard   85,
Faithfull, Geoffrey   298, 319
Falkner, Keith   102, 174, 196–7, 223, 225, 230, 238
Fancey, E. J.   293, 303
Fancourt, Darrell   247
Fanshawe, David   59
Farewell to Love (film)   26
Farmer's Wife, The (film)   17
Farnum, Dorothy   111
Farrar, David   274
Farrar, Gwen   2, 159
Farrell, Charles   193
Farrell, Charlie   146
Faust (opera)   29, 65, 151, 225
Fay, W. G.   194, 244
Faye, Randall   13
Feher, Friedrich   168

Feher, Hans   168
Feiner, Ruth   168
Feldman, Victor   300
Fellner, Herman   65, 158, 159
Fenn, F.   214
Ferrars, Helen   55
Feydeau, Georges   74
Fiddy, Dick   296
Field, Ben   83, 89, 100, 327
Field, Jonathan   320
Fielding, Daisy L.   234
Fielding, Guy   229, 308
Fields, Gracie   3, 24, 27–9, 46–7, 60, 71–3, 87, 89–90, 98, 106–8, 120, 127–8, 155, 170, 173, 174, 198–9, 232–4, 241, 244, 252–3, 268, 271, 290, 327
Fields, Tommy   128, 207, 244, 252
Finglass, Tom E.   295
Fiorello! (musical)   325
Fire Maidens from Outer Space (film)   307
Firth, Anne   305
Fisher, Daisy   119
Fisher, John   268, 285, 296
Fisher, Richard   305
Fitz, A. H.   320
Fitzgerald, Gerald (Jerry)   116, 220
Fitzgerald, Patricia   29
Fitzpatrick, James A.   218
Fitzsimmons, Maureen *see* O'Hara, Maureen
Five Charladies, The   157
Flanagan (Bud) and Allen (Chesney)   137, 197, 202, 225, 288, 300–1, 316
Fledermaus, Die (opera)   65
Fleming, Brandon   162
Flemyng, Robert   192
Fletcher, Jimmy   157
Flotsam and Jetsam   197
Flynn, Errol   36, 78, 268
Flynn, Howard   234
Fogwell, Reginald   13, 70, 91, 185, 186
Fol de Rols, The (concert party)   6
Foort, Reginald   316
Forbes-Robertson, Frank   101, 274
Ford, John   258

Ford, Victor   90
Ford, Wallace   223
Forde, Culley   308
Forde, Florrie   11, 83, 125, 239, 263, 295
Forde, Walter   8, 37, 43, 85, 102, 180, 235, 250, 272, 294, 308
Foreman Went to France, The (film)   271
Forest, Frank   79
Forever and a Day (film)   229
Formby, Beryl   87, 88, 123, 140, 173, 174, 250
Formby, George   3, 24, 87–8, 98, 123, 139–40, 170, 171, 173–4, 180, 195–6, 201, 212, 215, 229–30, 238, 241, 243, 250–1, 254–5, 261, 263, 268, 269, 271, 272, 275, 276, 280–1, 286–7, 289, 290, 296–7, 299, 301, 304, 305, 317, 318, 322–3
Forst, Willi   70, 73, 90
Forsythe, Seaman and Farrell   278
Foulke, Carl   116
Four Flash Devils, The   157
Four Franks, The   208
Four Mills Brothers, The   211
Fowler, Harry   313, 327
Fox, Roy   122
Foy, Nita   23
Frago, Sandor   244
Frakson, José   160
Francis, Bernard   222
Francis, Jack   209, 236
Franck, Paul   56
Frank Lee's Tara Ceilidh Band   194
Frank, Bruno   133
Frankau, Ronald   115, 286
Frankel, Benjamin (Ben)   115, 139, 276, 322
Franklin, Dave   309
Franks, Frank E.   252, 273
Fraser, Peter   305, 308, 322
Fraser–Simson, Harold   45, 77, 78
Frederick, Cecil   298
Freeland, Thornton   220, 239
French, Elsie   279
French, Harold   78, 79, 98, 137
French, Leslie   122

French, Percy   201, 234, 274
Freshman, William   19, 202, 239, 242
Friedman, Leo   266
Friese-Greene, Claude   4, 116, 138, 142
Friml, Rudolf   70
Fritsch, Willy   34, 47, 71
Fuller, Leslie   24–5
Funny Face (musical)   166
Furber, Douglas   36, 42, 43, 45, 49, 56, 60, 66, 76, 144, 155, 156, 221
Fyffe, Will   11, 87, 160, 165, 171, 308, 313
Fyffe, Will, Jnr.   11

Gaál, Béla   135
Gadd, Renee   87
Gaffney, Marjorie   93, 130, 141, 192, 200, 205
Gaiety Girls, The (film)   220
Gallone, Carmine   26, 27, 63, 75, 76, 79, 91, 113, 127
Galvani, Dino   37, 187
Gamble, Tom   273
Gangelin, Paul   121
Ganjou Brothers and Juanita   296
Garat, Henri   214
Garbo, Greta   105, 236
Gardiner, Reginald   63
Gardner, Joan   161
Garland, Judy   95, 280
Garmes, Lee   221
Garrick, John   82, 96, 102, 118, 121, 163, 180, 182, 218, 219, 238, 327
Gartman, Max   19
Gärtner, Henry (Heinrich)   15
Gatti, E.   211
Gaucho Tango Orchestra   39
Gawthorne, Peter   43, 260, 261
Gay Divorcee, The (film)   102
Gay, Noel   50, 52, 61, 63, 64, 77, 87, 119, 130, 152, 196, 239, 242, 250, 251, 255, 256, 261, 271, 278, 283, 312, 314
Geehl, Henry   101, 319
Geneen, Sasha   9
George in Civvy Street (film)   250
George, Henry W. *see* Lane, Lupino
George, Muriel   281, 297, 320

GENERAL INDEX

Georges Bizet (film)   218
Georgian Singers, The   260
Geraghty, Thomas J. (Tom)   139, 166, 173, 235
Geraldo (Gerald Walcon Bright)   151, 260, 291
Gerrard, Gene   31, 42, 106, 160, 188–9
Gershwin, George   146, 166
Gershwin, Ira   166, 256
Ghost Train, The (film)   43, 276
Ghoul, The (film)   101
Giacalone, Alberto   161
Gibbons, Carroll   7, 24, 46, 79, 109, 125, 198
Gibbs, Harry   285
Gibson, Kathleen   218, 219
Gideon, Melville   5–6
Gielgud, John   59, 60
Gielgud, Val   188
Gifford, Denis   189, 294
Gifford, Harry   174, 196, 212, 243, 250, 254, 263, 269, 272, 287, 317
Gigli, Beniamino   161–2
Gilbert and Sullivan   6, 71, 113, 142, 246–8, 3
Gilbert, Jean   45, 214
Gilbert, Michael   308
Gilbert, Olive   203, 327
Gill, Gwenllian   160
Gilliat, Sidney   4, 43, 66, 84, 85, 102, 113, 204, 270
Gillie, Jean   183, 214, 225, 226
Gilling, John   267
Gilman, Frank   202
Girl of the Golden West, The (opera)   232
Gish, Dorothy   16
Glamour Girl (film)   188
Glen, John   194
Glory, Marie   32
Glynne, Angela   287
Glynne, Mary   59
God in the Garden, The (film)   37
God's Clay (film)   275
Godal, Edward   230
Goddard, Alf   281
Goehr, G. Walter   138

Goldberg, Heinz   45
Golden Disc, The (film)   326
Golding, Louis   258
Goldini, Horace   149
Goldschmidt, Isidore   177
Goldsmith, Ralph   19
Gonella, Nat   184, 211
Goodhart, Al   124, 125, 135, 137, 141, 143, 144, 156, 158, 183, 190, 204, 205, 214, 219, 239
Goodner, Carol   132
Gordon Ray Girls   208
Gordon, Barbara   291
Gordon, Hal   155
Gordon, Leslie Howard   5, 19, 39, 222
Gordon, Mack   180, 192
Gorst, Eldon   206
Gossage, John   183
Gottfurcht, Fritz   214
Goulding, Alfred   8, 166
Goulding, Andy   263
Goulding, Edward   318
Gounod, Charles   64, 104, 151, 225, 232
Gow, Neil   177, 211
Gow, Ronald   207
Graetz, Paul   132, 135
Graham, Garrett   65
Graham, Harry   74, 78, 98, 239
Graham, Malcolm   218
Grahame, Margot   56, 69, 78, 79, 97
Grainger, Percy   172
Granger, Stewart   99
Granichstaedten, Bruno   88
Grant, Cary   50
Grant, Ian   298
Grant, James Edward   232
Granville, Sydney   247
Graves, George   95, 167, 168
Graves, Peter   292, 293, 299, 307, 313, 320, 324
Gravey, Fernand   70, 71, 88
Gray, Donald   291
Gray, Hugh   161
Gray, Sally   152, 153, 188, 217, 220, 239, 251
Greed of William Hart, The (film)   201

Green, Adolph   101
Green, Hughie   122, 222–3, 252, 253
Green, L.   271
Green, Martyn   247
Greenbaum, Mutz   68, 120
Greene, Barbara   193
Greene, Graham   78, 144, 162, 192, 203, 215, 309
Greenwell, Peter   113
Greenwood, Edwin   6, 33, 45
Greenwood, Walter   139, 286
Gregory, Charles   304, 305
Grenfell, Joyce   59
Gréville, Edmond T.   176
Grey, Clifford   37, 52, 53, 61, 63, 65, 73, 75, 77, 101, 109, 110, 129, 130, 131, 133, 138, 155, 179, 211, 239, 242, 243, 251, 255
Grey, Mary   119
Grey, Teddy   109
Grieg, Edward   304
Griffies, Ethel   194
Griffith, D. W.   182
Griffith, Robert   319
Grimaldi, Joseph   164, 300
Grossmith, George   91, 93
Grossmith, Lawrence   204, 214
Grosz, Wilhelm   119, 220
Groves, Fred   28
Grune, Karl   185
Grünwald, Alfred   150
Guest, Val   152, 154, 159, 167, 202, 261, 278, 280, 291, 299, 307, 320
Guissart, René   226
Gundrey, Gareth   17
Gunn, Gilbert   241, 248
Gwenn, Edmund   50, 59, 71, 86, 115, 240, 241
Gynt, Greta   270, 294

Hackett, Walter   114, 143
Hackney, W. Devenport   188
Hagen, Julius   23, 37, 38, 81, 82, 96, 100, 101, 112, 113, 125, 137, 145, 176
Hahm, Alfred   86
Haid, Liane   70, 73

Haines, William (Will E.)   28, 46, 90, 108, 128, 155, 198, 199, 214, 229, 244, 293, 303
Halamar and Konarski   318
Hale, Binnie   75, 110, 142, 143, 242
Hale, Robert   163
Hale, Sonnie   49, 60, 71, 86, 94, 104, 114, 140, 141, 163, 192, 214–15, 226, 228, 229, 277, 314
Hall Davis, Lilian   17
Hall, Henry   138, 145, 166
Hall, Stuart   14
Halliwell, Leslie   15, 85, 173, 180, 296, 318
Halman, Ella   247
Halstan, Margaret   34
Hambourg, Mark   210
Hamer, Robert   314
Hamilton, Neil   179, 184, 216
Hammerstein, Oscar II   146, 162, 228, 256
Hammond, Kay   31, 68
Hanbury, Victor   34, 52, 106, 115, 150, 159
Handl, Irene   298, 304, 319
Handley, Tommy   10, 11, 294
Hankinson, Michael   96, 216
Hanley, James F.   129
Hanley, Jimmy   319
Happiest Days of Your Life, The (film)   267
Harding, John F.   223
Harding, Lynn   191
Hardt-Warden, Bruno   131
Hardwicke, Cedric   172
Hardy, Sam   79
Hardy, Thomas   4
Hare, Doris   254
Hare, Robertson   120, 135, 158
Harker, Gordon   10, 68, 75, 114, 125, 143
Harling, W. Franke   144
Harlow, John   267, 308
Harmonica Band   151
Harper, Jimmy   46, 90, 108, 128, 155, 198, 199, 229, 244
Harris, 'Wee' Georgie   115, 220
Harris, Charles   185
Harris, Jack   146, 208, 209

GENERAL INDEX 361

Harris, Vernon   261
Harrison, Kathleen   254, 287
Harrison, Syd and Max   149
Hart, June   129
Hart, Lorenz   93
Hartley, Paul   146
Hartnell, Norman   102, 279
Hartnell, William   51
Harvel, John   33
Harvey, Al and Bob   232
Harvey, Lilian   34, 47–9, 64, 137, 167, 327
Harvey, Lola   24
Hassall, Christopher   202
Hastings, Warren   298
Havelock-Allan, Anthony   251
Hawkins, Jack   60
Hawtrey, Charles   222
Hay, Ian   52, 130, 173
Hay, Will   95, 115, 146, 195, 214, 266, 280
Haye, Helen   71, 73
Hayes, Patricia   297
Hayman, Joe   231
Hayward, Lydia   70
Hayward, Milton   264
Hazell, Derna *see* Hazell, Hy,
Hazell, Hy   297
He Loved an Actress (film)   223
He Wanted Adventure (musical)   190
Hearne, Richard   299
Hearts of Humanity (film)   83, 134, 265
Heimann *see* Heymann, Werner R.
Hellman, Sam   232
Hello London (film)   326
Helm, Brigitte   26, 35–6
Helmore, William   12
Henie, Sonja   326
Henley, Rosina   ?
Henry IV (play)   261
Henry, Ben   301, 308
Henshaw, Bobby   273
Henson, Leslie   75, 120
Hepburn, John   222
Hepburn, Katharine   236
Hepworth, Ronnie   101, 129
Herbert, A. P.   28, 65
Here Comes the Bride (musical)   23

Hermmann, Bernard   85
Herrmann, Willi   15
Heughan, William   210
Hewer, John   310
Heygate, John   64
Heymann, Werner R.   34, 45, 71, 177
Hi-De-Hi (revue)   316
Hilarius, A.   307, 313
Hildegarde   139
Hill, Helen   325
Hill, Ronald   40
Hill, Sinclair   5, 17, 39, 66, 143, 216, 237
Hippler, Fritz   103
Hippodrome Girls   151
Hirschfield, Ludwig   56
Hiscott, Leslie S.   105, 137, 145
Hislop, Joseph   16–17
History of Mr Polly, The (film)   167
Hitchcock, Alfred   3, 10, 12, 17, 28, 33, 39, 85–6, 114, 143, 270
Hitler, Adolf   45, 176, 179, 188, 203, 248, 252, 259, 263, 304
Hobbs, Jack   33, 135, 221, 243, 222
Hoey, Dennis   60, 82, 96
Hoey, Iris   96, 208
Hoffe, Monckton   4, 15, 57, 70, 88, 185, 189
Hoffman, Al   124, 125, 135, 137, 141, 143, 144, 156, 158, 183, 190, 204, 205, 214, 218, 219, 239
Hogan, Michael   88, 204, 235, 250
Holidays with Pay (film)   325
Hollaender, Friedrich   64
Holland, Jack   129
Holland's Magyar Band   186
Holles, Anthony   66, 69
Holloway, Dorothy   174
Holloway, Stanley   5, 6, 82, 108, 114, 119, 125, 204, 310, 312
Holmes, Leslie   40, 42, 79, 196, 151
Holmes, Phillips   127
Holy Matrimony (film)   27
Honey (film)   144
Honri, Percy   82, 89
Hooper, R. S.   139
Hope-Bell, Norman   204

Hope, Maidie   183
Hope, Vida   310
Hopkins Manuscript, The (novel)   118
Hore-Belisha, Leslie   191
Horton, Edward Everett   62
Hot Mikado, The (operetta)   247
Housing Problems (film)   107
Houston Sisters   160, 303
How Green Was My Valley (film)   258
Howard, Helen   197
Howard, Jenny   170
Howard, Keble   37
Howard, Norah   89, 135
Howard, Sydney   7, 252, 318
Howarth, Gyula   90
Howerd, Frankie   247
Howes, Bobby   13, 21, 24, 37, 53, 98–100, 110, 124, 190, 191, 226, 242, 243, 326, 327
Hueffer, Oliver Madox   40
Hughes, Gervase   70
Hughes, Harry   65, 78, 101, 112, 234
Hughes, Roddy   152, 154
Hughes, Spike   314
Hulbert, Claude   63, 74, 85, 124, 272, 297
Hulbert, Jack   10, 32, 36, 42–4, 45, 49, 60, 61, 66, 85, 157, 188, 204–5, 220–1, 270–1, 327
Hume, Benita   127
Humperdinck, Engelbert   64
Hunter, Alberta   116
Hunter, Ian   28, 47
Huntington, Lawrence   109
Hurst, Brian Desmond   202
Hutch (Leslie Hutchinson)   24, 129, 159, 298, 303
Hutcheson, David   109, 183, 255
Huth, Harold   204
Hutter, Richard   131, 211
Hutton, Clayton   221
Hyde, Pat   149
Hyden, Walford   187
Hylton, Jack   145, 146, 261, 305
Hylton, Mrs Jack   184, 273
Hyson, Carl   136, 152
Hyson, Dorothy   76, 272

I Lived with You (film)   73, 89
I Lost My Heart in Heidelberg (film)   131
I'll Turn to You (film)   319
Ilf, Elie   173, 304
Immortal Gentleman, The (film)   231
Imperfect Lady, The (film)   119
In an Old World Garden (film)   3
Infatuation (film)   10
Intolerance (film)   182
Ireland, Anthony   23
Irving, Ellis   295
Irving, Ernest   44, 243, 259, 312
Isabel and Emma   266
It Ain't Half Hot, Mum (TV)   7
It Always Rains on Sunday (film)   167
It's a Grand Life (film)   326

Jack Lewis's Singing Scholars   208
Jackley, Nat   306
Jackman, Hugh   188
Jackson, Freda   235
Jackson, Jack   209
Jackson, Jerome (Jerry)   40, 55, 123
Jacobson, Harry   314
Jacoby, Hans   106
Jacques, Hattie   267
Jaffé, Carl   322
Jail Birds (film)   123
James, Henry   324
James, Jimmy   149
Jaray, Hans   150
Jardine, Betty   291
Java's Tzigane Band   160
Jay, Harriet   156
Jazz Singer, The (film)   1
Jeans, Ursula   73
Jenbach, B.   211
Jenkins, Meg   304
Jenkins, Warren   122
Jenkinson, Philip   108
Jepson, Selwyn   75, 79, 143, 226
Jerome, William   129
Jessie James Meets Frankenstein's Daughter (film)   195
Jewell, Jimmy   301
Jill Darling (musical)   158

GENERAL INDEX

Johns, Mervyn   204
Johnson, Celia   59
Johnston, Arthur   226
Joie de Vivre (musical)   74
Jolly Roger (operetta)   40
Jolson, Al   80
Jones, Emrys   313
Jones, Griffith   141
Jones, Guy   161, 194, 235, 265
Jones, Hal   7
Jones, Howard   24
Jones, Jack   257
Jones, Mai   259
Jones, Trefor   88
Jope-Slade, Christine   67
Jordan, Herberte   298
Jory, Victor   203
Joshua, Lyn   259
Journey's End (play)   7
Joyce, Eileen   304
Juanita (film)   176
Judgement Deferred (film)   83
Julias Ladies Choir   260
Jumel, Betty   306
Junge, Alfred   68, 94, 95, 104, 111, 114, 131, 162, 163, 192, 226, 228, 276
Juno and the Paycock (play)   201
Justice, James Robertson   310

Kálmán, Emmerich   150
Kane, Robert T.   232, 252
Kanturek, Otto   131, 185, 217
Karina, Vadio and Hertz   157, 219–20
Karloff, Boris   101
Kate Plus Ten (film)   188
Kaufman, George S.   124
Kaufmann, Jonas   104
Kavanagh, Pat   218
Kavanagh, Ted   294
Kay, Katya and Kay   197
Keaton, Buster   77
Keller Hall Military Band   120
Kellino, W. P.   81
Kelly, Kathleen   133, 134
Kemble, Harry   269
Kemedi, Alexander   244

Kemm, Jean   15
Kendall, Henry   63, 73
Kendall, Marie   11, 84, 161, 327
Kendall, Victor   45, 51, 241
Kendall, William   183, 226
Kennedy, Hamilton   220
Kennedy, Jimmy   202, 208, 217, 220, 232, 235, 238, 309, 308
Kennedy, Margaret   301, 308
Kenney, Horace   129, 300
Kenny, Robert   194
Kent, Jean   294, 299, 307, 310, 312, 313
Kern, Jerome   70, 228
Kern, Sam   293
Kernel, W.   221
Kerr, Fred   52
Kerr, Geoffrey   167, 225, 236
Kester, Max   93
Ketèlbey, Albert   37, 38, 101
Keyes, Gladys and Clay   42, 129
Keys, Nelson   7, 156, 189
Kid from Spain, The (film)   50
Kidd, Bert and Michael   161
Kiepura, Jan   26–7, 28, 49–50, 70, 104–5, 113–14, 161
Kilgarriff, Michael   223, 232, 254, 286
Kimmins, Anthony   98, 118, 155, 173, 195, 198, 212, 229, 230, 243, 250, 254, 271
King of the Castle (film)   37
King Twist (book)   326
King-Hall, Stephen   52
King, George   78
King, Hetty   61, 141
King, Jack   65
King, Reginald   301
King's Rhapsody (film)   36, 76, 88, 202
Kirby, Joyce   196
Kirkwood, Pat   241, 242, 248, 254, 261, 318
Kiss Me, Sergeant (film)   24, 25
Kistemaecker, Henri   63
Kitchin, Jack   212, 254
Klaren, George   45
Knepler, Paul   142, 307
Knight, Esmond   86

Knight, June   211, 236
Knoblock, Edward   102, 111, 193
Knoles, Harley   2
Knowles, Patric   131
Knox, Collie   139
Koady, Harry   266
Königin, Die (operetta)   88
Korda, Alexander   74, 161, 220
Korda, Vincent   74
Korda, Zoltan   161
Korngold, Erich Wolfgang   86
Korris, Harry   269, 282, 288, 290, 298
Kortner, Fritz   102, 111, 112, 185
Koselka, Fritz   180
Krausz, Michael   47
Kreisler, Fritz   167
Kruger, Otto   203
Kyte, Sydney   157, 220

L-Shaped Room, The (film)   271
L'Africaine (opera)   161
L'elisir d'amore (opera)   161
la Fosse, Lorraine   162
La Rue, Danny   7
Labarr, Marta   150, 225, 236
Lachman, Harry   13, 21
Lady Vanishes, The (film)   270
Lai Founs   297
Laidlaw, Betty   219
Lambert, Constant   304
Lamont, Molly   42
Lancashire Luck (film)   207
Lanchester, Elsa   10
Land of Smiles, The (operetta)   102
Lane, Lupino   21, 22, 33, 45, 77, 78, 134, 136, 251, 302
Lang, Fritz   35, 94, 102
Langford, Gladys   50
Langton, Basil   218
Lantz, Adolf   15
Lanza, Mario   50
László, Vadnay   135
Latin Love (film)   19
Latta, Eddie   263, 275, 286, 297, 317
Lauder, Harry   3, 4
Laughton, Charles   10, 222

Launder, Frank   4, 13, 53, 65, 77, 84, 86, 95, 142, 270
Laurel and Hardy   77, 109, 268
Laurence, Margery   139
Lawrence, Brian   145, 211
Lawrence, Edwin   52
Lawson, Mary   122, 137
Lawson, Wilfrid   101, 274
Laye, Evelyn   28, 65, 91–3, 111–12
Layton, Turner   157
Le Breton, Flora   9
le Brocke, Betty   119
Le Brunn, George   320–2
Le Cocq, Stephanie   192
Le Gouriadec, Loïc   236
Lee-Thompson, J.   59
Lee, Alfred   312
Lee, Anna   51, 123
Lee, Bert   31, 42, 73, 75, 190, 199, 202, 234, 239, 242, 243
Lee, F. W.   297
Lee, Norman   115, 161, 194, 241, 242, 248, 280, 317, 322
Lee, Rowland V.   44
Lehár, Franz   52, 150, 182–3
Lehmann, Beatrix   308
Leigh, Rowland   34, 71, 142
Leigh, Vivien   128
Leigh, Walter   40
Leister, Frederick   291
Lejeune, C. A.   61, 65, 95, 127, 132, 135, 141, 158, 159, 163, 168, 180, 204, 211, 215, 226, 247, 250
Lengyel, Melchior   116
Lenner, Anne   268
Leno, Dan   320
Leon, Harry   28, 46, 108
Leoncavallo, Ruggero   185
Leroy, Irving   176
Leslie-Smith, Kenneth   174, 196, 223, 225, 230
Leslie, Dudley   167, 202
Leslie, Fred   53
Lest We Forget (film)   165
Lester-Smith, J.   297
Let's Be Happy (film)   326

GENERAL INDEX

Letting in the Sunshine (film)   171, 238
Leuthege, E. B.   98
Levis, Carroll   253–4
Levy, Benn W.   90, 93, 94
Levy, Louis   17, 52, 86, 272, 322
Lewin, J. D.   204
Lewis, Cecil   29, 40
Lewis, Idris   12, 103
Lewis, James E.   184
Lewis, Martin   19
Lewis, Ray   189
Leybourne, George   310–13
Liebmann, Robert   64, 71, 220
Life with the Lyons (film)   280
Lights Out at Eleven (play)   241
Lights Up! (revue)   283
Likes of Her, The (play)   28
Lilac Time (operetta)   103
Lipscomb, W. P.   6, 43, 59, 61, 130
Lipton, Dan   239
Lipton, Sydney   209
Lisbon Story, The (film)   103
Lisle, Lucille   218
Lister, Keith   203
Lister, Moira   315
Liszt, Franz   36, 176, 194, 325
Little Jean and John   109
Little Miss Somebody (film)   171
Little Tich   219
Little Tommy Tucker (musical)   31
Litvak, Anatole   50
Lively, Robert   219
Livesey family   122, 165, 244
Livre de Monsieur le Comte, La (play)   204
Llewellyn, Richard   258
Lloyd, Frederick   34, 74
Lloyd, Harold   280
Lloyd, Marie   21, 95, 111, 295, 320
Lloyd, Marie Jnr.   295
Locke, W. J.   177
Lockton, Edward   101, 133, 298
Lockwood, John   210
Lockwood, Margaret   151, 177, 199, 200, 222, 320
Loder, John   89, 108, 155, 172
Loftus, George   183

Löhner-Beda, Fritz   131, 150
Löhr, Marie   114, 129
London Melody (ice show)   229
London Philharmonic Orchestra   162, 304
London Symphony Orchestra   168, 247, 298
Long, Reginald   134, 150, 184
Longden, John   15, 16, 55, 110, 287
Longstaffe, Ernest   298, 302
Lonsdale, Frederick   45
Lopokova, Lydia   5
Loraine, Violet   28, 68–9, 75, 114–15, 327
Losch, Tilly   151
Loseff, Mara   221
Loss, Joe   209
Lost Empires (novel)   283
Loudon, Norman   122
Love Contract, The (film)   45
Love Lies (film)   33
Love Life and Laughter (Balfour film)   12
Love on the Dole (film)   83, 107
Love Your Neighbour (TV series)   78
Love, Bessie   182
Low, Rachael   4, 31, 33, 44, 45, 74, 75, 76, 77, 109, 144, 155, 156, 162, 171, 173, 174, 177, 185, 188, 211, 214, 234, 251
Lowe, Anita   303
Lubbock, Mark   122
Lubitsch, Ernst   32, 50
Lucan, Arthur   149, 170, 194, 201, 252, 264–7, 327
Lucas, Leighton   60, 93
Luce, Claire   208, 217, 327
Lucienne and Ashour   202
Lucky Number, The (film)   32
Ludwig, Otto   28
Lugosi, Bela   195, 267
Lupesco, Mme   203
Lupino, Antoinette / Toni / Tonie   283, 290
Lupino, Barry   268
Lupino, Stanley   24, 32, 33, 46, 50–1, 62, 64–5, 77, 78, 86–7, 107, 136, 152–4, 158, 171, 185, 188, 214, 216, 217, 220, 238–9, 255–6, 326, 327

GENERAL INDEX

Lupino, Wallace 33, 164
Lure of Crooning Water, The (film) 173
Luton Girls' Choir 267
Lynd, Della 131
Lynd, Eve 234
Lynn, Leni 307–8, 313
Lynn, Vera 290–1, 301, 308–9
Lyon, Ben 223, 280
Lyons in Paris, The (film) 280
Lyons, J. 281

M'Cullough, Donald 22
Macari and His Dutch Serenaders 208, 273
MacDonald, Jeanette 50, 232
Macdonald, Philip 12
Macdougall, Roger 249, 272, 275, 281
MacGinnis, Niall 234
Mackay, Barry 94, 120, 131, 188, 203, 215, 226
Mackeben, Theo 142
Mackenzie, S. P. 263
Mackey, Percival 75, 152, 218, 235, 265, 266, 269, 276, 287
Mackie, Marr 260
MacKinnon, Allan 249
Macphail, Angus 32, 37, 45, 235, 250, 263, 272, 310, 314
MacQueen-Pope, W. 151
Macrae, Arthur 145, 220, 271
MacWilliams, Glen 94, 141
Mad Girl (film) 226
Magistrate, The (play) 95, 214
Mahler, Gustav 232
Makeham, Eliot 171, 248, 272, 276, 308
Malleson, Miles 21, 26, 28, 35, 88
Malo, Gina 38, 62, 82, 104, 158, 177, 200, 217
Maltby, H. F. 66, 98, 155, 268, 276, 279, 285, 325
Man Who Knew Too Much, The (film) 142
Man with the Flower in His Mouth, The (play) 10
Mangan Tillerettes 17
Mankowitz, Wolf 113

Mann, Cathleen 199
Mannin, Ethel 159
Mannock, Patrick L. 4
Mantovani, Annunzio Paolo 211
Margetson, Arthur 42, 139, 142, 248
Marie Louise Sisters 208
Marischka, Ernst 86, 88, 104, 113, 161
Maritana (opera) 2, 110
Maritza, Sari 19, 44
Markham, Mansfield 65
Marks, Jack 71, 75, 286
Marksteiner, Franz 90
Marlock and Marlow 266
Marlowe, Charles *see* Jay, Harriet
Marriott, Moore 222, 261, 280, 320
Marriott, R. B. 228, 234
Marsh, Garry 221, 222, 236, 250, 263
Marsh, Marian 98
Marshall, Herbert 258
Marson, Aileen 104, 114, 136
Martin, Bob 28
Martin, Lorna 315
Martin, Paul 47, 49
Martos, Franz 91
Marvell, Holt *see* Maschwitz, Eric
Marvin, Johnny 301
Marx Brothers 77, 239, 254, 299
Mary Poppins (film) 19
Mary-Find-the-Gold (film) 11
Maschwitz, Eric 38, 40, 137–8, 180, 187–8
Mascot and Morice 208
Mason, Basil 171, 189, 211, 308
Mason, Elliott 275
Mason, Herbert 204, 303, 318
Massary, Fritzi 88
Massine, Léonide 35
Master Singers, The 240
Mather, Aubrey 44
Matthews, Jessie 3, 30–1, 52, 53, 59–61, 76, 79, 86, 93–5, 125, 140–2, 162–3, 184, 188, 189, 192–3, 214–15, 226–9, 238, 299, 308, 326, 327
Matthews, Lester 74
Maude, Arthur 182
Maude, Cyril 123

GENERAL INDEX

Maude, Joan   37, 38
Maxwell, John   13, 21
May, Hans   15, 98, 102, 110, 115, 131, 168, 177, 179, 184, 211, 294, 323–4
May, Joe   104
Mayerl, Billy   2, 135, 136, 152, 185, 217, 312, 313
Mayhew, Billy   208
Mayo, Sam   280
Mazzei, A. L.   166
McCarthy, Joseph   77, 129
McEvoy, Charles   28
McGrath Pat   290
McGrew, F.   208
McHugh, John   298
McKay, Claude   207
McKinney, Florine   168
McKinney, Nina Mae   113, 231
McLaglen, Victor   232, 234
McLaren, Ivor   61, 94, 105, 131
McLaughlin, Gibb   28, 69, 88, 106, 143, 239, 255
McNally, John   91
McNaughton, Gus   9, 42, 106, 115
McShane, Kitty   149, 194, 201, 252, 264–7
Me and My Girl (musical)   251
Mead, John   137
Meade, W. L.   240
Meadows, Bunty   298
Mear, H. Fowler   38, 71, 81, 83, 96, 113, 137, 145, 204, 209, 235, 236
Meehan Jnr., John   223, 230
Meehan, Elizabeth   217
Megrew, Janet   40
Meisel, Will   87
Melba, Dame Nellie   30, 171
Melford, Austin   78, 79, 85, 86, 104, 114, 120, 123, 135, 136, 157, 162, 195, 198, 212, 214, 229, 259, 263, 264, 272, 275, 276, 280, 288, 300, 307, 310, 313
Melford, Jack   136
Mellor, Tom   322
Melvin, G. S.   184, 273, 303, 327
Mendelssohn, Felix   259, 316
Mendelssohn, Felix, and His Hawaiian Serenaders   306

Mendes, Lothar   193
Mercanton, Louis   20
Mercer, Mabel   166
Meredith, George   106
Meredith, Lu Anne   150, 211
Merkel, Una   216
Merlini, Elsa   32
Merry Men of Sherwood, The (film)   231
Merryfield, Mathea   145
Merson, Billy   9, 230
Mertz, Arthur   88, 109, 123, 170, 207, 208, 240, 269, 282, 283, 288, 290, 306, 325
Merzbach, Paul   137, 138, 167, 168
Meseautó (film)   135
Messini, Jimmy   116
Metropolis (film)   94
Metzner, Ernö   102
Meyer, Joseph   76
Meyerbeer, Giacomo   161
Middleton, Guy   212, 236
Midgley, Walter   315
Mila, Bela   189
Milhaud, Darius   177
Military Pipers   210
Milland, Ray   75, 215
Millar, Dinah   220
Miller, Alice Duer   144
Miller, Frank   31, 42, 45, 78, 95, 109, 110, 134, 136, 166, 171
Miller, Max   60, 91, 93, 195, 282, 293
Miller, Ruby   276
Miller, Sonny   75, 302
Millions Like Us (film)   84
Millöcker, Karl   33, 142
Mills, Annette   301
Mills, Hugh   177, 275
Mills, John   52, 59, 68, 96, 125, 129, 135, 214
Milne, A. A.   6
Milton, Billy   79, 139, 220, 242
Milton, Ernest   314
Milton, Harry   167
Minipiano Ensemble of Fourteen Juveniles   210
Miss Charity (film)   37

Miss Hook of Holland (musical)   273
Miss Tulip Stays the Night (film)   180, 205, 271
Mitchell, Abbie   2
Mitchell, Julian   243
Mitchell, Oswald   101, 122, 129, 148, 149, 160, 163, 184, 201, 224, 225, 235, 252, 263, 265, 266, 287, 297
Mittler, Leo   152, 154, 182
Modern Times (film)   155
Modley, Albert   279
Moen, Lars   26
Moffatt, Graham   280
Moiseiwitsch, Benno   304
Mollison, Clifford   42, 78, 101, 102, 110, 115
Möme, La (play)   21
Monaco, Jimmy   77
Monckton, Lionel   2
Mondi, Bruno   15
Monkman, Phyllis   5
Montagu, Ivor   63
Montgomery, Doreen   239
Montgomery, John   268
Moon, George   248
Moore, Grace   79
Moore, Thomas   218
Mops (novel)   55
Morals of Marcus, The (film)   176
Morecambe and Wise   85
Moretti, Raoul   63
Morgan, Diana   312, 314
Morgan, Frank   119
Morgan, G. B.   182
Morgan, Joan   224
Morgan, Sidney   218, 224
Morris, Leonard   300
Morris, Lily   11, 95, 115, 122, 278
Morris, Phil   258
Morton, John Maddison   71
Mosheim, Grete   135
Mott, John   279
Mozart, Wolfgang Amadeus   304
Mr Abdullah (play)   42
Mr Britling Sees It Through (novel)   283
Mr Stringfellow Says 'No' (film)   184

Mr Whittington (musical)   190
Mrs Bradley's Formation Dancers   208
Mrs Dale's Diary (radio series)   30
Muir, Jean   160
Mulholland, Clara   194
Müller, Hans   44
Müller, Renate   32–3, 47, 56
Mundy, Hilda   240, 322
Munro, Ronnie   240, 260, 265
Murdoch, Richard   218, 261, 278
Murphy, C. W.   239
Murphy, Robert   287
Murray-Hill, Peter   301
Murray, Alan   298
Musical Medley (film)   109
Mussorgsky, Modest   5
My Fair Lady (musical)   142
My Friend the King (film)   40
My Old Dutch (film)   125
Mycroft, Walter C.   21, 78, 110, 115, 128, 131, 133, 137, 139, 142, 202, 208, 217, 239, 242, 255

Nagel, Conrad   150
Namara, Marguerite   29, 30, 162
Napier, Diana   79, 133, 179, 185
Nares, Owen   45, 52, 142, 198, 218
Nash, John Heddle   319
Nash, Paul   7
Natzler, Grete   131
Naughton and Gold   129, 303
Navarre   149, 164
Navarro, Dan   95
Naylor, Ruth   151
Neagle, Anna   16, 17, 36, 39, 57–8, 70, 88, 89, 144, 150–1, 189–90, 204, 272
Neal, Willer   266
Neame, Derek   211
Neame, Ronald   138
Neat, John   239
Neeld, Magda   145
Nell Gwynne (film)   16
Nelson, Billy   208, 240
Nesbitt, Robert   322
Nettlefold, Archibald   70, 91
Neubach, Ernst   109, 131

GENERAL INDEX

Neufeld, Max   116
Neumann, Ernst   131
Neuville, Pierre   160
New Empire Dancing Girls   273
New Moon, The (operetta)   46
Newall, Guy   173
Newell, Raymond   100, 197
Newman, Widgey Raphael   231
Nibelungen, Die (film)   102
Nicholas Brothers   198
Nicholls, Horatio   137, 297
Nichols, Beverley   111
Nichols, Dandy   267
Nicholson, Allan   254
Night Club Murder (film)   109
Night of the Demon (film)   234
Night to Remember, A (film)   164
Night Train to Munich (film)   270
Nightingale, The (musical)   134
Nikitina   35
Nipper, The (film)   20
Nirva, Dora   199
Nissen, Greta   188
Nit, Johnnie   125, 300
No Lady (film)   134, 251
Noble, Billy   23
Noble, Dennis   23
Noble, Ray, 51, 58, 93, 208
Noel, Art   276
Noni   9, 184, 273
Nordi, Cleo   188
Norman, Monty   113
Norris, Richard   252
Norton, Frederick   102
Norwich Trio   197
Not So Quiet on the Western Front (film)   24
Nothing Else Matters (film)   11
Noti, Karl   86
Novak, Peggy   242
Novello, Ivor   1, 10, 13, 36, 73, 89, 101, 111, 157, 202–3, 295, 314, 327
Novotná, Jarmila   182
Noy, Wilfred   112, 140, 162, 171, 204
Nugent, Frank S.   248
Nuttall, Jeff   326

O'Brien, Pat   149
O'Casey, Sean   201
O'Connor, Desmond   266, 267, 283, 288, 290, 291, 300, 308
O'Connor, Eily   81
O'Connor, Rory   194
O'Dea, Jimmy   133, 240–1, 249
O'Donovan, Harry   133
O'Farrell, Talbot   55, 194, 201, 202, 225, 235, 287
O'Gorman, Dave and Joe   184
O'Hara, Maureen   235, 245
O'Neal, Zelma   101, 102, 106, 115, 208
O'Neil, Denis   101, 122, 140
O'Neil, Nancy   302
O'Neil, Sally   194
O'Neill, Chuck   208, 240
O'Neill, Maire   203, 235, 241, 245
O'Regan, Kathleen   201, 287
O'Reilly, P. J.   101, 319
Oberon, Merle   96
Oh Rosalinda!! (film)   65
Okonowski, Georg   214
Old Mother Riley (film series)   134, 149, 152, 170, 195, 201, 252, 255, 264–7, 268, 301
Oldham, Derek   112, 162
Oliver, Vic   232, 276, 280, 320
Oliver! (musical)   325
Olivette (Nina Olivette)   24, 25
Olsen's Sea Lions   122
Once in a New Moon (film)   118
Ondra, Anny   39
One Hour with You (film)   50
Operette (operetta)   88
Opportunity Knocks (TV series)   122, 222
Orde, Beryl   115, 119, 211, 297
Orme, Geoffrey   151, 209, 266, 300
Orton, John (J. O. C.)   31, 50, 61, 85, 158, 230, 261, 280
Orton, Wallace   83, 151, 259, 297, 308
Oscar, Henry   140
Ostrer, Isidore   140
Oswald, Richard   109
Otello (opera)   79
Othello (play)   174

Oumansky, Alexander   14, 25
Owen, W. Armitage   241
Owens, Harrison   205
Oxenford, John   81
Oxley, Hylton R.   183

Paderewski, Ignace Jan   193–4
Palmer, Lilli   205, 216
Pape, Helene *see* Harvey, Lilian
Park, Phil   298, 305
Parker, Austin   144, 156
Parker, Ross   290, 298
Parkes, Ennis   303
Parkington, Gershom   100, 157, 325
Parr Davies, Harry   46, 73, 108, 127, 128, 140, 155, 174, 198, 199, 229, 234, 241, 243, 244, 253, 261, 271, 291, 298, 305, 308
Parr, Pamela   81
Parselles, Angela   185
Parsons, Donovan   20
Parsons, Roney *see* Mertz, Arthur
Pascha, Zeda   29
Passing of the Third Floor Back, The (film)   159
Passmore, H. Fraser   174, 185
Passport to Pimlico (film)   128, 270
Patch, Wally   60, 119, 231, 236, 260, 276, 279, 322
Paterson, Pat   37
Paul, Gerald   244
Payn, Graham   109
Payne, Jack   51, 151, 166
Payne, Tom   155
Peacock, Thomas Love   106
Pearce, Vera   57, 123, 124, 177, 190, 191, 192, 212, 242, 243, 327
Pearl Fishers, The (opera)   79
Pearl, Jack   2
Pearson, George   4, 11–12, 55, 125, 163, 216, 237
Pedelty, Donovan   76, 122
Peers, Donald   293
Pelosi, Don   276
Pendrell, Tony   325
Penn, W. H.   320

Penrose, Charles   171, 172, 239, 242
Pepper, Harry S.   1, 113, 131, 151, 261
Peppina   70
Perceval, Hugh   171, 274
Percy Athos Follies   208
Percy, Edward   320
Percy, Esme   138, 175
Perez, Paul   103, 115
Perfect Gentleman, The (film)   119
Perrins, Leslie   71, 82, 105, 151, 178, 179, 240
Perritt, Harry   156
Pertwee, Roland   235
Petrie, Hay   88, 138, 162
Petrov, Eugene   173, 304
Pettingell, Frank   71
Phantom Light, The (film)   75
Phillips, Eddie   313
Phillips, Gene D.   85
Phillips, Harry   297
Phillips, Van   236
Phipps, Tom   225
Piccadilly (film)   15
Piccadilly Circus (proposed film title)   234
Pickard, Lioni   133
Pierre ou Jack (play)   192
Pinero, Arthur Wing   95, 214
Pini, Eugene   198
Pirandello, Lyuigi   10, 261
Pirzinger, Steffi   51
Pitts, Archie   28, 46
Plater, Alan   59
Players' Theatre   5, 89, 310
Plough and the Stars, The (play)   201
Pola, Charlie   14
Pola, Eddie   146, 151, 199, 219
Pollock, William   51
Pommer, Erich   44, 49, 116
Pond, Arthur   109
Popplewell, Jack   291, 301, 309
Porter, Cole   31, 236
Porter, Uriel   276, 286
Portman, Eric   59, 143, 193
Posford, George   38, 60, 67, 78, 137, 138, 188, 280

GENERAL INDEX

Potter, Richard 172
Poulton, Mabel 186
Pound, Reginald 130
Powell, Dilys 258
Powell, Eleanor 215
Powell, Ellis 31
Powell, Michael 40, 53, 65, 120
Power, Hartley 56, 114
Power, Tyrone 280
Prador, Irene 208
Pressburger, Arnold 26, 90, 113, 127
Pressburger, Emeric 65
Previn, André 59, 60
Priestley, J. B. 59–61, 106–8, 127, 283–5, 300, 301, 304–5
Prince, Arthur 119
Princess Ida (operetta) 307
Princess Pearl *see* Roy, Mrs Harry
Prisoner of Zenda, The (novel) 12
Private Life of Henry VIII, The (film) 74
Procter, Adelaide 112
Producers, The (musical) 124
Provis, George 166, 301
Psycho (film) 85
Puccini, Giacomo 30, 232, 248
Pujol, René 176
Purcell, Harold 229, 276, 280, 308
Purdell, Reginald 44, 115, 264, 295, 304, 316
Purton, Norah 139
Pygmalion (play) 12

Quin, John 180, 231
Quinlan, David 23, 115, 127, 172, 211, 221

Rachmaninov, Sergei 30
Radford, Basil 79, 270
Radio Male Voice Choir 164
Radio Rogues, The 120
Radio Three, The 202, 273
Rambert, Marie 38
Rameau, Hans 193
Randall, Carl 199
Randle, Frank 268–9, 282, 288–90, 302, 325–6

Randolph, Elsie 56, 76, 183, 327
Random Harvest (film) 318
Raphaelson, Samson 88
Ratoff, Gregory 125
Rawicz and Landauer 200, 221, 325
Rawlinson, A. R. 79, 146
Rawnsley, David 98, 104, 115, 129, 142
Ray, Cyril 211, 219
Ray, Rene 55, 121, 159, 191, 234, 327
Ray, Ted 155
Raye, Carol 313, 324
Raymond, Fred 87, 131
Raymond, Jack 6, 51, 144, 156, 224
Rayner, Minnie 71, 203
Raynham, Glen 252
Reader, Ralph 51, 78, 100, 125, 151, 190, 200, 230
Reading and Grant 266
Real Bloke, A (film) 100, 165
Rebecca (film) 159
Reck-Mallaczewen, Fritz 44
Reed, Carol 229, 240, 241, 270
Reed, Langford 317
Reed, Phillip 245
Rehfisch, Hans 172
Reichert, Heinz 86
Reid, Billy 220
Reinert, Emil 176
Reisch, Walter 47, 64, 70, 73, 91, 127
Reisfeld, Bert 291
Reisie, Reginald 260
Reisner, Charles 180
Relph, Michael 310
Rennie, Alan 161
Rennie, James 57
Rennie, Michael 320
Retford, Ella 295
Reunion (film) 165, 300
Revel, Harry 180, 192
Reville, Alma 28, 86
Revnell, Ethel 140, 198, 293, 302, 303
Reynders, John 4, 14
Rhapsody (film) 35
Rhodes, Erik 102
Rhyder, Slim 296
Rhythm Sisters 232

Ricardo, Bertha   170
Richards, Jeffrey   199, 244, 268
Richardson, Frank A.   75
Ridgwell, George   81
Ridley, Walter   290, 291, 309
Riemann, Johannes   65
Rigby, Arthur   134, 255
Rigby, Edward   235, 284
Right Honourable, The (novel)   40
Rigoletto (opera)   2, 49, 161
Rigoletto Brothers   300
Ring o'Roses (novel)   276
Ring, The (film)   17
Rio and Santos   240
Rio Rita (film)   73
Riscoe, Arthur   24, 53, 75, 76, 79, 158, 200
Rise and Shine (musical)   74
Ritchard, Cyril   17, 229
Ritter, Alf   297
Road to Dishonour, The (film)   15
Robenis, The   202
Roberts, Arthur   310
Roberts, Leslie   136, 152
Robertson, Marjorie   150, 151
Robeson, Eslanda   207
Robeson, Paul   174–6, 184, 205–7, 258–9, 286
Robey, George   47, 69, 102, 165, 172, 177, 179, 186, 187, 295, 296, 324
Robins, Phyllis   186, 219, 273, 303
Robinson, Armin   180
Robinson, Percy   186
Robinson, Stanford   133
Robison, Carson   197
Roc, Patricia   264, 283, 291
Rock You Sinners (film)   326
Rock, Joe   166, 210, 219
Rode, Alfred   36, 116, 176
Rodgers and Hammerstein   31, 93, 94, 104, 190
Rodney Hudson Girls   171, 204
Roeg, Nicolette   315, 325
Roellinghoff, Charlie   106
Rogers, Buddy (Charles)   129, 208
Rogers, Gaby   297
Rogers, Ginger   51, 95, 154

Rogers, Maclean (R.)   16, 265, 267, 268, 275, 279, 285, 295, 298, 302, 307, 313, 319
Rolf, Tutta   174
Rolph, Dudley   303
Romberg, Sigmund   70, 131
Rome, Stuart   5, 116, 165
Rooney, Annie   109
Roosevelt, Eleanor   74
Root, Wells   177, 275
Ros, Edmundo   318
Rose, Fred   301
Rosen, Willy   87
Rosenfeld, H.   101
Rossier, Karl   324
Rossini, Gioachino   243, 316
Roth, Lillian   144
Rotha, Paul   108
Roundabout (musical)   318
Rourke, John   295
Rowland, William   223
Roy, Harry   166, 219
Roy, Mrs Harry   166, 219
Royal Kiltie Juniors   220
Royal Marines' Band   210
Royal Merry Four   109
Royal Tzigane Band   36
Royston, Roy   17
Rubens, Paul   111, 218, 220
Ruddigore (operetta)   246
Russell, Kennedy   134, 151, 195, 260, 264, 265, 266, 283, 288, 300, 304, 308, 313
Russell, Thomas   304, 305
Russell, Wensley   162
Rutherford, Billie   19
Rutherford, Robert   244, 261

Saint Joan (play)   2
Saint-Saëns, Camille   304
Salkind, Ilya   183
Salmony, G. F.   172
Salten, Felix   64
Samson and Delilah (opera)   2
Samuels, Lesser   215, 226
Samuelson, G. B.   23, 31
Sanders of the River (film)   174

GENERAL INDEX

Sanders Twins, The   236
Sanders, Ivy   247
Sanderson, Challis   101, 129, 148
Sandler, Albert   9, 324
Sandys, Oliver   55
Sapper (H. C. McNeile)   44
Sargent, Malcolm   29, 304
Sarony, Leslie   151, 196, 267
Saville, Victor   2, 32, 45, 59, 60, 61, 93–4, 111, 112, 130, 141, 162, 192, 214, 215, 226, 229
Schach, Max   156, 177, 180, 185
Schertzinger, Victor   246, 248
Schiaparelli, Elsa   143
Schildkraut, Joseph   35, 36
Schiller, Paul   199
Schilling, Ivy   53
Schlichting, Werner   15
Schmidt, Joseph   66, 98, 109–10, 161, 167–8
Schmitz, Oscar Adolf Hermann   179
Schneider, Magda   49, 75, 76, 101
Schofield, Johnny   219
School for Randle (film)   325
Schröder, Kurt   75
Schubert, Franz   90, 103–4
Schulz, Franz (Frank)   32, 44, 45, 103
Schumann, Robert   132
Schünzel, Reinhold   141
Schwabach, Kurt   87
Schwalb, Niklos   106
Schwartz, Arthur   31
Schwartz, Jean   129
Schwarz, Fred   87
Schwarz, Hanns   44, 69
Scotch Kilties   210
Scott and Whaley   84, 113, 219, 220
Scott, Janette   59
Scotti, William   218
Searle, Ronald   267
Sekely, Steve   150
Selpin, Herbert   45
Selten, Morton   119, 253
Seton, Bruce   158, 162
Seven Royal Hindustanis, The   240
Seven Thunderbolts, The   119

Seyler, Athene   50, 71, 104, 163, 179, 227
Seyler, Clifford   12
Seymour, James   219, 290, 298, 303
Seymour, Sid, and His Mad Hatters   17, 161
Shakespeare, William   10, 231
Shall, Theo   115
Shalson, Harry   19
Shannon, Ernest   273
Shaw, George Bernard   2, 12, 74
Shaw, Luanne   207
Sheils, Derek   290
Sheldon, Gene   255
Sheldon, Horace   160, 162, 164, 171, 265
Shelton, Anne   291, 292, 299, 307
Sheridan, Dinah   296, 319
Sheridan, Oscar M.   23, 24
Sherie, Fenn   174, 185, 207, 232
Sherkot, Leon   129
Sherman Fisher Girls   107, 122, 140, 164, 184, 202, 219, 240, 273, 303, 327
Sherman, Al   221
Sherriff, R. C.   7, 118
Sherwin, Manning   276, 280, 291, 293, 299, 300, 307, 320
Sherwood, Lydia   115
Shields, Ella   60, 123, 141, 165
Shiner, Ronald   125, 254, 281, 293, 307
Shipbuilders, The (film)   301
Shipman, David   27, 39, 61, 66, 76, 89, 150, 254
Shotter, Winifred   43, 45
Should a Doctor Tell? (film)   39
Shovitch, Vladimir   162
Show Boat (musical)   70, 174
Shuttlecoq (film)   35
Sieczyński, Rudolf   101, 133
Sievier, Bruce   174, 176, 183
Sigler, Maurice   124, 125, 135, 137, 141, 143, 144, 156, 158, 183, 190, 226, 239
Silver Soon, The (radio play)   208
Silver, Abner   221
Sim, Alastair   137, 222, 227, 284
Simon, Charles   30
Sinclair, Hugh   318
Singer, John (Johnny)   121, 282

Singin' in the Rain (film)   33
Siodmak, Kurt   142
Six Rose Petals, The   268
Six-Five Special (film)   326
Sixty Glorious Years (film)   190
Skating Avalons, The   297
Slaughter, Tod   60, 78, 82, 201, 268, 283
Sloan, Tot   170
Sloane, Olive   59, 61, 125, 188, 284, 297
Smart, Ralph   40, 55
Smiling Along (film)   244
Smith, Herbert   75, 84, 105, 119, 120, 129, 156, 197, 232
Smith, Paul Girard   166
Smith, Raymond   240
So This is Love (musical)   255
So You Won't Talk (film)   195
Somers, Debroy   113, 149, 219
Somewhere in Politics (film)   302, 325
Somio, Josef   246
Sondheim, Stephen   82
Song in Soho (film)   189
Song of the Flame, The (film)   146
Song of the Plough (film)   113
Sonja, Magda   168
Sonker, Hans   160
Sound of Music, The (film)   4, 103
Spear, Eric   175
Speedy   266
Spence, Ralph   180, 221, 225
Spider's Web (film)   205
Spoliansky, Mischa   49, 104, 109, 111, 135, 161, 221, 314
Spring in Park Lane (film)   144
Spring Song (film)   313
Squire, Ronald   144
St David's Singers   298
St Helier, Ivy   70, 185, 225
Stafford, John   33, 51, 106, 115, 159, 189
Stage Folk (film)   160
Stamp-Taylor, Enid   105, 122, 133, 134, 210, 236
Stanbury, Albert W.   208, 269, 283, 290
Stanelli, Edward   19
Stanley, Arthur   134
Stanley, Phyllis   288

Stanley, Ralph   87
Stannard, Eliot   12, 81
Stanwyck, Barbara   288
Stapenhorst, Günther   220
Stardust (film)   223
Starita, Rudy   209
Steed, Francis   304
Steele, Tommy   44, 326
Steffani, Arturo, and His Silver Songsters   170
Stein, Paul L.   73, 74, 103, 132, 133, 159–60, 188, 324
Steininger, Franz   75, 79, 146
Sten, Anna   44
Stern, Eric   310
Stevens, Alfred Peck *see* Vance, Albert
Stevens, Tod   302
Stevenson, Robert   19, 32, 45, 47, 49, 64, 66, 71, 157
Stewart, Donald   141, 157, 309
Stockfeld, Betty   26, 62, 177
Stokes, Sewell   67
Stoll, Oswald   152
Stolz, Robert   69–70, 74, 75, 90, 113
Stone, Christopher   63
Stone, Lew   200, 222, 254
Stone, Reg   7, 327
Storm, Lesley   318
Stothart, Herbert   146
Strange World of Planet X, The (novel and film)   159
Stranks, Alan   294, 323, 324
Stransky, Otto   106
Stratton, Eugene   113, 225, 295, 320
Straus, Oscar   88, 179, 182, 198
Strauss family   36, 45, 65, 86, 177
Straws in the Wind (film)   31
Strueby, Katherine   188, 318
Stuart, Binkie   171, 173, 193, 201–2, 235, 245, 287
Stuart, Jeanne   161
Stuart, John   21, 37, 198, 210
Stuart, Leslie   95, 225, 235, 295, 303
Styne, Jule   101
Suedo, Julie   231
Sullivan, Francis L.   314

GENERAL INDEX

Summers, Dorothy   294
Summers, Walter   12, 15, 139
Sumner, Frank   46
Superb Act, The   149
Supervia, Conchita   112
Sutherland, Duncan   102, 134, 139, 314, 316
Sutherland, Ian   184
Sutherland, Sally   118
Swan Lake (ballet)   65
Sweeney Todd (film)   283
Swinburne, Nora   224, 225
Swing Mikado, The (operetta)   247
Sydney, Basil   52
Sylphides, Les (ballet)   38
Székely, Hans   26, 71

Taking Ways (film)   300
Talbot, Henry   293
Tales of Hoffman, The (opera)   79
Taming of the Shrew, The (play)   77
Tara Troupe of Irish Dancers   194
Tate, Harry   87, 128, 157, 184
Tauber, Richard   40, 90, 103–4, 109, 132–3, 149, 161, 179–80, 185, 208, 221, 324, 327
Taylor, C. H.   297
Taylor, Donald   304, 305
Taylor, Dwight   192, 215
Taylor, Grant   274
Taylor, Rex   4
Tchaikovsky, Pyotr   304
Tell her the Truth (musical)   190
Temperance Fete, The (film)   186
Tempest, Marie   193
Temple, Shirley   120, 201, 209, 210, 245
Temple, Wilfred   8
Templeman, Harcourt   5, 143, 216, 237
Templeton, Alec   145
Temptress, The (film)   252
Tennyson, Pen   257, 258
Tennyson, Walter   140, 160, 171
Terrett, Courtney   184
Terror on Tiptoe (film)   186
Terry, Harry   97
Terry's Juveniles   145, 230

Teyte, Maggie   134
Thatcher, Heather   9
There Goes the Bride (film)   60
Thesiger, Ernest   102, 114
They Came to a City (film)   283
They Drive by Night (film)   102
Thiele, William   47, 65
Third Man, The (film)   270
Thirty Gypsy Revellers   240
This England (film)   31
This is the Night (film)   50
Thomas, Basil   291
Thomas, Dillwyn   200
Thomas, Howard   290
Thomas, Yvonne   193
Thompson, Fred   95, 139, 166, 183, 192
Thompson, Hal   235, 239
Thompson, Thomas   240
Thorndike, Sybil   2
Thornton, Michael   52, 74, 141, 228
Three Canadian Bachelors   198
Three Caskets, The (operetta)   113
Three Dots, The   236
Three Eddies, The   10
Three Gins, The   125
Three Jokers, The   252
Three Maxims, The (film)   190
Three Maxwells, The   260
Three Music-Hall Boys, The   240
Three Rascals, The   254
Three's a Crowd (proposed film title)   288
Threepenny Opera, The   65
Tidmarsh, Vivian   230
Tiller Girls   120
Tilley, Vesta   61, 141, 318
Tin Pan Alley Trio   232
Tipping, Annie Foy *see* Foy, Nita
Titterton, Frank   65, 101
Todd, Ann   101, 274
Todd, Thelma   77
Toeplitz, Ludovico   74, 177
Tolnay, Akos   150
Tom Thumb (film)   229
Toner, Anthony *see* Blakeley, John E.
Top Hat (film)   102
Tosca (opera)   113

Tottenham, Merle   322
Towers, Leo   28, 46, 90, 108, 317, 322
Toye, Geoffrey   246
Toye, Wendy   133, 300, 320, 322
Tracey, Bert   88, 109
Tracy, Arthur   150, 157, 199, 200, 208, 215, 237
Train, Jack   292, 293, 294, 299
Traitor's Gate (play)   21
Tranter, Florence   189, 205
Traubner, Richard   182, 323
Travers, Linden   281
Traviata, La (opera)   49, 111, 281
Tree, Lady (Viola)   53, 71, 74, 75
Trendall, Jack   168
Trent, Bruce   261
Trevor, Austin   97, 177
Trinder, Tommy   11, 241, 260, 271–2, 310–13, 314–15, 327
Tristan und Isolde (opera)   64, 74
Troise, Pasqual, and His Mandoliers and Banjoliers   151
Truex, Ernest   180
Trust the Navy (film)   134
Trytel, Victor   145
Trytel, W. L. (William)   19, 75, 82, 83, 96, 97, 100, 121, 137, 145
Tucherer, Eugène   214
Tucker, Sophie   105, 210
Tully, Montgomery   319, 324
Tunberg, Karl   252
Tunbridge, Joseph   33, 53, 124, 190, 242, 256, 261
Turner, John Hastings   101
Tussaud, Madame   12, 43
Twelve Aristocrats, The   198
Twelve Chairs, The (play)   173
Twenty Gordon Ray Girls   208
Twenty Tiny Tappers   230
Two Charladies   232
Two Cities (musical)   325
Two Leslies, The   196
Two Share a Dwelling (play)   135
Tyrone, Kathleen   287
Tzigansky Choir   188

Underneath the Arches (film)   197
Up with the Lark (musical)   12
Utopia Limited (operetta)   113

Vadnay, László   135
Vagabond King, The (operetta)   46
Vagabond Queen, The (film)   12
Vajda, Laszlo   52
Valentine, A. D.   154
Valentine, E. G.   198
Valentine, Val   13, 21, 23, 188, 195, 214, 244, 254, 293, 303, 320
Valentino, Rudolph   1, 50, 280
Van Straten's Piccadilly Orchestra   303
Vance, Albert   310, 312
Vane, Alma   3
Varconi, Victor   73, 74
Variety Follies (film)   160
Varley, Beatrice   298
Varnel, Marcel   128, 142, 158, 202, 261, 263, 276, 280, 286, 291, 296, 305, 317, 322
Vaughan, Michael   286, 296, 317, 322
Veidt, Conrad   34, 64
Velda and Vann   240
Velez, Lupe   176, 182, 223
Veness, Amy   160
Verdi, Giuseppe   104, 161, 248
Vergiss Mein Nicht (film)   161
Verno, Jerry   40–2, 176, 235
Vertes   247
Vesselo, A.   168–70
Vetchinsky, Alexander   32, 45, 119, 202
Vibert, Marcel   15
Victoria the Great (film)   190
Victoria, Vesta   84, 94, 112, 278
Vienna, Franz *see* Steininger, Franz
Vienna, Franz   146
Viktor und Viktoria (play)   141
Viktoria und ihr Husar (operetta)   32
Village Blacksmith, The (film)   204
Vincent, Gene   120
Vincent, Robbie   269, 282, 288, 298
Viragh, Arpad   26
Virginia (musical)   190
Vitéz, Miklós   135

GENERAL INDEX

Vokes, Stefan   298
Von Bolváry, Géza   91
von Cube, Irma   104
von Goth, Rolf   52
von Nagy, Käthe   71
von Trapp Family   104
Vorhaus, Bernard   26, 96–7, 121
Vosper, Frank   132
Vulpius, Paul   158

Waddington, Patrick   142
Wade, Hugh   23
Wagener, Kurt   324
Wagner, Richard   64, 149, 248
Wake Up and Dream (revue)   76
Wakefield, Douglas (Duggie)   71, 128, 207–8, 240
Wakefield, Hugh   162, 183
Wakefield, Oliver   208, 253, 284
Wakely, Jimmy   301
Waldock, Denis   128
Walker, Ian   224, 235, 244, 287
Walker, Norman   205
Walker, Syd   208, 218, 239, 259
Wall, Max   84, 210, 241
Wallace, Edgar   21
Wallace, Major Claude   174
Wallace, Nellie   115, 122, 297
Wallace, William   2, 110
Waller, Jack   33, 53, 124, 190, 242, 256, 261
Walls, Tom   131
Walmsley, Fred   170
Walsh, Kay   212, 229
Wanted for Murder (film)   109
Ward, Diana   146
Ward, Polly   14, 40–1, 51, 164, 171, 195, 239, 243
Ward, Ronald   112, 291
Ward, Warwick   22, 220, 241, 248
Ware, Irene   232
Waring, Barbara   118
Warner, Jack   285, 297
Warren, Betty   295, 310, 312
Warren, C. Denier   113, 137, 145, 204, 235

Warren, Harry   129
Warriss, Ben   301
Warwick, John   274
Water Gipsies, The (film)   19
Waters, Elsie and Doris   6, 63, 275–6, 279, 285–6, 293, 303–4
Watson, Norman   131
Watson, Wylie   53, 114, 192, 242, 274, 327
Watt, John   113, 115, 220, 261
Wayne, John   180
Wayne, Mabel   129, 139
Wayne, Naunton   75, 79, 270
Weatherley, Fred   108
Webster, Paul Francis   218
Wedding in Paris (musical)   15
Weddings Are Wonderful (film)   268, 275
Welch, Elisabeth   157, 175, 176, 198, 203, 206, 207, 314
Welch, James   156
Welchman, Harry   46, 78, 182
Welden, Ben   75
Weldon, Dan   176
Welleminsky, J. M.   142
Wellesley, Gordon   89, 98, 127, 139, 155, 301
Wells, Bombardier Billy   159
Wells, Cyril   163
Wells, H. G.   283
Went the Day Well? (film)   309
Werndorff, Oscar   5, 211
West, Con   113, 119, 129, 133, 151, 184, 252, 264, 266, 297, 302, 303
West, Gracie   140, 198, 293
West, Mae   105, 115, 122
Western Brothers   6, 110, 157
Weston, R. P.   31, 42, 73, 125, 190, 199, 202, 234, 239, 243
Whal, Chris   71
What Do We Do Now? (film)   171
What Would You Do, Chums? (film)   259
Whelan, Albert   149, 210, 274
Whelan, Tim   79, 80
When We Are Married (film)   301
When You Come Home (film)   325
Where There's a Will (film)   195

Whetter, Laura   150
Whidden, Jay   13, 17
Whiley, Manning   319
White Coons Concert Party   84
White Horse Inn (operetta)   45, 70, 74
White, Frederick   81
White, G. H. Moresby   66
Whitfield, David   50
Whiting, Jack   227, 228, 327
Whitman, Louis   75
Whitson, Beth Slater   266
Whittingham, Jack   324
Who's Your Father? (film)   134
Wicker Man, The (film)   69
Widdop, Walter   74
Wiene, Robert   168
Wiere Brothers   197
Wilcock, Frank   261
Wilcox, Herbert   1, 2, 6, 16, 17, 35–6, 38–9, 45, 51, 56, 57, 70, 76, 88, 89, 102, 144, 150–1, 155, 156, 160, 183, 189–90, 199, 200, 205, 272
Wilcoxon, Harry (Henry)   91, 93
Wild Rose (operetta)   134
Wild Violets (musical)   69
Wilder, Billy   47, 51
Wilding, Michael   17, 190, 272
Wilhelm, Wolfgang   101
William Tell (opera)   210
Williams, Bransby   61
Williams, Brock   124, 160, 225, 230
Williams, Campbell   23
Williams, D. J.   82
Williams, Emlyn   93, 104, 111, 114, 127
Williams, Hugh   37, 207
Williams, L. P.   183
Williams, Philip Martin   123
Williamson, W. K.   218
Willis, Constance   247
Willis, Dave   241, 248, 318
Willmott, Bertha   84
Willner, A. M.   86
Wills, Buntie *see* Wills, J. Elder,
Wills, Drusilla   69, 125
Wills, J. Elder   154, 175, 184, 185, 205
Wilson, Adam   251

Wilson, Ian   28, 62, 69, 204, 297
Wilson, Keppel and Betty   84, 119, 157, 296
Wilson, Maurice J.   9
Wilson, Sandy   203, 222
Wilton, Robb   89, 128, 137, 149, 230, 236, 273, 299, 327
Wimperis, Arthur   13, 74, 161, 177, 214
Windeatt, George   156
Windmill Revels (film)   189
Winn, Anona   57, 84
Winnick, Maurice   19, 232
Winter, Marius B.   40
Winters, Joan   296
Winters, Mike and Bernie   115
Wisdom, Norman   44, 229
Withers, Googie   167, 250
Wodehouse, P. G.   82
Woizikowski, Leon   145
Wolf, C. M.   158
Wolff, Ludwig   15
Wolfit, Donald   172
Wonderful Town (musical)   318
Wong, Anna May   15–16, 102, 163
Wood, Joan Wentworth *see* Morgan, Joan
Wood, John   217, 239, 327
Wood, Sir Henry   172
Wood, Wee Georgie   184, 236
Woodall, Doris   65
Woodforde-Finden, Amy   192
Woods, Arthur B.   101, 115, 174, 188
Woods, Harry   79, 85, 94, 110
Woon, Basil   301, 318
Words and Music (revue)   40
Workers and Jobs (film)   107
Workers' Playtime (BBC radio series)   220, 279
Wray, Fay   144, 156
Wright, Geoffrey   314
Wright, Hal, and His Circus   240
Wright, Hugh E.   4
Wright, Huntley   128
Wright, Josephine Huntley   189
Wright, Lawrence   128
Wyckham, Tony   230
Wylie, Julian   23

GENERAL INDEX

Wyndham-Lewis, D. B. 143
Wynne, Herbert 221, 235

Xenia and Boyder 218

Yaray, Hans 90
Yarde, Margaret 60, 125, 134, 135, 155, 176, 327
Yorke, Peter 244
Young Man's Fancy (film) 19
Young, Arthur 115, 116, 129, 272
Young, Dan 123, 170, 269, 282, 288, 306
Young, Howard Irving 278, 280, 294, 308, 317, 322
Young, Robert 163
Young, Roland 227

Youngest of Three, The (play) 98
Youth at the Helm (play) 157

Zágon, István 47
Zamecnik, J. S. 46
Zanuck, Darryl F. 232
Zeisler, Alfred 141
Zelnik, Frederic (Fred) 86, 110, 177, 211, 307, 313
Zerlett, Hans 33
Ziegfeld Follies (revue) 174
Ziegler, Anne 306, 323, 324
Ziereis, Barbara 205
Zimmerman, Louis 39
Zinkeisen, Doris 35
Zorlini, Max 306